Personality

Second Edition

Sara Miller McCune founded Sage Publishing in 1965 to support the dissemination of usable knowledge and educate a global community. Sage publishes more than 1000 journals and over 600 new books each year, spanning a wide range of subject areas. Our growing selection of library products includes archives, data, case studies and video. Sage remains majority owned by our founder and after her lifetime will become owned by a charitable trust that secures the company's continued independence.

Los Angeles | London | New Delhi | Singapore | Washington DC | Melbourne

Personality

Theories and Applications

Second Edition

Eric Shiraev

George Mason University

FOR INFORMATION:

2455 Teller Road
Thousand Oaks, California 91320
E-mail: order@sagepub.com

1 Oliver's Yard
55 City Road
London, EC1Y 1SP
United Kingdom

Unit No. 323-333, Third Floor, F-Block
International Trade Tower
Nehru Place, New Delhi – 110 019
India

18 Cross Street #10-10/11/12
China Square Central
Singapore 048423

Printed in the United States of America

Library of Congress Control Number: 2023040466

ISBN: 978-1-0718-5718-2

This book is printed on acid-free paper.

Acquisitions Editor: Mary Dudley

Product Associate: Latoya Douse

Production Editor: Vijayakumar

Copy Editor: Beth Hammond

Typesetter: TNQ Technologies

Indexer: TNQ Technologies

Cover Designer: Gail Buschman

Marketing Manager: Victoria Velasquez

23 24 25 26 27 10 9 8 7 6 5 4 3 2 1

BRIEF CONTENTS

DETAILED CONTENTS

PREFACE

Welcome to the study of personality in the 21st century—welcome to the field that is enlightening, intriguing, and promising. It is enlightening because of the superb quality and diversity of the research in which this field is rooted. It is intriguing because of the fascinating assumptions and unexpected answers this research into personality offers. And it is promising because of its significant practical applications in so many areas of our lives. This book will be your careful guide and a friendly companion in the journey to study personality.

Why do we need this book? Indeed, today we have unprecedented access to global information: social media postings, video clips, tweets, eyewitness reports, theoretical articles, statistics, research summaries, and sensational stories—all are just a click or tap away. Twenty years ago, it would have taken many hours to locate an article that today's reader can "Google" in seconds. And then you can find another article. And a new shorty on YouTube . . . and another one . . . and more . . . . How many of them should we read and watch? Which of these sources are valid? Which one is more accurate and trustworthy compared to others? This book is supposed to bring a measure of scientific certainty and confidence to your understanding of personality. This confidence is based on critical fact-analysis— the method that the author has already applied in his *A History of Psychology* (SAGE).

Main Features

First, the science about personality presented in this book is *interdisciplinary*. The book's core is about personality psychology, which is inseparable from basic science and social science and which welcomes the contributions from the fields of the humanities, history, culture studies, gender studies, and many other disciplines.

Second, this book emphasizes *diversity*. It has a significant cross-cultural and cross-national focus to emphasize the global nature of our knowledge about personality. The author has significant background and expertise in cross-cultural studies.

Third, the book introduces and applies *critical thinking* as a main method of analysis of facts and theories. One of the book's goals is to help students learn to deduce facts from opinions and to be informed skeptics.

Finally, the book pays attention to the practical *relevance* of our knowledge of personality to students' diverse experiences today. It introduces applications from the fields of medicine, therapy, education, training, criminal justice, business, and entertainment, to name a few.

Structure

The book contains 14 chapters. The first discusses main definitions and assumptions, the second turns to scientific foundations of personality studies, and the third one focuses on methodology to study personality. The next five chapters examine personality from the standpoint of several major psychological traditions. Then, the following five chapters discuss personality within the developmental, gender, clinical, adjustment, and digital domains. Finally, the concluding chapter asks students to use their critical and creative thinking while discussing contemporary research into personality.

You should notice the book's well-defined and consistent structure. After the first three introductory chapters, each following chapter is organized around three general themes related to our research journey into personality. These themes can be presented in the form of three questions:

What are the basic ideas and facts that we focus on?

How do we study these ideas and facts?

How do we apply them?

The coverage of classical and contemporary research in this text remains both comprehensive and chronological. Most research theories are presented as "products" of their own time, which are shaped by unique social circumstances. These theories and their applications, in turn, influenced society and the individual. Many earlier theories were making an instant and often lasting impact on later theories and their applications.

Academic traditions. The scientific knowledge about personality over the past 120 years developed within major academic traditions generally associated with psychology as an academic discipline. Such traditions brought together scholars—who often lived and worked thousands of miles apart, yet who shared similar views on a particular scientific approach, subject, or method. There are real associations involving interacting individuals, and there are traditions as convenient symbols to indicate a similarity in views across borders and times. To illustrate, consider these points:

- In studying personality, psychoanalysis of the early 20th century and later turned to the *conflicting and feeling individual.* Psychoanalysts focused on various unconscious motivational forces and believed in the crucial impact of early childhood on personality.

- Other scientists rejected psychoanalysis's assumptions and focused instead on the individual's reflexes, observable behavior, and learning mechanisms. To these scientists, the individual—who they studied—was seen mostly as *acting and learning.* The behaviorist tradition dominated academic and applied psychology for decades.

- While many researchers argued about the key sources of personality's features, others turned to measuring personality traits—the personality's most stable features. It was the tradition that emphasized the growing interest in the *structured individual*, which appeared as complex, interdependent, and—most importantly—measurable.

- The cognitive revolution in science in the middle of the past century meant a renewed interest in those inner mechanisms that define human experience. Again, the *thinking, information-processing individual* was back on the researchers' agenda. Cognitive science connected many disciplines together, including neuroscience, philosophy, and computer science.

- At the same time, many psychologists urged others to focus more on a different individual: the one that was mostly *loving, caring, and growing*. Humanistic psychologists emphasized the uniquely human core of personality and the individual's relentless search for happiness.

Although the book examines these traditions in seemingly a linear sequence, they have never been isolated from each other. They, like beams of light, were coming from different projectors and illuminating one object: personality. Each beam brightened only one side of the object, but together, they show a much clearer and detailed picture. Each tradition brought something new, something promising, as well as something controversial and exciting to our knowledge of personality. Using this analogy, we could see various traditions as relentless attempts to deepen and broaden our knowledge. It is about enlightenment and educated action, after all.

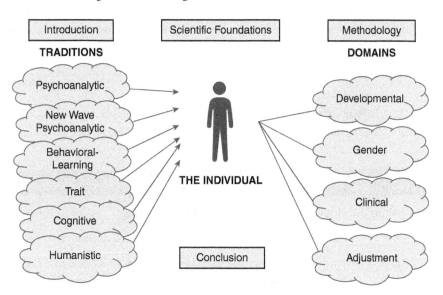

Domains. Our scientific journey in the fields of personality will be incomplete without a critical examination of knowledge in several specific "real-life" contexts or circumstances, which we will call for convenience *the domains*. The book examines personality within four of such domains: developmental, gender, clinical, and adjustment. This is how the next group of chapters is structured:

- Personality is never static. It is evolving, developing. We, as humans, are constantly growing, maturing, and changing. The *developmental domain* allows us to approach personality from the life span, dynamic perspective.

- Personality is gendered. For centuries, societal traditions, values, beliefs, and laws have been rooted in the male–female dichotomy, yet the concept of gender is evolving. The gender domain in the study of personality is an area of many discoveries and new, fascinating discussions.

- Personality can be described within the continuum of "normal" and "abnormal" features. The clinical domain approaches personality from the position of psychopathology and individual malfunction. True, there is always a way out of suffering. There must be. The chapter discusses them as well.

- Personality is about facing life's challenges and adjusting to them. We constantly cope with threats and sudden transformations, as well as long-awaited, life-changing events. Within the adjustment domain, we will focus together on the coping individual, who learns and adjusts—as the human being should.

- Personality has a digital dimension. This is a new context that stands for the digital reality of our online communications, YouTube channels, video games, and social networks—and within which an individual's personality unfolds, influences others, and thus can be studied. A field of passionate speculations a few years ago, this domain is now being examined in a growing stream of fascinating studies.

Pedagogy

- Each chapter begins with three learning objectives. For example, here are the objectives for Chapter 6 on the trait tradition:

LEARNING OBJECTIVES

After reading this chapter, you should be able to do the following:

- Identify the main principles and historic contexts of the trait tradition.

- Discuss several major approaches to personality from the trait tradition including Allport's' "four columns," Cattell's "16PF," and Eysenk's "E and N" and the Big Five research.

- Identify ways to apply the key principles of the trait tradition to individual experience and behavior.

Each chapter begins with a *vignette* or opening *case*, which serves as an informal introduction. Each vignette typically contains questions relevant to the chapter's contents. This is how Chapter 10 begins the discussion of gender, identity, and personality:

Kelsey has finally answered the question that most of us do not even have to ask: *Who am I . . . a boy or a girl?* Kelsey already knew that some people are born in female bodies but feel male inside, and some other people have male bodies but feel female. She also knew the meaning of the words *gay, unisex*, and *transgender*. They have become very common in the English language (although, frankly, many people still have only a superficial view of the meaning of these words). Today, more people speak freely about their true identity and overcome the fear of being condemned and discriminated against for their feelings. Yet Kelsey had a more complicated challenge—a feeling that neither *male* nor *female* categories were appropriate for her self-identity: She felt she was neither a girl nor a boy.

Growing up, Kelsey was always puzzled when she needed to cross the box on application forms that referred to male or female identity. Then there were the small but important choices at school: Which sports teams to play on? Which locker room to use? Which doors of gender-specific bathrooms to push? This struggle with self-perception was not about being straight or gay. This was not about being "boyish" or a "manly" girl. This was a matter of Kelsey being honest about yourself as a human being.

Meanwhile, Kelsey decided to use a pronoun that felt right when describing herself: *they*. By 2022, about one quarter of Americans said in surveys they personally knew at least one individual who went by gender-neutral pronouns such as "they" instead of "he" or "she." Younger people, more than 40% of them, are especially likely to know at least one person who uses gender-neutral pronouns.

- Several *Check Your Knowledge* boxes are placed strategically within chapters to help with immediate review of key points and facts. This is just one example of this feature from Chapter 13, which discusses the digital domain of personality:

CHECK AND APPLY YOUR KNOWLEDGE

1. Explain *personality lensing* in the digital context.
2. What are the key psychological and behavioral changes linked to the use of the web?
3. Who are (or what are) mindclones? Do you think you have your own mindclone? If yes, what is it?

- Each chapter has a *Self-Reflection* box, which typically presents a case in point, a life episode, or a research summary, and then asks students to apply the knowledge to themselves. This is just one example of this feature from Chapter 12, which discusses adjustment.

Self-Reflection

Every person has his or her own pathway to be optimistic. However, many people near you don't know how to find this path or whether the path is necessary to be optimistic. Some even say that being pessimistic is better than having a rosy view about life because pessimists are right in their judgment most of the time. One of psychology's main goals is to help people gain confidence, inner strength, and happiness. Do you think that cultivating optimism in people is a better way than to cultivate pessimism instead? Or is it better, from your personal view, to help people to lower their expectations rather than expect something great that is unlikely to happen?

Visual Summaries

Each chapter has a *Visual Summary* at the end of it. This will help students better prepare for exams and may serve as a reference as well. This is a sample of such summary from Chapter 11:

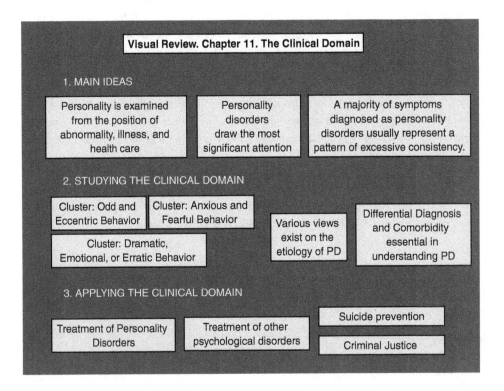

- In *On the Web*, additional support for the text can be found on the book website at www.sagepub.com/shiraev, where you can find practice and discussion questions, research updates, facts, and links. See the example here from Chapter 4:

New to The Second Edition

- Structure: The book has fewer chapters, compared to the first edition, related to theory (in particular, two chapters, Chapters 4 and 5, related to the psychoanalytic tradition in personality psychology are now combined into a single chapter).

- Structure: The book has a brand-new Chapter 13 on the digital domain of personality. This chapter is about examining a new "real-life" context of online communications, YouTube channels, video games, and social networks—and within which an individual's personality unfolds, influences others, and thus can be studied. A field of passionate speculations a few years ago, this domain is now examined in a growing stream of fascinating studies with far-reaching applications.

- Content: The book—based on the author's research and publications—significantly and critically expands the discussion of racism, sexism, antisemitism, and other forms of racial, religious, and ethnic prejudice. The new edition expands the coverage of LGBTQ+ issues including prejudice against and cultural stereotypes.

- Content: The book substantially expands its coverage of cross-cultural issues related to personality based on studies from various world's regions.

- Content: The new edition critically discusses a new subject related to empirical psychological research about the impact of the COVID pandemic on people's behavior and experience across the globe.

- Research: New data are added from the fields of neuroscience regarding longevity; pregnancy; drug use; and genetic foundations of individual features and traits such as stubbornness, openness to experience, adventurism, honesty, altruism, and pessimism.

- Research: New data from the complimentary to psychology field of behavioral economics are added to better understand the ways people make useful and healthy decisions as well as mistakes.

To the Student

Know thyself, says the ancient aphorism. *Learn about yourself,* encourages today's popular maxim. The journey to understand the individual's personality is as old as humankind. This book will help you navigate through a wide range of theories and empirical studies about personality. You will examine theoretical assumptions, research summaries, and critical-thinking exercises. You will take tests based on this text. True, it is very important to be informed, knowledgeable, and confident with this knowledge. Yet today's professional is not a passive observer or a wise guru judging the word from a secluded place. Your knowledge will require action. When you turn a page or when you finish a chapter in the book, ask yourself these questions. Start looking for answers today.

"How did this knowledge help me to understand myself?"

Reliable knowledge takes more than observing things unfolding in front of you at this hour. Experts who study personality do more than register this event or that fact. They analyze the inner logic of these events and the ways these facts are interconnected. Therefore, we will need serious analysis, or the breaking up of something complex into smaller parts, to comprehend their important features and interactions. Apply this knowledge to yourself. Ask others to share their views and help you. It too takes skill to ask for their help. Again, after turning another page, ask yourself this:

"How can I use this knowledge to help others?"

To answer this question, you will have to gain broader, critical knowledge about other people. To make conclusions, you ought to study, analyze, and generalize not only the headlines popping up on the screen of your mobile device but also the rich database of facts, opinions, and theories accumulated over the years. You will need to familiarize yourself with some general "rules" and patterns of human behavior as exceptions to these rules. You know that we, as individuals, are unique. There are many people who may be like you, but there is nobody else exactly like you.

"How can I use this knowledge to make a bigger difference in life?"

Do not be surprised if you realize that with each chapter, the more you learn about personality, the more you will realize that there are many things you don't know. This awareness of the limitations of our knowledge will be a sign that you are growing as a professional. Always patiently test your conclusions against the stubborn realities of this ever-changing, complex world. Whatever question, idea, or doubt you have, ask your professor, or email me, the author of this text. We will listen and, hopefully, provide you with a good answer. We also will learn from you.

Welcome to the journey, which we will undertake together.

ACKNOWLEDGEMENTS

I am very grateful for the insightful feedback and help of my colleagues and reviewers, the constant efforts of several research assistants, and the patience and understanding of my family members. Valuable contributions, help, and encouragement for this book came from many individuals. I certainly acknowledge Reid Hester for suggesting and supporting this project from the start. I appreciate the support of David Sears and Barry Collins from the University of California, Los Angeles, as well as my late mentors, James Sidanius from Harvard University and Cheryl Koopman from Stanford University. They gave me a jump start. I certainly thank David Levy from Pepperdine University who taught me about critical thinking in psychology during our time at UCLA and during our work on numerous publications. My special thanks to Sergei Tsytsarev from Hofstra University, Denis Sukhodolsky from Yale University, Phil Tetlock from the University of Pennsylvania, Martina Klicperova from the Czech Academy of Sciences, and Larisa Tsvetkova and Olga Makhovskaya from the Russian Academy of Educational Sciences. Thank you, my dear colleagues from our international research lab, especially Jennifer Keohane from University of Baltimore, Serge Samoilenko from George Mason University, and Martijn Icks from University of Amsterdam for your relentless critical analysis of my work. A word of appreciation to John and Judy Ehle, Vladislav Zubok, Dmitry Shiraev, Dennis Shiraev, Nicole Shiraev, Alex Shiraev, Sophie Shiraev, and Oh Em Tee. I can never thank them enough.

This book received constant attention and support from the dynamic, highly professional team at SAGE: Reid Hester (again, he initiated this project), Nathan Davidson, Jane Haenel, Sarita Sarak, Judith Newlin, Kassi Radomski, Beth Ginter, and Amy Harris. I thank them all for their professionalism and care.

A special word of appreciation is due to the administration, faculty, staff, and students at my academic institutions, where I have been consistently provided with an abundance of support, assistance, and validation.

Everything is to be continued . . .

ABOUT THE AUTHOR

Eric Shiraev is a professor, researcher, and author working and living in Virginia, near Washington, DC. He received his academic degrees at St. Petersburg University in Russia and completed a postdoctoral program in the United States at the University of California, Los Angeles. He has served in various teaching and research positions at St. Petersburg University, Northern Virginia Community College, Oregon State University, George Washington University, and at George Mason University. He has authored and edited 25 books, including several textbooks in multiple editions, such as *A History of Psychology* (SAGE). He has published numerous papers, essays, and reviews in the fields of cross-cultural psychology, political psychology, and individual reputation. He is a co-founder and head of Character Assassination and Reputation Politics Research Lab. His recent research involves the study—conducted together with a dynamic international scholarly team—of character attacks and defenses against them across times and cultures. He continues writing songs for pop singers in Europe, some of whom are famous. For updates and discussions of ongoing and new academic projects, follow him on LinkedIn, X/Twitter, and Facebook.

FOUNDATIONS

INTRODUCING PERSONALITY

iStockphoto.com /Image Source

LEARNING OBJECTIVES

After reading this chapter, you should be able to do the following:

- Define personality and explain the personality concept in psychology.

- Describe the four major types of knowledge relevant to the study of personality.

- Identify and critically discuss the major dichotomies of personality.

- Identify ways to apply knowledge of personality psychology in specific interpersonal and professional settings.

WHO ARE YOU AS A PERSON?

If you had just one opportunity, at this very moment, how would you describe yourself as a person? How would you present yourself to people who don't know you? What would you convey about yourself to those who will live on this planet 100 years from now? You have just 30 seconds and 280 characters, between 40 and 70 words, like on X/Twitter. This is not an epitaph nor is it an obituary. This is about you today and now. So, who are you? Nice to meet you.

To answer, you perhaps start with, "My name is . . . ." But do our names have anything to do with who we are as persons? Maybe yes. In 800 essays on the topic "My Name," 75% of college-age respondents considered their first names as very important to these individuals' identity. Yet 1 in 10 of them suggested they wouldn't mind changing their first names for good. When people change their names, do they also change their personalities?

Would you then mention your last name in your self-description? Our surnames often reveal our family origins. And yet we can change our names due to marriage and choice. We can change our gender. The same is true about our citizenship.

Perhaps you then reveal where you are from and where you live now. Have you noticed this is one of the most frequently asked questions when people meet for the first time? Why do they ask it? Hopefully not to make stereotypical judgments about you based on your birthplace. Same is true about the question, "What do you do?" Being a nurse, artist, teacher, or engineer identifies your occupation. But does it define you as a person?

Maybe you will mention your religion if you are a devout follower of faith. Perhaps you include your education. But all these facts above, how strongly do they represent who you are? Certainly, you are not just a complex blend of references to names, birthplace, height and weight, religious practices, educational institutions, and occupations. There is something special, unique, outstanding about you as a human being. For example, things accomplished and places visited. Something you have experienced or overcame. Your moments of pain. Things and events that made you happy or sad. By the way, could you tell, are you an ambitious person? Are you a procrastinator? Do you wait, or do you prefer to get everything now? Do you like the company of others, or prefer to be left alone? Are you mostly a talker or a listener? Are you one who mostly shares or takes? And all in all, do you like yourself?

So little time and so little space for this question, "Who are you as a person?" In fact, many people in the past, when I asked them, felt a bit puzzled when answering this question. Some asked for more time to think. Others would reject the imposed word limit: 280 characters? Professor, are you kidding? Yet others would say openly how little they know about themselves and how important it is to reflect on the things that matter to them.

Who are you? Maybe your life is a constant search for answers to this question. Let this book be a humble helper along this journey.

IDENTIFYING PERSONALITY

Defining *personality* is one of the most challenging tasks in psychology. Psychologists often view personality according to their main theoretical positions held within the discipline. So, if this is the case, and the views of personality are very diverse, what should we do? No matter how dissimilar the views of personality are, we need to have an initial point of reference. Let's suggest a working definition: **Personality** is a stable set of behavioral and experiential characteristics of an individual. These characteristics manifest in many forms and include interests, drives, values, self-concept, abilities, and emotional patterns (American Psychological Association Dictionary of Psychology, 2022a). We should also understand that this definition isn't carved in stone: During our learning journey, we will have more than ample opportunity to reexamine and clarify this initial definition. But we need to start somewhere.

Explaining the Definition and Asking Questions

Details are important when we finish our projects. Yet they are no less important at the beginning of the journey. To make sure that we are on the same page from the start, consider the following questions and answers about the personality definition and its interpretations.

Q. Which characteristics of an individual do psychologists associate with what they call personality?

A. The American Psychological Association refers to configurations of "characteristics and behavior" (APA, Dictionary of Psychology, 2022a). Our working definition here also refers to patterns of *thinking, feeling,* and *behaving* (experience in psychology traditionally refers to thinking and feeling).

Q. Do we need to study every behavioral act and every moment of experience of individuals to judge their personality?

A. Of course not. We are looking only at relatively *stable* patterns and *enduring* features of behavior and experience. These features manifest in various life situations. Psychologists try to describe, measure, compare, and explain such patterns. Later we will turn to the study of personality **traits** as distinct and stable patterns of behavior and experience (Chapter 6 specifically focuses on traits).

Q. Does every individual have a personality?

A. It is logical to assume that personality has to be associated with, or remains inseparable, from a certain material or physical carrier, such as a human body. However, in many parts of the book, and particularly in Chapters 7 and 13, we will discuss whether personality can be viewed and understood independently from such a carrier.

Q. Do stones, bridges, paper bags, or atomic particles have personalities? What about machines or artificial intelligence applications? They can display distinct characteristics, features, and patterns.

A. Probably not. Personality—let's get back to the definition—refers to behavior and feelings. Bridges and paper bags do not feel. We can assign in our imagination certain personality qualities to these and other objects like to software or literary figures, but these will be the imaginative features based on rather creative, artistic comparisons.

Q. But do pets have personalities? Cats and dogs can feel.

A.   This is an intriguing question to which we will turn in Chapter 5. For the sake of certainty, let's accept for now that personality is something related to human beings (we will call them persons, individuals, people, women, men, intersex, and so on) as carriers of personality features. But we will not ignore the questions about machines and pets and whether they "have" personality.

Q.   Do our personalities "exist" after we die?

A.   This is a difficult question. We remember people who are no longer with us; very often, we keep memories of their lives and their personalities. Furthermore, there is physical (their belongings, for example) or digital (their sites and online pics) evidence associated with such personalities. How many people who have already passed away still have their pages on social networks? On their pages, we can see the pictures of smiling, acting, and living individuals chitchatting about their lives and the world. Their profiles are there, but the hosts aren't. In Chapters 5 and 13 we will discuss the meaning of individual immortality.

Q.   Can a human being have two or more personalities?

R.   Probably yes. There are individuals who become impostors, pretending to be someone else for very long periods. Clinicians in the United States also recognize dissociative identity disorder (known as "multiple personality disorder"). But some psychologists across the globe disagree with their U.S. colleagues. Although there have been probably many thousands of individuals who have claimed to have or experience several personalities, the validity of their self-reported symptoms is often disputed. We will examine personality from the mental illness perspective in Chapter 11.

Q.   Is there another personality or personalities exactly like yours?

A.   Probably yes and maybe no. It depends how we interpret "exactly" and how many personality features we compare. But if we look at just a few features of you, we can suggest that a person with similar features may be located very near you—a step or a link away. Just look around.

Three Principles Explaining Personality

Although personality may appear as a theoretical concept, it is also very important in psychological practice at least for three reasons.

The first one has to do with *consistency.* The personality concept helps psychologists establish consistency in the individual's observable qualities and characteristics; based on that, they make predictions regarding the person's behavior. For example, consider a client who is never late for her appointments with a therapist, who writes down questions to the therapist before each therapeutic session, and who meticulously follows all the therapist's recommendations. Most likely, this person will be expected to exhibit these and similar patterns of behavior in the future therapeutic sessions.

The second reason is about the practical value of the personality concept, or the *causation* of behavior. Personality is a concept indicating that an individual's behavior, feelings, or thoughts are not just direct and random responses to various outside influences. These behaviors, feelings, or thoughts are, to a degree, originated "from within": We know that some people tend to be more secretive, open-minded, anxious, or aggressive than others. Personality features, for that reason, appear as an underlying force, influencing a person's interactions with the social environment. Some of these features can be very powerful causes of behavior, whereas others are only weak ones. For example, openness to experience, as a personality trait, may result in extremely promiscuous and dangerous behavior in one individual; although in another one, openness to experience may cause many helping, generous, and unselfish acts.

The third reason has to do with *organization*. People display thousands of seemingly unrelated characteristics. The systemic approach that has been used in psychological studies of personality helps psychologists delineate a few salient qualities of an individual, which are supposed to relate to each other. In a way, these qualities can represent a "summary" for what the individual is. Some characteristics are essential and central to the person. For example, five characteristics—neuroticism, extroversion, agreeableness, conscientiousness, and openness to experience—have been found by many psychologists to be the "core" or the most salient traits and were named the Big Five, which we will study later (Costa & McCrae, 1995). The more essential the quality is, the better it describes the essence of the individual's personality, the more it distinguishes this person from other people, and the more accurate it is in predicting the person's behavior.

Each of the central traits influences other secondary, less essential characteristics, which, in turn, affect a set of relatively stable behaviors, or habits (see Figure 1.1).

You can imagine that traits can be organized in "trees," with each salient trait (that represents an individual's personality) manifesting in secondary traits and then in very specific behavioral habits. Introversion (one of the most salient traits), for example, may lead to a person's continuous avoidant behavior of certain friends (secondary trait) and later may develop into a stable pattern of habits that involves enjoying a wide range of solitary activities at home, such as playing video games.

Studying personality is one of the most intriguing enterprises in psychology. In this journey, we will pursue at least two goals (Hogan & Bond, 2009). First, we will be trying to find out in which ways people are alike. Second, we will try to see in which ways each individual is different. Personality is the unity and competition of opposites, to which we turn in the next section.

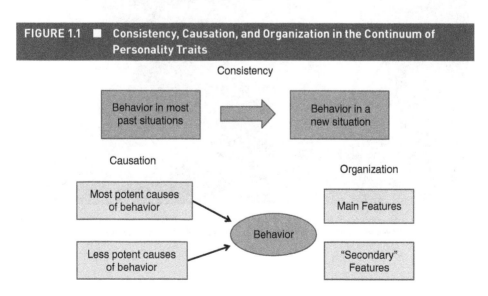

FIGURE 1.1 ■ Consistency, Causation, and Organization in the Continuum of Personality Traits

CHECK AND APPLY YOUR KNOWLEDGE

1. How does the American Psychological Association define *personality*? How would you define personality? How different is your definition from the one produced in this chapter? In what ways?
2. Explain consistency, organization, and causation—all as applied to personality.

PERSONALITY'S DICHOTOMIES

In many ways, personality can be described as a coexistence and interaction of at least two conditions that are opposite to each other. They are called opposites, or dichotomies. However, because they coexist, they are dependent on each other. As an example, the categories *big* or *kind* cannot be meaningful unless there are categories such as *small* or *mean*. In other words, the opposite is necessary for the existence of the other, and one manifests together with the other. Let's further explain this in the following illustrations. We will use examples from history, most recent research in psychology, and daily experiences.

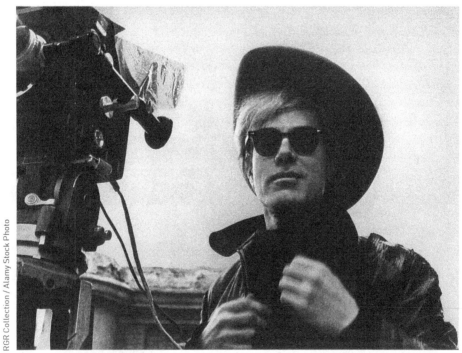

RGR Collection / Alamy Stock Photo

PHOTO 1.1 Most critics say Andy Warhol was a unique person. What does it mean to be unique? Are you a unique person? If not, why? If yes, which individual features or traits, from your view, make you markedly different from other people?

Personality Is Unique and Typical

Andy Warhol was and remains one of the most fascinating and internationally acclaimed artists ever and especially of the 20th century. He stood out because of his unique art, but he was also outstanding because of his personality (see Photo 1.1). Many who knew him claimed that his personality—a pattern of his actions, pranks, ideas, and emotional expressions—was unquestionably one of a kind. Warhol maintained the unique ability to surprise, shock, and inspire—all at the same time. One of his gifts was his ability to combine the incompatible just to see what happened. He had his mother sign his artwork. He asked other people to impersonate him on a lecture tour. He made movies of objects that never moved and used actors who could not act at all, and he made art out of boxes and cans that did not look like art (Menand, 2010). His personality was a spectacular bundle of positive energy, destined to shock and impress. And yet this type of behavior, this pattern of thinking, feeling, and acting, is not necessarily unique! His behavior and experiences exhibited a particular type of personality that, in theory and practicality, can be found in other people; someone's apparent uniqueness can be typical. Warhol belongs to a type of individuals who are predictable in their unpredictability: They are showy, flamboyant, and intriguing most of the time. There are many other people who think and act in a similar way. Being "typical" is, in fact, about combining or exhibiting the essential characteristics of many people.

We are similar to many other people because we share related genetic characteristics with them. We are also subject to comparable physical and environmental factors, such as geographic location or persistent weather patterns. Circumstances we all experience together may "produce" in us similar behavioral and emotional features, such as persistent despair, pride, or aggressiveness; however, most of these circumstances are interconnected (Astuti & Bloch, 2010), as we will see in Chapter 2. Sure, we shouldn't expect a 100% match of all personality features between any two individuals—even so-called *identical twins* are not necessarily identical since during their mother's pregnancy, they have different placement in the womb and tend to receive different quantities of nutrition and exposure to hormones (Segal, 2012)—but we all are different, and we all are similar to a certain degree.

Let's briefly summarize the topic of uniqueness. Our personality features are unique, and as distinguishable patterns of behavior and experience, they will be called personality traits. As strokes of a pencil or coal on a piece of paper define the important features of a portrait, traits help in defining personality (the term *trait* comes from the Latin *tractus*, which means "a stroke"). Taken together in a combination, our traits form a certain **type**. *Type* refers to a kind or category of elements or features sharing similar characteristics or qualities. Individuals thus displaying similar combinations of traits may be considered as belonging to the same type. We, as individuals, are unique. However, our apparent uniqueness can be . . . typical.

SELF-REFLECTION

Would you like to meet another you? Imagine that scientists have cloned a biological individual or produced a device empowered by artificial intelligence who (or that) looks, thinks, and acts exactly like you. This would be a bot or another individual displaying the same personality features that you have. Would you like to meet this person? What would you learn from this person? Would you be willing to have this person as your close friend, or would you rather keep your distance from this individual?

Personality Features Can Be Central and Peripheral

Do you think of yourself as mostly an optimist, pessimist, or somewhere in between? Are you pessimistic in some situations and optimistic in others? Or are you optimistic most of the time? Some personality features are **central** because they tend to be somewhat wide-ranging and present—to various degrees—in most people, most of the time. Consider, for example, openness to experience (mentioned earlier in this chapter), which includes a combination of imagination, aesthetic sensitivity, attentiveness to inner feelings, preference for variety, and intellectual curiosity. **Peripheral** personality features tend to be more specific and also tend to appear in particular individuals in specific individual or cultural circumstances. Also consider, for example, *sensitivity to humor*, which is a tendency to react angrily (or not to react) to actual or imaginable insults. Central features are not necessarily more important than peripheral, and the differences between them are not clear-cut.

Now let's talk about **pessimism**—a persistent, broad-spectrum belief in and anticipation of undesirable, negative, or damaging outcomes. Pessimism can be a central feature. It can be prevalent in some individuals (do you know some of them?) but not in others. Pessimism, however, may manifest in a range of peripheral features. One person with a strong propensity for pessimism may display persistent sadness or constant lack of initiative or chronic lack of self-discipline, which may affect individual performance. Research shows that such individuals are less likely to be successful in job searches compared to optimists with similar skills (Kaniel et al., 2010). Yet other people with a propensity for pessimism can display a very different pattern: They are always prepared for possible, undesirable outcomes and thus practice self-discipline and careful preparations to avoid them. Studies show, in fact, that pessimism encourages some people to live more carefully by taking serious health and safety precautions (Lang et al., 2013). Pessimism as a central feature or trait in yet another person may manifest as a secondary trait in the form of **cynicism**, which is persistent distrust of other people's motives. People prone to cynicism tend to question others' good intentions and believe that such intentions and actions are not altruistic but rather selfish. People who tend to be pessimistic are not necessarily cynical; however, a person who tends to by cynical is likely to be pessimistic. A cynical person does not have to be prone to sadness or display a lack of self-discipline. Such individuals tend to distrust others and treat them with suspiciousness (Stavrova & Ehlebracht, 2018).

As we will see later in other chapters, the interactions between central and peripheral traits tend to be extremely complex. At times they can seem puzzling.

Research helps clarify the interaction between central and peripheral personality features (see Figure 1.2). For example, people have been shown to have a general tendency to **self-enhance** or deem our self as superior to peers (in other words, we tend to believe that we are somewhat better, smarter, and more reasonable than others). Self-enhancement can be understood as a central trait. However, studies reveal that people in Western cultures (Western Europe,

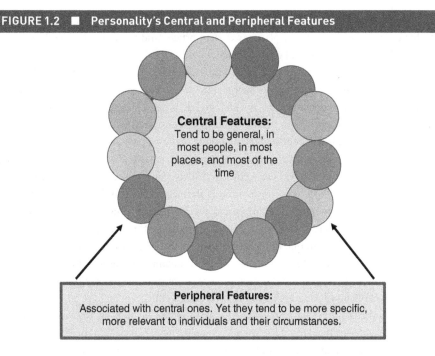

FIGURE 1.2 ■ Personality's Central and Peripheral Features

Central Features:
Tend to be general, in most people, in most places, and most of the time

Peripheral Features:
Associated with central ones. Yet they tend to be more specific, more relevant to individuals and their circumstances.

Australia, New Zealand, and North America) tend to self-enhance differently than people in East Asian cultures. Westerners were likely to self-enhance on traits relevant to individualism (being ambitions, decisive, etc.), and Easterners tended to self-enhance more on attributes relevant to collectivism, such as duty, responsibility, and the like (Gaertner et al., 2010). Will a similar study reveal the same tendencies in 2030? Some central personality features may be determined largely by biological factors (such as genetics), as research suggests, which may also affect their relative universality and constancy. Peripheral traits may appear as adjustments to specific social circumstances and can be associated with an individual's lifestyle. These peripheral features often change without affecting central features (McCrae & Costa, 1999). Imagine a woman who has been shy and withdrawn in her childhood. She felt most of the time uncomfortable being among strangers in her home country. In college, in The United Kingdom, however, she grows increasingly comfortable when interacting with most fellow students. Yet still, in most situations outside the campus, she remains largely shy and appears somewhat withdrawn.

Personality Is Stable and Evolving

A Christmas Carol is a masterpiece by the great English writer Charles Dickens. Its main character is Ebenezer Scrooge, whose personality is distinctively set early in the novel. He is consistent: He is mean, greedy, rude, cold, and full of envy. He is impolite to others, unhelpful, and lacks empathy. On Christmas Eve, Scrooge undergoes a miraculous and sweeping psychological transformation. After three spirits visit him at night and reveal to him how unhappy and meaningless his life is, he wakes up a different man. He suddenly turns into a kind, compassionate, generous, and caring individual. He dramatically changes his patterns of behavior and thought! Though Scrooge is a character in a fairy tale, you may find many examples of people who almost suddenly and swiftly change their behavior, their beliefs, and even their lifestyle. Change is part of our lives. Yet some changes take place faster than others, and some people experience them more often than others. Some tend not to change.

Stability is part of our lives as well. Research shows that people are inclined to challenge logic and math only to remain loyal to their stable, deep-seated values (Grant, 2021; Kahan, 2012). Do you know of people who have not changed their main habits for years? Some of them prefer to act in the politest way to avoid any form of confrontation. Others constantly seek action, engagement, and new conflicts. Some others prefer to pick the same type of a battle, like Jacques Vergèswas, an attorney who was always eager to defend "very bad guys." Among his defendants, almost exclusively, were accused terrorists, gangsters, dictators, bankrupts, and thieves. He defended the Nazi war criminal Klaus Barbie and the Cambodian dictator Khieu Samphan. He was a confrontational attorney and a feisty human being; his key strategy in life and in the courtroom was to accuse the accuser and challenge the challenger. His biographers say that he learned this technique in childhood, when his father taught him to throw stones at bullies. Vergèswas remained in a constant war of arguments with others. Big deal, one may say—he worked for money! Not necessarily. In very many cases, he worked *pro bono*, for free, just because he really loved what he was doing (McFadden, 2013).

Stability and change are based on many interconnected influences. Research has established that through our individual life span we keep many of our personality characteristics relatively stable: A challenger and troublemaker is likely to retain his or her "feistiness" for a long time. However, adults and children as groups, for example, tend to have a different sense of humor or the propensity to laugh about certain themes because our general perceptions of what is funny when we are children differs from our perception as adults (Stanley et al., 2014). Your parents may laugh at something you consider not funny at all. Studies also reveal that central features tend to change slowly, and peripheral ones may change faster. Change is susceptible to time. Most personality-related changes take place during childhood. Our personalities become relatively stable in middle age and are less changeable after we reach 50 (Roberts & Friend-DelVecchio, 2000). Yet many aspects of personality in older age, as research shows, are likely to relate to personality features in childhood (Harris et al., 2016).

Considering this research, should we assume that the transformation that has taken place in Scrooge's personality was rather atypical because older adults are not that susceptible to sudden personality changes compared to the young? It is probably so. But remember that our personalities are unique; statistical tendencies suggesting how we should feel or react in a certain type of situation are only expectations based on probabilities. Personality is supposed to be stable, and at the same time, it is evolving because stability and change are both adaptive features. As humans, we continually adjust to a changing social and physical environment. We often learn from our mistakes. We tend to grow wiser with age and better understand our personal boundaries (wisdom, among other things, is about knowing your own limitations). We tend to imitate other people's successful actions. We learn about connecting certain behaviors to the circumstances in which these behaviors occur. Some learn that being greedy is beneficial at times. Others, like Scrooge, learn kindness. Jacques Vergèswas, the lawyer who loved defending notorious individuals, saw his work as rewarding, thus allowing him to fulfill his individual skills and potential as an attorney.

Early Hindu writings (Chapter 2) from thousands of years ago suggest that some individuals are like "carvings" on a rock—their individual features are solid and long lasting. Other people are like "carvings" on the earth because their mental sates are fast passing. Yet others are compatible with marks on the water because they are extremely changeable.

PAUL J. RICHARDS / Staff

PHOTO 1.2 Connie Picciotto, who died in 2016 at the age of 70, carried on one of the longest continuous acts of political protest in the United States by keeping vigil, day and night, near the White House since the 1970s to protest nuclear weapons. Some personality features can be viewed as "normal" in some social situations and as "abnormal" in others. Could you suggest such features and situations? Discuss an individual's trait such as stubbornness, for starters.

Personality Can Be Viewed as "Normal" and "Abnormal"

Connie Picciotto (1946–2016) kept vigil near the White House for more than 30 years (see Photo 1.2). Day after day, she peacefully demonstrated there against nuclear weapons. Two large boards behind her with messages in all capital letters read "BAN ALL NUCLEAR WEAPONS OR HAVE A NICE DOOMSDAY" and "LIVE BY THE BOMB, DIE BY THE BOMB." She carried on one of the longest continuous acts of political protest in the United States: Five presidents resided in the White House since the first day of her protest. Thousands of tourists saw and photographed her there. Some stopped and talked to her. (The author of this book talked to her briefly, too.) Others smirked and passed by. Why did this woman spend more than half of her adult life in front of the White House? Why did she choose such an extraordinary method of activism? Was she . . . normal?

As you might know, effective activism requires a measure of unconventionality, but when nonconventional behavior is consistent and inflexible, it can be judged as deviant (Gibson, 2013). However, don't we all act in unconventional ways from time to time? And who is the judge of our actions?

We the people, as ultimate judges, create conventional rules to distinguish between acceptable and objectionable behavior. Moderation, modesty, honesty, and friendliness as individual traits are likely to be considered desirable and appropriate. Most people in most circumstances view these traits positively. In contrast, we recognize inappropriate, undesirable, or unhealthy patterns of actions and thought. We avoid, criticize, or reject them; for example, being a consistent liar is typically frowned upon. What other commonly undesirable patterns could you name?

Notice that judgments about normal (appropriate) and abnormal (inappropriate) traits of a person vary across circumstances, generations, and cultures. For example, flashy disco clothes at a "Remember the 70s" party would be expected, but wearing such clothes to an afternoon biology class lecture would be considered unusual and would definitely turn a few heads. Likewise, some personality traits may be seen as unusual, ambiguous, or even abnormal when you apply one set of social standards to judge them. **Tolerance threshold** is a measure of tolerance or intolerance toward specific personality traits in a society or within a cultural group. Tolerance thresholds can be high or low, and they are tested in specific situations. The musical personality David Bowie's eccentric behavior was largely accepted a couple decades ago and even admired because people, and particularly millions of his followers across the globe, expected him, as a creative person, singer, and performer to act in these unusual ways. High thresholds indicate relative societal tolerance to varying personality traits, whereas low thresholds signify relative societal intolerance against specific behaviors associated with certain personality traits.

Particular personality features are defined and categorized in medical terms. **Personality disorders** are enduring patterns of behavior and inner experience that deviate markedly from the expectations of the individual's culture. It is not just being different. It is a persistent behavioral pattern that leads to the individual's distress and impairment in one or several important areas of functioning (Akhtar, 2002). Clinicians today recognize personality disorders as a special diagnostic category, and there is growing consistency in the way these disorders are diagnosed in different countries. Overall, personality disorders represent a deviation (and there are various degrees of such deviation) from what is considered "standard" personality in a specific social and cultural environment (Yang et al., 2010). We will turn to this discussion in Chapter 11.

Is it accurate to assume that "what's typical is normal; what's normal is good," and therefore, "what's not typical is abnormal; what's abnormal is bad"? Notice how, in each case, a description of what exists becomes converted into a prescription of what we like or dislike. As Scottish philosopher Hume pointed out more than 200 years ago, values, ethics, and morality are based not on logic or reason but on the sentiments and public opinions of a particular society. Thus, no description of human behavior, however accurate, can ever ordain what is "right" or "wrong" behavior (Levy, 1997). It makes no difference whether we are studying cultural customs, religious convictions, political beliefs, educational practices, recreational activities, sexual proclivities, or table manners. If most people display a particular behavior, it does not necessarily make it right; if most people do not, it does not automatically make it wrong.

Personality Is Rooted in Nature and Nurture

Did you ever notice how quickly U.S. presidents age right before your eyes? Passing the middle of their 4-year term in office, they look tired, their faces are wrinkled, and their eyes signal fatigue. Their body language sends a desperate call for a long vacation. Science has established that aging is a biologically programmed mechanism. However, today's science also shows that non biological factors play a significant role in how the body ages. For example, chronic stress, overeating, or an inactive lifestyle accelerates aging (Epel, 2009, 2012). And this is true for every age group, including those who are in their 20s.

The debates about complex interactions of natural (biological) and social (cultural) factors have always been the focus of attention in social sciences and psychology. The essence of the **nature–nurture debates** was not necessarily about the dilemma of whether it is exclusively nature or nurture that makes us who we are as people. Some emphasized the importance of biological factors affecting human development, behavior, and experience. Others underlined the crucial role of social factors. Later, these views merged. A century ago, psychologists began viewing human beings as products of both the natural world and the social environment (Münsterberg, 1915). The assumption about the dual impact of natural and social factors on an individual's functioning is generally accepted today.

Consider the pseudobulbar affect, or PBA. This is a syndrome characterized by persistent, involuntary, and uncontrollable laughing and crying episodes or a combination of both (Ahmed & Simmons, 2013). Medical research indicates these symptoms are related to neurological disease or injury, which are natural factors. Yet these natural factors affect the behavior and experiences of a living, breathing, functioning person; they have a serious impact on the individual's social interactions, work, education, relationships, and the overall quality of life. It is common that individuals with PBA become socially withdrawn, shy, and overanxious over the years (Colamonico et al., 2012; Gordon, 2012). Why? People are aware of their symptoms, notice other people's negative reactions, and often feel embarrassed by strangers' remarks. Although this syndrome is a neurological condition, it can profoundly affect individuals' social behavior, self-esteem, and the way they see other people (Miller, 2021).

The question remains open about many specific mechanisms of nature–nurture interactions. Most debates focus on the extent or degree of the impact of such factors and on the ways our knowledge can be applied to practice.

Personality Refers to Body and Mind

Research showed that people who are ill but remain optimistic and strongly believe they will get healthy, tended to recover somewhat better than pessimists (Bryan et al., 2004). This may be a fine illustration of how the optimistic mind affects the body. Or does it? Could it be that healthy people tend to be more optimistic than those who are unhealthy? Understanding the mechanisms of the mind–body interactions has been one of the most challenging topics of research and intellectual debates in the history of science and one of the most intriguing problems in psychology (Gergen, 2001).

For centuries, many scholars believed that experimental science was incapable of studying the "higher" mental processes, including values, will, or beliefs. How could one, they argued, measure compassion? Others disagreed. They believed in the possibility of the scientific study of the mind through research on the nervous system and the brain. These opposing views stood for a global scientific and cultural divide between the two "camps" of thinkers. One often criticized the other for reducing the complexity of mental life to, practically, the movements of molecules through body fibers. The other camp, in response, accused its critics of backwardness and even ignorance (i.e., How can you not study the mind scientifically?). Nevertheless, using the most advanced methods of neurophysiology and computer science, today's researchers face a challenge in measuring the subjective elements of a person's experience. Yet they are firm in their assumptions that personality features are inseparable from our body. Neuroscientists have long associated personality with the functioning of the human brain (see Chapter 2). Leading researchers refer, for instance, to the functioning of the *brain stem* and the *hypothalamus* as key brain structures that has something to do with self-awareness, an important feature of personality (Damasio, 2012; Parvizi & Damasio, 2001).

The body and mind interact in remarkable ways. Remember the study showing that optimists who believe they will get healthier tend to achieve more positive results than bitter pessimists? Other studies reveal that optimism and high self-esteem contribute to healthy habits (Bryan et al., 2004). An individual's strong sense of personal control has a significant impact on health: If you believe that you are in charge of your life, you'll stay healthier than those who are not so sure about who is in charge (Johnson & Krueger, 2005). There is supportive evidence for the positive impact of our deep-seated positive beliefs, including love and faith, on health and behavior (Myers, 2008).

CHECK AND APPLY YOUR KNOWLEDGE

In the futuristic flick *Her,* the main character (Theodore) is a shy, bored, and frustrated man who is about to get a divorce. Driven by his loneliness, he purchases software that serves as his personal assistant. This thinking-and-talking operating system can self-advance and grow cognitively and emotionally. Theodore picks a gender for the system and calls her Samantha. Gradually, as they spend many hours "together," Theodore falls in love with Samantha (or what she represents): a kind, smart, gentle, and compassionate "being." At one point, Theodore becomes jealous of her for interacting with other clients who have purchased her services. The problem, of course, is that Samantha isn't human.

This film may be labeled as scientific fiction. Yet to some, *Her* is more than sci-fi entertainment. Technology guru and futurist Ray Kurzweil has already proposed that by 2045 humans will have achieved digital immortality by uploading their minds to computers. Humans, because of digital immortality, will overcome the need for a biological body for survival. Futurists who subscribe to this idea agree and argue that advances in neural engineering and modeling of brain function will make it possible to reproduce human minds in a digital medium even earlier than we think (Kurzweil, 2012). People will be able to create virtual bodies and virtual reality in which the virtual reality will be as realistic as the actual reality (we will turn to this discussion in Chapter 7).

Questions
Let's assume that Kurzweil's project is successful, and in 5 or 10 years, people can upload their personality features to computers. What benefits could this technological project bring to you personally? What ethical problems would you anticipate if such a project is implemented?

Personality Is Active and Reactive

Classical psychological experiments conducted in several countries in the past showed that children from wealthier families tended to see coins as smaller than they were, while children from poor families overestimated the size of coins (Bruner & Goodman, 1947; Dawson, 1975). This is just a small illustration that our minds and bodies work differently when we lack something and feel it. Anyone who has a shortage of money, time, food, rest, sleep, or emotional support from others is likely to think and behave out of so-called **scarcity mindset**: a reaction to a shortage of resources. People thus concentrate more on pressing threats and necessities and reassess the value of certain things that are in short supply. The chronically lonely, as research shows, become more aware of other people's feelings and become better interpreters of other people's emotions. People who are short on money pay greater attention, compared to people with money, to price tags in stores. This scarcity mindset may become a useful, adaptive mechanism of acting and thinking, but it may also produce less adaptive responses. People in need tend to process less information, weakening their self-discipline, and are likely to make more logical errors than those without scarcity mindset. As such, if you are temporarily low on cash, you will likely score lower on cognitive tests compared to the life periods when you have enough money (Mullainathan & Shafir, 2013).

These research data seem to make good sense. We respond to conditions in which we live here and now. We tend to adjust to changing circumstances. Our personality traits are formed under the complex interaction of natural and social factors. It seems plausible that personality is a "product" of circumstances, and every step we take is a response to these circumstances.

This position or view in psychology is called **determinism**: Psychological phenomena are causally determined by preceding events or some identifiable factors. In theory, the more such factors we identify, the more understandable and predictable psychological phenomena become (Kenrick et al., 2003). Determinism encourages personality psychologists to (1) study the factors that influence personality and its various features, (2) explain personality by referring to these factors, and (3) predict its development in the future.

Determinism faces at least two challenges. First, there are too many unknown factors affecting our behavior and experience, so we simply cannot take into consideration all of them to explain personality. Second, these factors are interconnected and thus are not clearly identifiable. Psychologists generally avoid **fatalism**, which states that humans are not in control of their lives because something or somebody else predetermines or "programs" them. It can be God, fate, or chance. Psychologists today are likely to support the position called **self-determination**, which means that we, as individuals, generally are in control of our plans, actions, responses, minds, and personality features. The key word here is *generally*, which means that there are exceptions for this expectation. Supporters of self-determination tend to be reasonably optimistic.

CHECK AND APPLY YOUR KNOWLEDGE

1. Define *personality traits*. Explain central and peripheral traits. What traits do you think you have? Could you name them?
2. How does the story of Ebenezer Scrooge relate to the study of personality? Could you provide examples of individuals who have significantly and rapidly changed their personality features.
3. Explain the tolerance threshold. Give an example.
4. Discuss the case of Connie Picciotto. Was her persistent behavior "normal" or "abnormal" from your standpoint?
5. Give an example of scarcity mindset. Give an example in which you or another person acted this way.
6. Explain the difference between determinism, fatalism, and self-determination—all referring to personality.

PHOTO 1.3 Why do people tend to view narcissism negatively? Can narcissism as a trait be useful or helpful? In which situations?

APPROACHING PERSONALITY

In an influential book, *The Mirror Effect* (2009), the doctor and TV personality Drew Pinsky and his colleague S. Mark Young provided an intriguing account of a personality feature known as *narcissism*. The authors reviewed stories of people who displayed the important signs of narcissism in their behavior and judgments (see Photo 1.3). What were those signs? In a nutshell, people labeled *narcissistic* were prone to vanity, which is the excessive belief in a person's own superiority, outstanding talents, or irresistible appeal to others; these individuals persistently craved being the center of attention; they believed they were entitled to enjoy special perks unavailable to other people; and they were manipulative and capricious. Based on these stories, the authors made several conclusions:

- Narcissistic people are trapped between their own imagined magnificence, on the one hand, and emotional disconnection with other people, on the other.

- People, especially the young, pay too much attention to celebrity narcissists and copy their behavior; this is how many new narcissistic personalities are likely to develop.

- Celebrities do not become narcissists; rather, most narcissists are driven to become celebrities.

- The behavior of modern celebrities, as individuals, is much more dysfunctional than it was a decade or two ago.

- Narcissism is more prevalent these days than it has ever been in human history.

But how do Pinsky and Young make these far-reaching conclusions? How did they study these personality types? How do we know that the knowledge we are gaining from the book about narcissism—as a personality feature—is accurate and the book's generalizations are correct? If our goal is to gain knowledge about personality, we have to pay attention to knowledge and the ways we select it.

Let's define a few key terms first. **Knowledge** is information that has a purpose or use. We are particularly interested in knowledge related to personality. This knowledge has certainly not been "set" or finalized once and for all. It is constantly evolving. Take, for example, what people knew about shyness and behavioral inhibition. Centuries ago, persistent inhibitive behavior was primarily associated in the minds of scientists and doctors with an imbalance of vital liquids in the body. Later theories of the 19th century referred to the nervous system and its weakness as a major cause of shyness. Many studies in the 20th century referred to shyness as a complex behavioral reflex, while others focused on introversion, an underlying psychological layer. Yet more recent studies focused on a dynamic combination of psychological, cultural, and hereditary factors as foundations of shyness. We can safely state that today's knowledge of shyness is evolving (Carducci, 2017).

To gain knowledge about personality, some of us read peer-reviewed psychological papers, while others discuss issues on social media, yet others browse through stories in online tabloids. Many people look for these and other sources. Which of these sources convey knowledge: a peer-reviewed academic journal or an online blog? Which of these contain knowledge: a research paper on narcissistic personality or a popular book on the same subject? In fact, they all do. Knowledge remains knowledge, regardless of whether you find it interesting or boring. Knowledge can be accurate and inaccurate. For centuries, different people and groups observed human behavior and experience, described them, and then used this knowledge to pursue their goals—academic, religious, social, political, educational, business, humanitarian, etc. As a result, several types of psychological knowledge have emerged (see Table 1.1).

TABLE 1.1 ■ Four Types of Knowledge Related to Personality: A Preview	
Type of Knowledge	*Sources of Knowledge*
Scientific	Knowledge accumulated through research, systematic empirical observation, and evaluation of a wide range of psychological phenomena. Facts are obtained with the help of scientific research methodologies and rigorous verification by multiple sources, typically including educated and trained peer reviewers. Scientific knowledge evolves with new scientific evidence.
Popular (or Folk)	Everyday assumptions about psychological phenomena and behavior. Such assumptions are often expressed in the form of judgments, assumptions, beliefs, evaluations, or prescriptions. Popular opinions change frequently based on new facts or assumptions.
Values	A consistent set of beliefs about the world, the nature of good and evil, right and wrong, appropriate or inappropriate behavior, and the purpose of human life. Human values tend to be stable and are based on a certain organizing principal or central idea, which is often accepted uncritically.
Legal	Knowledge encapsulated in the law and detailed in rules and principles regulating people's behavior. Legal authorities commonly establish these rules, change them, and enforce them.

Four Types of Knowledge

Scientific Knowledge

The type of knowledge to which we will pay most attention in this book is **scientific knowledge**. Its major source is science, or systematic empirical observation, measurement, and evaluation of facts. It is rooted in the scientific method, which uses cautious research procedures designed to provide reliable and verifiable evidence (Gergen, 2001). Scientific knowledge is accumulated through research, or systematic empirical observation and evaluation of a wide range of psychological phenomena. Facts should be obtained with the help of sound research methodologies, which require rigorous verification by multiple sources. However, relevance of these facts, as well as relevance of scientific knowledge, is continually changing with time because of new research evidence (Kendler, 1999).

Supporters of the importance of scientific knowledge saw it for centuries as the exclusive arbiter of truth in people's understanding of personality. However, what was accepted as scientific and what was not varied greatly throughout history, all based on religious, political, and cultural values of the time. Take the individual's emotional domain, for example. Over 2,500 years ago, the ancient Greek philosopher Democritus believed that the movement of atoms of different shape and speed should have influenced an individual's various emotional states. More than 400 years ago, René Descartes, the French-born scientist, associated emotions with the activities of "animal spirits" passing through the body's vascular system. Later, according to the James–Lange concept of the late 19th century, there were bodily reactions that evoked experiences that a person then labeled as *emotions*. The Cannon–Bard theory of the 20th century explained emotions as signals that cause an individual's bodily reactions. In the 1920s, the physiologist Ivan Pavlov in Russia (a Nobel Prize Winner) and the psychologist John Watson in the United States (the President of the American Psychological Association) insisted that emotions were an individual's learned reflexes. Can you guess which of these views developed by renown scientists represented scientific knowledge and which did not?

In fact, all of them represented science. All these theories attempted scientific yet incomplete, developing knowledge. New theories produced new scientific knowledge. This does not make the earlier views unscientific. They were just less scientific than modern views. Science is always a work in progress.

Popular Beliefs

Imagine you hear your friend saying, "Short people are enthusiastic, dynamic, and ambitious because they want to compensate psychologically for their height. They make great friends for the same reason: their height." How does your friend know about the connection between people's height and their behavior? Does this connection really exist?

Probably the most accessible type of knowledge to most people is **popular (or folk) beliefs**. They are assumptions that represent a form of "everyday psychology" created by the people and for the people (*folk* is an old Germanic word meaning "people"). It appears that the statement about short people belongs to this category. This judgment can easily be shared with other people who, in turn, may ignore, accept, or reject it. Popular beliefs related to personality are either individual or common assumptions about certain aspects of human behavior and experience. Some of these assumptions, such as the belief in the connections between people's height and their ambition, for example, are very broad. Others, such as how to ask for an extension of a paper's deadline in a psychology class, when the professor is in a good mood, could be very specific. Popular beliefs are, to some degree, our working assumptions about us and other people. These assumptions can be measured and tested. Yet often they are not. Many people simply believe them and use them as if they were based on facts. Popular beliefs refer to all areas of life. Consider important phenomena in our lives such as poverty. Bad things happen, and sometimes people struggle financially, but most get out of that tough situation. Yet why do some people remain chronically poor during their lives? And why do some people gain significant wealth even though they were not born rich? Think about the entrepreneurs like Jack Ma Yun in China or Elon Musk in the United States. People have different opinions on this subject. According to Pew Research, most Americans, for example, pointed to circumstances, not work ethic, for why people become rich or poor. Almost two thirds think the main reason for some people becoming wealthy is because they have had more advantages in life than most other people. More than 70% believed people remain poor because they have faced difficult obstacles in life. Yet almost one quarter of Americans maintained the belief that some people are poor because they have not worked as hard as others (Pew, 2020). Such views on poverty and wealth can affect many aspects of the individual's life: from choosing volunteer activities, to selecting hobbies, and voting in local and national elections. But how did these people get this knowledge? How do they know why people become rich and poor? What if their beliefs were wrong?

Many popular beliefs indeed tend to be accurate: They may be based on common sense, proven facts, or scientific research. This shouldn't be too surprising because people, as a group, tend to be careful and meticulous observers of behavior (Lock, 1981). For instance, from our own experience and from stories told by our friends, we know that people tend to become desperate during a lingering period of personal failures. We also learn that we all can have "good days" and "bad days" from time to time and that hope is often one of the greatest remedies against sadness and despair. We, as individuals, tend to distinguish between different kinds of popular knowledge. Some of us enjoy watching shows about vampires, yet we do not really believe in vampires roaming around. On the other hand, a streamed program on alcoholism may motivate some of us to make an intervention and to talk to a relative or friend in hopes of diverting them from excessive substance use.

It is also true that popular beliefs tend to be inconsistent. A person may have one opinion related to interpersonal skills of tall and short individuals but later agree with another person who has a different view. Popular beliefs can be inaccurate or simply wrong. Some people, for example, think that parental mistakes during early childhood can "cause" schizophrenia in children when they enter adulthood (science is skeptical about this belief). Or take, for example, popular assumptions about "permanent harms" of teenage masturbation—in particular, the belief that masturbation causes irreversible personality problems, intellectual decline, mental illness, or even blindness (Laqueur, 2004). Such unproven assumptions significantly impacted parental practices of millions of people around the globe and especially vast cultural prohibitions in many parts of the world related to women's sexuality (Kaur & Lindinger-Sternart, 2020).

Knowledge related to personality and designed for mass consumption is called *popular psychology*, or simply **pop psychology**. Pop psychology reaches people primarily through the media—television, streaming services, podcasts, social media, or popular books. This information tends to be simple and often sensational. Although professionals—who write for social media, popular blogs, or appear on YouTube—tend to have advanced degrees in psychology or medicine (and many of their ideas are valuable), it takes an average viewer's effort to filter sensational ideas or unproven generalizations from facts. Therefore, we will constantly need to learn and critically review many popular beliefs related to personality, human behavior, emotions, and the applications of these beliefs.

Values

In contrast to folk beliefs, **values** are rather stable perceptions about the world and the individual's place in it. Values refer to the nature of good and evil, purpose of human existence, life and death, right and wrong behavior, sexual practices, gender roles, and so forth. Values are different from popular beliefs because they are grounded on a set of unwavering principles, often accepted without critical evaluation. Tradition and authorities, including parents, often become sources of these principles. Values are deep-seated beliefs that do not necessarily require factual scrutiny. One person can hold a belief in the absolute necessity of being honest all the time and everywhere. This person is likely to practice this value. Another person believes that homosexuality is an abnormal

personality trait and a type of abhorrent behavior. This belief (if it is deeply held) may also be of value. In the history of human civilization, politics played a big role in promoting certain values related to individual behavior and traits while suppressing others (Dumont, 2010). In Germany more than 85 years ago, the Nazi ideology blended a mixture of radical nationalism and racism that affected the entire German society. During that time, the German educational institutions and the media actively promoted the "ideal" personality type: men and women that are physically fit, emotionally stable, morally pure, hard working, and uncompromising against Germany's domestic and foreign enemies. German psychologists were ordered by the government to provide research data to help the younger generations become physically and mentally strong; to learn Nazi principles advocating the supremacy of the Arian race; and to defend, as brave soldiers, the German state (Shiraev, 2015).

©iStockphoto.com/double_p

PHOTO 1.4 Are you a religious person? If yes, how did your beliefs influence your personality? If you are not religious, how did this view affect your behavior and in which ways?

Religion is one of the most powerful sources of values. People routinely use religion to navigate and explain their behavior and personality (Harrington, 1996). Behavioral prescriptions, such as moderation in needs, respect for strong family ties, frugality, discipline, and thrift, are common in the doctrines and practices of Christianity, Judaism, Confucianism, Hinduism, Sikhism, Islam, Buddhism, and other religions. Religious values also affected people's views of psychological illness. Within the Christian tradition, as an illustration, the core beliefs related to sin, confession, and repentance motivate many individuals to believe that some severe forms of mental illness are God's punishment for inappropriate behavior (see Photo 1.4; Shiraev & Levy, 2024).

How important is the impact of religious values on behavior? It depends on who you are and where you live. Some of us are religiously devout. Others are not. Some people do not practice religion, and it is not a source of values for them. Globally, back in 2017, 62% of people in the world defined themselves as religious. Three quarters of people globally believed in the existence of a soul in them, 54% believed in in life after death, and 49% believed in hell. In general, as education and income levels grow higher, religiosity levels tend to diminish. The most religious countries were Thailand (98% of the surveyed said they believed in God) and Nigeria (97%). China is the least religious country, where almost 7 out of 10 people said they were atheists, more than double than any other country (Gallup International, 2017). Most U.S. adults (81%) said they believe in God in 2022, compared to 90% in 2011 according to Gallup polls (Jones, 2022a).

Some religious values translate into actual behavior, but others do not. Indian psychologists admit the paradoxical nature of their society in which everyday life is conducted between profound mysticism and the spiritual nature of religious values on the one hand and ordinary, everyday lives on the other. The worship of goddesses and the abuse of women, unfortunately, coexist. Asceticism and modesty often are powerless against consumerism. The profound hope for fairness is numbed by daily corruption. These scholars maintain that spirituality and religious passion have not, unfortunately, played a crucial role in the improvement of the ordinary person (Chaudhary, 2010; Chaudhary et al., 2022; Ramanujan, 1989).

Legal Knowledge

Official prescriptions—including "this is allowed" or "this is not"—for centuries regulated behavior of individuals and groups. Law is a custom or practice of a community that is recognized as binding. **Legal knowledge** emerges in official prescriptions by authorities (ranging from tribal leaders to countries' governments). Legal knowledge may agree with or may contradict popular beliefs and values. The legal definition of mental illness, for instance, is country specific. Legal knowledge often produces labels to place people in special categories. The labels *lunatic* and *idiot* appeared until recently in the U.S. Code (the official compilation of federal laws), referring to individuals *non compos mentis* (not of sound mind). Existing legal categories such as *criminal* or *insane* can automatically create expectations that those who carry these labels presumably possess mainly undesirable personal qualities, including propensity to violence, disobedience, irrationality, perversion, and other forms of deviance.

Legal definitions provide strict guidelines about an individual's social status, such as formal maturity, as an example. In the United States, an individual becomes an "adult" and gains new rights, such as being able to vote or get married, at age 18. However, the official age allowing alcohol consumption is 21. Other legal rules define which acts of individual violence are allowed (like self-defense) and which are condemned or punished. Legal knowledge provides explanations for right and wrong actions related to marriage and divorce, people's ability to adopt children, an individual's choice of a sexual orientation, and so forth. From the legal standpoint, homosexuality was considered a pathological trait and illness in the United States for most of the past century. In 2015, the U.S. Supreme Court struck down all state bans on same-sex marriage, legalized it in all 50 states, and required states to honor out-of-state same-sex marriage licenses. In many countries, governments continue to criminalize people for their sexual orientation. Posting materials related to LGBTQ+ issues is likely to create serious legal problems for the author of such an article or video in Russia or Iran.

All in all, legal rules establish boundaries of acceptable human behavior and affect daily customs and practices globally. Legal knowledge directly affects many of our judgments, emotions, and thoughts.

How Different Types of Knowledge Interact

What is *character*? Define it in one sentence. Next, ask people near you to do the same. You will receive different answers. Probably you will receive quick replies, such as "Character is one's mental strength" or more evasive answers like "Character is something everyone has." These unrehearsed answers will probably reflect these respondents' popular knowledge. Other answers may be more sophisticated. Some people may refer to literary characters. Others will associate character with moral values. Some will cite definitions from academic books. You can imagine how many different answers you can get after collecting, for instance, 100 replies!

In our lives, the four types of knowledge are deeply interconnected. Common sense assumptions, such as how to be forgiving or resilient, have always been part of people's knowledge about their individual life. A continually moving flow of new facts and opinions constantly changes these views. At certain times in history, as we will see later in the book, values—often associated with religion or politics—have had a tremendous impact on other types of knowledge. Studies showed that individuals who are good at math and statistics tend to suddenly stop using reason when they discuss research results that threatens their values (Kahan, 2012). Values can affect scientific knowledge, and scientific knowledge influences values. All four types of knowledge remain inseparable parts of our inquiry into personality because we are learning not only what personality is but also how personality has been understood in the past, how people view it today, and how people apply their knowledge to their lives.

Let's return to *The Mirror Effect,* the book on narcissistic personality described early in this chapter. What knowledge does it convey to the reader? Many of the book's ideas are based on tabloid stories, radio and television interviews, and personal observations. However, this book is also rooted in science. The authors first published their research in the peer-reviewed *Journal of Research of Personality* (Pinsky & Young, 2006). The book also discussed values that lead so many young people to be obsessed with the lives of celebrities. Overall, the book is an important source of information about personality. Yet the challenge remains: We need to distinguish among scientific facts, popular ideas, value judgments, and legal facts.

Knowledge and Theory

We certainly hope the knowledge that we gain about personality has everything to do with facts. Facts, even the most comprehensive and accurate ones, have to be explained. Our knowledge also requires **analysis**, which is the breaking of something complex into smaller parts to understand their essential features and relations. This step is difficult enough, but even more is needed. If psychologists did only analysis, they would remain hopelessly confused by the multitude of research data, facts, numbers, and opinions. Which facts are accurate? Which facts are more important than others? To answer these and other questions, we have to look at the facts in light of broader ideas about personality. The ancient Greeks called this knowledge "from above" or theory (θεωρι'α). Applied to personality, **theory** is a type of comprehensive, scientific explanation about what personality is, how it develops, and how it functions.

- Theory is based on scientific knowledge and serves as a powerful tool in the studies of personality.

- Theory allows us to transform a formless heap of research data and opinions into a logical construction.

- Theory provides an explanation for a particular observation and through new assumptions suggests several hypotheses that can be tested to support or challenge the theory.

- Theory can then be applied to see if it explains many known facts and if new facts can be explained by the theory. Theorizing about personality requires both strong empirical knowledge and, of course, a measure of imagination (see Figure 1.3).

The scientific study of personality has a broad and varied history. We will take a critical look at many theories and their applications in the following chapters. We will also examine major psychological schools that have contributed and continue to impact our knowledge of personality.

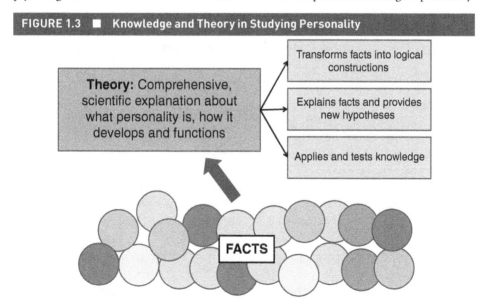

FIGURE 1.3 ■ Knowledge and Theory in Studying Personality

Theory: Comprehensive, scientific explanation about what personality is, how it develops and functions

Transforms facts into logical constructions

Explains facts and provides new hypotheses

Applies and tests knowledge

FACTS

We will study facts established by psychologists working in different countries and using different methods. We also look at a wide range of ideas created by those whose work did not necessarily fit into these convenient academic categories. As a famous ancient saying attributed to the Roman playwright Terence goes, *I am a human: I regard nothing human as foreign to me.*

Personality Theories and Academic Traditions

We can approach (or come near to) what we label *personality* from different angles. **Personality psychology**—a branch of psychology that studies personality—has been around for a relatively short period, about 100 years. However, personality psychology carries the influences of the knowledge accumulated for centuries within various approaches and scholarly disciplines.

Many theories of personality developed within **academic traditions**. These traditions bring together scholars that share similar views on a particular scientific approach, subject, or method. At least two types of such traditions exist. First, there are actual associations involving interacting individuals—the followers of an academic tradition. Second, there are traditions as convenient symbols to indicate a similarity in views among people who may or may not know one another. Some traditions remain short lived. They emerge, capture the imagination of their followers, and then lose their appeal. Other academic traditions remain influential for many years. Psychoanalysis since the beginning of the 20th century was a dominant field providing major views of personality approximately until the 1960s. It has generally lost its dominant position today (we discuss this tradition in Chapter 4). However, even though some theories have lost their leading role, we continue studying them today. Like pieces in a jigsaw puzzle, they are important elements of contemporary personality theory and its applications.

Academic traditions perform several functions. The first is organizational. Scientists have to exchange their ideas and discuss their research with one another. Discussion societies and clubs involving scientists were common in the past. In the 18th century, the famous French intellectual Paul-Henri Thiry (known also as Baron d'Holbach) established the *salon*: a regular get-together of progressive thinkers, authors, and educators. Liberal-minded philosophers discussed materialism and atheism and criticized the oppressive rule of the king. Psychoanalysts in the 20th century also formed groups to discuss new ideas, current research, and its applications. Researchers who study personality also belong to their academic organizations that conduct regular meetings, publish journals, and organize regular face-to-face meetings, podcasts, and webinars.

The second function is consolidation of knowledge. Quite often, several scholars working on the same problem or using the same theoretical approach can work more efficiently than individual scholars working separately. There are long-term informal associations, their purpose being to let their participants collaborate and share research findings. Such associations gain recognition among scholars of two or more generations. Many prominent psychologists of the past cared about their students, readers, and other followers—those who could and would continue or promote research of their mentors. Many psychologists actively and deliberately recruited their assistants, associates, and other colleagues to keep their research tradition thriving (Krantz & Wiggins, 1973). They do this today.

The third function of academic traditions is regulatory. Scholars themselves or through their academic associations render professional judgments and peer-reviewed opinions about the quality of research papers and books. On the one hand, such judgments are necessary because, for example, they can distinguish important, high-quality research from pop psychology. On the other hand, as it has been in the past in authoritarian countries, governments would support some academic traditions and reject others (Kusch, 1999). Formal academic associations thus played the role of censors. In the context of knowledge, **censorship** is a deliberate practice of selecting and disseminating what is deemed "appropriate" knowledge (from someone's point of view) and restricting knowledge deemed inappropriate. Censorship can be political, as in Russia or Iran, for example, where the law prohibits academic studies related to LGBTQ+ issues. Fortunately, censorship is rather a rare phenomenon in contemporary science in a democratic society.

In summary, certain academic traditions create favorable conditions for particular types of research of personality and development of scientific knowledge. A strong academic support of a theory, or its rejection, is crucial for this theory's survival and future impact. It is always important to examine which methodology is chosen to support a theory.

CHECK AND APPLY YOUR KNOWLEDGE

1. What is the difference between values and popular beliefs?
2. What discrepancies between values and individual behavior can you name as you observe people's everyday interactions?
3. Think about your day. Recall the situations in which you were using legal knowledge and scientific knowledge in making decisions or judging other people.
4. What is the book *The Mirror Effect* about?
5. Name the functions of academic traditions.
6. Ask your professors to which academic group or society they belong. Ask if this is an international or national group or whether it is local. What do they actually do as members of this group?

APPLYING KNOWLEDGE ABOUT PERSONALITY

Studying personality remains a theoretical endeavor as long as we do not pay attention to the practical value of the research into personality. Personality psychology as a discipline should offer solutions to many personal problems and social challenges of today's world. It also has to offer practical suggestions about how to unleash the psychological potentials that everyone has inside. In every chapter of this book, we will discuss the applications of personality psychology.

Areas of Application

Would you like to learn about your major strengths as a person? Do you want to learn what are your major individual weaknesses? Which job will be an ideal match for your personality type? What kind of a person will be an ideal match for you to create a family?

When I ask my students on the first day of class whether these questions interest them, practically everyone says that they do. Most of us are curious about who we are as individuals and how we can use this knowledge to help us pursue a healthy, happy, and successful life. In the past and today, philosophers and natural scientists, doctors and educators, and explorers and experimentalists have all attempted to bring the power of scientific knowledge to solve practical issues referring to the individual's personality. For starters, let's mention a few areas of applications.

To improve treatment procedures, doctors use research into personality to distinguish different patterns of their patients' behavior. Medical professionals recognize that different people understand their symptoms differently and that their personalities have a lot to do with how these symptoms are explained. *Personalized medicine* is an applied field in which clinical professionals use their knowledge about an individual's unique personality characteristics to choose effective treatments (Collins, 2010). As an example, a patient's critical thinking skills (either developed or not), motivation level (high or low), and general emotional tone (optimistic or pessimistic) can greatly affect the way this individual understands treatment recommendations and follows them (Bray, 2010).

A professional's knowledge about personality disorders (we will study them in Chapter 11), and measuring their symptoms, provides valuable knowledge about diagnoses, treatment, and prevention of other psychological disorders (Tyrer & Johnson, 1996). Even seemingly inconsequential behavioral features, like walking, may provide clues about potentially significant psychological problems. Japanese researchers, for example, found that people with symptoms of clinical depression tend to move differently than people without depressive symptoms (Nakamura et al., 2007). Our individual style of walking and moving can be used in diagnosing and monitoring neurodegenerative diseases or other problems related to aging (Otte et al., 2021).

Applied to clinical and counseling psychology, research into personality allows therapists to create new procedures and methods to help people recover from physical and mental abuse and discontinue their harmful habits and behavioral patterns (Jones, 2008). Knowledge of specific personality features of victims suffering from acute stress helps psychologists apply special therapeutic techniques in the aftermath of natural disasters or violent conflicts (Chung & Bemak, 2011). Knowledge about specific factors of individual decision-making in health-related areas helps psychologists make changes in people's behavior with respect to their daily nutrition choices, hygiene, and reproductive health (Leenen et al., 2008). Children diagnosed with autism spectrum disorders may benefit from specific recommendations related to the development of the ability to delay immediate impulse gratification—an important personality feature, which we will discuss in Chapter 2 (Faja & Dawson, 2013).

In education, many applications of personality psychology help improve educational effectiveness. Educational success is based, along with many other factors, on the type of motivation that teachers and students bring to classrooms. Successful learning is often about the ability to perform difficult, sometimes tedious tasks. Many factors influence this ability. However, individuals who have developed a strong sense of learning and who believe that they study for an important and socially meaningful goal perform better on many educational tasks, including the most boring ones. This knowledge allows psychologists to provide help in forming such traits in students (Yeager et al., 2014). Self-discipline can be improved not only by means of repetition but also through a deeper understanding of long-term, socially meaningful goals of studying. Psychologists assist educational professionals in many other areas, such as conflict resolution at schools, prevention of bullying, or addressing the deadly impact of substance abuse, including opioids, among the young.

Applied to business, research into personality provides knowledge about skills assessment, performance evaluation, and creative potentials related to various professional activities.

Psychologists suggest effective methods for job-related, competitive selection processes during hiring and promotion. Psychologists studying personality also make a strong contribution to *organization development*—planned changes targeted at improving organizational and individual performance and well-being in an established private business, a government institution, or a start-up (Frank et al., 2007). Psychologists also study common errors and individual weaknesses related to a wide range of professional activities. For example, if you are a defendant or witness in court, do you hope for fair judgments from the members of the court and jurors? Studies show that many factors can sway the jurors' perceptions and judgments, including their age, preexisting beliefs, and the appearance of the defendants. These findings were used in legal training of professionals as well as in jury-selection procedures (Quas et al., 2007).

In the forensic and security fields, studies into personality help practitioners better identify suspects, create their individual profiles, and compose various patterns of criminal behavior. Chapter 11, for example, discusses research into the personality of stalkers, or individuals engaged in persistent and unwanted pursuit of another person. National intelligence in the United States has long used help from professionals studying personality characteristics of foreign leaders (Post & George, 2004). The growing field of cybersecurity is in significant need of scientific data that explains the behavior of hackers. Studies into personality (including research of individual prejudice and intolerance) helped psychologists train specialists in conflict analysis, prevention, and resolution (Brewer & Pierce, 2005). Cooperation between personality psychologists and political scientists provided insight in the study of violence and martyrdom (Bélanger et al., 2014). Studies suggest that many radicalized youth could respond positively to reeducation and deradicalization efforts and return to violence-free life (Stern, 2010). See Figure 1.4 for a review of personality theories' applications. Which other application areas could you suggest?

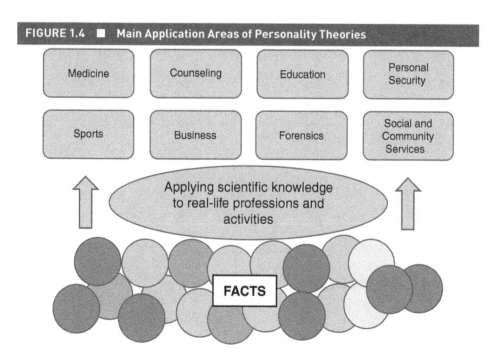

FIGURE 1.4 ■ Main Application Areas of Personality Theories

Steps in Applying Knowledge

Personality psychology—as a research and applied discipline—engages in an important mission of promoting science, reason, and educated social action. Psychologists expect that you will enrich and modify your view of yourself and others based on your analysis and evaluation of the facts developed in personality psychology. Psychologists also expect that you could make educated improvements in your life. What specific steps can you take to make these improvements?

There are at least three steps people can take to improve themselves in three different yet interconnected contexts of our lives: the individual, the interpersonal, and the global.

The Individual Context

Studying personality, you will learn critical judgments about yourself and other people. Studies show that many people wrongly believe they are competent enough to make good decisions about their lives. Unfortunately, scores of people have only limited knowledge about themselves and other people. People who are incompetent tend to make two kinds of mistakes. First (because of their lack of knowledge), they reach too many erroneous conclusions that guide them in making too many wrong choices in relationships, business, and education. Second, they develop and maintain overconfidence, which does not allow them to realize that they have already made too many logical mistakes, jumped to wrong conclusions, and ignored important facts (Dunning & Kruger, 1999; Sanchez & Dunning, 2021). Therefore, to avoid these mistakes, try to do the following:

- Apply the knowledge you gain from this book (and from the lectures) to self. Ask this question: How is this knowledge relevant to my life?

- Learn about your strengths and weaknesses. Evaluate your strengths and try to learn from your accomplishments. Examine your mistakes and try to explain why they occur.

- Examine which events or issues consistently make you (1) happy and (2) unhappy.

- After reading or summarizing a chapter or a part of it, ask two questions: How did this research help me in my development and growth? How can I use this research or this theory to become a better person?

The Interpersonal Context

Our goals in life can be self-oriented ("I want to be an interesting and attractive person") and socially oriented ("I want to make a difference in this world"). Studies show that people who set and then pursue their socially oriented goals can develop stronger will and a better ability to overcome difficulties compared to those who set mostly self-oriented goals (Yager et al., 2014). Your life should mean something to others. You can be more efficient and helpful because other people certainly need your knowledge and skills. You can apply your knowledge in social contexts of your life in the following ways:

- Think of your classmates, friends, and family members. There is always someone who needs help, advice, and guidance. Relate your knowledge to others.

- When *you* are in need, turn to others for guidance and help. They may know something that you don't.

- Specifically, after reading a chapter or a part of it, ask these questions: How can I use this knowledge to help others? How can I use this knowledge to ask others to help me improve and achieve?

The Global Context

Apply your knowledge to the global world and to your entire life. Psychologists today, at least most of them, have embraced a progressive view of their discipline and society in general: For years, based on surveys, most psychologists identified themselves as "liberal" and "progressive" (Aschwanden, 2018). Progressivism as a social position means that to improve the lives of people, concerned professionals and citizens should engage in an educated, deliberate, and planned intervention in many areas of our society. Today, we commonly call such a planned intervention "social policy." For psychology professionals, progressivism means an opportunity to apply scientific knowledge directly to social issues. Progressivism also emphasizes the importance of applied psychological knowledge in at least three areas: (1) health care, (2) education, and (3) social services. Therefore, you can apply your knowledge in global contexts in the following ways:

- Think about yourself and others from a greater perspective. What do you want to achieve globally? What is your role, your mission as an individual in this life, in this world?

- As a person, what are you bringing to the world? What do you want to be recognized for?

- Specifically, after reading a chapter or any part of it, ask this question: How can I use this knowledge to make a real difference in life? Ask others to answer this question. And then think, discuss, and do something useful.

CHECK AND APPLY YOUR KNOWLEDGE

1. What are the main areas of application of personality psychology?
2. Name at least one applied area or issue that you think should have been mentioned here.

Most of us probably will not be involved in national policymaking or global economic and social decisions. Yet we all can make a difference by promoting scientific knowledge and critically discussing and applying it. During class discussions and seminars, in articles and public lectures, in the media and social networks, or during face-to-face contacts, we can discuss both new and classical research findings, promote our original ideas, influence each other's opinions, change common stereotypes, and, most importantly, help other people. The first step is to gain knowledge. Let's begin.

SUMMARY

Personality is not easy to define, and there are several views on what personality is. We understand personality as a stable set of behavioral and experiential characteristics of an individual.

Personality refers to both unique and typical, distinguishable patterns of behavior and experience; together, they will be called personality traits. Taken together, in a combination, an individual's traits form a certain type. Type refers to a kind or category of elements or features sharing similar characteristics or features.

Some features can be called central because they tend to be broad and general. Peripheral personality features are associated with central ones, yet they tend to be more specific, more relevant to particular individuals and specific circumstances. Central features are not necessarily more important or valuable than peripheral.

Personality can be stable and evolving at the same time. Stability and change are based on many interconnected influences. Research has established that during the life span we as individuals keep many of our personality characteristics relatively stable. Most personality-related changes take place during childhood. Our personalities become more or less stable in middle age and are least changeable after people reach approximately age 50. Exceptions from these expectations are plenty.

Personality can be viewed as normal and abnormal. Tolerance threshold is a measure of tolerance or intolerance toward specific personality traits in a society or a cultural group. Tolerance thresholds are tested in specific social situations. Personality disorders are enduring patterns of behavior and inner experience that deviate markedly from the expectations of the individual's culture.

Our behavioral patterns and experiences that become a core of our personality are likely to be explained by a combination of biological and social factors. The debates about complex interactions of natural (biological) factors and social (cultural) influences have always been the focus of attention in social sciences and psychology.

Understanding the mechanisms of the mind–body interactions has been one of the most challenging topics of research and intellectual debates in the history of science and one of the most intriguing problems in psychology.

Personality is active and reactive. Determinism encourages psychologists to study how personality was formed (in the past) and how personality features affect behavior and experience now and in the future. Psychologists generally avoid fatalism, which states that we, as humans, are not in control of our actions and thoughts because something or somebody else (like God, fate, or chance) predetermines them.

At least four types of knowledge related to personality are relevant to our discussion: scientific knowledge, popular beliefs, values, and legal knowledge. These types constantly interact.

Knowledge requires analysis, which is the breaking of something complex into smaller parts to understand their essential features and relations. Applied to personality, theory is a type of comprehensive, scientific explanation about what personality is and how it develops and functions.

Many theories of personality developed within particular academic traditions. These traditions bring together scholars that help them share similar views on a particular scientific approach, subject, or method.

Personality theories find applications in many walks of life. Philosophers and natural scientists, doctors and educators, curious explorers and experimentalists, and then professional psychologists try to apply their knowledge of personality to a wide variety of human activities.

VISUAL REVIEW

Visual Review. Chapter 1. Introducing Personality

1. IDENTYFYING PERSONALITY

Personality: A stable set of behavioral and experiential characteristics of an individual	These characteristics are stable and organized; they influence an individual's behavior	Personality can be described as a coexistence of several psychological dichotomies

2. APPROACHING PERSONALITY

Four types of knowledge related to personality: Scientific, Folk, Values, and Legal.	Theory is a type of comprehensive, scientific explanation about what personality is, how it develops, and how it functions.	Many theories of personality developed within particular academic traditions.

3. APPLYING KNOWLEDGE ABOUT PERSONALITY

Knowledge is applied in personalized medicine, clinical and counseling psychology, education, business, forensic, and security fields, among others.	Three contexts of applications: Individual, interpersonal, and global.

KEY TERMS

academic traditions	determinism
analysis	fatalism
censorship	knowledge
central	legal knowledge
cynicism	nature–nurture debates

peripheral

personality

personality disorders

personality psychology

pessimism

pop psychology

popular (or folk) beliefs

scarcity mindset

scientific knowledge

self-determination

self-enhance

theory

tolerance threshold

traits

type

values

EVALUATING WHAT YOU KNOW

Define *personality*.

Explain the three principles referring to personality.

Explain personality's dichotomies and give examples.

Describe the four types of knowledge related to personality; provide examples.

Explain how the four types of knowledge interact.

Describe the areas of application of knowledge about personality.

Describe the steps in applying knowledge.

A BRIDGE TO THE NEXT CHAPTER

Studying personality should be interesting yet challenging. We are not the first to start this journey. Early philosophers, doctors, and scientists have laid the foundations for personality theory. Year after year, decade after decade, psychologists, like prospectors, tried to gather different theories, concepts, methods, and approaches to find valuable "nuggets" of knowledge about personality. Offering their findings for critical peer review or other forms of evaluation, psychologists began to "filter" and accumulate the best, most successful, and effective methods of investigation and psychological intervention. Travel and publications made this knowledge available to more psychologists globally. More scientists began to combine methods received from different schools to critically examine personality and then apply this knowledge. Psychologists gain their knowledge from other disciplines, including biology, medicine, social sciences, computer sciences, sociology, behavioral economics, and philosophy. This list can easily be continued.

We are at the beginning of our journey. Our next step, in the following chapter, will be to examine how science, social sciences, and humanities throughout their long history have contributed to our knowledge of personality today.

2 SCIENTIFIC FOUNDATIONS TO STUDY PERSONALITY

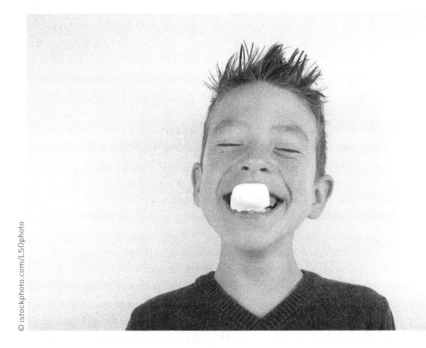

© istockphoto.com/LSOphoto

LEARNING OBJECTIVES

After reading this chapter, you should be able to do the following:

- Explain the role of the scientific method in studying personality.

- Summarize the major influences of the sciences, social sciences, and the humanities on the study of personality.

- Identify ways to apply scientific knowledge about personality to self, to others, and to the world.

What would you prefer to receive as a gift: a 2017, preowned electric car right now or a brand-new electric car in 2 years? Consider another choice: a $500 prize today or a $3,000 one the year after your graduation? Of course, your choice will be based on many factors. Yet in general, are you a person who usually waits to carefully select your choices? Or are you a person driven by your immediate calculations?

The phenomenon known as impulse gratification (IG) has been discussed for centuries, as we shall examine this in the chapter. Psychologists studied IG as well, and studied experimentally. In the famous **marshmallow experiments** at Stanford, researchers asked individual children if they wanted to eat a marshmallow now or wait 15 minutes and then eat two. Some children waited; others ate the marshmallow immediately. Many years later, those who waited, on average, had better grades and higher SAT scores, made more money, had a lower body mass index, showed greater psychological well-being, were less likely to misuse drugs, and had fewer behavioral problems, such as drug abuse (Mischel et al., 1972). Other researchers found a strong correlation between impulse control and achievement tests scores at age 15 (Watts et al., 2018). Another study showed that inmates with low IG control were more likely than others to commit new crimes and return to prison (Malouf et al., 2012). In Sweden, children with lower IG control were 32% more likely to be convicted of a crime as adults than the group with higher IG control (Akerlund et al., 2014). These and many other studies show that the ability to control one's own impulses can be an important individual feature related to a host of other factors, including individual qualities and behaviors.

How does impulse gratification develop in life? Are we born with it? Studies show that impulse control is associated with the functioning of the brain's prefrontal cortex, which is responsible for logic and patience, and the brain's ventral striatum (a cluster of neurons in the forebrain), which regulates reward mechanisms (Casey et al., 2011). Yet impulse control is not determined by biology alone. Nature perhaps sets only the general course for our individual features—not the final destiny. Research shows, for example, that economic and educational problems significantly affect IG: People who face poverty and economic uncertainty and people who are less educated tend to be more impulsive in their decisions than the educated and those who grow up facing certainty (Chiraag & Griskevicius, 2014; Mischel, 2014; Perez-Arce, 2011). Adults' reputation matters, too: If children trust adults who are around them, like parents or neighbors, and expect that the grownups' promises will be kept, the studied children display stronger impulse control (Ma et al., 2020).

We may be born with certain predispositions for stronger willpower and impulse control, but our life and experiences contribute as well. We learn from our own victories and mistakes. We absorb from successful and unsuccessful behaviors of others. We follow cultural customs. Our lives are often a lasting discovery of the worth of waiting. Such discoveries differ from person to person.

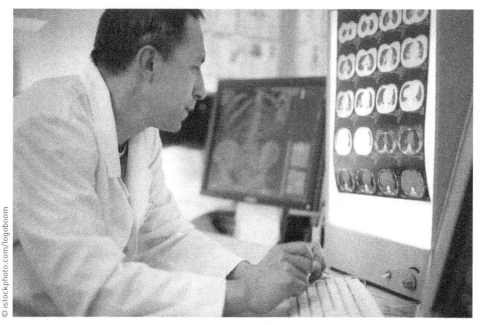

© istockphoto.com/logoboom

PHOTO 2.1 A researcher examines a CT scan. Do you mostly rely on scientific knowledge to make decisions? Think of situations wherein you relied on popular beliefs instead. Can you describe these situations?

SCIENCE AND THE SCIENTIFIC METHOD

Personality psychology draws on various types of knowledge (see Chapter 1). Scientific knowledge is the focus of our attention throughout the book. This knowledge is accumulated through research, systematic empirical observation, and critical evaluation of facts. Personality psychology is a scientific discipline rooted in the **scientific method**, which uses careful research procedures designed to provide reliable and verifiable evidence (Gergen, 2001). This method is about critically checking and judging, rather than simply believing or uncritically accepting, knowledge (Shermer, 2015).

Scientists created various methods to gather facts and theories to explain personality. What is the difference between a scientific theory and just a series of logical assumptions about personality? A theory should be considered scientific if it is falsifiable—it is testable to prove if it is correct or wrong (Popper, 1992). In personality psychology, many theories are falsifiable (that is, testable), as we shall see throughout the book, and some are not. They may become testable in the future. In any case, if personality psychology is based on the scientific method, in which scientific fields does it obtain its facts? We now turn to a brief description of the three major sources of knowledge: basic science, social science, and humanities.

In very general terms, **natural science** is concerned with the description, prediction, and understanding of natural phenomena. Natural science has two key branches: physical science and biological science (often called life science), which focus on living organisms, including human beings. Biological science includes many branches of biology involving anatomy, physiology, evolutionary sciences, genetics, and neuroscience. Personality psychology constantly receives new empirical data from life sciences. Which of them are most valuable for psychologists? Let's mention and briefly preview several.

For example, genetics is the field of biology involving multidisciplinary studies of heredity through genetic transmission and genetic variations. The term *genetics* has its roots in the ancient Greek word "origin." Indeed, genetics seeks out the "origins" of the bodily structures, physiological processes, and behavioral and cognitive functions of living organisms, including human beings. Behavior genetics studies how genetic differences among people contribute to differences in their psychology and behavior (Harden, 2021). We will discuss the research into behavioral genetics on many pages in this book.

Another field of life sciences that contributes to personality psychology is **neuroscience**, which is a scientific study of the nervous system. This is a vast field examining the molecular, structural, functional, medical, evolutionary, and many other aspects of the nervous system. **Cognitive neuroscience** also has a special importance for personality psychology. It examines the brain mechanisms that support the individual's mental functions and subsequent behaviors. This field also includes neurochemistry, which examines how various neurochemicals, such as neurotransmitters, influence the network of neural operations.

Personality psychology also receives feedback from **evolutionary science**, which explains how large populations of organisms—plants, animals, and human beings—evolve over time. In very broad terms, evolution is transformation of the heritable traits of species and humans over successive generations. Evolutionary science contributes to personality psychology by providing assumptions about the roots of personality traits and behaviors, especially those that are common in large populations and social groups, such as men and women or the young and the middle-aged, or people in general.

Social science is concerned with society and the relationships among individuals within it. This discipline includes anthropology, economics, political science, and sociology, among others. The goal of *anthropology*, for instance, is to provide scientific knowledge about human beings. Anthropologists are interested in such dissimilar topics as the biological roots of humans, the common grammars of languages, or gender biases in religious rituals (Nanda & Warms, 2009). Yet as a vast field, anthropology provides an uninterrupted stream of knowledge to personality psychology about the universal and culture-specific roots of human beliefs, customs, rituals, and practices.

Sociology is the study of society and the social action of humans. This field is generally concerned with associations, groups, organizations, communities, and institutions, both large and small. Sociologists study social development, organization, and change. Personality psychologists obtain facts and new applications from sociology. For example, psychologists learn from urban sociology about the impact of big-city communities on the adolescent lifestyle, from sociology of age about the patterns of habits and attitudes of people of different age groups, or from environmental sociology about how religious or secular beliefs affect individual environmental conservation efforts. These were just a few examples.

Research in economics also contributes to our understanding of personality. Economics analyzes and describes the production, distribution, and consumption of resources. Personality psychologists are especially interested in research findings of **behavioral economics**, which studies the effects of individual factors on individual economics and other decisions. We will be turning to research in behavioral economics in most chapters of this book.

Personality psychology also relies on the humanities. In very broad terms, the **humanities** study human culture. **Culture** is a set of beliefs, behaviors, and symbols shared by a large group of people and usually communicated from one generation to the next. Sociology and anthropology are also interested in culture, but the humanities tend to use methods that are primarily critical and have a significant historical and creative element. The humanities study ancient and modern languages, literature, philosophy, religion, and visual and performing arts such as literature, music, and theater. Later in this chapter, we will look at the impact of the humanities on the study of personality.

We shall not forget about philosophy either. In Greek, **philosophy** means "love of wisdom." It is the study of the most general and basic problems of nature, human existence, mind, and society. Philosophy is based on rational argument in contrast to faith, belief, or trust, which all do not have to be rational. Most of us, as human beings, think about the meaning of life. Philosophers try to provide answers.

> **Question.** Read and identify a few common features that these religions share in their reference to the individual's personality.

The expression of human imagination through creativity is called **art**. It typically includes, among many other forms, visual arts, such as painting and sculpture, and performing arts, such as music, theatre, film, and dance. Artists can be scientists, yet most of them aren't. They do not intend to convey scientific knowledge through their artistic designs. Artists create something that is supposed to be beautiful or carry emotional power and requires an act of judgment from the listener or viewer (Kandel, 2012). By studying art, we learn about history, culture, and of course, individual lives.

Personality psychology is rooted in the **humanist tradition** (or humanism) in science, which emphasizes the subjective side of the individual—the sense of freedom, beauty, creativity, and moral responsibility. Humanism encourages self-understanding and improvement, openness, and sharing of skills and experience (Dilthey, 1910/2002). A typical humanist is a person of virtues, knowledge, and passion. Humanism is also based on science and tends to be secular but respectful to religion. Art gives personality psychologists a treasure trove of materials to enrich their scientific outlook of human beings, their behavior, and their inner world. *Ramayana*, the ancient Indian epic, or *Dream of the Red Chamber*, an 18th-century Chinese classic, provide great accounts of the complexities of human behavior and individual choices. Writers such as Shakespeare in England and Tolstoy in Russia have created a long line of literary characters that millions of people continue examining today. Scores of artistic sources that originated in the Middle East, Iran, and central Asia also deal with the individual's personality. Creations of Firdawsi, Umar Hayyam, and

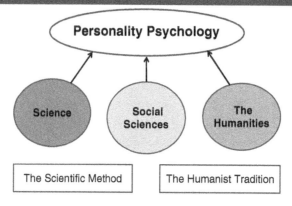

FIGURE 2.1 ■ The Scientific Traditions to Study Personality

Nizami teach us about passion and romantic love, anger, jealousy, pride, and generosity of people living centuries ago.

Science, social sciences, and humanities interact when we study personality. Without science, personality psychology would certainly lose the power of the scientific method. Without social sciences, personality psychology would overlook the importance of social factors in shaping who we are as people. The humanities provide personality psychology with moral strength and encourage care about one another and the world around us (see Figure 2.1).

CHECK AND APPLY YOUR KNOWLEDGE

1. What is cognitive neuroscience? How does it contribute to the study of personality?
2. Explain behavioral economics and why it is important for the study of personality.
3. Compare the scientific tradition and the humanistic method to study personality. Consider two assertions:
   a. Social sciences, for example, provide evidence about the impact of education on reducing violence and crime.
   b. The French novelist Victor Hugo (1802–1885) wrote, "He who opens a school door, closes a prison." Do scientists and poets tend to convey ideas that essentially are the same? What are the differences in their approach to facts?
4. When scientists appeal to reason, artists inspire imagination. Think about and suggest the cases in which science appeals to imagination and art refers to reason.

We are now turning to a more detailed discussion of major contributions to personality psychology from life sciences, social sciences, and humanities. These disciplines' intellectual legacy is diverse and vast. What did they bring to our understanding of personality? How can we apply this knowledge?

CONTRIBUTIONS TO THE STUDY OF PERSONALITY

Genetics

Genetics is the study of heredity through genetic transmission and genetic variations. For centuries, scientists tried to understand **inheritance**, or how certain traits in living organisms were handed down from parents to offspring. Many researchers looked for the most elementary bodily "units" responsible for inheritance of such traits. Charles Darwin (1809–1882), one of the world's most famous naturalists, for example, believed that acquired characteristics are inherited: If a person developed strong willpower in life, this person's children are supposed to have strong willpower. Darwin thought that gemmules, some identifiable particles in the body, could transmit such individual characteristics. To test his hypothesis, he transfused blood from different breeds of rabbits (he could not conduct similar experiments on people) to examine the resulting characteristics of the offspring. To his disappointment, he did not confirm his hypothesis related to gemmules. Instead, the 20th century science began to use molecular biology to explain hereditary transition processes and patterns. These days, the union of genetics with molecular biology has created a powerful new science that provides personality psychology with a constant stream of new facts. What do we learn specifically from genetics research about heredity and its role in the individual's personality?

PHOTO 2.2 Have you met any identical twins? If yes, how different or similar did their behavior appear to you?

©iStockphoto.com/rachasuk

Some Personality Features Are Inherited

When scientists discuss heredity, they usually talk genetic transmissions and genes. In a simple way, a **gene** is a segment or portion of the DNA (a complex molecule) that contains codes or "instructions" as biological information about how to build new protein structures. Genetics, the scientific study of genes and heredity, offers several important facts and assumptions about the biological factors affecting many personality features—including traits, skills, emotional patterns, personality disorders, and so on.

The following summative arguments can help us better understand the impact of hereditary factors on personality:

- An individual's personality features, including traits, subsequent behaviors, and psychological experiences, are often influenced by genetic factors. Genetic information activates particular physiological "mechanisms" in the individual's body, thus affecting their physical development, as well as a wide range of behavioral, cognitive, and emotional features. The consistency of our behaviors and inner experiences has something to do with our genetic makeup.

- Genetic factors can explain many variations in personality traits and behaviors, including the similarities and differences among individuals. At the same time, we should accept that some personality features have a stronger genetic component compared to others.

- The individual's personality features, however, develop in a complex and constant interaction between genetic and environmental factors. Genes do not directly create or "build" individual traits or other features. Genes are responsible only for "building materials," which, in the process of active interaction with the environment, influence the development of certain behaviors, thought patterns, and other personality qualities.

Research spreading over several decades in various countries shows the role of hereditary factors in the individual's life, behavior, and specific traits. Consider a few examples for starters. Our genes significantly affect our life expectancy. If your grandparents are alive and they are in their 80s, your parents and you are very likely to live as long and possibly even longer. Genetic factors have something to do with our susceptibility to many illnesses, such as certain cancers, heart diseases, or diabetes (Dubal et al., 2014). Genetic factors also affect our predisposition to serious psychological disorders, such as schizophrenia, bipolar disorder, and depression (Paul, 2014). A child's early measures of activity, emotionality, and sociability (these are major components of temperament and foundations of our personality) have a significant hereditary component (Zwir et al., 2020). Genes influence a person's cognitive abilities as well as play a very important role in triggering intellectual disabilities (American Psychiatric Association, 2022). Our musical skills are rooted in genetic factors, too. Research shows that practicing music without the "right genes" to back up that practice could be unproductive (Mosing et al., 2014). While it is also true that Mozart and Lady Gaga spent long hours in training (in Salzburg and in New York, respectively) before they became famous, they also most likely had those "musical genes." Researchers keep identifying genetic links to complex behavioral traits. Genetic factors are also responsible for aggressiveness, inhibition, or propensity for anxiety (Krueger & Markon, 2006). Patterns of coffee and tea consumption, chronic sleep disturbances, tendency for tiredness, and even whether an individual is a "morning" or "night" person—they all have a genetic component (Plomin, 2018).

Genetic factors also contribute to physiological variations among large groups. For example, ethnic groups living in Tibet developed a genetic variant that allows them to function at high altitudes, where most other people suffer because of the lack of oxygen (Wade, 2015). In countries that have no chronic shortages of food, people's height is determined mostly by their heredity (Bilger, 2004). Genetic factors also affect the stability of individual traits during the process of development (Hopwood et al., 2011). In other words, some of us are predisposed to have stable personality traits; others should expect their traits to change during their life span (the stability and change of personality traits is the focus of Chapter 9). However, our genetic "building blocks," or predispositions for developing stable psychological features of our personalities, should always be considered in the context of environmental conditions within which we develop and live.

Genes and the Environment Interact

Thirty years ago, personality studies borrowing from genetics focused mostly on specific genes that correlate to specific personality traits (Davies, 2014). Today's understanding of genetic transmission is more complex: Genes provide numerous options for varying cells to be expressed, but the environment determines which of these are activated. A fine illustration comes from the studies of twins: Despite sharing similar genetic backgrounds, their actual physical features (such as fingerprints) are extremely diverse. Identical twins—even those raised in the same environment—are not perfect replicas of each other; their experiences can make them very distinctive from each other as personalities (Harden, 2021).

Studies of animals also provide ideas about the behavior of humans. Genetically identical mice, for example, are different in terms of the amount of activity in which they engage—some are active explorers, and some are not. In a study using microchips, scientists measured the amount of active and exploratory behavior in mice. Over the course of 3 months, the brains of the most explorative mice were building more new neurons in the hippocampus (a process called neurogenesis), which is the center for learning and memory, than the animals that were more passive. So even though these mice were genetically identical, their brains became different due to the differences in their experiences (Bergmann & Frisén, 2013).

Research shows that some genetic factors under certain environmental conditions can result in particularly advantageous traits that help individuals in their lives. For example, parental choices to constantly engage a child at home, read books together, organize trivia, do puzzles, and visit museums might be conditioned by their temperamental features rooted in their genes, yet such activities produce important *educational* effects (Wertz et al., 2019). Certainly, some people are genetically predisposed to be more socially sensitive and anxious compared to others. Sensitivity is positively correlated with religiosity: People who tend to be emotionally sensitive also tend to be religious. Religiosity is also connected in surveys with the person's sense of happiness. However, people feel happier when they find opportunities for social connectedness and affiliation with others, which they often find in their temples, churches, and mosques (Sasaki et al., 2011). It is not enough to have certain inherited conditions for being happy. There must be a social environment that influences the individual's ability to be happy or unhappy. To reiterate, people's genetic predispositions for developing psychological features should always be considered in the framework of their social conditions (Davies, 2014; Wade, 2015).

Neuroscience

Recall that neuroscience is the scientific study of the nervous system. At least three disciplines within neuroscience contribute to personality psychology: electrophysiology, clinical pathology, and brain imaging studies. In university- and hospital-based laboratories, researchers use increasingly sophisticated methods and experimental devices to learn more about the mechanisms of neurophysiological processes and the brain's chemistry. The brain has about 86 billion neurons, 16 billion of which are in the cerebral cortex, the seat of many behavioral, emotional, and cognitive functions affecting an individual's personality (Jabr, 2015).

Clinical studies of brain pathology provide valuable knowledge about the brain's normal functioning as well as its dysfunctions. One of the many efficient methods involves studies of lesions in people who suffered brain damage that examine if or how their personality traits were affected by the trauma. For years, scientists using the **clinical–pathological method** compared clinical observations of a patient's abnormal symptoms with reliable data about brain pathology, most likely obtained during an autopsy on the deceased patient's brain (Taves, 1999). Ideally, this method helps to establish cause-and-effect relationships between pathology of certain areas of the brain and various psychological functions and dysfunctions (Seitelberger, 1997). In reality, such cause-and-effect relationships are extremely complicated.

The rapidly developing methods of brain imaging added to the clinical–pathological method and provided cognitive neuroscientists with remarkable new facts. For example, by examining the location of neural activation generated by a behavioral or cognitive task, researchers learn more about the role of brain processes in thinking, emoting, and decision-making. Electroencephalography (EEG) was introduced gradually around the 1920s and 1930s and has been used in clinical settings ever since. This method allows doctors and researchers to study the dynamic aspects of brain activity under changing functional conditions. Computerized tomography (CT) used since the 1970s helps to identify the precise location of a brain lesion while the patient is alive, and for the past 20 years, magnetic resonance imaging (MRI) and functional neuroimaging have allowed us to see direct changing psychological conditions. The advances in EEG help study the neural dynamics associated with mental events at the millisecond level (Solms & Turnbull, 2011). Although almost 90% of neuroimaging studies were performed a decade and a half ago in Western countries (Chiao, 2009), this situation is changing recently to include more culturally diverse subjects (Martinez-Tejada et al., 2020).

These are several summative and key assumptions of neuroscience relevant to personality psychology:

- Identifiable brain structures contribute to particular behavioral, cognitive, and emotional functions of the individual and his or her personality traits. Specific neurophysiological mechanisms in the brain are associated with particular behavioral, cognitive, and emotional functions of the individual. These physiological mechanisms can explain differences in personality features.

- The relations between neurophysiological functions and behavioral responses are not that simplistic. Specific personality features can have something to do with different brain mechanisms; similarly, different features could be associated with similar physiological mechanisms. Brain centers do not operate independently, and their functions are continually influenced by the activities in other parts of the brain.

- To better understand the individual's personality using research in neurophysiology, we should always understand human physiology in its constant interaction with the environment (both social and physical).

Brain Activities Are Associated With Specific Behaviors

The functioning of a brain's frontal lobes has been associated with the individual's style of planning, the style of responses to reward and punishment, tendencies to procrastinate, and a wide range of executive functions related to decision-making (Carver & Harmon-Jones, 2009). Studies of traumatic brain injury of the prefrontal cortex show serious changes in several areas of the individual's activities and emotional states involving disturbances in executive functions (lack of planning and indecisiveness), disconnect between emotions and behavior, changes in emotional responses including anxiety, and lack of stamina (Barrash et al., 2018). Studies involving brain tomography showed a significant underdevelopment of the frontal lobes, compared with the control group, in individuals convicted of serious violent crimes such as murder (Raine, 2014). The frontal lobes contribute to individual self-control, including the ability to regulate anger and other emotions that contribute to violence.

The size and functioning of the **amygdala**, the almond-shaped part of the brain crucial for processing emotions, is also apparently correlated with the individual's violent traits (Raine, 2014). The hypothalamus function has something to do with our style of attachment and bonding as well as our predisposition to lying (Shalvi & De Dreu, 2014). **Neurotransmitters**, or endogenous chemicals that enable neurotransmission between two cells, are associated with regulation of a wide range of behavioral and psychological functions (Zmorzyński et al., 2021) including propensity to depression, anxiety, and even social delinquency (Raine, 2014; Rang, 2003).

Cognitive neuroscientists proposed various models of the brain process, largely comparing it to the way computers process data. In a nutshell, the brain receives information from the senses, encodes it, stores it, and then exercises decision-making and response selection (Hilger & Markett, 2021). But how and where does all this information travel within the brain? Cognitive neuroscience comes to help and uses the model of neural networks to explain these dynamics. What are these neural network models? The brain neurons can be presented as "nodes." A node is like a communication device of some sort that is connected to other nodes and attached to a larger network. Such a node is able to send, receive, block, and forward information through various communication channels (Glynn, 1999).

The Nervous System Interacts With the Environment

From the opening vignette, you should remember that impulse gratification has something to do, among other factors, with the person's insecurity and the lack of resources. Studies show that poor children as a group are prone to opt for immediate rewards compared to other kids (Mischel, 2014). Educational experience makes young people value their future more and contributes to patience (Perez-Arce, 2011). Asian immigrants in North America tend to emphasize impulse control more than other families do—the fact that some researchers suggest may partly explain the educational and professional success of Asian Americans as a group compared to others (Baumeister & Tierney, 2012). Family background, early cognitive ability of the child, and the home environment matter, too (Watts et al., 2018). Young children can learn to be patient by simply knowing that people around them, especially their family members, are also patient in the way they approach small or big challenges (Doebel & Munataka, 2018).

Psychologists need to be careful, however, and critically review the data they obtain from neuroscientists. An experimental fact that, for instance, one portion of the brain is more active than several adjacent areas during a certain mental operation could be interpreted in too many ways. Leading physiologists of the past conveyed to future generations of scientists that the higher level mental processes, such as making an important decision, or psychological traits, such as openness to experience, cannot be reduced to physiological processes, even the most complicated ones (Sperry, 1961). A mental function is more than a combination of billions of neurons firing. To understand an individual's inner world, one has to acknowledge the complexity of multilevel interactions of physiological processes and mechanisms by which they interact. Most importantly, these physiological processes and mechanisms take place within specific environments, both physical and social. This constant interaction has created us, human beings.

Certain animals have very large brains. Billions of neurons in such brains support very sophisticated functions. But just the size of the brain does not make such a large animal a human being with intellectual and personality features. Humans do not have the largest brains, compared to some animals, yet they have the most cortical neurons of any species on Earth. Although it makes up only 2% of body weight, the human brain consumes about 20% of the body's total energy at rest. In contrast, the chimpanzee brain needs only half that (Jabr, 2015). In addition to the brain functions, human bodies also have certain advantages that are likely to distinguish human beings from other species. Dolphins have demonstrated elements of self-awareness. They can cooperate, plan ahead, and use simple elements of a language. However, dolphins don't have hands or can't build tools, like humans. Apes can mimic human behavior, perform complex operations, and understand words from human language. Yet their vocal tracts lack the ability to produce speech, which humans can do. Continuing the same logic, some parrots and crows have the vocal anatomy to imitate human speech, but their brains are not large enough or wired in the way to master complex reasoning (Jabr, 2015).

What made human beings who they are is a sophisticated combination of biological, physical, and environmental conditions in the context of human evolution. About 1.8 million years ago, human brains became larger. Humans stared walking upright. They had transformed themselves from tree-climbing apes that needed to spend a lot of time searching for food to upright, meat-consuming hunters that could roam large distances. Learning to cook with fire, searching for water, making tools, and using the vocabulary cord to make sounds and develop the language were several crucial circumstances among many other conditions that were shaping the minds of our ancestors (Finlayson, 2014).

Evolutionary Science

Personality psychology receives important feedback from evolutionary science. Evolution, in very general terms, is transformation in the heritable traits of species over successive generations. Evolutionary science generally explains how large populations of organisms—plants, animals, and human beings—evolve over time. **Evolutionary psychology** combines the knowledge of evolutionary science and psychology and explores the ways in which complex evolutionary factors affect human behavior, experience, and personality features

(Confer et al., 2010). Particular adaptive mechanisms of thinking and acting allowed humans to survive and adjust to challenging environmental conditions. These mechanisms have been transmitted—most likely genetically—from one generation to the next. It was a long process: Human beings were evolving during hundreds of thousands of years as a result of competition and natural selection.

Several summative assumptions of evolutionary psychology are most suitable for the study of personality:

- The individual's personality features can be explained as useful, adaptive functions of the individual interacting with the physical and social environment.

- Natural selection principles can explain similarities and differences in personality traits between different groups of people. Principles of natural selection are not necessarily useful in explaining individual differences between two individuals.

- To better understand how evolutionary factors influence the individual's personality, it is crucial to consider them in close interaction with other factors, including individual genetic variations, physiological mechanisms' underlying behavior, and specific social conditions within which an individual lives.

Evolutionary Factors

Today's evolutionary psychologists explain a diverse array of features, including people's curiosity and shyness, openness to new experiences, friendship and aggression, propensity to lie or suspiciousness to strangers, and many other behaviors—all by evolutionary mechanisms. The main assumption of evolutionary psychology is that most patterns of human behavior should have a biological, evolutionary meaning. People survive, while competing for resources and safety, while cooperating and helping—because the things they do make sense (most of the time). People, for example, are supposed to approach with caution all new, untested obstacles in their lives. Indeed, infants show a very early tendency to be wary of certain unknowns to them like animals and plants. It should make good evolutionary sense to be afraid of plants when we are young and ignorant about which are useful and which are harmful (Wertz & Wynn, 2014). People are supposed to support and protect the members of their families, their neighbors, and friends. On the other hand, other behaviors and habits, such as drug use, overeating, smoking, or constant reckless driving, are harmful to evolution. Individuals who practice such behaviors are likely to risk their health and die prematurely, reducing their chances of having offspring.

The "logic" of the evolutionary theory can be further illustrated with several examples. Let's turn, for instance, to the similarities and differences between men and women as large groups. Throughout history, especially during the early stages of human civilization, the **alpha males**, which are the strongest and most aggressive, were able to reproduce better than other, weaker males. Therefore, to survive, men in the past had to develop habits of aggressive and dominant behaviors to compete against one another. Thus, strong, dominant men created a particular culture to benefit the most competitive and the most aggressive. In history, such conditions certainly benefited strong men, who maintained this culture. Today, despite massive changes, men as a group continue to dominate the upper echelons of business and politics. Yet men also suffer because of this evolutionary male-dominant culture: Far more men than women die in on-the-job accidents, are detained for crime, and are killed on the battlefield. For these and other reasons, men's life expectancy is constantly lower than women's: It is between 5 and 7 years, depending on a country's conditions and several other social and environmental factors (Baumeister, 2010; Thornton, 2019).

Furthermore, as evolutionary scientists suggest, men's desire for a variety of partners and women's desire for one committed partner (promoted by customs and even religious practices) also played a major role in the evolution of human behavior. Evolutionary "strategies" for men and women were different in some ways. Men throughout sought variety and tried to multiply the number of their offspring. Women's evolutionary strategies were mostly oriented toward protecting resources, selecting reliable partners capable of protecting their offspring, and fighting ways to avoid violence and protect their children. Therefore, men and women, as groups, are engaged in "virtue signaling" (communicating own great personal qualities) differently: Men tend to signal they can provide and protect; women tend to signal they are ready to share and care (Confer & Cloud, 2010; Miller, 2019). Although such ideas of evolutionary psychologists remain assumptions, they are worth discussing.

Social Behavior

Evolutionary theories also attempt to explain stable patterns of social behavior. For example, according to an evolutionary argument, humans can be seen as driven by at least two natural needs: The first is a need for assimilation and inclusion, a desire for belonging that motivates immersion in social groups; the second is a need for differentiation from others that operates in opposition to the need for immersion (Brewer, 1991). Both such needs could be a cause of prejudice and intolerance against other groups (Brewer & Pierce, 2005).

Greed also can be a useful feature when it demonstrates that the individual can protect valuable resources (Miller, 2000). Yet evolutionary theories do not claim that human beings are supposed to be exclusively greedy and violent. On the contrary, people also learned during evolution about kindness and cooperation. How did this happen? The significant changes in our ancestors' environment associated with farming and expansion of communities created new evolutionary demands. People had to show less aggression; greater patience, which was especially vital for farmers; and display greater willingness to trust people from other groups. Then societal pressures made people develop skills required for craftsmanship, commerce, management, and so on (Cochran & Harpending, 2010). Altruism (selflessness) and kindness as individual features should be biologically useful because they serve as a demonstration to others that the person can share resources. An act of self-sacrifice or an act of forgiveness on behalf of the family or community was in many cases evolutionarily useful. Just like violence and greed, human kindness could be a "product" of natural selection as well.

Evolutionary theories tend to remain speculative because we cannot go back in time and demonstrate how certain individual features (such as greed or kindness) emerged and developed in humans. There are some studies, however, that help better explain how evolutionary factors probably worked. For example, researchers in Russia successfully bred silver foxes for many years to create a line of animals that would be, like pets, nonaggressive and playful. In each generation, they would select for breeding only the "friendliest" species. The result of this project involving more than 40 generations of silver foxes was a line of friendly pets. They displayed behavioral, physiological, and anatomical characteristics that were difficult to find in the wild population of foxes. These sociable and friendly foxes had significantly lower levels of adrenaline (associated with reactions to stress), rounder skulls and flatter faces with smaller noses, and shorter muzzles compared to their wild counterparts The features seen in specially bred foxes—including flat faces and smaller jaws, as well as a large space between the height of the cranium and face—tend to be the same features that humans of various cultures find by researchers as both friendly and beautiful (Goldman, 2010; Mehrabian & Bloom, 1997).

SELF-REFLECTION

Studies show that people tend to attribute positive personality characteristics, such as kindness or high intelligence, to physically attractive individuals. Mothers tend to unintentionally treat attractive children more favorably than unattractive ones. As evolutionary psychologists maintain, a friendly face is seen as attractive and beautiful because friendliness is an important evolutionary feature (Elia, 2013).

Questions

1. Just for the sake of this exercise, contemplate for a minute whether other people find you (a) very attractive, (b) somewhat attractive, or (c) not very attractive—based only on your "external" physical characteristics. How did these perceptions of your physical characteristics affect your view of self or your individual features? We will revisit this issue in Chapter 7.
2. Discuss if other people, in your experience, tend to associate a person's physical characteristics, such as attractiveness, with their kindness.

CHECK AND APPLY YOUR KNOWLEDGE

1. Explain this statement: *Genes and environment interact.* Describe yourself and some of your physical and behavioral features, as an example, to illustrate this statement.
2. Have you ever heard phrases such as "the gene for the diabetes" or "the gene for thinness" or "the gene for alcoholism"? We know there are significant genetic factors involved in certain illnesses and behaviors, but we should be very careful not to oversimplify the findings. Search the web using all three words together—*gene, aggression,* and *found.* You will probably find several links to articles about the genetic foundation of human aggression. Pick one article. What is its conclusion? Most likely, if this is a peer-reviewed publication, it will point to an interaction of biological and social factors that affect human aggression. If the article is posted for entertainment

purposes, it will likely try to persuade us that "the gene for aggression has been found." Sensationalism is good for headlines but not necessarily for personality psychology.

3. Explain the meaning of clinical–pathological method.

4. Identify a function of the brain's (a) frontal lobes and (b) the amygdala that is related to an individual's behavior.

5. At least three particularly crucial evolutionary adaptations took place and dramatically affected our ancestors' development: bipedalism (moving by means of two rear limbs or legs), which freed up human hands for tool making; fire building and hunting; and the development of a vocal tract that allowed humans to speak and communicate. Discuss how these three adaptations could have helped our ancestors to build and develop their IG (impulse gratification) control.

6. Define evolutionary psychology.

7. Explain who the alpha males were and their assumed role in human evolution.

8. Why can altruism and kindness be viewed as evolutionary "products"?

What knowledge does personality psychology gain from social sciences and humanities? Here we will start with some important highlights and discussions of such contributions.

Social Sciences

Both natural and social sciences provide evidence about the dual impact of natural and social factors on an individual's functioning (Pickard, 2011). Individuals are not just passive "recipients" but rather active participants in the process of interaction with the natural and social environments. We learn that individuals are dynamic beings who interact with such environments and are constantly transforming themselves in this process (Bronfenbrenner, 1979; Harkness, 1992). Yet understanding the mechanisms of the mind–body and nature–nurture interactions has been and remains one of the most difficult scientific challenges (Gergen, 2001).

Studying the individual in social contexts, social scientists acknowledge that the individual is an integral part of society. People create their social environment and depend on it. Personality psychologists put forward three key summative assumptions:

- The quantity and quality of resources available to the individual and the quality of surrounding physical and social conditions all affect the individual's personality.

- Specific interactions of the individual with the environment (both physical and social) affect the individual's specific traits, which develop as a result of these interactions.

- Individual differences and group differences can be explained, to a significant degree, by the variations in their social environments.

Abundance or scarcity of resources profoundly affects human behavior and an individual's personality features. Research shows that poverty, for instance, is distinctly linked to a shorter life span and poorer health (Canudas-Romo, 2018). The poor tend to live in more harmful environments and are more likely to be exposed to diseases and other risks than those who are not poor (Wairaven, 2013). Malnutrition in childhood, particularly during the first year of life; childhood infections; social instability; and exposure to accidents and injuries all make chronic and sometimes disabling diseases more likely in adult life, causing substantial changes in individual activities. Poverty affects the way people make decisions, form habits, and see themselves and others (Banerjee & Duflo, 2019). Research related to the impact of social and economic factors on individuals will be addressed throughout the text.

Climate and environmental changes and trends both have a tremendous impact on the individual. Harsher climates involve a wide variety of risks and challenges, including severe food shortages, limited diets, air pollution, unclean water, and resulting health problems. People living in regions exposed to harsh climatic conditions persistently face greater risks compared to people living in mild climates and safer environmental conditions (Van de Vliert, 2006). Some remarkable facts have emerged. Consistent levels of pathogens (infectious agents such as microbes) could partly explain people's propensity to interconnectedness and collectivism. How? Groups facing high prevalence of local pathogens (to which they develop resistance) tend to protect themselves from strangers (who— who knows?—possibly carry new germs). Therefore, such groups develop behavioral norms to be more inward-oriented, protective, and collectivist (Cashdan & Steele, 2013). Moreover, in areas with pathogen prevalence, both men and women place greater value on a potential mate's physical attractiveness (Gangestad et al., 2006). Certain parasites tend to degrade physical appearance. Therefore, a person's looks may quickly suggest (correctly or not) this person's health status.

Social scientists suggest that particular personality features develop in certain historic conditions. The American sociologist Fredrick Turner (1920) argued that while facing the challenges of the frontier, Americans developed their frontier spirit and individualistic features because they were mainly conquerors and builders. Similar speculative assumptions were common in social sciences in the past. More recent research, however, produces some intriguing conclusions. Japanese scholars (Kitayama et al., 2006) found that people in Hokkaido, the northern island of Japan with a history of frontier spirit, showed a greater degree of individualism than did mainland Japanese who don't have such a history. Another well-known study published in *Science* examined agricultural practices, such as rice and wheat growing. Both required significant cooperation among farmers; however, farmers who grew rice (before mechanization of agriculture) had to expend twice as many hours doing so as those who grew wheat. Therefore, rice-growing communities such as those in India, Malaysia, and Japan had to develop more "cooperative" labor practices and thus collectivist traits compared to Europeans or some other farmers, such as in northern China, who mostly grew wheat (Talhelm et al., 2014). Wheat-growing societies also required cooperation and mutual help, yet to a smaller degree, compared to rice-growers. These societies have developed less collectivist behavior and outlook in their members.

The Economics Dimension

Economists make their contribution to personality psychology because they study and try to explain the connections between economic factors and the individual's personality and behavior. Consider several illustrations.

Do you think wealthy individuals are different from poor ones in terms of their personality features? Would you say the thinking patterns and everyday habits of the super rich are different from those in the middle class? Economist Karl Marx (1818–1883) and later his many followers called "communists" suggested that there are "higher" and "lower" classes based on their access to resources, and ultimately, power. How does people's social class affect their behavioral and psychological features? Social classes, according to Marx, pursue their fundamental class interests: The *haves* (the wealthy) want to keep the resources and power in their hands, and the *have-nots* (the poor) want to redistribute power and resources to have their share. Thus, social classes create their own values, customs, and even individual habits that serve their class interests! One of the most important ideas for personality psychology to examine is that individuals tend to develop **class consciousness**, a set of core beliefs and perceptions about their life and the world around them based on their social (class) position in the society. In practical terms, people born to luxury or privilege or those who are surrounded by poverty and injustice are expected to develop different personality features relevant to their socioeconomic status. Arrogance and greed, to name a few, as behavioral patterns, would be attributed to the *haves* and kindness and cooperativeness would be attributed to the *have-nots*.

What specific personality features are developed, and how can researchers prove that individuals have different qualities because they belong to different social classes? Sociologists and psychologists have tried to study and answer these questions for years. Studies in the former Soviet Union and in China conducted some 40 years ago showed that people in egalitarian societies (where private property was outlawed so that people were in theory economically and socially equal) tended to be more collectivist, honest, altruistic, generous, and optimistic than people living in capitalist countries, who were described as more greedy, individualistic, and pessimistic. However, the results of such studies are questionable because they haven't been properly peer reviewed by independent scholars. Also, many researchers who conducted such studies received financial and professional incentives, and they were even required by the government to demonstrate in their research the superior features of people living in communist countries (Shiraev, 2021). These criticisms should not diminish the importance of the economic dimension of academic research into personality. Access to resources (money, housing, education, and employment) affects many aspects of individual behavior, habits, and beliefs. Studies showed that social and economic inequality, as well as discrimination of one group against others, could affect a host of psychological features in individuals living under those conditions (Fowers & Richardson, 1996; Jenkins, 1995).

Economists and personality psychologists share common interests: They study people's behavioral patterns as well as how people make decisions. Which factors influence their decisions? These factors include reasoning, mistakes of judgment, habit, group pressure, and so on. These are our daily choices, for example, when we are buying an app for our phone, declining a wedding invitation, or choosing a roommate. The cooperation between psychology and economics has been very productive. For instance, the 2002 Nobel Prize in economics went for the first time in history to psychologist Daniel Kahneman (b. 1934) for his research on systematic biases of individual decision-making. We will turn to his research later in this chapter.

Social Science and Typology

Social scientists also study individual types based on their **social status**, or position within society. Social status can be a measure of an individual's access to privileges and power. Sociologists most often put people in categories according to their income, education, gender, age, and occupation and then try to see similarities and differences in their behavior, opinions, and personality features. Studies show that an individual's perceived social status affects other people's perception of this individual as a person. People tend to perceive and respond differently to a perceived low-status person compared to a high-status person (Fiske, 2010). Social scientists also study **stereotyping**, a generalization of others' behaviors and traits based on their social status or membership in a particular gender, age, ethnic, or professional group. On these pages, you will see many examples of stereotyping as well as suggestions for ways to reduce it.

CHECK AND APPLY YOUR KNOWLEDGE

1. Name the two key summative assumptions (related to the study of personality) of social sciences.
2. Explain the phenomenon known as the "frontier spirit" in America and Japan.
3. What is class consciousness? How does it relate to the study of personality?

The Humanities

Personality Psychology Learns From Studying Philosophy

Philosophy is rooted in a global intellectual tradition spreading its roots across continents and millennia. Across regions and times, philosophers emphasized the importance of education, friendship, cooperation, hard work, and the ability to persevere in difficult circumstances. "How should we live?" asked Aristotle (384–322 BCE), who lived in Ancient Greece. He, like many other philosophers, believed that the individual should develop the capacity for virtue—a stable set of character traits to think, feel, and act in the right way (Pickard, 2011; Warburton, 2012). Moderation in desires and actions was valued by many European, Indian, and Chinese philosophers since hundreds of years ago. Many philosophers searched for the essence of moral behavior, which we call these days the "golden rule": Act according to your rational will but assume that your action, to be considered moral, should become a universal law for others to follow. In other words, treat others as you would like others to treat you (Gensler, 2013; Kant, 1956/1785).

Most philosophers endorsed **enlightenment**, which is the view and action of validating knowledge and education based on science and reason rather than on religious dogmas. Philosophy celebrates the educated individual. The propensity to learn and reason is the essence of humans. Ancient Indian philosophers compared education with personal liberation from fear and despair. Chinese thinkers, such as Confucius (c. 551–479 BCE), emphasized the importance of education for an individual to become an efficient member of society. Although philosophers expressed different ideas about how the individual should learn, they emphasized the necessity for the learned to apply their knowledge in the right, ethical way. The ability to think critically was also enthusiastically desired (Collins, 1990).

Philosophers initiated the discussion about the interaction between the natural tendencies, or inborn factors, and the quality of the learning process. These thinkers commonly associated the lack of education with the inability to live a productive, fulfilled, and happy life. Most modern philosophers agree with social scientists that a deliberate, planned intervention in many areas of society should be beneficial to human growth and improvement (Nugent, 2009).

Many philosophers wrote about various personality types and produced some interesting and detailed descriptions of such types. At least two clusters of their assumptions are important in the context of personality psychology. In vertical hierarchical typologies, philosophers placed the types in a particular ranked order to indicate the strength, purity, skills, or other features of the individual, such as social status (like in social sciences). For example, the Greek philosopher Plato (427–347 BCE) believed in different quality of the souls. According to his classification, philosophers and public officials are likely to possess the highest quality rational souls. Warriors have strong affective souls. Others should have dominant desirous souls. In horizontal typologies, the types appear as somewhat loose clusters assembled by the philosopher's creative imagination. For example, the English philosopher David Hume (1711–1776) described four personality types: The Epicurean type displays elegance and seeks pleasure; the Stoic is a person of action and virtue; the Platonist type regards philosophical devotion; and the Skeptic is the critical thinker (Hume, 1777/1987). Such characteristics and types, are, of course just assumptions—they may be intriguing—but still, they remain untested assumptions.

Personality Psychology Learns From Studying Religion

Beliefs, practices, and prescriptions relevant to the supernatural and the relationships between the individual and the supernatural are commonly called **religion** (Smith, 1982). Religion is different from philosophy. When philosophy relies mostly on science and logic, religion turns to faith. When philosophy embraces critical reason, religion turns to prescriptions and trusts in tradition. As you should remember from Chapter 1, religious knowledge commonly appears in the form of human values usually supported by custom. Religion does not necessarily reject science—it embraces it. However, it requires putting faith before science when there is a contradiction between the two. We should keep in mind that for centuries religion's influence on science, social sciences, and humanities was significant.

For a psychologist, religious values are a rich source of knowledge about the individual's inner world, behavior, and personality. Religious knowledge is both descriptive and perspective. It describes various individual features and explains the individual's inner world and behavior. It also prescribes the rules and directions of thinking and action.

First, religious beliefs reflect the **transcendental** (spiritual, nonphysical) side of human experience. Religious beliefs contain the idea that something larger and more important than human beings should exist and govern our behavior (Park, 2005). Good and bad things can happen to us beyond our control. Research shows many individuals share the view that several aspects of our lives are out of our personal control or that our control is almost inconsequential. We return to these studies and the phenomenon called *locus of control* in Chapter 5.

Second, religious beliefs offer people a distinct possibility of extending their life beyond the time of their physical existence. This can happen because, according to religious teachings, people have a soul. Across religions, the soul is perceived as immortal, indivisible, active, and existing independently of the body (Collins, 1990; Fernandez et al., 2010).

Third, religious teachings often embrace mysticism—a belief in the existence of realities beyond rational reflection or scientific scrutiny, but accessible by feelings. Mysticism is reflected in many teachings, including the Sufi tradition in Islam, the Kabbalah tradition in Judaism, and in the Christian tradition in general (Shiraev & Levy, 2024).

Fourth, religions teach that happiness is possible. Individuals can achieve this stage through their own effort. For example, Buddhism and Hinduism teach about pursuing and reaching nirvana, or a state of profound peace of mind and perfect enlightenment (Collins, 1990). We shall return to these views when we discuss the Humanistic views in personality psychology.

Finally, religious teachings tend to prescribe particular behaviors and urge the development of certain desirable personality traits, such as kindness, humility, and self-control. Behaviors such as learning, sharing, and helping others are also strongly encouraged. Religion postulates behavioral taboos—actions and behaviors individuals should eliminate or repress, which often cannot be negotiated or traded (Saroglu, 2011). For example, anger, impulsivity, and jealousy are criticized across faiths. People should not consider wealth and power as the main goals of their lives. Vanity is sinful. Religious knowledge contains detailed descriptions of desirable and undesirable individual types. Some religious teachings provided a clear dichotomy: They separated divine beings (such as saints) from profane beings (such as demons). In other religions, such as Hinduism, the divisions appear more complex because good and evil are usually viewed as intertwined. We will discuss this in some detail in Chapter 6.

In prescribing behaviors, religious teachings introduce two interconnected types of action. One requires our individual effort and engagement of others. The other path is inaction and even disengagement based on self-limitations. These paths (for example, in Christianity or Buddhism) are not mutually exclusive. They both can lead toward moral behavior and happiness (see Table 2.1).

TABLE 2.1 ■ Religious Prescriptions of Engagement and Disengagement		
Prescriptions	*Action and Engagement*	*Inaction and Disengagement*
Positive prescriptions and values	● Become an activist; volunteer. ● Engage others. ● Make a difference.	● Do not impose your views. ● Grow inside through self-discipline, knowledge, and mediation.
Negative prescriptions and taboos	● Abstain from harmful substances. ● Abstain from sex before marriage. ● Confront evil temptations involving greed, vanity, or anger.	● Reject excessive wealth, greed, and do not consider material success as your ultimate goal. ● Pursue a simple life; embrace asceticism wherever you can. ● If in position to help others, help

Sources: Ellens, 2011; Graham & Haidt, 2010.

What does personality psychology gain from the study of religion? Just for starters, psychologists are interested in how religious values and habits affect individual traits and other features, such as self-esteem, altruism, or conscientiousness. Psychologists working in alcohol and drug rehabilitation programs can also apply their knowledge about religious beliefs affecting moderation, temperance, and other forms of impulse control. Most important, religious teachings that encourage self-improvement certainly interest psychology theorists and practitioners (Dahlsgaard et al., 2005). In summary, religious beliefs and prescriptions suggested valuable information about the individual's inner features such as self-cognition, self-growth, the psychological nature of good and evil behavior, and overt behavioral features such as moral and volunteer behavior.

Arts

How do those artistically created objects help our study of personality psychology?

The Greek author Homer, about 3,000 years ago in approximately 800 BCE, immortalized Odysseus, the famed traveler, who overcame the temptation of the lure of the beautiful yet deadly Sirens. In today's terms, Odysseus had strong IG control. Poets and novelists masterfully described patience and endurance. Chinese scholars 2,000 years ago and European and Middle Eastern philosophers of past centuries praised restraint and moderation as most appropriate personality features and denounced impulsivity and immediate gratification of desires. Being a good person was almost always meant to be self-controlling.

Writers and sculptors are not scientists. Unlike researchers, they artistically reflect their observations of other people, they encourage new reflections of human beings, and they are influencing those who enjoy their art.

Describing

In the 1951 book *Catcher in the Rye* by J. D. Salinger, we learn about the insecurities, identity struggles, alienation, depression, and personal growth of the novel's main character, Holden Caulfield. A stream of his experiences creates in our memory an image of a unique individual personality. Art, at its simplest, is a form of communication. Artists express their vision of human beings—their looks, postures, actions, and characters—and then convey it to their audience. Artists also attempt to portray, reflect, and even creatively explain the inner world of others—their thoughts, desires, uncertainties, and emotions. Artists depict specific and recognizable individuals as well as create images of certain individual types. Some artists try to be as close to reality as possible, while others turn to imagination. We learn from them.

Artists (such as actors, directors, and writers) also convey to us their thoughts, beliefs, emotions, moods, and intentions. An artist's creation is often a window into the artist's mind and personality. By studying their creative works, we learn about artists' personality traits as well. For example, in the classic film *Forrest Gump* (1994), we learn from the character played by Tom Hanks about the extraordinary power of kindness and forgiveness. In another example, the contemporary Norwegian author Karl Ove Knausgård, who began his six-book series *My Struggle* in 2009, masterfully reflects on the most complex and profound inner psychological battles of the individual living in the 21st century.

Encouraging New Reflections

Artists also give the reader or viewer an emotional impulse to look around, ask questions about their lives, revisit the dilemmas they face, and think about the moral choices they make. Their work can encourage us to think critically and analyze other people's behavior, scrutinize their choices, and even speculate about their possible actions. A stroke of a brush or a poetic verse makes us think about others and search for some yet unknown features of human experience and behavior. Art can also serve as a source of entertainment and relaxation by stimulating curiosity, joy, and positive mood.

Images and words can also bring about individual action by encouraging us to look inside our own minds and think about the meaning of our own lives, the decisions we make, the differences and similarities among humans, or the nature of good and evil within us. Art provides a means to express the imagination and bring about inner changes. People do not necessarily copy the behavior of literary characters. The changes may be subtle but produce new perspectives on self and the world (Fairhall, 2012). And as we change our views, habits, and personality features, those individual changes may bring social action, which can bring about social change (see Figure 2.2).

Affecting an Individual's Personality

How can we understand the impact of art on an individual's personality? Several influences should be considered. The first one is socialization, which can be direct and indirect (as is noted earlier in the chapter). Studies show that reading books and stories, sharing these stories, and thinking about them are all important elements of socialization and growth (Thorne & Nam, 2009). When parents read stories to children, the latter learn about the characters from these stories and their personality features. This knowledge may affect individual behavior and personality traits: After watching a film or reading a book about other people, we often self-reflect about ourselves. Then a behavioral change is possible. A person may start thinking and acting differently; habits can change, so do several personality features.

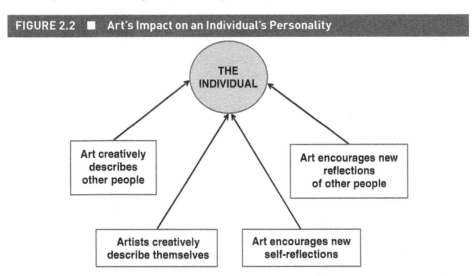

FIGURE 2.2 ■ Art's Impact on an Individual's Personality

There is also evidence that suggests literary works had an impact on scientists who have contributed to personality psychology. To illustrate, literary creations of Ancient Greeks and Romans influenced scores of social scientists and psychologists of modern times. Tragedies by Sophocles gave inspiration to Sigmund Freud—one of the most prominent psychiatrists of the past century (see Chapter 4). Epicurus's ideas about friendship were highly regarded by the philosopher Nietzsche (Dumont, 2010). Nietzsche also credited the influence of Dostoyevsky, whose impact on today's views of personality, on the nature of good and evil, is noteworthy. Petrarch influenced Renaissance humanist philosophers for at least a couple of centuries and beyond. Psychologist Lev Vygotsky, author of impactful theories of the child's development, was deeply inspired by Shakespeare's *Hamlet*. Other examples will follow in later chapters.

CHECK AND APPLY YOUR KNOWLEDGE

1. Explain the transcendental side of human experience.
2. How would you explain *nirvana*?
3. Does religion affect your behavior directly? Discuss a few examples illustrating the impact of your religious beliefs on your daily habits and behavior.
4. How does art impact an individual's personality?
5. Which literary or film character has had at least some impact on your ideas or behavior? The impact does not have to be direct and overwhelming. It can be limited and subtle.

HOW DO WE APPLY KNOWLEDGE?

Sciences, social sciences, and humanities celebrate knowledge over ignorance, care over indifference, and moral values over indecency. The process of learning, as the Greek philosopher Aristotle believed, should essentially give us the capacity for *virtue*, a stable set of character traits to think, feel, and act in the right way (Pickard, 2011). Scientific knowledge provides personality psychologists with a vast arsenal of theories and facts to search for virtues in us and other people and apply them to various areas of life.

Applying Knowledge to Self

Know Yourself

Do you know yourself? Just describe your basic physical and social features. How well do you know them? Use Table 2.2 to answer a few simple questions. To answer them with a measure of accuracy, we probably have to turn to measurements (to check weight, for example), pause for a second and think ("Do I really have health concerns?"), and even contemplate for some time when the question asks about your personal satisfaction with your individual features.

These simple questions about some of the most obvious individual characteristics are not as superficial as they may seem. They can encourage us to pay more attention to our health, habits,

TABLE 2.2 ■ Knowing Own Individual Features	
Individual Features	**Assessments**
Physical features: Describe your height, weight, body shape, and so on.	**Are you satisfied with your physical features?** Mostly satisfied Not sure Mostly dissatisfied
Health: Describe if you have health issues or concerns today (including psychological health).	**Are you satisfied with your health?** Mostly satisfied Not sure Mostly dissatisfied
Social status: Describe your income, living conditions, and education today.	**Are you satisfied with your social status?** Mostly satisfied Not sure Mostly dissatisfied
Personal relationships: Describe your friends, relatives, and people with whom you are close today.	**Are you satisfied with your personal relationships?** Mostly satisfied Not sure Mostly dissatisfied
Daily habits: Describe the things you do regularly, the daily routines.	**Are you satisfied with your daily habits?** Mostly satisfied Not sure Mostly dissatisfied

or lifestyle. For instance, have you seen a doctor lately to judge with confidence about your health? Did you discuss lately your educational or work plans with someone? With whom did you discuss these plans? Who are your friends now? Are most of your habits healthy and helpful? The study of personality psychology ought to start with simple self-evaluation of the facts about you.

Improve Yourself

Behavioral economists suggest that to be successful as an individual, you have to make the most reasonable decisions by (a) maximizing your gains and (b) minimizing your losses (Levitt & Dubner, 2005). Psychologists in cooperation with other scientists propose effective techniques to improve the effectiveness of our decisions and life in general. For example, do you worry about your frequent inability to focus on tasks and difficulty finishing projects in time? There are great suggestions on how to improve your ability to focus. The "deep work" method should allow you to ignore all those distracting emails, texts, postings, and videos and focus on your immediate task instead (Newport, 2016). However, these improvements require knowledge, critical thinking, and hard work. And, of course, you have to make a decision first: Do you want to improve yourself? Do you want to be a better person? Start with a simple step: Keep a daily journal to list all of the things for which you are grateful. Research shows people who keep such a journal reported significantly increased feelings of happiness and increased healthy behavior, which are interconnected (Emmons & McCullough, 2003). Contemplating and sketching a plan should be helpful (see Table 2.3).

©iStockphoto.com /Orbon Alija

PHOTO 2.3 Do you exercise regularly? If you do, how does being active affect your individual traits? If you do not exercise, does this inactivity reflect your personality?

TABLE 2.3 ■ Changing Own Individual Features	
Individual Features	*Areas of Change*
Physical features: Describe your height, weight, body shape, and so on.	Do you want to change your physical features? In which way? How soon? What will you likely do?
Health: Describe if you have health issues or concerns today.	Do you want to change your health status? In which way? How soon? What will you likely do?
Social status: Describe your income, living conditions, and education today.	Do you want to change your social status? In which way? How soon? What will you likely do?
Personal relationships: Describe your friends, relatives, and people with whom you are close today.	Do you want to change your personal relationships? In which way? How soon? What will you likely do?
Daily habits: Describe the things you do regularly, the daily routines.	Do you want to change your daily habits? In which way? How soon? What will you likely do?

We can change our minds and bodies and make more effective decisions if we commit to an effort to achieve this. Consider **yoga**, for example, a system of beliefs and practices to facilitate the transformation of body and consciousness (Flood, 2012). It is rooted in various religious traditions, especially in Hinduism and Buddhism. Yoga is used these days in the West as well as globally as a comprehensive exercise program, focusing simultaneously on body and mind (Sutherland, 2014). Research showed that learning and practicing yoga helps individuals in addressing their emotional problems, such as depressed mood and excessive anxiety (Sathyanarayanan et al., 2019; Streeter et al., 2010). Yoga is a source of positive changes in behavior and thinking, staying focused, avoiding excessive stress, and learning about your own body and mind (Deshpande et al., 2009). Yoga also teaches us to be ethical, honest, and nonviolent (Broad, 2012). It is important to practice concentration and self-discipline. An important role in self-improvement, attributed to meditation, is a broad range of principles and techniques of self-reflection, concentration, and contemplation. We will return to this subject in Chapters 8 and 12.

Strive for Happiness

Some scientists and philosophers (we will learn more about them in Chapter 9) predicted a major crisis in the middle of every person's life—a crisis at which we all seriously question our life and accomplishments halfway through our lives (Camus, 1951/1992). Contemporary sciences and humanities tell us that such "inevitable" crises in the middle of someone's life are more uncommon than common. Moreover, they are avoidable. The Dutch professor Ruut Veenhoven (2008) showed that happiness is largely built on three factors: positive emotion (the pleasant life), engagement (the engaged life), and meaning (the meaningful life). These three factors are very much under our control. Psychological research shows that our own educated individual efforts are significant factors of happiness (Lyubomirsky, 2007, 2014). Notice the word *educated* here: Our self-improvement should start with self-knowledge first. The Greek philosopher Socrates's famous assertion remains meaningful today: *There is only one good, knowledge, and one evil, ignorance.*

Practicing psychologists use a therapeutic procedure called **positive psychotherapy**. It is based on the scientific premise that the human mind is capable of changing itself through behavior. The right state of mind affects behavior; the behavior then produces changes within the mind (Seligman et al., 2006). To some people, their meaningful life is associated with their work. To others, meaningful life is their family. Yet to others, the meaning is in their faith. Cross-cultural studies show that religiosity is positively correlated with life satisfaction (Sabatier et al., 2011). The key is to acknowledge that human beings can have many ways to achieve happiness, and they have the right to choose their personal way. Scientists offer many visions of the role that the individual should play in search for and building of happiness. Some suggested an active engagement in daily affairs. Other teachings discouraged too much engagement (Bhikkhu, 2002).

Applying Knowledge to Others

Help People Understand the Sources of Their Problems

Many scientists for centuries emphasized the moral side of human behavior. It was assumed that if people knew the good, they would always do the good. Moreover, people go astray because they do not really know how to act correctly. Many contemporary therapeutic techniques support these assumptions. Psychologists help other people recognize the causes of their behavior, the sources of their pleasure and suffering. Based on this knowledge, professionals help people reevaluate their lives and make a change, if necessary. Modern techniques of cognitive–behavior therapy provide insight into the causes of suffering (Farmer & Chapman, 2007).

Social sciences often view people as members of certain groups or types. We can further learn from sociologists and economists that there are group differences between various social, national, ethnic, age, and gender groups in terms of certain aspects of their preferences, beliefs, and so on. Yet these disciplines also help us see and celebrate the individual beyond these social categories. It is imperative therefore that we avoid biases of **categorization**, which entails a variety of mental shortcuts, or heuristics, that tend to reduce complex and time-consuming tasks of describing and analyzing to seemingly more simple, manageable, practical, and efficient labeling strategies. We all have a repertoire of such shortcuts that we tend to use automatically, without necessarily considering their accuracy or validity in each situation.

Renowned psychologists Tversky and Kahneman (1973, 1982) identified several such shortcuts, the most basic of which they termed the *representativeness heuristic*. Essentially, this involves judging the likelihood that something belongs to (i.e., "represents") a particular category. One of the most common uses of the representativeness heuristic involves judging whether a person belongs to a specific group based on how similar he or she is to the "typical" member of that group. In this way, we may conclude, for example, that Ted (A) is an Asian because he looks like your prototype of an Asian person (B). Or that Jane (A) is a gay because she behaves like your stereotype of a gay (B). In like manner, we use the representativeness heuristic for identifying almost everything about individuals (Tversky & Kahneman, 1974).

How would you interpret, for instance, the results of a study showing that people living in nations with dominantly Protestant cultural histories had more promarket economic attitudes than people from other, non-Protestant, countries (Hayward & Kemmelmeier, 2011)? Would you assume that your fellow student from Denmark (mostly Protestant country) should have different views of free trade compared to another fellow student from Ireland (mostly Catholic country)? The results of such studies present general data about the samples representing large communities but tell us little about specific individuals. As you can readily see, this simple act is fundamental to all subsequent inferences and behaviors: Before any other cognitive task can be addressed, we first must answer this: "What is it?"

Social scientists warn about the categorization error. They teach us about the impressive variability of social and religious groups and identification. These groups and communities may be small or large in size, old or new in history, exclusive or inclusive in membership, strict or weak in affiliation, horizontal or vertical in structure, and even real or virtual (Saroglou, 2011).

Applying Knowledge to the World

Progressivism is a general way of thinking and a social movement based on the deep belief that human beings and their society can be improved through social reform, education, and opportunity available to all people. An increasing number of psychologists historically embraced progressive values (Shiraev, 2015). For psychology professionals, progressivism means an opportunity to apply scientific knowledge to social issues. Progressivism also emphasizes the importance of applied psychological knowledge in at least three areas: (1) health care, (2) education, and (3) social services. There is nothing wrong with seeing yourself as a social reformer who is interested in pursuing the expansion of your professional role in social life and the increased role of psychology as an applied field. Yet to become reformers, we need to gain knowledge first.

CHECK AND APPLY YOUR KNOWLEDGE

1. What is yoga, and what can it do for self-improvement?
2. Explain positive psychotherapy.
3. What is social categorization? Give examples.
4. How different and how similar are religions and their followers? Read about similarities and differences below.

Similarities. Religiosity stands for a degree or depth of one's cognitive, emotional, and behavioral dedication to a religion. There are levels or dimensions of religiosity, which involves believing, emotionally bonding with religious knowledge, behaving, and belonging (Saroglu, 2011). Religious teachings may have relatively similar impact on individuals regardless of a specific religion. Religious rituals and the experience of related emotions seem rather universal across cultures (Saroglu, 2014). Religious teachings may have a different impact on individuals simply because these individuals are already different when they turn to their religions.

Differences. The very specific forms, predictors, and outcomes of religion and personal religiosity should vary as a function of many factors referring to specific geographic region, climate zone, ethnicity, history, politics, and so on. Consider a simple example: Religious groups endorse a great variety of beliefs and rituals regarding food. Jews and Muslims don't eat pork, and Hindus don't eat beef. Catholics don't eat meat on Fridays during Lent. What other important differences—such as food, clothing, and rituals—among different religions can you name?

Questions

Studies show that different religious teachings tend to inspire similar individual features in us, including honesty, goodwill, modesty, and kindness. In other words, if two people belong to different religions yet they are equally bright, kind, and generous, what is the difference then between their religious beliefs in your view? Does their actual everyday behavior make it relatively unimportant what they eat and how they pray? Or do the diet and style of praying matter in our scientific understanding of individuals?

SUMMARY

- Personality psychology is a scientific discipline rooted in the scientific method, which uses carefully designed research procedures to provide reliable and verifiable evidence. Personality psychology is rooted in science, social sciences, and humanities.

- Personality psychology learns from genetics. An individual's personality features, including traits, subsequent behaviors, and psychological experiences, should be influenced by genetic factors. Genetic information activates particular physiological "mechanisms" in the individual's body that affect his or her physical development as well as a wide range of behavioral, cognitive, and emotional features. Genetic and environmental factors interact.

- Neuroscience is another important source of knowledge for personality psychology. Identifiable brain structures contribute to particular behavioral, cognitive, and emotional functions of the individual and her or his personality traits. Specific neurophysiological mechanisms in the brain are associated with particular behavioral, cognitive, and emotional functions of the individual. These physiological mechanisms can explain differences in personality features. Physiological and environmental factors interact.

- Personality psychology learns from evolutionary science. The individual's personality features can be explained as useful, adaptive functions of the individual interacting with the physical and social environment. Natural selection principles can explain similarities and differences in personality traits between different groups of people.

- Social sciences contribute to personality psychology. The quantity and quality of resources available to the individual and the quality of surrounding physical and social condition all affect the individual's personality. Specific interactions of the individual with the environment (both physical and social) affect the individual's specific traits, which develop as a result of these interactions.

- Social science—including anthropology, economics, political science, and sociology— concerns with society and the relationships among individuals within it. The humanities, including philosophy, religion, and art, examine human culture.

- Human beings cannot be understood apart from social bonds and interpersonal relationships, yet they are part of nature as well. Individuals are not just passive "recipients" but rather active participants in the process of interaction with their natural environment. Scarcity, availability, and quality of resources, specific natural factors, and the types of interactions between humans and their environment all affect an individual's behavior, experience, and traits.

- Economists make their contribution to personality psychology by explaining several ways to link economic factors and the individual's personality and behavior. Economic features and individual behavior are interconnected.

- Philosophy is the study of the most general and basic problems of nature, human existence, mind, and society. Philosophy is based on rational argument in contrast to faith. Across regions and times, philosophers emphasized ethical imperatives, the importance of education, honesty, friendship, cooperation, hard work, and the ability to persevere in difficult circumstances. Philosophers endorse enlightenment by validating knowledge and education based on science and reason rather than on dogmas.

- Religion relates to beliefs, practices, and prescriptions relevant to the supernatural and the relationships between the individual and the supernatural. Religious beliefs reflect the transcendental side of human experience, its spiritual or nonphysical realm, and they offer believers the distinct possibility of extending their life beyond the time of their physical existence. Religious knowledge contains detailed descriptions of desirable and undesirable individual types.

- The expression of human imagination through creativity is art. The acts of artistic creation and reflection are important processes in understanding personality. Artists describe themselves, other people, and encourage within us new reflections of others, as well as new self-reflections. Art affects individuals via socialization processes and through the psychologists' new knowledge and its transformation inspired by art.

- In the application fields, social sciences and humanities—for the most part— celebrate knowledge over ignorance, care over indifference, and moral values over indecency. We are encouraged to know more about ourselves, understand our actions, and improve from within. Personal enlightenment should lead us toward a better understanding of others and the world around us. This will lead to an educated action.

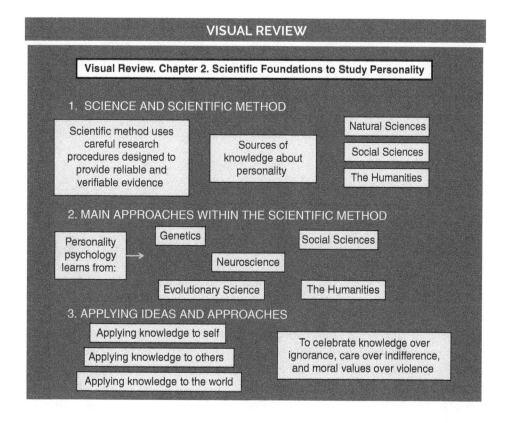

VISUAL REVIEW

Visual Review. Chapter 2. Scientific Foundations to Study Personality

1. SCIENCE AND SCIENTIFIC METHOD

Scientific method uses careful research procedures designed to provide reliable and verifiable evidence

Sources of knowledge about personality

Natural Sciences

Social Sciences

The Humanities

2. MAIN APPROACHES WITHIN THE SCIENTIFIC METHOD

Personality psychology learns from:

Genetics

Social Sciences

Neuroscience

Evolutionary Science

The Humanities

3. APPLYING IDEAS AND APPROACHES

Applying knowledge to self

Applying knowledge to others

Applying knowledge to the world

To celebrate knowledge over ignorance, care over indifference, and moral values over violence

KEY TERMS

alpha males

amygdala

art

behavioral economics

categorization

class consciousness

clinical–pathological method

cognitive neuroscience

culture

enlightenment

evolutionary psychology

evolutionary science

gene

genetics

humanist tradition

humanities

inheritance

marshmallow experiments

natural science

neuroscience

neurotransmitters

philosophy

positive psychotherapy

progressivism

religion

scientific method

social science

social status

sociology

stereotyping

transcendental

yoga

EVALUATING WHAT YOU KNOW

Define *scientific method.*

Explain the role of sciences in personality psychology.

Explain the role of social sciences in personality psychology.

Explain the role of humanities in personality psychology.

Give examples of the three areas of application related to self, others, and the world.

A BRIDGE TO THE NEXT CHAPTER

Year after year, decade after decade, psychologists, like prospectors or gold seekers, tried different theories, concepts, methods, and approaches to advance their knowledge of personality. Offering their findings for critical peer review or other forms of professional evaluation, psychologists "filter" and accumulate the best, most successful, and effective methods of investigation of personality. First travel, then paper publications, and now online articles make this knowledge available to more people globally. Besides psychology, other disciplines now provide reliable and relevant facts. Yet how do psychology and other disciplines supply these facts? How do they obtain them? The next chapter turns to studying the methodology of personality psychology.

3 RESEARCH METHODS

Peter Dazeley/Photographer's Choice/Getty Images

LEARNING OBJECTIVES

After reading this chapter, you should be able to do the following:

- Identify the primary research methods used in personality psychology as well as common biases in collecting and interpreting research data.

- Describe the key steps in conducting research into personality.
- Identify ways to apply critical thinking skills in conducting research into personality.

They will first check your identification documents to verify your birth date, birthplace, and your current address. Then they will measure your weight and height. Then they will verify your education and employment history. Your parents will be visited to learn about their parenting style. Then they will ask you to tie a necktie. Can you cook a meal? Please do. They will taste it. After reviewing your meal, they will ask you about your dating history. They will verify your answers. They will ask you about how you manage your money. More questions will address the breadth of your general knowledge and your formal intellectual skills. A few questions will evaluate your life experience, attitudes about marriage and family, and plans. Next, they will ask you how much money you would give to a beggar on the street. Finally, they will look at your self-introduction video.

Who are *they*? Maybe a government institution or a casting agency for a reality show? No, they are neither. In fact, they are a matchmaking agency in the Hunan province, China. The agency does an exhaustive background check and personality assessments of their applicants. This is not a dating service, which are plenty in China (in fact, matchmaking businesses make one billion dollars a year). The company selects potential brides for very rich, single Chinese entrepreneurs. These entrepreneurs pay tens of thousands of dollars to prepare their "wish lists" of personality characteristics in an ideal bride. Although most of the potential grooms are looking for a "good woman, good wife, and good mother" (as they put in their applications), the specific requirements, as you can imagine, vary greatly.

If this service were available to you now, would you apply as a candidate to be matched with a successful entrepreneur and professional man or a woman?

Critics view the methods of this "matchmaking" service as vague and superficial. Yes, a person's height, weight, memory, and intellectual skills can be measured, but how can an individual's compassion, empathy, or piety be quantified? Supporters argue that the methods are good enough and in line with what we do daily. We all are engaged in spontaneous matchmaking: We seek and find new friends, business partners, intimate friends, and spouses. The difference between our daily "searches" and matchmaking services is that the latter does it seemingly professionally, with the use of psychological science.

Is it possible to design a research method to predict whether two people will fall in love? Do your weight, height, moderate openness to experience, and good creative skills make you a better candidate to marry Person A but not B? Or, looking from the other point of view, if the assessment methods were to measure personality features and predict future behavior with some precision, would you be curious to see if someone is the best match for you?

As one of the candidates in China said, "What's wrong with wanting to love a rich guy? I am young, pretty, and smart, and I deserve someone who can match me." Besides, China is a country of more than 200 million singles.

Source: Coonan, 2012; Kuntz, 2019; Moore, 2015

PERSONALITY RESEARCH METHODS

This chapter deals with research assessment methods in personality psychology. Some of these methods and critical procedures should be familiar to you from introductory psychology classes. This chapter will provide a critical overview of several research strategies and offer critical suggestions about gathering, analyzing, and interpreting facts in research into personality. Here, as an introduction, we will review several most important methods and outline some of their critical assessments. Further discussions of specific methods will follow in every chapter. There is no "one-size-fits-all" standard research strategy and procedure that every psychologist must follow. In fact, almost every research procedure is unique. Psychologists who study personality pursue different goals, have different resources available to them, and work in different social and cultural circumstances. Researchers' strategies often relate to the specific methods they use and the interpretations of the results they collect. In many ways, they can determine what the final product will be and what practical conclusions it will bring.

What do psychologists try to achieve in studying personality? They pursue at least two general strategies proposed by more than 100 years ago and later developed by the American psychologist Gordon Allport (1897–1967): nomothetic and idiographic (Hurlburt & Knapp, 2006). The **nomothetic** strategy, or approach, uses the same method to compare many people or subjects to a certain average, standard, or norm. This approach focuses on comparisons and generalizations. It pays attention to characteristics in which individuals may be similar to one another or vary. The **idiographic** approach is person-centered and focuses on many characteristics integrated in a unique person. It refers to specific features within an individual and uses various assessments and measurements. In the 20th century, several prominent psychologists, such as American Henry Murray or Boris Ananiev from Russia, believed that the ideographic approach should be the central approach in personality studies: Psychologists would coordinate research of many other specialists, such as doctors, anthropologists, sociologists, and neuroscientists, to study the individual. Today, most psychologists acknowledge the importance of both approaches and the advantages of combining them. For example, studying the prevalence of depressive disorders in first-generation immigrants, a psychologist can gather statistical data and analyze them in the context of individual interviews in which they would share their unique experiences dealing with depression (Borge, 2020).

What type of data would you need to collect? The American psychologist Raymond Cattell (1905–1998), a pioneer in the scientific study of personality, proposed at least three types of methods, which should produce three kinds of data. The first one is so-called L-data, which includes subjective assessment of biographical (life record) data, including age, sex, nationality, education, occupation, work, volunteer experience, and so forth. The second kind of data is produced in self-reports or questionnaires (often called Q-data). In such self-reports, individuals express their views of various real or hypothetical situations and give assessments of their own individual features in specific situations or in general. And finally, T-data, which include descriptions of people's behavior in standardized experimental situations, can be gathered through experimental methods. We will return to these methods again in Chapter 7.

If you look back at the opening case, you will notice the trained staff used all three types of Cattell's methods as well as nomothetic and ideographic strategies to obtain comprehensive data about the individuals they examined.

What specific research methods do psychologists use?

Observation

Scientific **observation** involves acquisition of information about identifiable variables from a primary source. Observation is not just spontaneous witnessing of something or somebody (it could be, of course, in some cases). As a research method, though, observation requires serious preparation. Observation can be of two types: naturalistic and laboratory based. In the laboratory observation, the participants or subjects are brought in, and you—as a researcher—prepare tasks or assignments for them to perform. Researchers in both natural and laboratory cases typically focus on certain manifestations of an individual's behavior. If you are observing from a distance how children share toys in the sandbox, this procedure is likely to be called naturalistic observation. A group of British psychologists, for example, conducted naturalistic observation and focused on the incidents of individual aggression on the streets. The researchers used CCTV street cameras, which are now commonplace in the United Kingdom. Using the camera footage, the scientists spent many hours observing various, although rare, street confrontations. They found that an individual's quick and decisive intervention into a potentially violent street confrontation tends to deescalate this conflict (Levine et al., 2011). Other studies of real-life behavior captured on CCTV cameras also showed that people's decisive peacemaking actions should make a difference in stopping violent behavior. These data have been used in violence reduction training programs dealing with prevention of sexual and domestic violence (Levine et al., 2019).

Direct observations such as these are often difficult or sometimes impossible. How can one examine the facts that took place some time ago and the individual is not available for the study? In this case, the researcher turns to eyewitnesses. Sigmund Freud and William Bullitt (1966) published a study of the personality of the U.S. President Woodrow Wilson. Although the authors did not examine Wilson, who died in 1924, this work was based on other people's observations of the president and many biographical facts. Historians can particularly assist psychologists. The Canadian-born historian Margrett Macmillan at Oxford University provides unique and detailed description of individual personalities of queens, emperors, presidents, and prime ministers—all based on archival documents and eyewitness counts (Macmillan, 2014). Of course, research data about an individual can be collected over various periods ranging from a few seconds to a life span. Observations can be both unstructured and structured. In an unstructured observation, the researcher plays the role of an observer to identify and describe various behavior manifestations involving an individual under observation. The method may be used, for instance, for preliminary investigation into a subject. To illustrate, before conducting a detailed assessment of an elementary school student's behavioral problems, a school psychologist can spend some time observing the student's conduct during recess. In such a case, the psychologist observes as much as possible with no specific behaviors in mind. Whatever seems important for the observer is recorded. Nonstructured procedures are often necessary, especially if the psychologist has no other means to obtain information about behavior in general or specific individual traits (Hintze et al., 2002).

A combination of observation and self-reporting was described in a study in the Philippines (Ho, 1998). The procedure is called *pagtatanung-tanong*, and it can be used in relatively small and culturally homogeneous communities. Researchers avoid making people feel they are "subjects" in a survey. Although researchers ask many questions, they are discussed in a very informal context. Researchers ask prepared and memorized questions in sequence, but the answers they get may lead to the formulation of new questions and further clarifications if needed. Conducting this type of research does not alert or frustrate people, and it allows some personal or other sensitive issues to be discussed. Answers to questions are gathered as research data. The method, in fact, has been assessed as a reliable tool for creating an atmosphere of trust between the interviewer and the respondent. The method can be adjusted to specific conditions or combined with several indigenous research methods to study individuals in unique cultural communities (Wilson, 2017).

Structured observations are based on a plan. You first identify the behaviors or individual features you want to observe. Then you define the specific characteristics of each behavior or feature you want to observe. And then, you register the frequency and duration of the established characteristics under observation (American Psychological Association Dictionary of Psychology, 2022a). Structured observation requires **observer ratings**, or assessment of these observed actions and features. Studies show that observer ratings of other people, by and large, can produce quite reliable assessments. Such ratings should be, however, well-defined and explained to reduce subjectivity of the observation. One study examined data obtained from more than 40,000 people; it showed that personality ratings (evaluations) by friends, family members, or unrelated observers can somewhat accurately predict behavior of the rated individuals based on their observed personality features (Connelly & Ones, 2010).

Observer ratings can be used in various situations and settings. For example, the members of a sorority could assess each other's leadership qualities and rank them. Each sorority member ranks every other member. Then two people with the highest scores become candidates for an office election. This method has been already used in the past in well-known studies when subjects knew each other relatively well, such as family members (Costa & McCrae, 1988). It is also effective in clinical settings when relatives and friends assess psychological features of individuals undergoing treatment—for example, the patients recovering after stroke, or the individuals with different forms and stages of dementia.

Psychologists also need to take into consideration a possible cultural bias of observation methods even in those cases when observer ratings are based on clear, measurable criteria. A cross-cultural study in Japan and Germany researched several applications of a medical protocol to observe and assess motor symptoms in patients with multiple sclerosis. But first, the researchers wanted to create statistical "norms" by measuring motor activities of young and healthy adults in both countries. With the use of such norms, they then could make assessments of patients with abnormal symptoms. Observations showed that despite some similarities between the two groups, in stand-up and sit-down tasks, healthy Japanese subjects, at group level, transitioned faster between sitting and standing, used a smaller range of hand motion, and showed higher knee movement amplitudes compared to healthy German subjects. What was before considered "standard" or "universal" in measures of healthy movements, should be, most likely reevaluated to adjust to the "norms" characteristic of national or ethnic groups. Quantification of motor performance has a promising role in diagnosing and monitoring neurodegenerative diseases or other problems related to aging. Ethnic differences in normative data for motor function have been obtained in the United states as well and several other countries (Otte et al., 2021).

Of course, observation can produce inaccurate and biased data and for different reasons. A school psychologist can assess a boy as hyperactive and inattentive, yet the child's parents disagree and assess him as "spontaneous." One of the remedies is to use multiple observers who are likely to produce a more balanced record of observations of some enduring characteristics of individuals (Kenrick & Funder, 1988). Another remedy is to use, when possible, other research methods in addition to observation (Wrzus & Mehl, 2015). Whenever it is achievable or appropriate, the researcher should verify the facts and check for sources of the received information—for example, when analyzing simple judgments about an individual or detailed written biographies and autobiographies.

Self-Reports

Written opinions, posted comments, videos, pics, emails, and private diaries may become sources of information about people even though they do not necessarily expect or plan that other people will study these materials. Today, many employers study their job applicants' or employees' posted messages and public profiles on social networks to gather information and form impressions about applicants. Although these "impressions" tend to be biased (remember the discussion of *popular knowledge* from Chapter 1), they are increasingly common, everyday ways of personality assessments by non-psychologists.

Other types of self-assessments, such as diaries and memoirs, are often the only sources that allow professionals to make judgments about personality features of individuals, including famous, historic figures. Psychology's history contains many such examples. For instance, Cardano (1501–1576), known also as Jérôme Cardan, was an Italian physician, mathematician, and astrologer. Cardano wrote a detailed autobiography filled with meticulous details about his daily activities, habits, and psychological experiences. From his unique self-report, we learn that he was an optimistic, hardworking, and conscientious person, yet he was bothered by occasional yet unpleasant obsessive ideas (it looks somewhat like a contemporary profile!). In clinical settings these days, clients often provide detailed self-descriptions to help their therapists diagnose and treat their psychological problems. In cases involving legal judgments, psychologists in various countries often use personal statements to better describe individual features of defendants or plaintiffs (Krauss & Lieberman, 2016).

Among self-assessment methods, self-report questionnaires have become dominant in studies of personality (Boyle & Helmes, 2009). For decades, the

Girolamo Cardano. Stipple engraving by R. Cooper. Wellcome Collection. Public Domain Mark

PHOTO 3.1 More than 500 years ago, Jérôme Cardan, a respected Italian mathematician, wrote a very detailed autobiography. How is such a biography different from any individual's Facebook profile today? What kind of information could you gather studying someone's Facebook page?

written questionnaire and the pencil were the most common methods of assessment. Today, these methods are increasingly computerized. Questionnaires typically consist of several statements for a person to evaluate or a list of questions to answer. Respondents, for example, assess whether each statement applies to them, or they express the degree to which they agree or disagree with certain assertions related to their daily habits, moods, and views of self or other people.

Among the most typical forms of questions used in self-assessment are dichotomous, open-ended, and multiple-choice ones. Dichotomous questions give the subject only two choices: to respond *yes* or *no* or *true* or *false*. Open-ended questions typically begin with *What do you think . . .* or *Describe . . .* and give subjects an opportunity to express themselves, explaining some nuances of their thoughts and feelings. However, the answers to open-ended questions are difficult to analyze. Multiple-choice (or close-ended) questions are easier to analyze than open-ended ones. Nevertheless, these questions limit the choices from which the respondent can select.

Psychologists use some questionnaires to examine as many people as possible to establish common trends in the answers. (Remember the nomothetic approach?) Other questionnaires examine several features or traits of one person. (Remember the idiographic approach?) Any set of questions within a personality questionnaire that is designed to measure a particular personality trait is called a *personality scale*. Most personality questionnaires contain several different scales, which means they attempt to measure several personality traits (Archer & Smith, 2014; Johnson, 2001).

Studies conducted over the years suggest that many questionnaires used by professional psychologists can generally predict behavior of an individual based on the questionnaire assessment of his or her traits. However, self-reports are not bias free. Be aware, for example, of **social desirability bias**, which is the tendency of respondents to give answers that are supposed to be received favorably by others. As an illustration, in answering the question *Do you acknowledge your own mistakes?*, many people could be tempted to give a positive answer. To appear humble and self-critical is commonly viewed as a virtue (Levy, 1997; 2009). You should also be aware of a **self-serving bias**—people's tendency to assess their own features as better or more advanced than those of the "average" person. On the other hand, some people tend to diminish their accomplishments or potentials; respondents from Chinese, Korean, and Japanese samples commonly evaluate themselves among the least hard-working in the world. In self-reports, people from Western cultures (e.g., Australians, Americans, Canadians, or Germans) were far more likely to describe their individual traits in terms of internal psychological characteristics and were less likely to describe themselves in terms of roles and relationships than are people from non-Western populations (Heine, 2008; Schmitt et al., 2007). Self-assessment studies show cross-cultural differences between European Americans and Hong Kong Chinese. The Americans displayed higher levels of well-being and positively biased view of the self, compared to Chinese subjects. Living conditions, wealth, education, and certain political factors could have contributed to the differences between the two groups. Another possible factor is that North American culture tends to foster positive evaluations of the self to enhance self-esteem and to feel positive emotions, compared to East Asians (Kim et al., 2016).

Respondents also tend to present themselves in a socially appropriate way. For example, parents tended to be reluctant to admit certain practices, such as spanking and grounding their children (Iusitini et al., 2011). On the other hand, people tend to answer that they would definitely report child abuse committed by others (LeCroy & Milligan-LeCroy, 2020). Studies also reveal that people's concerns about privacy affect the answers (Mills & Singh, 2007). With the spread of Telemental Health Therapy (TMHT), especially during and after the COVID pandemic, the benefits of this long-distance method have been noticeable. However, despite the benefits from these relatively new services, many clients express concerns about their confidentiality when they answer questions from a psychologist online. Digital privacy is an important concern in modern psychological research (Lustgarten et al., 2020). One area of careful attention is research or assessment questions referring to sexuality and sexual behavior. There are cultural, political, age-related, or personal reasons why people give either "appropriate" answers or refuse to answer (Alexander & Fisher, 2003; Shirmohammadi et al., 2018). And then there are selective memories; for example, in testimonies, clinical interviews, or other personal recollections, people tend to remember better the facts that support their point of view and tend to forget others (Browder, 2000; Fine, 2006).

In the following chapters, we will study some of the prominent, cross-culturally tested self-assessment methods, such as the Sixteen Personality Factor Questionnaire (16PF), Minnesota Multiphasic Personality Inventory (MMPI), Clinical Analysis Questionnaire (CAQ), and others.

Experiments

Experimental methods allow psychologists to determine how an individual's behavior and experience vary across different situations (Johnson, 2001). Experiments should give the researcher transparent and often replicable procedures. Not only do researchers ask individuals about, for example, how well they feel after a meditation session, the experimenters design various conditions in which they try to measure the cognitive and emotional changes that take place in participants after meditation. One of such experimental studies showed that mindfulness meditation positively influences the individual's motivation to repair harm caused to others, increases pro-social behavior, and tends to reduce guilt (Hafenbrack et al., 2022).

By varying experimental conditions, psychologists try to detect specific changes in the subjects' behaviors, judgments, opinions, or emotions. In an experiment, the condition(s) that are controlled—that is, can be changed by you, an experimenter—are called the **independent variable**(s). The aspect of human activity that is studied and expected to change under influence of the independent variable is called the dependent variable. As an experimenter, you control the independent variable: You may change the conditions of the experiment.

Researchers using the experimental method should try to avoid many of the biases often found in observations and self-reports. In other cases, experimental procedures allow researchers to design conditions that are difficult or impossible to "assemble" in reality. A group of British and other European scholars, for example, wanted to study why and when individuals intervene in a violent confrontation (the topic was also briefly discussed early in this chapter). Previous research paid the most attention to several outside factors, such as the size of the group. Yet under what individual conditions will a bystander attempt to stop a violent attack of one person against another (Slater et al., 2013)? Obviously, psychologists may not, just out of curiosity, stage real fistfights and brawls on the street. What they may do in addition to observation is design an experimental procedure: a virtual-reality experiment in which the participants were asked to watch several versions of an animated confrontation between an attacker and a victim. The researchers found that at least two factors played a role in the behavior that stops a violent confrontation: the victim's direct pleas for help and whether the victim and the witness shared some common identity features, such as being followers of the same sports club. This work suggests that when it really matters, bystanders can and do intervene (Liebst et al., 2019).

In the following chapters, we will illustrate and critically discuss many other experiments to study personality (see Figure 3.1).

Content Analysis

Content analysis is a research method that systematically organizes and summarizes both the manifest (what was said or written) and latent (the meaning of what was said and written) content of communication. The researcher usually examines transcripts of conversations or interviews, speeches, postings, television or radio programs, letters, newspaper articles, and other forms of communication. The main investigative procedure in content analysis consists of two steps. Initially, the researcher identifies coding categories; these can be nouns, concepts, names, or topics. First-level coding involves identifying properties of data that are clear in the text. Second-level coding involves categorization and interpreting what the first-level categories mean.

To illustrate, Elker Weber, a leading specialist in psychology of risky behavior, compared and content-analyzed thousands of American and Chinese proverbs and popular expressions to study wisdoms related to an individual's risky behavior as well as risk aversion. She assumed initially that in Chinese culture the number of proverbs related to the individual's cautious behavior would be significantly greater than in the West (in the English language). In fact, she found

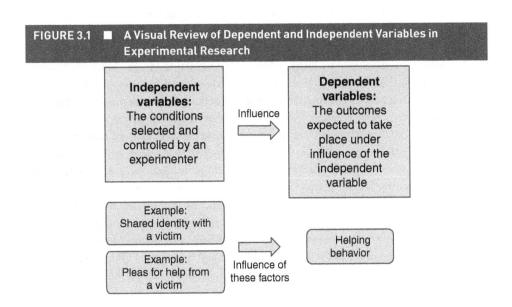

FIGURE 3.1 ■ A Visual Review of Dependent and Independent Variables in Experimental Research

that in Chinese language, sayings related to risk-taking behavior (such as "Seize an opportunity and make good use of it") are more prevalent than similar expressions in English (Weber, 1998).

Projective Methods

If you were a tree, what kind of a tree would you be? Which character in Harry Potter are you likely to be? If you are skeptical of such questions because they seemingly provide little information about the respondent's personality, you are not alone. Some psychologists would argue, however, that these types of questions, if properly designed, could in fact generate valuable information about many individual features, such as a person's interests, concerns, imagination, and even some personality traits. **Projective methods** in personality psychology require the respondent to answer questions or perform tasks—the results of which are expected to reveal certain meanings that are typically concealed from a direct observation (Konnikova, 2014). These tasks include interpreting pictures, drawing sketches, completing stories or sentences, describing other people, and so forth. The ways we describe other people, often called *perceiver effects*, tend to be linked to several stable individual characteristics of the perceiver. In other words, a person's judgment of other people can reveal to psychologists valuable information about this person (Wood et al., 2010).

It is assumed that projective methods can have an advantage over traditional questionnaires because the direct questions may encourage the respondents to give socially desirable answers (as we have mentioned earlier in this chapter). For example, by asking the question *Do you have violent thoughts and how often?*, you are unlikely to register exactly how often the respondent has those thoughts; many people do not want to appear violent. However, asking a person to propose an ending to a short story may not necessarily make the respondent think that she or he has violent tendencies (a respondent may think, "It is just a story after all"). Psychologists study the responses to projective tests and look for their meanings that may reflect certain consistent emotions or motivations that the respondent is unwilling or unable to reveal when preparing a self-report or answering a questionnaire.

One of the classical examples of a projective test is the **Thematic Apperception Test** (TAT), which was developed by Henry Murray with Christina Morgan (Murray, 1938). In its original form, TAT contained 19 pictures creatively selected from popular magazines. A person undergoing testing was asked to tell a story about each of these pictures, which were sufficiently vague to leave enough to the imagination of the person taking the test. Murray's main idea was that the test taker in the process of picture interpretation would reveal specific psychological needs that are difficult to identify by other methods. Murray used the term *themas* to describe stories or interpretations projecting fantasy imagery onto an objective stimulus, such as a picture. When a person experiences a press (an external influence) on his or her needs, a thema is activated to bring this person satisfaction and the sense of power, affiliation, and achievement. By studying these themas, a trained psychologist could reveal the true nature of this person's hopes, wishes, or specific psychological problems (Murray, 1938). TAT received global recognition and was translated into many languages. Different versions were created and became particularly effective for use with Hispanic populations and children of color (Bendi & Garcia, 2015).

The Swiss psychiatrist Hermann Rorschach (1884–1922) authored one of the best known projective techniques known as the **inkblot test** (see Photo 3.2). An inkblot is a spot or stain of ink that has no geometrical pattern or meaning. In the procedure, an individual is shown several pictures (there were 10 in the original version) with symmetrical inkblots on each. The person is asked to generate associations or tell what he or she sees in these pictures. The researcher then analyzes the answers, the commentaries the person makes, the time of response, and other variables. Among the features to analyze can be the person's originality of thought, thinking patterns, aggressive or suicidal tendencies, and a range of clinical features (Weiner, 2003). Over

decades, psychologists and psychiatrists in several countries offered and developed several assessment systems, allowing them to take into consideration cultural and socioeconomic backgrounds of subjects, quantify the answers, and create statistical norms (Allen, 2004). The inkblot test remains particularly popular in clinical assessments in assessment of psychopathological symptoms and executive functions (Theoduloz, 2017).

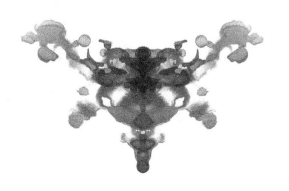

© iStockphoto.com/4khz

PHOTO 3.2 This is an example of a scoring card from an inkblot test. An inkblot is a stain of ink that has no particular geometrical pattern or meaning. The person is asked to generate associations or tell what he or she sees in these pictures.

Mixed and Holistic Methods

In psychological research and practice, most researchers are likely to use several methods of assessment of an individual: self-reports, observations, experiments, and biographical data. To illustrate, Chapter 8, Chapter 12, and others, will discuss individual features associated with happiness. This is not just about feeling good. Happiness is typically described as a complex feature that contains several interconnected states, such as stable subjective experiences and also decisions and actions involving other people. Therefore, to study happiness, researchers commonly use self-reports (to examine individual experiences), observers' ratings (to study a person's impact on other people), and the subjects' accomplishments in life, such as their impact on other people—which is studied by biographical methods (Csíkszentmihályi, 1990, 1997, 2014).

Increasingly often, personality psychologists implement holistic methods of research. In this context, **holistic** refers to the study of systems with multiple interconnected elements. Applied to personality psychology, holistic methods are based on the principle that scientific knowledge of personality cannot be obtained only from studying various features of an individual taken separately from one another—such as experiences, traits, actions, motivation, emotions, and so on. They must be studied together, as a "whole."

Some psychologists use the term *holistic* to refer to intuition, folk knowledge, or rituals in studying an individual. Holistic psychology, in their view, emphasizes spiritual healing,

FIGURE 3.2 ■ Research Methods in Studying Personality

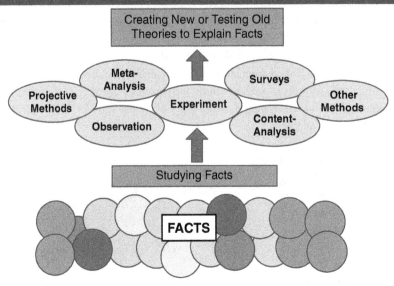

multicultural counseling, and community interventions in case of problems. It stems from the spiritual and wisdom traditions that should be applied to combating illness, injustice, violence, and other problems prevalent in contemporary society (Edwards, 2013).

Yet holistic methods are not necessarily an "alternative" (or nonscientific) type of research in personality psychology. In science, holistic methods attempt to combine different scientific methods and thus produce a comprehensive set of data that can be analyzed on different levels. For a summary of research methods, see Figure 3.2.

CHECK AND APPLY YOUR KNOWLEDGE

1. Describe the differences between nomothetic and idiographic approaches (strategies).
2. What are observer ratings?
3. Give an example of self-serving bias.
4. What is the difference between dependent and independent variables in an experiment?
5. What are projective methods in psychology?
6. You have only 1 minute to draw an image of yourself—the one that would represent your personality in the best way (use a piece of paper or a tablet's screen). Imagine, this image will be preserved for future generations to remind them about you. Use no words. What would you draw or assemble on paper (or on a screen)? When the image is ready, write down specific personality features you wanted to reflect in it. Ask other people to tell their interpretations of the image. What are the most obvious weaknesses of this projective technique?

PHOTO 3.3 How often do you use Wikipedia to get facts? What is an essential weakness of Wikipedia as a source of scientific knowledge?

HOW DO WE PREPARE AND CONDUCT RESEARCH?

We have reviewed several methods of assessment for studying an individual's personality, so the next step is to find the right method for the study. How do we choose the "right" methods of assessment and the correct number of them? Before starting your research, you will need to formulate and describe a problem you need or want to investigate. Why does this problem interest you? For example, you can study something that nobody has studied before. You can continue somebody's incomplete research. Or you can seek a solution to a certain practical problem. In the beginning, you should always ask, *What do I want to achieve by studying this problem?*

Reviewing Your Sources

Now you have identified the problem, and you are about to begin your research; first, you need to determine if anyone has done similar research before. Often, a simple web search will reveal that someone else has already approached your problem. This finding should not discourage you. You may conduct your own study with different methods, and you may obtain different results. Ask these questions: *What methods did the researchers use? What were the other studies' findings? Do you find these findings convincing?*

It is also important, whenever possible, to examine the sources in other languages, other than English. Between 2006 and 2016, English speaking publications made up 97% of the papers in the Science Citation Index Expanded, 95% of the papers in the Social Sciences Citation Index (SSCI), and 73% of the papers in the Arts & Humanities Citation Index (Tindle,

2021). Although English is the key language in personality psychology and the most prominent psychological publications appear in English, we need to avoid this bias and turn to sources in non-English language publications, too.

Describing Your Goals

What do you want to show and achieve by the research? At this stage, you identify what you want to accomplish as a result. At least three goals exist. The first one is discovering. To *discover* is to find something new, previously unknown, unclear, or unresolved. For example, as a researcher, you found the existing studies showing that the divorce rates among same-sex couples were somewhat higher than the rates among different-sex couples and the presence of children increase chances for marital stability in both cases (Allen & Price, 2019). Yet the question you are interested in is to find what personality features are most common in successful different-sex and same-sex marriages. You can also pursue confirmatory strategies, in which the goal is to find support for an assumption that, for example, both spouses' mutual tolerance, respect, and sense of togetherness are connected to marriage stability in both types of marriages. Your research can either support or disprove this assumption.

The second goal is explaining. To *explain* is to show how various elements of reality work. In our case, your research might show why certain individual features help in building successful marriages. You may explain that couples in the most successful marriages, because of their mutual tolerance and respect, tend to resolve a minor problem emerging between them by engaging in a dialogue before this problem grows bigger and leads to a serious conflict. In fact, you also find research supporting your explanation and pointing at mutual commitment as a factor preserving marriages in critical situations (Karimi et al., 2019).

The third goal is predicting. To *predict* is to estimate whether something will happen in the future or if it will be a consequence of something. The art and science of predicting is about applying the results of your research to real-life issues.

Formulating Hypotheses

At this stage, you formulate your research **hypotheses**, which are expectations or proposed explanations for something that you study. Your research should either support, partially support, or reject the proposed hypotheses. Preferably, your hypotheses should be *testable* and *falsifiable*. To make your hypothesis testable, you need formulate it in such a way that allows an empirical verification of it. For example, you wonder why most computer science majors are men and why not many women major in computer science. Indeed, in the mid-1980s, about 40% of computer science graduates were women in the United States. Recently, although there are more women than men graduating from college, they earned only 19% of the computer science degrees awarded in 2016.

You might then propose this hypothesis: Women do not pursue this major because they tend to have low expectations of success in this field. Here, you should design a method to see if the expectations affect the choice of major. By doing this, you prove or disprove your hypothesis and discuss other assumptions, such as whether this gender gap was initially due to a trend to market personal computers almost exclusively to men, and families were more likely to buy computers for boys than girls (Computer Science, 2022).

Falsifiability is the assumption that a research hypothesis should be disprovable, which means that you or somebody else should have an opportunity to test it and, as a result, reject it or support it. For example, the hypothesis that people who are born in April have a higher GPA compared to the ones born in other months is falsifiable because you can test it empirically (you can do it in your class for starters).

Choosing a Sample

Next, you identify the research sample of your study: a single individual's traits or traits of a group of people. It could also be artifacts and other products of human activities, including newspaper reports, children's drawings, posted comments, songs, and so on.

Choosing a sample is usually a challenging task. A **sample** is a part of a larger group so that by studying this sample the researcher generalizes the results to that larger group. Not every sample would allow the researchers to generalize about the larger group. This sample should be **representative**. In a representative sample, its characteristics should accurately reflect the characteristics of the population. There are several ways to assemble a representative sample. One of the most reliable methods is random sampling. In a random sample, everyone is chosen randomly, by chance. A random sample is expected to be representative. The average score received for a representative sample is likely to be a good estimation of the score for the entire population that this sample represents. However, this is just an assumption. Even random sampling may produce an unrepresentative sample.

How big should your sample be? The determination of the size of a representative sample is another challenging task of psychological research. Several statistical methods help determine accurately the size and type of the sample (Heiman, 1996). The **sampling error** indicates the extent to which the sample is different from the population it represents. In general, the smaller the sample, the greater the sampling error. Conversely, the larger the sample, the lower the sampling error. For example, a key study examining leadership characteristics used a sample from 39 countries. This study should have had a lower sampling error compared to a similar hypothetical study that would have engaged samples from only five countries (Offermann & Hellmann, 1997).

On the companion website, you will find an abstract (a summary and conclusions) of a study. Individuals from several countries were selected for the study's research sample. What were the age, education, and nationality of the subjects in this study? What would you do to make this sample more representative?

Choosing Specific Methods

On this stage, you choose a specific research method or several methods. You may use some known methods or design an original one. Research in personality psychology often requires participants to make judgments in response to hypothetical situations, answer questions referring to laboratory tasks, or recall and generalize events and experiences. Every research method chosen for the study should be done in accordance with the requirements of the Human Subjects Review Board (most universities and big research institutions have such boards). This is the administrative and decision-making body that has responsibility for review and approval of research involving human subjects. The purpose of this review—which is a standard practice today in most countries where professional psychologists work, including India, South Africa, or Brazil—is to guarantee that the rights and welfare of human beings participating as subjects in a research study are protected. The European Union (EU), for example, established the Office for Human Research Protections for scholars involved in human subject research in any country of the EU.

By and large, research methodology to study personality can be divided into two categories: quantitative and qualitative. This division is imprecise because these categories of assessment usually overlap. **Qualitative research** does not involve measurement or statistical procedures. Qualitative procedures apply when psychologists study variables that are difficult to measure, such as examining a patient's traumatic experiences, studying children's drawings, or examining the content of folk songs. There are also situations in which standardized measures are not suited or unavailable: Imagine you work with subjects who are illiterate and cannot use answer scales. In such cases, qualitative methods become suitable, as this happened in psychological research in the past (Tutty et al., 1996). One form of qualitative studies is biographical research, or an in-depth analysis of individuals. For example, how can we learn about people's emotions in Ancient Rome? The British scholar Mary Beard examined ancient manuscripts on the art of rhetoric, transcripts of speeches, and jokes (Beard, 2014). She concluded that there were no exact words in Latin for *smile*. Of course, the Romans smiled out of joy; however, Beard suggests, they did not smile to indicate greeting or one's willingness to help.

As it has been mentioned, qualitative and quantitative methods are not mutually exclusive, and psychologists often choose both to use in one study. For example, it is common to use a qualitative method to better understand the studying sample and then design applied quantitative procedures to measure individual psychological features (Roer-Strier & Kurman, 2009).

Quantitative research is about systematic investigation of behavioral or psychological phenomena by means of statistical or mathematical data and various computational techniques. This research is based on measurement and involves recording, measurement, classification, assessment, and interpretation of data. As an illustration, using quantitative methods, the researcher can measure the emotional stability of an individual, compare the strength of organizational skills in a group of applicants for a job, or compare collectivist habits of two or several age or cultural groups. Individual features can be compared and quantified in different groups within a country. For example, some major psychological differences were found in China. A well-known study, already mentioned in Chapter 2, published in *Science* (Talhelm et al, 2014), tested more than a thousand of Han Chinese and found, based on quantitative data, that rice-growing southern China is more collectivist, interdependent, and holistic-thinking than the wheat-growing, more individualistic north.

Being Aware of Biases

One important issue in evaluating personality assessment instruments involves the actual items and how they are phrased. Psychologists carefully approach subjects such as religion, race, sex, ethnicity, religion, and politics. Questions are supposed to be gender-neutral unless the method is designed specifically for a particular group. Psychologists often use focus groups and independent "judges" to check the words used in their methods.

If psychologists try to avoid bias, can they assume that some people deliberately lie or provide careless, inaccurate answers? True, some questions or items on the psychological test can be very difficult or ambiguous, and some subjects give random answers without thinking. Another reason is social desirability, which we have mentioned earlier in this chapter. There is widespread recognition of the nature of social desirability as an important personality variable (Boyle & Helmes, 2009). There are certain procedures that help avoiding the negative impact of deliberately inaccurate, deceptive, or wrong answers to questionnaires. The question *Have you ever driven your car above the speed limit?* may be one of such questions addressed to a driver. The answer *no* will likely indicate that a person may tend to lie. Another reason for providing inaccurate answers is deception—the individual wants to obtain something, such as medical treatment, or avoid a punishment. During a mandatory psychological assessment, a suspect who has been charged with a sexual crime may deny having had any sexual fantasies over the last 20 years. Therefore, many personality questionnaires have so-called *correction scales*. They measure inconsistency or deception in the individual's answers and provide the psychologists who administer tests with valuable information about the subjects.

Checking Reliability and Validity

Reliability is the extent to which a particular method gives consistent results. Each new method typically undergoes a reliability inspection. Several types of such inspection exist. Test–retest reliability is a measure obtained by administering the same test twice over a certain period (a day or a week) to the same person or group. Parallel–forms reliability is checked by giving two or several versions of the test to the same person or the same group. The scores from the two versions are then compared to evaluate the consistency of their results. Sometimes it is possible to check the method's split-half reliability. After "splitting" or dividing in half all items of a test, the researchers then administer these two halves and compare the results. Inter-rater reliability assesses the degree to which different observers or raters agree in their assessments of someone's behavior or other variables. Observers do not necessarily interpret facts the same way; however, the closer their assessments are, the higher the method's reliability is.

Validity of an assessment is the degree to which it measures what it is supposed to measure and not some other variables (Bailey & Burch, 2017). For example, if you want to assess leadership skills of children working on a group task, you have to make sure that you measure these leadership skills and not only children's knowledge of the task or their propensity to speak loudly. In most cases, the method you are using is supposed to measure a relatively stable personality trait and not some responses caused by the situation or other passing influences.

Different types of validity exist. Construct validity is used to ensure that the method assesses what it is intended to measure according to a theory. For example, you measure social dominance orientation (SDO) in a group of trainees. SDO is a personal and stable tendency to accept or prefer circumstances that sustain social inequalities, combined with a general preference for hierarchical social structures (Sidanius & Pratto, 1999). The questionnaire you are using should measure SDO according to how psychologists understand this phenomenon. Using a panel of "experts" familiar with the construct is a way in which this type of validity can be assessed. Convergent validity is the extent to which a method yields the results obtained by other methods when they measure the same phenomenon. To make sure that the results of the study reflect a particular trend and are not due to chance alone, the researcher should repeat the same study to accept the data with confidence or find out about other similar studies. External validity of a method refers to the degree to which the results obtained by this method can be generalized to other individuals, groups, or conditions. Predictive validity is the degree to which a method accurately predicts something that will occur in the future with the phenomenon it studies. Recall the famous marshmallow experiments (Chapter 2) to measure willpower in children. The test might have demonstrated some predictive validity because it could predict general behavioral tendencies in the future.

Analyzing Your Data

Measuring a certain individual personality trait or someone's assessment of other people often requires several attempts. Therefore, among the most used data are measures of central tendency. They indicate the location of a score distribution on a variable; that is, it describes where most of the distribution is located. The most convenient and frequently used measure of central tendency in personality psychology is the mean. The mean indicates the mathematical central point of a distribution of scores.

Scales

When you measure distance, weight, volume, motion, or temperature, the results represent quantity, magnitude, or degree. Individual features can be measured along these dimensions, too. Choosing a correct measurement scale becomes a crucial factor for the overall success of any psychological research. There are four types of measurement scales: nominal, ordinal, interval, and ratio (Stevens, 1946). A *nominal* scale is primarily used for identification purposes. Each score on it does not indicate an amount. This scale does not measure any rank or order and is used mostly for identification purposes. In an *ordinal* scale, the scores designate rank order. A rank order may indicate the subject's preference, accomplishment, or opinion. In an *interval* scale, each score indicates some amount. There is presumably an equal unit of measurement separating each score. With a *ratio* scale, the scores reflect the true amount of the present variable, and zero truly means that zero amount of the variable is present (see Table 3.1).

Correlation

In studying personality, we often need to establish correlations, or the relationships between two or among several variables. If in one set of data, when Variable X is low, Variable Y is

TABLE 3.1 ■ Types of Measurement Scales		
Type of Scale	*Descriptions*	*Examples*
Nominal	The differences between items are based only on their names.	What is your major? Psychology___ Business___ Government___ Communications___ Other___
Ordinal	Each item on the scale allows for a certain rank order.	What do you value the most in other people? Rank these five features: honesty, physical strength, intellect, sense of humor, kindness.
Interval	Items on the scale allow for relatively equal intervals between them.	Which year of your college life was the happiest? First Second Third Fourth
Ratio	This scale possesses an identifiable "zero" value.	How many hours did you sleep last night? 0 1 2 3 4 5 6 7 8 9 10 11 12 13 14

also low, and when Variable X is high, Variable Y is also high, we have a positive correlation between the variables. If, according to another data set, when Variable A is low, Variable B is high, and when Variable A is high, Variable B is low, we have a negative correlation. A measure of correlation—correlation coefficient—contains two components. The first is the sign that indicates either positive or negative linear relationship. The second is the value. The larger the absolute value, the stronger the relationship. For example, the classical study showed that intelligence scores of identical twins raised either together or apart are highly correlated: +0.88. The intelligence scores of nonrelatives raised together are relatively low: +0.20 (Bouchard et al., 1990). Does correlation establish a cause-and-effect relationship between the variables? A psychologist who, for example, finds a positive cross-cultural correlation between (1) violent crime and (2) level of poverty in a particular country, in most cases, would not be able to make a conclusion about which, if either, factor was the cause and which, if either, was the effect or result. In other words, poverty may cause crime, crime can contribute to poverty, or a third variable—unknown to the psychologist—may contribute to both.

Factor Analysis

Factor analysis is a statistical method for identifying clusters of items that tend to be answered the same way. This method, like the empirical method, begins with a large set of items that are administered to a group of respondents. If respondents who agree with Item A also tend to agree with Items B, C, D, and so forth, these items are deemed to measure the same psychological trait. We will return to this method in Chapter 6.

A special statistical method allows psychologists to do quantitative analysis of a large collection of scientific results and integrate the findings. It is called **meta-analysis,** or the analysis of analyses (usually called "combined tests") of a large collection of individual results to make sense of a diverse selection of data. One of the attractive features of this method is the reliance on statistical formulas and an imperative to include a large selection of studies, not just those that appear to be "good" and "interesting." This method often shows results that are difficult to see in individual studies. For instance, meta-analysis of rewarding behavior such as praise, encouragement, and so on across cultures (25 studies altogether) has shown that results yielded by student samples differed from those collected from samples of employees (Fischer & Smith, 2003).

We need to be persistent and patient in the way we apply our knowledge. Yet we cannot simply take one study, read one report, examine one or even several theories, and start applying them immediately. First, we have to learn how to think about the facts we are learning, *think critically*. We have heard this term before. But what is critical thinking, and why is it important to learn its skills?

CHECK AND APPLY YOUR KNOWLEDGE

1. Name the four goals of research.
2. Explain construct validity.
3. Explain one or two "reliability inspection" procedures.
4. Name and explain the four measurement scales.

5. Give examples of a positive and a negative correlation.

6. Research has shown, time and again, that estimates derived from large samples are more reliable than those derived from small samples. Nevertheless, when forming judgments, we typically do not take this principle into account. Consequently, despite the fact that data collected from small samples cannot be counted on as trustworthy predictors of a population's characteristics, we often are prone to commit the error of overgeneralizing from too small a sample. Let us illustrate. What do you think? Does "7 out of 10" look like better odds than "60 out of 100"?

Answer. Yes, it looks as if the first one is better. However, the more reliable indicator is "60 out of 100" because it is drawn from a larger—that is, more reliable—sample. [This is the answer that I would like printed upside down or hidden some way on the page.]

©iStockphoto.com / targovcom

PHOTO 3.4 Imagine a person says to you that she has the personality of a mermaid. Is it intriguing? Maybe. Yet this statement (hypothesis) is unscientific because it is not falsifiable. Explain why.

APPLYING CRITICAL THINKING TO RESEARCH METHODS

Critical thinking is not all about passing skeptical judgments on everything. **Critical thinking** is an active and systematic strategy for understanding knowledge on the basis of sound reasoning and evidence (Levy, 2009). It is rather a set of constructive skills that you can improve and master. Critical thinking is about curiosity, doubt, and intellectual honesty. Curiosity guides in searching for and finding new facts. Doubt helps in producing new ideas and offering new solutions. Intellectual honesty helps in distinguishing facts from opinions and recognizing our own biases.

Imagine a test suggests that A has a higher score on a curiosity scale compared to B. What does this difference in scores mean? Does it say that A is a more curious person than B? So what? Assessments like this should not lead to quick generalizations and judgments about individuals or groups. Tests scores can be important indicators of how an individual thinks, decides, and acts. However, tests do not necessarily allow psychologists to hire or fire an individual. Just 80 years ago in the United States, many psychologists believed that in educational placement, employment and promotion should rely exclusively on psychological tests. However, a certain test performance might not necessarily and accurately predict this person's professional or social potential in the future (Vernon, 1969). Moreover, factors such as a test-taker's language proficiency and motivation, test content, and various contextual factors significantly contribute to people's test performance (Sternberg, 2007). Psychology's history teaches us that the tests created in one social and cultural environment (upper-middle class) tend to be biased against other groups (middle and lower class). Cross-cultural studies reveal that children tend to have many advanced practical and social skills that are not recognized on academic tests (Shiraev & Levy, 2024).

Psychologists seldom, if ever, take test responses and scores at face value. Extra procedures are necessary. For example, there is no shortage of online tests that ask you to answer a few questions and then quickly evaluate your mind skills, personality traits, and even predict your future. Are these conclusions convincing? Such tests are likely to be based on nonrepresentative samples and produce invalid assessments. Although many online tests are entertaining, they do not provide reliable scientific knowledge about personality (Konnikova, 2014).

Distinguish Facts From Opinions

Scientific knowledge (discussed in Chapter 1) is rooted in procedures designed to provide reliable and verifiable evidence based on facts. We need to separate facts from opinions. On the surface, it appears easy: Facts are supposed to be verifiable. Something either happened or did not. On the other hand, opinions are speculations or intuitions about how and why such developments may have taken place. Yet distinguishing facts from opinions can be complicated. Some facts are hidden: How do we know what a person is thinking about now? Other facts can be distorted: People routinely misrepresent their intentions ("Oh, I didn't mean to say that") or feelings ("Oh, I am fine"). Sometimes such distortions are deliberate; sometimes they are not. Yet other facts can be in dispute. One research study suggests that children growing up with one parent develop more psychological and behavioral problems than those with two parents;

another set of studies disputes these findings. In 2020, about 15 million children in the United States lived with a single mother, compared to about 3 million children living with a single father. These families, as families with both parents, have different circumstances, income, educational background, health issues, and community support (U.S. Census Bureau, 2021).

Many people tend to embrace the facts they like and events they approve of but ignore information that appears to challenge their views. A passionate supporter of one theory would select scientific facts to support the idea that Dissociative Identify Disorder (often called *multiple personality*) is linked to an early emotional trauma of childhood. The same person may easily ignore other facts challenging this assumption. The period of the global COVID pandemic between in 2020–2021 showed that significant proportions of the world population believed in government conspiracy behind this global challenge and tragedy. A study in Turkey, for example, showed that beliefs in such conspiracy were not likely to be passing judgment. They were correlated with personality features such as higher faith in intuition, impulsivity, generic conspiracy beliefs, religiosity, and conservative ideology (Alper et al., 2021).

The opinions and beliefs that we hold toward other people can—with or without our intent—actually "produce" or encourage the very behaviors that we expect to find. In other words, a perceiver's assumptions about another person may lead that person to adopt those expected attributes. This phenomenon is known as the **self-fulfilling prophecy**. In what is probably the most famous—and still controversial—study of the self-fulfilling prophecy, Rosenthal and Jacobson (1968) informed teachers at a San Francisco elementary school that on the basis of a reliable psychological test, some of the pupils in their classroom would show dramatic spurts in academic performance during the upcoming school year. In fact, there was no such test, and the children designated as "intellectual bloomers" were chosen at random. Nevertheless, when the children's performance was assessed several months later, those students who had been earmarked as "bloomers" did indeed show an improvement in their schoolwork; even more remarkably, their IQ scores had increased. The teachers thus unwittingly created the very behaviors that they expected.

Separating facts from opinions should help you navigate the sea of information related to personality. It can start with looking for new and more reliable sources of facts. Some facts may appear more plausible on their surface than others. Whenever possible, try to establish as many facts as possible related to the issue you are studying. Check the credibility of your sources. If there is a disagreement about the facts, try to find out why the differences exist. What are the interests and motivations behind these disagreements? The more facts you obtain, the more accurate your analysis will be. If individuals who indicate that they suffer from anxiety score as high as other people known to have anxiety problems, those individuals can also be viewed as suffering from anxiety. If a person indicates in a questionnaire that she is "very generous" yet disagrees with statements such as "I regularly donate to other people," this person is unlikely to be considered generous (Wolfe, 1993).

We need to avoid quick generalizations, which often appear tempting. Although personal testimonies and vivid cases may be very persuasive, they are not inherently trustworthy indicators of fact. Also, when we generalize about research findings, we will remember that the best basis for drawing valid generalizations is from a representative sample of relevant cases. We can generalize, but we should do it carefully.

SELF-REFLECTION

Are you a happy person? On a scale from 1 to 10, how happy are you most of the day? According to surveys by Blue Zones over more than 20 years, the happiest people live in Scandinavia and Singapore (Buettner, 2017). They score the highest on the scale, around 8. Knowing this, if you met a person from Denmark, Finland, or Singapore, would you expect them to be happy? Although some people might be tempted to make such a generalization, we should think critically about this. Just because surveys indicate that people from Denmark and Singapore are the happiest people in the world, that doesn't mean *all* people from these countries are happy. This is true in other instances as well.

Questions

Try to generalize how many people around you are generally happy. A small proportion? About one half? A majority? What will be their average number be on a scale from 1 to 10? Ask people in class to define how happy they are using the same scale. Compare their actual scores with your prediction. How accurate were you?

Describe, Not Prescribe

Language serves many functions. Certainly, one of its most common and most important purposes is to help us describe events, situations, and people. We constantly ask, *What is it?* Another purpose is to evaluate these same phenomena: *Is it good or bad?* or *Is this habit useful or harmful?* Typically, we consider descriptions to be objective, while we consider evaluations to be subjective.

However, the distinction between objective description and subjective evaluation is not always clear. Words both describe and evaluate. Whenever we attempt to describe something or someone, the words we use are almost invariably value laden in that they reflect our own personal likes and dislikes. Thus, our use of any term serves not only to describe but also to prescribe what is desirable or undesirable to us (Shiraev & Levy, 2024).

This problem is not so prevalent in describing objects as compared with people. Take, as an illustration, the terms *cold* and *hot*. For material substances, both terms refer literally to temperature: *That coffee is very cold*, or *That tea is very hot*. When we use these same terms to describe an individual, however, they take on a distinctly evaluative connotation: *J. J. is very cold*, or *E. E. is very hot*.

Our best attempts to remain neutral are constrained by the limits of language. When it comes to describing people (e.g., in conducting research or clinical interviews), it is nearly impossible to find words that are devoid of evaluative connotation. Incredible as it may seem, we simply do not have entirely neutral adjectives to describe personality characteristics, whether of an individual or group. And even if such words did exist, we still would be very likely to use the ones that reflect our own personal preferences. You may be described as *idealistic* by your close friends, while other people may label you *naïve*. You can call someone *obsessed*, but someone else will call this person *committed*.

Not only are we seldom aware of the extent to which our expectations can influence the behavior of others, but we probably are even less aware of how the expectations of others can influence our behavior. It is thus important to remember that our actions are shaped not only by our own attitudes but also by the expectations of those with whom we interact. Put another way, we are continually cultivating the constructions of each other's social realities.

Remember that descriptions, especially concerning personality characteristics, can never be entirely objective, impartial, or neutral. Become aware of your own personal values and biases and how these influence the language that you use. Avoid presenting your value judgments as objective reflections of truth. Recognize how other people's use of language reveals their own values and biases (see Figure 3.3).

Do Not Always See Correlation as Causation

As was mentioned earlier in this chapter, correlation does not establish a cause-and-effect relationship between two variables. A **correlation** is a statement about the relationship or association between two (or more) variables. Correlations thus enable us to make predictions from one variable or event to another. That is, if two events are correlated (or "coappear"), then the presence of one event provides us with information about the other event. However, a correlation does not necessarily establish a causal relationship between the variables. In other words, causation cannot be proven simply by virtue of a correlation or coappearance.

As an example, let us consider the correlation between creativity of artists and performers and their psychological disorders (see, e.g., Andreason & Canter, 1974; Andreason & Powers, 1975; Jamison, 1993). Great Dutch painter Vincent van Gogh, Russian novelist Fyodor Dostoyevsky, and American writers Virginia Woolf and Ernest Hemingway, among many others, all suffered from psychological disorders that seriously disrupted their lives. The late U.S. comedians John Belushi and Chris Farley developed serious (and ultimately fatal) drug addictions. Based on these observations, what may we conclude? That psychological disorders cause creativity? Perhaps. But maybe creativity causes psychological disorders. Then again, isn't it possible that creativity and psychological disorders reciprocally affect each other? To complicate

FIGURE 3.3 ■ On Evaluative Bias of Language

The same person as described from two perspectives

From Jenny's Value System	From Lee's Value System
irresponsible	spontaneous
troublemaker	feisty
cheap	frugal
spineless	cooperative
naive	idealistic
old	mature
weird	interesting
obsessed	committed
dependent	loyal
paranoid	vigilant
manic	enthusiastic
psychotic	creative
bum	vocationally disadvantaged
sociopath	morally challenged
reckless	brave
dead	ontologically impaired

matters further, what about the possibility that some other variable, such as a genetic predisposition, causes both creativity and psychological disorders? Put another way, given a correlation between A and B, does A cause B? Does B cause A? Do A and B cause each other? Does C cause A and B? Could there be some combination of these causal relationships? Unfortunately, a correlation alone does not (in fact, cannot) provide us with the definitive answers to these questions.

The following are some examples of correlated variables about which some people may erroneously infer causality. You can do an exercise to interpret the following correlations found in research in the past.

CHECK AND APPLY YOUR KNOWLEDGE

1. Research has established a strong and positive correlation between aggression and meteorological conditions. For example, rates of homicide and rape were generally higher in warmer than in colder climates (Anderson, 1987). Do these findings suggest that only the climate (and not other factors) affected violence? Suggest factors that could affect incidents of violence.
2. Another study found that smoking cannabis, such as marijuana, is correlated with schizophrenia: People who smoke pot are found to be more likely to have symptoms of this illness (Power et al., 2014). Does this study suggest that smoking cannabis is a contributing cause of schizophrenia? Is it also possible that the drug can set off short-term psychotic episodes—such as hallucinations and delusions—in those already suffering from the condition? Or is it possible that people who have already been diagnosed with schizophrenia are more likely to smoke pot, compared to the nonsmoking?
3. A study conducted in four countries—France, Germany, Poland, and the United States—examined more than 1,000 adolescents. The study showed that a person's religiosity was correlated with this person's family orientation, which is also correlated with life satisfaction. The correlations were stronger in cultures with a high overall religiosity (Poland and the United States) as compared to one of the two cultures that places the least importance on religion, Germany (Sabatier et al., 2011). How would you interpret these results? Which factors should affect which, in your view?

One particular type of faulty, uncritical reasoning, the **post hoc error**, refers to the mistaken logic that because Event B follows Event A, then B must have been caused by A. This error, also known as parataxic reasoning (Sullivan, 1953), may be seen as a kind of "magical thinking" because events that occur close together in time are construed as causally linked. As it turns out, most superstitions are based on parataxic reasoning. For example, if a football coach does not shave before a game and his team then wins, he might assume that not shaving somehow caused the success. As a result, he may adopt this superstitious behavior for future games.

Look for Multiple Causes

Let's return to research on happiness. Which factors affect happiness in individuals? Why do some people report that they tend to be happy most of the time when others do not feel the same? There are many reasons why. First, people who say they are happy may have good things happen to them more often than to others. Second, it is also possible that people feel they are happy because they have material resources and good health. In fact, these reasons can be true, as several studies show. For example, researchers Lyubomirsky (2007) and Veenhoven (2008) have shown that many people tend to judge their happiness based on economic factors, such as money or good jobs. Yet studies in Southeast Asia show that despite steady economic growth in their countries, people on average tend to score somewhat low on happiness surveys. They complain about competitiveness, strict education, excessive conformity, and the emphasis on outward appearance (Ng, 2022). There are also many individuals who were probably born with either strong or weak neurophysiological predisposition to be happy. Further, many of us learn how to feel happy and how to maintain a positive outlook on life despite difficulties. In other words, there are many other factors affecting happiness. What should make us happy often doesn't, and what shouldn't make us happy often does (Luybomirsky, 2014). Cross-cultural studies also show that people tend to assess their happiness based on cultural patterns. In predominantly individualistic cultures, people, on the average, tend to rely on their emotions when they assess their own happiness. In predominantly collectivist cultures, people tend to carry negative attitudes toward enjoyment (as possible sign of selfishness) or seek social cues or other people's opinions to make a judgment about their own happiness (Suh et al., 2008).

Virtually anything in an individual behavior and experience has at least several underlying reasons or causes. As critical thinkers studying personality, we need to consider a wide range of possible influences and factors, all of which could be involved to varying degrees in the shaping of certain traits. Although we typically tend to think of causal relationships as being unidirectional (Event A causes Event B), frequently they are bidirectional (Event A causes Event B, and Event B causes Event A). In other words, variables can, and frequently do, affect each other. Also consider the bidirectional relationship between psychological disturbance and one's social environment. Specifically, it is probable that cold, rejecting, and hostile parents can cause emotional and behavioral problems in their children. At the same time, do not ignore the possibility (even the likelihood) that children with emotional and behavioral problems also might cause their parents to become colder, more rejecting, and even hostile. Virtually every significant behavior has many determinants, and any single explanation is inevitably an oversimplification. Thus, in this case, we would need to consider a wide range of possible factors (e.g., genetic, dietary, stress, family norms, and cultural traditions), all of which could, to varying degrees, be involved.

In sum, when facing an issue or problem that is presented in terms of *either/or*, try replacing either/or with *both/and*. For example, the statement *Prejudice is caused by either ignorance or hatred*, becomes *Prejudice is caused by both ignorance and hatred* (and probably many other factors as well).

Critically Compare

Without comparisons, there is no study of personality. When comparing any two phenomena, initially they may "match" with respect to their mutual similarities. But no matter how many features they share, there is no escaping the inevitable fact that at some point there will be a "conceptual fork" in the road, where the phenomena will differ. Two people that seem to be completely different may share many similar features, just as two individuals who appear to be similar may be different in many ways.

We make judgments based on comparisons. Consider human height. Who is a tall person? A 5-foot, 10-inch person is likely to be seen as tall in some contexts (e.g., compared to most 7-year-old children) and short in others (e.g., compared to professional basketball players). Individual characteristics of one person are compared to the similar characteristics of others. Yet our comparisons tend to be incomplete and narrow. For example, Chinese people tended to evaluate themselves in comparison with other people in China, while people in the United States tended to evaluate themselves with reference to Americans (Heine et al., 2002). As we discussed earlier in the book, in surveys, Japanese and Koreans tend to evaluate themselves as less hardworking compared to people in other countries. To understand why people in these countries give themselves such lower evaluations, we should realize that hard work and conscientiousness are usually estimated with respect to larger social cultural norms. Speaking hypothetically, if everyone is expected to be hardworking, punctual, and reliable, many people may see themselves as not meeting the standards of "ideal" set by cultural norms. As a result, most people report in surveys that they are less organized and less determined than they ought to be. These are examples of cultural response bias (Schmitt et al., 2007).

Whenever we learn facts about a person or a group of people, it is important to compare these facts, if possible, with other facts. When comparing any two phenomena, we should ask ourselves, "In what ways are they similar?" and "In what ways are they different?"

Recognize Continuous and Dichotomous Variables

Some phenomena may be divided into two mutually exclusive or contradictory categories. These types of phenomena are **dichotomous variables**. For example, when you flip a coin, it must turn up either heads or tails—there is no middle ground. Similarly, a text message that you have typed is either sent or not. An individual next to you was either born in the United States or she wasn't. Other phenomena, by contrast, consist of a theoretically infinite number of points lying between two opposites. These types of phenomena are **continuous variables**. For example, consider such variables as an individual's weight and height. Many features that we will use to describe personality are likely to be continuous phenomena, such as masculinity, femininity, abnormality, consistency, conscientiousness, collectivism, individualism, and so forth. In Chapter 6, we will study the trait called *openness to experience*, which stands for, among other characteristics, a person's preference for variety and intellectual curiosity. Is openness to experience a dichotomous or continuous variable? Can you be totally "open" to experience and another person totally "closed" to it?

People around us (hopefully, not us) often confuse these two types of variables. Specifically, people have a natural tendency to dichotomize variables that, more accurately, should be conceptualized as continuous. Most person-related phenomena are frequently presumed to fit into one of two discrete types (either Category A or Category B), rather than as lying on a continuum (somewhere between End Point A and End Point B). In most cases, however, continuous variables are more accurate and therefore more meaningful representations of the phenomena we are attempting to describe and explain.

When comparing large samples, do not forget that these groups are far from homogeneous. Among them are individuals who are educated and those who are not, who are wealthy and poor, and who live in cities and small towns. It is always useful to request additional information about the groups that you study. For example, the diversity or homogeneity of the population and people's experience of such diversity may affect observation procedures. According to Matsumoto (1992), individuals from homogeneous societies (Japan, for example) detected and identified other people's emotions less accurately than people from heterogeneous societies did (the United States, for example).

Learn to differentiate between variables that are dichotomous and those that are continuous. Remember that most person-related phenomena—such as traits, attitudes, and beliefs—lie along a continuum. To practice, see Figure 3.4.

Be Aware of Possible Ethnocentrism

The view that supports judgment about other ethnic, national, and cultural groups and events from the observer's own ethnic, national, or cultural group's outlook is called **ethnocentrism**. Ethnocentrism is the tendency (often unintentional) to produce knowledge about personality from a specific national or cultural point of view. Let's illustrate. Imagine you develop a new method to assess "online shyness"—a tendency to feel awkward, worried, and tense while interacting on Zoom or social networks. You studied this type of shyness in a large sample of college students in the United States. Can you be sure that your method could measure shyness in individuals living in China, Mexico, or South Africa? We know that social and cultural factors may impact the way people act, think, and feel. Sometimes this impact is great, and sometimes it is not. Before testing a method on samples from different social and cultural environments, the researchers may not conclude that their study describes some psychological phenomenon or personality feature. If a study is conducted on just one ethnic or national sample, the results of this study should not be extrapolated onto the entire global population.

To avoid ethnocentrism, personality psychology should rely on **cross-cultural psychology**, which is the critical and comparative study of cultural effects on human psychology (Shiraev & Levy, 2024). Cross-cultural psychology examines psychological diversity and the underlying reasons for such diversity. Cross-cultural psychology inspects—again, from a comparative

---

FIGURE 3.4 ■ Dichotomous and Continuous Variables

Which of these variables would you consider dichotomous?
And which appear to you as continuous? Explain your choices.

feminine-masculine: ___
married-single: ___
conscious-unconscious: ___
prejudiced-unprejudiced: ___
liberal-conservative: ___
enemy-ally: ___
racist-nonracist: ___
guilty verdict-not guilty verdict: ___
tolerant-intolerant: ___
politically correct-politically incorrect: ___

perfect-imperfect: ___
young-old: ___
present-absent: ___
rich-poor: ___
gay-heterosexual: ___
licensed-unlicensed: ___
dead-alive: ___
power on-power off:
subjective-objective: ___
right-wrong: ___

perspective—the links between cultural norms and behavior and the ways in which particular human activities are influenced by different, sometimes dissimilar social and cultural forces (Segall et al., 1990). Cross-cultural psychology attempts not only to distinguish differences between groups but also to establish psychological universals and phenomena common to all people and groups (McCrae & Costa, 1997; Schmitt et al., 2007). For example, cross-cultural psychology seeks to identify commonalties regarding personality traits, the relatively enduring patterns of thinking, feeling, and acting.

CHECK AND APPLY YOUR KNOWLEDGE

1. Describe continuous and dichotomous variables.
2. Explain ethnocentrism.
3. Until very recent times, more than 90% of research samples in psychology came from a small sample of countries representing only 12% of the world's population (Henrich et al., 2010a). Most people who participate in psychological surveys, experiments, and other studies come from the United States, Canada, the United Kingdom, Germany, France, and Australia. Because psychology has been focusing so far on only a narrow sample of the population coming from only a few countries, what should be done, in your view, to correct this trend and, most importantly, how?

SUMMARY

- Studies of personality are based on nomothetic and idiographic approaches, quantitative and qualitative studies rooted in a variety of research methods, including observation, surveys, experiments, content analysis, and many others.

- Personality psychology uses observation, self-reports, experiments, content analysis, projective methods, and holistic methods (among others). In many studies, researchers use mixed methods.

- Before starting their research, scientists need to formulate and describe a problem to investigate, review the available sources, and describe the goals of their study.

- Hypotheses are expectations or proposed explanations for something that you study. They should be testable and falsifiable.

- A sample is a part of a larger group, and by studying this sample, the researcher generalizes the results to that larger group. The sample should be representative.

- By and large, research methodology to study personality can be divided into two categories: quantitative and qualitative. This division is imprecise because these categories of assessment usually overlap.

- Reliability is the extent to which a particular method gives consistent results. Validity of an assessment is the degree to which it measures what it is supposed to measure and not some other variables.

- Measuring a certain individual personality trait or someone's assessment of other people often requires several attempts. Therefore, among the most used data are measures of central tendency. They indicate the location of a score distribution on a variable; that is, it describes where most of the distribution is located.

- Studying personality, researchers often need to establish correlations, or the relationships between two or among several variables.

- Factor analysis is a statistical method for identifying clusters of items that tend to be answered the same way.

- Meta-analysis allows psychologists to do quantitative analysis of a large collection of scientific results and integrate the findings.

- Critical thinking is an active and systematic strategy for understanding knowledge based on sound reasoning and evidence. As a critical thinker, you will be encouraged to distinguish facts from opinions, critically generalize about facts and compare them, look for multiple causes of facts, avoid prescriptions, and see both continuous and dichotomous variables in many things you learn about.

VISUAL REVIEW

Visual Review. Chapter 3. Research Methods

1. RESEARCH METHODS

> There are nomothetic and idiographic approaches in personality research

> Psychologists use observation, self-reports, experiment, content analysis, projective methods, as well as mixed and holistic methods to study personality

2. PREPARING AND CONDUCTING RESEARCH

> Review your source. Describe your goals. Suggest a hypothesis. Choose a sample. Choose a method. Be aware of biases. Check for reliability and validity. Analyze your data using interpretive procedures.

3. APPLYING CRITICAL THINKING TO RESEARCH METHODS

> Be cautious about quick conclusions. Distinguish facts from opinions
> Describe, not prescribe. Do not always see correlation as causation
> Look for multiple causes. Critically compare. Recognize continuous and dichotomous variable. Be aware of ethnocentrism.

KEY TERMS

continuous variables

correlation

critical thinking

cross-cultural psychology

dichotomous variables

ethnocentrism

factor analysis

holistic

hypotheses

idiographic

independent variable(s)

meta-analysis

nomothetic

observation

observer ratings

post hoc error

projective methods

qualitative research

quantitative research

reliability

representative

sample

sampling error

self-fulfilling prophecy

self-serving bias

social desirability bias

the inkblot test

Thematic Apperception Test

validity

EVALUATING WHAT YOU KNOW

What are the key research methods in personality psychology?

What are advantages and disadvantages of self-evaluation?

Explain holistic methods.

Name and describe the steps in preparing research.

What are potential types of biases in research?

Explain reliability and validity.

Name and describe at least three rules of critical thinking to interpret research data.

A BRIDGE TO THE NEXT CHAPTER

As you should remember from Chapter 1, many theories of personality and their applications developed within so-called academic traditions. These traditions bring together scholars who share similar views on a particular scientific approach, subject, or method. Some traditions remain relevant for a short period. Others remain influential for decades. In the next chapter, we will be examining psychoanalysis—a dominant field that provided major theoretical views of personality until approximately the 1960s. Today, it has generally lost its major role and influence, yet its impact on psychology and personality psychology is present and remains strong, and it is constantly reevaluated across countries.

PSYCHOLOGICAL TRADITIONS

4 PSYCHOANALYTIC TRADITION

LEARNING OBJECTIVES

After reading this chapter, you should be able to do the following:

- Identify the main features of the psychoanalytic tradition in its historical context as relevant to the study of personality today.

- Summarize the key theories of Sigmund Freud, Anna Freud, Alfred Adler, and Karl Jung.

- Identify ways to apply the main principles of the psychoanalytic tradition to individual experience and behavior.

Some years ago, journalist Stephen Glass wrote false stories for more than 40 articles for the *New Republic, Rolling Stone,* and other popular magazines in the United States. He didn't just add a few creative details to those stories: He simply fabricated them. He made up his interviewees and created fake business cards, websites, and fictitious letters—all to make his articles appear legitimate. When his superiors uncovered his lies, he confessed. Then he was immediately fired.

A lie is an intentional false statement. Studies show that most of us tell small lies daily. But why do we lie? There are certain external incentives to lie, for example, to get ahold of a thing or to avoid or delay something unpleasant. But can it be that the incentives to lie come not from the outside world but from within an individual? Psychological studies reveal that people lie especially when they try to impress others. Others are driven by ambition because they desperately want to achieve something big. What if these incentives to lie reflect unresolved personal issues from the past?

Some psychologists who studied the case of Stephen Glass (and some of them argued on his behalf in court when he tried to restore his damaged reputation) explained that his lying was a result of his traumatic childhood experiences. Allegedly, his parents put immense psychological pressure on him, which was intense and often subtle. His parents cultivated in him a strong need for approval. As a result, he developed a powerful drive: To feel happy, he did not necessarily need to achieve; what he needed was to please his parents. How? It didn't matter. Even when he grew up and was working for a prestigious magazine, his parents were dismissive of his successes as a journalist. And that's when he began making things up in order to impress. As Stephen describes it, "I was anxious and scared and depressed. Outwardly I was communicating fun, but inside all I felt was anxiety." His work was a desperate attempt to impress his parents.

Many psychologists maintain that we all have a propensity to act in a certain way to address unresolved psychological conflicts from the past. Such conflicts may have deep roots in early family experiences and most people are unaware of them. At any rate, something happened in the past, and we try to address those issues and conflicts through some of our present actions. Some of us fight for personal or social causes; others write poetry; yet others turn to lying. The question of who is "good" or who is "bad" in these cases is a matter of value judgment.

Sources: Dolan, 2014; Feldman et al., 2002; Glass, 2003; Rosin, 2014

THE ESSENCE OF THE PSYCHOANALYTIC TRADITION

The psychoanalytic tradition, or *psychoanalysis,* as we call it for convenience, is probably the most scrutinized and controversial of all traditions in personality studies and in psychology in general. Supporters praise psychoanalysis for its early contribution to the scientific knowledge of the individual. Critics see psychoanalysis as a misleading speculation, brilliantly disguised in a fake academic uniform. Yet both critics and supporters acknowledge that the influence of psychoanalysis on psychology in general and personality psychology in particular was vast and lasting (Karlsson, 2010).

Social and Cultural Contexts

The emergence of psychoanalysis can be traced to the end of the 19th century. It was the time of early globalization—the massive exchange and cross-influence of various products, services, and ideas. More people could move internationally without visas. Studies and research abroad were common, and psychologists often traveled across borders. Psychological literature was increasingly popular among non-specialists. An unprecedented number of people turned to higher education. Telephones, telegraphs, daily newspapers, popular magazines, indoor plumbing, and orders by mail—all were bringing a relative and increasing comfort to the daily lives. Old policies and customs were changing. Women were fighting for and gaining their basic political rights. The traditional way of life was seemingly under pressure from almost every direction. In science, new views of nature rapidly developed. The emerging quantum physics challenged the traditional Newtonian understanding of the world as a mechanical unity. The seemingly undivided atom now contained numerous particles. Albert Einstein formulated the theory of relativity (Einstein, 1905). Time and space, according to this theory, are not absolute but relative to the observer. Matter appeared as a form of energy. This was the time of impressionism, cubism, symbolism, abstract painting, and conceptual poetry, as well as an era of bold experimentations with form, sound, and color (Kandel, 2012). Artistic imagination and the scope of creative genres appeared limitless.

But these developments were only one side of the ongoing changes. Paradoxically, the first 15 years of that century were also a period of boiling nationalism, militarism, and violence. World War I (1914–1918) took more than 19 million lives and left another 21 million wounded worldwide. Although social scientists portrayed human life as based on reason, the assumption of the irrational core of human existence gained support among many commentators. It was the time when the writings of the German philosopher Friedrich Nietzsche (1844–1900) introduced the idea that irrational forces dominate human motivation. The rationality of a capitalist society and its reliance on orderliness was a sign of weakness and future defeat. Only the strong and the power driven should rule the world, Nietzsche believed.

Within this mixed social atmosphere of optimism and doubt, enthusiasm and pessimism, and irrationality and reason, psychoanalysis emerged. The followers of the psychoanalytic tradition—mostly psychiatrists during early periods—wanted to remain on a solid scientific foundation. They innovatively borrowed from psychology and psychiatry, biology and medicine, history, and anthropology, among many other disciplines. Based on these diverse sources, psychoanalysts offered their own original ideas about the individual's personality. These ideas have been evolving for more than 100 years.

Psychoanalysis has many contributors yet one indisputable founder: Sigmund Freud (1856–1939). He was born in Freiberg (today the city is in the Czech Republic) in the Austrian Empire. His parents were Jewish, and his native language was German. An excellent student during his school years, he studied neurology in college and chose psychiatry as a profession. It took him many years of practice and research before he developed his own approach to the understanding of personality and to mental illness. His ideas, which were as controversial as they were influential, brought him global exposure and recognition in the 20th century and beyond. Freud called his views and his method **psychoanalysis**.

EXAMINE FREUD'S BRIEF PERSONALITY PROFILE, HIS CONTRADICTIONS, AND PARADOXES

Questions

Are you aware of any contradictions when you think of the ways you usually make your decisions and resolve your problems? If yes, what are your contradictions? List them and discuss them with a close friend. Could you or would you discuss them with others in class?

Key Assumptions

What is psychoanalysis? Let's highlight the four most important points relevant to the study of personality.

First, psychoanalysis emphasizes the dominant role of unconscious processes in human experience, motivation, and behavior. To psychoanalysts, a feeling, thinking, and acting individual is governed by concealed, inner forces, which, nevertheless, should be available for scientific scrutiny. Psychoanalysis did not discover the unconscious side of the human mind; it sustained and advanced an already rich intellectual tradition in science, art, humanities, and the philosophical tradition of hedonism, which says the main energy source of human activities is pleasure (Boring, 1950).

Second, psychoanalysis stresses the importance of sexuality in an individual's life. Sexuality should affect all aspects of life, including motivation, cognition, emotion, as well as creativity, health, and psychological abnormality. Although sexuality was already a subject of growing academic interest, research, and publications in the 19th century (Ellis & Symonds, 1897/2006), psychoanalysis elevated the significance of sexuality in all areas of human life. Like no other tradition in psychology, psychoanalysis turned to the study and interpretation of sexual drives, orientations, and practices.

Third, psychoanalysis emphasizes the importance of early childhood experiences in the individual's life. Child psychology was already taking shape early in the 20th century as a research subdiscipline (Hall, 1904). University-trained psychologists wrote about what they called *critical periods* of the child's development. However, psychoanalysis is different because it placed childhood in the center of psychologists' attention. Most adults are unaware of the meaning of their early childhood events and experiences and cannot link their personality features today to their childhood. The goal of psychoanalysis is to discover, analyze, and then explain the significance of those experiences in the life of the individual.

Fourth, psychoanalysis is a type of treatment, or a method of interaction between a professional therapist and a client. According to this method, the therapist and the client together identify the sources of the client's psychological problems and then find ways to recover from these problems. Psychoanalysis assumes that only through persistent and critical analysis of psychological problems will people who suffer from psychological maladies identify their inner conflicts and find the way to recovery using help of trained psychoanalysts.

DPST/Newscom

PHOTO 4.1 Freud remains one of the most controversial thinkers of all time. Yet which of Freud's ideas would you find today applicable to your personal experiences and why?

To discuss the contributions of psychoanalysis to personality psychology and its applications, we will combine the chronological method with a critical review. First, we will examine the views of Sigmund Freud, Anna Freud, Alfred Adler, and Carl Jung. We will summarize their theories in the end by considering their applications and the overall impact on our knowledge of personality.

DISCUSSING SIGMUND FREUD'S PSYCHOANALYSIS

Freud accepted the prevailing scientific outlook of the 19th century that multiple forces, external and internal, cause humans to think, feel, desire, and act. The individual seeks gratification of inner drives, and the act of gratification should bring pleasure (Freud, 1905/2000). However, immediate gratification is difficult or often impossible because an individual's inner barriers block this gratification. Such barriers (or defenses) are associated with moral judgments and social imperatives, such as prescriptions about how to act and think (we examine these defenses later in the chapter). Thus, the drives become repressed or "shoved" inside the individual. In contemporary terms, "out of sight" should not mean "out of mind."

Freud and his followers claimed the existence of mental energy. Can an observer see it? No, the observer can only register some effects of it (Slife, 1993). When Isaac Newton in the 17th century proposed the laws of gravity, he could not show what gravity was. People saw only gravity's effects, such as apples falling from trees. Freud then turned to the ideas of energy conservation proposed in the 19th century by the physiologist Alexander Bain (1818–1903), who also believed that the nervous system should somehow discharge surplus energy or excitation. This discharge is pleasant and should impact all activities of individuals, including their mental acts. Could a researcher describe and measure such energy discharges, like a physicist measuring electrical impulses in the lab? Not always, not immediately, and not directly. Only educated and trained psychoanalysts can approach these phenomena, which Freud called the **unconscious**—the psychological activities that are not open to direct rational scrutiny but that influence an individual. The unconscious is a complicated dynamic of wishes and drives fighting against numerous blockings (Freud, 1920/1990).

Freud formulated and described two major mechanisms that regulate mental activities: the **pleasure principle** and the **reality principle**. The first is the demand that an instinctual need be immediately gratified. The second is the realization of the demands of the environment (which is, mostly, the social world) and the adjustment of behavior to these demands. Driven by the pleasure principle, people cannot postpone their desire to gratify their immediate impulses. Controlled by the reality principle, they continue to live in the state of constant delay of their desires (see Figure 4.1).

Human Desires Are Repressed

Freud gained his experience as a researcher in his clinical work with patients seeking treatment for their psychological problems. He hypothesized that an individual's early disturbing or traumatic experiences, primarily of a sexual nature, might cause some forms of challenging psychological symptoms later in life. These disturbing events may cause an accumulation of unreleased energy, which later manifests in a variety of forms such as elevated anxiety, phobias, obsessive behavior, or depressive symptoms. Whatever is revealed in seemingly insignificant behaviors

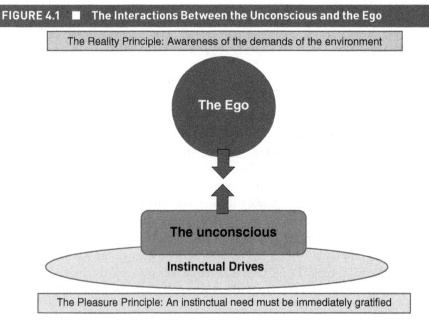

FIGURE 4.1 ■ The Interactions Between the Unconscious and the Ego

The Reality Principle: Awareness of the demands of the environment

The Ego

The unconscious

Instinctual Drives

The Pleasure Principle: An instinctual need must be immediately gratified

such as a mispronounced word, a misspelled name, a lost key, a forgotten appointment, an angry reaction, or procrastination—all these could be reflections of an individual's unconscious inner struggles (Freud, 1901/2009b). The problem is that we, as individuals, typically deny the existence of these repressed conflicts.

Yet why are certain experiences and drives repressed? Pain and pleasure are the first feelings to remain in the memory of an infant. The child tends to secure pleasurable moments in the memory and reexperience them. However, this is difficult for two reasons. First, society restricts many pleasure-related activities—such as sexual excitement or a violent outburst, especially in children—by imposing moral taboos and social regulations. A child who out of joy destroys a sandcastle being built by another child is taught to experience guilt for this act, not pleasure. Second, some pleasurable activities are deemed shameful. Children are also pressured not to have sexual fantasies. These repressed feelings usually surface later—for the most part unconsciously—in various experiences and activities, including dreams, jokes, fantasies, hobbies, attachments, and, often, abnormal psychological symptoms such as excessive anxiety, depression, or obsessive thoughts (Freud, 1901/2009b).

What is this force that causes inner conflicts? Freud called it **libido**, which is the energy of the sexual drive or an erotic desire common in all people (English & English, 1958). Not only people who are passionately in love but also individuals who care, dare, cure, design clothes, write songs, strive for perfection, or seek new experiences and friends are influenced by their libido. Freud later connected libido with the universal *life drive*, often called **Eros**. Eros defines all the tendencies that strive toward the integration of a living substance. As with libido, Eros manifests in love, friendship, courtship, altruistic help, kindness, and the creative work of carpenters and artists, among others. Eros is responsible for love, bond, and the survival of the individual.

Freud was developing his views of personality during the first quarter of the 20th century. World War I (1914–1919) brought death, disease, and starvation. They all appeared to Freud as a collective suicide by human civilization. His worldview grew increasingly pessimistic. The years after 1914 provided Freud with ample evidence to contemplate the reasons behind human's seemingly self-destructive behavior. He adopted the concept of the **death wish**—the repressed instinctual tendencies that lead toward destruction, pain, and death. A contrarian term to Eros is **Thanatos** ("death" in ancient Greek), which, according to Freud, means striving for destruction, humiliation, pain, and death. Death wish manifests in direct violent acts as well as in offensive jokes, jealous outbursts, envious comments or thoughts, racial slurs, character attacks, or contemptible responses—in anything that involves competition against another person or advancement at the expense of others.

The Id, the Ego, and the Superego

An individual's psyche (we can label it the *inner world* or *personality*) is made up of three levels (features). The most "primitive" feature of the personality is the **id**. This term was borrowed (and modified) from the German philosopher Friedrich Nietzsche. The id is the component of the psyche that contains inborn biological drives (the death wish and the life instinct); the id seeks immediate gratification of its impulses. The id, like unmanaged will, operates exclusively

according to the pleasure principle. It represents a constant struggle between love and destruction (Freud, 1920/2009a).

Neither Nietzsche nor Freud should get credit for identifying the good and the evil sides of
an individual's psyche. Religious knowledge of the past has contained these assumptions since
centuries ago. For example, Manichaeism, a religion formed about 2,000 years ago on the ter-
ritory of today's Iran, teaches that the individual is a perpetual "battleground" of good and evil
forces. Christian theologian Augustine (354–430 CE) formulated the principle of two wills
within the individual: the virtuous *caritas* and the sinful *cupiditas*. They divide the self into
struggling entities: lust versus chastity, greed versus self-control, and cravings versus moderation
(Hooker, 1982). What makes Freudian ideas different from the religious assumptions is that in
religion, the potential for a moral action is based on God's will. In Freud's system, the potentials
for thoughts and actions are imbedded in the individual.

Making compromises between the id and the outside world is the ego, which is guided by
the reality principle. During a child's development, the ego starts within the id but gradually
changes to accept reason. Children learn to be "good" by accepting moral rules as inner regula-
tors of their behavior, emotional expressions, and thinking. The pleasure principle guides the
child's behavior, but they gradually learn how to restrict themselves. Society imposes especially
strong restrictions on the child's sexual interests, which are labeled as indecent. Children are
unaware yet of what decency means but learn it during the first few years of their lives. This
is associated with the development of the superego, the moral guide passing on imperatives
regarding appropriate or inappropriate actions, emotions, and thoughts.

Among the first lessons children learn is what clothes they have to wear at home and in
public. They also learn about circumstances when they should cover certain body parts (for
example, children learn to cover their mouth when sneezing). Children then learn how to experience embarrassment when they accidentally appear naked in front of a stranger. The child also
acquires knowledge about appropriate and indecent words. Some words related to their body
parts—such as *nose* or *knee*—are appropriate and may be spoken freely. Others—like *butt*—
appear as inappropriate. Later, the child learns how to talk about "appropriate" topics, such as
friendship or toys, and avoid "inappropriate" themes discussed in front of adults, such as talking
about poop or toilet activities. Overall, the superego, transmitted to the child by parents, older
siblings, family members, and teachers, represents the values and the customs of society (see
Figure 4.2).

Developmental Stages

Children go through several developmental stages in which the libido focuses ("fixates" in the
psychoanalytic language) on different tactile experiences from the body. Children and adults
enjoy a wide range of tactile experiences, such as touching, fondling, scratching, tasting, and
kissing. Such early fixations tend to manifest later in attempts to repeat those experiences in various patterns of behavior and thought. Because children experience such fixations differently,
as adults, they display different behavioral and thinking patterns. One child enjoys their own
experiences and thus desires to repeat them in the future. Another child may dislike experiences
and thus tries to avoid them in the future. These experiences develop in stages.

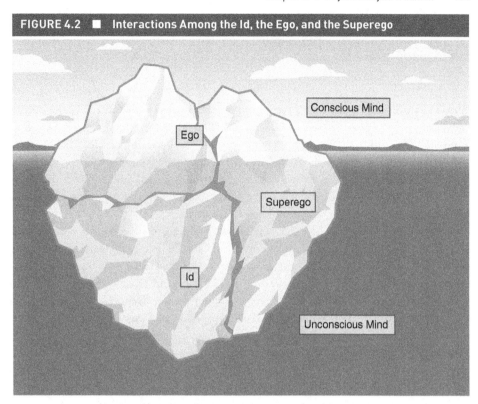

FIGURE 4.2 ■ Interactions Among the Id, the Ego, and the Superego

The first developmental stage, called the *oral stage*, begins in infancy and is linked to an infant's nursing and eating. The infant who fixates on these activities, many years later as an adult, will likely be prone to overeating, drinking, smoking, and excessive talking. The infant deprived of joy coming through the mouth is likely to show angry and envious tendencies as a grownup.

The next stage, which lasts until the age of 4, is called the *anal stage*. During the period of toilet training, the child should use the bathroom regularly, follow the rules, and develop self-discipline. The child who develops a fixation during this stage (referred to in popular literature as an *anal fixation*) later is likely to show obsessive tendencies, preoccupation with rules, orderliness, and delayed gratification (we discussed delayed gratification in Chapter 2). The child who felt miserable during toilet training will likely later rebel against restrictive societal norms.

At the *phallic stage*, which lasts up to six or seven years, the focus of pleasure is the genitalia. According to Freud, at this point some boys may develop the castration complex, or an irrational fear of losing their penis (boys see people with missing limbs or teeth and assume that the penis can be "lost" too). Later in life, these boys tend to become indecisive and lack initiative. Some girls tend to develop *penis envy*, an unconscious desire to have a penis. Such girls later tend to become submissive and dependent on men. Other girls will develop opposite tendencies rooted in unconscious hostility to boys and then to men. During the *latency stage*, which lasts until puberty, the child combines individual responses that they developed during the previous stages. The fifth stage is the *genital stage*, which lasts through adulthood. During this stage, the ego is formed. Many adults are now capable of gratifying the drives through society-approved activities, such as friendship, creativity, education, travel, and so forth.

Views of Women

Freud's views of women were controversial and reflected the prevailing discriminatory norms and sexist perceptions of the time. Although most of Freud's patients were women, a majority of his original postulates related to males and were only later modified to describe women as well. Freud tended to see women as "failed" men because they do not develop the same anatomical organs that men have. Freud considered women as sexually more passive than men. Freud acknowledged though that such passivity was the result of social inequalities and cultural restrictions that have been for centuries imposed on women.

Some women who learned psychoanalysis from Freud maintained similar views. Helene Deutsch (1884–1982) was Freud's favorite student and a follower as a researcher and professional. After working in Vienna as a therapist, she moved to the United States in 1935 to escape her imminent arrest and death due to the unfolding political terror in her country. She became well-known for her two-volume book *The Psychology of Women* (Deutsch, 1944, 1945). This book was a major early contribution to the field of psychology of women (Chapter 10), and it received attention from many professionals, from whom she received significant support and at the same time faced criticisms for her vision of the woman's role in contemporary society. She described women as affected by the unconscious desire to overcome psychological pressures associated with their realization as young girls that their destiny is as a wife and mother. Deutsch believed that women must challenge and overcome many psychological problems associated with their biological and social roles. Critics dismissed these ideas and believed Deutsch focused on the wrong causes, claiming problems that women faced were not about their psychological complexes but rather about social injustice and gender inequality.

Freud encouraged women to demand a greater access to sex education, learn about contraceptives, and seek own rational choices in marriage. He also believed that women should have the right to divorce. He encouraged women to become psychoanalysts and to pursue further education and training. One of the best illustrations of his position was his enthusiastic support of the professional advancement of his youngest daughter, Anna, who became a world-renowned psychologist.

CHECK AND APPLY YOUR KNOWLEDGE

1. Compare and contrast the pleasure principle and the reality principle.
2. What is the opposite drive to the death wish?
3. Using Freud's psychoanalysis, how would you explain the motivation of the person who sacrifices her safety and well-being on behalf of another person? In your view, is this a manifestation of the death wish or the love instinct?
4. The id is the component of the psyche that contains what?

5. What is the superego? Is it conscious or not?
6. Choose one developmental stage and describe it.
7. If you were a psychoanalyst, how would you apply these developmental stages to explain the lying behavior in the opening case?
8. From your personal standpoint now, suggest at least two strengths and two weaknesses of this Freudian classification.

Studying Anna Freud's Views

Anna Freud (1895–1982) was the youngest of Sigmund Freud's six offspring. Born and raised in Vienna, she expressed her interest in psychoanalysis very early in her life. She started reading her father's articles and books at the age of 15 (some commentators considered this inappropriate because of the strong sexual context of these works). She chose a career as a schoolteacher, for which she received professional training. She later received training as a psychoanalyst and began therapeutic work with children. She published several influential research papers. Anna escaped persecution by the Nazis and emigrated with her parents from Austria to London in 1938. There she founded a child therapy clinic, which is still in existence and is now called the Anna Freud National Centre for Children and Families. She continued to work in the United Kingdom for many years, earning many awards and honorary degrees.

Anna could not escape the fact that she was the daughter of an internationally famous researcher and therapist. Nevertheless, it wasn't her father's reputation alone that brought Anna worldwide recognition and a place in psychology textbooks. She was above all a talented scholar, a dedicated teacher, and a successful therapist. Her training as a teacher and work with children influenced her later work as a therapist. She emphasized that children could not explain their psychological problems as efficiently as most adults could. Medical and educational professionals working with children, she argued, should develop special skills to understand children's symptoms and interpret them (Bruehl, 1990).

Her most influential book was *The Ego and the Mechanisms of Defense* (1966), in which she focused on the inner struggles of the individual. It was above all the struggle of the ego with the overwhelming demands of the id, on the one hand, and powerful restrictions imposed by reality, on the other. Ego defenses or **defense mechanisms** are specific unconscious structures that enable an individual to avoid awareness of unpleasant, anxiety-arousing issues. The function of the ego is to defend itself from these issues. Such a defense is set to protect a person's ego against anxiety, shame, guilt, or other emotional challenges. The defense is launched automatically and remains mostly unconscious. This means that a person's defenses occur without this individual's awareness of them.

Anna Freud suggested 10 basic defense mechanisms (there are other defense mechanisms, the exact number of which has always been disputed): repression, regression, reaction formation, isolation, undoing, projection, introjection, turning against, compensation, sublimation, rationalization, and displacement (Cramer, 1991; see Table 4.1).

How can one detect and study defense mechanisms within an individual? A trained analyst can do so in the process of a clinical interview and by examining a person's everyday behavior

TABLE 4.1 ■ Examples and Brief Descriptions of Defense Mechanisms	
Defense Mechanism	*A Brief Illustration*
Repression: Shoving thoughts and urges—socially unacceptable or distressing—into the unconscious. The exclusion of certain psychological activities from conscious awareness.	Not remembering, thinking, or talking about a violent incident that took place years ago.
Regression: Reversion of the ego to earlier, "childish" or infantile ways of acting or feeling even though more mature responses have been learned.	Instead of planning his wedding, the fiancée spends all day long under the blanket playing video games.
Reaction formation: Establishment of a trait or behavioral pattern that is exactly opposed to a strong unconscious trend. Typically, such unconscious trend is anxiety provoking and, therefore, appears as a threat to the ego.	A person who dislikes little children (especially noisy ones) volunteers to be a babysitter in the neighborhood.
Isolation: Manifesting a mental gap or a period of inactivity between a strong unconscious impulse and subsequent other thoughts and behaviors.	A client takes a long pause during a therapy session before talking about this person's traumatic experience 10 years ago.
Undoing: Overcoming or taking back threatening thoughts or actions by engaging in behavior or thinking that new ideas or deeds are supposed to "undo" the threatening actions or thoughts.	Turning to cooking dinner after feeling guilty for a particular act or a thought.
Projection: Self-denial and unwittingly attributing one's own unacceptable thoughts and impulses to others.	People who are jealous of their friend's success accuse other friends of being jealous.
Introjection: Bringing external events or other people's experiences and behaviors to own mental processes and actions.	An individual imitates the voice or manners of a particular movie character.
Self-Harm: Turning against oneself in words and actions.	Individuals are spreading disparaging yet unwarranted remarks about themselves.
Compensation: Exclusion of awareness of any anxiety-provoking deficiency by engaging in some activities or excelling in some way.	After a breakup, a woman turns to songwriting.
Sublimation: Transforming unacceptable ideas and impulses into socially acceptable ambitions and actions.	Instead of breaking up with his partner, an unhappy man begins studying yoga and meditation.
Rationalization: Giving improbable (or other) excuses for own shortcomings and mistakes, thereby avoiding responsibility.	A person says to her family members who ask her to make an important life decision: "I am a thinker not a decision-maker!"
Displacement: Redirecting impulses, emotions, fears, and so on from the real Person A to a "substitute" Person B.	A person is frustrated with a demanding boss at work and, after returning home, kicks their family dog.

Sources: English & English, 1958; Freud, 1966

and decisions. All they need is paper and a pen or pencil to record their dialogues with an individual, write down observations, and suggest their interpretations.

Many psychologists used the concept of the defense mechanism in their research and practical work. For this and many other reasons, Anna Freud has earned respect among several generations of psychologists.

CHECK AND APPLY YOUR KNOWLEDGE

1. Who was Anna Freud? What did she do as a professional?
2. What is ego psychology's main subject?
3. Explain a defense mechanism.
4. Give an example of regression using your personal observations.

Studying Alfred Adler's Views

One of Freud's most outstanding followers was Alfred Adler (1870–1937), who was born near Vienna. His father was a middle-class grain merchant. Young Alfred had to deal with numerous health problems as he grew up. Yet he overcame them, went to medical school, became a doctor, and established a practice in Vienna. After meeting Freud, Adler became a dedicated follower of his teacher's ideas. However, they never became close friends, and disagreements between Adler and Freud surfaced early. Adler, for example, particularly emphasized the importance of the relationships among siblings, not between the parents and the child, as Freud did. Adler also questioned sexuality as the most dominant force in human life and one of the central points of Freud's psychoanalysis. Their disagreements deepened. Until the end of his days, Freud criticized Adler's work. Their critical exchanges became personal sometimes. Researchers often get passionate about their ideas.

SELF-REFLECTION

Adler first (1930) and then others (Sulloway, 1996) studied birth order and argued that it makes a difference on a person's behavior and personality features. Adler believed that firstborn children, because of the responsibilities imposed on them by the family, should be more serious, conscientious, aggressive, conservative, organized, responsible, independent, fearful, high achieving, and competitive than their younger siblings. The youngest, because of the support they tend to receive from their families, should be more outgoing, spontaneous, selfish, irresponsible, dependent, more challenging yet less competitive, and less achievement-oriented than other siblings. Children who are born in the middle are "mediators"; they need to take care of the conflicts between other siblings, take middle ground, and find compromises. The single child can assume features of both categories and is likely to be selfish.

According to Sulloway's (1996) research, firstborn children tend to be more supportive of status quo and the existing social and political establishment than their younger siblings (*later-borns*). For example, during the French Revolution, royalists (supporters of the king) were largely firstborns. Later-borns, on the other hand, as challengers, tended to conduct most groundbreaking scientific discoveries.

Questions

- Identify from their biographies the birth order of the past 10 U.S. presidents. Were they older or younger brothers in their families? What was their party affiliation? According to theory, older siblings are supposed to be more conservative and younger ones are supposed to be more liberal.
- Select 20 of the most successful women in modern history and today from your point of view (choose fields such as politics, business, science, etc. Feel free to ask your professor to suggest their choices). Were these women firstborns, younger siblings, or single children? Of course, a sample of 20 won't be representative, but it may reveal a few interesting tendencies.
- Discuss in class if the assumptions of Adler and Sulloway about birth order are applicable to you personally and your siblings (if you have them).

Organ Inferiority and Its Consequences

Out of this assumption came one of Adler's central concepts called **organ inferiority** (Adler, 1930). The term stands for the sense of being inferior compared to others because of negative feelings about a real or imagined abnormality of organ function or structure. Organ inferiority refers not only to organs as such (for instance, the eye, the hand, the heart, etc.) but also to the nervous system. Organ inferiority manifests in many ways. For example, a very short boy does not play rough games at school, so children tease him for being short and reject him. Thus, his height is the source of his organ inferiority. Similarly, a girl with a mild learning disability, which is an obvious weakness in the classroom, feels embarrassed for scoring lowest on the test. In this case, the girl's learning disability is the source of her organ inferiority. According to Adler, a "malfunctioning" system sends signals to the brain suggesting that something is wrong or insufficient. Based on lengthy observations of children, Adler concluded that organ inferiority is particularly common in the physically weak and in those with poor learning or adaptation skills.

However, the person cannot suffer continually because they need to compensate for an emerging insufficiency, find energy resources to address the problem, and reduce the unpleasant feelings. The person thus attempts to overcome the discomfort caused by their inferiority. These attempts are called **compensation**. Compensation can bring different outcomes.

There are three general outcomes of an individual's compensatory efforts. The **genius** overcomes the old inferiority problems and achieves success and happiness. Compensation in this case brings success and delivers a new life free from the pain of inferiority. The second outcome is *neurosis*. A neurosis is a person's failed attempt to compensate for a real or imaginary imperfection. This happens when an individual is sliding from comfortable to difficult times. Imagine a 12-year-old girl who suddenly begins to think she is unattractive when someone jokingly tells her she has a big nose and pointy ears. Now the girl looks in the mirror and feels ugly for the first time in her life. As a result, this girl who was once an outgoing and happy person becomes anxious and withdrawn. She loses interest in many activities she previously enjoyed. She turns to fantasies. In her dreams, she becomes a supermodel, creates her own fashion line, and returns to her school years later to confront her peers who all turned out to be stupid and ugly losers. Fantasy is a temporary substitute for real action. Adler explains why the famous Cinderella fairy tale remained popular across generations: It was an example of a powerful childish expectation of a better outcome, a form of personal liberation from humiliation and pain caused by Cinderella's mean stepmother.

In the case of **degeneration**, which is the third outcome, the attempted compensation is unsuccessful. The person falls out of the normal course of life and is unable to adjust to social rules, thus becoming incapable of social functioning. Others may turn to violence to address their hostile fantasies against their real or imaginary abusers. Adler, in fact, described children who compensate by engaging in violent acts, which can manifest in many ways and in people of all ages.

People tend to develop their own ideal world of fantasy because there, in that world, not necessarily in real life, they achieve redemption. In some cases, fantasies may cause action because the person realizes the difference between the dream and the reality. Such actions may, in some cases, lead to a change in habits, a different view of self and others, self-improvement, growth, and eventual success.

Self-Ideal

Adler was particularly impressed with the work of Hans Vaihinger, who published *The Philosophy of As If* (1924/1952). In this fascinating book, the author maintains that people live primarily by a fiction that does not correspond with reality (Vaihinger, 1924/1952). Some of us, for example, believe that the world is disorderly. Yet we reject this belief and behave as if the world were well-ordered. Similarly, people create God, ignoring the idea that God could be fiction. Why do people create and live by such falsifications? One of the reasons is that to achieve an ambitious goal, we have to believe in it. We also have to know how to achieve it. While Freud was interested in his patients' past, Adler believed that people are motivated primarily by future expectations. By forming them, people pursue their fictional final goal, called *self-ideal*. Self-ideal can be achieved if an individual engages in **striving toward superiority**. It is not about domination of others. It is about striving for security, improvement, and control in all activities. Whether you and I win or make mistakes—it doesn't matter. What matters is the great upward drive, as Adler put it. The human feeling of imperfection is never ending, which should be accepted. But people should constantly seek for a solution to this problem by using the imperatives, "Achieve! Arise! Conquer!" (Adler, 1930). Those psychologists who today study Adler's work always remember these words of his.

Social Interest

Recall that Adler viewed the power drive within individuals as a response to feelings of inferiority. He later modified his view, adding another important motivational feature to his views of personality: **social interest**, or the desire to be connected with other people and to adapt positively to the perceived social environment. Adler realized that while people strive for self-advancement, they have to take into consideration other people's interests (because these people are striving for power, too). There are three major and interconnected social ties appearing in social interest.

The first social tie is *occupation*. People engage in activities that provide food, water, safety, and comfort. People then create a division of labor. *Society* is the second tie. People join different groups based on their occupation or other interests. The third tie is *love*. People are attracted to one another. The division of labor and social requirements influence love.

People thus create their own **style of life**. This concept is helpful in summarizing Adler's views. Every person's style of life develops in stages. First, a child has inferiority issues. Second, this child is set to overcome inferiority by means of compensation. Compensation can manifest in behavior, imagination, or both. Pursuing compensation, this individual strives toward superiority and self-enhancement by engaging in social life and establishing social ties. Altogether, these elements form a unique style of life for each one of us (see Figure 4.3).

Although Adler (1930) acknowledged factual inequality between men and women, he also believed that mistakes of the history of civilization must be corrected and the social gap between men and women should be narrowed. However, as a man of his time, Adler accepted the long-established, traditional construction of gender roles. He used his theory to explain social and political aspects of gender inequality. He believed, for example, that women's protest against sexism and discrimination was misguided because, in reality, as he insisted, it was a protest against women's natural roles as mothers and caregivers.

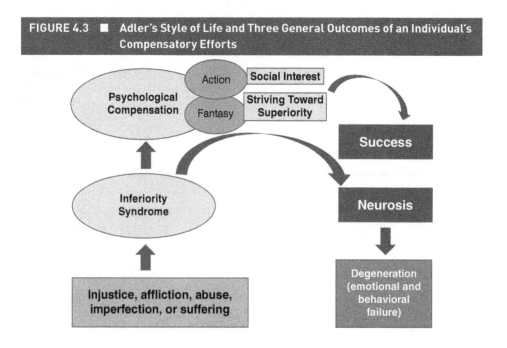

FIGURE 4.3 ■ Adler's Style of Life and Three General Outcomes of an Individual's Compensatory Efforts

CHECK AND APPLY YOUR KNOWLEDGE

1. What is organ inferiority?
2. What is compensation, according to Adler? Give examples.
3. What is the self-ideal, according to Adler?
4. What is your personal self-ideal? What difficulties do you have to overcome to achieve this self-ideal?

Studying Carl Jung's Views

Carl Jung (1875–1961) was frequently called the "crown prince" of psychoanalysis. For several years early in his career, like Adler, Jung was a firm and loyal supporter of Freud, his theory, and his method (Eisold, 2002). Their friendship lasted for several years. Their academic and personal breakup has become one of the most discussed stories in psychology's history. The uncrowned prince of psychoanalysis would never be king. Yet Jung's own original theory and his view of personality would attract a growing posse of dedicated followers across the world.

The son of a Protestant pastor in Switzerland, Jung suffered from anxiety and obsessive symptoms early in life. Carl grew imaginative and creative, showing early interest in self-analysis. After getting a medical degree, he worked as a psychiatrist in a mental asylum where he turned to study mental illness. Jung was supportive of Freud's ideas about unconscious processes. Yet he was hesitant to embrace the Freudian concept of sexuality and libido. Jung considered *mental energy* as a better term (Jung, 1961).

PHOTO 4.2 Adler believed that adversities in our lives could spark the development of our previously hidden talents. Are you able to apply this theory to your life? Were there any significant difficulties helpful in developing some of your personality traits?

© Sueddeutsche Zeitung Photo / Alamy

Collective Unconscious and Archetypes

Jung used the term **analytical psychology** to distinguish his views from Freud's psychoanalysis. In one of his earlier works, Jung explored the idea that human dreams contained experiences beyond conscious awareness (Jung & Hinkle, 1912). He thought of dreams as a multistory house in which the basement represents the most fundamental and ancient features. Contradicting Freud, Jung insisted that dreams do not necessarily reflect a child's unrealized wishes but are rather mythological images from the experiences of our ancestors. Fantasy, too, like dreams, serves as a connector between our ancestors' experiences hundreds and thousands of years ago and our experience at this moment. As a trained medical doctor, Jung was fascinated with mysticism and spirituality. Jung turned to folklore: fairy tales, myths, legends, drawings, and rituals. He was inspired by the ideas of the Christian Middle Ages, Greek philosophy, and alchemy. Later in his career, he incorporated into his theory the thoughts of Eastern philosophy, theology, and mythology. This was an eclectic combination of many designs. Yet they were shaped around a central assumption: The individual's unconscious contains mental relics from earlier generations (Drob, 1999).

He believed that there must be an impersonal layer in human psyche, which he called the **collective unconscious.** It is different from the individual unconscious. It is inherited and shared with other members of the species. The collective unconscious consists of **archetypes**, or images of the primordial (elemental, ancient) character. These are people's ancestral experiences, which appear in three universal ways: dreams during sleep, fantasies, and delusions. Jung believed that certain delusions of his patients (e.g., a belief that the sun has wings or that a giant animal can swallow the patient) resemble mythological beliefs of the past. While our ancestors did not separate these beliefs from their everyday experience, we, in modern times, view them as unusual or even abnormal symptoms. How many archetypes are there? Jung and his followers did not attempt to give the exact number because the archetypes tend to combine with each other. There is considerable confusion in literature about specific issues related to archetypes, and Jung's position on archetypes evolved throughout his career. Therefore, the following are examples of a few categories of archetypes.

An archetype called the *shadow* contains the unconscious aspects of the self. The shadow obeys instinctual forces. It manifests in a person's romantic attachments, aggressive acts, fears, obsessions, avoidant behavior, and so forth. Another archetype called *persona* appears as a symbolic mask to trick other people into the belief that the carrier of the mask is playing a particular social role. The persona represents an individual's public image (the word *persona* comes from the Latin word for "mask"). Men have an inherited collective image of the feminine human essence called *anima.* In contrast, women possess an inherited image of masculine essence, called *animus.* Anima represents the man's unconscious expectation of women but also is a symbol of a man's feminine potentials. Animus is the analogous image of the masculine that occurs in women (Odajnyk, 2012). Every individual has fundamental unconscious feminine and masculine features. Anima and animus, as archetypes, according to Jung, serve as an unconscious guide to an individual's love life. People often fall in love with little rational reason because the archetypes take over and direct the individual's feelings and subsequent behavior.

Jung hoped that his theory could help people become aware of the existence of their archetypes. This, Jung also believed, could be accomplished through an interpretation of cultural symbols, dreams, and fantasies (Jung, 1967). These patterns of cultural symbols appeared to Jung consistently across similar cultures and times. If people in the past created images and artifacts that are comparable to the images and artifacts created today, then the mental patterns of people today are similar to the mental patterns of people in the past. It was an optimistic outlook.

CHECK AND APPLY YOUR KNOWLEDGE

1. What is the collective unconscious?
2. What are Jung's archetypes? Name any two and explain them.
3. Why is it important to us to be aware of our archetypes?
4. How did Jung explain the mandala?
5. How would you personally interpret your own circular patterns on a piece of paper?
6. What are primordial fears? Are you aware of having primordial fears? What are they? How difficult will it be to discuss these fears with somebody else? How about in class? (If this is too difficult, you don't have to do this.)
7. Have you ever wondered how it would feel if a giant animal swallowed you? Think about it. Does this idea scare you or fascinate you?

Jung believed that fear of being swallowed is one of the universal human fantasies related to death and rebirth through the act of eating. Jung compared the dreams and fantasies of his patients with different fairy tales. He turned to several such tales. One was the famous Red Riding Hood story, in which the wolf eats the grandmother, who is later rescued by the huntsman. Jung also considered ancient myths in which the sun is swallowed by a sea monster. The sun rises again in the morning. The story of Jonah in the Christian tradition and of Yunus in the Islamic tradition both contain the plot element in which a man is swallowed by a giant fish but then rescued. We can find many similar examples. In the *Adventures of Pinocchio* by the 19th-century Italian author Carlo Collodi, a giant fish swallows the little wooden puppet, who later escapes. In a famous Russian fairy tale by Kornei Chukovsky, a giant crocodile swallows the sun. In the ensuing darkness, the distressed people force the crocodile to spit out the sun. In the film trilogy of *Pirates of the Caribbean*, Captain Jack Sparrow is swallowed by a giant sea beast in the second film, only to reappear in the third.

Using these examples, Jung's followers maintain that the similarities in these stories are based on the common human archetypes attached to fears and fascinations. Critics maintain that children (and adults as well) hear such stories about beasts swallowing a character first and then develop fantasies and fears related to these stories, not the other way around.

Could you suggest other tales or films involving the act of swallowing and rebirth or reappearance? How do these stories end? Discuss a possibility to test Jung's ideas about primordial fears experimentally or by other methods.

Psychological Types

Jung did not conduct laboratory experiments. He relied on his encyclopedic knowledge and, as a psychiatrist, on clinical observations. The idea of psychological types came to Jung earlier in his career when he compared the experiences of patients with schizophrenia with those of patients with hysteria (Jung, 1924). In Jung's view, the patient with hysteric symptoms attaches his or her energy to other people. Jung termed this behavior **extroversion**. Conversely, most patients with schizophrenic symptoms turn energy back to themselves. Jung called this **introversion**. In fact, in Jung's view, all people can be described along these directional lines. Extroversion and introversion, he argued, are about an individual's sense of direction (Odajnyk, 2012).

Extroverts, or individuals prone to extroversion, spontaneously embrace the world. Extroverts stream their libido (you should remember this Freudian term) outward, toward external objects. They commonly turn to other people and their ideas. Extroverts, however, can be shallow and their interests lie in the outside world. They are often inconsistent. Their many projects often do not materialize. Extroverts may start a new project because they see potential rewards and seldom anticipate failure. Yet they frequently miscalculate their options because they are too optimistic and don't clearly see potential problems arising.

On the other hand, introverts tend to shy away from the world and turn their attention and interest to themselves. The introvert's libido streams inward, toward a subjective realm of thoughts and fantasies. Introverts tend to seek internal resources to act. Introverts make mistakes too because they often see things from a gloomy, pessimistic perspective. Introverts tend to be reluctant to start new projects because they anticipate few rewards in the end and forecast difficulties ahead. In the end, both types, introverts and extroverts, can fail or win, but for different psychological reasons.

Jung believed, that to an introvert, the world appears too challenging, pushy, annoying, and demanding. These critical perceptions are uncommon in the mind of an extrovert. Extroverts agree that the world is demanding, but as they argue, who says it shouldn't be? Introversion is not necessarily about the soul's depth. Some of their inner worlds are not that sophisticated and complex; they can be dull and banal (see Table 4.2).

TABLE 4.2 ■ Features Associated With Extroversion and Introversion (Jung, 1924)	
Features Associated With Extroversion	**Features Associated With Introversion**
Generally directed to others.	Generally directed to self.
Tries to participate in social events; joins many groups and feels comfortable when there are many people around.	Stays away from participating in social events; doesn't join many groups and feels uncomfortable when there are many people around.
Most tasks and problems appear easy, manageable, positive, and rewarding.	Most tasks and problems appear too demanding, overpowering, negative, and menacing.
Tends to trust people, to avoid envy, and to feel competent and confident.	Tends to be distrustful, envious, and often prone to inferiority feelings.
Has a generally positive attitude about other people and the world in general; tends to see the world in rosy colors.	Tends to be critical about other people and the world in general; always finds "a hair in every soup."
Self-criticism is infrequent and insignificant.	Self-criticism is frequent and significant.
Relations with other people do not require a guaranteed safety. In relationships, trust prevails.	Relations with other people tend to be warm only if safety is guaranteed. In other cases, defensive distrust is common.
Views of others and group pressure frequently affect judgments and actions.	Views of others and group pressure only infrequently affect judgments and actions.

Jung also believed that people have access to four ways to deal with reality: thinking, feeling, intuition, and sensation. These features help the individual organize and evaluate experiences. Sensation and intuition provide knowledge. Thinking organizes this knowledge and sorts it out in terms of its significance, but thinking is not equal to high intelligence. Feeling brings evaluation, including moral judgments, likes and dislikes, and attachments to people and things. Extroversion and introversion are different orientations, in the same way that thinking and feeling as well as sensation and intuition are opposite in function. Sensation focuses on details, while intuition embraces the whole; thinking is about connecting ideas and structuring them, while feeling is about value judgments. Overall, Jung introduces eight psychological types. In these dyads, both functions have to be compatible, not contradictory. For example, a thinking type cannot simultaneously be a feeling type (see Table 4.3).

Jung believed that such categories should help psychologists in their theoretical and practical work. However, he warned against overusing the psychological types. Human beings are different from one another not only because of their types but also because of their distinctive individual qualities, strengths, and weaknesses (Odajnyk, 2012).

Criticisms of Ethnocentrism

Jung was among the first psychologists to critically review the ethnocentric worldview of Western psychology. He confronted in his works a widespread opinion of the time that the European type

TABLE 4.3 ■ Jung's Function Types

The Extrovert			
Thinking Type	**Feeling Type**	**Sensation Type**	**Intuition Type**
Rejects most things based on feelings or intuitive or irrational ideas, including religious beliefs and experiences. Common among men. Jung considers Freud to be in this category.	Feelings are based on the impact of external circumstances and less on subjective experiences. This type tries to do the right things. Pleasure seeking is typical. Common among women.	Lacks an intellectual potential and tries to find pleasure under any circumstances.	This type cares about relationships among several things and tries to exploit social situations. Common among entrepreneurs, politicians, and women.

The Introvert			
Thinking Type	*Feeling Type*	*Sensation Type*	*Intuition Type*
Less concerned with new facts and more preoccupied with new ideas. Follows own way of thinking and tends to ignore criticism. Frequently is impractical.	Cares about personal experience and often appears negative or indifferent. Common among women and creative artists.	Behavior is guided less by the object than by the intensity of own, subjective experiences.	Focuses on the background process of consciousness. This type is common among musicians, dreamers, or artists. Jung considers himself in this category.

of thinking (such as pragmatic, analytical, and science-oriented) was far superior to other cultural patterns (such as intuitive, holistic, and spiritual). Jung was not insisting on pure geographical differences. He compared the world of technology and science on the one hand to the world of tradition and intuition on the other. Consider two examples. In present-day terms, college-educated people from New York or Tokyo who catch a respiratory infection and thus become sick may attribute this health problem to their "bad luck" during the pandemic. A person who lacks formal education may explain the fever and coughing because of a malevolent act committed by "evil forces" (whatever they are). Both these assumptions claim that infection is only the means for delivering harm. In both cases, these people are satisfied with their explanation of why they got sick and turn to various remedies—prescribed or not—for help. In the other example, people in many places of today's world believe in evil spirits and ghosts. Most educated people in London or Seoul consider such beliefs wrong, yet they often make similar and seemingly misleading judgments. Like most of us, we point out, for example, parental mistakes or unfortunate circumstances for our own flops or failures when we have little evidence that these causes are true! Jung hoped that the *Eastern type of thinking* (a term for non-Western cognition) would be gradually accepted in the West.

Summarizing the Psychoanalytic Tradition

Sigmund Freud and his many followers wanted to build a solid scientific background for their theories. Unfortunately, persistent researchers' attempts to identify physiological mechanisms to explain psychological constructs of psychoanalysis, such as Thanatos or archetypes, were inconclusive so far (Goldberg, 2014; Meissner, 2006). Jung vigorously defended the idea of the collective unconscious. But where is evidentiary support in neurosciences for this idea? Evolutionary and archaeological studies identify one common geographical origin of the entire human species. Most probably, our ancestors appeared first in Central Africa and later spread in three different directions (Oppenheimer, 2003). However, this fact does not necessarily support the idea about genetically transmittable and universal mechanisms regulating human unconscious experiences. Researchers also have been critical of Jungian assumption that the historical and cultural development of human beings appears in the individual's developmental history (Ritvo, 1990). Does the mind of a developing child resemble the dynamics of human cultural history? If it does, psychology needs supportive evidence.

Psychoanalysts were more like creative storytellers than careful researchers and collectors of unbiased facts. See, for example, how Sigmund Freud built his theoretical discourses. First, an analyst collects and records observations from his or her own experience or from a clinical case. Then, the analyst compares the selected facts from several cases. Relevant literature is a useful source of information. Next, the analyst interprets the selected facts from a psychoanalytic perspective. A psychoanalytic conclusion follows, and this is constructed as fact. Freud paid attention to infantile conflicts of a sexual nature. Adler focused on an individual's unconscious effort to compensate for deficiency and inferiority. Jung turned to dreams and suggested their links with ancient myths and cultural artifacts.

Another critical point is that psychoanalysts were designing a self-fulfilling prophecy (Chapter 3): They created their own facts to support their own theory (Levy, 2009). Their method of gathering information resembled the principle "I see only what I like to see," which is probably suitable for creative artistic expression but not for unbiased scientific research. When new historical and archaeological facts challenged most Freudian assumptions, he insisted that a psychoanalyst was entitled to choose any theory suited to support his or her own assumptions and reject those that disproved them (Dufresne, 2003). Although Freud presented himself as a scientist, he did not send his works for independent peer review and had little interest in publishing in academic psychological journals, except those under his control. It is not surprising that psychoanalysts drew significant criticisms. Look at the following critical epithets attached to psychoanalysis in modern sources: *grotesque, weird, sheer nonsense, uncanny, a religion* (alluding that it was not a science), *idiotic, uncomprehending, deplorable, "old wives' psychiatry," wildly conjectural,* and *unproven* (Esterson, 2002; Gay, 1998; Hornstein, 1992; Shorter, 1997). This is just a small sample.

Despite fundamental problems associated with psychoanalysis, Freud remains one of the most prominent representatives of modern thought. He is frequently compared today with the most prominent thinkers—the naturalist Charles Darwin, the economist Karl Marx, and the physicist Albert Einstein. Adler, Jung, and Anna Freud also remain in the ranks of the most celebrated minds in psychology. Their ideas continue to generate interest today. The overall cultural impact of psychoanalysis is immense: It influenced and inspired many writers, journalists, theater critics, artists, and millions of people interested in psychology, psychiatry, the theory of arts, cultural studies, linguistics, and anthropology. Interest toward psychoanalysis and its methods is growing today in China and other countries that created a psychology major in their universities (Shariff, 2021). Psychoanalysis also embraced *epistemological optimism*, which is better understood as "know yourself better"! Studies show that the desire to understand and self-improve continues to be a reason that so many people read psychology books and take psychology classes (Campbell, 2006). It remains to be seen if this is applicable to today's young generation.

Psychoanalysis earned a reputation as a theory and method valid primarily within the Western culture (Da Conceição & De Lyra Chebabi, 1987). Over the years, however, many psychoanalytic ideas were critically examined in the context of different countries (Devereux, 1953; Kakar, 1995). The psychoanalytic tradition has been open to cross-cultural examination. Jung clearly focused on non-Western cultural traditions and inspired studies of African witchcraft, social customs of Australian aboriginal natives, the impact of mainstream culture on African Americans, or ego defenses in people from Buddhist communities (Tori & Bilmes, 2002). Contemporary psychology has accepted Jung's encouragements to develop an inclusive, cross-cultural approach to psychological knowledge (Shiraev & Levy, 2024). Some ideas of psychoanalysis have universal significance, others do not. There are papers examining the successful applicability of psychoanalysis to Chinese contexts (Xiubing, 2021). The psychoanalytic tradition has difficulty interpreting, for example, the complexity of gender relations in Muslim communities, the importance of male bonding common in South Asia, or the role of religious identity in a person's life (Kurtz, 1992). Criticism is also directed at the cultural applicability of psychoanalysis as a therapeutic method. For many years, the principles of interaction between the therapist and the client in the West were generally based on the assumption that patient and analyst were essentially equal, although the analyst was more knowledgeable. It is not always the case in other cultural environments. Research showed that many immigrants from traditional cultures, for instance, expected a great deal of advice and direct guidance from the therapist, much as they expected guidance from the authority figure or family elders (Roland, 2006).

Today, one of the most important legacies of psychoanalysis is its ability to constantly generate fascination about us, as human beings—about how we develop, feel, and act.

CHECK AND APPLY YOUR KNOWLEDGE

1. Compare the characteristics of extroverts and introverts. Are there any similarities between them?
2. Compare the feeling and the thinking types (according to Jung).
3. Which type do you feel resembles your personality features the most and why?
4. What is **individuation**? Give an example.
5. Why did Jung call the Western psychology's worldview *ethnocentric*?
6. Why was psychoanalysis often labeled as a *self-fulfilling prophecy*?

APPLYING THE PSYCHOANALYTIC TRADITION

Understanding Self

Psychoanalysis would have probably remained an obscure and even an elitist theory known to a few educated enthusiasts had it not found its way to the hearts and minds of millions of people globally. It offered them a choice and an educated opportunity to investigate the depths of consciousness, to examine a world of experiences hidden from direct observation.

Freud taught psychologists to be careful and critical observers. They should apply their theoretical knowledge to interpret their own experiences as well as experiences of others. From the early days of psychoanalysis, many of its educated followers believed they were skilled practitioners capable of understanding the deep-seated individual problems hidden in the murky waters of unconsciousness, covered with a thick layer of resistance. Only trained psychoanalysts could finally reveal the "truth" about other people's personalities as well as causes of their problems. The professional language of psychoanalysis was straightforward: *It is not your bad luck that made you lose; it is your repressed fear of your mother!* or *You are not just late for the online test. Your tardiness reflects your hidden dislike of the professor!* Despite such apparent simplification in explaining human behavior, psychoanalysis encouraged the observer's curiosity, constant attention to details, and a relentless search for answers. Would you agree that these are fine qualities of a true psychology and health care professional today?

Freud legitimized the distinction between "higher," prosocial structures of the individual personality and "lower," primitive, and largely antisocial formations. The problem in the patient was not in the prevalence or deficiency of certain personality traits (as Greek and many later thinkers would refer to deficiency or surplus of bodily fluids), but in the individual's inability to adequately resolve an inner conflict. Attempts to resolve a conflict lead to the formation of behavioral traits that were deemed inappropriate, inept, and harmful within a social context. A person who consistently exhibits outrageous childish behavior—such as someone who *regresses*, (in Anna Freud's terminology)—attempts to gain attention and love from others, which, unfortunately, does not happen because others not only refrain from expressing love but also reject or even condemn this childishness. This conceptual understanding of dysfunctions of personality as unresolved conflicts had a significant impact on contemporary views on personality disorders, which we will study in Chapter 11.

Although psychoanalysis was often incorrect about the mechanisms of the individual's unconscious actions, it has brought significant attention to what we label today *spontaneous reactions*. For example, experimental studies show that individuals too often make quick, spontaneous, yet seemingly illogical decisions about complex and sophisticated products, such as buying kitchen furniture or a car (Dijksterhuis, 2004). There are certain "mechanisms" within the individual's mind that may explain why such decisions take place. What are the lessons of such studies? We have to be aware of this and sometimes wait longer, check again, or ask a friend or a family member to help us with certain decisions, especially if they are personally important or costly (Dijksterhuis et al., 2006). The ability to wait, take time, and reflect on certain events or circumstances is another practical lesson that we learn from psychoanalysis. Very often our reactions are spontaneous or, as we sometimes call them, "natural." Experimental studies display, for example, that aggressive humor (when a person on a caricature, for example, punches someone in the face) usually distracts people so that they are not fully aware of the content they are laughing at. When people are asked to first explain an aggressive joke or a cartoon, they consider them not as funny as other people do when they are not asked to pay attention to the violent content of a joke (Gollob & Levine, 1967).

PHOTO 4.3 Do you have individual skills and traits that could make you a fine therapist who can help people with their psychological problems? What are these skills and traits?

Helping Others: Therapy

Perhaps one of the most noteworthy applications of psychoanalytic theories is the method (or rather a range of methods) of treatment of psychological problems. Psychoanalytic ideas and practical work helped in making psychotherapy a legitimate occupation early in the 20th century. People began to understand mental illness better, thus challenging the stigma of mental illness (Shiraev, 2015). Jung's therapy also won global recognition. Many people from different countries sought his treatment. They paid significant sums of money and settled in hotels near Jung's lakeshore residence in Switzerland, devoting weeks and months of their lives to therapy. In addition to individual sessions, Jung offered lectures and seminars attended by groups of his patients, who could receive an abbreviated course in his analytical psychology. Adler was also a sought-after therapist who believed that mental health was inseparable from the problem of social inequality. Anna Freud is known for her work with children.

In the past century, most practicing psychiatrists in the United States were not psychoanalysts. Yet many studied psychoanalysis in medical schools and freely applied its principles in diagnosis and therapy of mental illness. The first edition of *The Diagnostic and Statistical Manual of Mental Disorders (DSM)*, published in 1952, was filled with psychoanalytic terminology and arguments. By the third edition of the *DSM*, published in 1980, psychoanalysis and psychoanalytic theory were excluded from its pages (Menand, 2014). Psychoanalysts, however, did not give up and continued improving the scientific foundation of their theory. They modified their research and practical work to pursue three principles or imperatives: (1) use clinical data to generate testable hypotheses, (2) test these hypotheses by scientific methods, and (3) look outside the discipline to exchange data with other fields in psychology (Bornstein, 2001; Mills, 2001). Many analysts began to implement these principles in their studies. Jonathan Metzl (2005), for example, in the book *Prozac on the Couch*, provides evidence of the effective use of psychoanalysis in combination with prescribed medication. Other researchers analyzed the effectiveness of psychoanalysis as a therapeutic method using controlled methods and statistical analysis (Karon & Widener, 2001). Studies of the American Psychological Association (Gerber et al., 2011) and other clinical studies (Hilsenroth, 2007; Leichsenring et al., 2005) show that psychoanalysis as a therapeutic method can be as effective as other popular forms of therapy.

Some researchers turned to psychoanalysis to apply some of its ideas of unconscious processes to the scientific study of the spiritual side of human existence. **Transpersonal psychology**, for example, is a theoretical and applied field that focuses on spiritual and transcendent states of consciousness (Vich, 1988), and it continues to attract attention today. Overall, the contemporary view of spirituality is that spiritual factors such as strong religious beliefs, prayer, meditation, and combinations thereof affect at least four interacting physiological systems: (1) the brain, (2) the endocrine system, (3) the peripheral nervous system, and (4) the immune system. These data have been published in top peer-reviewed psychology journals (Powell et al., 2003; Ray, 2004).

Applying to Art

Freud applied psychoanalysis to study personalities of historic figures; one of the most famous cases he studied was Leonardo da Vinci (1452–1519), the creator of the *Mona Lisa*. Freud explained Leonardo's scientific and artistic creativity as the result of his repressed inner conflicts. The *Mona Lisa*'s smile, according to Freud, reflects the artist's repressed love for his mother and stepmother. Repressed conflicts produced anxiety, which resulted in imagination, a form of symbolic alteration of reality. Studies show that artists used canvas, oil, and marble to reexperience their fantasies. Many contemporary researchers in the fields of neuroscience and art, including Nobel Prize winners, use the psychoanalytic tradition to reflect on personalities of artists (Kandel, 2012).

Applying to Neuroscience

Many psychoanalysts believed that the structure and functions of the human mind were intimately related to the structure and functions of the brain. For example, an individual's obsessive or avoidant behavior or defense mechanisms that make one individual different from another were supposed to be explained by the brain's functioning. Yet for decades in the past century, brain researchers did not have the tools to explore these relationships. One of several intriguing applications of psychoanalysis is **neuropsychoanalysis**, the discipline that provides a link between psychoanalysis and the neurosciences. Neuroscientists have begun to investigate various topics that have traditionally been an "intellectual sanctuary" of psychoanalysts. Neuropsychoanalysis generated many new insights into numerous problems of vital interest to psychoanalysis (Solms & Turnbull, 2011).

Some results have been encouraging. Researchers found that certain malfunctions in the right-parietal lobe can be associated with narcissistic tendencies and the individual's tendency to launch defense mechanisms (Kaplan-Solms & Solms, 2000). These patients also appeared to have disrupted cognitive processes and the diminished ability to tolerate powerful negative emotions.

Clinicians are now applying psychoanalytic methods to the study of individuals with neurological problems (Solms & Turnbull, 2011). Studying brain injury and examining the effects of new medications in pharmacological probes, some therapists have turned to psychoanalytic theories to describe several neurophysiological mechanisms. Research has demonstrated the powerful influence of unconscious cognitions, including defenses, on the formation of false beliefs. For example, the patients with specific damages in their cortex show excessive attention to words that refer to paralysis and disabilities, despite denying that they are themselves disabled and paralyzed (Nardone et al., 2007).

Psychoanalytic theories inspired some researchers to study the limbic system and the processes that are likely associated with anger and rage (which is anger out of control), panic, separation distress, lust, and seeking behavior. The latter is often compared to libido (see Chapter 4) as the most powerful force responsible for an individual's activities. It was shown that stimulation of certain areas of the midbrain in mice caused their unusual investigative, searching behavior—even food could not distract them from exploring (Panksepp, 1998). Is this the area generally responsible for similar behavior in humans? Could this "seeking drive" be compared to libido? Some researchers believe so (Solms & Turnbull, 2011). Others show that the activities in this zone correlate with behavioral phenomena such as intense love, lust, and obsession with love figures, especially after being rejected by them (Fisher, 2004).

Applying to Political Behavior

Psychoanalysts try to explain behavior of political leaders. One of Freud's subjects was U.S. President Woodrow Wilson (1856–1924), though Wilson was unaware of this. Freud's coauthored work on Wilson wasn't published until 1967, so Freud, who died in 1939, could not read the book's poor reviews. Nevertheless, the genre of historical biography based on psychoanalysis—often called **psychobiography**—flourished. Many authors adopted psychobiography as their key method.

Another noticeable application of the psychoanalytic view belongs to Henry Murray (1893–1988). Murray built foundations for **political psychology**—the field examining psychological factors in politics as well as an individual's political behavior. Murray and his colleagues wrote a psychological profile of German dictator Adolf Hitler (Murray, 1943). Their report was a detailed psychological examination of the facts known about Hitler combined with psychoanalytic discussions about the causes of his cruelty and erratic behavior. Murray gave specific recommendations for anti-Hitler propaganda that could have been launched via mass media and leaflets. This analysis of a political leader was one of the earliest attempts at "long-distance" psychological profiling—a method that is used today, especially with Zoom sessions— by practitioners.

Political psychologists apply psychoanalysis to explain war and violence. They argue that violent, radical leaders can attract attention and support of many individuals who are like worshippers and treat these leaders as minigods (Berman, 2004). The leaders mobilize their worshippers, who are predominantly young, to sacrifice their lives on behalf of an idea or an illusion. These leaders also appeal to a fundamental unconscious desire of the individual to avoid or block unpleasant information (Koenigsberg, 2014).

Erich Fromm (1900–1980) researched **authoritarian personality**—a complex pattern of behavior and thought based on the individual's faithful acceptance of the power of authority, order, and subordination (see Figure 4.2). Discussions about authoritarian personality drew significant attention and sparked new research on this subject for many years (Adorno et al., 1950). The interest in these studies continues today. One of the main assumptions of this line of research, which used methods including psychobiography, surveys, and laboratory experiments, was that some individuals develop a stable pattern of authoritarian traits due to their childhood experiences. Such individuals are prone to mystical thinking and prejudice against other individuals and social groups, especially ethnic minorities, and LGBTQ+ community. They are obedient to authority figures, such as parents, teachers, and political leaders, and resistant to social innovation while rejecting new societal trends. These individuals are also prone to anger and violence. The most remarkable finding of early and later studies was that the authoritarian personality type is very common in ordinary people. These individuals tend to endorse authoritarian methods of government and enthusiastically support dictators. They also tend to welcome injustice, oppression, and discrimination because they feel comfortable discriminating and oppressing. High scorers on authoritarianism have been associated with a punitive parenting style that had adverse consequences for parent–child relationships (Peterson et al., 1997).Today, political psychology is an influential field of studies and applications based on a wide variety of psychological theories and empirical research.

CHECK AND APPLY YOUR KNOWLEDGE

1. What is psychobiography?
2. Which edition of the *Diagnostic and Statistical Manual of Mental Disorders (DSM)*, published in 1952, was filled with psychoanalytic terminology and arguments?
3. Answer these questions from the standpoint of psychoanalysis: Why do people often turn to violence on behalf of an idea or myth? What forces motivate these people to willingly sacrifice their lives to kill others?

SUMMARY

- Psychoanalysis is one of the most prominent traditions used to understand personality. Supporters praise psychoanalysis for its significant contribution to the scientific knowledge of the individual. Critics see psychoanalysis as an immense yet misleading speculation, brilliantly disguised in a fake academic uniform.

- First, psychoanalysis emphasized the dominant role of unconscious processes in human experience and behavior. Next, psychoanalysts stressed the importance of human sexuality in an individual's life. Then psychoanalysis emphasized the significance of early childhood experiences in the individual's life. And last, which is not least important for us, psychoanalysis was a type of treatment, or a sophisticated method of interaction between a professional therapist and a client.

- Freud accepted the prevailing scientific outlook of the 19th century that multiple forces, external and internal, cause humans to think and act. Some of these forces are instinctual drives. The individual, of course, seeks their gratification. Freud formulated and described two major mechanisms that regulate their activities: the pleasure principle and the reality principle.

- Freud advocated that boys and girls mature in similar ways but also differently. They both develop emotional attachment to their parents. The boys, however, are attached to their mothers, and girls are attached to their fathers. These conflicting attachments create a foundation for future psychological problems and influence every element of the child's and family's functioning.

- An individual's psyche (we can label it the *inner world* or *personality*) is made up of three levels (features). The most primitive part of the personality is the **id**. The **superego** is the moral guide passing on imperatives of appropriate or inappropriate actions and thoughts. Making compromises between the id and the environment is the **ego**, which is guided by the reality principle.

- Anna Freud's **The Ego and the Mechanisms of Defense** focused on the inner struggles of the individual. She wrote about the struggle of the ego with the overwhelming demands of the id, on the one hand, and powerful restrictions imposed by reality, on the other.

- Ego defenses can be described as defense mechanisms, or specific unconscious structures that enable an individual to avoid awareness of unpleasant, anxiety-arousing issues.

- Adler was Freud's follower, yet he emphasized the importance of the relationships among siblings, not between the parents and the child as Freud did. Adler also questioned sexuality as the most dominant force in human life and one of the central points of Freud's psychoanalysis.

- Adler emphasized the importance of concepts such as organ inferiority and compensation. There are three general outcomes of an individual's compensatory efforts. The genius overcomes the old inferiority problems and achieves success and happiness. Compensation in this case brings success and delivers a new life free from the pain of inferiority. In the case of degeneration, the attempted compensation is unsuccessful. The person falls out of the normal course of life and is unable to adjust to social rules. The third outcome is neurosis.

- Adler assumed that people are motivated primarily by future expectations. By forming them, people pursue their fictional final goal, called **self-ideal**. This is the unifying principle of an individual's personality. Self-ideal can be achieved if an individual engages in striving toward superiority. People have social interests, or the desire to be connected with other people and to adapt positively to the perceived social environment.

- Jung used the term *analytical psychology* to distinguish his views from Freud's psychoanalysis. Jung suggested an impersonal layer in human psyche, which he called the collective unconscious. The content of the collective unconscious consists of archetypes, or images of the primordial (elemental, ancient) character. These are people's ancestral experiences, which appear in three universal ways: dreams, fantasies, and delusions.

- Jung theorized about extroversion and introversion. Extroverts, or individuals prone to extroversion, spontaneously embrace the world. Extroverts stream their libido outward, toward external objects. They commonly turn to other people and their ideas. Introverts tend to shy away from the world and turn their attention and interest to themselves. The introvert's libido streams inward, toward a subjective realm, thought, and fantasies. Introverts tend to seek internal resources to act.

- Jung was among the first psychologists to critically review the ethnocentric worldview of Western psychology.

- One of several intriguing applications of psychoanalysis is neuropsychoanalysis, the discipline that provides a link between psychoanalysis and the neurosciences.

- Henry Murray and other psychoanalysts built foundations for political psychology— the field examining psychological factors in politics as well as an individual's political behavior.

- Erich Fromm researched authoritarian personality—a complex pattern of behavior and thought based on the individual's faithful acceptance of the power of authority, order, and subordination. Discussions about authoritarian personality drew significant attention and sparked new research on this subject for many years.

- Over the years, mainstream personality psychology based on experimental research developed unsettled relations with psychoanalysis. Some of its assumptions have been accepted. Many others have been criticized and rejected. Nevertheless, psychoanalysis offered them a choice and an educated opportunity to look into the depths of consciousness, to examine a world of experiences hidden from direct or superficial observation.

VISUAL REVIEW

Visual Review. Chapter 4. Psychoanalytic Tradition.

1. THE ESSENCE OF THE TRADITION

Unconscious processes play the dominant role in human experience and behavior.	Sexuality plays an important role in an individual's emotions and behavior.	Early childhood experiences significantly affect the individual's life	An individual can seek cure and relief in psychoanalysis as a therapeutic method

2. DISCUSSING PSYCHOANALYSIS

S. Freud emphasized the repressed instinctual drives and suggested the id, the superego, and the ego as the personality's features	A. Freud emphasized defense mechanisms. Adler taught about inferiority, psychological compensation, and striving toward superiority	Jung taught about collective unconscious, archetypes, and described psychological types

3. APPLYING PSYCHOANALYSIS

Understanding self and others	Using psychoanalysis in psychotherapy	Explaining social events

KEY TERMS

analytical psychology
archetypes
authoritarian personality
collective unconscious
compensation
death wish
defense mechanisms
degeneration
ego
Eros
extroversion
genius
id
individuation
introversion
libido

neuropsychoanalysis
organ inferiority
pleasure principle
political psychology
psychoanalysis
psychobiography
reality principle
social interest
striving toward superiority
style of life
superego
Thanatos
transpersonal psychology
unconscious

EVALUATING WHAT YOU KNOW

Describe the essence and the sources of the psychoanalytic tradition.

What were its major assumptions related to an individual?

In three or for sentences, describe the major views of S. Freud, A. Freud, A. Adler, and K. Jung related to personality.

What are the most noticeable similarities and differences among these scholars?

Explain the id, the ego, and the superego.

Explain the inferiority complex.

Explain and give an example of an archetype.

Explain defense mechanisms and give a couple of examples.

How did psychoanalysis contribute to scientific psychology?

How did psychoanalysts contribute to therapy?

A BRIDGE TO THE NEXT CHAPTER

Over the years, mainstream psychology based on experimental research developed unsettled relations with psychoanalysis. Two opinions related to personality psychology coexist:

● *Positive.* The works of psychoanalysts had a notable impact on personality psychology. Psychoanalysis paid serious attention to the unconscious side of the individual's experience. Psychoanalysis also focused on early childhood and its role in the development of the individual's personality and elevated human sexuality as a legitimate research topic. Psychoanalysis had a big impact on modern psychotherapy as a key method of treatment of psychological problems.

● *Critical.* Psychoanalysis grossly exaggerated the role of unconscious processes in the individual's life. The impact of sexuality on individual development and interpersonal relationships was also overestimated. Psychoanalysts' focus on early childhood was valid, but many of their assumptions were wrong: It is clear now that infantile unconscious experiences do not play the central role in an individual's life.

Because of their belief in the possibility of improving humanity through social changes, psychoanalysis shared progressive ideas. Supporters of progressivism, as you should remember from Chapter 2, believed in the opportunity to apply scientific knowledge to improve many spheres of social life. Progressivism in psychology also emphasized the importance of applied knowledge in three areas: health care, education, and social services. Psychoanalysts believed in their science as a new force, capable of changing society and providing people with a new vision of a peaceful and healthy life. It is probably true that psychology today is rooted in the same genuinely progressive view.

Yet psychoanalysis was most likely missing, as its critics insisted, a few important features. It did not embrace measurement. It did not accept the audacity of carefully crafted experimental research. It was somewhat indifferent to the rational person's acting, judging, and making decisions. Of course, there were other angles from which psychologists could examine personality.

At this point, we are ready to study another remarkable and highly influential tradition in psychology that focused exclusively on the individual's overt behavior.

5
THE BEHAVIORAL-LEARNING TRADITION

iStockphoto.com /anouchka

LEARNING OBJECTIVES

After reading this chapter, you should be able to do the following:

- Identify the main principles and historical contexts of the behavioral learning tradition including operant conditioning and social learning theories.

- Discuss the principles of operant conditioning and social learning theories.

- Identify ways to apply the principles of the behavioral learning tradition to individual experience and behavior.

First, an international flight, then a few hours on a bus through the serpentine of mountain roads—and finally I had a chance to see this amazing place for the first time. It was a small town, conveniently located at the foot of the hill near a beautiful lake.

"How many people are living here?" I asked my guide.

"About 700," she replied. "There are more moving in this year. The COVID pandemic slowed the process down. But now we have more applicants than we can accommodate."

"Tell, me, what attracts people to this place?"

"Just see and learn…"

After spending 2 days, I have learned that people here own property collectively. Their economy is small. Residents, based on the bylaws, work for only 4 hours daily. All people here have been trained to recycle, consume only what is necessary, and not to overproduce. Most marriages are monogamous and same sex unions are common. The residents educate children together. Each family must take turns spending time with other children: Children spend each month with a new family. Parents treat every child with care and affection.

Everyone goes to school, and education is separate for boys and girls. Children begin their vocational training at age 16. Boys learn engineering, science, medicine, and manufacturing, while girls learn cooking, home management, child rearing, health monitoring, and sex education. Adults and children alike learn daily useful habits. Mistakes are recorded and discussed in weekly community meetings.

There are no police in town because people train themselves to respect and enforce the rules. Occasional behavioral problems (like a verbal assault) are corrected by imposing mandatory training in the reeducation camp nearby. There are no elected officials or office bureaucrats. There are no prisons either. The power in the community belongs to a few people called *behaviorists*. They are trained to observe, judge, and pass on decisions—all of them are based on science—so that other people follow them with confidence. Most individuals in this community are happy, virtuous, and they all look forward to a new day. Those who are unhappy must attend special behavioral correction programs.

You have probably figured out that this is not a true story. This is actually a short summary, with a few modern touches, of the futuristic projects by two influential American psychologists of the past century, John Watson (in 1929) and B. F. Skinner (in 1948). Watson and Skinner, as well as a handful of scientists of their time, believed that psychological science, if used in the right way, could help in creating an ideal person: happy, educated, productive, nonviolent, creative, and moral. Skinner held that most human problems were because people put too much trust into incompetent, sinister, and self-centered politicians. As soon as trained psychologists replace such incompetent bureaucrats and then scientists offer a list of useful conditions for people's moral growth and professional improvement, a new society, and a new type of people will certainly emerge.

Many psychologists in the past and today defended a research position that we, as individuals, are essentially "products" of environmental and social factors. Social and psychological problems can be explained if we find the causes of those problems. All in all, right people, in right places, using right methods could change our society for the better. Imagine a community that is just, green, prosperous, and people in it tend to realize most of their potentials.

Would you prefer to live in such a community? What would be the advantages and disadvantages of giving professional psychologists the opportunity to train the best individual features in specially organized communities? If such communities existed today, hypothetically, would you like to work in one of them, as a psychologist? Explain your choices. If you have children, would you agree to educate your own children there, in that community? Why or why not?

THE BEHAVIORAL-LEARNING TRADITION

This tradition in personality psychology is closely connected to **behaviorism**, which is an incredibly rich and diverse interdisciplinary tradition. It focuses on observable behavior. Behaviorism gained strength at the beginning of the 1900s within a favorable social and research climate. The rapidly developing industrial societies needed more technocrats and scientists—educated, trained, and skilled individuals. Social progress was increasingly seen as rooted in experimental science and technology. Behaviorists can be seen today as, perhaps, technocrats of psychology; they turned to science to measure and explain people's behavior.

PHOTO 5.1 There is a monument to the unknown dog in St. Petersburg (Russia), near the Institute of Experimental Medicine, where Ivan Pavlov headed the physiology laboratory for many years about 100 years ago. The monument commissioned and partially designed by Pavlov himself to honor the animals that died for the sake of scientific progress. May animals to be used in psychology research? Dogs, for example, play a big therapeutic role in helping people with psychological problems. Are there other areas in which animals can be studied and used?

Catriona Bass Russian Images/Alamy Stock Photo

For more than 100 years, behaviorists supported a somewhat unpretentious, yet clear and intelligent view of personality: We, as individuals, live and learn. Our actions are learned behaviors. Because people are not completely identical at birth, because they are exposed to different physical conditions, and because they live in different social and cultural environments, their learning experiences result in different responses and habits. Such habits then evolve and become stable behavioral patterns (Banks & Rose, 2010). In the mind of the behaviorist, personality is something that "occurs" between behavior and the environment (see Figure 5.1; Mischel, 1993). Providing knowledge about the universal learning principles and the different conditions in which this learning takes place is a key contribution of behaviorism to the study of personality. Behaviorism grew and evolved within psychology, biology, and physiology. Unlike thoughts, perceptions, and will, which psychologists struggled to study experimentally, behavior and learning appeared observable and quantifiable. More scientists saw human life and mental activities as measurable. Many portrayed human and animal behavior as reflexes

FIGURE 5.1   ■   The Behavioral-Learning Tradition: An Illustrative Model

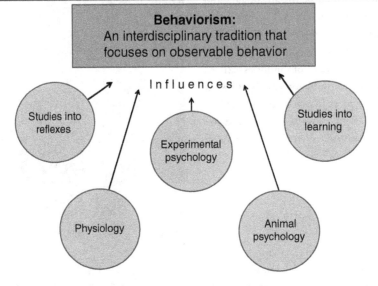

and in mechanical terms. Mechanics meant measurement. Simple reactions and movements of individuals, as well as complex actions of the crowd, were appearing suitable to be explained by mathematical formulas. Behaviorists' logic was strikingly simple: We may have difficulty explaining the subjective side of, for example, embarrassment, but we can measure a person's behavioral responses in an embarrassing situation.

When psychologists apply behavioral principles to study personality, they tend to emphasize the importance of situational, environmental, and developmental factors in an individual's learning. They also study habits, traits, and the ways people change and develop them. Some traits are leaned early and remain stable during an individual's life span. Studies show, for instance, that personality traits and stable patterns of behavior measured in childhood are a strong predictor of adult behavior (Nave et al., 2010). Many behavioral patterns, like habits, change with age due to a person's life experiences (Damian et al., 2019).

Several factors contributed to behaviorism's rapid development. The first was the success of animal psychology early in the 20th century. Researchers studying animals believed in the principle of continuity: Both humans and animals represent one natural world and must be subject to at least some similar laws. The second development was the accomplishments of physiology. The success of general physiology in the early 20th century encouraged psychologists to turn to neuroscience. Researchers looked for measurable facts that are subject to verification and further experimentation. As with physics and the study of the atom, psychologists hoped to find physiological "atoms" of human behavior. Finally, there was the development of new research methods. Psychology was turning to a new generation of experiments, which many behaviorists called "objective methods" to distinguish them from introspection and other forms of self-observation.

A noteworthy contribution of behaviorism to personality psychology was in the former's emphasis on education and learning. To optimize them, three conditions should exist, as leading behaviorists were proposing (Skinner, 1938). First, behaviorism as a scientific discipline should provide knowledge in explaining how and under what circumstances habits and other personality features develop and change. Second, successful learning takes place under specific conditions that must be created. Remember the discussion about special communities at the beginning of the chapter? And finally, there should also be a group of highly educated and properly trained behavioral specialists, or *behaviorist physicians*. They should plan, manage, and protect human society in the same way that physicians conduct preventative care and treatment. These tasks are difficult; therefore, behaviorist physicians must be licensed. They will carry special observational devices to carefully examine every person's daily behavior. Behaviorists will correct deviant behavior and heal mental illness. Behavioral errors should be fixed; excellent behavior will receive recognition and rewards. Behaviorists encouraged psychologists to exclusively use behavioral terms in describing the individual's psychological features.

CHECK AND APPLY YOUR KNOWLEDGE

1. Describe yourself from a "behavioral" standpoint. Compose five short statements containing five verbs that best describe you as a person (it is a challenging task, but it should help you in grasping the essence of behaviorism). Emphasize things you do and not how you feel or what you like and dislike. Compare your profile with one composed by another person. How different or similar are these profiles?

2. Who were behaviorist physicians? Imagine this profession existed today and you got a job as a behaviorist physician. What would you ideally want to do? Be creative and discuss in class.

UNDERSTANDING PERSONALITY BY STUDYING ANIMAL BEHAVIOR

Comparative psychologists pioneered behavioral research into personality. Although the term *comparative psychology* became broadly accepted only in the 20th century (Johnston, 2002), studies in this field go deep into history. Comparative psychologists embraced the evolutionary ideas of Darwin and Spencer (Chapter 2), believed in the adaptive nature of animal behavior, and argued that animals and humans should be subject to many essentially similar laws. To understand complex phenomena, a scientist should seek the simplest explanations. This principle, known as **parsimony**, became a working rule in comparative research. Studying animal behavior and comparing it to human actions, scientists often assumed that many basic mechanisms of learning should be similar. Humans, like animals, seek safety, and comfort. Animals, like humans, try to avoid discomfort and suffering. Studying animals, we ultimately study humans.

Anthropomorphism

More than 60% of Americans own at least one pet, according to the American Veterinary Medical Association (AVMA) and the National Pet Owners Survey (American Pet Products

Association, 2022; AVMA, 2016). You probably watch videos or hear (or maybe even tell) stories about the surprisingly "human" behavior of some of those animals. In these stories, dogs display "stubborn" and "clever" personalities, cats have introverted tendencies, or parrots project a superb sense of humor. Portraying animal behavior in human terms is **anthropomorphism**. Among the most vivid examples of anthropomorphism are fairy tales, cartoons, and, of course, children's animations. Early comparative psychologists were anthropomorphists to some degree. They often elevated popular beliefs to the level of scientific knowledge. A pioneer ethnographer of Native American culture, Lewis Henry Morgan (1818–1881), argued that animals, like individuals, possess reason, creativity, and moral judgment. He maintained that the differences between humans and animals are based on the sophistication of their habits and the difficulty of their projects: In fact, both humans and beavers build dams! Animals too could develop their mental abilities if only they had access to special training (Johnston, 2002).

The British physiologist George J. Romanes (1848–1894) published *Animal Intelligence* in which he argued that sophisticated emotional dilemmas regulate animal behavior, and animals can display fortitude and patience (Romanes, 1882). Contemporary research shows how animals, such as dogs, react to other people's emotions and display their emotions through muscular movements (Caeiro et al., 2017; Nagasawa et al., 2013). However, this and similar studies do not suggest that animals can experience deep moral conflicts and struggle with complex ethical predicaments.

Social Instincts

Supporters of anthropomorphism also found a convenient concept to explain behavior and individual traits: the **instinct**, which is the inherent pattern or a complex behavior. Humans belong to social groups in which they acquire social instincts as automatic and unconscious responses. The French psychologist Gustave Le Bon (1841–1931) believed, for instance, that aggressiveness as an individual gets stronger in a large crowd. A typically nonviolent person can act aggressively in a crowd simply because social groups are akin living "organisms" emulating magnetic impulses of some sort (Le Bon, 1896). Gabriel Tarde (1843–1904), another Frenchman, focused on the mechanism of imitation. He believed that the entire learning process is rooted in imitation (Tarde, 1903). The English scholar William McDougall (1871–1938) argued that human behavior could be linked to initial animal instincts, such as parenting (people, like animals, tend to take care of the young), self-display (individuals and animals tend to show off to gain support), or hoarding (people, like animals, tend to congregate in groups; McDougall, 1908).

Of course, some of these assumptions appeared intriguing. Yet science does not consider human behavior as rooted in animal instincts. Take **deindividuation**, for example, which is a behavioral shift taking place when people assume they cannot be personally identified, especially being in a group. Experimental research shows that some people indeed tend to abandon the sense of responsibility when they act in a group: They can commit immoral and violent acts and only later express the remorse for what they have done. Group members tend to become less critical of one another (Lea & Spears, 1991). The Stanford psychologist Philip Zimbardo (b. 1933) claimed that factors such as diminished self-observation, reduced concern for social evaluation, and weakened controls—often weakened by alcohol or other substance—all can predictably lead to irresponsible and evil acts. Zimbardo's research also showed that seemingly "good people" can be placed in social conditions under which they can be provoked by others and initiated into behaving in evil ways (Zimbardo, 2007). But these reactions are not instinctual. Today a once popular term, "social instinct," is used mostly in a metaphorical way. Our behavior is learned, as behaviorists claim, and we can empirically study how people learn.

Learning Laws

Comparative psychologists believed that animals learn according to some uniform principles that are generally applicable to all humans. Researchers turned to the study of **habit formation**, the process by which new behaviors become automatic. They offered a simple yet intriguing hypothesis that favorable conditions stimulate one type of behavior, and unfavorable conditions suppress this behavior. For example, a dog may learn to bark and then receive a treat after the dog's trainer says, "Speak!" Or a person learns to be honest because honesty is a habit, which develops in situations when honesty is required. Similarly, another person learns how to lie because lying in some earlier situations helped this person avoid punishment.

The American scholar Edward Thorndike (1874–1949) introduced a new method, a "puzzle box," which was a specially designed small cage or enclosure. An animal could escape by tripping a latch mechanism that opened a door or lifted a small barrier. Using this method, Thorndike observed and measured the behavior of his experimental animals (Thorndike, 1911). Thorndike showed the improvement of learning with experience. He called it the **learning curve**. He showed that with each new trial, the animal was spending less time in the puzzle box and making fewer trials before escaping from the box or solving a problem. The experience of an animal, its familiarity with the experimental situation, the quality of the reward, and the presence of distracting signals, such as noises, all may affect learning. Humans, according to Thorndike, are supposed to learn and unlearn in the same way.

Thorndike suggested several **laws of learning**, which are the most essential principles on which behavioral learning is based. For example, the *Law of Exercise* stated that the more one repeats an action, the better it is retained. Describing the *Law of Effect*, Thorndike showed that people tend to learn faster if the reaction is associated with pleasure. This is a mechanism explaining how people acquire harmful habits. For example, overeating or drinking alcohol may bring immediate satisfaction, but the long-term harmful effects can be devastating.

It should be mentioned that Thorndike's biography remains controversial. Back 100 years ago, as a professor at Columbia University in New York City, he often applied his work and his name to make sexist and anti-Semitic statements that contributed to a discriminatory environment at the university in the early 20th century (Umanah, 2020).

In perspective, studies of animal behavior made an important contribution to the study of personality. This research encouraged some psychologists to consider humans and animals similar in principle yet different in complexity. The differences between them seemed substantial but not profound. Humans appeared more sophisticated than primates; monkeys appeared more advanced than cats and dogs, which in turn seemed more sophisticated than turtles and fish; and so forth. These specialists believed that animal research could help in the understanding of human individual traits and complex behavior.

CHECK AND APPLY YOUR KNOWLEDGE

1. What is parsimony? Recall an important decision you have made recently. Explain this decision in a few sentences, using the parsimony principle. Which factors have influenced your decision?
2. On YouTube (or on any other platform), watch a sample of commercials. Describe in a short sentence every display of anthropomorphism in these commercials (such as talking dogs, dancing cats, etc.). What exactly did the animals do or say? In which social activities is anthropomorphism also common?
3. Give an example of the learning curve using a recent episode from your life.
4. Which life situations involving humans should resemble, in your view, the "puzzle box"? Have you ever been in such situations, and what did you do?
5. Assume you have a video of seven people stuck in the elevator for 15 minutes and later freed. As a behaviorist who could examine the video, what would you learn about these seven individuals?

STUDYING REFLEXES

Psychology's interest in reflexes stemmed from the teachings of doctors and physiologists who understood reflexes as automatic responses of the organism. Psychologists assumed that studying human reflexes should help to better understand human action and experience. At least two theories deserve our attention.

Reflexology and Personality

Vladimir Bekhterev (1857–1927) was a Russian physiologist and doctor. He was among the first to use the term *personality* in his research (Strickland, 1997). He was among the most active promoters of the idea that science must study the individual from a multidisciplinary perspective, at the center of which he saw **reflexology**, which is a unifying science to study reflexes. He also hoped that one day reflexology would resemble biology or physics.

He hoped that reflexology could explain practically all aspects of human behavior as transformations of energy in the brain and nervous system (Bekhterev, 1904). He believed that human emotions, thinking, and consciousness are all modifications of energy within the brain (Frost, 1912). He discussed simple reflexes, like blinking or yawning, and complex social reflexes, like courage or honesty, which emerge as responses to signals and events in the social world (Bekhterev, 1921/2001a; Strickland, 2001).

What is personality, according to Bekhterev? At least two points are important. Personality is, first, a "foundation," or an inner core of reflexes that integrates and manages an individual's thoughts, actions, and complex behavior. Second, this core is interacting with the environment. Personality should be understood as an individual's unique characteristics that are self-organized in relation to the outside world. He believed, as a doctor, that a person's physical health, psychological soundness, and moral values were inseparable. Bekhterev liked to quote an ancient principle, *Mens sana in corpore sano* (a sound mind in a healthy body). A quite contemporary vision!

SELF-REFLECTION

Bekhterev used the concept of energy to explain immortality. Because people are afraid of death, he argued, many turn to religion as a great source of hope. Many believe in the immortal soul or the resurrection of the dead. However, in his view, it is science that could provide the most valid justification of immortality. According to the principle of energy conservation (he borrowed it from physics), energy cannot disappear without a trace, and it cannot appear without being caused by another source of energy (Bekhterev, 1916/2001b). Human internal energy transforms into the energy of muscles, thoughts, and actions. According to Bekhterev, our personality continues into new forms of energy, including the thoughts, emotions, and actions of other people. Our lives still influence the lives of other people! This is, in fact, the life cycle of immortality (Bekhterev, 1908/2017; Dobreva-Martinova & Strickland, 2001).

Questions

1. Animals don't seem to care how their offspring will remember them. Why do people care about how they will be remembered? Do you personally care about being remembered? Why or why not?
2. If our immortality is predetermined by our actions, as some behaviorists have proposed, would you agree that some people become more "immortal" than others because they have accomplished more and impacted more people during their lives?
3. As a behaviorist, discuss and suggest an "index of immortality," which is a composite measure of a person's impact. What criteria would you suggest for this index (for example, the number of Google "hits," social media "likes," or followers related to this person's account, or a frequency measure in ChatGPT and similar platforms)?

Conditioned Reflexes

The son of a provincial priest, Ivan Pavlov (1849–1936) became one of the world's most influential scientists and the first Russian ever to win the Nobel Prize. Although Pavlov used dogs in his experiments, his real passion was studying human behavior. Pavlov was a doctor, a physiologist, and a psychologist. He called his research an objective study of reflexes, or physiological activities of the brain's cortex, the "highest nervous activity." He believed that his knowledge of reflexes would allow him to learn about personality, its traits, the most significant types, and even allow him to measure them with precision. What role do reflexes play in an individual's personality?

Pavlov recognized two categories of reflexes. Those of the first category are associated with the direct influence of a signal; they are inborn. This category received the name unconditioned reflexes. For example, dogs as well as humans do not learn how to salivate when the food enters their mouth—it just happens. Similarly, we (and animals) remove our hand (or paw) quickly when we touch something very hot. Altogether, unconditioned reflexes provide for the most basic biological functions: food (search and consumption), procreation, and self-protection. The reflexes in the second category are acquired only under certain conditions, which gave them their name, **conditioned reflexes**. A classic example of this reflex is when a dog starts salivating after hearing a bell; for a week prior to this, the sound of the bell preceded every feeding. Similarly, a child who is scared by a big crow at the playground displays a fearful reaction when going back to the same playground the next day even though there are no crows there.

To explain the dynamics of reflexes, Pavlov turned to physiological excitement and inhibition. He hoped that a better understanding of these processes could be a key to understanding human behavior and personality. Excitement and inhibition can override each other. Consider the reaction of group panic: In fast-developing, difficult, or dangerous situations, many people lose self-control and act erratically because they are influenced mostly by excitement, Pavlov reasoned. Others, affected by inhibition in their brain, freeze. Still others do not panic and act rationally. Their inhibition and excitement are balanced. Excitement related to one type of behavior may also inhibit other behaviors. Inhibition in one part of the brain may excite other parts of the brain. This is called *induction*.

Induction takes place almost constantly in our lives when a situation associated with joy is paired with a situation associated with pain or suffering. In such situations, one activity is inhibited, and another is likely to be carried out. For example, some people can spend tedious, long hours trying to buy tickets online to see their favorite performer. An individual's "suffering" during the waiting period is inhibited by an anticipation of the excitement of the future show. Imagine now a person who is consistently capable of conditioning the self to inhibit some immediate impulses to gratify them later. The ability to sacrifice now for the sake of something in the future is an important personality feature, which is often referred to as self-control. As we discussed in Chapter 2, people with high levels of self-control tend to do better than people with low levels of self-control in many areas, including employment, income, health, and social interactions (Baumeister & Tierney, 2012). Self-control has a strong genetic component, yet people can develop this feature in themselves through their own efforts (Willems et al., 2019).

Types of Personality and the Nervous System

Pavlov understood the nervous system's dynamics in individual personality types from the standpoint of three functions: strength, balance, and agility. The **strength of the nervous system** reflects the functional ability of the neurons to maintain the state of activation or excitement without developing self-protecting inhibition. A strong nervous system can respond to strong, frequent, or unexpected signals. The weak system exhausts itself quickly responding to long and strong signals. The **balance** characteristic refers to equilibrium between excitement and inhibition within the nervous system. The system may be balanced or unbalanced. Finally, the **agility** characteristic refers to the quickness of the activation of excitement or the quickness of change between inhibition and excitement. There are different types of nervous systems based on a combination of these features. People develop personality types—Pavlov called them "character types"—based on the particular type of nervous system interacting with the environment.

Compare two types of individuals, for instance. One is constantly in a hurry, talkative, emotionally explosive, and pushy. The other one is slow, quiet, and thinks before making decisions. According to Pavlov, these two are different because each has a different type of nervous system. The first is strong and imbalanced; the other is strong, balanced, and inertial. If this is correct, then physiological types, as Pavlov believed, could apparently predict behavioral types (see Figure 5.2).

Pavlov's message was that personality types should be described along simple conceptual lines. In some ways, these ideas make sense: Some individuals appear strong mentally, while others appear weaker; some are quick and fast, while others are slow. Do you think that these criteria are sufficient to describe your personality?

For today's critical observers, Pavlov's research shortcomings are almost obvious. When he measured physiological characteristics in certain parts of the brain, he did not take into consideration that various parts of the cerebral cortex might function differently. An organism may show signs of strength in one receptor (e.g., the tactile receptor) and at the same time show weakness in another (e.g., taste). The second substantial weakness of Pavlov's theory was that he and his followers could not identify specific physiological mechanisms in the brain that would stand for the strength, balance, and dynamics of the nervous system. His personality model based on these conceptual features of the nervous system is thought-provoking, but it rests on weak scientific foundation.

Pavlov understood personality from the standpoint of reflexes, behavior, and learning. He clearly understood that the complexity of human life couldn't be reduced to simple reflexes. But, as a researcher, he had to begin somewhere; he had to study those basic "elements" of human behavior.

FIGURE 5.2   ■   Pavlov: Types of the Nervous System and Their Behavioral Profiles

Types of Nervous System and Personality			
Strong	Balanced	Agile	Strong, balanced, and agile type. Inhibition and excitement are balanced. The person adjusts quickly to changing conditions and can stand up to difficulties. Makes quick decisions and changes strategies when necessary.
		Inertial	Calm and slow type. Able to resist significant pressure. The person can handle difficult situations by ignoring them or by making carefully planned decisions. Changes in habits and behavioral strategies are difficult to make.
	Imbalanced		Strong and imbalanced type. Excitement dominates over inhibition. Explosive and temperamental, feisty and energetic. The person can stand up to difficulties but often cannot control emotion. Frequently and in various situations may lose self-control.
Weak			Weak type. Experiences difficulties under the pressure of challenges, including lack of time. Highly avoidant and sensitive to external signals such as other people's opinions. The person often has a hard time making quick decisions or selecting among choices.

CHECK AND APPLY YOUR KNOWLEDGE

1. Let's assume Bekhterev was right about energy transformation. Now recall the activities that consumed your "energy" today. Consider two variables such as (1) the time spent on these activities and (2) the effort (small, significant, very significant) you have used in these activities. Which activity has drained most of your energy and why? How could you—or not—save more energy next time around?

2. Choose a character from a book or a movie. Design a brief behavioral profile of this character using Pavlov's three functions of the nervous system: strength, balance, and agility. How strong or weak, balanced or imbalanced, and agile or inertial is this character?

3. Write a brief behavioral profile of yourself (your behavioral characteristics) using Pavlov's three functions of the nervous system. What type are you likely to be? Strong, balanced, and agile? Or imbalanced and inertial? Or will it be weak? Maybe you will discover another combination.

WATSON: STUDYING AND APPLYING BEHAVIORISM

The American psychologist John Watson (1878–1958) took the discipline of psychology by storm. Ambitious and hard-working, he was at the helm of the American Psychological Association at the age of 38. After that, his academic career did not last long: He was forced to resign his professorship when he was 42 due to an extramarital affair. Despite this personal turmoil, Watson's influence on psychology was substantial. Essentially, Watson's (1919) views can be summarized as follows:

1. Behavior is a set of responses to specific signals.

2. Behavioral responses become useful and thus retained.

3. Some simple reactions develop into complex acts.

Simple and complex reactions, shaped by circumstances, form habits. Different habits then integrate into functions of an individual's organism. Functions are organized, integrated habit systems, such as writing or swimming. Functions may be explicit and observable, like speech, or implicit, like thinking. They too are activated under specific conditions. Psychologists (Watson often called them *behaviorist physicians*) should study various stimuli and conditions under which habits are formed. Then they help people improve, strengthen, or change certain habits. Psychology's goal was to develop principles that would explain, predict, and control behavior (Watson, 1919). Remember the opening case to this chapter? Watson believed a knowledgeable and skilled behaviorist physician should have the right to "shape up" other individuals' personalities and change human lives for the better (Buckley, 1989).

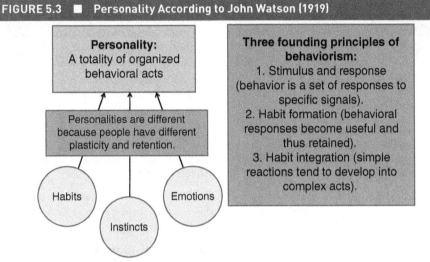

FIGURE 5.3   ■   Personality According to John Watson (1919)

Personality, in Watson's view, is a totality of organized behavioral acts, such as habits, instincts, emotions, and their combinations (see Figure 5.3). Personalities are different because different people have different **plasticity**—a capacity for new habit formation or change of old habits. People are also different because some keep their habits ready to be used in a new situation, while others lose them. He called this **retention**.

Habit Formation

How do habits—the foundation of personality—develop? John Watson considered emotions as conditioned responses or habits learned during childhood. Emotion formation thus is a process of habit formation. To examine it, Watson, together with Elizabeth Rayner studied the development of conditioned reflexes in a 9-month-old baby. The researchers using experiments and observations wanted to show that emotions created in a laboratory were retained later in life (Watson & Rayner, 1920). Watson paired unconditioned stimuli that should cause initial alarm and fear in the child (e.g., a very loud noise) with live animals and toys that initially did not cause any emotional reaction. In his experiments, Watson attempted to experimentally develop fearful reactions in children. Although the procedure was questionable from the ethical standpoint, Watson argued that behaviorists could use habit formation techniques to help children develop positive emotions and useful behaviors.

Like Bekhterev and Pavlov, Watson rejected the "subjective" side of an individual's personality. Watson was skeptical about so-called "mental tests," which were popular during the time. He wrote that by judging someone's answers on a piece of paper, he would not be able to detect whether this person is a liar or if this individual can effectively work with other people (Watson, 1927). Only individuals' observable behavior, such as their responses, decisions, and habits, could provide reliable facts, in his view (see Table 5.1).

TABLE 5.1 ■ Psychology's Objectives and Their Applications to the Study of Personality	
Psychology's Objectives	*What It Means in the Study of Personality*
All speculations about the subjective mechanisms of the mind must be abandoned and replaced by behavioral terms.	People are better understood when psychologists focus on what people do and how they do it.
All experiments should be replicated and controlled. Specifically, introspection should be ruled out because it is not a method of scientific investigation.	New experimental procedures should be developed and implemented. Psychologists should not ask, "How do you feel?" but measure an individual's observable actions.
Psychology should become an experimental branch of natural science. Psychology should resemble biology.	It is desirable to compare an individual's behavior to the behavior of an animal, especially in experimental situations.
The goal of psychology should be to describe, predict, and control human behavior. Psychologists should play a bigger role in society.	Studying personality is also about applying the received data in various fields, including work, education, communications, advertisement, health care, and so on.

Habit Disturbances: Abnormal Behavior and Deviance

Watson argued that a healthy personality consisted of well-functioning habit systems in most situations. Abnormal features were characterized by an individual's inability to get rid of old habits and old emotions in new situations in which those old habits were no longer efficient. Mental illness, therefore, according to classical behaviorism, was a kind of **habit disturbance**. Watson interpreted abnormal symptoms differently than most clinical psychologists of the time. Symptoms of hysteria or neurosis (popular terms early in the 20th century), defensive reactions, guilt, irrational fears—all these and scores of other symptoms—were maladaptive reflexes in his view. How did they develop? There must have been a situation or condition in the past, an emotional trauma, physical or sexual abuse, masturbation (scores of psychologists 100 years ago viewed masturbation as an abnormal, immoral, even pathological behavior; Laqueur, 2004), or something else—as Watson believed—that triggered the development of a dysfunctional habit. This habit, in a chain reaction, then triggers the development of other progressively maladaptive behaviors. Watson believed in treatment, such as behavioral training and retraining of individuals, to help them acquire new habits (Wozniak, 1993).

Watson also connected the individual's criminal behavior and maladaptive habits (Watson, 1919). Psychologists, in Watson's opinion, could provide treatment for such people through special behavioral programs funded by the government. Subsequently, after spending some time in such a program under a behaviorist's supervision, a troubled individual would form new, pro-social behavioral habits. This could reduce the prison population and result in crime reduction. Such views were met with enthusiasm by some psychologists but were also criticized as naïve. Yet contemporary cross-national studies of hundreds of rehabilitation programs for criminal offenders show their effectiveness today (Beaudry et al., 2021). Watson had the right ideas about the reduction of recidivism, yet he had very limited behavioral methods as well as public support at his disposal.

Watson's ideas were simple, understandable, and attractive to many specialists in education, business, and psychology. He gave psychologists inspiration and built their confidence as researchers, educators, and other practitioners. He influenced a large and enthusiastic audience, professionals, and ordinary people alike, who were ready to learn, support, and apply his ideas.

STUDYING BEHAVIOR FROM DIFFERENT ANGLES

While supporting behaviorism in general, many psychologists wanted to alter its focus. Edwin Holt (1873–1946), who served as a professor at Harvard and later at Princeton, argued that in real-life situations, behavior is more complex and must be understood as a complex unity of many behavioral acts. Holt introduced the concept of **molar responses**. The responses require interpretation. The concept of "interpretation" signaled a departure from a traditional behaviorism that generally ignored the concepts of goal or purpose. Individuals are different because they pursue different goals. One of Holt's supporters and students was Edward Tolman (1886–1959).

Working as professor of psychology at the University of California at Berkeley, Tolman was often called a *purposive behaviorist*, and his views were labeled **purposive or operational behaviorism**. Tolman suggested an expansion of the traditional S → R (stimulus–response) model of behaviorism and added S → O → R, in which O stood for measurable processes or variables within an organism. These variables are heredity (some animals or individuals have certain inborn abilities), age (e.g., strength of responses may decline with age), quality of previous training (some of us develop specific habits), features of stimuli (responses depend on various signals), and an organism's drive (Tolman, 1932). Drive is caused by frustration; although we cannot see it, we can perfectly describe frustration in operational terms as a degree of tension caused by an inability to reach a goal. The more time you spend or the more unsuccessful attempts you make to achieve your goal, the stronger your frustration is felt. It will direct your behavior for some time. Studying rats, Tolman believed that animals could learn the connections between stimuli and did not need any biologically significant factor, like hunger or fear, to make their learning occur (see Figure 5.4).

Tolman introduced the concept called a **cognitive map**, which refers to internal processing by which individuals code, store, recall, and decode information about elements of their experience. It is not just a memory of vivid events. Cognitive maps represent a complex pattern that guides a person's behavior based on learned behaviors. New learning experiences, either successful or not, build new cognitive maps. Tolman and his followers believed that individuals constantly learn and develop new cognitive maps, which should result in new behaviors (Tolman, 1948).

FIGURE 5.4   ■   Tolman's Modification of the Behaviorist Formula

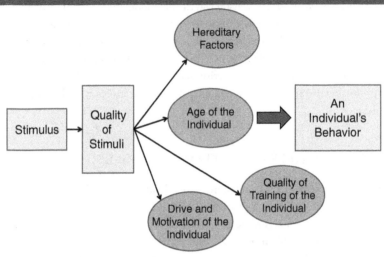

CHECK AND APPLY YOUR KNOWLEDGE

1. Could you improve your own plasticity? Recall what Watson meant by it. Think of one habit (a) you do not particularly like in yourself (like procrastination) or (b) you think needs development (like being more punctual, for example). Think of the circumstances in which this habit appears. Without delay, prepare a plan to change this habit. Start today. Monitor the changes.

2. Imagine a dilemma. You can get a B+ as a final grade in this class now, and then you do not have to attend this class any longer. If you reject this offer, you stay in this class, but no grade is guaranteed. What will you do? Explain your decision by using Tolman's cognitive map concept. What factors did you include in your decision?

OPTIMISTIC BEHAVIORISM OF B. F. SKINNER

One of the most dynamic devotees of behaviorism in the mid-20th century was Burrhus Frederick Skinner, who is commonly known as B. F. Skinner (1904–1990). His theory and applications have generated enthusiastic support, heated debates, acceptance, mockery, and outright rejections. Today, his name and his ideas (often simplified and sometimes misinterpreted) still appear in popular literature and scholarly journals around the world. Although he continued the line of research by John Watson, Skinner moved farther ahead of his prominent predecessor.

He embraced the idea that psychologists in their experiments need not rely so much on physiology (as Pavlov did) but could focus on overt behavior instead. He was not really interested in what was going on "inside" the brain. Accurate measurement of behavior was a key challenge, which he recognized. To study behavior, Skinner designed many devices, but one, often referred to as the "Skinner box," was particularly successful. A mouse placed inside a specially made box was free to move around in it. As soon as the animal pressed a lever (at first accidentally), a small food pellet was automatically released on a tray so the mouse could eat it. In behaviorist terms, the mouse's lever-pressing act was reinforced by the food being delivered immediately afterward. Skinner next realized that he could measure many elements (or variables) of the process: the time elapsing before the mouse pressed the lever, the number of repetitions before the animal learned a habit, and so forth.

Skinner turned to study *behavioral reinforcements*, the term he borrowed from Pavlov. People always learn about the consequences of their behavior because they receive rewards and punishments. This type of learning is called **operant conditioning**. The word *operant* means activities producing effects. Like the rat in the box presses the button (an activity) and then receives food (an effect), the individual engages in the same type of learning and habit development based on operant conditioning (Skinner, 1938).

Skinner came up with the idea of **schedules of reinforcement**, or conditions involving different rates and times of reinforcement. By changing the schedules of reinforcement, Skinner was able to measure behavioral responses. For example, at the beginning of an experiment, the rat received food every time it pushed the button. Next, Skinner gave reinforcement precisely in 1-minute intervals, regardless of how many times the rat pushed the button. Or he released food exactly after the rat pushed the button three consecutive times. Now he believed he could measure the behavior of his experimental animals with more precision and sophistication. The key question remained: What if humans learn the same way?

From Animals to Humans

Skinner always believed it would be just a matter of time before everyone could see the practical value of his behavioral research (Skinner, 1960). His goal was to apply his studies to humans. If we know, for example, that certain conditions influence the formation of certain habits, why can't we design such conditions? In 1944, Skinner built the **Aircrib**—a thermostatically controlled crib with a safety-glass front and a stretched-canvas floor—for his second daughter, Deborah. The boxlike crib contained soundproof walls and a window. If the baby cried, the insulation would reduce the noise, yet the parent could hear the baby. It had warming and moistening devices as well as air filters to control the quality of the air inside. Skinner believed that his invention would provide both safety and freedom of movement for a baby, a secure, controlled environment for the child, and better opportunities for parents to develop useful habits in their children. Yet both manufacturers and consumers remained skeptical about the safety of his invention. Many people who saw the promotional materials about Aircrib immediately called it a small "jail" for babies. Critics rejected the idea of "building" habits in their children as if they were robots responding to external signals and commands. Skinner was very disappointed to read such critical reviews. More than 75 years have passed. Today, numerous patented devices and gadgets simplify infant care and communications with the child—disposable diapers (they did not exist in 1944), video monitoring devices, portable cribs, developmental interactive gadgets based on AI, and multifunctional strollers—they may all serve as reminders that Skinner's idea was not necessarily wrong.

Social Engineering

From the behaviorist's view, animals and humans learn a habit not because they "understand" the purpose of learning. They retain useful habits because they are likely to secure their access to food, shelter, pleasure, or safety. People and animals alike adapt to changing conditions by constantly modifying their reflexes. Skinner believed his research, if it was properly applied, could change the individual and society. Two of his books, *Walden Two* (1948/2005) and *Beyond Freedom and Dignity* (1971), brought him worldwide fame and sparked heated discussions. In *Walden Two*, Skinner returned to the question posed by the philosopher and writer Henry D. Thoreau (1817–1862). In the first *Walden*, published in 1854, Thoreau argued for the psychological and moral benefits of a simple lifestyle. Skinner went even further. He claimed that humans could build an entire society that embraces a simple and healthy lifestyle by applying positive reinforcement. Who would manage such an enterprise? Politicians? No. In Skinner's version of the new world, only when educated behaviorists take over, they would help other people develop many useful, socially approved personality features. People would be honest, modest, and hardworking, and they would live in harmony with one another. Individuals will be conditioned to live in harmony with nature.

Skinner's ideas, as you can imagine, received criticism. Some even criticized him for being a misguided scientist who believed in conditioned slavery (Jessup, 1948). Critics also pointed out that this utopian theory was no more than a disguised attempt to give power to unelected scientists. Who would guarantee that they would not use behavioral methods to advance their own selfish interests? To others, *Walden Two* was a harmless fiction written by a respected Harvard professor.

Skinner's biggest publishing "hit" was *Beyond Freedom and Dignity* in which he applied behaviorism to explain the modern individual of the time. People, he wrote, were misguided in their overconfident belief in individual freedom. In fact, what is called "freedom" had been defined by the ruling elites, such as government and powerful corporations, who tend to treat us, ordinary citizens, like experimental rats. The elites use behavioral reinforcement to make us love and buy certain products, order particular services, watch shows, join associations, and vote for certain political parties. We, as individuals, according to Skinner, uncritically follow these pressures, mistakenly calling them freedom to choose. In fact, we are trapped by the pursuit of material goods, services, and money. Only behaviorists could effectively teach self-control and moderation. (see Figure 5.5).

Criticism of his book came from scholars and philosophers, including a champion of progressive ideas, Noam Chomsky (b. 1928), and an influential conservative intellectual, Ayn Rand (1905–1982). They both criticized Skinner for his alleged disbelief in the individual's freedom. Skinner, of course, fought back. He claimed that the alleged freedom that modern people thought they possessed was merely a set of their conditioned reactions

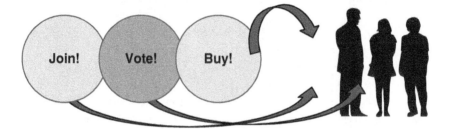

FIGURE 5.5 ■ Skinner's Views of Personality, Freedom, and the Societal Role of Behaviorists

called *consumerism*. True freedom can occur only when people use behavioral science to identify the morally "right" kinds of conditioning based on restraint, rational choice, and common good. All in all, Skinner wanted to free the individual from the abusive forces of ignorance and selfishness.

CHECK AND APPLY YOUR KNOWLEDGE

1. Skinner's Aircrib today appears outdated and even odd. Yet was his idea of a monitoring and conditioning system odd? Search the web to see what kind of apps and devices are available today to monitor, entertain, or educate a child. Suggest your own device or an app that would provide a kind of positive reinforcement to a baby. Your creative ideas are welcome.

2. Spend about 10 minutes online looking at ads and commercials. Select five of them. Record them, take screenshots of them, or write down their contents. What is being pitched to you? Which of these ads, if any, reflect your shopping preferences or interests in the past? Make an argument for or against Skinner's viewpoint that the "system" in which we live "dictates" what you should buy, watch, and how you should spend your time.

SOCIAL LEARNING THEORY

While some behaviorists were studying reinforcements and conditioning, other researchers turned to social factors in learning as the process of acquisition of new knowledge and habits. **Social learning theory** is a general term to outline, among other things, that learning does not necessarily need reinforcement and conditioning. An individual learns and makes decisions within a particular social environment. Learning can take place through observation of other people's behavior, personal curiosity, through direct and deliberate instruction from one person to another, or through exposure of an individual to certain events.

Psychologist Julian Rotter (1916–2014) focused on an "inner" factor regulating human behavior: the expected outcome. A person's anticipation of a particular result, such as success or failure, produces specific motivation to act or not to act. People tend to avoid defeats or penalties and seek victories or rewards (of course, there are exceptions from this tendency). We tend to engage in behaviors in which we anticipate a successful outcome. If we experience success or victory, we are likely to repeat this behavior. Of course, success is based on many factors and conditions, which may or may not be under an individual's control. Think of the weather, for instance: Can we change it by working harder on a research paper? There are also events that appear beyond our control because of the complexity of the world around us. We don't know what's causing those events, but even if we don't know what's causing a specific event, just explaining connections between events will lead to more predictability, which will give the appearance of more control (Kelley, 1967).

Rotter (1966, 1990) further developed this idea about control in experiments that showed consistent differences among individuals in the degree to which they attribute or explain personal control. Rotter categorized them into two groups. One group tends to explain events as influenced by somewhat controllable, internal, relatively permanent characteristics such as skill, preparedness, will, and the like. This group is labeled *internals* because they mostly display an **internal locus of control**. Those with an **external locus of control** (*externals*) tend to explain events as influenced by uncontrollable external factors, such as powerful others, luck, the great complexity of the "outside" forces, and so on. Rotter's research sparked significant interest and follow-up studies. For example, people with an external locus of control are more likely to engage in gambling (Hock, 2013). People with an internal locus of control tend to be "difficult" patients because they are less likely than externals to follow the doctor's recommendations. Strangers do not easily persuade internals, who tend to have stronger achievement motivation than externals (Rotter, 1990). We will discuss achievement motivation further in Chapter 9 and Chapter 12.

Early publications about locus of control inspired interest in testing its cross-cultural applicability. Do people from a particular cultural group tend to display a particular locus of control? Are members of predominantly collectivistic cultures more likely to develop an external locus of control than those who live in predominantly individualistic cultures? We need to think critically, of course. Research shows, with some exceptions, that individuals from Western countries are more likely to display a strong internal locus of control than individuals from non-Western countries. Studies also show that "Westerners" as a group (1) are generally more suspicious of authoritarian leaders (which are seen as "external" forces and thus rejected); (2) possess a measure of material resources (such as stable jobs and social security benefits); and (3) grow up in predominantly individualistic communities emphasizing individual effort. These and other factors make people in the West, seemingly, less dependent on external factors. If we follow this logic, can we expect that most city dwellers who have a relatively high socioeconomic status should have an internal locus of control? Conversely, how accurate are our predictions if we suggest that a person with a low socioeconomic status will likely have an external locus of control? Apparently, such assumptions are inaccurate and have been challenged by most comparative studies (Nowicki, 2016). Only small differences were found in studies of locus of control in the context of age and gender; yet positive life events in the life of an individual tend to be associated with more internal locus of control (Hovenkamp-Hermelink et al., 2019).

CHECK AND APPLY YOUR KNOWLEDGE

1. Based on what you know about Rotter's research, do you think you are more external, internal, or somewhere in between?
2. After you've made your best guess, go to the companion website to find the original Rotter scale to measure your locus of control. Does your score reflect your expectation about your locus of control? As in previous examples and self-evaluations, use the knowledge about yourself critically and wisely.

The Canadian-born psychologist Albert Bandura (1925–2021) worked at Stanford University and published the influential book *Social Learning and Personality Development* in 1963. In the early 1960s, Bandura and associates conducted a series of experiments that gained global recognition as the *Bobo doll experiment* (Bobo was a 5-foot, inflatable toy made from vinyl; when pushed or hit, it would fall and then return to an upright position). In this experiment, children between the ages of 3 and 6 were told they could play with various toys, including the Bobo doll, that were presented to them. In some experimental scenarios, the children were in the room with an adult (a member of the team). In some cases, the person would do nothing. In others, the adult would kick, punch, and verbally assault the doll. Yet in other cases, the children would watch a film in which an adult would assault the doll. As a result, the children exposed to direct and indirect violence were significantly more likely to quickly express aggression toward the Bobo doll than those boys and girls who did not see violent acts during the experiment (Bandura et al., 1961, 1963). The experiment was replicated many times and produced similar results: Children learned violence through imitation, just by observing the behavior of an adult. This study sparked a discussion among both professionals and the public about violence in the media and its impact on actual behavior of children and adults.

©iStockphoto.com / RapidEye

©iStockphoto.com / John Sommer

PHOTO 5.2 The Bobo doll experiments sparked a discussion about the role of imitation in behavior. Do you find that people tend to imitate "bad" behavior easier than they imitate "good" behavior? Why?

The Bobo doll experiment, replicated in many countries, showed that the children exposed to direct and indirect violence were significantly more likely to express aggression toward the Bobo doll than others who did not see violent acts during the experiment.

This experiment was only one in the series of studies in which Bandura showed that learning occurred by observing a person's behavior and its consequences (Bandura, 1977). Learning takes place through demonstration (when we witness an event or behavior of other people), verbal instrumentation (like the safety instructions aboard a plane), and symbolic demonstration (such as watching a movie). The learner, however, is not a passive observer. People are active thinkers, paying and not paying attention to the information, retaining it in memory, forgetting it, or being able to recall it or not. According to **reciprocal determinism**, individuals influence their environment and vice versa. Bandura referred to his research as *social cognitive theory* to emphasize the importance of cognitive processes in social learning. In 1986, he published research showing that individuals were not passive agents of social influences but rather active, enthusiastic, stubborn, developing, and self-regulating (Bandura, 1986).

Based on his research, Bandura formulated the principle of **self-efficacy**, which is people's belief in their ability to manage their lives and to exercise control over events that affect their lives (Bandura, 1997, 2001). People who have developed self-efficacy tend to believe they have enough power to produce desired outcomes in most cases. Therefore, they tend to persevere when facing difficulties or disagreements. They also tend to resist stress, stand up to misfortunes, and overcome bad moods. People with low self-efficacy tend to lose motivation and interest in fighting for their happiness. Instead, they succumb to despair when facing serious challenges.

WHAT BEHAVIORISM ACCOMPLISHED AND WHAT IT MISSED

Behaviorists provided a solid foundation for future research into personality. Their followers agreed on the major principles of behaviorism but differed in the ways they interpreted it. They were often called neobehaviorists, although very few of them wanted to accept this one-dimensional label. Besides the differences among them, at least two issues unified neobehaviorists: their unrestrained belief in the possibility and necessity of objective measurement of behavior and their support for the reductionist belief that psychology should be a science of behavior and conditioning. Several researchers distinguished themselves because of valuable theoretical and practical innovations they added to the mainstream assumptions of behaviorism and learning.

Instead of describing self-observed feelings, behaviorists turned their attention to learned reactions, reflexes, reaction times, and emotional responses. Many of their findings were presented with amazing clarity. There were clear suggestions about where and under which circumstances behavioral research should be applied to education, therapy, work, and other areas. Many conclusions about human behavior and personality were almost commonsensical, as well as clear and often encouraging. They converted the language of common sense into the language of experimental research and vice versa. To many people, behaviorism appeared as a straightforward and simple theory in an increasingly confusing world. It was an unambiguous statement of clarity in a world of ambiguity. It was also an honest promise of confidence in a world of skepticism. Behaviorists emphasized that psychology could have done more to contribute to education, health care, professional training, and many other areas of life.

What did behaviorism miss? Psychologists working within the behavioral-learning tradition, despite their optimistic promises, did not produce a simple "magic" formula to describe an individual's personality in behavioral terms. Critics predictably describe behaviorism as reductionist and simplistic. The behavioral-learning tradition viewed reflex as an important physiological model; however, this model had only limited applicability to an individual's personality. Behaviorism rejected subjectivity, yet only few psychologists today agree that psychology must abandon "subjectivity" altogether and switch to behavioral or physiological models.

CHECK AND APPLY YOUR KNOWLEDGE

1. Self-efficacy is not a dichotomous (one either has it or not) but rather a continuous variable (see Chapter 3 on methodology). Self-efficacy can be high and low and anywhere in between. It can be stable, or it can change. Pick a difficult life situation you have encountered either recently or some time ago. How would you evaluate your self-efficacy in that situation? Describe your self-observations in a paragraph.
2. Who among your friends or family members has high self-efficacy? Briefly describe this person's behavior indicative of his or her self-efficacy.

©iStockphoto.com / subman

PHOTO 5.3 Behavioral economists bring an individual dimension to the study of economic decisions. Think about yourself. Do you have the particular personality features of a good entrepreneur or not? Explain why.

APPLYING THE BEHAVIORAL-LEARNING TRADITION

Behaviorism carried an optimistic message about the possibility to form, shape, and change skills, habits, and personality features through exercising, training, and organized learning. Therefore, there was no shortage of attempted applications of behaviorism to practical fields, including education, business, law enforcement, and health care. Animal psychologists showed that proper training could "override" instinctual drives. For example, Zing-Yang Kuo (1898–1970), who worked in the United States and in China, raised kittens and rats together to demonstrate that the cats did not chase and kill the rats as they normally would in natural conditions. Doctors applied the key principles of learning to help people get rid of bad habits such as smoking and drinking (Bekhterev, 1918/1933). Criminologists insisted that criminal behavior is not inborn but rather learned and thus could be corrected through special training with proper reinforcement (Burgess & Akers, 1966). Some applications were effective, yet others were not.

For example, *Taylorism* was a short-lived behavioral training program named after Frederick Taylor (1856–1915), an engineer by education and occupation (Taylor, 1911). According to the program, every worker's movement must be regulated—every simple operation should be effective, every movement should be useful. No long lunch breaks. No meaningless conversations or jokes at the workplace should be allowed. Initially, this program was met with enthusiasm. Soon, however, the euphoria about the Taylor method evaporated. Managers and workers alike hated the "sweatshop" atmosphere imposed by Taylorism. This system ignored the role of individual motivation, pride, and interpersonal relationships at the workplace and focused exclusively on production. As psychologists gradually realized, an individual's sense of comfort at the workplace and good relationships with coworkers and management were far more important for efficiency.

Other applications of the behavioral-learning tradition were more successful.

Behavioral Economics

Behavioral principles find significant and promising applications in behavioral economics. As was noted in Chapter 2, personality psychology uses research into economics that focuses on how various individual factors affect people's choices. Behavioral economics is an experimental field and, like behaviorism, studies observable outcomes of human actions. It studies the effects of individual factors, such as reasoning, emotional stability, or habit, and group factors, such as traditions, group pressure, or competition, on individual economic decisions. These are our daily choices—for example, buying a product online, accepting a birthday invitation, or purchasing a nonrefundable airline ticket. Economists and personality psychologists find common interest in studying typical, consistent decisions that people make in their daily routines. In fact, the cooperation between psychology and economics has been extremely productive. For instance, the 2002 Nobel Prize in economics went to psychologist Daniel Kahneman for his research into biases of individual decision-making, as it was mentioned earlier. Esther Duflo, Abhijit Banerjee, and Michael Kremer won the 2014 Nobel Prize in economic sciences for their experimental approach to alleviating global poverty. In fact, they and their associates conducted and continue to organize many behavioral experiments around the globe.

Consider chronic poverty. So far in this century, 1 billion to 2 billion people have remained chronically poor. The researchers investigated poverty from the position of an individual and this person's daily actions (Banerjee & Duflo, 2011). Researchers have demonstrated that (besides social and political factors) many people remain poor because they do not have (or did not learn) the necessary behavioral habits and skills to climb out of poverty. For example, across countries, the poor consistently make similar mistakes in starting and operating small businesses. They tend to make bad decisions about their own health. Also, the poor tend to give up easily when they believe they cannot succeed (when, in fact, they can). One of several common denominators of these constant errors was the people's lack of patience. It is poverty that makes people more impatient because they have not been conditioned in the past to receive rewards for being patient. So what is the behavioral remedy? The remedy is education and learning new and useful skills that emphasize patience and perseverance in business, in education, and in health decisions. "Intelligent interventionism" (Banerjee & Duflo, 2019) can transform a society to be built on compassion and respect. However, this type of learning requires qualified and motivated teachers. You can be one of them.

Now consider deviant behavior. Why do some people engage in extremely risky behavior while others do not? Tolman's ideas about the individual's "inner variable" find applications in safety policies. Studies show, for example, that most people tend to avoid unnecessary risk. However, in simple terms, we tend to act more carelessly when we feel more protected, and we act more cautiously when we don't feel safe. We know that riding a bike or a scooter without a helmet is dangerous, so why don't we initiate a policy to make helmets mandatory and thus reduce the number of injuries? The outcome of this policy is less than certain. People tend to immediately reevaluate their risks. They tend to think because they are wearing a helmet, they are better protected, and they can ride faster and make more dangerous moves on the road. This is an example of risk compensation as a behavioral adaptation that may diminish the impact of safety rules.

Economist Sam Peltzman studying human behavior showed how risk compensation works (Peltzman, 2011). People in general show a consistent tendency: They tend to act more dangerously *today* if they feel they are safer than *yesterday*. For example, one of the most significant medical breakthroughs in human history for fighting infections was the development of antibiotics—people know they no longer face inevitable death because of scarlet fever or tuberculosis. Yet this knowledge lets some people take more risks, such as not washing their hands before meals, eating unwashed products, and so on. The discovery of new treatments for heart disease and the development of the anti-AIDS medication have saved many lives, yet they could have triggered even riskier behavior in many individuals. Why so? An individual falsely assumes that his or her behaviors—unhealthy eating, overeating, smoking, or unprotected sex—are no longer harmful because there are great medical products and procedures that could easily provide a cure for any health malady. As mandatory car safety belts have saved many lives, their positive impact would be greater if there were no risk takers. They falsely believe they can drive faster and more recklessly because they are safer with a seatbelt. This also means that a safety ruling or policy by itself may not produce a desirable effect. It must be explained to people time and time again that it's necessary to always follow safety rules and reduce risky behavior.

Nudging

However, we all know that often we do not like to be told what to do, right? Modern behavioral research, in fact, tries to avoid this obvious psychological obstacle in teaching and interpersonal communications. Consider, for example, the concept of **nudging**—the influencing of behavior without coercion (Thaler & Sunstein, 2021). In their daily decisions, most people tend to make many mistakes based on individual biases, logical errors, miscalculations, and in the inability of many of us to judge ourselves critically. We often are influenced by the actions of others and emotional considerations. To teach people how to make good, useful, or healthy decisions, there is no necessity to force them to accept what is told. (No mandatory trainings!) Behavioral economists and psychologists suggest noncoercive options than can lead to desirable outcomes to improve health, increase wealth, and prolong lives. For example, people are more likely to choose a particular option on the list or on the screen if it is the default option (Campbell-Arvai et al., 2014). People tend to buy small snacks that are closer to the cash register than a bit further (Van Gestel et al., 2018). Knowing such and many other tendencies of human behavior, can we promote healthier and safer behavior by "nudging" people into accepting better choices? In fact, many scholars agree and are exercising different types of nudging. For example, the Dutch scholar Christina Gravert (Gravert & Collentine, 2021) does behavioral research to understand better how people make good decisions and how they can be motivated or nudged to "do the right things." She specifically focuses on environmental sustainability, charitable donations, healthy choices, and the use of public transportation instead of individual cars to reduce pollution.

Coping With Traumatic Events

Traumatic experiences are part of life. Serious accidents, terrorist attacks, sexual assaults, natural disasters, military combat, and other traumatic events cause significant impact on millions of people. Many people continue having painful psychological symptoms long after the traumatic events took place. Such symptoms include elevated anxiety, sleep disturbances, nightmares, irritability, emotional detachment, and profound behavioral disengagement. Behaviorists such as Bandura and colleagues have found that building up self-efficacy is instrumental in overcoming the most painful post-traumatic symptoms (Bandura, 1997). Psychologists these days put together therapeutic procedures to help the sufferers build confidence and inner strength in dealing with their painful symptoms. People who suffer post-traumatic symptoms learn that taking charge of their own lives is the beginning of the healing process (Benight & Bandura, 2004). These methods help tens of thousands of natural disaster survivors, refugees, accident victims, and returning veterans (Bemak & Chung, 2004). We will return to several coping methods in Chapter 12 related to adjustment.

Behavior Therapy

Classical behavioral studies showed that **extinction**—which can involve abandoning a bad habit or a decrease in a fearful reaction—is not only a disappearance of something previously learned but is also a form of learning (Myers & Davis, 2002). Behavioral principles have found important applications in today's behavioral methods of treatment for a wide range of psychological disorders. Behavioral theories generally suggest that certain circumstances, such as stress, may lead to constant anxiety or depressive symptoms because they reduce the number of positive stimuli in a person's environment. Certain conditions in our lives may either increase or decrease the probability of abnormal or dysfunctional emotional symptoms. Overall, behavior therapies based on principles of operant conditioning have often been effective (Lewinsohn et al., 2003; Nolen-Hoeksema, 1991; Spiegler, 2016).

Self-control therapy is used in dealing with emotional problems. It contains three phases. During the first phase—*self-monitoring*—the person receives a homework assignment, which consists of monitoring positive activities with immediate and delayed reinforcement value (Craighead et al., 2013). In the second phase—*self-evaluation*—clients are taught to use self-monitoring data to define realistic and reachable goals in behavioral terms. For example, people describe the specific steps that they should take to solve specific life situations. In the third phase—*self-reinforcement*—people are helped to create self-administered reinforcement programs. Behavioral distraction techniques, such as blocking negative thoughts, are sometimes used as well to help individuals avoid ruminations (or constant focusing on one's negative emotions). Patients learn that their behavior is controlled by rewards and punishments, and that is the way to control their own actions, too. They also learn that people tend to self-punish too much and self-reward too little. At the end of therapy, patients construct individual self-reinforcement programs aimed at maintaining and increasing the level of positive activities in which they should engage. It results in an inventory of activities that contains various kinds of reinforcement.

Education

Many teaching strategies use principles of social learning. These strategies aim at enhancing students' knowledge acquisition and retention. Rather than just explaining things to their students, teachers could try using the technique of *guided participation*. For example, the teacher says a short statement and then asks the students in class to repeat it. While repeating aloud, the students imitate their teacher and retain the information. Then the class and the teacher exchange opinions about the statement. The teacher delivers positive reinforcement to those students who participate. The students are encouraged to make evaluations themselves, and they begin playing a more active role in the process. By encouraging the students to adopt the position of active observers, the teacher, as research shows, improves the students' retention and their learning outcomes (Kumpulainen & Rajala, 2017; Kumpulainen & Wray, 2002).

CHECK AND APPLY YOUR KNOWLEDGE

1. Taylorism is psychology's convenient target to criticize, yet you can find some of its ideas applicable to our daily lives. For example, how much time do you waste every day on something that's under your control? Reflect on your day today. Identify the moments that you consider a waste of time (it could be anything, like chatting with someone, spending time on social networks, browsing the web aimlessly, just hanging out, etc.). Now make an authoritative decision: Tomorrow, try to regain at least some of the time that you think you wasted today. Shorten, cut, or avoid just one of the activities you

listed. Do the same the next day. Make *saving time* a habit. After 2 or 3 days of such habit formation, describe your impressions. Discuss them in class. Was Taylor right or wrong for "pushing" us to change our habits? Will you continue practicing your time saving? Why or why not?

2. Behavioral economics teaches about rational and irrational choices. Return to the example on subjective safety and risky behavior. These days, car accidents are down, and cars are getting safer. However, one of the biggest risks now is the use of electronic devices when driving. Just 2 seconds of taking your eyes off the road may lead to a tragedy.

   a. In the following practicum, for 1 week, conduct a self-monitoring exercise: Join with two or three people and pledge not to use a smartphone while driving—the driver shall not text or browse the web while sitting behind the wheel.

   b. During this week, recall the episodes when you were really tempted to use the device. What were the occasions? Did you use the phone or not? Did you stop your car first before using it?

   c. Discuss your observations with others. Has your pledge helped you not to use the phone and to what degree?

   d. How would personal examples help persuade others not to text or browse while driving?

SUMMARY

- Behaviorism is the psychological and interdisciplinary tradition that focuses on observable behavior. Behaviorists offer a clear view of personality: An individual's development, actions, complex behavior, and traits are all based on the underlying learning processes. Behaviorism as a tradition primarily grew within psychology. It also evolved together with other disciplines, including biology and physiology.

- A behavioral-learning approach emphasizes the importance of situational, environmental, and developmental factors in an individual's learning, choices, habits, traits, and the ways they change and develop.

- Comparative psychologists accepted the evolutionary ideas of Darwin and Spencer and believed in the adaptive nature of animal behavior. To understand difficult, complex phenomena, a scientist should seek the simplest explanations. This principle, known in science as parsimony, became a working rule for comparative researchers. Portraying animal behavior in human terms is called *anthropomorphism*. Early comparative psychologists tended to support anthropomorphism to some degree and sought scientific data to connect animal and human behavior. Supporters of anthropomorphism also found a seemingly convenient concept linking animal and human behavior: the instinct, or the inherent pattern, or a complex behavior.

- The learning process of animals was called *habit formation* and means the process by which new behaviors or responses become automatic. Thorndike, using new experimental methods, described the learning curve: the improvement of learning with experience.

Thorndike's experiments provided him empirical data to suggest several laws of learning, which are the essential principles on which learning is based.

- Researchers' interest in studying reflexes has been consistent and stemmed from the teachings of René Descartes and the physiologists of the 19th century. Bekhterev suggested reflexology, a unifying new science to study reflexes. Reflexology used the principle of energy transformation. Personality, in his view, was an integrative core of reflexes.

- Pavlov turned to an objective study of the highest nervous activity (i.e., behavior) referring to physiological activities of the brain's cortex. He recognized two categories of reflexes: unconditioned and conditioned. He introduced the concept of physiological associations to explain an individual's complex behavior. Pavlov introduced behavioral types from the standpoint of three functions of the nervous system: strength, balance, and agility. According to Pavlov, there are four types of personalities based on four types of nervous systems: (1) strong, balanced, and mobile; (2) strong, balanced, and slow; (3) strong, unbalanced, and spontaneous; and (4) weak. Within this structure, psychopathological syndromes could be defined as exaggerations of the normal traits.

- Watson considered behavior as actual movements of the body: legs and arms, glands, and specific muscles. Watson saw any complex behavior as containing numerous smaller behavioral elements. Watson suggested three founding principles of behaviorism: stimulus and response, habit formation, and habit integration. Watson saw personality as a totality of organized behavioral acts, such as habits, instincts, emotions, and their combinations. Personalities are different because individuals have different capacity in new habit formation or change of old habits. Watson argued that a healthy personality consists of well-developed and efficient habit systems. Abnormal features are characterized by an individual's inability to get rid of old habits and old emotions in new situations in which those old habits are no longer efficient. Mental illness was a kind of *habit disturbance.*

- Holt followed Watson but argued that in real-life situations, behavior is different, more complex, and must be understood as a multifaceted unity of many behavioral acts. He introduced the concept of molar responses. Tolman offered key ideas of purposive or operational behaviorism. He also suggested an expansion of the traditional S → R (stimulus–response) model and added S → O → R, in which O stood for measurable processes or variables within an organism. Tolman moved further away from traditional behaviorism by introducing the concept called a *cognitive map.*

- Skinner believed psychologists should focus on overt behavior instead. He was not really interested in what was going "inside" the brain. He turned to descriptive behaviorism and the study of behavioral reinforcements. Learning through reward and punishment received the name operant conditioning. Skinner came up with the idea of schedules of reinforcement, or conditions involving different rates and times of reinforcement. By changing the conditions of schedules of reinforcement, the researchers were able to measure behavioral responses. Skinner, a social designer, applied his research to address human problems and explain the modern individual. People, according to his works, are misguided in their overconfident belief in individual freedom.

- *Social learning theory* is a general term that means, among other things, that learning does not necessarily need reinforcement and conditioning. Instead, an individual's experiences and social environment play a powerful role in learning.

- Julian Rotter showed consistent differences among individuals in the degree to which they attribute or explain personal control. Alfred Bandura showed that learning occurred by observing a person's behavior and its consequences.

- Behavioral-learning principles can be used in many fields of applications, including behavioral economics, organizational development, education, and coping with traumatic stress.

VISUAL REVIEW

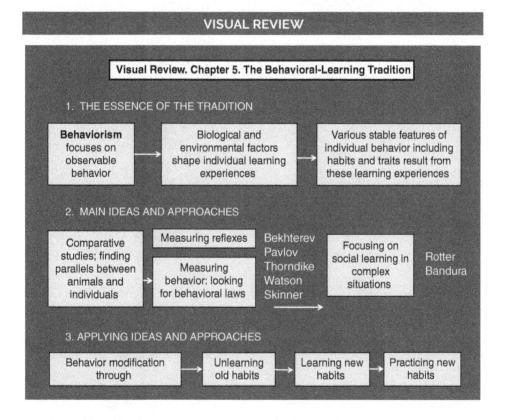

Visual Review. Chapter 5. The Behavioral-Learning Tradition

1. THE ESSENCE OF THE TRADITION

| **Behaviorism** focuses on observable behavior | Biological and environmental factors shape individual learning experiences | Various stable features of individual behavior including habits and traits result from these learning experiences |

2. MAIN IDEAS AND APPROACHES

Comparative studies; finding parallels between animals and individuals

Measuring reflexes

Measuring behavior: looking for behavioral laws

Bekhterev
Pavlov
Thorndike
Watson
Skinner

Focusing on social learning in complex situations

Rotter
Bandura

3. APPLYING IDEAS AND APPROACHES

| Behavior modification through | Unlearning old habits | Learning new habits | Practicing new habits |

KEY TERMS

agility
Aircrib
anthropomorphism
balance
behaviorism
cognitive map
conditioned reflexes

deindividuation
external locus of control
extinction
habit disturbance
habit formation
instinct
internal locus of control

laws of learning
learning curve
molar responses
nudging
operant conditioning
parsimony
plasticity
purposive or operational behaviorism

reciprocal determinism
reflexology
retention
schedules of reinforcement
self-control therapy
self-efficacy
social learning theory
strength of the nervous system

EVALUATING WHAT YOU KNOW

What are the main principles of the behavioral-learning tradition?

What is anthropomorphism?

Explain the learning curve.

What was Watson's view of introspection?

Explain Tolman's cognitive map.

Define *operant conditioning*.

Give an example of schedule reinforcement.

What were the major ideas of *Walden Two* and *Beyond Freedom and Dignity*?

Explain Taylorism.

What is nudging? Give an example.

Explain self-control therapy.

A BRIDGE TO THE NEXT CHAPTER

Skinner was probably the most recognizable representative of the behaviorist-learning tradition and should have taught us several valuable lessons. First, in our continuing quest to understand personality, we certainly need to learn more about behavior and its reinforcement. However, we must not ignore the complexity and the beauty of an individual's experiences. Our personalities are not necessarily combinations of reactions and reflexes—no matter how sophisticated these reactions can be. Your traits are not simply a selection of habits. The supporters of psychoanalytic tradition have already presented their case in favor of the "subjective" side in the previous chapters. Their arguments are intriguing but vague. At this point, we are ready to study another "side" of personality using the methods of contemporary science.

6 | THE TRAIT TRADITION

LEARNING OBJECTIVES

After reading this chapter, you should be able to do the following:

- Explain the main principles and historic contexts of the trait tradition.

- Discuss several major approaches to personality from the trait tradition including Allport's "four columns," Cattell's "16PF," Eysenk's "E and N," and the Big Five research.

- Identify ways to apply the key principles of the trait tradition to individual experience and behavior.

Imagine you need to interview and then hire a new employee for in important position in your company. Would you rather rely more on the candidate's resume, or standardized psychological tests, or just your personal observations? Let's assume that in addition to the submitted resumes, you also have modern psychological tests available to you, and you also think you are an excellent psychologist because you know how to judge people. Which method would you choose in the selection procedure to hire the best person?

In fact, opinions about the best selection methods vary. One large group of experts maintains that in the modern world of facts and statistics, we need to rely mostly on them. There are ways to obtain verifiable evidence from past performances. As a simple example, how did we judge the success of Simone Biles in gymnastics or the Williams sisters in tennis? By their accomplishments. In sports, you use undisputable statistics when you recruit athletes for a college team or draft for a professional franchise. Some big teams even reduced their scouting staff to turn to pure statistical evidence related to their potential recruits. In the same manner, a good teacher, a doctor, or an engineer also can provide those "numbers" to prove their past accomplishments for a hiring committee.

Another group of experts understands the importance of past performances but suggests that no objective facts—about the buildings built or videogames designed—can tell you about the person's individual qualities, such as openness to experience, emotional stability, stamina, creativity, dependability, their ability to be patient, or even their ambition and honesty. Therefore, psychological tests that can reveal these and many other qualities are crucial in the process of selection of the best candidate. Moreover, these tests are already widely used in modern, especially high-tech, businesses.

Yet another group criticizes both previous arguments. Some people "beef up" their resumes. People also may give deliberately misleading or socially desirable answers to test questions. Ask an applicant, "are you hardworking?" or "are you honest?" and you know the answer you are likely to receive, right? A person can also say, "I am creative" or "I am extremely organized," but would these answers reflect on this individual's pet peeves, moral features, or good character? Some candidates produce prepared standard answers and even "coached" to give certain replies. To avoid all of these, the critics suggest more spontaneous interaction with a candidate and questions like, "Are you an ambition person?" or even, "Which windows are open on your laptop at the moment?" They believe such spontaneous questions provide more "natural" and insightful answers, which could be a perfect criterion for a better hiring judgment.

All these views have a strong point. Which one would you prefer? Could you rank them based on their effectiveness, based on your judgment?

Psychologists are likely to defend and promote all three methods while considering them mutually complimenting. How well they have been adopting these methods and tests to real life situation—you will judge from this chapter.

Sources: Cowen & Gross, 2022; Pethokoukis & Cowen, 2022.

PHOTO 6.1 Which specific personality traits would you like to develop or change in yourself to be more competitive in the job market?

THE TRAIT APPROACH

The trait tradition in personality psychology focuses on identifying and measuring **traits,** which are distinguishable and stable patterns of behavior and experience. Recall from Chapter 4 that the psychoanalytic tradition focuses on unconscious mechanisms directing the inner world of the individual. The behavioral-learning tradition discussed in Chapter 5 brings our attention to the individual's observable behavior. Psychoanalysis underlines the subjective side of the individual's life, while behaviorism mostly diminishes it. The trait tradition focuses on both behavior and experience and pays some attention to their causes. Yet it is mostly interested in identification and measurement of individual traits. These traits, as you remember from Chapter 1, include stable patterns of physical actions, decisions, emotions, and thoughts. The combination and interaction of various traits form a personality that is unique to each individual. The trait tradition to personality also focuses on differences between individuals and describes such differences as quantifiable, or measurable.

Like behaviorists and psychoanalysts, psychologists working within the trait tradition generally accept several common principles or general expectations related to their research and applications. First, traits are not just single behavioral manifestations or isolated emotional reactions. If you are a clinical psychologist, your client may appear nervous and timid during your first clinical interview and therapy session. Or a new acquaintance of yours appears outspoken and funny in the afternoon during lunch and then quiet and reserved in the evening. Which situation was more telling about these individuals' traits? Probably neither because we haven't examined their behavior over a longer period. Traits are supposed to be stable, or relatively unchanging over a relatively significant time. Traits are different from what we call "states." In our daily English vocabulary, we sometimes describe ourselves or other people as being in a particular emotional or motivational state. We say, "I don't want you to be in such as sad state," or "She is going through a state in which she is only focused on her work." Or a person may go through a period of dysphoria, such as exaggerated sadness, lack of motivation, fatigue, and the like. However, states are likely to evolve with or without an individual's deliberate effort or an outside intervention. Psychologists usually understand states, compared to traits, as more transitory or dynamic (Steyer et al., 2015).

Second, traits should also impact the individual's actions, emotions, and overall experiences. In other words, if we recognize and measure a particular trait in a person, we should anticipate that this individual should react, think, or feel in a certain way in many other situations. For example, if somebody displays a trait such as openness to experience (we will look later at it as a trait), then we anticipate that this individual is likely in most situations to tend to eagerly learn, explore, study new materials, read, meet new people, take chances, and seek novelty in life.

Third, traits are expected to be dichotomous, or in many cases, measured as a point on a continuum. It is not very common that a person either "has" or "does not have" a particular trait, such as impulsivity; there are times when nearly all of us will do some things impulsively, without giving much thought to the actions. Some of us are more impulsive than others. It is likely that we each have certain "strength" of individual traits somewhere along this spectrum (see Chapter 3 for the discussion of continuous and dichotomous variables).

Yet how many traits are there? In the past 100 years or so, psychologists proposed, studied, and measured a significant number of individual personality traits. Some psychologists suggested dozens of traits to describe an individual, while others offered just a few (Corr & Matthews, 2009). Some psychologists, as we will see in this chapter, also offered their own original scales to measure the traits. They have proposed these and their **taxonomies**, which are descriptive models or classifications based on similarity, functioning, structure, size, origin, and the like. Taxonomies are supposed to be scientifically based, of course, and provide opportunities for further examination and careful review for replication and cross-cultural applicability. These models ought to be understood in a relatively simple way. Furthermore, to examine the similarities and differences among individuals, psychologists have to examine a relatively small (or at least manageable) number of individual traits rather than go through hundreds and maybe thousands of characteristics that may describe individual features that make us, humans, different. A "good" taxonomy should also allow psychologists to efficiently compare their findings with other psychologists' research, use a common language to describe these traits, and improve communication among other researchers (John & Srivastava, 2001).

The trait tradition is not a lone theory but a way, using which psychologists and their colleagues think about and conduct research related to personality traits. It is a distinct type of research that recognizes and measures the strength or salience of personality traits. The degree or similar measure referring to these traits should indicate an "identification card" of each individual's personality.

Ancient Philosophies

The ideas about personality as a distinct combination of traits appeared in many ancient philosophical teachings. Buddhist thinkers referred to an individual uniqueness as a combination of various traits. Five constituents of personality (*khandha*) exist: body, perception, feeling, mental formations, and consciousness (Collins, 1990). The ancient Greek philosophers believed that individual traits should refer to the work of different parts of the body, such as the heart, the liver, or the brain; the heart and the liver had something to do with courage, lustfulness, stamina, and awareness; and the brain had something to do with judgment, patience, and intellectual skills. Many early classifications described the individual's bodily humors as foundations of stable traits. A misbalance in bodily humors—either due to inborn factors or other natural forces—likely caused this person to be either persistently and unreasonably elated or constantly withdrawn and grumpy, or stubbornly belligerent and unpredictable or persistently sad or easily disturbed.

In the teachings of Hinduism, people had obligations regarding their position in society and to their stages of individual development. They had to act and think according to the prescribed models. The Brahmins (the highest class) taught religion; the Nobles practiced defense; the Commoners plowed, tended cattle, and lent money; and the lowest class served the upper ones. The caste system has had a profound impact on India's society, as well as on the individual behavior and thinking of many generations of Indians. It is outlawed in contemporary India, but its prescriptions are likely to be embedded in customs and subsequent thought and behavior of many individuals today. According to surveys, caste segregation remains prevalent in India these days still (Sahgal et al., 2021). Hinduism suggests various combinations of traits based on an individual's phases of growth. For example, one can be labeled *the moral student* for combining good learning habits of religion with obedience. Another can be labeled *the dreamer* for combining faith and affection, but pursuing only little knowledge and obedience (Robbie, 2014).

In the Islamic tradition, there are several "levels" or qualities of personality traits distinguished according to the quality of *nafs* (self or soul): The lowest is characterized by the tendency toward evil; the middle level is associated with conscience and concern with moral rectitude; the highest level is associated with gradual movement toward perfection in thought and action (Kasule, 2000).

Astrological explanations of personality traits appeared in ancient times and remained very common for centuries (they remain very popular today as part of popular beliefs). According to these explanations, specific personality traits largely depend on celestial bodies. For example, the planet Jupiter was associated with an individual's predominant happiness and optimism. The impact from the planet Saturn could make certain people constantly bitter or sardonic. Mars as a planet affected traits such as bravery and conscientiousness. Did you know that the meaning of the term *lunatic* (in Latin, it is *lunaticus or lunatica*) comes from the belief that the moon could negatively influence a person's behavior, which becomes unpredictable and irrational under the moon's influence?

Further Research in Philosophy and Psychology

It is hard to find a philosopher from the past who didn't write about personality traits. The prominent English thinker David Hume (1711–1776) described at least four most significant traits: pleasure seeking (which is a commitment to fun, variety, and entertainment), virtue seeking (a commitment to good deeds and action), philosophical devotion (a commitment to thinking), and critical thinking (a commitment to skepticism and evaluation). Another English philosopher, David Hartley (1705–1757), distinguished two groups of traits. The first group includes imagination, ambition, and self-interest. The second group includes sympathy, theopathy, and the moral sense. *Imagination* refers to objects as sources of pleasure or displeasure. *Ambition* is the realization of one's own status in the eyes of other people. *Self-interest* manages the demands of imagination and ambition. *Sympathy* refers to the feelings of other people. *Theopathy* refers to the individual's moral sense and connection with spiritual issues, such as religion. Although Hartley's theory of personality is based on theoretical assumptions, his approach shared common ground with various trait theories of personality developed during the 20th century by Gordon Allport, Raymond Cattell, and others. As in Hartley's writings, these theories state that individuals tend to possess relatively stable and unique characteristics.

Early experimental psychologists were looking for empirical descriptions and explanations of individual traits. The German psychologist Wilhelm Wundt (1832–1920), one of the founders of experimental psychology, believed that language had a big role in forming individual traits. When an individual speaks a particular language, this person then follows a particular custom and thus acquires a specific order of thinking. Wundt described Greek and Latin languages as relatively loose in terms of the positioning of words in comparison to the German language, which, according to Wundt, requires discipline, precision, and order. Thus, people who spoke German beginning in childhood were more likely to become most organized, orderly, and responsible compared to others who do not speak German (Wundt, 1916).

Recall from Chapter 4 that Carl Jung studied personality traits such as introversion and extroversion, and he provided detailed descriptions about them (these are described in Chapter 4). Jung used a pure observational method in describing personality traits, but other researchers were turning to more empirical methods. German-born psychologist William Stern (1871–1938), who is also known for his early studies of intelligence, studied personality as a unique, active, and self-contained entity. According to his research, individual traits are formed in the process of constant interaction among the environment, the individual's characteristics, and the individual's motivation, intellectual skills, and personal goals. He also gave a classification of individual types.

The American psychologist James McKeen Cattell (1860–1944) coined the term *mental test* in 1890 to indicate the procedures used to measure "mental energy" of the participants in psychological experiments. Attention was paid to the difference between (a) an individual's performance and (b) the performance of large populations on the same test. The goal of such measurements was mostly educational: Cattell believed that university counselors would use mental testing to make speedy assessments of students' potentials and give professional advice about their future. He first began to administer tests in 1894 to students at Columbia University, where he worked as a professor. In the early 1900s, many universities and private businesses asked psychologists to help them with assessments of individual traits of students, potential employees, and workers (von Mayrhauser, 2002).

Most of the teachings in philosophy and early psychology about individual traits were speculative and based on some popular beliefs, a particular doctrine, or ideological values. However, early psychologists were determined to bring science to their study of traits. They often disagreed about the sources of their knowledge and about the theory and methods of their investigation.

The History Collection/Alamy Stock Photo

PHOTO 6.2 The German psychologists Wilhelm Wundt (1832–1920), one of the founders of experimental psychology, believed that language had a big role in forming individual traits, like punctuality or spontaneity.

CHECK AND APPLY YOUR KNOWLEDGE

1. Define *traits*.
2. What are taxonomies?
3. Who were lunatics, and why were they called this?
4. Find any astrological horoscope online. What does the horoscope tell you about your personality traits? How accurate or inaccurate is the description of your traits? Is the description equally accurate in describing other people, such as your friends?

SELF-REFLECTION

Meyer Friedman and his coworkers (Friedman & Ulmer, 1984) defined what they called *Type A* and *Type B* patterns. Type A traits include impatience and assertive competitiveness; people with these traits tend to challenge other people. They are intense and hard driving and do not mind engaging in conflicts. Type B people, on the other hand, tend to be patient and less competitive, possessing traits that help them be kind to others. They are not intense and prefer to avoid conflicts. There was also a *Type AB*, which is a mixed profile of traits that are between the Type A and Type B. Type AB people are likely to be intense and hard driving in some situations and less intense in others.

Questions

Which type of traits are you likely to have: A, B, or AB? How do you know that? Would you like to change these traits in yourself? Why or why not?

TRAIT THEORISTS AND PERSPECTIVES

Several prominent psychologists have contributed to the trait tradition. Unlike psychoanalysts or behaviorists, they did not call themselves *trait psychologists*. The label arrived later, mostly out of convenience, when other psychologists began their evaluation of this rich legacy of studies of individual traits. Several prominent psychologists have contributed to the trait tradition. Unlike psychoanalysts or behaviorists, they did not call themselves *trait psychologists*. The label arrived later, mostly out of convenience, when other psychologists began their evaluation of this rich legacy of studies of individual traits. Several prominent psychologists have contributed to the trait tradition. Unlike psychoanalysts or behaviorists, who preferred to be called that way, they did not call themselves *trait psychologists*. The label arrived later, mostly out of convenience, when other psychologists began their evaluation of this rich legacy of studies of individual traits.

Gordon Allport

The American psychologist Gordon Allport (1897–1967) was a pioneer psychologist who created a new field of study dedicated to the measurement of personality. He was born in Indiana and from the beginning of his life he appreciated the hard work, perseverance, and dedication of his parents. As a Harvard social ethics student, Allport was genuinely committed to science. A formative experience for Allport was his postdoctoral fellowship in Germany in the fall of 1922. He was influenced by the works of the German psychologist William Stern, especially by Stern's attempts to measure and categorize an individual's traits (Allport, 1937; Nicholson, 2000).

Allport argued that "character" and "personality" were distinct and different entities. Borrowing this idea from the behaviorist John Watson, Allport maintained that character was a moral category associated with societal prescriptions and the manner with which people follow these directions. Personality, on the other hand, referred to the objective self, or the fundamental adjustment patterns that an individual forms over the course of his or her life and in various situations. Allport described both internal and external forces that influence an individual's personality traits. Two of them included genotypes and phenotypes. **Genotypes** are our individual forces that relate to how we keep information and use it to interact with the social and physical world around us. **Phenotypes** reflect the way individuals accept their environments and how others influence their behavior. He maintained that there was a stable but heavily interconnected core of traits in every person (Allport, 1924, 1937). Allport also believed that only experimental procedures and measurements (as was done with intelligence testing) could bring psychology a new understanding of personality, free from theoretical speculation and bias.

Allport and his colleagues wanted to find one or more unifying principles that could help them create a reliable, science-based taxonomy of personality traits. Yet to study such principles and create a classification, they had to have a comprehensive list of personality traits. Where could such a description be obtained? One of Allport's assumptions was that the daily language we speak and write should contain a very exhaustive database of labels, tags, and markers that people historically and commonly attached to other people's behavior, feelings, and other manifestations. A few psychologists before them had already studied dictionaries in search of the words that would describe mental states and had identified thousands of such words related to traits in German and English (Klages, 1929). Yet what should be done with these words to study personality? Allport and Odbert (1936) identified 17,953 unique terms used to describe the individual's personality, behavior, feelings, and so on. Next, they separated these into four categories (or columns) based on their own criteria for classification (see Table 6.1).

This placement of traits into columns appears logical yet somewhat arbitrary. The researchers were aware of the subjectivity of such a classification and used several research assistants for independent reviewing to increase the consistency of their evaluations. Yet the

TABLE 6.1 ■ Gordon Allport's Classification of Personality Traits			
Column I	*Column II*	*Column III*	*Column IV*
Descriptions of seemingly stable personality traits such as polite, extroverted, assertive, aggressive, kind, and so on	Descriptions of passing emotional states referring to a period, and attitudes such as frantic, calm, and so on	Reflections of other people regarding an individual's character, such as valuable, respectable, and the like	Important personality descriptive terms that did not fit into the other three columns, such as physical abilities or skills

degree of consistency among different assistants was relatively low. Allport also realized that many individual traits are too complex to be limited to single words. Moreover, he was also aware that the words related to personality meant different things in different languages and cultural groups.

Allport presented personality traits as cardinal, central, and secondary. Cardinal traits dominate an individual's personality and should explain most of this individual's important decisions or actions. These traits stand out. For example, rejection of violence (or propensity for nonviolence) would probably be Mohandas Gandhi's cardinal trait (he was the preeminent leader of the Indian independence movement). We easily recognize some people among our friends and relatives because of their cardinal traits.

Next, individuals have several central traits, which are viewed as basic building blocks of an individual's personality. In the case of Gandhi, it could be his openness to experience, his kindness, and his resilience. It is expected that cardinal traits influence central traits, and their influence is mutual.

Finally, there are more than several secondary traits. They are not unimportant because they are labeled "secondary." They tend to appear as patterns under circumstances. Take, for example, Gandhi's self-reliance traits. They were more dominate in some situations and less in others: Even professing self-reliance, he was eager to help assist and help as well (Sarnobat, 2020).

Allport's research into personality was inspired by a deep belief in social progressivism: He believed in the transformational power of the educated action. Like many of his colleagues at the time, he also believed that the solutions to problems such as poverty, crime, and violence should be found in the works of scientists—psychologists in particular. He understood, however, that psychology as a discipline could not change social institutions easily and at will. Psychology provides knowledge, yet this knowledge, if applied correctly, should change many people's traits, and subsequently, their behavior for the better of society.

Raymond Cattell

Raymond Cattell (1905–1998) was a British American psychologist who joined the ranks of many colleagues and contemporaries in his belief that only science and the scientific method could explain human behavior and experience. He received his undergraduate and advanced college degrees in the United Kingdom. After moving to the United States, he was invited by Gordon Allport to join Harvard University in 1941. As did most American psychologists during World War II, he contributed to the war effort, working on various tests for selecting officers in the armed forces. After the war, he joined the University of Illinois, where he worked for almost 30 years. He is considered among the most quoted psychologists of the 20th century and beyond (Tucker, 2009).

Like Allport, Cattell felt that psychology should distance itself from speculation and embrace measurement (Cattell, 1965, 1983). Such measurements should be available for verification, or retesting by other scientists (peer review), and the results should be explained in an open discussion. Earlier in his career, Cattell was working with Charles Spearman, who studied human abilities and with whom he learned about factor analysis (see Chapter 3)—a method to deal with large numbers of observed variables that are thought to reflect a smaller number of underlying variables (Cattell, 1978). Factor analysis performs complex calculations on the correlation coefficients among the variables within a particular domain (personality features) to determine the basic, primary factors for the particular domain. This method gave him confidence that a long list of human traits (different psychologists provided various lineups of traits) could be shortened and not necessarily by subjective reasoning and prejudgments. He believed that factor analysis could identify basic "building blocks," such as honesty or aggressive tendencies (like molecules in chemistry) of human personality (Cattell, 1946).

To apply factor analysis to personality, Cattell used three kinds of data: life, experimental, and questionnaire-based. He taught that to obtain life data (or L-data) the researcher should gather facts from the individual's behavior patterns in the real world. This could include jobs she or he has held, number of friends, frequency of visits to a doctor, and even eating and sleeping habits. Experimental data (or T-data) are about responses to standardized experimental situations created in a psychology laboratory where a subject's behavior is investigated and measured. And finally, questionnaire data (or Q-data) are about self-assessments or answers to a series of questions about specific behaviors or experiences.

He reexamined the largest compilation of words representing personality traits available to him (Allport & Odbert, 1936) and collected adjectives related to human personality. He then organized the list of adjectives into fewer than 200 items by eliminating redundancies, and then he asked subjects to evaluate people they knew with each of the adjectives on the list. Using data from three of the measurement domains (L-data, Q-data, T-data) and then applying factor analysis, Cattell identified a number of trait factors within the personality (Cattell, 1978). He used a technological device that was new at that time—the computer—to conduct a programmatic series of factor analyses on the data derived from each of the measurements (Cattell, 1983). In the end, Cattell was able to reduce the list of hundreds of psychological traits into 16 basic groups or dimensions that he believed were the core of the individual's personality (Kaplan & Saccuzzo, 2013). It appeared to observers that because of Cattell's background in the physical sciences he saw personality traits as fundamental underlying elements—like molecules— of daily human behavior and experience. To reiterate, Cattell believed that as chemical elements in the periodic system, psychological and behavioral features of individuals should be measurable and placed in categories (see Table 6.2; Cattell, 1965).

Cattell developed a test known as the Sixteen Personality Factor Questionnaire (16PF) to measure these personality features. This self-report method was revised at least four times, translated into several languages, and adopted (which is not easy to due to translation challenges and cultural differences among studied populations) for use in many countries. This has been one of the most popular psychological methods of personality assessment used globally for clinical, educational, business, and other purposes (Cattell & Mead, 2008; Shiraev & Levy, 2024). Just browse a few introductory psychology books, and you will see that Cattell remains one of the most referred-to psychologists.

TABLE 6.2 ■ Sixteen-Factor Structure of Personality by Raymond Cattell		
Factor	*High-Degree Manifestations*	*Low-Degree Manifestations*
Warmth	Outgoing	Reserved
Reasoning	Abstract	Concrete
Emotional stability	Stable	Volatile
Dominance	Forceful	Submissive
Liveliness	Spontaneous	Restrained
Rule-Consciousness	Conforming	Nonconforming
Social boldness	Uninhibited	Shy
Sensitivity	Sensitive	Tough-Minded
Vigilance	Suspicious	Trusting
Abstractedness	Imaginative	Practical
Privateness	Discrete	Open
Apprehension	Anxious	Confident
Openness to change	Flexible	Inflexible
Self-Reliance	Self-Sufficient	Dependent
Perfectionism	Controlled	Undisciplined
Tension	Impatient	Relaxed

Hans Eysenck

Hans Eysenck (1916–1997) was a German-born psychologist who lived and worked in the United Kingdom. He is known for his work on a wide range of topics within psychology, including intelligence. One of his most significant contributions to psychology was in personality psychology. Like Cattell, he used empirical data and factor-analytic research to design and develop his theory. He emphasized two major personality dimensions: extroversion and neuroticism (Eysenk, 1948). Psychologists frequently refer to these dimensions as **Eysenck's E and N.**

Extroversion (E) is characterized by talkativeness, positive emotions, and the need to seek external sources of stimulation. Eysenk believed that traits should have a strong biological background (of course, this is not the only background, see Chapter 2), and he maintained that extroversion, for example, is based on brain activities that determine a person's level of arousal. People who are prone to extroversion tend to be underaroused (bored) so they need to seek new experiences to achieve the optimal level of arousal. Introversion, on the other hand, is characterized by quietness, doubt, and the need to stick to inner experiences. People who are prone to introversion tend to be overaroused (jittery) and thus need calm and peace to achieve their optimal level of arousal.

Neuroticism (N) refers to an individual's level of emotionality. People who measure high in neuroticism have the tendency to see danger in many people, events, and developments around them. Their brains are activated quickly when they face a new situation or encounter a new problem. They tend to experience negative reactions associated with fear or anger. They tend to be easily upset and are also prone to depression and anxiety. People who measure low in neuroticism tend to be emotionally stable. Their brains are not activated quickly in new circumstances. They tend to control their negative emotions and are likely to be calm and collected under pressure. Depression and anxiety are not typical among them (see Table 6.3).

Eysenck underlined that these two dimensions were somewhat similar to the four personality types (commonly called *temperaments*) first proposed by the Greek physician Hippocrates, who lived 2,500 years ago: the Choleric (high N and E), the Melancholic (high N and low E), the Sanguine (Low N and high E), and the Phlegmatic (both N and E are low). The famous Greek speculated about the individual; Eysenck provided empirical research of individual traits.

Later on in his career, Eysenck added another dimension to his model of the individual's personality. He called in **psychoticism**, which is a personality pattern that manifests in persistent aggressiveness and hostility to others (Eysenck & Eysenck, 1976). Specifically, people with a predisposition to psychoticism (Eysenck believed that psychoticism has a significant biological component) tend to be tough-minded and nonconforming, as well as prone to recklessness, unfriendliness, anger, and impulsiveness. They tend not to experience remorse. Psychoticism also stands for impulsive tendencies in behavior (such as speaking before thinking or deciding quickly before assessing the decision's consequences) and **sensation seeking**, which is the constant tendency to search for new experiences and feelings. People who measure high on psychoticism tend to be sensation seekers. They need adventure. They tend to like noisy parties and unusual activities. They also feel bored in the company of "ordinary" people (Zuckerman, 2007a). This trait also positively correlates with artistic creativity (Eysenck, 1993). Unfortunately, they also tend to look for new psychological experiences using additional "boosters," including alcohol and other substances.

TABLE 6.3 ■ Extroversion–Introversion and Emotional Stability–Instability, According to Eysenck (1948)

Extroversion	High Neuroticism	Low Neuroticism
High	A person tends to be quick-tempered, restless, edgy, changeable, impulsive, irresponsible	A person tends to be outgoing, talkative, responsible, friendly, carefree, and tends to display leadership
Low	A person tends to be quiet, reserved, pessimistic, solemn, rigid, anxious, and moody	A person tends to be calm, even-tempered, consistent, controlled, peaceful, thoughtful, careful, and passive

CHECK AND APPLY YOUR KNOWLEDGE

1. Explain Gordon Allport's four columns.
2. Where did Gordon Allport obtain significant empirical data for his research into personality?
3. What are cardinal, central, and secondary traits? What would be your cardinal trait or traits? What traits would you like other people to recognize in you?
4. What is factor analysis and why is it used?
5. What is the number 16 in 16FP?
6. Describe briefly Eysenck's E and N.
7. Define *sensation seeking*. Suggest two situations in which sensation seeking has (a) a negative impact on the individual life and education and (b) positive impact.

THE BIG FIVE

For many years in the 20th century, research of personality traits was associated with the original theories by Gordon Allport, Raymond Cattell, Hans Eysenck, and a few others. A new generation of psychologists offered their own versions of these theories, as well as their own new theories. One approach developed by several psychologists caught some attention, and once additional research was conducted, this approach eventually received global recognition (Goldberg, 1993). In fact, it is a data-driven analysis of verbal descriptors of human behavioral patterns that tend to cluster together. This theory is often called the **Big Five**, or as some call it OCEAN, a convenient acronym to outline and better remember these traits.

There is no single researcher who "originated" and developed the Big Five model. Rather, there were several independent or collaborating individuals and groups who began to empirically study relationships among verbal and written descriptions of human behavior, appearance, emotional expressions, and the like. Then they reduced redundancies in such descriptions using multiple "judges" and then used factor analysis to statistically determine the underlying factors or traits of personality.

This five-factor structure of personality traits has been measured and discussed in numerous studies in different countries for many years (McCrae & Costa, 1997), and there are several versions of the test measuring these traits (Soto, 2019). The traits can be labeled *openness, conscientiousness, extroversion, agreeableness*, and *neuroticism*. According to the theory, other individual traits are likely to fall within these five. All five factors are rather continuous because they measure a certain degree for the manifestation of each trait. The opposite characteristics are often labeled as *dogmatism, irresponsibility, introversion, unfriendliness*, and *emotional stability* (see Figure 6.1).

Openness to Experience

People who score higher on this measure tend to be curious, inventive, and exploratory. A person with high scores here is open to new experiences and tends to be intellectually and emotionally

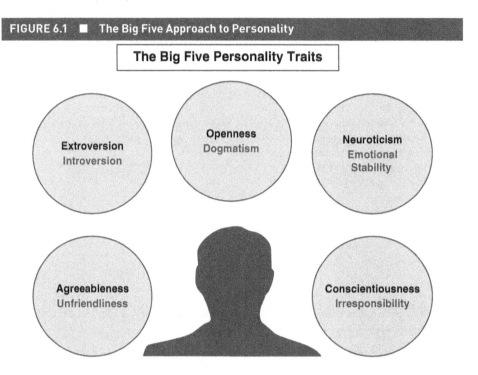

FIGURE 6.1 ■ The Big Five Approach to Personality

The Big Five Personality Traits

Extroversion
Introversion

Openness
Dogmatism

Neuroticism
Emotional
Stability

Agreeableness
Unfriendliness

Conscientiousness
Irresponsibility

curious, likes to travel to new places, is sensitive to beauty, and is willing to experience new things. Be careful, though. These features are not supposed to be judged as unconditionally "good" or most desirable. We should consider them in specific circumstances. Sometimes people who are open to various experiences are viewed as lacking focus. On the other hand, those who score lower on openness tend to be more consistent in their interests and goals. Such people also tend to have more conventional, traditional interests in life. They prefer to plan things in advance and avoid ambiguity, rather than go with the flow. They prefer things that are familiar to them, while new things take some time to accept, if ever. They tend to be more resistant to change compared to those who are open to experience (McCrae & Costa, 1987). This may change with age and evolving social circumstances. We will discuss this later in Chapter 9.

Conscientiousness

People who score high on this measure tend to be organized, industrious, and efficient compared to those who display lower scores and tend to be less efficient and more carefree and blithe. Highly conscientious people strive for achievement and base their behavior on a plan. They tend to be less spontaneous and prefer an articulated strategy rather than improvisation. Nevertheless, high scores on conscientiousness may also indicate a person's stubbornness, making them sometimes unreasonable and prone to mistakes because they tend to resist changing their initial course of action. On the other hand, low scores on conscientiousness may indicate an individual's lack of a reliable plan or behavior pattern. Low scores on conscientiousness may also indicate a person's ability to change and to be spontaneous. A high level of conscientiousness is often related to the propensity to control, regulate, and direct desires and tame exciting ideas. People who scored high on conscientiousness do not necessarily follow the rules prescribed by government or other authorities—all for the sake of orderliness. A study in Spain, for example, showed that during the first year of the COVID pandemic people who scored high on this measure did not necessarily wear masks in higher numbers compared to other people (Barceló & Sheen, 2020). On the other hand, conscientiousness has been correlated with other forms of healthy behavior, such as wearing sunscreen under the sun, or healthy eating (Kouzes et al., 2017).

Extroversion

A person who scores high on this variable tends to seek new contacts and attention, as well as be outgoing, full of energy, talkative, and dominant. People with low scores on extroversion tend to be more reserved, not seek much attention, and not look for new contacts. They are more reflective and less talkative compared to others. Extroversion is usually about the scope and number of activities in which you are engaged. The opposite side of the spectrum is about depth and often attention to the quality of relationships and activities. Extroversion is associated with high levels of social interaction, along with being constantly energetic and action oriented. People who are in this category are relatively visible simply because their presence is usually detectable: They talk more than listen, often sit in the front row during a presentation, ask questions, or make frequent comments. People low on extroversion (often called *introverts*—but remember, labels usually attempt to describe the entire person, and such simplistic descriptions are often inaccurate) display less intense social engagement and lower energy levels compared to others, especially to "extroverts." They tend to seem quiet, low-key, deliberate, and less involved in the social world. Their lack of social involvement should not be interpreted as shyness or depression; instead, they are more independent of their social world than extroverts. Introverts need less stimulation than extroverts and more time alone. This is not to suggest that they are unfriendly or antisocial; rather, they tend to be reserved in social situations (Laney, 2002). Studies show that children with high scores on extroversion tend to be energetic, talkative, and more dominant in their play with children and interaction with adults. Children who score low on extroversion tend to be quieter, calmer, and appear more reserved than other children (Shiner & Caspi, 2003).

Agreeableness

People who rank high on this measure tend to appear friendly, cooperative, and compassionate to other individuals and to other people's concerns and problems. Lower scores on this measure are associated with an individual's detachment from other people's issues, a tendency to be unfriendly and even antagonistic. Agreeableness is also about a tendency to trust people, make new friends, listen to others, and cooperate with them. It is about an individual's desire to get along with neighbors, coworkers, and even strangers. It is about a tendency to seek approval from others and compromise by considering other people's plans and interests. Agreeableness may also appear to some as a negative, socially undesirable trend in an individual because it may be seen as a tendency of being weak, spineless, and "soft." On the other hand, low levels of agreeableness embody competition, challenge, skepticism, and a general tendency not to trust others. Trusting or not trusting others is not about being a good person or a bad one—it is highly contextual. Based on specific conditions, low and high levels of agreeableness may be useful or not for certain professions or activities.

Neuroticism

A person who scores high on this variable tends to be more sensitive, concerned, and anxious compared to others. High scores indicate that the individual is passionately aware about people and circumstances. Low scores are associated with being calm, confident, and "sturdy." Neuroticism typically refers to an individual's degree of emotional stability and the ability to handle incoming information and address real and imaginary threats. Neuroticism is also associated with a tendency to frequently experience negative emotions, such as anger and fear, and a tendency to experience anxiety or depression. High measures of neuroticism are associated with emotional instability—that is, the propensity to move back and forth from being in a good mood to being in a bad one (Jeronimus et al., 2014). Individuals who score high in neuroticism are likely to be vulnerable to stress, compared to other people. They are also more likely to interpret many everyday situations as threatening, difficult, or simply bad. Neuroticism is usually connected to a somewhat cynical (bitterly contemptuous and pessimistic) approach to work, relationships, and social life (Fiske et al., 2009). For people who score high on neuroticism, life usually appears as filled with negative events and new daily threats. At the other end of the scale, individuals who score low in neuroticism tend to be emotionally stable.

Why are there five and only five factors and not four or 10? Supporters of this approach to personality maintain that they are not using any theoretical assumptions, based on which they try to collect facts to prove or disprove these assumptions. Rather, they are, as psychologists, deploying a data-driven method of analysis, which reduces the element of subjectivity. The five factors (no more or less) appeared because they are an empirical fact, as some suggested (Costa & McCrae, 1992). The mathematical method, supporters also say, gives them confidence they are learning the basic dimensions of personality that can be replicated in other studies (Block, 2001).

The five-factor theory has received significant empirical support. Studies have been conducted on various groups and in more than 50 countries. Twin studies suggest that both heritability and environmental factors influence all five factors to the approximately same degree (Bouchard & McGue, 2003; Jang et al., 1996). Studies of longitudinal data, which correlate people's test scores over time, and cross-sectional data, which compare personality levels across different age groups, show a high degree of stability in personality traits during adulthood (McCrae & Costa, 1990). Cross-cultural research also strongly suggested that personality trait structure is likely to be cross-cultural (Costa & McCrae, 1992; McCrae & Costa, 1997). The data obtained from comprehensive studies conducted in 28 languages and administered to almost 18,000 individuals from 56 nations showed that the five-dimensional structure was present, with some variations, across major regions of the world. Moreover, psychologists found some differences in groups on certain measures. For example, on average, people from the geographic regions of South America and East Asia were different in openness from those inhabiting other world regions (Schmitt et al., 2007). Sure, it will be wrong to make far-reaching conclusions based only on these data.

A study of gender differences in more than 50 countries found that women, again, on the average, tended to be somewhat higher than men in neuroticism, extroversion, agreeableness, and conscientiousness. Gender differences in personality traits tended to be larger in prosperous, healthy, and more gender-equal–based cultures. Perhaps, as a possible explanation, women's behaviors and traits in free and egalitarian countries are more likely to be attributed to their personality, rather than to certain ascribed gender roles within more collectivist or traditional communities (Costa et al., 2001). Regarding parenthood, people tend to become less open to experience and less extroverted after they became parents (Asslemann & Specht, 2021).

Certainly, the Big Five model has weaknesses. One common criticism is that the theory explains an individual only superficially without looking at deeper structures and inner experiences. In addition, people tend to describe their own behavior differently than they describe other people's behavior (Piekkola, 2011). Psychologists also criticize the Big Five model for failing to include many other important features of human beings, such as honesty, sense of humor, cynicism, selfishness, and so forth (we will return to these features in later chapters). Cross-cultural applicability was also an issue in several studies. For instance, as a study of farmers in the Bolivian Amazon showed, some of the abstract concepts in the translated versions of the Big Five tests were incorrectly understood by the locals (Gurven at al., 2013). Perhaps this model will not fully describe neither one of us as individuals. However, this model provides one of the best empirical models available to psychologists these days. The search for a better one will continue.

CHECK AND APPLY YOUR KNOWLEDGE

1. Why is the theory of personality called the Big Five?
2. Pick any trait from the list of the Big Five and describe yourself from the view of this trait.
3. Briefly explain why the Big Five model does not adequately explain your personality or a personality of a person you know very well.

HUMANITIES AND PERSONALITY TRAITS

Studies in the humanities reveal that written knowledge across cultures contains detailed descriptions of desirable and undesirable individual traits and types. These are not just individual acts or states; they are somewhat stable behavioral traits. Some writings, especially religious teachings, reflect on a pure dichotomy: They separate divine beings (such as saints or other heroes) and profane beings (such as demons and villains). In other writings (and religions, such as Hinduism, for example), the divisions often appear more complex because good and evil can be intertwined in one being.

The Perfect. The sacred figures of saints, angels, and prophets provide a collective portrait of ideal, desirable individual qualities. Many religions distinguish an individual entity who carried the holiest, most divine, and important message from the supernatural entity. Muslims were taught to use the life of the prophet Mohammed as the touchstone for proper thought, decision, and action. Christians admire the life, the thought, and the deeds of Jesus Christ, which represents to them ultimate kindness, justice, wisdom, and compassion. Similarly, Siddhartha Gautama, or Buddha, appears to Buddhists as reflecting the complete set of virtuous personality traits. Angels in most religious teachings usually appear as innocent and helpful transcendental beings who are universal helpers and rescuers. People attribute great, yet unexpected events to the work of angels. The saints are generally people who are believed to have holiness, which is a very high measure of perfection, purity, and righteousness. Saints commonly (1) sacrifice themselves for the sake of many, (2) refuse material possessions and bodily pleasures, and (3) inspire many followers to think, act, and feel in a positive, uplifting way (Hawley, 1987).

National heroes (take any country's written history) typically appear in books, stories, films, and songs as mostly infallible, honest, brave, and dedicated to their cause. Children are taught to admire them, be like them, think, and act like these heroes. The historical cases of Lenin or Stalin in Russia, as well as Mao in China, or Kim Il-Sung in North Korea are just few examples of such "training" of the young to model their personalities after these leaders.

The Cursed. In religious teachings, the devil is the ultimate evil; in fact, the most repulsive traits and individual features are often attributed to the devil. Evil characters appear in many shapes and forms, and they are labeled differently across cultures and religions. *Demons* and *ghosts* in Christianity; *jinn* in Islam; *vetala, bhoot,* and others in Hinduism; *dybbuks* in Judaism; and *mara* in Buddhism all possess evil "human" traits such as greed, trickery, ire, jealousy, and pride. The cursed, such as demons and ghosts, often (1) interfere in and obstruct human affairs, (2) evoke fear and other negative emotions such as jealousy, and (3) provoke people to commit evil deeds. They lie, seduce, destroy, and spoil. In the folklore tradition, the most undesirable traits appear in descriptions of witches. Belief in witches was widespread in many countries in early medieval society and continued through the centuries. People learn about witches through the description of witchcraft, which is the alleged practice or art of witches, including their use of supernatural power, sorcery, enchantments, and trickery.

In national historic accounts, opposite to national heroes, there are unconditional evil individuals, whose lives and deeds are seen as cruel, trickery, abhorrent, and overall, unconditionally repulsive. This is a major personal insult to an individual to be compared with such a villain (such as Hitler among others), as cross-national studies of character assassination show (Shiraev et al., 2022). Of course, as history shows, the judgments about who remains a hero or a heroine and who becomes a villain can change because such decisions—like many other traditions—are often based on value judgment and a historical perspective. Historical perspectives tend to change with new generations.

As it was discussed in Chapter 3, some people tend to dichotomize variables that, more accurately, should be conceptualized as continuous. Continuous variables are more accurate and therefore more meaningful representations of an individual's personality. Therefore, to present individuals in world's written sources as reflecting either "good" and "bad "qualities will be inaccurate. Both dichotomies can reveal themselves on a continuum and can alter each other. Just one example follows.

The Mingled. Dr. Henry Jekyll and his alternative personality, Mr. Edward Hyde, are fictional characters in Robert L. Stevenson's famous book *Strange Case of Dr. Jekyll and Mr. Hyde*, published in 1886. After drinking a special potion, Dr. Jekyll changes from a nice, friendly man to his alter-personality, Mr. Hyde, who is nasty, violent, and bad. Two personalities lived in one individual, changing control of the body's behavior and the mind's functioning. This story and its characters have become widely recognized icons symbolizing "good" and "bad" individual types—one oriented toward respect and peace, the other toward lust and violence. Dr. Jekyll, who has a "good" personality, was very unhappy and felt guilty for having an evil side within him. On the other hand, Mr. Hyde, who was a "bad" person, was thrilled to be engaged in violent and illegal acts. (Based on Eysenk's classification, we can suggest that Dr. Jekyll would have scored low on psychoticism. Mr. Hyde's score, on the other hand, would have been very high.)

There is a plethora of other examples—from books, films, TV series, etc.—showing contradictions, inner struggle, or even confusion within mythical and literary heroes. Could you provide such examples?

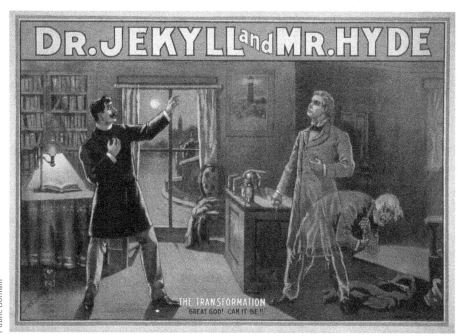

Public Domain

PHOTO 6.3 In Stevenson's book, Dr. Jekyll had good traits, while Mr. Hyde had evil ones. Yet can a "bad" person still have several "good" traits?

A CROSS-CULTURAL APPROACH TO PERSONALITY TRAITS

During a relatively short period of scientific cross-cultural research, scientists and practitioners focused on the question of whether certain personality characteristics are typical of citizens of particular countries. You can imagine the degree of speculation and stereotypical judgments these researchers had to examine. Most national characterizations remain speculative (Shiraev & Levy, 2024). Yet the idea behind the existence of culture-bound or specific "national" or "ethnic" personality traits was explored by many intellectuals of the past and present. From the times of the Greek philosopher Aristotle (5th century BCE), who claimed that the Greeks had an inclination to philosophy while people of other nations developed skills, there were numerous written statements or scientific theories about personality traits developed on entire peoples and cultural groups (Cooper, 2003). Little empirical evidence, of course, was produced to back up the theories espousing the existence of a distinct Greek, Babylonian, or any other "collective" personality. Even in more recent times at the dawn of scientific psychology, there has been no shortage of such stereotypical theories about the prevalence of specific personality traits in national or cultural groups.

Many, if not most, popular assumptions were established about the differences between European and Asian cultures. Karl Jung, for instance, believed in substantial differences between Eastern and Western types of individuals based on their traits. The Western type is rooted mostly in reason but has less connection to intuition and emotion, which is more common in the Eastern type. The Western type is mostly an extrovert, while the Eastern type is mostly an introvert (Kleinman & Kleinman, 1991). While evaluating Chinese and European personality types, other authors focused their attention on the peasant roots of the Chinese civilization associated with pragmatism and down-to-earth considerations, as well as mercantilism of Europeans with their love of numbers and abstract theories (Fung, 1948).

Jung worked and published many decades ago. Yet the discussions about the existence of specific traits associated with countries continue. National character is a perceived set of predominant behavioral and psychological features and traits common in most people of a nation. Very often these features are rooted in people's assumptions. Many of these assumptions are passing and relate to specific events. Others have a long history. Some of them can be offensive. Yet others are perceived as humorous.

Some scholars made sweeping assumptions about fundamental cultural differences that shaped different types of behavior in individuals who are brought up in different countries (Li, 2003; Mahbubani, 1999). Most of these assumptions—although intriguing—were not accompanied by strong empirical evidence or support. Searching for empirical evidence, psychologists often turn to opinion polls, which reflect people's perceptions.

However, politics often plays a major role in how people see other nations and cultural groups. For example, People in Japan and China (close to 80% in both countries), according to surveys, have had very negative views of each other for years (Pew, 2016b). A large share of people (45%, compared to 25% in 2013 when Barack Obama was president) around the world saw U.S. power and influence as a "major threat" to their country, and these views have been connected to attitudes toward Donald Trump and the United States as a country (Gramlich & Devlin, 2019). International surveys consistently show that Americans, for the most part, were described as assertive, hardworking, and open minded, but antagonistic. The Pew Research Center (Gao, 2015) found in international polls that more than close to 50% of people around the world rated Americans as industrious and inventive but also greedy and violent. Americans are seen as high in competence and low in warmth. Americans' perceived emphasis on individualism and work ethic stands out in surveys of people around the world. Americans themselves tend to believe that hard work pays off and consider themselves hardworking (Gao, 2015). Canadians tend to emphasize multiculturalism, diversity, and inclusion as key features of their nation and their country's most notable contribution to the world (Canada World Survey, 2018). In 2019, almost 60% of U.S. citizens believed that the world sees Americans favorably (Gallup, 2019).

However, do these perceptions have a basis in reality? How do people learn about other nations? Are most people in Switzerland excellent planners? Are most people in China exceptionally polite? Are most people in Britain efficient and emotionless? If you are an American, would you personally agree that Americans tend to be hardworking but emotionally cold?

It is very difficult to validate assumptions about the existence of distinct "national" or "cultural" personality types. The most substantial cautionary argument here is that there is a tremendous diversity of personality traits within every ethnic or national group. Furthermore, studies already showed with consistency that the variation of characteristics within national samples is typically greater than the differences between any two national samples (Barrett & Eysenck, 1984; Zuckerman, 1990).

CHECK AND APPLY YOUR KNOWLEDGE

1. Describe the most common personality traits of saints.
2. What are the Eastern and Western types of traits, according to Jung?
3. What is a "national" character and how accurate, in your view, are people's perceptions about people from other countries and cultures?

APPLYING THE TRAIT TRADITION

Individual traits are studied and measured for a reason. Major goals for learning about, measuring, and interpreting individual traits are (a) making decisions about people in terms of their professional selection and promotion, (b) helping people make better decisions, and (c) helping people in finding their unrealized potentials (Johnson, 2001). In decision-making, personality assessments are used to predict how an individual will think, feel, behave, or be perceived by others in various life situations.

Marriage and Individual Traits

Marriage is supposed to be an interaction, as both spouses have their own unique traits. At least two hypotheses based on common sense can be suggested here. First, in a successful marriage, both spouses should have similar personality traits, and the more they match, the more stable the marriage. For example, it is better for a relationship if both individuals are open to experience, they both are conscientious, and friendly. The second assumption is rooted in the theory that opposites attract—in other words, the most stable marriage is the one in which individual traits of both spouses are different so that they compensate each other. In this case, both spouses find attractive in their partner the traits that they lack. Which of these two hypotheses is more scientifically accurate?

Numerous dating sites boast the ability to help people find others with compatible personality traits; one such site is *eHarmony*. Customers fill out a lengthy questionnaire; then responses are evaluated, traits are identified, and finally, a match is (hopefully) found. *Match.com* also asks personal questions, yet it suggests finding people from a broader spectrum, as if suggesting "opposites attract." So what do personality psychologists say about the effectiveness of these two models?

At least two problems exist. The first is methodological. Although many dating sites claim they have a scientific model or an algorithm for partner matching, their methods do not allow for an independent verification or peer review, as is common in academic research. Only by offering their findings for critical peer review or other forms of evaluation can psychologists test their methods and select the most successful and effective methods of investigation and psychological advice (Finkel et al., 2012).

The second problem is factual. Research-based psychology so far is skeptical about the claims that certain personality traits reliably predict compatibility and lead to more satisfying relationships in marriage. Specifically, research suggests that in a relationship, two people need not be similar (but, of course, they can be) in personality traits in order to have a successful, happy, and long-lasting union. Other factors, especially related to people's mutual attraction, trust, and their ability to communicate, can be more important (Orbuch, 2015).

So why do millions of people look for personality profile matches online? According to studies, about 52 million Americans were using online dating sites in 2022 (Statista, 2022), about 30% more than in 2016 (Pew, 2016a). Communicating online can nurture intimacy, bring excitement, and build affection between two people who may not have met otherwise. Others, of course, look for entertainment. There are many people who find happy, stable relationships from an online dating service—if there weren't, these services wouldn't exist. However, as studies show, hoping that an online company can help find an ideal mate with identical or best-fitting characteristics can lead to unrealistic expectations and disappointment when potential partners meet in real life. Unrealistic expectations rapidly turn to frustration; frustration becomes impatience; and impatience cultivates negative emotions that grow and ruin relationships and marriage. (There are also online predators and trolls; we address these issues in Chapter 13.) There is no single magic key to a successful relationship or marriage; contexts, circumstances, financial issues, intrusive in-laws, and many other small details—all can matter (Finkel et al., 2012; Orbuch, 2015). One of the most important things in any relationship is the *mutual* willingness and ability of two people to communicate and create a healthy, exciting, and long-lasting relationship (Orbuch, 2015). Still, the ability to communicate can be an individual trait that we can develop in ourselves and look for in others.

Which Personality Traits Are Most Important to Employers?

If you don't already have one, someday you will be looking for a job based on your education, qualifications, and personality features. During our professional careers, statistics show, we are likely to apply for new jobs several times. Certainly, exceptions exist, yet most of us will have to compete for a job opening, hoping that our qualifications and skills are better than the qualifications and skills of other candidates. How do we figure out which of our individual traits are considered the most desirable to give us the advantage over others competing for the same job? Which individual traits do employers look for most of the time regardless of the profession? Many factors determine the answers to these questions, as you remember from the introductory vignette to this chapter.

Today, companies increasingly use personality measures to decide whether a candidate is a good fit. According to a survey from the Society for Human Resource Management, almost 20% of employers report they use some personality test or a similar assessment procedure as part of the hiring process. Some experts estimate that almost 60% of potential employers are now asked to take some form of workplace assessments. The assessment industry was recently a $500-million-per-year business, and growing (Meinert, 2015). Globally, according to an analysis by Emergen Research (2022), the global revenue for assessment services is expected to reach $11 billion by 2027. Of course, not everything in this business is about individual assessments, yet the role of psychologists in this field is increasing.

In a study published in *Perspectives in Psychological Science*, psychologists reviewed a database on hiring and job performance information to discover which personality characteristics companies value most (Sacket & Walmsley, 2014). The researchers chose to use the Big Five model to examine personality traits, and they investigated the materials of structured job interviews in which employers ask questions and evaluate candidates' responses to find out more about particular personality traits. The researchers' goal was to identify those traits that were chosen consistently and were considered "better" than others for particular job openings.

Most companies looked for conscientiousness as the most desirable trait. Agreeableness was the second-most sought-after trait. The researchers also examined how significant a factor conscientiousness was in determining an employee's success in the workplace. The researchers looked at the relationship between personality traits and three work performance criteria: whether an employee was able to satisfactorily complete work, how often an employee went above and beyond at work, and how often an employee engaged in negative behaviors. In this case, too, conscientiousness and agreeableness were the top two traits. These two traits were also listed in the Department of Labor Database (2016)—along with emotional stability—as the top three traits most important for professional success in the American workforce, regardless of experience and training. However, keep in mind that some professions and job descriptions require different traits. Most importantly, with many significant changes that took place during the pandemic after 2020, when millions of people began to work from home, new questions arise about which individual qualities will be most valuable in the ongoing and changing working conditions.

Politics

Are there any distinct personality traits that determine political orientations and party preferences? Political scientists assume that our personalities motivate us to develop certain political attitudes later in life, and we will vote according to our personality traits (Gerber et al., 2010; Mondak et al., 2010). This assumption is founded on the simple correlation between the two constructs and the observation that personality traits are genetically influenced and developed in infancy, whereas political preferences develop later in life. Table 6.4 provides a brief summary of some studies and their validation in further research.

The relationship between personality traits and political preferences in voting is more complex than it seems. Although there are some correlations between personality traits and political beliefs

TABLE 6.4 ■ Studies of Traits Related to Political Behavior		
Research	*Interpretation*	*Validation*
Radicalism (R-factor) and tender-mindedness (T-factor)	People are likely to be divided into political categories based on their acceptance of toughness and force, on the one hand, and tolerance and consensus, on the other.	Partial support has been found.
Psychoticism, social desirability, and neuroticism	Psychoticism is substantially correlated with conservative defense and social attitudes; social desirability (a tendency to respond in a manner consistent with perceived social norms) is related to liberal social attitudes; and neuroticism is related to liberal economic attitudes.	Limited evidence has been found.
Authoritarian personality	Some people develop a set of corresponding traits such as intolerance, obedience to authority, mystical view of life, rejection of new experiences, superstition, and propensity for violence.	Limited evidence has been found. New research continues to study terrorism and radicalism.
Openness to experience, emotional stability, extroversion, and conscientiousness	Openness to experience is related to liberal political views; emotional stability is correlated with conservative views; conscientiousness is negatively correlated with liberalism; and extroversion is not correlated with conservatism or liberalism.	Some supporting evidence has been found in cross-national studies, except for emotional stability.
Political preferences	Political preferences develop in childhood and are influenced by genetic factors, which means an individual has certain predispositions to be either liberal or conservative.	Limited evidence has been found.

Sources: Eysenck, 1956; Gerber et al., 2010; Mondak et al., 2010; Verhulst et al., 2010.

(Phillips, 2021), personality traits, in most cases, do not necessarily "cause" people to develop specific political attitudes and not others (Verhulst et al., 2012). Personality traits may direct a child to develop certain activities within which the child learns about particular political ideas and values, and some traits are associated with political ideologies. For example, being conscientious increases your chances of being conservative (this is only a probability). Being highly open to experience is likely (but not certainly) to put you in the "liberal column." At the same time, these ideas and the experiences associated with them develop an individual's traits further in many unpredictable directions. An outgoing person is equally likely to be conservative, liberal, or neither. However, people who tend to display radical or violent behaviors may share similar traits regardless of their political orientation (such as liberal or conservative). In fact, studies suggest that the most active and vocal supporters *and* opponents of the death penalty or abortion rights may share similar personality traits. Studies also show that people form their political beliefs early in life, strengthen them during socialization, and further enhance them during their lives (Sears & Funk, 1999). In other words, we evolve individually and politically, yet this change is mutual.

Do "Stupid" People Have Certain Traits?

Is there a list of traits in a person we label *stupid*? Psychologists from the University of Budapest (Aczel et al., 2015) gathered a sample of stories from the web and other publicly available literature in which an action of a main character was described as stupid. The stories were then presented to reviewers who were asked to fill out a questionnaire. According to their responses, the psychologists suggested a short list of traits that are associated with stupidity.

The worst type of stupidity is **confident arrogance**. This is behavior and thinking to support people's *belief* that their ability to do something outweighs their actual ability to do it. Think of drunk drivers, who tend to erroneously believe they can manage driving and then, contrary to what they thought, crash their cars. Or think of a burglar who steals a smartphone, then calls several friends using it, and then posts selfies on Instagram bragging about a new phone.

Lack of control is the second "stupid" trait. In this case, someone is supposed to be doing something important but becomes engaged in some other unimportant activity instead. For example, a person misses a flight at the airport because this individual cannot resist an urge to eat at a favorite fast food restaurant just before it is time to board the plane. Lack of control often refers to particular forms of obsessive, compulsive, or even addictive behavior (Aczel et al., 2015).

The third type is labeled **absentmindedness**, which in behavioral terms can be called lack of practical skills, common sense, or simply attention. People fail because they do not pay attention to something they should have, or they are unaware of their surroundings. How many people have fallen, crossed the street without looking for an approaching car, or bumped into a tree while texting? When this low awareness becomes constant, it becomes a trait.

There are individual traits and social conditions that contribute to the "stupid" traits. Having many supporting friends who constantly "like" your social media postings may contribute to confident arrogance. A habit of multitasking can contribute to absentmindedness. Intense feelings, both positive and negative (such as love or jealousy), can contribute to lack of control (Aczel et al., 2015). In other words, always be careful and thoughtful.

Are There Criminal Traits?

For many years, social scientists and psychologists attempted to find out why some people commit crimes or engage in serious forms of antisocial behavior. Psychologists frequently turned to individual characteristics and traits. The Italian criminologist Cesare Lombroso (1835–1909) attempted to empirically study and then explain the individual factors that affect criminal behavior. In 1876, he published a pamphlet in Italian, setting forth his theory of the origin of criminal traits. Lombroso believed that the most violent criminals have a biological predisposition, which is an **atavism**, or a reversion of behavior to some earlier developmental stages when theft, rape, and pillage contributed directly to male reproductive potential. Lombroso also argued that heredity interacts with the environment to produce individuals with various potentials for criminality. These views brought his book popularity and respect (Gibson, 2002). Another book, *The Female Offender*, translated and published in English (Lombroso & Ferrero, 1895/1959), was based on Lombroso's observations of female convicted criminals and women of deviant behavior, such as prostitutes. One of Lombroso's contributions to psychology was his typology of criminal behavior. He believed that some individuals have serious predispositions to

TABLE 6.5 ■ Traits in Relation to Criminal Behavior	
Personality Traits	*Links to Criminal Behavior*
Agreeableness	Low scores associated with criminality
Conscientiousness	Low scores associated with criminality
Self-control and impulsivity	Lack of self-control associated with criminality
Novelty-seeking	High scores associated with criminality
Empathy and propensity to be remorseful	Research evidence inconclusive
Reward dependence	Research evidence inconclusive

Sources: Gottfredson, 2007; Kenny, 2015; Miller and Lynam, 2001; Reid, 2011.

break the law and be violent; others are less predisposed—willing to break the law but without resorting to violence (a certain prototype of what we now refer to as *white-collar crime*).

In the 20th century and today, psychologists worked and continue to work on theories to provide some evidence for particular traits associated with criminality. Can modern personality psychology identify some traits associated with criminal behavior? Table 6.5 provides a summary of research referring to individual traits.

Consider just a few interesting research findings. Criminal behavior is linked to high novelty seeking, low harm avoidance, and low reward dependence (Reid, 2011). Brain imaging studies showed the connection between frontal lobe executive functioning and impulsivity (Eme, 2008; Moffitt, 1990). Hyperactivity and a poor ability to perceive potential consequences of actions may result in antisocial behavior (Farrington, 2002). A tendency toward intense excitement in response to novel stimuli and the temptation for short-term pleasures in the face of escalating long-term risks are also those traits (Kenny, 2015).

There is no single cause or causes that shape the traits associated with criminality. Some causes are genetic; others are social. As we have learned in previous chapters, we are typically looking for a combination of biological, social, and situational factors to explain most psychological phenomena:

- Genetic factors alone do not "create" traits associated with criminality and do not "produce" criminal behavior.

- In addition to personality traits, a wide range of social conditions contributes to violent behavior—among them poverty, unemployment, discrimination, injustice, social instability, lack of education, and many others.

- There are also many factors (associated with social psychological factors), such as the impact of friends, group pressure, obedience to authority, and others, that affect deviant and criminal acts.

- There are important contextual and individual factors associated with crime, including the level of intoxication of the offender, emotional condition of the offender, misperceptions, opportunity, impulsivity, perceived low risk, and the like.

SUMMARY

- The trait tradition in personality psychology focuses on identifying and measuring traits, which are distinguishable, and stable patterns of behavior and experience.

- Like behaviorists and psychoanalysts, psychologists working within the trait tradition generally accept several common principles or general expectations. First, traits are not just single behavioral manifestations or isolated emotional reactions. Traits are different from what we call "states." Second, traits should also impact the individual's actions, emotions, and overall experiences. Third, traits are expected to be dichotomous or, in many cases, be measured as a point on a continuum.

- Psychologists also offered their own original scales to measure the traits they have proposed and their taxonomies. Taxonomies are descriptive models or classifications based on similarity, functioning, structure, size, origin, and so on.

- Studies of personality traits have a long history in philosophy, the humanities, and early psychological studies.

- Allport argued that "character" and "personality" were distinct and different entities. He identified 17,953 unique terms used to describe the individual's personality, behavior, feelings, and so on. Next, they separated these into four categories (or columns), based on their own criteria for classification. Allport also presented personality traits as cardinal, central, and secondary.

- Cattell used factor analysis—a method to deal with large numbers of observed variables that are thought to reflect a smaller number of underlying variables. To apply factor analysis to personality, Cattell used three kinds of data: life, experimental, and questionnaire-based. Cattell developed a test known as the Sixteen Personality Factor Questionnaire (16PF) to measure these personality features. This self-report method was revised at least four times, translated into several languages, and adopted for use in many countries.

- Eysenck used empirical data and factor-analytic research to design and develop his theory. He emphasized two major personality dimensions: extroversion and neuroticism. Psychologists frequently refer to these dimensions as Eysenck's E and N. Later on in his career, Eysenck added another dimension to his model of the individual's personality. He called in psychoticism.

- The Big Five is a five-factor structure of personality traits that appears in most studies in different countries. The traits can be labeled *openness, conscientiousness, extroversion, agreeableness,* and *neuroticism.* As far as this theory goes, other individual traits are likely to fall within these five. All five factors are not dichotomous but rather continuous.

- The five-factor theory has received significant empirical support. Studies have been conducted on various groups and in more than 50 countries. Twin studies suggest that heritability and environmental factors both influence all five factors to approximately the same degree.

- Studies in the fields of humanities reveal that written and other forms of knowledge contain detailed descriptions of desirable and undesirable individual traits and types as well as cultural and political prescriptions to develop some and avoid having other traits.

- Trait theories find applications in many practical fields, including assessment for employment, dating services, political behavior and elections, and criminal behavior, to name a few.

VISUAL REVIEW

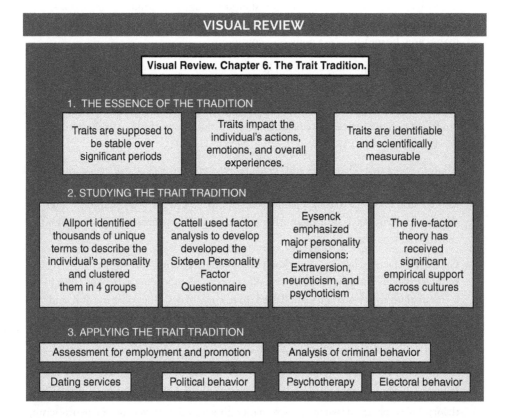

Visual Review. Chapter 6. The Trait Tradition.

1. THE ESSENCE OF THE TRADITION

Traits are supposed to be stable over significant periods

Traits impact the individual's actions, emotions, and overall experiences.

Traits are identifiable and scientifically measurable

2. STUDYING THE TRAIT TRADITION

Allport identified thousands of unique terms to describe the individual's personality and clustered them in 4 groups

Cattell used factor analysis to develop developed the Sixteen Personality Factor Questionnaire

Eysenck emphasized major personality dimensions: Extraversion, neuroticism, and psychoticism

The five-factor theory has received significant empirical support across cultures

3. APPLYING THE TRAIT TRADITION

Assessment for employment and promotion

Analysis of criminal behavior

Dating services

Political behavior

Psychotherapy

Electoral behavior

KEY TERMS

16PF
absentmindedness
atavism
Big Five
confident arrogance
extroversion (E)
Eysenk's E and N
genotypes

lack of control
neuroticism (N)
phenotypes
psychoticism
sensation seeking
taxonomies
traits

EVALUATING WHAT YOU KNOW

What is the trait tradition about?

What are common principles or general expectations that psychologists working within this tradition share?

Describe the major ideas of the studies into personality by Gordon Allport, Raymond Cattell, and Hans Eysenck.

Describe the main idea of the Big Five approach.

How do the humanities approach the individual's traits?

Explain the main idea of the cross-cultural approach to the individual's traits.

Explain several areas of applications of the trait domain, including marriage, employment, politics, criminal behavior, and others.

A BRIDGE TO THE NEXT CHAPTER

Perhaps the biggest strength of trait theory is that it's fairly understandable and straightforward. It appears unambiguous and finds support among practitioners around the globe. Trait theories usually rely on significant and comprehensive data, as well as statistical analysis. In contrast, as you remember, psychoanalysts relied mostly on personal interpretation of subjective factors. The subjective experiences of the theorists affect the theory.

Trait researchers know that many unanswered questions still remain. For example, people do not always act according to their traits. Next, trait theories do not say enough about how our traits develop and change. It is still a challenge to understand how traits change and how people adjust their traits to face and address big and small challenges in their lives. We need to know more about this to help people strengthen their "positive" traits and correct the "negative" ones. Is this possible?

Finally, there is the big issue of self-reporting. If the trait theories we have studied on these pages claim they are "objective," why did they rely on "subjective" self-reporting? Are we as individuals to remain the best interpreters of our own behaviors and traits? And if we are not, who can judge the process of our experience and self-reflection?

The next chapter will discuss this "subjective" factor in personality psychology and the importance of the cognitive factors in studying personality.

7 THE COGNITIVE TRADITION

Martin Puddy/Photonica/Getty Images

After reading this chapter, you should be able to do the following:

- Identify and explain the main features of the cognitive tradition in the study of personality.

- Critically describe attitudes, the self, constructs, and self-esteem as key cognitive features of the individual.

- Apply the key principles of cognitive tradition to individual behavior.

Are you a wise person? How do you know? Can you make a judgment about how wise you are or is this totally "in the eye of the beholder"? Most importantly, do you want to get wiser? There is no shortage of online instructions, videos, questionnaires, and even seminars promising to measure how wise you are and promising to get you wiser. For starters, it probably won't be wise to rush and check them out without first clarifying what wisdom is.

Wisdom has many definitions, but most of them point out the ability to feel, judge, and act based on reason, common sense, vast knowledge, and ethics. It is different from intelligence, which is mostly about the efficiency of mental operations leading to successful results. Wisdom is likely to be about impartiality, balance, and moderation. There is a difference between "acting wise" and "being wise." The difference is not necessarily pure semantic. Wisdom can be a state of your mind, emotions, and behavior in a single situation or during a short period. It also can be a "trait," a feature that is stable, long-lasting, and cross-situational.

Psychologists associate with wisdom cognitive processes like accepting uncertainty, accepting the inevitability of change, understanding own limitations, or seeing things in perspective. Some definitions of wisdom appear timeless and universal. Others are evolving as a response to historical, political, and cultural changes. Therefore, it has been a long-lasting opinion among psychologists that empirical research of wisdom was too vague to pursue it.

Canadian psychologist Igor Grossman disagreed. His experimental research of wisdom produced interesting and promising results. For example, according to his model, wisdom is expectedly correlated with high scores on recognizing own intellectual limitations (intellectual humility), recognizing uncertainty, striving for compromise, and taking the perspective of others. To improve these scores, Grossman, among other methods, suggests practicing illeism: referring to self in the third person, not of first person. Try this method in class or individually. For the sake of learning experience or curiosity, set up a discussion and deliberately try to refer to self as "he," or "she," or "they." Practice this method alone when you are thinking about a challenging problem or personal conflict. Will these exercises help you understand self and others better and make better decisions?

By the way, high scores on the "wisdom scale" are found to be fine predictors of emotional well-being and relationship satisfaction. If only for these, wisdom is worth practicing.

Sources: Grossman, 2017; Robinson, 2022

THE PSYCHOLOGY ROOTS OF THE COGNITIVE TRADITION

The word *cognitive* refers to cognition, which relates to senses, experience, and thought. In the middle of the 20th century, psychology as a discipline was under the significant influence of psychoanalysis and behaviorism. Then it underwent a substantial change in its course called the **cognitive revolution**. This was a gradual yet major shift of focus within university psychology from being primarily behavioral to being increasingly cognitive—that is, increasingly studying the work of the mind. Of course, the term *revolution* is used as a convenient label here to describe several decades of studies in psychology as a discipline. Personality psychology also began paying more attention to cognitive processes.

In cognitive theory, behavior is generally explained as guided by cognitions (e.g., memories, reflections, understandings, and expectations) about the world, other people, and the self. Cognitive theories of personality emphasize cognitive processes, such as thinking, imagining, and judging. It is about the functioning of an individual experience. It is about many experiences.

The cognitive revolution, of course, had its roots and causes. Psychology's great scholars—from its early days as a research discipline in the 19th century—tried to find a way to measure the ever-elusive "internal" mechanisms of the mental life of individuals. Psychologists wanted to measure mental life like physicists and chemists can measure molecules and electromagnetic fields; quantifying or explaining in precise terms the inner experience of a person seemed an intriguing and rewarding task.

PHOTO 7.1 Supporters of experimental introspection believed in a scientific measurement of inner experiences, such as sensations. Yet can we measure the subjective side of our personalities?

©iStockphoto.com / tizkes

An Era of Introspection

The founders of experimental psychology used the methods of **experimental introspection** by asking subjects to focus on their personal reflections and then relate them to outside signals. A subject (in the 19th century, it was most likely a male student or professor) was usually asked to rate his experiences on a 1- to 10-point scale while looking at a light or listening to a sound within a dark research lab. The subject rated his experiences based on their quality, intensity, or duration.

It seemed to researchers that introspection had brought them a sense of validity to their experimental studies. Psychologists believed that by studying mental elements such as sensations and feelings they would collect enough data to examine many sophisticated mental acts, such as thinking, memory, decision-making, and even some lasting emotional states. It also appeared that using experimental introspection to examine immediate experiences by breaking them up into mental elements, such as feelings and sensations, would help in studying complex psychological processes and long-term states such as pride and envy or even some personality traits, like will power.

Although the hope was that self-reported assessment numbers and mathematical formulas to interpret them would be suitable to describe the mind's action, they failed to provide sufficient and reliable information about the mind's work. Such assessments were imprecise and subjective.

Studying the Self

Psychologists understood the limitations of introspection. Some of them turned to the subjective side of the individual—or the self—from a different angle. One such psychologist was Mary Calkins (1863–1930), the first female president of the American Psychological Association. She maintained that psychology was supposed to become the science of "selves" (Calkins, 1906), closely related to its environment, both physical and social. Calkins's self-psychology had three founding concepts: (1) the self, (2) the object, and (3) the self's relation or attitude toward that object.

She described the self on two levels: The first is contents of consciousness, and the second is the environment in which the content unfolds. As an illustration, an individual's direct experiences appear as a conscious process of sharing this experience of several other "selves" that are attached to memories, imagination, anticipation, etc. Calkins's view of the self generally reflected a Western cultural tradition that usually connects the self with the environment. Observation and reflection usually function together. This approach is different from those common in Indian philosophical traditions in which the psychological act of reflection (as opposed to observation) is about the removal of all sensory content to access a person's inner consciousness (Rao et al., 2008).

The Gestalt Tradition

Behaviorism (see Chapter 5) has been a mainstream orientation in Western psychology for many decades since the beginning of the 20th century. Nevertheless, studies of the "subjective" element of the individual's life have never stopped. The Gestalt tradition in psychology developed by the European psychologists Max Wertheimer, Wolfgang Köhler, Kurt Koffka, and others advanced the experimental study of individual experience (Mandler, 2007). The main thesis taught in German universities in the first quarter of the 20th century was that an individual's experience consists of unrelated inert elements. The mind, from the traditional view, was a builder that collects multiple elements of experience and puts them together in an organized fashion under the laws of association (Köhler, 1959). Gestalt psychologists challenged this view and showed in their experimental research that it is not the elements but the integrated and constant patterns, or "wholes," that are likely to be the fundamental features of our psychological experience. A psychologist trained in the 19th century was likely to report this looking at a portrait: "I perceive a pattern of sensations that is occurring because I am engaged in the act of perception of a child's face." Now, a Gestalt psychologist would likely put it very simply: "I see a child."

Gestalt ideas were a significant departure from the ideas of the traditional psychology of perception. Subsequently, supporters of Gestalt psychology applied its principles to thinking, learning, making decisions, and behavior in general. This was an important step in the development of personality psychology—it meant that our subjective "self" was not necessarily a bunch of elements bundled together. Instead, our inner world is a whole, or a coherent system with its own inner logic that interconnects all these elements. The challenge for psychologists was to understand this inner logic.

Gestalt theory had an initial impact on **Gestalt therapy**, a theoretical and practical field in clinical psychology. Gestalt therapy uses the ideas about the holistic nature of human experience, the disruption of its structure, and the emphasis on the actuality of the moment (Perls et al., 1951). One of the founders of this method was Fritz Perls (1883–1970), a German American doctor who escaped from Germany in 1933. Borrowing from the classic Gestalt theory, he proposed that individual's experience is a dynamic summary that reflects needs, hopes, strengths, and weaknesses. Both satisfied and unsatisfied needs interact as "figures" and "grounds" of perceptual experience. Psychological problems arise when the form and structure of this interaction process are distorted. Gestalt therapy focuses more on the process of individuals' experience than on its content—that is, the emphasis is on what is being felt now rather than on memories (Perls, 1968). To summarize,

Gestalt therapy focuses on a here-and-now method (how are you feeling now?), embracing immediate experiences rather than recollections. Gestalt therapists promote the necessity of people heightening their awareness of themselves and exploring their needs (Levine, 2011).

Field Theory

Kurt Lewin (1890–1947) was one of the most prominent German American psychologists whose research legacy is constantly reevaluated (Foschi & Lombardo, 2006). His **field theory** has been a noteworthy contribution to personality psychology (Lewin, 1943). According to field theory, the acting and thinking individual lives in a dynamic field of interdependent forces. Life appears as a giant diagram with opposing forces, energy fields, obstacles, goals, conflicting interests, supportive aids, and obstructive opponents. To understand or predict someone's behavior (Lewin labeled it B), the researcher must understand the psychological, cognitive state of a person (labeled P) and of the psychological environment (E). In this system, P and E are interdependent variables. Behavior becomes a function (labeled f) of an individual's personality characteristics and of specific environmental or situational conditions.

$$B = f(P, E)$$

Field theory holds that an individual's choices depend on the characteristics of the present field at a particular moment. An individual's goals and past experiences all fit into the field characteristics of the moment. To describe the field, Lewin introduced terms such as *life space, field, existence, locomotion, force, valence, goal, conflict, interdependence*, and many others (Lewin, 1944). Many psychologists, as you can see, attempted to quantify human behavior and experience, following the approaches and methods of basic sciences.

In field theory, the individual becomes a calculating, conscious organism that constantly evaluates the options available now and reevaluates new options available next. Field theory assumed that if the psychologist understands most of the variables surrounding the individual and considers most of this individual's rational calculations, then psychologists can have an effective explanatory model of the individual. The problem, of course, is that functioning in the world of reality, we don't understand how many variables affect us every second. In addition, everyone's style of responses depends on a greater variety of other inner variables, rational and not, such as thoughts, expectations, beliefs, fears, prejudice, attraction, and so on.

Lewin was also an author and coauthor of studies of **level of aspiration**, or the degree of difficulty of the goal toward which a person is striving. Whether or not a person will become successful is deeply influenced by that person's wish to aspire. In most cases, a person's history of successes and failures determines a particular level of aspiration. In turn, they influence the expectation for the outcome of the future action and increase or decrease the level of aspiration accordingly (Lewin, 1942). For example, good students, in general, tend to keep their level of aspiration slightly above their past achievement, while less successful students tend to show excessively high or very low levels of aspiration—that is, ineffective students have not learned to be realistic in evaluating their past achievements and failures and today's opportunities. Today, studies of aspiration, its importance, and its impact on educational and professional success are conducted in many countries (Kim et al., 2016)

What was specifically innovative in the new wave of research within the cognitive tradition in the 20th century and after? What was its impact on personality psychology? Let's first examine a few principles of this tradition. Next, we will consider cognitive psychology in the context of a larger field of cognitive science. After that, we will turn to the specific discussions within the cognitive tradition in personality psychology.

COGNITIVE SCIENCE

Several great scholarly minds working in various fields of science contributed to the development of the cognitive tradition in psychology. The American professor George Miller (1920–2012) was one of them. In 1960, Miller and his colleagues founded the Center for Cognitive Studies at Harvard University. This was also the year when George Miller, Eugene Galanter, and Karl Pribram published their groundbreaking work *Plans and the Structure of Behavior* (1960). In this book, the authors explained the key principles of their approach to psychology. At least four of these principles are important for personality psychology.

First, anything we refer to as "mental" (which is traditionally viewed as subjective, even immeasurable) should be studied from the standpoint of information, which is measurable (Miller et al., 1960). While many psychologists underlined the importance of traditional variables—such as behavioral habits, traits, learning principles, unconscious motivation, or complex biochemical mechanisms—to explain the individual, Miller and colleagues turned to information processing, which is the exchange of information in any way detectable by an observer. Consider the trait *openness to experience*, for example. According to the cognitive approach, this should be understood as a quantifiable, or measurable, amount of information that an individual receives, stores, and processes.

Second, Miller and colleagues (1960) believed that individuals should be understood as extremely complex computing devices. If the nature of all mental aspects of our lives is information processing, then human beings should be natural processors of such information. If we know how machines process information, then by analogy, according to Miller, we could use this knowledge to understand the work of the individual's mind.

According to the third principle, understanding personality is like understanding computers: Computers conduct operations based on a set of instructions or programs, so if there is no program, there is no corresponding operation. The program compels the device's every operation in solving a particular problem or performing a task. When programming instructions change, the operations change accordingly. In general terms, every operation of the device refers to an underlying program, or a set of commands. Therefore, applying this analogy to personality, we can propose that every element of behavior—any thought, emotion, or trait—can be explained as information processing based on a set of specific instructions or programs.

Fourth, such instructions underlying the work of the mind are very sophisticated and part of a multilevel plan, or long chain of operations. Each operation can be described as either *action* or *inaction*. Every psychological phenomenon—such as an act of thinking or an aggressive act, for example—is a complex process, giving individuals special tools to control the schedule according to which chain of operations takes place.

CHECK AND APPLY YOUR KNOWLEDGE

1. What was the cognitive revolution?
2. Explain experimental introspection.
3. How does Gestalt therapy refer to the individual's cognition?
4. Explain field theory.
5. What is your level of aspiration: high, moderate, or low? Would you like to change your level of aspiration and why?

PSYCHOLOGY AND COGNITIVE SCIENCE

Cognitive psychology belongs to the line of research that is commonly regarded today as part of an interdisciplinary field of **cognitive science**. This vast field includes studies in many areas, particularly cognitive neuroscience, computer science, philosophy, and linguistics, among others. To better understand cognitive psychology and the cognitive tradition to study personality, let's briefly examine some key studies involved in the early development of cognitive science.

Cognitive Neuroscience

As an academic field, cognitive neuroscience examines the brain mechanisms that support mental functions (we also reviewed this field in Chapter 2). At least

Antoine Taveneaux / CC BY-SA 3.0

PHOTO 7.2 Alan Turing believed it would be possible in the future to mathematically describe and simulate virtually all operations taking place in a person's brain.

three areas of study should be mentioned. The first is experimental research in neurophysiology conducted in university- and hospital-based laboratories. Next, is research into the brain's pathology. Finally, rapidly developing methods of brain imaging provide cognitive neuroscientists with remarkable new facts. By examining the location of neural activation generated by a cognitive task, researchers can learn more about the brain's role in the processes in thinking, emotions, and decision-making. Take free will, for example—historically, whether we have free will was a question philosophers examined. However, contemporary studies see free will as the result of special electrical activity in the brain—that is, "background noise," or patterns of brain activities that can be detected before a person makes a "freewill" decision. In other words, a person's brain seems to commit to certain decisions *before* the person becomes aware of having made them (Bengson et al., 2014). For instance, at this very moment you may believe you can think about anything you want, yet it appears that a new thought or one you want to bring back at this moment has already been determined by a set of random activities in the brain. It may be that our conscious "self" gets involved at a later stage, not at the beginning of the decision-making process (Roskies, 2010; Smith, 2011). Conscious awareness about an intention to act, in other words, probably comes after specific neural activities have already begun in the brain (Soon et al., 2013).

Computer Science

After the advent of computers in the 1950s, for psychologists the most important assumption of the rapidly developing new discipline called *computer science* was that computers and human beings process information similarly. In a way, computer science represents a computational approach to psychology. One of the most prominent pioneers of the computational approach was the British scientist Alan Turing (1912–1954). Science historians agree that Turing's work was the theoretical and practical basis of the development of computer science (Hodges, 1983).

Turing's theoretical quests and remarkable practical accomplishments convinced him that human judgment, or the sophisticated work of the mind, could be explained with absolute certainty from the standpoint of mathematics and logic. Although he was not a psychologist, several of Turing's ideas were essential to the young field of cognitive psychology (Turing, 1950; Weizenbaum, 1976). What were these fundamental ideas?

First, Turing put forth that the brain must use information from a variety of sources inside and outside the body to operate. The brain then must store this information. A crucial point here is that this information is not as infinite or incalculable as it may appear; it is limited and measurable (Turing, 1950).

Second, the brain uses this information to solve problems. Therefore, mental functions can be viewed as problem-solving operations, programs, or procedures. If the information is finite and measurable, Turing proposed, then every problem the brain solves using this information is essentially mathematical.

Next, according to Turing, each problem-solving method is based on a particular rule or algorithm. Each algorithm can be viewed as a computable operation. All mental operations are computable, and computable operations should be sufficient to explain all mental functions the brain performs (Turing, 1950).

Turing believed that if these assumptions were correct then computer science could provide new insights into the mechanisms of the central nervous system. Sometime in the future, he thought, it would be possible to mathematically describe and simulate virtually all operations taking place in a person's brain. It also occurred to him that if problem-solving was a computable operation, such operations should be available for a machine only if it was given a sufficient algorithm—ultimately, he was proposing a machine capable of thinking. Today, researchers and philosophers ponder whether we can create an artificial, digital personality. We will discuss this in Chapter 13.

Philosophy and Consciousness

In addition to computer science, cognitive psychology secured another source of knowledge and inspiration. It was philosophy. As you remember, since the end of the 19th century, experiment-oriented scientists representing a "new" psychology had pursued a peaceful separation with philosophy. For a number of years, experimental and then, to a large degree, mainstream psychology ignored and avoided philosophical discussions about the activities of the rational mind and the awesome power of human will. The situation started to change in the 1950s, when psychology as an experimental discipline became more confident and secure. One of the most difficult questions coming from the philosophers was, *How exactly do neurobiological processes in the brain result in consciousness?* Now, supported by neuroscience and computer science, philosophers turned again to a holistic perspective on the functioning of the mind. There is a view believed that an individual's consciousness could be studied perfectly by physics or biology. Above all, consciousness is a biological phenomenon. However, it has some important and unique features that cannot be understood by biology alone. The most important of these features is "subjectivity." Searle used a specific example to demonstrate subjectivity. If somebody asked him what it feels like to give a lecture in front of a large audience, he could answer that question. But if somebody asked what it feels like to be a stone, there is no answer to that question because stones are not conscious. At least two crucial relationships between consciousness and the brain can be established. First, lower level neuronal processes in the brain cause consciousness. Second, consciousness is simply a higher level feature of the system that is made up of lower level neuronal elements (Searle, 1992, 1998).

Further Studies

Further research into the fields of memory, decision-making, and thinking inspired psychologists' work on theories and practical applications that were then widely used in schools, universities, business selection, job training, design, psychological counseling, and rehabilitation therapy, among others. New facts were obtained in the areas, such as the impact of aging on general cognitive functions, the effectiveness of cognitive and motor rehabilitation after illness or injury, eyewitness memory in testimony, or decision-making in engineering and driving. Applied cognitive psychology is perhaps one of the fastest growing fields in global psychology today.

At the same time, critics emphasized that cognitive psychologists were turning to computer science but losing psychology. Critics also maintained that cognitive psychology did not pay enough attention to emotion and motivation. Therefore, studying personality, many psychologists turned to the symbolic activities that human beings employed in constructing and making sense of the world and themselves, especially to the issues involving ultimate "human" attributes of people's existence and experience: attitudes, ideals, moral choices, and values.

STUDIES OF ATTITUDES

An individual's personality can be viewed from the standpoint of **attitudes**, which are the cognitive representations and evaluations of various features of the social and physical world. The study of attitudes gained significant popularity and research support in psychology and social psychology, especially from the second half of the past century. Attitudes are the psychological links, or associations between various cognitive images and their evaluations (Fazio et al.,

2000). Attitudes are based on personal experience. An individual's memory retains a particular image along with its positive, negative, or ambivalent appraisal.

Attitudes are not directly observable. Therefore, any description of attitude is an act of creative imagination. The question is *How do we bring measurable variables to the study of attitudes?* Consider physics. We cannot see electricity, but we can observe its effects by turning the lights on in your room. The same is true with attitudes: Although we do not visibly see attitudes, we can judge them from people's behavior, their verbal or written responses, as well as infer them by means of experimental procedures. An individual's personality can be described based on what this person says and does. Unlike in the trait tradition, psychologists who study attitudes are interested in describing psychological "types" based on complex and interconnected features and traits. They turn to the mechanisms that "connect" and "separate" attitudes and the ways by which attitudes regulate individual judgment and behavior (Brinol et al., 2019).

It is assumed, based on the long tradition in psychology, that there are two general features or components of attitudes: cognitive and affective.

1. *The cognitive component*: This is characterized by an individual's knowledge about a certain object, person (for instance, a fiancé, a presidential candidate), or issue (such as raising speed limits on the interstate), including learned facts, experiences, and assumptions about various aspects of reality.

2. *The affective component*: Often known as the emotional component, this is an evaluation of an object or issue linked to one or several basic human emotions, such as joy, fear, disgust, sadness, anger, and surprise. In general, the emotional component may not be only a dichotomous "positive-or-negative" evaluation of a particular object. Ambivalence, or presence of both positive and negative valuations, may coexist in many attitudes (Lavine et al., 2000). Both emotional and cognitive components are likely to affect the individual's behavioral readiness to act in a certain way with respect to an object or issue under evaluation (Allport, 1935).

An attitude can be measured on a scale as being "weak" or "strong." Strong attitudes are enforced by the emotional-cognitive links that are based on a substantial amount of knowledge and reinforced by a sound emotional commitment to an object or issue the individual evaluates (Kallgren & Wood, 1986) and are likely to influence individuals' behavior. For example, industrious behavior and traits are linked to the strong attitude and knowledge about how to be an organized, conscientious, and effective professional and a desire to be or become one. Weak attitudes tend to change because the emotional-cognitive connection is weak, and they are not based on important knowledge or a strong emotional commitment. For example, "I don't like carbonated drinks, but I will take one now."

Cognitive processes such as perception, memory, recognition, and decision-making play a critical role in attitude formation and expression. People's attitudes depend on the presence of other attitudes and specific cognitive mechanisms by which individuals receive, understand, and interpret the incoming facts. The studies in attitude accessibility, balance, and dissonance should help us understand this tradition better.

Attitude Accessibility

Individuals can easily access some of their attitudes while others make an effort to retrieve. Think about your life: Certain facts and their evaluations are easily retrievable from your memory. For example, "Do you like your major?" Other facts and their assessments are not as easy to access if you can access them at all. Several reasons have been studied. The first is the frequency of the attitude's expression (Fazio, 1989). Research showed that if someone has a chance to explain or defend an attitude, it should be more easily accessible from memory in the future (Boninger et. al., 1995). Attitudes that are more accessible are more likely to be expressed and more likely to affect behavior than attitudes that are less accessible (Roese & Olson, 1994; Snyder & Swann, 1978). In addition, people are less likely to hold onto attitudes that are accessible to them if these attitudes conflict with the individual's other attitudes.

An attitude becomes more accessible if it contains a strong emotional evaluation of an issue—either positive or negative—but not both (Bizer & Krosnik, 2001). Attitudes with a single composition of the affective component are called **single-evaluation attitudes**. Attitudes that contain an ambivalent emotional component are called **dual-evaluation attitudes**. If you develop a dual-evaluation attitude, the process of responding to a question should require the integration of positive and negative evaluations. Thus, the process of retrieving ambivalent components should be more time-consuming and requires a greater cognitive effort than a single-evaluation attitude. Therefore, as research showed, ambivalent attitudes are usually less accessible than single evaluation attitudes (Lavine et al., 2000).

Attitude Balance

The ideas of Gestalt psychology described earlier made a distinct impact on the research of an individual's attitudes. One of these ideas was that people need a balanced, noncontradictory, and consistent view of the world around them. Fritz Heider (1896–1988), an Austrian-born American psychologist, was among the first to demonstrate that people seek consistency among their judgments. They do not necessarily do this deliberately; rather, it is the nature of human experience to be "balanced" (Heider, 1944, 1958). To maintain their perception in "good form," people tend to seek explanations for their judgments, thus creating perceptual distortions. For example, if Person A has a good friend (Person B) and they both have a good opinion of a third individual (Person C), this situation is balanced because there is no tension or contradiction between Person A's attitudes. However, if Person A and Person B like each other but they have different views of Person C, this creates tension, or a lack of balance, in Person A's attitudes. Person A must now bring the attitudes to a balanced state: Two people who like each other are supposed to see things in similar ways or, if they do not, they should like each other less. In general, a balanced cognitive system is one in which individuals agree with people they like or differ with people they dislike. This theory also proposes that we attach a greater value to things we like and lesser value to anything we dislike (Davison & Thomson, 1980; Pratkanis, 1988).

Cross-cultural research demonstrated that cognitive consistency varied across cultures. For instance, in the United States, people, on the average, are more concerned about the consistency of their attitudes than individuals in Japan, where the ability to handle inconsistency is considered a sign of maturity (Shiraev & Levy, 2024). In traditional Islamic communities, being consistent in one's religious attitudes requires a more complex behavioral reaction than the religious behavior of people in other societies. For instance, such consistency requires regularity of prayers, abstention from alcohol, paying of Islamic taxes, and following the suggestions of religious leaders (Moghaddam, 1998, 2019). This variance in cognitive consistency across cultures is likely positively linked to various cultures' level of uncertainty avoidance (see Chapter 1). Cross-cultural research overall shows that cultural contexts make an impact on how people balance their attitudes (Baker & Carson, 2012).

Attitude Dissonance

The idea that an individual is supposed to maintain a cohesive, noncontradictory view of the self and of the world was further developed in the studies of the American psychologist Leon Festinger (1919–1989), the author of the theory of **cognitive dissonance**, which is one of the most recognizable theories in psychology. The term refers to an unpleasant psychological state experienced by an individual who performs an action that is contradictory to his beliefs and ideas or is confronted by new information that conflicts with his beliefs or ideas. Festinger maintained that people tend to experience tension, an unpleasant emotional state, caused by the perceived mismatch (dissonance) between the following:

- Their judgments (or two elements of knowledge, two facts)—for example, "I like this person, but I have been told that she had lied to me on several occasions."

- Their judgment and behavior—for example, "I know I have promised to study for the test today, but I have also promised my parents to spend some time with them on Zoom now."

Whenever an individual must decide between two or more alternatives, the final choice is likely to be inconsistent and contradict some of this person's attitudes or previous decisions (Should I forgive and ignore my friend's lying? Should I conveniently "forget" about a promise I made?). This inconsistency generates dissonance (Festinger, 1957). Because this is an unpleasant state, to avoid it and to reduce or eliminate the tension, people have several choices. They can change their judgments to bring them back to harmony, they can modify their behavior somehow so that there is no longer an unpleasant dilemma, or they can avoid the unpleasant information or address their dissonance (Festinger et al., 1956). This theory generated significant research and found many applications, especially in psychotherapy, marketing, and electoral campaigning.

Why do most people strive to balance their attitudes and behavior and avoid dissonance? The main motive is to avoid unpleasant emotions caused by cognitive tensions. A simple, harmonious, consistent, and meaningful view on issues is normally free of tensions. To achieve a harmonious view, people tend to use the **least-effort principle**: They minimize the number of cognitive operations to reach a goal. In other words, "bad" people are supposed to do bad things, while "good" people are most likely to do good things. If you have developed a set of beliefs about the world that is mean and unfair, you are likely to interpret most of the events around you from a pessimistic standpoint. The facts that contradict our attitudes are ignored, critically dismissed, or outright rejected (see Figure 7.1).

Studies indicate different cultural values trigger different expressions of cognitive dissonance. Individuals in predominantly individualistic cultures in Western countries tend to experience dissonance when their behavior violates either a personal or a social standard. Meanwhile, people in predominantly collectivistic cultures, are much more concerned about violating social standards, out of fear of challenging social harmony, and thus being rejected by others (Boucher et al., 2009).

Attribution

Every second, something happens around us, and every second, people around us make decisions, judge, and act. Most people tend to explain other people's behavior in a consistent way. This assumption is common in the cognitive tradition. Consistency is also an important adaptive function: We have to make sense of this world and explain most things that are relevant to us. We do this through **attribution**, or the process by which individuals explain the causes of behavior and events. Attribution involves an act of judgment, so the attribution approach shows from a particular angle how we explain the world and other people's actions. The UCLA psychologist Harold Kelly (1921–2003) showed in his research that people use attribution in a rational, logical fashion, and they assign the cause of an action to the factor that is connected (or appears connected) most closely with that action.

FIGURE 7.1 ■ A Case Explaining Cognitive Dissonance

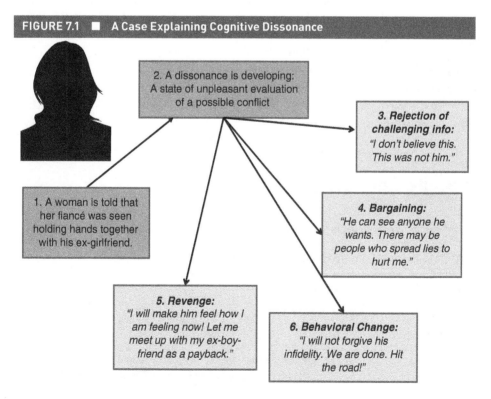

Kelley's (1967, 1979) research showed that people judge other people's behavior from at least three standpoints. The first one is consistency. Imagine that your professor expresses anger and disappointment when students come late to class. How do we explain this reaction? We ask the question *How frequent is this professor's behavior observed with a similar stimulus (such as when someone is late) but in different situations?* The second is distinctiveness, for which we ask *How does the individual respond to different stimuli?* For example, you observe this professor in different situations during the day, at the cafeteria, or in the parking lot, and in those situations, you find that this professor is mostly outgoing, cordial, and pleasant. And the third is consensus for which we ask *Do most professors express anger and disappointment when students come late to their class?*

People usually attribute their actions either to their personality or to their circumstances. They are called *dispositional attributions* or *situational attributions*. Dispositional attributions involve explaining the causes of behavior to people's personality traits, characteristics, or attitudes, that is, to "internal" influences. Situational attributions, in contrast, involve assigning the causes of behavior to people's circumstances or surroundings, that is, to "external" influences. In arriving at causal attributions, we tend to overestimate people's dispositions and to underestimate their situations. In other words, we are prone to weigh internal determinants too heavily and external determinants too lightly. We are likely to explain the behavior of others as resulting predominantly from their personality, while we tend to minimize the importance of the context or situation. This mistake is so prevalent, in fact, that social psychologist Ross (1977) termed it the **fundamental attribution error.**

The fundamental attribution error can explain why some people often blame other people for situations over which they usually have no or little control. The term "blaming the victim" is used by social psychologists to describe a phenomenon, in which people blame innocent victims of crimes for what happened to them (Felson & Palmore, 2018). To take another example, consider the dilemma of the homeless. Some people are prone to explain a homeless person's condition in terms of personality factors, such as laziness, moral weakness, drug abuse, or mental illness. These attributions, however, fail to consider the situational factors that perpetuate homelessness, such as a lack of affordable housing, job scarcity, discrimination, and economic difficulties.

CHECK AND APPLY YOUR KNOWLEDGE

1. Describe the three fields of cognitive science. What are their impacts on personality psychology?
2. What are dual-evaluation attitudes?
3. Explain the fundamental attribution error. Give examples.
4. Consider the following example: A man walks into a bar and sees a beautiful woman smiling at him. How does the man attribute her behavior? Does it mean she likes him? Or is it all in his mind? Research into this scenario has shown that, in general, men tend to misjudge a woman's romantic intent, particularly after a few drinks. Studies also show that a man's attachment style influences his attribution of a woman's interest. There are secure, anxious, and avoidant styles of attachment. Those higher in attachment anxiety have a need for love and reassurance and a fear of rejection. People

higher in attachment avoidance typically are reluctant to trust and rely on others, and they fear intimacy. Men on the higher end of the attachment anxiety spectrum are most likely to imagine a woman being romantically interested in them. Conversely, men higher in attachment avoidance felt the opposite (Hart et al., 2015). Explain the result of this study from the standpoint of cognitive balance or cognitive dissonance.

THE PERSONAL CONSTRUCTS APPROACH

Our inner world, the world of cognition, is an interconnected structure in which every element or function is attached to another element or function with a somewhat predictable connection. This means that certain ideas we have are likely to predict the existence of other ideas so that our inner world of experience is, in fact, a somewhat foreseeable or expectable system. To illustrate, the psychologists David Palermo and James Jenkins (1964) amassed a huge database of word associations, which are the first thoughts that come to mind when people are asked to comment on a specific word. The researchers discovered that most of these associations were extremely predictable. If we say one word, most people who fluently speak the same language are likely to respond with a certain word. For instance, when people are asked to free-associate about the word *blue*, the most likely first answer is *green*, followed by *sky* and *ocean*. When asked to free-associate about *green*, nearly everyone says *grass* (Lehrer, 2012). The same principle refers to more complex cognitive structures: We tend to assume what is coming next.

The American psychologist George Kelly (1905–1967) is one of the most recognized psychologists who combined the principles of cognitive psychology and applied psychotherapy to approach the individual personality. He believed that people, for the most part, can make reasonable and rational judgments. People design and use, like associations, cognitive constructs about themselves and the world around them. Constructs should provide a certain order, clarity, and prediction to a person's world. People then approach daily events and take steps as reasonable decision-makers. In fact, people can be seen as scientists of sorts. Although most of them do not apply the scientific method all the time to make their decisions, they still try to rely on evidence available to them and facts that they learn from other individuals. In fact, people are likely to be **naïve scientists**—individuals seeking rational and reasonable answers yet lacking scientific knowledge and critical judgment. This is how Kelly generalized about human beings (Kelly, 1963).

To make quick and hopefully correct judgments about the world, other people's behavior, and ourselves, we create a system of expectations, based on our own experiences and beliefs. In science, each hypothesis put together by the researcher is supposed to be carefully verified and scrutinized by independent peer reviewers. Yet because most of us are in actuality "naïve scientists," we tend to rely on our own reviews or on the reviews that are easily available to us. Very often we use the views and ideas that we simply like or with which we are comfortable.

As a clinical psychologist, Kelly (1955, 1963) maintained that we constantly engage in coping with the psychological stresses of our lives, using our judgments from previous experiences that we think should help us now. However, our past experiences often have very little to do with our current challenges and problems.

Yet how do individuals make sense of the world based on their constructs? Most of us pay attention to the words we use, and we tend to attach different meaning to these words based on the different experiences we have while learning these meanings. Recall from Chapter 3's discussion of studying the rules of critical thinking: One description of someone's behavior often means different things to different people. For example, consider the adjective "assertive" when referring to a person's individual traits. In some cases, and for some individuals, this adjective should represent people who are strong, decisive, and effective in their decisions. However, to another person, being assertive means being pushy, forceful, and even rude.

It is probably expected that we all have different views of the world and attach different meanings to words. What is especially important about human beings is that they tend to establish stable patterns of such assessments and use these patterns to judge small events, such as taking an exam, as well as significant developments, such as permanent relocation, marriage, or college graduation. In a certain way, people develop their own complex cognitive systems to filter the information about the world and make good judgments. Such systems or **constructs** are stable assumptions that the individual develops about other people, the self, and the world in general. Such assumptions tend to focus on two opposing sides of the spectrum. For example, if you believe that the world must be stable and predictable, you will want the world to be well-organized and "nice": Busses should arrive on time, people should not lie or steal things, and politicians should always deliver their promises. However, every day we often encounter a different world—one that is unstable, unpredictable, and unfair. Busses are late, people lie and cheat, and the world of politics is apparently getting nastier. As a result, we develop a dichotomous view of the world: One is the view about how the world should be, and the other is about the world that is. This construct is filled with frustration: We want to live in a "nice" world yet realize this is impossible to do.

These constructs affect the individual's life, and they may or may not be adaptive. If a construct can be successfully applied to a situation and it is useful at predicting events, then it is adaptive. Adaptive people are continually revising and updating their own constructs to match new information they encounter. All constructs are not used in every situation because they have a limited range of predicting power. To summarize, our world is cognitively constructed by the ways in which we anticipate events (Kelly's constructs are summarized in Table 7.1).

People use in their daily lives 11 common and interconnected types of significant, basic assumptions, or corollaries. The first assumption (construction) means that each one of us anticipates events in the future by perceiving a similarity with a past event. Events do not necessarily repeat themselves, yet we still construct something cognitively that allows us to perceive many events as similar: "I have seen people like this before! I can easily explain their behavior." Another option is the commonality corollary—we often make judgments simply because most people around us see them as "normal," "expected," and even "required." These choices affect our choice of lifestyle, friends, occupation, and faith, among others.

Most constructs are useful, and they help us adjust to the changing conditions of our world, yet there are "disordered constructs" in which the system of construction is not useful in predicting social events and fails to change to accommodate new information. If a person has many disordered constructs, then psychological and behavioral problems may be considered a mental illness. Kelly's **fixed-role therapy** was designed to change the individual's perception of self during a relatively short period. In a simple way, the person gives a self-description

TABLE 7.1 ■ George Kelly's Personal Constructs Approach to Personality	
Corollaries or Interconnected Assumptions	*Description of the Assumptions*
Construction	We assume, anticipate, and "construct" events that are supposed to happen based on our experience with past events.
Individuality	Each person constructs an internal model of external events, and those models differ from one person to another.
Organization	Each person develops a model or roadmap of external reality built upon their theories about external reality.
Dichotomy	The constructs that make up our personal maps of reality are paths between two polar opposites.
Choice	People "invest" in these constructs and are dependent on them; they will make choices that promise to develop the usefulness of these constructs.
Range	People establish a convenient zone within which the construct can be applicable.
Experience	People's construction systems change and develop as they successively construe the replication of events.
Modulation	Constructs are different in their ability to change people's circumstances.
Fragmentation	Constructs compete with one another. Each person may successively employ a variety of constructions that appear incompatible with each other.
Commonality	Most constructs are gathered through common learning in common situations. Individuals tend to share many common experiences.
Sociality	Interpersonal relationships matter. Together, people can change others' constructs.

while emphasizing problems. Then the psychologist rewrites this self-description but instead of focusing on negative characteristics and mistakes, emphasizes helpful behaviors and positive self-evaluations. The individual is then asked to perform a new role with new behaviors and perceptions (Maltby et al., 2013).

CULTURE AND THE SELF

The term self refers to the representation of one's identity or the subject of experience. People make distinctions between the world within them and the world outside. Both these internal and external worlds shape our self-perception in a variety of ways that can reflect the most prominent, individual characteristics of ourselves and the culture in which we live. We have been turning to various aspects of the self throughout the book. We will turn to this again in the later chapters, but now we will look at certain cultural aspects associated with the self.

Perceiving the Self

Our ability to recognize self or "I" as something separate from the environment and other individuals is called **self-awareness**. Self-awareness is similar yet different from consciousness, which is a state of awareness of your existence. Self-awareness is, in fact, a reflection of this awareness; it allows us to perceive our existence with a sense of consistency—you are likely to remain the same "you" when you wake up tomorrow, right? We also see ourselves with a sense of distinction—you are indeed different from other people!

Awareness can be viewed from two interconnected sides: private and social (public). Cross-cultural research on self-perception over the years showed distinctions between the "private" and "public" self (Benedict, 1946; Shiraev & Fillipov, 1990; Triandis, 1994). The private self indicates feelings and thoughts about oneself for oneself. The public self is the concept of self in relation to others for others. Research shows that many characteristics of self-perception are consistent across countries and cultures.

People from collectivistic cultures produce more group-centric (public) and fewer self-centric (private) descriptions of self than people from individualistic cultures. In collectivistic—and therefore more interdependent compared to the West—cultures (e.g., China, Japan, and South Korea), people tend to identify their self not as an independent entity but rather as part of particular social groups (Tafarodi, et al., 2004; Triandis, 1989, 1994). On the other hand, when U.S. subjects describe themselves, they tend to identify a greater number of individual traits—relatively unrelated to particular social groups.

In self-reports, online postings, and other communications, men tend to exaggerate their height—they prefer to appear taller (Cheryan & Markus, 2020). Women, on the other hand, tend to lower their weight. On online dating sites, people routinely portray themselves as taller, younger, more athletic, and healthier than they are (Levitt & Dubner, 2009). Similar tendencies, especially related to younger women, were found in South Korea (Park, 2019). Several studies showed that men also tend to overestimate their own intelligence level, while women tend to underestimate it (Furnham & Baguma, 1999; Furnham et al., 1999; Reilly et al., 2022).

The individual's identity is not formed at once. It is a long process that goes through childhood and continues into adulthood. (We will discuss some aspects of this process in Chapter 9 and Chapter 12.) We change in the way we see, understand, and evaluate ourselves due to the natural aging process, the social roles we have to follow, and the transitions we go through.

Self-Esteem

A person's general subjective evaluation, both emotional and rational, of his or her own worth is called **self-esteem**. There are findings that point to a correlation between individualism and collectivism on one hand and self-esteem on the other. Studies across 2 decades show that people in East Asia, such as Japan or China, tend to report lower self-esteem than do Westerners (Tafarodi et al., 2011; Tafarodi and Swann, 1996). Perhaps in icollectivistic cultures—which require sensitivity to the needs of others and subordination of personal goals to collective needs—it is expected that individuals develop self-liking. However, these cultures also promote restraints on feelings of self-competence due to high demands toward an individual's performance. In individualist cultures, on the contrary, independence and high self-esteem of the self are prioritized.

In fact, many studies conducted over the years have established lower self-esteem scores in East Asian countries compared to North America and Europe (Boucher et al., 2009; Brown & Cai, 2010). The findings do not suggest that Chinese, Japanese, or Korean individuals perceive themselves more negatively than their U.S. or Netherland counterparts. Rather, these lower scores are a form of expressed self-criticism, derived from a pervasive and complex cultural tradition of self-restraint. For example, the linguistic and behavioral emphasis in Japan on *kenson* (modesty) and *enryo* (reserve or restraint) lack analogous terms in Western culture. This emphasis constrains those who are Japanese from speaking or writing that which might be perceived as arrogant, presumptuous, or impudent (Tafarodi et al., 2011). More recent studies also show the stronger emphasis placed on the cultivation of positive self-esteem in Western cultures compared to non-Western cultures like those in East Asia particularly (Hamamura, 2017).

Culture and Identity

Our **social identity** refers to our perceived membership in one or several social groups. It is a fluid category: We change our professions and earn different incomes; we migrate. We are getting more accustomed to the idea that people can permanently change their physical characteristics, their religion, or their sex. Further, your answer to the question *Who am I?* may be different based on who asks it and when. We are aware of the contexts in which we speak and act. We also learn from the social sciences and the humanities that the (1) ability and (2) willingness to change your socially prescribed self—the way you identify yourself—is probably a relatively recent cultural development.

Just several hundred years ago, people faced significantly fewer choices for their social identity. Most of their roles were prescribed to them by society through strict custom and law. The Indian religious caste system, the feudal Japanese system, the European structure of the so-called *estates of the realm*, or sectarian and tribal divisions in Islam typically prescribed people by their social category at birth. In the past, most individuals were typically born into their social class. These "spots" were inherited and changes in social position, if possible, at all, occurred slowly (Huizinga, 1924/2013). For centuries, the predominant form of social organization in India was the caste system, which reinforced inequality and hierarchy among India's citizens. The caste system is formally outlawed, yet it continues in customs and beliefs, as it was mentioned earlier. Accordingly, Indians tended, at least in the past, to view themselves and their interpersonal relationships as more hierarchically structured than U.S. citizens (Sinha & Verma, 1983). A study conducted by Biswas and Pandey (1996) compared the self-perceptions of male members of three social groups in India. The respondents were asked to evaluate their quality of life, followed by which each respondent's answer was matched with his socioeconomic status. The researchers found that socioeconomic upward mobility—measured as an increase in income and occupational status—did not substantially affect the respondents' self-image or perception of their social status. In other words, a respondent may earn more money than he or she did several years ago, have a better job, and have a higher academic degree but still perceive her- or himself as a person of lower status. What can be concluded from these findings is that socioeconomic change alone did not necessarily bring about changes in the way people perceive themselves as members of higher and lower castes. One can comment that these studies were conducted some time ago and many changes must have taken place. However, more recent studies also revealed that status distancing and devaluation of others based on their caste has probably diminished, but not disappeared (Sindhuja et al., 2017). Because many societies are still divided along historical class, gender, ethnic, and caste lines, "older" identities may be more salient than "newer" ones, despite significant changes that have taken place in people's lives.

As an educated person living in the 21st century, you have a significantly wider scope of options for social self-identification. You can even invent and accept your own identity free from the most common social categories. Yet most people adapt to changes in response to economic and cultural globalization, though many people develop new self-perceptions based on old and "local" customs, ideas, and symbols, as well as new, cross-cultural ones (including new fashions, foods, leisure activities, and educational principles). However, for some people the process of change is more difficult than it is for others. The new values, norms, and behaviors may seem frightening and challenging when compared to old and "convenient" cultural images and norms.

There are people who feel excluded from both their local culture and the global culture, finding themselves belonging to neither (Arnett, 2002). Psychologists describe the phenomenon of **ethnic disidentification**—detaching an individual's self from the ethnic group with which they've been previously or currently associated. The reasons for such detachment range from misperceptions, concerns about being looked down by members of other groups, dissatisfaction with personal life, or practical consideration (David, 2013). In your view, what other factors and conditions (social and psychological) can trigger ethnic or national disidentification?

LITERATURE AND THE INNER WORLD

Artists create characters, or fictional images of human beings. Most writers are not scientists. However, just as artists do, they use words to describe either extraordinary (unusual or improbable) or ordinary (common, everyday) characters in extraordinary and ordinary circumstances (see Table 7.2). Poetry, literary novels, fairy tales can encourage us to think about the minds of others, and in turn might shed light on our own lives (Koriat & Ackerman, 2010). Extraordinary events and extraordinary characters are the most recognizable sources of knowledge about personality.

Heroes and villains defying social order have always been popular literary characters. From the Spanish playwright Miguel de Cervantes (1547–1616), you will experience Don Quixote, an ultimate idealist, a social misfit, and a hopeful dreamer driven by optimism, honesty, and

TABLE 7.2 ■ Characters in Different Circumstances: What They Convey About Personality Features		
Characters and Circumstances	**Extraordinary Situations**	**Ordinary Situations**
Extraordinary characters	Outstanding characters with amazing abilities who are searching, fighting, and rescuing in unusual situations	Outstanding characters in everyday situations facing the circumstances and challenges that the average person usually faces
Ordinary characters	Ordinary individuals placed in extraordinary situations and showing outstanding personality qualities	Average, "next door" individuals acting and thinking in a typical, average way in everyday situations

honor. In contrast, the Russian writer Dostoyevsky in *Crime and Punishment* (1866) created a remarkable character of a young man (Raskolnikov) who thinks of himself as a villain "superman" and whose actions must not be judged by moral rules.

Then listen and think to the rhyme and musical rhythms of the poetry written by Maya Angelou (1928–2014). Enrich your soul through learning about her love, loss, happiness, pain, and struggle. Next turn to the Colombian writer Gabriel García Márquez (1928–2014). His most famous novel, *One Hundred Years of Solitude* will guide you and the characters through several time dimensions. You will feel the past diminished into a single moment, and then the future becomes present and twisted in a mysterious way. Analyzing Marquez's work, you can find elements of Catholic traditions, Spanish cultural practices, and Native Indian beliefs.

Fairy tales produced by our ancestors from five continents—are all fine examples of the works in this genre—have been embedded in many people's vocabulary, memories, teachings, and daily associations. Just take one for starters: Scheherazade—a key female character of the Middle Eastern collection of fascinating tales about adventure, honor, intrigue, deception, and wit. The tales are called *One Thousand and One Nights*. Then reread *The Little Mermaid* and *The Steadfast Tin Soldier* by Hans Christian Andersen (1805–1875). Very few could write better about love and dedication.

Empower yourself when reading Jhumpa Lahiri (b. 1967) and her elegant but powerful stories about daily anxieties, victories, prejudices, and discoveries through which she conveys a narrative about the nuances of modern immigrant psychology and behavior. Then read the works by the Spanish playwright Lope de Vega (1562–1635). In his plays and essays, he reveals the complexity of human emotions and behaviors, mistakes in the pursuit of individual choices, and the power of human greed. And last, but not least, on this list is Kazuo Ishiguro (b. 1954). Begin with his *Remains of the Day*. A wonderful lesson about individual duty, the self, and the ideas upon which we often and faithfully build our lives.

CHECK AND APPLY YOUR KNOWLEDGE

1. Why did George Kelly call people "naïve scientists"?
2. What are Kelly's constructs, and how do they function? Think about and identify two or three constructs within your personality. Describe them.
3. Explain self-awareness and self-esteem. How would you describe your self-esteem? How does your self-esteem help you in dealing with your daily issues? Would you rather change your self-esteem or keep it as is? Why?
4. Extraordinary events and extraordinary characters are probably the most recognizable sources of knowledge about personality. Suggest a few of such characters that you think most other people should name as well. Discuss in class.
5. Name a book or a story that has had an impact on you and your understanding of other people. Discuss in class.

APPLYING THE COGNITIVE TRADITION

How does our knowledge within the cognitive tradition help in practical matters related to personality? We will first consider an example from psychotherapy. Then we will turn to applied spirituality. And in the end, we will consider cognitive roots of specific examples of maladaptive behavior.

Cognitive Therapy

Cognitive therapy is not a single method of treatment; rather, it is an approach to psychotherapy rooted in the assumption that certain psychological disorders and many difficult psychological problems come from an individual's unique view of the world and the self. This is not about either accurate or inaccurate perceptions of the world (Whose perceptions are actually accurate?). The problem is that some individuals maintain perceptions that are linked to their emotional and behavioral problems and thus contribute to their disorders. In short, some individuals develop wrong information-processing styles and habits, so the goal of cognitive therapists is to help individuals change those styles (Beck, 1964, 1991). People who need help have to evaluate and change certain beliefs about self and others. Three essential concepts in cognitive therapy that help them to do this are collaborative empiricism, Socratic dialogue, and guided discovery (Beck & Weishaar, 2013).

Collaborative empiricism refers to a therapeutic alliance between a therapist and a client in which they become coinvestigators as they examine the evidence to accept, support, reevaluate, or reject the client's thoughts, assumptions, intentions, and beliefs. The therapist sees the client as a partner, a collaborator. This process is conducted as a dynamic partnership between the patient and the therapist—they both learn from each other.

Socratic dialogue is named after the Greek philosopher Socrates. This method aims at helping the individual arrive at new, more logical conclusions by encouraging discussion—every argument is questioned and supposedly weakened by additional questions, and contradictions are emphasized. The Socratic method does not necessarily aim to demonstrate a person's ignorance or mistakes; instead, it encourages him or her to seek new solutions to the problems that appear unsolvable (Clark & Egan, 2015).

Through *guided discovery*, the individual modifies maladaptive beliefs and assumptions. The therapist serves as a critical but helpful "guide" who elucidates the person's errors in logic by designing new experiences (by means of behavioral experiments) that lead to the acquisition of new skills and perspectives (Beck & Weishaar, 2005). This aspect of therapy is based on the notion that the old reality could be reinvestigated, and some new answers found.

Cognitive therapy is commonly combined with other therapeutic interventions. This combination should make sense: To change our thinking, it is necessary for us to perceive life differently and develop new habits. For example, ACT (acceptance and commitment therapy) is supposed to help individuals increase their psychological flexibility by changing their mode of judging as well as behavioral habits. It contains six principles: Individuals learn not to dwell on their negative emotions, to allow bad thoughts to come and go, to be more open to new experiences, to better understand and accept self, to set new goals, and carry them out with new plans. Empirical studies show the effectiveness of this form of therapy in the United States (Davis et al., 2015) and in other countries, such as Iran (Heydari et al., 2018), among others.

PHOTO 7.3 Psychologists are often increasingly turning to spirituality as a positive factor in therapy. How can spiritual beliefs help individuals with their emotional problems?

"Applied" Spirituality

Psychologists are increasingly turning to spirituality as a possible mediating factor in therapy and as a tool in helping individuals recover from deep emotional problems, psychological traumas, and many other personal problems. The key strategy is to apply principles of thinking (they can be religious, philosophical, or just associated with belief in a "higher power," which we typically call *spirituality*) to the process of individual growth, improvements, and healing.

Religious scholars in the past provided interesting suggestions about self-healing and growth. In Christianity, Ignatius of Loyola (1491–1556), the founder of the Society of Jesus (known as the Jesuits), published a book under the title *The Spiritual Exercises*. The book described 370 such exercises by which people could advance their individual willpower. For example, the book teaches how to use meditation to focus on specific experiences of the past, as well as imagination about the future. During meditation, people focus on the memories of their own sinful behavior or imagine painful experiences they could encounter in hell. By focusing on the negative, individuals were supposed to find the way to their own individual growth. Clinicians in the past incorporated spirituality into their therapeutic techniques. In the United States, the Emmanuel Church Healing Movement gained popularity between 1906 and 1910. This practice made an impact on the subsequent rapid development of psychotherapy in the United States and focused the attention of millions of people to self-knowledge and self-improvement. People would attend private or group sessions with medical doctors and members of the clergy. Through dialogue and prayer, people learned how to gain access to their psychological problems. Using the power of scientific knowledge and their religious faith, they were gaining moral self-control, better self-knowledge, and willpower to overcome their emotional problems. Scores of individuals sought help from the Healing Movement for their substance use problems. Some experts consider this as a prototype of future Alcoholic Anonymous, a global peer-lead fellowship (Caplan, 1998; Dubiel, 2004).

Key principles of Buddhist philosophy, their focus on human mind, for decades impacted psychotherapy (Gold & Zahn, 2018; Mathers et al., 2009). The teachings of the **Four Noble Truths** are most central to the Buddhist tradition. First, Buddhism maintains that suffering (*dukkha*) is an inseparable part of life. Several types of suffering exist. One is everyday physical and psychological suffering that is inevitable and associated with physical pain, discomfort brought by illness, loneliness, aging, and dying. Another type of suffering is based on anxiety or stress caused by people's desire to hold onto things that are constantly changing (people often try to possess something that will not be there for them tomorrow). The third type of suffering is rooted in the lack of satisfaction about things not measuring up to our expectations or desired standards. Does this all mean that humans are destined to suffer? No. Moreover, acknowledging the existence of suffering is not about giving up. In fact, there is a way to avoid suffering (Gethin, 1998).

To find this way, one must understand the true origins of suffering, and this is the Second Truth. People mistakenly believe that they need pleasurable experiences and to get what they want: status, power, money, admiration, fame, and physical comfort. Their attachment to such pleasurable experiences is the key source of suffering, but realizing that there is an escape from cravings and ignorance is learning the Third Truth of Buddhism.

The Fourth Truth is about acting to reduce and eliminate suffering. This is essentially about becoming a moral person by looking at things carefully and critically, speaking truthfully, trying not to harm by deeds or words, making constant attempts at self-improvement, understanding self, avoiding being influenced by cravings, and practicing concentration and meditation.

Contrary to a common misperception, Buddhism does not encourage people to turn to poverty and social disengagement. There is a path between two extremes of human existence: People should not succumb to greed and self-indulgence, but at the same time, they should not practice self-punishment and total asceticism (a lifestyle of restraint or abstinence from various worldly pleasures). Instead, people should adopt the Middle Way, a concept that has also become a distinct feature of Buddhism. It means that people should avoid the excesses of self-indulgence and self-punishment. Moderation and nonviolence should be constantly practiced (Mathers et al., 2009). But everything starts in the individual mind first.

Specialists find a useful overlap between Buddhist psychology and many modern therapeutic methods involving mindfulness or based on holistic principles. This is particularly relevant to the work of clinicians using Gestalt therapy theory and method, which were examined earlier in the chapter (Gold & Zahn, 2018).

Gambling Fallacies

Although gambling in the United States is restricted, according on each state's policies, it is not prohibited. Scores of people each year legally buy lottery tickets, scratch cards, and play in casinos. Since 2018 states were allowed to legalize sports betting, which immediately turned a few million people to online gambling. Gambling involves risking (wagering) something valuable, usually money (the stakes), in an episode, which involves an uncertain outcome: a card game or a sports game, for example. The key goal of gambling is to win additional value, such as money, if the gambler's prediction or choice is correct. Most gamblers often rely on luck to win. Those who place a bet on a single event once a year, such as a college basketball tournament, often have personal attachments to a certain team. Regular gamblers, however, place their bets differently: They believe they can design a strategy that should allow them to beat the odds, or probabilities, to win. One such strategy involves observations of several repetitive events and then placing their bets on several such events consecutively.

Most gamblers also know that over the long-term, odds cannot be beaten. However, there are "hot hands" or long winning streaks—you win once, twice, and you continue to bet. Conversely, many also believe bad luck is not forever either—you lose once, twice, and you may win soon. In the end, losing gamblers feel certain they will recoup their losses. This is known as the *gamblers' fallacy*, or the false belief that if something happens more frequently than usual during a period, it will happen less frequently in the future. Conversely, if something happens less frequently than typical during a period, it surely will happen more frequently in the future (Xu & Harvey, 2014).

A study of more than 565,000 sports bets made by 770 online gamblers showed that people who won were more likely to win again, but apparently this was not happening because they believed in their "hot hands" and luck—it was because they chose safer, less risky odds than before. Yet those who lost were more likely to lose again because they tended to choose riskier odds than before. Being cautious after winning and riskier after losing indicates that online sports gamblers suffer from the gamblers' fallacy—both winners and losers expected their luck to reverse. But winners' winning streaks increased in length because they started choosing safer odds, which led them to win more often (though less money). In contrast, those who had experienced a losing streak chose ever-riskier bets, making it more likely the streak would continue (Xu & Harvey, 2014).

In fact, cognitive psychologists suggest that the propensity for gambling can be rooted in the person's mind. Perhaps what are called "hot hands" and "losing streaks" in gambling are real, yet they are created by the powerful cognitive fallacies of the gambler. Imagine that such fallacies are persistent in the person's mind, and as a result, this individual is back to betting on a regular basis, weekly or even daily. In fact, gambling disorder is an addictive disorder included in *DSM–5–TR* as a diagnosable condition. This is a persistent and recurrent problematic gambling behavior leading to clinically significant impairment or distress. It could be that one of the ways to address this issue is to make sure that the person with this problem is explained the cognitive fallacies involved in gambling behavior. This section of the chapter can be a good starter.

SUMMARY

- The term *cognitive revolution* refers to the shift of focus within university psychology that went from being primarily behavioral (regarding action) to being increasingly cognitive (regarding the mind). In cognitive theory, behavior is explained as guided by cognitions (e.g., understandings and expectations) about the world, other people, and the self.

- The cognitive revolution, of course, had its roots and causes. From its early days as a research discipline in the 19th century, psychology's great scholars tried to find a way to measure the ever-elusive "internal" mechanisms of mental life of an individual's personality. They used experimental introspection, studied the self, and applied the principles of Gestalt psychology and field theory to bring cognition to the study of personality. Gestalt therapy uses the ideas about the holistic nature of human experience, the disruption of its structure, and the emphasis on the actuality of the moment.

- Cognitive psychology belongs to the line of research that is commonly regarded today as part of an interdisciplinary field of cognitive science. This field includes studies in several fields, particularly cognitive neuroscience, computer science, philosophy, and linguistics.

- Philosophy and its studies of consciousness and the self brought new inspiration to personality psychology.

- An individual's personality can be viewed and assessed from the standpoint of attitudes, which are the cognitive representations and evaluations of various features of the social and physical world. The study of attitudes gained significant popularity and research support in psychology and social psychology, especially in the second half of the past century.

- Attitudes are not directly observable; yet they can be measured with various methods of assessment and self-assessment. We can judge them from people's verbal or written responses or infer them from people's behavior. The individual holds attitudes in a particular fashion, and the connections between attitudes and behavior can be studied and measured.

- There are relatively strong and weak attitudes. An individual has some attitudes easily accessible, while others make an effort to retrieve. This is a measure of availability and easiness of expression of the individual's attitude.

- Attitudes with a "unipolar" composition of the affective component are called *single-evaluation attitudes*. Attitudes that contain an ambivalent emotional component are called *dual-evaluation attitudes*.

- Balance theory maintains that people seek consistency among their judgments. They do not necessarily do this deliberately. It is the nature of human experience to be "balanced." To maintain their perception in "good form," people tend to seek explanations for their judgments, thus creating perceptual distortions.

- Leon Festinger, the author of the theory of cognitive dissonance, maintained that people tend to experience tension—an unpleasant emotional state caused by the perceived mismatch dissonance between their attitudes and behavior. The dissonance causes people to change either behavior or attitudes. To achieve a harmonious view, people tend to use the least-effort principle—they minimize the number of cognitive operations to reach a goal.

- The attribution approach shows from a particular angle how the individual explains the world and other people's actions. Attribution involves an act of judgment and is the process by which individuals explain the causes of behavior and events. Harold Kelly proposed that people judge other people's behavior from the standpoints of consistency, distinctiveness, and consensus.

- The American psychologist George Kelly combined the principles of cognitive psychology and applied psychotherapy to approach the individual personality. He believed that people for the most part are "naïve scientists" capable of making reasonable and rational judgments. Such construct systems or constructs are stable assumptions that the individual develops about other people, the self, and the world in general. Such assumptions tend to be "bipolar," or focus on two opposing sides of the spectrum. Constructs should provide a certain order, clarity, and prediction to a person's world. We as individuals develop our "construct systems" to filter the information about the world and make stable judgments.

- A disordered construct system does not accurately predict events and does not help the person adjust to new circumstances. Kelly's fixed-role therapy was designed to change the individual's perception of self. In a simple way, the person would describe self and emphasize various problems that he or she has at present. Then the psychologist would rewrite this self-description and, instead of focusing on negative characteristics and mistakes, would emphasize helpful behaviors and positive self-evaluations.

- The term *self* refers to the representation of one's identity or the subject of experience. The cognitive tradition assumes that people make distinctions between the world within them and the world outside.

- Consciousness is a state of awareness of our own existence. Self-awareness is, in fact, a reflection of this awareness that allows us to perceive our existence with a sense of consistency. Identity can be private and social. Social identity refers to the individual's perceived membership in one or several social groups.

- A person's general subjective evaluation, both emotional and rational, of his or her own worth is called *self-esteem*.

- Writers are not scientists, but as artists, they use words to describe either extraordinary (unusual or improbable) or ordinary (common, everyday) characters in extraordinary and ordinary circumstances. Extraordinary events and extraordinary characters are the most recognizable sources of knowledge about personality. Reflections about everyday people in ordinary situations bring valuable knowledge to the study of personality.

- Cognitive therapy is an approach to psychotherapy rooted in the assumption that certain psychological disorders and many difficult psychological problems are established in the individual's particular view of the world and the self. Three essential concepts in cognitive therapy are collaborative empiricism, Socratic dialogue, and guided discovery.

- Psychologists use spirituality as a mediating factor in therapy and as a cognitive tool in helping individuals to recover from deep emotional traumas and personal problems. The key strategy is to apply principles of thinking (they can be religious, philosophical, or just associated with the belief in a "higher power") to the process of individual growth and healing.

- Cognitive psychology studies cognitive errors related to gambling. Psychologists suggest that "hot hands" and "losing streaks" in gambling are real, yet they are created by the cognitive fallacies of the gambler.

VISUAL REVIEW

Visual Review. Chapter 7. The Cognitive Tradition

1. THE ESSENCE OF THE TRADITION

"Cognitive" to an individual's senses, experience, and thought	The cognitive traditions gains knowledge form introspection, studying the self, the Gestalt tradition, and the cognitive science

2. STUDYING THE COGNITIVE TRADITION

The cotemporary Cognitive Tradition: The cooperation of cognitive neuroscience, computer science, and philosophy of the self	Studies of attitude accessibility, attitude balance, attitude dissonance, and attributions have enriched or knowledge about personality	Studies of personal constructs and the self, within cultural contexts added a new dimension to our understanding of personality

3. APPLYING THE COGNITIVE TRADITION

Cognitive therapy	Applied knowledge about cognitive errors	Applied Spirituality	Applied artificial intelligence

attitudes

attribution

cognitive dissonance

cognitive revolution

cognitive science

collaborative empiricism

constructs

dual-evaluation attitudes

ethnic disidentification

experimental introspection

field theory

fixed-role therapy

Four Noble Truths

fundamental attribution error

Gestalt therapy

least-effort principle

level of aspiration

naïve scientists

self

self-awareness

self-esteem

single-evaluation attitude

social identity

EVALUATING WHAT YOU KNOW

What is the main idea of the cognitive tradition in personality psychology?

Summarize the contribution of early studies in psychology to the cognitive tradition.

What did cognitive science give to this tradition?

Describe the role of cognitive science in the study of personality.

What do studies of consciousness bring to personality psychology?

Explain attitude accessibility, attitude balance, and attitude dissonance. Give examples.

How do attributions and personal constructs affect behavior?

Explain the self, self-esteem, and social identity.

Identify several areas of applications of the cognitive tradition including therapy, spirituality, gambling problems, and others.

A BRIDGE TO THE NEXT CHAPTER

Critics of the cognitive tradition in personality psychology often claim that it overemphasizes cognition, rational choice, wisdom, identity, or pays significantly less attention to emotion and motivation, especially to the issues involving ultimate "human" attributes of people's existence and experience: ideals, moral choices, and values. In the next chapter, we turn to a tradition in psychology that holds a hopeful, constructive view of human beings and of their substantial capacity to be self-determining. It is guided by a conviction that ethical values are strong determinants of human behavior. This belief leads to an effort to emphasize human qualities such as choice, imagination, and the capacity to be free and happy.

8

THE HUMANISTIC TRADITION

iStockphoto.com/Susan Chiang

LEARNING OBJECTIVES

After reading this chapter, you should be able to do the following:

- Identify the main principles and historical contexts of humanistic psychology.

- Discuss the four assumptions of existentialism and May's ideas about fear.

- Discuss Maslow's hierarchy of needs and what it means to be autotelic.

- Explain Rogers person-centered approach and the principles of positive psychology.

- Identify the achievements and shortcomings of the humanistic tradition.

- Identify ways to apply the key principles of the humanistic tradition to individual experience and behavior.

The purpose of life is a life of purpose.

The difference between ordinary and extraordinary is that little extra.

These are the words of a young girl named Athena Orchard who died at age 13 after a brief, stoic battle with cancer. Following her death, Athena's parents uncovered an unusual diary written on the back of her bedroom mirror. With whom did Athena want to share the 3,000 words written in marker? Maybe with her parents, siblings, and friends. Or maybe with all of us.

Happiness is a direction not a destination.

Thank you for existing.

Be happy, be free, believe, forever young.

Athena was first diagnosed with cancer when she was 12. She underwent a long emergency operation, which was followed by months of chemotherapy. The chances of survival were slim, but she fought. She gave everything to this battle, in which the illness prevailed. Despite all the treatments attempted, the doctors could no longer do anything for her.

Love is not about who you can see spending your future with; it's about who you can't see spending your life without.

Athena—before her illness—was very athletic and strong. She loved to write. The illness took away her physical abilities. She lost her hair. But she never lost her positive outlook. She always believed in the best outcome. She believed in life. She left behind her six sisters and three brothers.

People gonna hate you, rate you, break you, but how strong you stand, that's what makes you . . . you!

Don't we all sometimes feel sorry about how life treats us? There are those days when we feel gloomy and desperate. Life seems unfair. There are nights when we dread the upcoming morning. We wish our tasks were easier, people nicer, workdays shorter, and vacations longer. Maybe today is that day. However, the next time you feel sad, think of Athena. She never gave up. She inspired others. She reminded us about dignity and hope. We can *feel* down sometimes, yet we should not let ourselves *be* down. We can be happy. It is up to us.

Happiness depends upon ourselves.

Maybe it's not about the happy ending—maybe it's about the story.

Maybe happiness is a state of mind. Maybe it is ephemeral. Yet happiness can also be a trait. There are happy people around us, and you may be or become one of them. You can also make other people happy. The humanistic tradition in personality psychology focuses on happiness— not only does it tell us about happy individuals, but it teaches us how to be and remain happy.

Sources: Perry, 2014; Spillett, 2014.

THE HUMANISTIC TRADITION: SOCIAL CONTEXTS

The humanistic tradition in personality psychology took shape during one of the most turbulent and uncertain periods in history. At least two major global developments contributed to this worldwide uneasiness. The first was World War II (1939–1945) and the massive international devastation that resulted. The second was the Cold War—a period of dangerous ideological and political struggle between capitalism and communism that lasted until the end of the 20th century. Scientists, politicians, and ordinary people alike were increasingly aware of the dangers of nuclear war, which they knew could bring death to human civilization.

In the second half of the past century, the United States became a powerful center of education and science. Colleges and universities in the United States were in much better shape compared to educational institutions in other parts of the world. A significant influx of immigrants from all over the world brought to America a fresh new wave of educated specialists.

Let us examine how all of these events relate to the humanistic tradition that we study in this chapter.

New and intriguing debates about the role of psychology emerged in the 1950s. When behaviorists studied a person's useful habits and psychoanalysts scrutinized early childhood problems, more psychologists began to argue that their discipline must change its focus and embrace something more human, such as happiness, self-improvement, inner growth, and compassion instead of just studying "reactions" and "defenses." Psychologists reasoned that the mathematical precision of most behavioral studies was running a risk of losing the purpose and focus of psychological research. The attention should turn toward the individual: the comprehending, compassionate, and ever-evolving person who is not necessarily "responding" to stimuli but rather "growing" (Aanstoos et al., 2000). In the early 1960s, many psychologists began to emphasize the importance of moral issues in psychology. Research into healthy relationships and training seminars on self-esteem became popular.

Furthermore, more psychologists wanted to pursue progressive goals to make society better. These arguments drew in the changing political culture of the 1960s and beyond. The focus of their attention was shifting toward civil rights and social ills, including discrimination, prejudice, racism, sexism, and bigotry. Many professors and students shared a popular opinion that psychology as a discipline should bring scientific wisdom, compassion,

©iStockphoto.com / Cylonphoto

PHOTO 8.1 Humanistic psychologists believe that psychology should pursue an ambitious social goal to make society better. Suggest two or three specific social areas in which you think psychologists can help today the most and why.

and action to addressing lingering societal problems, especially in the fields of education, mental health, individual development, and global peace.

THE ESSENCE OF HUMANISTIC TRADITION

The term *humanistic* is somewhat imprecise. It has several interpretations, which multiply in foreign translations. Applied to psychology, the humanistic tradition calls for renewed efforts to study the phenomena that distinguish human beings—love, happiness, and self-growth. It also focuses on "being and becoming somebody" rather than "having and accumulating something." Those who called themselves **humanistic psychologists** wanted to focus less on experimental procedures and statistics and more on the individual's care and self-growth. They wanted to celebrate the uniqueness of individual experiences and share them with others.

Humanistic principles are extraordinarily diverse and have deep roots in several academic disciplines. Almost every contributor to personality psychology in the past had somehow addressed humanistic ideas (Greening, 2011). Looking at their contributions, we will focus primarily on a few that have influenced personality psychology.

The Critical Aspect

The humanistic tradition is rooted in critical examinations of other traditions, especially behaviorism and psychoanalysis. Humanistic psychologists claimed that psychology was losing its main subject: the individual.

Behaviorism was the first target of criticism. Behaviorists, representing the "first force" in psychology, focused on reinforcement and learning. In essence, an individual's personality is a complex "ensemble" of learned responses and habits. Critics argued that behavioral experiments, measurements, and correlation quotients could provide some knowledge about an individual. However, this knowledge would be grossly incomplete because it would convey little about the individual's subjective experience.

Psychoanalysis was another target of criticisms. Many humanistic psychologists studied and practiced psychoanalysis early in their careers (Greening, 1971). They agreed that psychoanalysis encouraged self-discovery and a sustained mental effort. However, they also criticized psychoanalysis for focusing primarily on psychological anomalies. Psychoanalysis, as they claimed, had overemphasized the importance of unconscious processes, and had devalued the meaning of conscious, purposeful acts. The individual in many psychoanalytic theories appeared overwhelmed with the heavy weight of traumatic unconscious experiences stemming from childhood. The individual appeared helpless dealing with the "demons" of the past (Schneider et al., 2014).

The Positive Aspect

Humanistic psychologists also claimed that the intriguing, provocative, controversial, and inspirational core of human existence was seemingly disappearing in the "forest" of technical terms to describe learned reactions and defense mechanisms. They challenged behaviorism and psychoanalysis by emphasizing the importance of individual responsibility, free choice, and intellectual

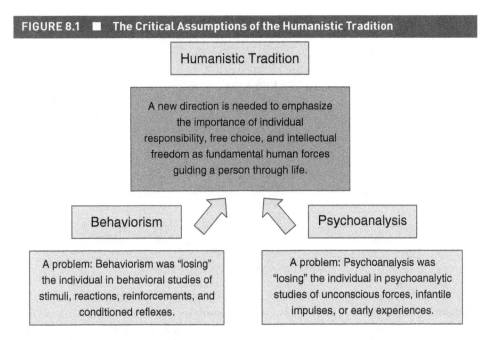

FIGURE 8.1 ■ The Critical Assumptions of the Humanistic Tradition

Humanistic Tradition

A new direction is needed to emphasize the importance of individual responsibility, free choice, and intellectual freedom as fundamental human forces guiding a person through life.

Behaviorism

Psychoanalysis

A problem: Behaviorism was "losing" the individual in behavioral studies of stimuli, reactions, reinforcements, and conditioned reflexes.

A problem: Psychoanalysis was "losing" the individual in psychoanalytic studies of unconscious forces, infantile impulses, or early experiences.

freedom as fundamental human forces guiding a person through life. It was a very optimistic orientation, assuring people of the strength of their own unrealized power (see Figure 8.1).

PRINCIPLES OF HUMANISTIC PSYCHOLOGY

In a nutshell, **humanistic psychology** treats individuals as uniquely human. Humanistic psychologists themselves define this tradition as a value orientation that holds a hopeful and constructive view of people and of their substantial capacity to be self-determining (Association for Humanistic Psychology, 2023). The humanistic tradition is based on five theoretical principles (see Figure 8.2).

Five Theoretical Principles

The first principle of the humanistic tradition states that people should be viewed from a holistic perspective. Each individual is more than the sum of their habits, reflexes, mental operations, or decision-making strategies. This point may seem trivial because it would probably be difficult to find any psychologist in the 1960s who would state that a human being is "just a sum of several parts." Nevertheless, the focus on holism within the humanistic tradition was another way to express criticism of behaviorism. The message was as follows: In our humanistic study, we will focus on all aspects of an individual's existence and not necessarily on isolated behavioral acts, no matter how complex they are (Bugental, 1964).

Second, individuals are aware of their existence. Moreover, they are aware of being aware, which means they are conscious. This statement was a direct challenge to psychoanalysis and its fundamental assumption about the supremacy of the unconscious side of human experience.

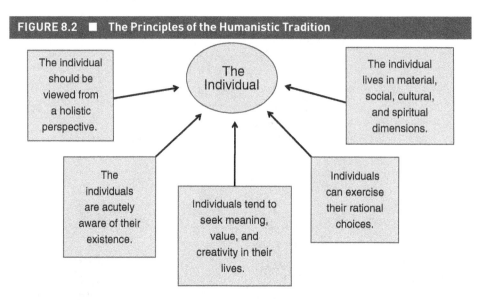

FIGURE 8.2   ■   The Principles of the Humanistic Tradition

The individual should be viewed from a holistic perspective.

The Individual

The individual lives in material, social, cultural, and spiritual dimensions.

The individuals are acutely aware of their existence.

Individuals tend to seek meaning, value, and creativity in their lives.

Individuals can exercise their rational choices.

Although many humanistic psychologists, as you know, were trained within the psychoanalytic tradition, their focus was shifting toward consciousness and reason. The focal point of their interest was the knowledgeable, thinking individuals who are aware of their inner world.

The third principle asserts that human beings live in a uniquely human context that is not limited to their immediate surroundings, such as an office, classroom, or coffee house. To better understand a person's inner world, psychologists must examine an individual's "cosmic ecology" involving its material, social, cultural, gender, and spiritual dimensions. Ethnicity and race are important dimensions, too. Not surprisingly, humanistic psychology has been interconnected from its early days with Hispanic and Black psychology (Jackson, 2019). Both these disciplines focus on how people of Latin American and African descent know and experience the world.

Fourth, rational and knowledgeable individuals can exercise their choices through action. With those choices, however, comes individual responsibility. People make mistakes and learn from them. Humanistic psychologists—contrary to the assumptions of their critics—did not believe in total, unconditional freedom of the individual to do whatever they please. Choice comes with accountability. Humanistic psychology embraces tenets of multiculturalism and social justice.

And finally, because human behavior is generally intentional and deliberate, people can control the outcomes of their behavior. Being aware of their goals, people seek meaning, value, justice, and creativity in their lives, which can become a foundation of happiness.

As you can see, taken as a whole, the main message of humanistic psychology was constructive. People are generally rational and logical in setting their goals and choosing the methods to achieve them. Humanistic psychology is also inherently optimistic. Circumstances can affect all of us, but we, as humans, have the power to overcome these challenges.

Yet what if we fail to achieve our goals despite a sustained effort and good intentions? Sure, a person can choose a wrong method or strategy. Sometimes circumstances stand in our way. We fail, and this causes suffering; persistent failures cause persistent suffering. Fortunately, humanistic psychology shows the individual several ways out of this suffering.

Methods and Humanistic Psychology

Humanistic psychologists focus on the actual experience of an individual (Greening, 1971). They generally prefer qualitative research methods to quantitative procedures and stress the importance of in-depth examinations of an individual's concerns, memories, plans, feelings, and actions taken together in unity. Although humanistic psychologists acknowledge several limitations of the experimental method and, above all, the restraints of its formalized, statistics-based view of the individual, they do not reject experiments. In their view, experiments should be conducted in combination with nonexperimental methods such as observations, interviews, content analysis, and so forth. For example, let's assume that some patients have shown improvements in their symptoms after undergoing a certain kind of psychotherapy. Does this finding say anything about what these individuals felt, how they understood their own symptoms, and whether the changes in their behavioral symptoms affected their overall psychological state? Not always, not necessarily.

> Half a century ago, as well as today, new ideas required promotion, including professional incorporation, publications, and other steps. Learn more about the first steps of humanistic psychology and its later developments on the companion website.

CHECK AND APPLY YOUR KNOWLEDGE

1. What were the "first" and "second" forces in psychology?
2. What is humanistic psychology?
3. Explain humanistic psychology's five points.
4. Imagine that you have founded a new field of research in personality psychology. What would you do today to promote this theory (besides having your own website or blog)?

The role of humanistic tradition in personality psychology is significant and is better explained if we study it from several angles and see its connections to philosophy, the social sciences, and the humanities (Chapter 2).

EXISTENTIAL PSYCHOLOGY

The term *existential* refers, above all, to existence and being. **Existentialism**, as an intellectual tradition, focuses on individual existence, its uniqueness, free will, and responsibility. A central proposition of existentialism is that human beings, through their conscious efforts, create their own meanings, roles, prescriptions, and values. The problem is that as individuals, we do not necessarily fit well into these meanings and roles (Olson, 2017).

Existentialism puts forward several candid and contentious assumptions. For convenience, let's put them in sequence:

- Human existence is tragic.

- Life is painful and absurd.

- Life is full of anxiety and depression.

- Steps can be taken to address the tragic nature and absurdity of our lives.

Why Is Our Existence Tragic? Existential philosophy celebrates and mourns the heartbreaking uniqueness of each individual's experience. People are free, yet every moment they struggle with the demands of society (Berdyaev, 1931/2009). People are free, yet most individuals have little idea what to do with their freedom. Every moment of our lives, we are breathing, acting, hoping, willing, and . . . getting closer to death. No matter what we do and how hard we try, the final results do not match our expectations. We are left sad and disoriented, according to existentialism.

Why Is Life Absurd? Existentialism holds that there is no true meaning in life, and our attempts to find it are fruitless (Sartre, 1943/1969). This futility adds to a sense of confusion, which existentialists call the *existential attitude*. The struggle to comprehend reality often leads to an **existential crisis**, or a period at which an individual questions the very foundations of life and asks whether life has any meaning, purpose, or value. The weakening of religious faith and moral values reinforces the existential crisis (Camus, 1951/1992). In psychological terms, many people encounter anxiety and depression.

Why Is Life Full of Anxiety and Depression? Existentialists say that there is little certainty in life except death. We fear death and look for superficial distractions to reduce this fear (Sartre, 1943/1969). Some people are working harder, others are making more money, yet others are earning more power. The irony is that these actions make the individual even more unhappy (Kierkegaard, 1843/1992). Uncertainty mounts and anxiety grows. Depression, often called *despair*, takes over.

Are There Solutions? Existentialists differ in the way they see despair. Some advocated action and celebrate the power of human will (Nietzsche, 1901/1968). Others encouraged people to revolt against their own daily existence (Camus, 1951/1992). Yet others encouraged people to reconsider their prescribed social roles and standards (Kierkegaard, 1843/1992; Sartre, 1943/1969). Some thinkers and practitioners continue to discuss a personal, subjective realm of existence in which an individual lives and extracts pleasure from life only for their own sake. They maintain that people can grow spiritually, embrace the shortness of their lives, and thus reduce their worry and despair (Menand, 2009). Other psychologists-supporters of existential views turned to psychotherapy to address the individual's anxieties (Frankl, 1959).

Rollo May and Existential Psychology

Existentialism influenced personality psychology in several ways. **Existential psychology** is a system of views and practices based on existentialist principles that the individual's existence and experience are unique, exceptional, and unrepeatable. Each one of us is a universe in itself. When you die, there will never be another "you." This fact is both inspiring and tragic: We simultaneously celebrate our uniqueness and bemoan the shortness of our existence. Existential psychology emphasizes the importance of individual free choice. However, it comes with a price: When we make decisions, we need to take responsibility for them. For existential psychologists, every person has a unique entity in the context of their circumstances, relationships, conditions, influences, and internal forces (Binswanger, 1963).

Unlike existential philosophers—most of whom considered the world and individuals in it as disorganized, tragic, and confused—existential psychologists tend to be more optimistic. True, the world seems chaotic. But it only seems this way. It happens because many people feel trapped in their daily routines and cannot break some of their habits: We study, work, pay bills, buy property, save for retirement. Yet we tend to forget to be human beings. Our lives are short, but we can discover the path that will lead us to confidence and happiness. This discovery can come naturally through the process of our individual growth. Self-improvement can take place under guidance and deliberate effort.

Existential psychology echoes and often borrows from—sometimes deliberately by the design and sometimes not—the Indian classical philosophical tradition (Chapter 2). One of many applications stemming from this tradition is that self-improvement can be achieved not through disengagement, but by developing self-awareness. A self-improving person overcomes selfish aspirations and self-destructive pride. Existential psychology does not encourage people to self-isolate. Instead, it suggests that by focusing on awareness of others and self-awareness, a person can pursue spiritual growth and, ultimately, happiness (Rao et al., 2008). Moreover, the principles of existential psychology, which are rooted in compassion and the pursuit of dignity, are important these days in the process of empowerment of people struggling against social injustice and discrimination (Hoffman et al., 2016).

Anxiety and Personality

One of the leading representatives of existential psychology was the American psychologist Rollo May (1909–1994). His personal health problems early in life and his constant search for inner strength contributed to his relentless and creative insight into personality psychology. As a theorist and practitioner, May considered anxiety one of the most fundamental psychological features of the modern individual.

Anxiety is a psychological phenomenon provoked by the fundamental technological and social changes taking place in the global world. The individual was caught amid an epic conflict between the old world of tradition and the new world of change. Tradition represented stability and certainty; change was rooted in uncertainty and instability (May, 1950; May et al., 1958). The individual feels increasingly insignificant, which can lead to excessive worry, anger, and violence (May, 1969).

Certainly, according to May, people seek remedies against anxiety. Some remedies may bring only temporary relief. For example, some people seek self-isolation. They build psychological shelters of selfishness, disengagement from social life, and apathy: Such individuals disregard other people's interests (Why do I have to care about other people?) or stop pursuing their own goals and dreams (Why do I have to take chances?).

May was not the only thinker who called anxiety the most profound feature of his time. The expression "the age of anxiety" had been discussed in literature (Auden, 1949). But May did not want to focus on negativism; he encouraged people to reduce their anxiety by rediscovering the importance of caring for one another. Only then, he postulated, can people overcome the emerging "bankruptcy of inner values" (May, 1969). Specifically, he taught about the necessity to distinguish between anxiety and fear. Fears usually have an unidentifiable source. Therefore, fears are more manageable than anxiety.

May believed there were two different ways to cope with fear: by avoiding it or confronting it (May, 1969). Yet there is another, third way to manage fear: We can accept it. For example, how do we overcome fear of death? An individual's awareness of death is essential to life, but can we deny death? It is better to accept the existential inevitability of death rather than being afraid of it. As if supporting May's views, Arthur Koestler, a Hungarian British author and journalist who fought with his pen against political oppression, wrote in *Dialogue With Death* (1942) that when he and the other political prisoners knew that they were going to die and no longer feared dying, "at such moments we were *free*—men without shadows, dismissed from the ranks of the mortal; it was the most complete experience of freedom" that can be granted a person (see Figure 9.3; Menand, 2009).

As we could see, May believed that anxiety could be reduced if we understood it as a certain fear. Another way to overcome anxiety is love. There are different types of love, however. Sexual love is the "lowest" type because it is rooted in predominantly natural impulses. May argued that when a person gives into the impulses of sexual promiscuity, it does not actually make that person free. Instead, resisting these impulses is about being free. He believed that love can be unselfish and manifested in friendship and dedication to others (May, 1969, 1994). May's publications and lectures about anxiety, fear, love, and the possibility for self-improvement drew a significant reading and listening audience.

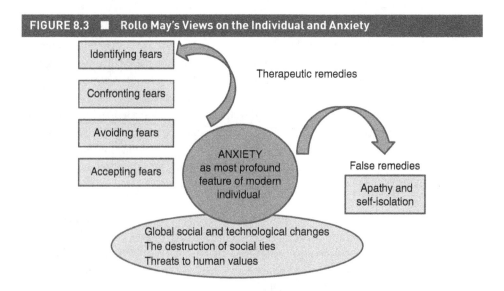

FIGURE 8.3 ■ Rollo May's Views on the Individual and Anxiety

CHECK AND APPLY YOUR KNOWLEDGE

1. What is existentialism? Explain an existential crisis in an individual.
2. What does the expression "the age of anxiety" mean?
3. How can the individual reduce anxiety, according to Rollo May?
4. How is today's "age of anxiety" different, in your view, from the period described by May?

ABRAHAM MASLOW AND HUMANISTIC PSYCHOLOGY

A noteworthy contribution to personality psychology came from Abraham Maslow (1908–1970), whose name is among the most recognizable in modern psychology and social sciences. Born to a family of poor immigrants from Russia, Maslow developed an early love for learning and chose psychology for his major and career. He did experimental research before turning to humanistic psychology.

Bettmann/Getty Images

PHOTO 8.2 Maslow described the individual's needs as arranged in a hierarchy in terms of their potency. Can you apply your own life experiences to this hierarchy?

Hierarchy of Needs

One of the most quoted works by Maslow was his research into motivation. For Maslow, motivation is a force within an organism that initiates and maintains behavior (Maslow, 1970). How does this motivation work? Hunger, for example, is an indicator of food deficiency. An individual will consume food to reduce or eliminate this deficiency, which will end the subjective experience of hunger. There are other needs, however, that are distinctly human. They are not necessarily related to food, water, or something material. These are needs related to being or becoming. For example, there are needs of becoming a better person, a caring family member, a decent human being, and more. Maslow described the individual's needs as arranged in a hierarchy in terms of their potency. He grouped these needs into five categorical levels: physiological, safety, love, esteem, and self-actualization (Maslow, 1970).

The concept of hierarchy of needs has an intriguing analogy in the Indian spiritual tradition. To illustrate, Hinduism introduces *kama* (pleasurable activity), *artha* (activity related to pursuit of a livelihood), and *dharma* (spiritual duty) as a hierarchy of critical guiding principles of life. However, there is no indication that Maslow knew about these ideas before he published his works on motivation (Collins, 1990).

Not only did Maslow introduce a hierarchy of needs, but he suggested how this hierarchy functioned. In particular, he proposed that once an individual has satisfied the cluster of needs at a particular level, he or she is able to progress to the next hierarchical level (see Figure 8.4).

People typically tend not to seek safety and security until they have met their needs for food, water, and shelter (Level 1). After individuals secured their immediate access to basic resources, then they try to meet their safety needs by making sure these recourses remain available in the future (Level 2). For example, if a former student is looking for and then finding a stable job, this activity is likely to refer to this person's satisfying the safety needs. Then, on Level 3, individuals are likely to seek social affiliation with other people and groups and pursue affection from others. Then comes Level 4, associated with esteem needs: People now pursue approval and appreciation from others. People of all walks of life and professions seek respect and recognition. For example, not only is it important for the teacher to teach classes according to a lesson plan; now, on this level, the teacher needs feedback—preferably positive—from the students who are satisfied with the quality of their education.

Maslow gathered most of his data more than 55 years ago. Yet contemporary studies show that many of his conclusions are very much applicable to today's word (Konnikova, 2014). Maslow was also aware about cross-cultural applications of his research. During his life, he was applying some principles of Daoism—a religion, a philosophy, and lifestyle originated in China in the 6th century BCE—to his research including teaching, counseling, psychotherapy, and parenting. Cross-cultural psychologists today maintain, for example, that Maslow's research into growth-centered mentorship (with an emphasis on individual progress) contrasted with skill-centered mentorship (with a focus on specific skills only)—echoes Daoist teachings (Hoffman & Compton, 2022).

A Harvard University project to study digital behavior showed that with a rapid expanding and fragmentation of television, blogs, and social networks, young people tend to find the

---

FIGURE 8.4   ■   Maslow's Hierarchy of Needs

Level 5:	*Self-Actualization Needs* Completion, sufficiency, morality, etc.
Level 4: ⬆	*Esteem Needs* Achievement, self-esteem, respect by others, etc.
Level 3: ⬆	*Belonging and Love Needs* Friendship, family, intimacy, etc.
Level 2: ⬆	*Safety Needs* Security of the body, health, resources, the family, etc.
Level 1: ⬆	*Physiological Needs* Homeostasis, breathing, water, food, sex, etc.

way to strengthen their identity. They don't want to get lost in the ocean of information and personal posts. They want to identify self in a special way and find like-minded individuals online (Level 3). Finding like-minded others may be more important than ever before in history (Gardner & Davis, 2013). Studies show that online contacts, in fact (despite many setbacks), can foster a strong sense of identity in a person, stimulate meaningful relationships, and fuel creativity. Esteem and respect (Level 4) received from others can come quickly or it can last—it all depends on how vast and lengthy the impact of the online "self" is.

Maslow's needs on the first four levels are labeled as *deficit needs* or **D-needs** because they are rooted in a scarcity of something, such as food or esteem from others. Maslow noted that as one gradually ascends the hierarchy of needs, this person becomes less animal-like and more human. The highest human function is being achieved on Level 5. If a woman, for example, has been able to satisfy adequately, step by step, the needs on the first four levels, she is able to fulfill the highest order needs—namely, to actualize her unique potential. According to Maslow, once she enters the top level of the hierarchy, the realm of **self-actualization**, she becomes qualitatively different from those who are still attempting to meet their more basic needs. However, she does not necessarily reach the self-actualization level routinely, simply because she satisfied all other needs. Achieving self-actualization requires time, certain conditions, and, most importantly, significant inner work.

Self-Actualization

Maslow's interest in self-actualizing people began with his great admiration for Max Wertheimer (1880–1943), one of the pioneers of experimental psychology, and Ruth Benedict (1887–1948), the renowned American cultural anthropologist and one of the most ardent critics of the early-20th-century racist theories in social sciences. After learning that these two individuals—a man and a woman—had many characteristics in common, such as optimism, efficiency, kindness, and generosity, Maslow began to search for other people with similar qualities. The group he finally selected for a more detailed study included European or European American people from different historic periods: American presidents Abraham Lincoln and Thomas Jefferson, physicist Albert Einstein, First Lady Eleanor Roosevelt (wife of President Franklin D. Roosevelt), philosophers Benedict Spinoza and Albert Schweitzer, politician Adlai Stevenson, and educator Martin Buber.

Based on his research, Maslow developed a composite, impressionistic profile of an optimally functioning, mature, and healthy human being. Maslow concluded that self-actualizing persons exhibit a number of similar characteristics, including the following:

- Accurate perception of reality
- Continued freshness of appreciation and openness to experience
- Spontaneity and simplicity
- Strong ethical awareness
- Philosophical (rather than hostile) sense of humor

- Need for privacy

- Periodic peak experiences

- Democratic (nonauthoritarian) leadership traits

- Deep interpersonal relations

- Autonomy and independence

- Creativeness

- Problem-centered (rather than self-centered) orientation

- Resistance to enculturation

- Acceptance of self, others, and nature

The self-actualizing person's life is governed by the search for *being-values*, or **B-values**, such as truth, goodness, beauty, wholeness, justice, and meaningfulness.

Maslow's research drew criticism, however. Maslow, as you could notice, focused on a sample of individuals in his research that was not necessarily representative of the global population. Maslow selected people who shared his moral code and his conception of fulfillment and assigned them the honorific status of self-actualizers (Kendler, 1999). Maslow's critics wonder if Maslow simply selected his "personal" heroes and heroines and offered his impressions of them (Smith, 1978).

Indeed, Maslow's idea of a specific values hierarchy with self-actualization on top was innovative, yet not necessarily universal. The traditional Chinese hierarchy of values, for instance, includes the promotion of interconnectedness, in contrast to the emphasis on self-development in Maslow's version. Nevis (1983) examined Maslow's hierarchy of needs and argued that one of the most basic needs of people in China was the need to belong, rather than safety or physiological needs. Interconnectedness among people continues to be an important variable affecting people's motivation (Jasielska et al., 2018). Moreover, self-actualization could manifest not in self-centered behavior, but rather as a person's devoted service to community. If a person self-actualized by means of contributing to the group, this individual was realizing the value of collectivist self-actualization (Shiraev & Levy, 2024).

THE AUTOTELIC PERSONALITY

One of the distinct features of a self-actualizing individual is **peak experiences**—periodic and profound episodes of happiness, optimism, inner harmony, and creativity. These are the most significant, happiest moments of discovery, understanding, accomplishment, or intimacy. Is it possible for a non–self-actualizing person to have peak experiences? It is possible, yet such experiences are likely to be infrequent (Maslow, 1962). Peak experiences can be achieved through training and meditation. They are common in teachings and practices of Hindu or Buddhist traditions. However, meditation techniques generally encourage self-focus and detachment from the outside word. Peak experiences require social engagement instead. These experiences typically involve other people and consistent social engagements.

Years after Maslow described peak experiences, his ideas found support in the studies of so-called **flow**—a state of complete concentration and joyful immersion in the situation or activity (Csíkszentmihályi, 2014). Flow is a feature associated with the key (Car, 2011). This is a general term (*auto* in Greek means "self" and *telos* means "goal") to describe a person who tends to be engaged in activities that are naturally rewarding and not necessarily associated with material goals such as money, fame, or high social status. It is also associated with the person's ability to find enjoyment in everyday activities that many people can find tedious (Csíkszentmihályi, 1990). Authentic personality is associated with traits such as curiosity, purposeful behavior, and modesty. **Autotelic personalities**—compared to others—tend to seek and create situations in which they experience flow states. Compared to other people, autotelic personalities have a greater capacity to initiate, sustain, and enjoy such experiences (Baumann, 2012).

People can be called *autotelic* because they find the right balance between serious activities and play. However, finding this balance is difficult. The individual must learn at least two important things: how to stay focused and how to set realistic goals. This also requires a willingness to learn about one's own limitations. In other words, individuals create their flow experiences because they know that they are achievable. Where avoidant individuals see obstacles and problems, the autotelic person believes opportunity is not only fun but also builds skills (Baumann, 2012). This person also has a capacity for disinterested interest, which means the performance may be valued higher than the result of this performance (Csíkszentmihályi, 1997, 2014).

SELF-REFLECTION

If somebody has had recurrent and powerful flow experiences, this does not necessarily mean this person has developed traits of an autotelic personality. Some people have flow experiences and have never been challenged in life. They are simply lucky: Good things just happen to them, and great friends find them. Most probably, the dichotomous division "auto-telic–not autotelic" is rather inaccurate. It should be that every person has to have at least some measure—either significant or not—of features or traits of the autotelic personality.

Questions

Read again the definition of the autotelic personality. Which features of an autotelic person-ality do you think you have? Have you found in your life the right balance between serious activities (such as work and studying) and play? Is it possible and even necessary to make certain tedious activities in your life (such as studying for the test) more enjoyable?

Source: Kang, 2015.

HUMANISTIC TRADITION AND ACTIVISM

Should psychologists be impartial observers of facts, or should they bring their values to their research? Should they focus on "what is" in the world, or should they pay attention to "what should be" instead? Should they study individuals, or should they change them? Many humanistic psychologists prefer an activist position. Maslow's critics maintain that his theory was not necessarily a depiction of a fully functioning person, but instead reflected Maslow's own activist value system and beliefs about how people should feel and act. Did Maslow mix ethical considerations with his research logic? Consider, for example, his portrayal of self-actualizing people as open, realistic, spontaneous, possessing democratic leadership traits, resistant to enculturation, and accepting of self, others, and nature. Is this an objective description of human fulfillment? Or is it a prescription of what Maslow wanted people to be?

Maslow (1970) acknowledged that his theorizing and research on self-actualization lacked the rigor of strict, quantitative empirical investigation (Chapter 3). He fervently believed, however, that it was imperative to begin the process of rounding out the field of psychology by attending to "the highest capacities of the healthy and strong man as well as with the defensive maneuvers of crippled spirits" (p. 33). Maslow wanted to inspire others by his research and give them the right knowledge and skills to be liberated and happy. Furthermore, he maintained that science is not value-free because its methods and procedures are developed and used for human purposes.

CHECK AND APPLY YOUR KNOWLEDGE

1. What is self-actualization? Are you a self-actualizer now? If not, do you want to be one? If you do, how soon?
2. What are B-values?
3. Give an example of peak experiences.
4. Explain the autotelic personality.
5. Consider a case: Alex did not like his high school and struggled academically. Maybe he was failing because of his chronic attention problems, or maybe he simply didn't have passion for studying. Few activities interested him, except just two—he loved skateboarding and video games. After finishing high school and changing several jobs, Alex finally found his niche: He now plays video games on an online gaming platform. People from all over the world—for a small subscription fee—log on and watch him play, read his comments, and leave their feedback. Alex has hundreds and sometimes thousands of observers, who are also his paying customers; they are watching Alex's moves, kicks, and other spectacular tricks. Alex is a virtual performer with a salary that is probably less than any minimum-wage job would bring him, so he needs more viewers. This is a challenging task. The viewers can leave as easily as they came to watch. Yet Alex is determined to stay in business, develop his skills, entertain, teach, and inspire others because he loves what he does. Sometimes he works (plays) for 12 hours consecutively or more. He says his performance is not about making money—at least, the material side is not his top priority. By playing video games professionally, he hopes, as he says, to win the battle against his past failures and childhood insecurities. Even though nobody believed he could succeed in anything, he says he is finally doing something he truly loves and gets attention from others. Some people encourage him to stay in business; one comment said, "I hope this guy makes it." Others suggest getting a "real" tech job, mocking him and his work: "The only thing that is a bigger waste of time than constantly playing video games is watching someone else play."
   a. Does Alex, in your view, have features of an autotelic personality?
   b. Does Alex's work help him to experience flow?

    c. Do you think he is happy? His work is an emotional rollercoaster: He is happy when he has new spectators and miserable when they leave. The work makes him anxious and often sleepless. He lives in a busy world with successes and failures, relationships and strategies. He loves what he does because his activity apparently makes him uniquely human if you apply Maslow's theory. Yet from your personal standpoint, do you want to experience the same type of happiness that Alex has?

6. Although these days most students suggest that a psychologist should combine the rigor of a researcher and the passion of an activist, they disagree about the extent. What is your view on this? Choose one statement and explain your choice:

    a. Psychologists should be researchers, not necessarily activists.

    b. Psychologists should be researchers first and activists second.

    c. Psychologists should be equally researchers and activists.

    d. Psychologists should be activists first and researchers second.

    e. Psychologists should be activists, not necessarily researchers.

Maslow's views were innovative for his time. In contrast to many psychoanalytic theorists preceding him that focused on clinical cases, Maslow created his theory by studying healthy and successful people. His influence in personality psychology was significant. Instead of asking, "What does it mean to be mentally ill?" he asked, "What does it mean to be mentally healthy?" His approach stimulated the development of numerous studies into personality and the creation of several therapeutic methods. Carl Rogers did both.

CARL ROGERS AND THE PERSON-CENTERED APPROACH

The American psychologist Carl Rogers (1902–1987) was another influential psychologist of the 20th century, and his views remain influential today globally. He was born near Chicago, obtained his PhD at Columbia University in New York, and worked in several universities, including the University of Chicago and the University of Wisconsin.

Rogers (1947) maintained that all of us exist in a changing world of their experience. This experience becomes reality for us. The organism responds to the outside signals and satisfies its needs, but all this happens within this organism's individual experience. Most of the behaviors we learn are consistent with the subjective concept of self. All living organisms strive to make the very best of their existence. Above other things, people tend to value positive regard, which is love, warmth, attention, and care from others. People also value **positive self-regard**, which refers to high self-esteem and positive emotions toward the self. However, human society sets special conditions for positive regard. We as individuals are raised to understand that only certain behaviors and certain conditions could lead to rewards from others. For instance, as children, we need to wash our hands before meals, speak politely to adults, and do our homework. We grow older and, according to Rogers, develop the belief that our personal self-regard also should be conditioned by certain things we do or decisions we make. In other words, we see ourselves in a positive light only when we behave according to certain expectations and accomplishments, not because we realize our potential or simply exist. Because most of us cannot maintain the high standards set for us by our parents, teachers, supervisors, and society in general, we experience incongruity between who we are and who we are supposed to be. This incongruity is the source of our psychological tensions. Here, Rogers echoes assumptions of the prominent German psychologist Karen Horney (Boeree, 2006).

Like Maslow, Rogers saw self-actualization as the highest level of psychological health. Self-actualization, however, does not occur simply because people want it to arrive. To achieve self-actualization, they have to make a conscious and sustained effort (Rogers, 1961). Specifically, they must try to be open to new experiences, learn, live each day fully, have trust in their own decisions, enjoy freedom to choose, remain creative without the feeling of conformity, balance their own needs, and participate in the opportunities that life constantly offers. For Rogers, fully functioning people are well adjusted, well balanced, and interested in learning and knowing. Such people tend to be high achievers.

Rogers's critics rightly suggested that the profile of fully functioning people is more likely to fit into predominantly individualist cultures (see Chapter 2). In other, more collectivist and traditional cultures, individual achievement is valued, yet not as much as the achievement of the group. Furthermore, in mostly traditional cultures, conformity to group norms is valued more than making individual decisions or being open to new experiences.

As a therapist, Rogers proposed a person-centered (often called *client-centered*) approach to an individual, and it has become famous and has found many applications in therapeutic practice worldwide. We will discuss this approach later in this chapter when we turn to applications of humanistic psychology.

POSITIVE PSYCHOLOGY

Humanistic psychologists contributed to its "sister field" called **positive psychology**, which studies the strengths and virtues that enable individuals and communities to thrive (Compton, 2004). As you remember, Maslow and Rogers encouraged psychologists to study success and accomplishment, nurture talent, support great initiatives, and set examples of happiness. Thus many psychologists turned to studies of happiness, meaningful life, and achievement. Psychology professionals used methods of positive psychology in the classroom and workplace. The main focus of their work was not problems or weaknesses, but mostly growth and improvement. Practical applications of positive psychology included helping individuals find their strength and assisting organizations to identify their potential (Smith, 2019).

An important contribution of humanistic psychology was the concept of positive mental health. Instead of studying, almost exclusively, psychopathological symptoms and traumatic conditions causing such symptoms, humanistic psychologists turned to the healthy side of an individual, the optimal state of functioning and experience. The concept of self-actualization has become a widely accepted idea in contemporary psychology.

Studying Happiness

Happiness, which we already briefly discussed in Chapter 3, is an important measure of social and economic development of a country—the higher the indexes of happiness are, the higher the position of that country on quantitative global scales used by diplomats and businesspeople. Happiness statistics are becoming an important social and economic yardstick. The humanistic tradition, like no other tradition in personality psychology, pays attention to happiness and the ways to reach it. Within this tradition, psychologists are not necessarily interested in an emotion of joy or related emotional states. The focus is on the happy person. How does one become a happy person? How can one be a happy person? By asking these key questions, psychologists share their knowledge with others and help them learn how to be happy.

Critical Assessments of Happiness Approaches

Before offering their research-based visions of happiness, psychologists working within the humanistic tradition critically examined other views of happiness common in the humanities. These views were also rooted in popular beliefs that existed in various cultures for centuries.

According to the materialist view, an individual can become happy through the accumulation of material wealth, such as money and products. Happiness is also about possessing power and social status. Things that make an individual's life more comfortable—a cozy home, an impressive savings account, an Instagram account followed by thousands, a new car, or the latest version of a smartphone—are important "triggers" of happiness. The higher the social status of an individual, the more power she or he has, and somehow, that status and power translate into happiness. Most of us are aware that although material possessions can make a person happy, this emotional state does not last long. Studies show that happiness and wealth (economic success) are not always strongly correlated (Harari, 2014). In the United Kingdom, for instance, different indicators of happiness haven't changed much for the past 4 decades, even during good and bad economic periods; overall, people in Britain score consistently higher on happiness than people in most other countries (Buettnerr, 2017; Suh et al., 2008).

A slightly different view—the progressive view—adds an important element to the recipe for happiness: social care. Supporters of this view argue that if every individual is guaranteed and given basic social services—including health care, affordable housing, a living wage, paid vacations, and free tuition (to name a few)—then there will practically be no external factors that should contribute to this individual's unnecessary suffering. If the basic needs are secured, the individual ought to be happy. Indeed, people in Denmark or Finland, the Scandinavian countries with seemingly the most developed social welfare systems, receive very high scores on the measures of happiness. However, surveys also show that the amount of social welfare does not necessarily affect people's happiness. Iceland, based on studies conducted a few years ago, spent significantly less on social welfare than Sweden, but people were happier there (Buettnerr, 2017; Suh et al., 2008). In the past, many psychologists, including Freud and others, were already skeptical about the idea that social welfare reforms alone would make people happy (Menand, 2014).

The situational view maintains that happiness is not necessarily about vast material possessions or generous social services. The entire life situation in which individuals find themselves should determine how happy they are (Lyubomirsky, 2007, 2014). The presence or absence of major tragedies in their lives, the quality of their relationships, especially within the family, the existence of opportunities—all should contribute to happiness. Yet other psychologists argue that even if the life conditions are favorable, people still tend to compare themselves to others.

The comparison view suggests that happiness is a state of mind based on appraisals and evaluations of self and others. If we are doing better than others, we tend to feel better about life. Yet what if others do better than us? Comparisons, unfortunately, often lead to envy: "I wish you did not have it," we may say about others who have more than us (Fiske, 2010). Envy leads to scorn and contributes to unhappiness. Studies also show that in individualistic cultures, people rely on their emotions when they assess their own happiness. In predominantly collectivist cultures, people tend to seek social cues or other people's responses to make a judgment (Ng, 2022; Suh et al., 2008). In other words, other people may play a role in how we evaluate our happiness.

The expectation view refers to the goals an individual had in the past and the degree to which the individual accomplished those goals. Happiness depends less on material conditions or other people, but rather on what we expect from our lives. If our experiences today match or exceed our expectations yesterday, then we feel happy. However, our expectations do change. When life is getting better, expectations tend to increase, thus increasing our dissatisfaction if our goals aren't met—the better outcomes we expect, the less happy we become if we don't achieve them.

The biological view suggests that people can be happier or less happy primarily because of their genetic and biological makeup. The brain and the body are basically responsible for pleasant sensations, and some people are predisposed to have more of such sensations than others. Evolutionary psychology maintains that happiness is a temporary state that organisms try to achieve. Yet it is quite normal that individuals remain mostly dissatisfied; they always try to survive and always strive to achieve more (Harari, 2014). In sum, with the biological view, unhappiness is biologically predetermined, so some individuals could be happier than others due to their genetic makeup.

The spiritual view stresses the importance of inner factors and emphasizes the search for the higher power within the individual. Philosophers, religious scholars, pundits, and social scientists in many cultures and regions have discussed the ideas about the passing nature of our sensations and emotions. Buddhist and Hindu teachers, philosophers of ancient Greece and Rome, and Central Asian and Chinese philosophers, for example, consistently referred to the possibility for the individual to become and stay happy after turning to inner strengths. Pleasant sensations from the body come and go, a source of happiness tomorrow may disappear today, and people we love may depart, so the path to happiness is in limiting the influence of the world of sensations and cultivating wisdom as well as an introspective mind (Harari, 2014).

The moral view teaches that the secret of happiness is in a person's constant pursuit of virtue. Virtuous deeds ultimately give humans a chance at happiness: to know it, to experience it. Happiness is likely to emerge from a life well lived, filled with moral pursuits (Birkhaug, 2022). See these views summarized in Table 8.1.

The Humanistic View

Psychologists working within the humanistic perspective embrace many views on happiness but also suggest their own version of how an individual can become and remain happy. There are differences among psychologists, but the most important similarities can be summarized as follows.

TABLE 8.1 ■ Views of Happiness		
View	*Brief Description*	*Practical Steps*
Materialist	The individual's happiness is about material possessions, including money and social status, that lead to more possessions and power.	Pursue material values, money, and high social status.
Progressive	Happiness is not about wealth or status. It is about social welfare or guaranteed opportunities and basic necessities, such as health care, jobs, and education.	Make sure that there is a guaranteed level of social support and social services.
Situational	Individuals become happy or unhappy mainly because of favorable and unfavorable circumstances in their lives. Most of these conditions, yet not all, tend to be outside the individual's control.	Life outcomes are basically out of our control, yet we have some power to avoid unfavorable ones.
Comparison	Happiness is based on perceptions. It is relative to the results of comparisons made by the individual between self and other people.	Make sure the comparisons are favorable or avoid comparisons with other people.
Expectation	The individual feels happy or unhappy based on what she or he expected from self.	Make sure your expectations have been met or ignore such expectations.
Biological	Some people are biologically programmed to be either happy or unhappy.	If you believe that you have been "born" unhappy, adjust and work on yourself.
Spiritual	Passing emotions are too shallow to bring happiness. Happiness should be found within yourself.	Happiness is the state of your soul, which should be cultivated through detachment and meditation.
Moral	Happiness is a person's constant pursuit of virtue. Virtue ultimately gives humans a "shot" at happiness.	Perfect happiness cannot be found without virtue. We need to constantly pursue virtuous goals.
Humanistic	Happiness is a result of many factors. It requires self-growth, hard work on self-improvement, and social engagement.	Think critically, engage socially, practice peace, and provide positive feedback.

It is quite possible that some individuals are born with a propensity to experience certain emotional states. There are individuals who tend to be happy or sad due to their hormones or the functioning of their brain and the nervous system. It is also possible that material possessions, social protection, and comparisons to other people can bring joy to some individuals. Yet joy is a passing emotion and is not necessarily the *state* of happiness. Happiness is a state of mind, and individuals can be in control of it. So the first point of the humanistic argument is that happiness is achievable and can be learned.

The second point refers to social and interpersonal engagement. Contrary to some religious teachings that encourage self-reflection coupled with (often suggested) detachment and self-isolation, the humanistic perspective encourages interpersonal action, critical thinking, and engagement in social affairs. The humanist view is rooted in the modern philosophical view that scientific knowledge, reasoning, rationality, empiricism, and skepticism have profoundly changed the way individuals perceive morality, justice, and happiness (Shermer, 2015; Lyubomirsky, 2014). Findings indicate, for example, that autotelic individuals are not necessarily happier than other people but more often involved in complex activities, which, in turn, make them feel better about themselves and increase their self-esteem (Csikszentmihalyi, 1997).

The third point is about positive feedback. We, as individuals, need to receive persistent positive feedback about ourselves. Encouragement and praise from others are valuable to us. People often turn to horoscopes for the same reason—to receive validation. As in a fortunate tarot reading, the happier the assessment, the more likely we are to believe it and the more likely we will feel better about ourselves (Konnikova, 2014). Positive assessments encourage optimism in us; optimism stimulates short-term joy; and joy adds to long-term happiness.

Self-growth, described earlier, is one of several applications of the humanistic perspective's approach to personality. Self-growth is difficult to achieve without the practical steps of learning, dedication, and perseverance to the goals one has set. The bottom line is this: The individual can achieve happiness through self-growth.

CHECK AND APPLY YOUR KNOWLEDGE

1. Explain positive regard.
2. What are the similarities and differences between Rogers's and Maslow's views on self-actualization?
3. Explain positive psychology.
4. Choose and explain at least two of the approaches to happiness presented earlier.
5. The English philosopher and writer Aldous Huxley (1894–1963) in Brave New World (1932) imagined a global society of the future in which people live in harmony and are conditioned to work hard and respect their government. They also take a hallucinogenic substance called *soma*. This hangover-free drug makes everyone who takes it happy. Stress and anxiety go away. So do envy and jealousy—after taking soma, people feel content and grateful for what they do and have. They do not experience existential crises. Soma helps everyone experience a high self-esteem. Soma also substitutes for religious feelings and interpersonal attachments; they are no longer needed because the only attachment that people have is their work and their government. Brave New World is a satirical, fictional book full of sarcasm and exaggerations; however, one of Huxley's points is clear: People can be manipulated. Either powerful authorities or scientists can create a reality for them and make them happy while they remain slaves.
   a. Do humanistic psychologists, in your opinion, propose another Brave New World?
   b. Instead of prescribing a drug like soma, psychologists suggest humanistic methods of self-growth. Do you agree or disagree that they simply teach individuals to change

their view of life and largely ignore the problems that surround them? Explain why or why not.

6. Is bitter truth better and healthier than sweet lies? Explain your choice using a specific example from your life.

7. Studies show that people who are pessimistic tend to see reality more accurately than optimistic individuals, who tend to see things in rosy colors; however, similar studies show that optimists are happier than pessimists (Konnikova, 2014). What is your position in a difficult alternative: (A) to see the world as it is, with all its pains and tragedies, and be a bit unhappy or (B) to see it from a more optimistic view and remain a bit happy? Explain your choice.

ACCOMPLISHMENTS AND LIMITATIONS OF THE HUMANISTIC TRADITION

Humanistic principles attracted the attention of professionals studying personality and encouraged many dedicated followers around the world for years to come. The overall success of this tradition was due to many innovative ideas and their practical applications.

Accomplishments

Humanistic psychologists refocused attention back to the individual, to the human factor, and to the issues that are ultimately unique to an individual's experience. This was quite a reasonable and timely shift. Although most professional psychologists in the end of the 20th century did not switch their research interests dramatically in favor of humanistic principles, many of them turned their attention to the questions that were central for humanistic psychology. In fact, personality psychology today is inseparable from the humanistic principles on which it is based.

The ideas and values of the humanistic tradition became very popular first in Western countries and later around the world. Humanistic psychologists offered an optimistic vision of human beings, their nature, and their experiences. The emphasis on a free, rational, and ever-growing individual was innovative and promising, compared with the widely accepted psychoanalytic assumption about the predetermined trouble hidden in the dungeon of an individual's unconscious mind. The behaviorist assumptions about the value of rewards and conditioning were challenged, too, as the humanistic tradition offered a new set of humanistic values for understanding, teaching, and healing of the individual.

The humanistic tradition offered a hopeful, constructive view of individuals and challenged social injustice. Ethical values should be strong determinants of human behavior. This belief leads to an effort to emphasize human qualities such as equality of opportunity, choice, imagination, self-improvement, the interaction of the body and mind, and the capacity to become free and happy.

Some existential philosophers claimed that human beings would inevitably become lazy, complacent, and satisfied because of the enticing power of material possessions (Žižek, 2015). As a challenge to these and other pessimistic assumptions, the humanistic tradition in psychology claimed that the individual path to equality, happiness, and care for others should always activate in human beings new individual traits full of passionate intensity.

Shortcomings

One of the obvious shortcomings of humanistic psychology was its relatively poor record of experimental, quantitative research. You remember that the founders of this tradition were disappointed with the status of what appeared to be mainstream psychology of the day. Psychology as a discipline, they believed, was losing the "tree" of the person in the "forest" of experimental procedures and statistical methods. Unfortunately, humanistic psychology had somewhat distanced itself from empirical studies and statistical interpretations of experimental data. As a result, most empirical facts obtained in this field are based on individual observations, stories, and interviews—all very important, yet imprecise and probably biased. Like the introspection method popular in the 19th century, most research methods of humanistic psychology were very subjective.

Critics also maintained that humanistic psychology was not necessarily scientific. The central argument was that a theory's hypotheses (Chapter 3) should be falsifiable (Popper, 1992). What does that mean? Consider, for example, the following statement: Every person has the right to be happy. It is an unfalsifiable statement because it would be almost impossible to demonstrate its falsehood and prove, for example, that "this person or that individual does not have the right to be happy." A falsifiable statement would be that "this therapeutic method provides successful outcomes 70% of the time" because it is possible, hopefully, to verify empirically. If major statements and findings of humanistic psychology are not falsifiable, the discipline is likely to be just a set of inspirational ideas that exist at the mercy of their creators and supporters. Furthermore, the validity of their assumptions is probably a matter of individual position or social perspective.

Humanistic principles attempted to bring psychologists' attention back to the individual's subjectivity. Cognitive psychology, which we studied in Chapter 7, pursued a relatively similar goal. But despite this common strategic interest, cognitive and humanistic psychologists were very different in how they approached subjectivity. In short, they asked different questions, and this was the crucial difference between the two groups. Psychologists who supported the humanistic tradition were mostly interested in *why* people do what they do. The cognitive tradition in psychology was studying *how* the individual processes information. Not surprisingly, the first group (humanistic psychologists) turned to moral values and ethical prescriptions. The other group (cognitive psychologists) paid most attention to formal operations, or various models describing cognitive processes.

©iStockphoto.com / Silvia Jansen

PHOTO 8.3 According to client-centered therapy, psychologists show their clients unconditional positive regard. Can you suggest situations when psychologists should criticize and even confront their clients?

APPLYING THE HUMANISTIC TRADITION

Despite criticisms, humanistic ideas find many applications in clinical practice, education, and other applied fields. One important application is in psychotherapy.

Psychotherapy

Existential Therapy

Most theoretical assumptions of existential psychology find their applications in **existential therapy** as a method of psychotherapy. It is based on the assumption that we, as human beings, make our own choices and should assume full responsibility for the outcomes of our behavior, experiences, and feelings. It is hard to argue that we often feel unhappy because life too often treats us in a very unkind way. Still, every individual possesses the freedom to create his or her own goals. This freedom could generate in every one of us the sense of purpose and meaning. As soon as we have our goals and achieve this sense of purpose, we need to start working on reaching our goals. The responsibility of the psychotherapist is to understand the four basic dimensions of human existence (the physical, the social, the psychological, and the spiritual) and help people set, reset, and eventually achieve their ultimate individual goal, which is happiness (Rogers, 1951).

A critical thinker would quickly comment that this is all easier said than done: Who does not want to be happy? It is a valid critical question. However, existential therapists insist that happiness is not reached overnight or simply because we want to be happy. A fundamental change in our attitudes toward life is needed and it is achieved through therapy. We need to stop thinking of what we expect from our lives and think of what our lives expect from us. Life challenges us every moment, and we must respond to these challenges by taking charge of our thoughts and actions and engage in right conduct. Life ultimately means taking responsibility, which is an important condition on the path to happiness (Frankl, 1959). Overall, many clinical trials involving existential therapy have demonstrated their relative effectiveness in helping people overcome their setbacks, limitations, and difficulties, and to lead more meaningful lives (Wong, 2015).

Client-Centered Therapy

Carl Rogers' theoretical ideas were applied to what he called **client-centered therapy**, which brought him global recognition. According to Rogers, therapists show their clients genuineness, empathy, and unconditional positive regard and create a supportive, nonjudgmental environment in which clients are encouraged to think about their own problems, discuss them, prepare a course of action, and then reach their full potential (Cooper et al., 2013; Rogers, 1959). A healthy, friendly relationship between the client and the therapist must be achieved, based on openness, trust, and mutual respect. The therapist accepts the client without disapproval or approval; this attitude should facilitate increased self-respect in the clients, which they often lack when they enter therapy. This method has gone through a couple of name changes along the way. Rogers originally called it *nondirective* therapy because he felt the therapist should not lead the client, but rather be there for the client while the client directs the progress of the therapy. As he became more experienced, he realized that even being "nondirective," he still influenced his client by his very "nondirectiveness." In other words, clients look to therapists for guidance and will find it even when the therapist is trying not to guide (Arnold, 2014; Rogers, 1961).

Care With Dignity

Life and Death Decisions

Humanistic ideas have meaningfully affected contemporary discussions related to end-of-life issues. A philosophical and legal question is, *Does an individual have the right to die when this person suffers due to incurable illness?* Many philosophers and writers of the past, such as Locke in England and Dostoyevsky in Russia, discussed this question and appealed to religion, science, critical thinking, and common sense to offer quite different opinions. For centuries, most countries' laws and religious traditions rendered negative views on the right to die or strictly prohibited an individual's choices of the matters of death. Governments would commonly put their convicted criminals to death by means of capital punishment yet denied the right to die to citizens if they asked for it. The discussion reemerged in the past decades in the contexts of individual rights and humanistic principles.

In the late 20th century, the term *assisted suicide* was used to identify a suffering person's decision to end life with the help of another individual, usually a doctor. Opponents of assisted suicide offered a long range of legal, religious, moral, and psychological arguments to oppose assisted suicide. They argued that legalization of assisted suicide would place the most vulnerable and afflicted in an even more susceptible position because someone else makes the decisions for them (Yuill, 2013). Proponents prefer to call the procedure *assisted dying or death with dignity* (instead of assisted suicide). They also argue that the goal of any treatment is to reduce the individual's suffering and that individuals have the fundamental right to make decisions about their lives (Docker, 2013; Lepore, 2009). Several countries as well as some states in the United States have legalized this procedure under specific conditions (Death With Dignity, 2022).

Humanistic principles are nonpartisan, and they do not encourage or discourage certain legal or political decisions on the matters of assisted dying. However, these principles simply direct our undivided attention to the individual and his and her right to dignity and a pain-free existence. It is absolutely important that making any end-of-life decisions requires openness, honesty, and complete disclosure of medical information to the patient and the family members. All options should be discussed, and multiple opinions should be sought. The individuals making such decisions must be knowledgeable and free to make the right choice. According to the American Medical Association, every patient ought to "come to the end of life as free as possible from suffering that does not serve the patient's deepest self-defining belief" (AMA, 2022). Still, disagreements persist, and assisted dying remains one of the most controversial issues in medical care today. However, there are other applied areas in which significant progress has been made. Such decisions have affected the lives of millions of people.

Hospice Care

Humanistic principles in psychology contributed to a global discussion as well as decisions about the right to be treated humanely. Humanistic psychologists championed the idea that all human beings have the right to be treated with dignity regardless of age, gender, or a social group to which they belong. Moreover, not only do people have the right to live with dignity, but they also have the right to decline with dignity (Lepore, 2009). Humanistic principles of the necessity of care and dignity in an individual's existence were crucial in the development of **hospice care**, a complex medical and psychological system that is focusing on palliative and other humane principles of medical care. The major goal of **palliative care** is to prevent and relieve the suffering and distress of individuals affected by a serious illness and to improve their well-being when it is possible (Berger & O'Neal, 2021; Callanan & Kelley, 1997). Today, hospice care in the United States and many other countries has become a very important part of the health care system.

Holistic Health Movement

Humanistic principles have contributed to the **holistic health**, a multidisciplinary applied field focusing on the fundamental assumption that physical, mental, and spiritual factors contributing to an individual's illness are interconnected and equally important in treatment. In fact, the holistic approach in medicine elevates the importance of psychological factors in medical treatment and the prevention of illness (Remen, 1996). Under the influence of humanistic and holistic ideas, during the past 50 or so years, many new centers of holistic treatment appeared, first in North America and Europe, and then across the world. Many trained professionals with medical and psychology degrees work in the fields of spirituality, classic literature, folklore, and traditional methods of healing (in Africa, Asia, and Latin America) to identify and use the effective methods of treatment involving both body and mind. Supporters of holistic treatment used humanistic principles and no longer saw their clients and patients as "sets of symptoms" but rather emphasized the uniqueness of every individual's history of illness and every therapeutic method used in each case (Ventegodt et al., 2006).

Basic humanistic principles found another application in **narrative medicine**, a clinical field that helps medical professionals recognize, absorb, interpret, and be moved by the stories of illness (Charon, 1992). Several medical schools and residency programs train physicians and nurses to treat patients and their medical issues not as problems to be solved but to take into account the specific psychological and personal history of the patient. Narrative medicine helps doctors, nurses, social workers, and therapists improve the effectiveness of care by developing the capacity for attention, reflection, representation, and affiliation with patients and colleagues (Charon, 1993).

Some fields of research turned to empirical studies of specific mechanisms of socialization and development. For example, **narrative psychology** focuses on how told, posted, or published stories and essays shape lives (Murray, 1985; Vassilieva, 2016). Narrative psychology also uses storytelling as a part of psychotherapy: The therapist is listening and recording a story. The story can be retold later. There is no interference and instruction. Telling their stories and hearing the stories of others help promote better understanding and better interaction between therapists and clients. Quantitative methods, such as content-analysis, can be used to analyze such narratives.

Narratives can contain powerful generational memories. The psychologist James Liu, who was born in Taiwan and now works in New Zealand, showed in his cross-national studies that despite popular assumptions about the existence of profound differences in the way people of different cultures perceive history and major world events, the similarities among individuals are overwhelming (Hilton & Liu, 2017; Liu et al., 2005).

Peace Psychology and Public Diplomacy

Principles of humanistic psychology influenced **peace psychology**, a theoretical and applied branch that studies ideological and psychological causes of war and develops educational programs to reduce the threat of violence in international relations and domestic policies of some countries (Greening, 1986). Psychologists working in this field conducted research on a wide range of social issues and topics, including forgiveness, social awareness, altruism, and conflict resolution. Specifically, peace psychology teaches that most causes of war and violence are preventable. It takes both political leaders and ordinary people to give up their old images of the enemy and try to find possibilities for dialogue with their adversaries.

Humanistic principles found applications not only in health care but also in other areas. One of them was a global field of **public diplomacy**, which is the organized interaction among citizens of different countries to establish a dialogue intended to find solutions to international disputes or other issues. Public diplomacy is about helping politicians, experts, students, and ordinary people to communicate, understand, and ultimately, reduce international tensions.

Several pioneers of peace psychology, including Thomas Greening, made an important contribution to the U.S.-Soviet relations during the Cold War, especially in the 1980s (Greening, 1986). Psychologists organized face-to-face meetings between officials, students, teachers, and other professionals in the United States and the Soviet Union to "deconstruct" the old enemy image and promote the new atmosphere of trust. Carl Rogers was also actively engaged in public diplomacy. He conducted multiple seminars and face-to-face meetings between representatives of conflicting groups, including Northern Ireland and South Africa. He traveled to Brazil, Russia, and other countries to conduct seminars of creativity, goodwill, and mutual understanding (Cohen, 2000).

You may ask, "How is it possible to affect international relations by conducting interpersonal group seminars?" Peace psychologists believe that psychological changes should influence policy and global outcomes in large contexts. Although the direct impact of such interpersonal interactions is difficult to measure, public diplomacy receives high marks from many professionals who acknowledge that a gradual reduction of international tensions is possible to achieve by turning to, among other issues, individual contacts between opinion leaders, including scientists, journalists, and business leaders (Hart, 2013).

Skeptics, of course, disagree. They have long maintained that we must pay attention to fundamental social and political processes that cause psychological transformations in political leaders and in public opinion, not the other way around. To achieve peace, for example, one side must propose or impose it first, and then people change their attitudes and behavior to adjust to the reality of peace (Kaplan, 2012).

Which side would you support in this argument? If psychologists had enough resources, would they have enough intellectual power to resolve social conflicts? Time will tell.

CHECK AND APPLY YOUR KNOWLEDGE

1. Explain client-centered therapy.
2. Explain narrative medicine and narrative psychology.
3. What is peace psychology and how can it be effective in today's world?

SUMMARY

- In the second half of the 20th century, researchers shared a popular opinion that psychology as a discipline should bring wisdom and compassion in addressing lingering societal problems, especially in the fields of education, mental health, and individual development. Applied to psychology, the humanistic tradition calls for renewed efforts to study the phenomena that distinguish human beings—love, happiness, and self-growth.

- The humanistic tradition is rooted in critical examinations of other traditions. Humanistic psychologists challenged behaviorism and psychoanalysis by emphasizing the importance of individual responsibility, free choice, and intellectual freedom as fundamental human forces guiding a person through life.

- Humanistic psychologists focus on the actual experience of an individual. They generally prefer qualitative research methods to quantitative procedures and stress the importance of in-depth examinations of an individual's concerns, memories, plans, feelings, and actions taken together, in unity.

- Humanistic psychologists based their views, in part, on existentialism in philosophy and on existential psychology. One of the leading representatives of existential psychology was the American psychologist Rollo May, who, like many existential psychologists, believed in self-awareness and self-growth as two important goals that the individual should pursue.

- One of the most notable contributions of Abraham Maslow to personality psychology was his hierarchical theory of motivation and human needs.

- According to Maslow, the highest level of the hierarchy of needs is self-actualization; he concluded that self-actualizing persons exhibit a number of similar behavioral and psychological characteristics.

- One of the distinct features of a self-actualizing individual is peak experiences, which are periodic and profound episodes of happiness, optimism, inner harmony, and creativity. Years after Maslow described peak experiences, his ideas found support in the studies of so-called *flow*—a state of complete concentration and joyful immersion in the situation or activity. Flow is a feature associated with the autotelic personality.

- Carl Rogers saw self-actualization as the highest level of psychological health. Self-actualization, however, does not occur simply because an individual wants it. To achieve self-actualization, he or she has to make a conscious and sustained effort.

- Humanistic psychology influenced positive psychology, the discipline studying the strengths and virtues that enable the individual and communities to thrive. Positive psychology as well as the humanistic tradition in general pay significant attention to happiness and the ways to reach it.

- Most theoretical assumptions of existential psychology find their applications in existential therapy. Carl Rogers's person-centered theoretical ideas found applications in his famous client-centered therapy.

- Humanistic ideas find significant applications in health care in general, hospice care, the holistic health movement, people's diplomacy, and many other fields.

VISUAL REVIEW

Visual Review. Chapter 8. The Humanistic Tradition.

1. MAIN IDEAS

Humanistic psychologists focus on the individual's care and self-growth	Human beings should be viewed from a holistic and optimistic perspectives.	Rational and knowledgeable individuals are can exercise their choices and be responsible for their actions

2. STUDYING THE HUMANISTIC TRADITION

Existential psychology celebrates the uniqueness of human existence, self-growth, and happiness	Maslow's system offered a hierarchy of human needs and focused on self-actualization and the autotelic personality	Rogers' person-centered theoretical ideas found applications in his famous client-centered therapy

3. APPLYING THE HUMANISTIC TRADITION

Psychotherapy	Hospice care	Holistic health movement	Peace psychology

KEY TERMS

autotelic personality

B-values

client-centered therapy

D-needs

existential crisis

existential psychology

existential therapy

existentialism

flow

holistic health

hospice care

humanistic psychologists

humanistic psychology

narrative medicine

narrative psychology

palliative care

peace psychology

peak experiences

positive psychology

positive self-regard

public diplomacy

self-actualization

EVALUATING WHAT YOU KNOW

Describe the key ideas of the humanistic tradition.

Explain the "five points" related to humanistic psychology.

Explain existentialism and existential psychology.

Explain Rollo May's views on tradition, change, and anxiety.

What is Maslow's hierarchy of needs and self-actualization?

What are peak experiences? Who usually has them?

What is the essence of the person-centered approach?

What are the key views of happiness?

Explain existential therapy.

What is nondirective therapy?

Explain the holistic health movement.

What is narrative psychology?

A BRIDGE TO THE NEXT CHAPTER

In the previous chapters, we have examined five different traditions of research into personality. Among them were the behavioral-learning, the psychoanalytic, the trait, the cognitive, and the humanistic traditions. It is time now to investigate how these major traditions, as well as other approaches, explain the individual personality within several major contexts. We will call such contexts domains. They are circumstances or conditions without which major personality traditions cannot be fully understood and assessed. These domains or fields include gender, psychological abnormality, and adjustment. But first, we will turn to the developing person.

PERSONALITY DOMAINS

PART

III

9 THE DEVELOPMENTAL DOMAIN

Steve Glass/Getty Images

LEARNING OBJECTIVES

After reading this chapter, you should be able to do the following:

- Discuss the major milestones in human development and the impact of nature-nurture as well as consistency-openness models to study personality.

- Explain cultural influences as well as social, economic, and political factors that affect the developing personality.
- Identify ways to apply knowledge about personality psychology in the developmental domain.

How different is your generation—your collective interests, values, and habits—from your parents' generation? Just compare the clothes fashion dominant 30 years ago or the music people liked then to what you tend to wear and listen to today. Do you see, feel, and hear the differences? Of course, as an old saying goes: *Times change; we also change.* But can we state with confidence that we as individuals are different from our parents simply because we belong to different generations? And what is a "generation" from personality psychology's standpoint?

An average 45-year-old is different from an average 15-year-old not only because of expected physical changes taking place in the body due to aging. What other factors can suggest the differences between these two individuals? Of course, these must be their health histories and life experiences. There may be different countries and cultures in which they grew up. The experiences might also be shaped by their race, gender, social class, their education, and a host of political factors. And even though two individuals were born in the same year and grew up within similar social circumstances, they can be completely different as individual personalities. Yes, a tendency to put human beings in distinct age or generational groups is overwhelming in social sciences and in psychology as well.

A few decades ago, journalists and then social scientists began assigning similar personality traits to entire American generations—the large groups of individuals born and living at about the same time. The baby boomers came first. They were the people born after World War II, approximately between the late 1940s and the early 1960s. Their personalities were described as mostly open-minded, optimistic, family-oriented, resilient, and hardworking.

Then came the hippies. They appeared very much different than the generation before them. They had long hair, wore tie-dyed T-shirts, and spoke a different English full of slang (imagine how terrified their parents were). They challenged the old traditions and allegedly preferred "peace, love, and rock 'n' roll" to hard work and sacrifice.

The 1980s was the decade of the yuppies. These young professionals challenged the counterculture of their hippie generation. Yuppies were mostly about education and business; they appeared hardworking, rational, and industrious.

After that was generation X with a "softer" view of life. They were described as balanced, happy, tolerant, and family-oriented.

Next came the millennials, whose birth years ranged from the early 1980s to the early 2000s. They seemed community-oriented and supersensitive to injustice. They tended to be more upbeat and happy than their parents. They were mostly detached from official institutions, as well as being family-oriented and networked among their friends.

And then came generation Z (called by some the *app generation*). Most adults older than 30 these days are "app-enabled," and people between 18 and 25 today are mostly "app-dependent." Psychologists, based on their research, guess that individuals within the Z generation tend to be balancing between two extremes: They vary between a weak and strong sense of identity; they tend to maintain superficial relations with others *and* develop very deep relationships; and they either have little creative imagination or extremely high levels of creativity. Sociologists also indicate that this generation, on the one hand, expresses more progressive views of life than their predecessors. On the other hand, many others within this generation have tendencies toward nationalism and populism.

Questions

- To which generation do you think you belong?

- How would you describe yourself in comparison to your parents or other (20 or 30 years older) members of your family?

- How would you describe yourself in comparison to your peers? How different are you from most of them and how similar?

- Are you a different person compared to 5 years ago? Does our age have anything to do with our personality features?

Sources: Dawson, 2011; Eatwell and Goodwn, 2018; Gardner and Davis, 2013; Twenge, 2017

THE ESSENCE OF THE DEVELOPMENTAL DOMAIN

This chapter describes personality in the context of development, or a specified state of growth or advancement. Together, we will focus here on **human development**—the changes in physical, psychological, and social behavior that individuals experience across the life span, from conception to their last days. Studying these changes, we will also recognize **socialization**—the process by which an individual becomes a member of a society and takes on its ideas and behaviors.

People accumulate new knowledge and thus develop their beliefs, habits, and individual traits. We dress in certain clothes, enjoy or avoid specific foods, engage or keep away from certain situations, pursue distinct goals, and evade discussing some topics because of the way the socialization process works: We tend to behave in the ways that others consider appropriate and normal (Henrich et al., 2010a). The experiences that we have every day can be different from those of the generation that came of age just 20 years before us. Typically, the characteristics that come to define a generation appear gradually, and along a continuum (Twenge, 2017).

Socialization refers to social factors that shape the behavior of individuals and can affect their personality traits. People too, can influence the socialization process by changing the social world around them according to their own perceptions, ideas, and voting chances. As processes, human development and socialization overlap, and neither stops at a particular age. Regardless of how mature you are, you continue to develop, and your socialization continues as well. Yet remember, not only human development involves growth. It involves decline, too.

Nature and Nurture Interact

Psychologists have long maintained that the individual's development and socialization depend on the interplay of nature and nurture. Specifically, the development of the child's personality is rooted in the child's natural features and direct interaction with other individuals, as well as general environmental factors. But how does the developing individual learn and acquire individual traits? Two interconnected concepts have emerged in psychology (Whiting & Whiting, 1975).

The first one, which we call "the natural," assumes that the developing individual should have certain natural predispositions to think, experience emotions, and act in particular ways. How individual personalities are built is certainly dependent on many natural factors. Social conditions can only modify whatever nature potentially "prescribes" to individuals (see Chapter 2).

The other concept, which we will call "the social," states we, as humans, are not destined to follow the prescriptions of genetic codes from DNA. Although humans have different natural predispositions, their development is largely based on the challenges and opportunities they encounter in life. Throughout history, especially in the past several decades, psychologists have maintained a progressive view that a deliberate, comprehensive, and psychologically sound "intervention" of qualified educators in the developing individual's life could bring significant and positive results (Cravens, 2002).

Quality of Life Is Essential

Development and socialization should be understood in the context of the **quality of life**. This is the general well-being of individuals measured by the availability of resources, physical and financial security, quality of living conditions, quality of education and health care, presence or absence of violence, and a number of other factors—all of which significantly affect the individual's development and socialization. To illustrate, countries vary in overall density of population and number of close family members living under the same roof. The child's development and socialization depend on the people with whom the child interacts, the places where they spend time together, and the roles children play (Whiting & Whiting, 1975). Access to resources and educational opportunities are likely to provide an advantageous environment for the developing child. Poverty also directly affects relationships within the family. In relatively poor regions—because most people have only limited access to resources—close cooperation within families is necessary for survival. In wealthier regions, people tend to be less interdependent simply because they are already secure enough.

©iStockphoto.com / franckreporter

PHOTO 9.1 Contemporary families become significantly smaller across the world. Fertility rates in countries such as Iran, Saudi Arabia, or Brazil are similar or even lower than in the United States. The rates are falling in Africa. Why do women, on average, have fewer children than their mothers had 20 years ago? What does a smaller family today, in your opinion, mean for a child's development?

Global Changes Affect the Individual

To state that the world today is changing is meaningless. Every generation in the past could make a similar statement: Do you think your parents were not talking about a rapidly changing world when they were much younger? This is important for a science-minded person not to declare that the world is changing, but to focus on specific changes. For example, one of the most significant changes that affects our lives is a rapid global decline in fertility rates during the past 25 years. This trend continues today. General demographic trends in Europe, North and South America, and Asia show fertility rates of slightly above two children per woman across practically every country except several countries in Africa (Alvarez, 2022; Winter & Teitelbaum, 2013). Increasing living standards and educational levels, changing societal norms (especially those concerning women's rights and their reproductive health), plus several other global factors are likely to contribute to the decreasing fertility rates around the world. What do these changes mean in terms of our study of personality?

Smaller families are likely to mean more material resources available to children of the new generation. The focus of the family is seemingly shifting toward the child. Yet smaller families could mean the end of the traditional family, in which members of several generations lived under the same roof. Smaller families also mean differences in socialization patterns in the family: If a child has just one or no siblings at all, does this fact affect this child's development compared to situations when a child had several siblings? Research in this field is necessary and timely (Mussino et al., 2021).

Social scientists have long predicted that the changes taking place in the world these days would likely affect many individuals' ethnic and religious identities. In what way? Globalization, at least the processes that were happening during the past 20 years or so, often promoted universal standards for all people in all places. In a way, the message "We are all humans, we have similar values of equality and justice, and we do not need wars to resolve our problems" even emphasizes similarities among humans. Thus, billions of people living during this period of globalization felt they were losing their sense of cultural identity. There were too many things appearing to them as universally faceless and domineering, like Hyundai cars, McDonalds hamburgers, or Fly Emirates airlines. A trend was predicted some time ago—that more individuals would become conservative or traditional in their judgments and decisions, including people's turn to religion and nationalism (Huntington, 1993).

Other scientists disagree with such assumptions and discuss the weakening of the influence of local cultures on the individual and the development of a new global culture. The ongoing social, economic, technological, and political realities transform traditional cultures (Draguns, 2009; Faiola, 2003). This new global culture with its emphasis on consumption and the Internet was supposed to create similar lifestyles and produce somewhat "uniform" personality traits in most people (Ho-Ying Fu & Chiu, 2007). Today we can discuss if people's individual identities are becoming increasingly dynamic, absorbing, and tolerant, or if we are entering an era of global confrontation and bigotry.

Developmental Stages

Across cultures, an individual's development is commonly understood in the context of developmental stages. In the process of development and socialization, individuals go through these

developmental stages, which are definite periods in the individual's life characterized by certain physical, psychological, behavioral, and social characteristics. Contemporary scholarly books on human development distinguish several stages within the life span: prenatal period, infancy, childhood (divided into early and middle childhood), adolescence, and adulthood, which is subdivided into three stages, early adulthood, middle adulthood, and late adulthood (see Figure 9.1).

Classifications of Stages

Most life span classifications across cultures include the birth and the death of the individual. Cultural beliefs in immortality and reincarnation—in some cultures—uphold the understanding of the life span as an endless cycle. In addition, the views about the beginning of life (i.e., does it start at conception or at a later period?) vary cross-culturally and are based on people's educational background, religion, and their political and ideological values. There can also be slightly different categorizations of the life span. For example, according to Hindu tradition, infancy, early childhood, and middle childhood are not necessarily separate stages (Valsiner & Lawrence, 1997). In the Judeo-Christian tradition, life is represented somewhat linearly; it begins at conception and its end is death. In Hinduism, life is represented circularly: People live and die many times (Fernandez et al., 2010). In more than half of the societies in the 20th century studied by Schlegel and Barry (1991), there was no special term for adolescence. Indeed, adolescence is a transitional stage between childhood and adulthood in relatively affluent societies, which can afford the existence of a large segment of the population who may look and feel like adults and yet are not allowed to take on adults' duties, roles, and responsibilities (see Figure 9.1).

In some traditional religious teachings, people acquire social status, develop behaviors, and shape personality traits according to prescribed roles. For example, in traditional Hinduism,

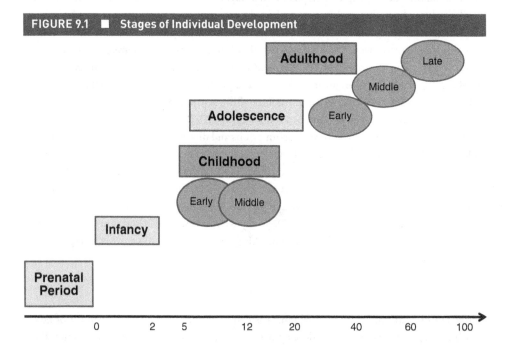

FIGURE 9.1 ■ Stages of Individual Development

people have obligations regarding their position in society and to their stages of individual development. Societal positions and the roles attached to them are called *castes*, and they are hierarchical. The Brahmins (priests) hold the highest position, followed by the nobles or warriors, then the commoners, and, finally, the serfs, who are the lowest. The Brahmins teach religion; the nobles practice defense; the commoners plow, tend cattle, and lend money; and the lowest class serves the upper ones. Every person is supposed to come through developmental stages, such as the celibate student, householder, forest dweller, and renouncer. During the first stage, which lasts to approximately the mid-30s, the person learns about religion. After this, the person gets married, starts a family, and becomes a householder. The next stages come after the person retires and returns to the life of self-discipline and ritual. Compassion and giving should dominate this stage. During the last stage, the renouncer gives up daily pleasures and reaches spiritual liberation. These classifications and rules refer to traditional beliefs, which most members of today's Hindu community do not practice today.

Most classifications of the life span focus on transition points of the individual's development. Birthdays, initiation rituals, weddings, school graduations, divorces, the birth of children and grandchildren, retirement, and other significant life events mark the most important points of human transition. Legal knowledge matters, too (see Chapter 1). Reaching the voting age or drinking age, which is 18 and 21 respectively in the United States and 18 in both cases in other countries, for example, could also be interpreted as a sign of legal maturity. It is common to attach developmental labels to other people who reach a transition point in their lives. For example, a person's high school graduation is likely to be considered a sign of maturity. Several biological, behavioral, and physiological changes are also recognized cross-culturally as indicators of reaching particular life stages. Among these natural events are emergence of permanent teeth, first words, first menstruation or menopause in women, growth of facial hair in young men, and so forth. Across cultures, gray hair is commonly viewed as a sign of maturity, despite tremendous individual variation with regard to hair pigmentation. Changes can be gradual, as well as sudden and abrupt: In many cultures, it took just a special ritual or ceremony to "transfer" from a child into an "adult" (McDowell, 1988). In other words, the transition from one state to another was a matter of social custom.

In the contemporary world, the amount of education required for young people to enter the workforce is expanding. As these people pursue education for longer periods (to obtain a law degree usually takes, for example, at least 7 years of college education and training in the United States), they also postpone transitions into adult roles. The median ages for these adult transitions were the late 20s in every industrialized society, and it was rising in developing countries (Arnett, 2008; Settersten & Ray, 2010). The fact that transitions into adult roles have become somewhat delayed in many societies has led to the spread of a new period of life, called **emerging adulthood**, that extends from the late teens to the mid-20s (and even later) and is characterized by self-focused exploration of possibilities in work, relationships, interests, and values.

Is There a Midlife Crisis?

You have certainly heard about the midlife crisis. In popular literature, this is described as a period in people's lives when they are believed to realize the pressures of age, question their accomplishments, experience excessive anxiety about the future, and have doubts about their life plans. This period typically occurs, according to popular beliefs across cultures, in a person's age between 35 and 50. In popular novels and movies, this midlife crisis sometimes is also associated with the unusual, unexpected things people do, such as buying flashy clothes and cars, digging into some strange projects, falling in love with a seemingly "wrong" person, or giving up a successful career for a "questionable" lifestyle. Popular stories make it appear that every person should go into this crisis. Does research support this popular belief? In fact, psychological research remains skeptical. Several empirical studies find little evidence about the existence of such a crisis. For example, a study in Canada, one of the most in-depth analyses ever conducted in this field, followed the fortunes of two groups—specifically, 18-year-old Canadian high school students and 23-year-old university seniors—for the period of more than 25 years (Galambos et al., 2015). Participants were regularly asked to report their assessments of happiness, relationship and employment statuses, and how their health fared. Both groups were found to become, on average, happier most quickly when they hit their 30s, largely thanks to job and personal relationship upturns, and the 40-year-olds were mostly happy as well. Measures of happiness took a slight downturn by age 43, but this was only in the high school sample. In general, the results of this and most other studies question the myth that there must be a midlife crisis. True, crises take place in our lives, but they are not necessarily confined to any age period.

Research also suggests that the midlife crisis is often confused in some people's views with *awareness of aging*, which incorporates all aspects of individuals' perceptions, behavioral experiences, and subjective interpretations related to their process of growing older (Dutt et al., 2018). This can be relevant to the experiences of a 10-year-old as well as to the perceptions of more mature individuals. Many people see their midlife positively. Instead of a perceived crisis, it can be an opportunity for growth. At any moment of our lives, we can reevaluate how we are moving toward our goal and make changes if we feel we need to make them (Nindl, 2019).

Earlier Stages Affect Later Ones

It is generally assumed that early stages of individual development should influence later ones—that is, whatever happens early in our lives should somehow affect our experience and our personality features later. Ancient philosophers in India, China, or Greece were aware of the impact of a person's early experiences on later developing traits (Pickard, 2011). Psychological theories developed in the past 100 years maintained this view, too: As was discussed in earlier chapters on psychoanalysis and behavioral traditions, despite their substantial differences, theories were essentially in agreement that an individual's early experiences and habits play a significant role in an individual's personality traits and habits during the later stages of life.

Stability and Change: Consistency and Openness Models

One of the most important questions developmental psychologists ask is whether individual personality features change during the life span. The common view is that these features do change. However, how significant are these changes? Two models—**consistency** and **openness**—attempt to explain the process of stability and change in personality features and how they change (Renshon, 1989). According to the first model, consistency, most people acquire (or learn) behaviors and develop stable traits early in life and tend not to change them later. For example, if a person grows up in a conservative, religious family in Morocco, this person will likely be religious and will not tend to seek new experiences later in life. The other model, openness, suggests the opposite: People do constantly change their behaviors, encounter new experiences, and adjust to changing life situations. Early childhood and adolescent experiences do not necessarily determine who you are today as a person. Your traits and habits evolve (Sigel, 1989).

Overall, we need to see human development in a context of a continuum: Some personality features remain stable during the life span, while others change. The most important question is how stable a person's specific individual features are and how they develop and change.

Persistence and Change

Personality traits' stability and change should be assessed from different angles. Research shows that most individuals have relatively enduring attributes and that the changes across the life span are somewhat predictable. Stability of personality features is shaped by a complicated interaction between individuals and their social environments. The stability of traits can also be associated with completely different social environments. Consider two examples.

Social and political developments in Afghanistan during the last 45 years have been marked by several overwhelming developments. Among them were the revolution and dismissal of the king, the Soviet invasion in 1979, the war against the occupation, the emergence of radical religious groups, a new foreign occupation, the end of it, and then the new period of uncertainty. Think of an Afghani girl born in a village near Jalalabad in the1980s. During practically all stages of her life, she was likely to be exposed to continuous stress, challenges, and fear for her life and the lives of her loved ones. She had to constantly adjust to the changing conditions and at the same time develop a stable set of personality features necessary to deal with the daily stress of her life (we will learn more about individual coping mechanisms in Chapter 12). The second example sees another girl born in the 1980s in a small Norwegian town, likely able to live a life relatively free of cataclysms, significant economic downturns, and unexpected turns. Norway is a country that has one of the most developed social welfare systems and one of the highest life expectancy rates in the world. In both cases, individuals are likely to develop relatively stable personality features in response to completely different social and political conditions. In the first case, the stability of traits helps with the changing dangerous circumstances. In the other, the stability of traits can be associated with social stability (Shiraev & Levy, 2024).

The relationship between many personality features and social conditions is a two-way street. We, as individuals, with all our qualities and traits, seem to shape environmental contexts, within which we live. In turn, those contexts often accentuate and reinforce our beliefs, habits, and individual traits. Studies show, for instance, that some of our political beliefs—such as being conservative or liberal—are somehow correlated with certain basic personality features. However, some people do not change their beliefs during their life span, while others do change their values because of changing social conditions (Caprara & Vecchione, 2009; Sears & Funk, 1999). Personality traits change or other transformations are possible because individuals "respond" to their environments and adjust to them. Yet we also change due to our own individual efforts or by turning for help or advice to our family members, friends, or professional psychologists (Donnellan & Robins, 2009).

Of course, important life experiences may change our beliefs, values, and subsequent behaviors as well as personality features and traits. The following case in point, which is borrowed from history, is just one example of a sudden change that takes place in our lives out of a single event or experience.

A Life-Changing Experience

How do we become who we are right now? Contemporary science suggests that changes tend to be gradual and come from different directions. However, we also know from our own experiences and the lives of others that there are some moments in our life that change our values and expectations. Consider an example. Back in 1893, a young lawyer named Mohandas Gandhi (1869–1948) traveled from England to South Africa on business. While on the train, he was removed from a Whites-only carriage on a train because South African law assigned each carriage according to race. Appalled by this act of racial discrimination, Gandhi wanted to return to England immediately. However, the night he spent in a cold waiting room in the train station probably, as he recalled, changed his life forever. This act of dishonor was one of the most inspiring experiences of his life. From that hour, he refused to accept injustice. Known to the world today as Mahatma (Sanskrit for "great soul"), Gandhi has become a living symbol for peaceful resistance for the sake of justice.

CHECK AND APPLY YOUR KNOWLEDGE

1. Explain human development and socialization.
2. Name the key developmental stages.
3. What is a midlife crisis? Ask a person who is over 40 if he or she has experienced a major crisis; if yes, what was its cause(s)?
4. Explain the consistency and oppress models of development.
5. Have you experienced significant changes in your views of life and other people due to a major event in your life? If yes, what was the event, and what were the changes?

STUDYING THE DEVELOPMENTAL DOMAIN

An Individual's Development and Life Sciences

Personality psychologists learn from life sciences about the important biological foundations that affect personality traits and other stable behavioral and emotional characteristics during a life span.

Hayley Okines was just 17 when she died. This beautiful English girl with blonde hair and blue eyes had a rare premature aging disorder, which gave her the body of a 104-year-old woman at her death. The syndrome, known as *Hutchinson-Gilford progeria syndrome* (HGPS), a genetic condition characterized by the dramatic, rapid appearance of aging beginning in childhood. Children age about 10 times faster than the normal pace (Harley, 2015). There have been about 200 known cases of this illness on the planet (Hall, 2020). Hayley was one of them.

We, as human beings, have a naturally determined pace of aging. It is genetically programmed. This means we are supposed to go through physical developmental stages at certain times, but our lifestyle and the events around us can change the pace that nature has set for us. Hayley was born a unique genetic program that made her skin look aged, her face small, and her height short. She also suffered from serious and increasing health problems associated with aging, including bone and cardiovascular issues. Yet even though her body had physically aged, she remained a 17-year-old in her soul. In the book *Old Before My Time* (Okines, 2012), we learn more about Hayley's life, her interests, and her daily routines. Despite the physical aging, she remained a girl just like millions of other girls around her: She was interested in music, games, and was very much involved in thinking about her future—she believed her future would be bright and happy.

Nature has substantial control over the aging process. Age-related physiological mechanisms control the development of our traits, behaviors, stable emotional states, and even the ways we relate to reality and understand it. Nature sets the length of the **prenatal period,** or the time between conception and birth, which is 38 weeks for humans on average. Yet from conception, the developing embryo in a mother's womb is exposed to different conditions: Some of them are favorable, while others are not. Across the world, physical violence, exposure to chemicals or radiation, and air and water pollution, to name a few, can cause various complications in pregnancy and serious birth defects. In addition, a lack of professional prenatal care is also a crucial factor affecting children's future development and a variety of their personality traits. Psychologists already researched and published their findings more than 170 years ago about the harmful impact of extreme poverty, hunger, domestic violence, and parents' alcohol consumption on the developing child (Morel, 1857/1976).

Numerous studies show how early physical traumas, illnesses, exposure to toxic substances and other body- and health-related factors affect the development of stable psychological features in younger individuals (Rauh & Margolis, 2016). Consider just one example involving studies of children who become addicted to glue at a very early age. Mostly homeless and suffering from hunger and abuse, these children use glue—easily available on the streets—as a narcotic. As it reacts to glue (and may similar toxins), the brain releases endorphins that on the psychological level produce joy, excitement, and, for a brief period, comfort. Unfortunately, children quickly develop glue dependency. As a result of this dependency, not only do they suffer from chronic, long-term kidney problems, but they also have brain seizures, memory loss, and serious intellectual delays. There are also significant personality changes—the child becomes consistently angry, violent, and depressed (Bergmann & Frisén, 2013).

Advanced age, of course, means a higher probability of illness affecting every area of an individual's functioning. There is no escape: Most individual functions naturally decline with age. Physical aging is akin wear and tear: The skin becomes less elastic, the hair loses its pigmentation, the muscles begin to atrophy, the bones become more brittle, and the cardiovascular system declines. Brain maladies such as cerebral degenerative disease or stroke are more common in people over 70 compared to people 30 years younger. Notice that most CEOs of the biggest companies retire around 65. This is hardly a capricious custom. Any "normal" aging means a host of predictable psychological changes: the decrease of the speed of information-processing, diminished working memory capacity, reduced verbal learning, and the ability to ignore irrelevant information—these all take place regardless of the person's lifestyle or attitude, according to massive longitudinal studies (Schaie, 2012). Of course, as we learned in previous chapters, it is wrong to state the process of aging is all about decline and loss.

Cross-Cultural Approach

Another approach to studying personality within the developmental domain comes from cross-cultural psychology. Psychologists study how different cultural influences affect the individual's personality. They look for similar personality features as well as cultural differences among personality traits. Social scientists and psychologists generally assume that cultures can be described in terms of continuums placed between cultural dichotomies, such as high- versus low-power distance, high- versus low-uncertainty avoidance, and collectivism versus individualism.

Power distance is the extent to which the members of a society accept that power in institutions and organizations is distributed unequally (Hofstede, 1980). People in high-power distance cultures tend to accept inequality between the leaders and the led, the elite and the common, the managers and the subordinates, and breadwinners and other family members. A traditional caste-based Indian society was one of high-power distance. Studies reveal that people in hierarchical, high-power distance cultures tend to assign stricter behavior rules associated with social status (e.g., "A father should always act like a respectable head of the family"). On the other hand, people in egalitarian, low-power distance cultures are less preoccupied with the behavioral rules attached to the status (e.g., "A father can be a caring friend above all"). In many studies, it has been shown, for instance, that the United States is viewed as a relatively egalitarian, low-power distance culture. Alternatively, Japan and South Korea were commonly viewed in the past as more hierarchical and higher in power distance (Matsumoto, 2007).

Uncertainty orientation refers to common ways used by people to handle uncertainty in their daily situations and lives in general. Uncertainty avoidance is the degree to which the members of a society feel uncomfortable with uncertainty and ambiguity. People in high-uncertainty avoidance communities tend to support beliefs promising certainty and to maintain institutions protecting conformity. Likewise, people in low-uncertainty avoidance cultures are apt to maintain nonconformist attitudes, unpredictability, creativity, and new forms of thinking and behavior. People who are certainty-oriented tend to defer to rules, customs, or opinions of other people, including authority figures, to resolve uncertainty (Sorrentino et al., 2008).

Finally, the third dichotomy refers to individualism and collectivism. **Individualism** is a complex pattern of cognition and behavior based on concern for oneself and one's immediate family or primary group, as opposed to concern for other groups or society to which one belongs. On the other side of the spectrum is **collectivism**, which is complex behavior based on concerns for other individuals and care for shared traditions and values (Triandis, 1996).

Key processes by which individuals learn cultural norms are socialization and education. School, the family, peers, and social groups provide individuals with knowledge and skills to adjust to the rules and demands of the society or change them (see Figure 9.2). Not only do people adjust to their cultural environments they transform them, too. Sometimes such transformations take decades to take place. Sometimes changes come overnight.

FIGURE 9.2 ■ Cultures Can Be Described in Terms of Continuums Between Dichotomies

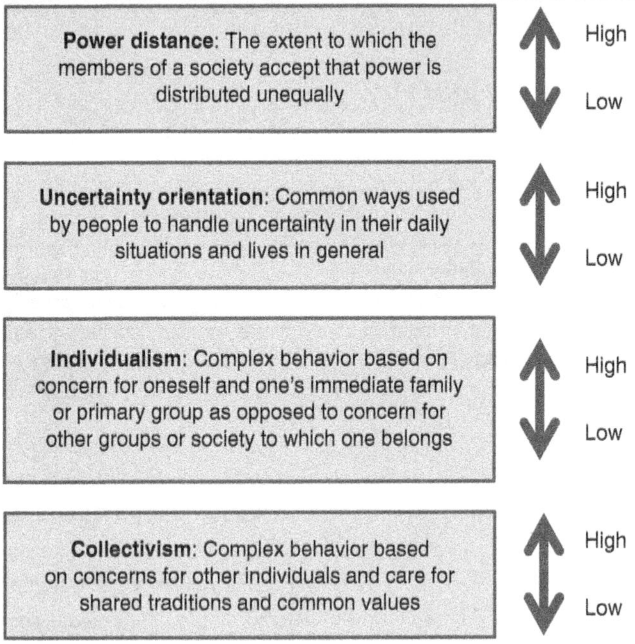

Power distance: The extent to which the members of a society accept that power is distributed unequally

High
Low

Uncertainty orientation: Common ways used by people to handle uncertainty in their daily situations and lives in general

High
Low

Individualism: Complex behavior based on concern for oneself and one's immediate family or primary group as opposed to concern for other groups or society to which one belongs

High
Low

Collectivism: Complex behavior based on concerns for other individuals and care for shared traditions and common values

High
Low

Collectivism and individualism are not static categories. Consider, for example, their vertical and horizontal dimensions (Triandis, 1996). In the vertical dimension, people tend to refer to one another from power and achievement standpoints. They tend to consider their relationships as employees and managers, teachers, and students, or as leaders and the led. In the horizontal dimension, people are engaged with one another as friends, family members, and coworkers. Thus, equality is a crucial feature within the horizontal dimension. Authoritarian regimes, for example, are likely to emphasize equality (horizontal level) but not necessarily freedom. Western and other modern democracies tend to emphasize freedom (vertical level) but not necessarily equality (Kurman & Sriram, 2002). It is important to understand that our local cultures undergo rapid transitions because of today's travel, new opportunities, and people's increased willingness to move away from their birthplaces. People's views of equality and power change with time. They also are based on many socioeconomic and psychological factors. Sustained economic success in a country or long-term difficulties in another country tend to make people change their views of equality and authority (O'Neal, 2019).

In general, psychologists are aware of a methodological obstacle they face in their research: Even though they study children from different countries and cultures, their samples are comprised mostly of educated and economically secure families. Parents with the time, resources, and motivation are more likely to bring their infant in to participate in a developmental study at a university laboratory compared to the poor. Many hundreds of experiments in recent years exploring basic cognitive capacities of the young have almost all focused on middle-class participants (Fernald, 2010). This situation is changing today, and the samples in psychological studies are becoming more diverse and representative (Best, 2018).

CHECK AND APPLY YOUR KNOWLEDGE

1. Explain collectivism, power distance, uncertainty orientation, and individualism.
2. Explain vertical and horizontal collectivism and individualism.
3. Do you personally want to look younger or older? Ask your friends, too. Do people want to look older sometimes? Why do so many people want to look younger? What do most people do to look younger? Use your personal observations or other sources to discuss in class how people in different families and cultures cope with aging. Which businesses are interested in creating hype about the "younger image"?

Erik Erikson's Tradition

When you see a psychological study showing that young adults tend to accept and laugh at offensive jokes more often, compared to older adults, how would you interpret such findings (Stanley, Lohani, & Isaacowitz, 2014)? Ok, young adults endorse a more aggressive humor style than older adults. But why? There could be different explanations. And then you hear that the differences between the young and the mature are rooted in the strengths of their super-ego: The young have a weaker super-ego, which allows them to accept violent and offensive impulses. As a person studying psychology, what will this explanation remind you about? Of course, this is a view from psychoanalysis (Chapter 4).

Recall from that chapter that the psychoanalytic tradition in psychology emphasizes the importance of early childhood experiences in the future development of the adult. This vision of the individual's development does not seem to be unique. Many psychologists in the past emphasized the importance of the earlier stages of development on the later ones. At least four important points make the psychoanalytic tradition different.

First, the psychoanalytic tradition emphasizes that only the earlier stages of human development are especially important. They have a crucial impact on the future personality traits of the individual.

Second, during the process of individual development, a person goes through several stages. Every stage is characterized by a particular conflict, contradiction, or a set of distinct features that the individual acquires. Recall that Freud emphasized human sexuality, Jung discussed archetypes, while Adler paid attention to human imperfection and inferiority. Erik Erikson (1902–1994), an immigrant to the United States and one of the most quoted psychologists globally, believed—based on his research and clinical practice—that at each stage the ego faces a developmental conflict or crisis. If the crisis has been positively resolved, the person's ego strengthens by gaining greater adaptation (Erikson, 1950). But if the crisis has not been resolved, the ego loses strength, which results in poor adaptation and many psychological problems including anxiety and depression.

Third, most likely, the impact of the earlier stages remains outside of the individual's aware-ness. Only trained psychology professionals are capable of understanding the deep-seated roots of adult behavior and individual traits. Our life is a constant development. If somebody is undergoing psychotherapy, this is, in fact, the act of learning and growing. The individual seeing a therapist is developing new virtues that were missing earlier in life (Erikson, 1968). Parents and adults have to play the important role, too. If growing children, for instance, are not allowed to discover their own talents, as adults they will probably lack strong motivation, have low self-esteem, and prefer passivity to action.

Fourth, and probably the most important assumption, is that we, as individuals, have the capacity to understand our own problems and weaknesses and then address them to become better people. These views correspond in many ways with Indian, Muslim, Christian, Buddhist, and several religious and philosophical traditions aimed at self-transformation through insight into the nature of self (Paranjpe, 1998). Moreover, Erikson and others wrote about the necessity for developing adults to focus increasingly on others, helping in the community, and society in general. Personal growth is not only about focusing on self but most likely is about the well-being and happiness of others.

Laurence Kohlberg's Tradition

Psychologists and social scientists for years tried to address an important question: How do chil-dren learn moral values? **Morality** is commonly defined as a complex cognitive, emotional, and behavioral construct associated with the person's understanding of right and wrong based on societal norms. A common view prevails that the developing child should be "ready" to under-stand morality and virtue before the adults teach it to them.

The works of the American psychologist G. Stanley Hall (1844–1924) suggested that the child's development advances through critical periods. Before age 6, for example, the child is unable to make sophisticated theoretical judgments and is generally insensitive to moral values. There is no reason at this age to teach the child complex theories about morally right and wrong actions. Once the child reaches the next stage at age 8, formal learning can begin. The child is ready to understand moral issues, such as kindness, love, and justice. It is generally accepted in modern psychology that the child has to develop first certain cognitive and emotional skills— for example, understanding compassion and empathy—to adopt moral values. This process is likely to take place in stages. Yet what are these stages?

One of the most prominent theories about moral values and their role in individual develop-ment came from the American psychologist Lawrence Kohlberg (1927–1987). He studied and described six stages of moral development (Kohlberg, 1981). In brief, children develop their moral judgments from "lower" stages of reasoning, in which they prefer to avoid punishment for wrongdoing, to the "higher" stages, where they choose social contact and then universal prin-ciples to guide their moral assessments and actions (see Table 9.1).

In the past, several empirical cross-cultural studies provided support for the initial Kohlberg's assumptions. As an example, a comparative study took 45 psychological projects of moral judgment development conducted in 27 countries and showed that the first four stages appeared to be very similar in the subjects of all countries studied (Snarey, 1985). However,

TABLE 9.1 ■ Kohlberg's Stages of Moral Development

Stage 1. Preconventional level I: Judgments about what is right and what is wrong are based on fear of punishment.

Stage 2. Preconventional level II: Moral conduct produces pleasure, whereas immoral conduct results in unwanted consequences.

Stage 3. Conventional level I: Any behavior is good if it is approved by significant others.

Stage 4. Conventional level II: The existing laws determine what is moral and immoral.

Stage 5. Postconventional level I: Moral behavior is based on individual rights and underlying social circumstances.

Stage 6. Postconventional level II: Moral conduct is regulated by universal ethical principles that may rise above government and laws.

Comment: The term "conventional" is vague; it should be understood as "average" or "regular" and not necessarily as "good" or "required."

critics expressed skepticism about the cross-cultural validity of this theory. The methodology used in cross-cultural studies on moral development was based on hypothetical stories about moral choices that a person was making. Critics suggested that these stories were more likely to be related to U.S. and other Western subjects, compared to people living in other countries (Rook et al, 2021; Shweder et al., 1990).

Other studies pointed out that the individual's moral judgments are influenced mostly by specific circumstances; the values are not necessarily based on a certain "developmental" level of the person's moral development (Matsumoto, 1994; Vassiliou & Vassiliou, 1973). One of the most compelling arguments was that moral judgments are difficult to examine in a laboratory. Have you heard about the **trolley dilemma**? In the well-known thought exercise, people (imagine yourself in their place) are asked to visualize a runaway trolley, rapidly moving down the railway tracks. You, as a participant, have two options: (1) You do nothing, and the trolley kills the five people in it after an inevitable collision with the wall; or (2) you pull the lever, thus diverting the trolley onto the side track where it will kill just one person, who just happens to be there—however, your act will save the lives of the five. Which will be your choice?

Studies show that most people, from 80% to 90%, prefer to save the lives of five people and sacrifice the life of one. However, studies show that we also pay attention to the circumstances and the specific characteristics of the people involved surrounding this hypothetical situation. Significantly more people found it acceptable in general to sacrifice a perceived low-status person than a high-status person. And it was significantly more acceptable to save the lives of seemingly "good" people (such as children) by sacrificing a seemingly "bad" person (such as a drunk man). Also, people were unwilling to sacrifice the life of a person who is their relative or the loved one (Fiske, 2010).

The trolley dilemma examines the human capacity for rational justification of moral and immoral decision-making: Is it appropriate to save the lives of five people by sacrificing the life of one? It also shows that people pay attention to the circumstances surrounding the experimental conditions. Moreover, people's decisions are not attached to their developmental levels. In fact, our moral decisions are caused by a great range of mediating factors. Researchers also found that personality traits such as optimism, conscientiousness, and openness to experience are strong predictors of certain moral decision-making (such as constantly practicing physical distancing behavior during the COVID pandemic). Positive mood also is associated with moral behavior, while negative affect predicts less moral behavior (Alivernini et al., 2020).

CHECK AND APPLY YOUR KNOWLEDGE

1. Describe in three sentences the key points of the psychoanalytic approach to an individual's development.
2. Describe the six stages of moral development, according to Kohlberg.
3. Explain the "trolley dilemma" using a different example.

Developmental psychologists emphasize the interaction of the developing individual with the environment. Jean Piaget from Switzerland and Lev Vygotsky from Russia—two outstanding psychologists of the 20th century—further developed this view. Vygotsky's observations of parent–child interactions led him to a conclusion about an active and adaptive role of the child's adjustment to the changing conditions and demands of life. Piaget's theory emphasized the child's inner developmental mechanisms and their adaptive role. Both theories gained major international recognition.

Jean Piaget's Developmental Approach

The Swiss psychologist Jean Piaget (1896–1970) believed that the process of development progresses in stages determined by the child's developing brain, skills, and social environment. The movement from one state to another is primarily a natural process. A main lesson we learn from Piaget is that an individual's features are predetermined due to a variety of natural factors that are unfolding within particular interactions and social circumstances. These views had an important impact on personality psychology.

Piaget believed that human development is a process of adapting to the changing contexts of life. Perhaps the most substantial contribution by Piaget was his ideas of **assimilation** and **accommodation**—the two sides of the process of adaptation or learning. Assimilation is adopting operations with new objects into older mind patterns. Accommodation is modifying one's mental structures to fit the new demands of the environment. Assimilation and accommodation are both fundamentally biological processes and work in tandem to help individuals advance their understanding of the world.

Stages of Development

In Stage 1, the *sensorimotor* stage, infants learn about their interaction with their immediate environment through immediate experiences. Around the age of 18 months, children develop the increased ability to hold an image in their mind beyond the immediate experience. During Stage 2, the *preoperational* stage, children acquire language, develop imagination, learn the meaning of symbols, and develop creative play. Children remain generally egocentric, which means they have a diminished capacity to see the world from another person's viewpoint. At this stage, which lasts until approximately age 7, children tend to be animistic in their judgments; for example, they can assign personality features to objects and animals or tend to believe in fairy tales.

At the third stage of *concrete operations*, children learn the rules of logic and begin to comprehend the laws of physics related to volume, amount, and weight. They become more mechanical in their judgments about nature and things around them. From age 7 to 11, children acquire *operations*, or logical principles to solve most problems. At this stage, the child not only uses symbols to make them represent something but can also logically manipulate those symbols. A child learns to classify and put objects in a series or group according to various rules. The final stage, *formal operations*, which begins at age 11 or 12, indicates the time when adolescents develop the ability to think abstractly. This involves using complex logical operations and hypothetical thinking.

In the process of development, one stage must be accomplished before the next can emerge. The process may resemble construction of a building: Each new level is impossible to build without constructing the lower ones. As soon as the child has constructed the operations on a new level, then the child learns about more complex objects and performs more complex operations. Thus, children continually renovate the ideas they formed earlier.

Do all children develop thinking and move through developmental stages in the way Piaget proposed? Summarizing results from a handful of studies, Dasen (1994) showed that the stage sequence (preoperational, operational, and abstract thinking) appears to be similar across countries. Children tend to move from one stage to another as Piaget predicted. However, other studies contradicted Piaget's belief that children go through the animism stage before age 7. Studies of indigenous people (Gardiner et al., 1998) showed that the animistic view of life developed much later, and that children up to age 7 were really thinking more like natural scientists (Shweder, 2010).

Piaget's original ideas about the stage-by-stage development of the child have found applications in educational programs in many countries. Critics pointed out that Piaget provoked a temptation to interpret some higher developmental stages as more "valuable" than others. In reality, though, social success, satisfaction, and adaptation strategies, as well as certain activities and professions, do not require that the individual function on the level of advanced formal operations. Piaget also believed, based on his experimental research, that children made moral judgments based on their own observations of the world. According to Piaget, children can construct their own moral worldview and form ideas about right and wrong, and fair and unfair, that are not the direct product of adult teaching.

©iStockphoto.com / triloks

PHOTO 9.2 According to Vygotsky, a child is typically ready to learn more and understand better than a teacher or parent assumes. Taking on the role of a parent or a teacher, explain this statement in practical terms.

Lev Vygotsky's Developmental Approach

The works of Lev Vygotsky (1896–1934) remained generally unknown for many years. However, his research has had a significant impact on educational and developmental psychology. Many of his ideas related to child development have influenced personality psychology. Like Piaget, he promoted the child-centered approach. His studies directed the attention of parents and teachers toward the child's personality: the child's rational thinking, creativity, individual choices, and nonconforming attitudes.

Vygotsky's research methods were largely observational. His students recalled that he had a habit of coming to the room where preschoolers played and sitting there for hours. After some time, the children in the room would stop paying attention to the man sitting there and begin to act "naturally." This was exactly what Vygotsky wanted to see (Shedrovitsky, 2009). Most of his ideas came from such observations, like the idea about the child's developmental periods. A child's development is not a steady process of a consistent, uninterrupted transformation and change. Periods of gradual change are followed by rapid transitions, sudden transformations, and even crises. Vygotsky suggested five stages of such transformation, occurring at birth, at the end of the first year, and then at the ages of 3, 7, and 13. At each stage, new situations and crises occur, and every new situation is a new source of development.

Parents and teachers have to understand the entire social situation surrounding the child. The goal of upbringing is not to emphasize a child's inabilities or deficiencies, but to pay attention to what this child has already achieved or developed. Finding new potential in a child is a top priority of an educator and parent (Vygotsky, 1933).

Vygotsky also introduced the idea of cultural mediation. Every psychological function, such as thinking, appears twice. First, it is an "outside" social activity or learning. Next, this learning is internalized as thinking. Human consciousness therefore should be understood in the context of interaction of an individual with the outside world. In fact, Vygotsky, in a symbolic way, placed the soul outside the human body. This was a new theoretical way to understand the most difficult question about the nature of consciousness. The essence of human consciousness is in its unity with the cultural environment (Vygotsky, 1934/2005).

Vygotsky introduced and developed the concept of **zone of proximal development**, understood as the difference between a child's learning progress with help or guidance and this child's learning achievement without the guidance of an adult. Children usually have potential, a latent reserve for their intellectual growth. This means that the child is typically ready to learn more and understand better than a teacher or parent assumes. Vygotsky challenged a common belief of the time that the child has to be prepared to understand certain concepts (e.g., a 3-year-old is not ready to study something that only a 4-year-old is capable of knowing). In his view, the child can learn more if teachers or adults stimulate the child's intellectual advance within the zone of proximal development (Vygotsky, 1934/2005).

Vygotsky thus argued that the task of education is not to offer something that the child is ready to perform. Such task is greater. Children, as well as adults, have hidden potential that can be developed with some external help. Two tasks should be pursued here. The first one is to provide detailed information about what specifically each child's "zone" is—some kids may have a greater potential than their peers in some areas but not in others. Second, both psychologists and teachers should create new tasks, exercises, and programs to assist children in developing their skills.

Vygotsky originally developed the concept of the zone of proximal development to argue against the use of standardized tests as a means to gauge intelligence. Vygotsky believed that rather than examining what students already know to measure their intelligence, it is better to examine their ability to solve problems independently and with the assistance of an adult. In Vygotsky's view, ideally, teachers and parents should not only follow and accommodate children but also accelerate, improve, and enhance their potential in as many areas as possible.

He maintained that creativity and discipline are not mutually exclusive phenomena and that educational programs can promote both imagination and orderliness in the growing individual. Educators should focus on their students as individual personalities, as learners. They add new concepts to prior knowledge and construct, build, and understand themselves—the process that is intrinsically human.

Vygotsky believed that when we study what a child can do alone at this moment, we actually study his or her development as of yesterday. When we study what this child can do in cooperation, we look at the developments of tomorrow. This was a new, optimistic, and obviously progressive view of human development. An individual, in his view, is not a mere product of social environment (a popular thesis partially supported by behaviorists). To him, people are independent and active thinkers. He believed that education should involve the process of the child's interaction with teachers and peers and not necessarily memorization and repetition. Vygotsky's ideas years ago already resonated well with educational researchers working on advancing teaching techniques to stimulate the child's unknown or underdeveloped potential (Bruner, 1960).

Vygotsky's views also found a reflection in so-called "narrative therapy," based on the assumption that an individual's identity reveals itself in certain symbols as short accounts or narratives about their life (Charon, 1993). To correct a person's psychological problem is to investigate such narratives and then restructure them to explain new potentials and possibilities for improvement. An externalization of a problem makes it easier to investigate and evaluate it.

Specific Traits

How do individual traits change during the life span? Do they tend to change in the same direction in most individuals? What changes in us, as individuals, and what does not? Early in this chapter, we discussed stability and change of personality traits in the context of consistency and openness models. These questions related to openness and stability have intrigued philosophers and scientists for centuries. Ancient Greek philosophers saw consistency of traits in adulthood as a virtue (Donnellan & Robins, 2009). More than 100 years ago, American psychologist William James wrote that personality characteristics (they were called *character*) are set firmly after the age of 30 and do not change. Psychologist Gordon Allport emphasized the biological basis of individual traits—personality traits can be traced to certain features of the child's temperament, or a general and stable set of behavioral and emotional responses (Allport, 1937). Behaviorists, however, maintained that personality traits are learned behaviors and thus they can change with circumstances surrounding the individual. As you can see, the views varied.

The Big Five, and other approaches to studying personality, provide some specific answers to the issue of trait stability and change (Anusic et al., 2012; Donnellan et al., 2007). We have already looked at the theory that organizes most personality traits into five categories—extroversion, agreeableness, conscientiousness, neuroticism, and openness to experience (see Chapter 6). Studies show that certain consistent behaviors and responses appear early in life and tend to correlate with some personality features developed later. Extroversion seems to be correlated with the general style of approaching behavior (whether the child is interested in exploring a novel object—such as a new toy—or not) and the direction of incentive motivation. (For example, do other people motivate the child to act? Or does the motivation come from within?) Research also shows that extroversion is correlated with the balance of the child's inhibited and uninhibited behavior. For instance, children who appear to be inhibited tend to be shy, timid, and fearful in the future, but those who tend to be uninhibited later tend to display more sociable and outgoing behaviors (Kagan & Herschkowitz, 2005). Neuroticism seems to correlate with withdrawal behavior, anxiety, and the ability to recognize threats. Children pay different attention to other people and situations that appear to be different from their normal, everyday experiences; one child feels apprehensive even threatened by a new situation while another does not (Kagan & Snidman, 1991). Adults with elevated levels of neuroticism tend to respond poorly to stressful situations and often interpret ordinary situations as threatening. Studies establish connections between neuroticism's manifestations during childhood and adolescence, on the one hand, and during adulthood, on the other (Widiger & Oltmanns, 2017).

Agreeableness is associated with enjoyment of social attachments and affection toward others. Conscientiousness is likely to be associated with the brain's frontal lobes and is correlated with the ability to plan, predict, and anticipate. A few studies agree that openness to experience, as a trait, is likely to be formed a bit later in life and is related to the person's educational and life experiences (Lucas & Donnellan, 2009, 2011).

How stable are these five characteristics within the life span? Table 9.2 summarizes several studies conducted in different years. Studies show that average levels of extroversion, especially the attributes associated with self-confidence and independence, tend to increase with age. Agreeableness and conscientiousness appear to increase with age, while neuroticism appears to decrease with the passage of time (Roberts et al., 2006). Studies also show that childhood conscientiousness can predict health behaviors of adulthood, which can have an impact on life expectancy (Widiger & Oltmann, 2017). This finding should make sense: The more careful we are about our body and our health, the more persistent we are in maintaining our healthy schedules, and the more likely we are to maintain a healthy lifestyle and seek medical attention when necessary.

More conscientious children, compared to others, tend to grow up into more conscientious adolescents and adults. Psychologists tend to see such dynamics in personality traits as positive trends. For example, higher levels of agreeableness and conscientiousness and lower levels of neuroticism are associated with stability and quality of relationships, greater success at work, better health, a reduced risk of criminality and mental illness, and even decreased levels of mortality (Hampson et al., 2015). This pattern of positive average changes in personality attributes is known as the maturity principle of adult personality development. The basic idea is that attributes associated with positive adaptation and with the successful fulfillment of adult roles tend to increase during adulthood in terms of their average levels. It is also interesting to notice that

TABLE 9.2 ■ The Big Five Personality Traits and the Life Span	
Extroversion	• Average levels tend to slightly increase with age, especially attributes linked to self-confidence and independence.
	• Variations remain less significant with age.
Agreeableness	• Average levels gradually increase across the life span.
	• Variations remain less significant with age.
Conscientiousness	• Research is inconclusive. Some studies show that average levels gradually increase across the life span until midlife or old age when they tend to decline.
	• Other studies find this relatively stable across the life span.
Neuroticism	• Level gradually declines across the life span but has a tendency to increase in old age.
Openness to experience	• Average levels increase during adolescence and then gradually decline after midlife and across the life span.

Sources: Donnellan and Robins, 2009; Hampson et al., 2015; Specht et al., 2011

openness (e.g., openness to new experiences) increases during adulthood and then declines with more mature age, especially after 60 (Roberts et al., 2006; Specht et al., 2011). It looks as if most of us develop it for a particular view of life that is increasingly difficult, or even unreasonable, to change during adulthood. Some people develop a stable worldview and feel comfortable with that, but others may feel less comfortable with the way they see the world yet don't find a way to accept new experiences because of their profession, social networks, or their family.

Overall, personality attributes are relatively enduring and become increasingly consistent during adulthood. The most changes are taking place in either younger or older age periods. Personality developments (stability and change) result from the dynamic interplay between individuals and their environment (Donnellan & Robins, 2009). Personality traits are associated with specific responses that promote personality continuity. People with particular personality traits often develop and sustain behaviors relevant to their traits. For example, people who are friendly are likely to evoke more pleasant and supportive responses from other people. This is helpful in other social interactions. Such positive interactions reinforce the disposition to be friendly. In addition, personality traits shape how people construe social situations. A long business meeting involving many heated discussions may have a particular effect on an extrovert and a different effect on an introvert. For example, introverts may feel less comfortable speaking out during business meetings, so they don't make an effort to be active and engaged participants. Finally, individuals play an active role in selecting and manipulating their own social experiences. Many people have a tendency to seek out, modify, and even create certain social environments that are consistent with their individual personality characteristics. For instance, people who are shy and anxious may be less likely to look for careers that require significant social interaction.

CHECK AND APPLY YOUR KNOWLEDGE

1. Describe the stages of development, according to Piaget.
2. What is the "zone of proximal development"? Which one of your personal features do you think was overlooked when you were a child? What can you do to develop and advance this feature today?
3. What was William James's view of an individual's personality characteristics?
4. Describe how extroversion, agreeableness, openness to experience, neuroticism, and conscientiousness change during the life span.

APPLYING THE DEVELOPMENTAL DOMAIN

Personality psychologists study human development to gain scientific knowledge about the dynamics related to the formation of personality traits. In a simple way, the individual's personality is understood from the standpoint of age and the age-related features that human beings develop in various social contexts. Human beings are seen as developing, changing, and dynamic individuals. This means that every stage of human development has certain features that make this stage somewhat different from all other stages. This also means that our knowledge about human beings should be applied carefully because each person is unique. People have different natural backgrounds (such as genetic makeups) and social conditions, but they also evolve going through developmental stages. The following text will consider several applications of the studies with the developmental domain. We will look at suicide, criminal behavior, and the approaches to educational practices.

© David Corby

PHOTO 9.3 Suicide is the second-most common cause of death in adolescents. Suicide-prevention centers are always looking for volunteers and qualified professionals.

Developmental Factors and Suicide

More than 700,000 people commit suicide globally every year (World Health Organization [WHO], 2022. Approximately every 15 minutes, somebody in the United States takes his or her own life. According to the Centers for Disease Control and Prevention (CDC), 35,000 to 40,000 lives are cut short every year in the United States alone. More than 6,000 of them will be individuals who are over 65. Some countries, such as Estonia and Russia, have higher suicide rates than in the United States. Others, like Mexico, have lower rates (WHO, 2022). In the Western world, males die up to significantly more often by means of suicide than do females—both adults and adolescents—although females *attempt* suicide more often (Miranda & Jeglic, 2022). In the United States, the suicide rates among males are approximately 4 times higher than the rate among females. Males represent nearly half of the population but commit nearly 80% of suicides. People over 85 have the highest rate of suicides, according to government statistics (CDC, 2022a).

Suicide is the second-most common cause of death in adolescents, and in young males, it was second only to accidental death (Värnik, 2012; Yip et al., 2012). It is also the fourth-leading cause of death among young children. Between 2007 and 2017, the number of children aged 10 to 14 who took their lives in the United States more than doubled (Solomon, 2022). In the United States, veterans, LGBTQ+ groups, middle-aged adults, individuals living in rural areas, and tribal populations disproportionately experience factors linked to suicide (CDC, 2022a). While suicide rates among Blacks in America remain twice as low as the national average, suicide remains the third-leading cause of death among African Americans ages 15 to 19 (CDC, 2022a; CDC, 2015). Suicide is a serious problem that requires research and social action. Psychological research shows that individuals who attempt suicide tend to use different reasons to make this fatal decision. Around the world, scores of suicide cases go unreported. People tend to maintain a negative view of suicide or prefer not to discuss this problem with researchers (WHO, 2022). In this section, we will focus on how to apply our knowledge about age-related factors of suicide to suggest and provide, as psychologists, better preventive measures.

Personality Traits

Experts tend to agree that there is no "suicidal personality," and there are no personality traits that signal with certainty that the person having them is at risk of taking own life. However, there are indicators that can send a signal that a person may be contemplating suicide. There are risk factors associated with suicide. Psychologists and medical professionals identify several common warning signs referring to psychological disorders, including schizophrenia and anxiety disorders. At least two are the most common globally: depressive illness and substance abuse. Depressive illness remains the most serious contributor to suicide. A combination of depression (a mood disorder) and substance abuse is a lethal blend, leading to a high probability of suicidal behavior (Esang & Ahmed, 2018; Goldston et al., 2008). Depression almost never leads to suicide by itself. People who attempt or die by suicide can have a variety of additional problems: losing a job, having problems at school, having relationships breaking down, physical illness, pain and disability, financial or legal difficulties, or alcohol and drug abuse. Sometimes many of these or even all these problems come together.

Suicidal ideation (such as persistent discussion of death or statements made personally or on social networks) is a factor, too. The presence of a specific plan is considered an additional predictor of suicide. Access to lethal means (such as firearms or sleeping pills) also increases the probability of suicide. It has been found that borderline personality disorder (Chapter 11) is associated with suicidal acts. In addition, suicide is more likely to occur during periods of economic difficulties and family and individual crises (e.g., loss of a significant other, unemployment, or bankruptcy). However, preliminary data published by the U.S. government didn't show an increase in suicides during the first year of the COVID pandemic (Bryan, 2021). An opinion that during a major crisis, more people tend to stick together and help one another may be valid but requires more research.

One of the most important skills psychologists can learn is to identify suicidal risk and to urgently take measures to help at-risk individuals.

Age Factors

There are two critical ages during which most suicides take place in countries where reliable statistics are available. The first critical age period is between late adolescence and young adulthood; younger people are also significantly more likely than those in other age groups to *attempt* suicide and survive. The other period is late adulthood. In the United States, for example, men over 85 years old are especially at risk (CDC, 2022a).

Young People. The most at-risk individuals to attempt suicide among the young are likely to have depressive illness plus substance abuse. Compared to adults, teens and younger adults are also likely to have the symptoms of adjustment disorder, which is a serious and distressful inability to cope with life circumstances (Sunesh-Kumar et al., 2015). We will pay more attention to adjustment disorder in Chapter 12. Studies also have found that impulsivity can be a factor, too—a person focuses on immediate outcomes instead of delayed ones and neglects important information in making decisions. In teens and young adults, several additional risk factors can play a role in suicidal behavior: previous suicide attempts, presence of mental illness, preoccupation with death, family history of mental illness among parents or siblings, and bullying against the child. Harmful social and environmental factors also play a role in childhood suicidal behavior (Tishler et al., 2007). One of the most serious factors affecting suicide among children remains depression and associated with it suicidal thoughts. According to the National Institute of Mental Health, three million American adolescents experienced major depression in 2020. *The Lancet*, one of the top medical journals reported that among 9-10-year-olds, one in twelve suggested having had suicidal thoughts (Solomon, 2022). A global study involving 82 countries showed significant levels of anxiety and suicidal ideation among 12-17-year-olds ranging from 9 to 14% (Biswas et al., 2020). Unfortunately, many parents and caregivers have a vague knowledge about depression, especially in children, and cannot recognize its symptoms. Some people remain simply dismissive of such symptoms wrongly assuming that children cannot have depression.

The Elderly. Unlike the young, older individuals tend to have extensive medical issues that contribute to suicide. A significant number of people in the elderly group have a current diagnosis of depression and might consider themselves (and report to their psychology professionals) a burden to their families. Physical illness and family burden of psychiatric illness are important at-risk predictors in comparison to younger populations (Sunesh-Kumar et al., 2015). The inability to function well in daily life, the failure to do what has been done for years with ease, and fear of social disconnection have become significant risk factors that can predict suicide among older age groups (see Table 9.3; CDC, 2022a; Span, 2009).

Crime as a Developmental Problem

For centuries, social scientists and psychologists were looking for specific personality features associated with criminal behavior, especially with violent crime. Scientists identify certain personality traits such as lack of remorse, aggressiveness, low anxiety levels, and antisocial personality disorder as factors predicting crime.

Studying the individual's personality and combining this research with various economic models can produce intriguing results and applications. Some time ago, American economist Gary Becker (1968) wrote that most criminals act as if they were "rational actors"—they, like ordinary citizens, seek to maximize their own well-being, but they use criminal acts instead of legal means. Becker suggested that if society teaches individuals the tough lesson they will spend some time in prison if they commit a crime, then people should learn to choose better options, such as freedom (in fact, this is an approach that behavioral psychologists would likely suggest). Indeed, it makes sense that being punished for bad behavior with a significant prison term would cause this behavior to change, and after the 1980s in the United States, there were significant increases in sentence length. In Becker's theory, this should have reduced crime,

TABLE 9.3 ■ Risk Factors of Suicide: A Developmental Comparative View		
Risk Factors	*Older Individuals*	*Younger Individuals*
Depressive illness or other mental illness	A significant factor	A significant factor; not common in young children
Substance abuse	A significant factor, especially in combination with depression	A significant factor, especially in combination with depression; not common among young children
Suicidal ideation	A significant factor	A significant factor
Chronic illness	A significant factor	A possible but not common factor
Significant life stressor	A significant factor	A significant factor
Impulsivity, risk propensity	A factor due to the loss of reasoning	A factor due to undeveloped reasoning
Lack of social interaction	A substantial factor	Typically not a factor
Loss of social or professional status	A substantial factor	A factor, but insignificant among young children
Bullying	Typically not a factor	A significant factor
Physical decline	Can be a common factor	Usually not a common factor

diminished the costs of law enforcement, and resulted in *fewer* people in prison. But in reality, it simply led to more spending on crime control and many more people in prison (Becker, 1968; Tabarrok, 2015). Longer sentences did not reduce crime—why not?

The "Child" Personality?

One of the hypotheses as to why longer sentences didn't reduce crime is rooted in developmental theory. As you should remember from this chapter, Piaget and Vygotsky (and scores of other psychologists) argued the following:

- Individuals have to develop certain psychological skills and functions before they can perform certain operations.

- If we give the child the necessary conditions and encourage the child to act and think, the child is likely to develop better intellectual skills and more adaptive behaviors.

Applied to criminal behavior, the logic can be as follows: What if certain individuals (let's call them "criminal types" for the sake of the argument) have problems forecasting and difficulty regulating their emotions and controlling their impulses? They have these problems not because they're bad people; on the contrary, we label them *bad* because they cannot control their impulses and commit theft or burglary. Why can't they control their impulses? Because their specific personality features are not developed enough to let them judge their behavior and the consequences of their behavior to avoid trouble. In the heat of the moment, the threat of future punishment is just not strong enough to deter their act.

Instead of thinking about criminals as rational individuals, we should think about criminals, at least some of them, as resembling children. This means that the punishment for the crime they commit should be quick, swift, and consistent. Inconsistencies in sentencing are detrimental. Studies also show that inconsistencies in the parent's sanctions against the child's misbehavior, in fact, contribute to this misbehavior in the future.

In a brief summary, the developmental reasoning is that when punishment is not quick, children who misbehave have difficulty learning cause and effect—they begin to believe that they can get away with those small bad things that they do. Many adults act the same way, with several types of crime committed on the spur of the moment. We must give people a small opportunity to reflect and consider the consequences of their behavior. They must learn to associate crime with punishment (Scott et al., 2010). This approach remains controversial. Yet not only does it emphasize the importance of crime prevention, it also suggests the increasing role of psychologists, counselors, and community organizers in learning about, addressing, and reducing crime.

Education: Discipline Versus Freedom

For decades, philosophers believed that rigorous discipline, drill, and repetition were key factors in the academic success of a child. Many professionals referred to the studies of 19th-century German psychologist Ebbinghaus to emphasize the special importance of relentless repetition and constant effort (Young, 1985). However, a different viewpoint on education was based on an assumption that children should receive a variety of opportunities and equal choices at school so they can fully develop their intellectual and emotional potential (Vygotsky, 1934/2005). A young child's personality is not fully developed and still unable to manifest a stable set of traits. Therefore, to help the child achieve his or her personal potential, the teacher and the parent should be given more freedom and creativity in the classroom. In a way, according to Vygotsky, the child should learn according to his or her individual "schedule." The more creative the educational environment is, the more efficient the process of education is. Children need guidance, not drill or punishment. A child's potential skills should be facilitated, not left alone.

This point of view has been challenged by other theories and popular beliefs, which mainly argue that children can be easily trapped in the continual search for gratification of their wishes. To avoid this endless quest for pleasure, children should learn discipline and respect the demands of teachers. The educational system in China, for example, historically emphasized learning and discipline as important tools that help the individual to function properly in society.

There is a third way, however. As the legendary UCLA basketball coach John Wooden said, "Drilling creates a foundation on which individual initiative and imagination can flourish." This means that our individual creativity flourishes only within a certain system of rules; we can improvise with these rules once we understand the systems (Lemov, 2014).

These three views summarize the centuries of intellectual debates about the most appropriate way to raise and educate an individual. Which strategy is the best? Is it mostly about creativity, freedom, and spontaneity? Is it mostly about drill, repetition, and following the rules? Or maybe we can combine the two approaches?

CHECK AND APPLY YOUR KNOWLEDGE

1. Describe the development factors of suicide. Which age groups are the most susceptible to suicide?
2. Explain why crime can be viewed as a developmental issue.
3. According to your personal view, what is more important in your educational success: drill and memorization or creative discussion? Or maybe both are equally important?

SUMMARY

- Human development—the changes in physical, psychological, and social behavior that individuals experience across the life span, from conception to their last days.

- Socialization—the process by which an individual becomes a member of a society and takes on its ideas and behaviors.

- Psychologists have long maintained—and it has been discussed in previous chapters—that the individual's development and socialization depend on the interplay of influences involving nature and nurture.

- The general well-being of individuals is measured by the availability of resources, physical and financial security, type of living conditions, quality of education and health care, presence or absence of violence, and a number of other factors—all of which significantly affect the individual's development and socialization.

- Global fertility rates and global migration affect the processes of development and socialization.

- In the process of development and socialization, individuals go through developmental stages, which are definite periods in the individual's life characterized by certain physical, psychological, behavioral, and social characteristics. Contemporary scholarly books on human development distinguish several common stages within the life span.

- It is generally assumed that early stages of individual development should influence the later one. Two models—the **consistency model** and the **openness model**—attempt to explain the process of stability and change in personality features and their changes. According to the consistency model, most adults acquire (or learn) behaviors and develop stable traits early in life and tend not to change them later. The openness model suggests the opposite: People do constantly change their behaviors and adjust their traits to changing life situations.

- Nature has substantial control over the aging process. Personality psychologists learn from life sciences about the important biological foundations affecting personality traits and other stable behavioral and emotional characteristics during the individual's life span.

- Social scientists as well psychologists generally assume that cultures can be described in terms of cultural dichotomies, such as high- versus low-power distance, high- versus low-uncertainty avoidance, and collectivism versus individualism.

- The psychoanalytic tradition in psychology emphasizes the importance of early childhood experiences in the future development of the adult.

- Kohlberg described six stages of moral development in which children and adults are able to make several types of moral judgments. In brief, people go from lower stages of reasoning, when they prefer to avoid punishment for wrongdoing, to the higher stages, when they choose social contract and then universal principles to guide moral actions.

- The Swiss psychologist Jean Piaget believed that the process of development goes in stages determined by the child's developing brain, skills, and social environment.

- According to Vygotsky's view, a child's development is not a steady process of consistent, uninterrupted transformation and change. Instead, periods of gradual change are followed by rapid transitions, sudden transformations, and crises.

- Vygotsky introduced and developed the concept of zone of proximal development, understood as the difference between a child's learning progress with help or guidance and this child's learning achievement without the guidance of an adult.

- Studies show that average levels of extroversion—especially the attributes associated with self-confidence and independence—tend to increase with age. Agreeableness and conscientiousness also appear to increase with age, while neuroticism appears to decrease with age. Studies also show that childhood conscientiousness can predict health behaviors of adulthood. This can also have an impact on the person's life expectancy.

- Several applications of theories within the developmental domain can be described in the studies of suicide, criminal behavior, and the approaches to educational practices.

VISUAL REVIEW

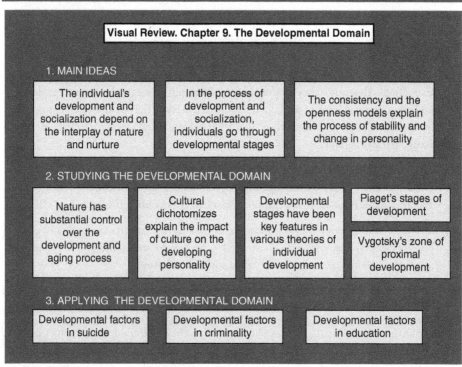

Visual Review. Chapter 9. The Developmental Domain

1. MAIN IDEAS

The individual's development and socialization depend on the interplay of nature and nurture	In the process of development and socialization, individuals go through developmental stages	The consistency and the openness models explain the process of stability and change in personality

2. STUDYING THE DEVELOPMENTAL DOMAIN

Nature has substantial control over the development and aging process	Cultural dichotomizes explain the impact of culture on the developing personality	Developmental stages have been key features in various theories of individual development	Piaget's stages of development
			Vygotsky's zone of proximal development

3. APPLYING THE DEVELOPMENTAL DOMAIN

Developmental factors in suicide	Developmental factors in criminality	Developmental factors in education

KEY TERMS

accommodation
assimilation
collectivism
consistency model

developmental stages
emerging adulthood
human development
individualism

morality
openness model
power distance
prenatal period
quality of life

socialization
trolley dilemma
uncertainty orientation
zone of proximal development

EVALUATING WHAT YOU KNOW

What are the key ideas of the developmental domain in personality psychology?

Describe the main developmental stages.

Explain the consistency and openness models.

What do life sciences teach us about individual development?

What is a cross-cultural approach to individual development?

Explain the views of individual development from Piaget, Kohlberg, and Vygotsky.

Describe the application of the developmental domain to studies of education, criminal behavior, and suicide.

A BRIDGE TO THE NEXT CHAPTER

Developmental factors certainly have a substantial impact on the individual's personality. First, as individuals, we have a number of genetic features that significantly affect our future development. We inherit certain temperament: life expectancy; the propensity to be tall or short, or skinny, or overweight; or the predisposition to have certain psychological problems.

As we know, however, biology is not always our destiny. We live and develop in certain cultural conditions. We are influenced by culture and develop patterns of behavior associated with collectivism or individualism, the acceptance or rejection of power distance, the embrace of certainty or uncertainty, and many other cultural factors. Our society, with its customs and norms—through teachers and parents and recently often media and social networks, as well as a wide variety of other influences—shapes our individualities in a certain way. One of the most intriguing factors in this process is gender, to which we will turn in the next chapter.

10 THE GENDER DOMAIN

Kelsy has finally answered the question that most of us do not even have to ask: *Who am I . . . a boy or a girl?* Kelsy already knew that some people are born in female bodies but feel male inside, and some other people have male bodies but feel female. She also knew the meaning of the words *gay, unisex,* and *transgender.* They have become very common in the English language (although, frankly, many people still have only a superficial view of the meaning of these words). Today, more people speak freely about their true identity and overcome the fear of being condemned and discriminated against for their feelings. Yet Kelsey had a more complicated challenge—a feeling that neither *male* nor *female* categories were appropriate for her self-identity: She felt she was neither a girl nor a boy.

©iStockphoto.com /FatCamera

PHOTO 10.1 From birth, human beings typically follow the perceptions that are expected to match the behavioral and other standards of the assigned sex. Why is it (or isn't it) important to maintain such standards in the 21st century?

Growing up, Kelsy was always puzzled when she needed to cross the box on application forms that referred to male or female identity. Then there were the small but important choices at school: Which sports teams to play on? Which locker room to use? Which doors of gender-specific bathrooms to push? This struggle with self-perception was not about being straight or gay. This was not about being "boyish" or a "manly" girl. This was a matter of Kelsey being honest about yourself as a human being.

Meanwhile, Kelsey decided to use a pronoun that felt right when describing herself: *they.* By 2022, about one quarter of Americans said in surveys they personally knew at least one individual who went by gender-neutral pronouns such as "they" instead of "he" or "she." Younger people, more than 40% of them, are especially likely to know at least one person who uses gender-neutral pronouns.

Sources: Hesse, 2014; Pew, 2019; Smoot, 2022; YouGov, 2022

THE ESSENCE OF THE GENDER DOMAIN

Society traditionally divides individuals into large categories. *Women* and *men* are perhaps the most common categories of all. People usually use these words in their immediate verbal descriptions of others. Most of us think of ourselves as either a woman or a man. The "male" and "female" boxes commonly appear on various forms and surveys. In almost every sphere of our lives, we encounter the *gender* category. Gender has been a very important factor affecting people's knowledge of personality (Riger, 2002).

What does the gender domain mean to our study of personality? Given the complexity of the topic, it is not surprising to discover a great variety of views and opinions. We will discuss three main facets: sex, gender, and sexual orientation. The chapter will outline the most important applications of our knowledge of such facets.

The Sexes and the Intersex

In the context of personality, the term **sex** refers to anatomical and physiological characteristics or features of males and females, the two typically assigned sexes. These features include at least four commonly recognized clusters, such as external genitalia (the body's reproductive organs), glands, hormones, and chromosomes. For example, females have a uterus and ovaries, and males have a prostate gland and testicles. These anatomical structures are present, by and large, when an individual is born. By looking at a newborn's external genitalia, a designated person (often a doctor) "pronounces" a newborn either a boy (male) or a girl (female). This act of judgment becomes an official assignment of a sex to a newborn individual. The child's parents or caregivers are expected to accept the assigned sex (these days, due to advancements in scanning technology, many parents choose to learn about the sex of their future baby before the child is born). The child is immediately referred to linguistically as "he" or "she."

As soon as a certain sex is assigned to a newborn, people start acting toward the child in accordance with the popular norms and expectations. What is expected and in which ways do they act? Consider a simple question: In the United States, would most people select a blue or a pink baby blanket as a gift for a newborn boy? Consider the names parents give their babies—most are sex-specific. Now try to visualize people whose names are John and Joan, or Kuldeep and Kuldeepa. Would most people imagine them as men or women? There are exceptions, of course. In every culture, there are certain names that can be assigned to both sexes, but such names are somewhat rare.

Once a particular sex is assigned, boys and girls often begin wearing gender-specific clothes, usually chosen by the parents or the family members who follow the specific cultural prescriptions of their communities. As babies grow up, their toys tend to be different, too. Many activities, such as child's play, are often chosen to match what is considered a typical, "expected" male or female activity. The growing child and then the mature individual are expected to follow the rules, customs, and perceptions that match (or at least are *expected* to match) the behavioral and other standards of the assigned sex.

However, this common sex dichotomy (either–or) does not accurately represent reality. Some individuals are born with sexual anatomy or reproductive organs, and often chromosome patterns, that do not fit the typical definition of *male* or *female*. This evidence may be apparent at birth or become so later in life (United Nations [UN] for LGBT Equality, 2015). In other words, sex is not strictly dichotomous, but rather a continuous variable. If this is the case, there should be a combination of sex characteristics, such as anatomical structures, that are not exclusively male or female. The **intersex** category is based on the features that are between distinct male and female characteristics. For example, a person can be born with *ambiguous* outer genitalia—those that do not have the typical appearance that allows a child to be assigned immediately to a particular sex. Other people, even if they were born with certain characteristics assigned to a particular sex, choose a different sex at will and accept a surgical and physiological transformation of the body to achieve the physical appearance of their chosen sex (UN Free & Equal, 2022).

In a brief review, scientists and medical doctors these days commonly identify a "third" category in between the two known sex dichotomies. Moreover, some researchers suggest that the third category can be further expanded into subcategories so that there could be at least five sexes: the two traditional ones and three in between (see Table 10.1; Fausto-Sterling, 2012).

Gender as a Social Construct

Sex as a category is rooted in biological, physiological, and anatomical factors. **Gender** is a complex set of behavioral, cultural, cognitive, and other psychological features associated with an individual's sex. Gender as a concept has a significant social component: It is the state of being male or female and practicing informally prescribed cultural norms (such as customs); following expectations about what a person should do as a member of a particular sex; and adhering to formal legal rules (the law) that mandate, regulate, limit, or prohibit particular actions. If gender is a social category, it can be viewed from two gender dimensions: the internal and external. The internal, or psychological, dimension refers to the degree of experiencing being male or female. The external, or social, dimension refers to the roles that society assigns to each sex. These dimensions, of course, are interconnected and actively interact with each other within us.

Let's look at the internal dimension first. **Gender identity** is an individual's self-determination (or a complex self-reflection) as being male, female, intersex (between male and female), both, or neither. The opening vignette introduced the "neither" identity. Or, for example, consider **androgyny**—a combination, a coexistence, a blend of both male and female behavioral characteristics, features, and reflections. Studies show that for most of us, a gender identity tends to remain stable after we establish it as children. American Psychological Association suggests the term, **gender consistency**, which is the understanding that maleness or femaleness is fixed across situations, regardless of superficial changes in appearance or activities (APA, Dictionary of Psychology, 2022b). Yet gender identity can change. This is a process rather than a "product." Gender identity can strengthen (when an individual feels stronger about this identity than before), and it may weaken. It can get stronger again. Although most children refer to

TABLE 10.1 ■ Traditional and Changing Sex Categories		
Traditional Categories	*New Categories*	
	Three	*Five*
Male or female	Female, or intersex, or male	Female, or "leaning" female, or neither, or "leaning" male, or male

self as "I am a boy" or "I am a girl" at a very early age, their understanding or acceptance of the meaning of these words is likely to develop over a period. They may never stop evolving; people constantly learn more about themselves, about gender, and gender identity. It may be rediscovered again.

Why does it change or evolve? Many life circumstances influence the ways we identify self: They include physiological factors (like, during puberty), our interactions with our parents when we grow up, our experiences with family members, our friendships, or travels—they all matter. Activities such as play or education, exposure to the media, and other life experiences also affect our gender identity in so many ways.

Most individuals develop a specific gender identity that matches their biological sex assigned at birth. However, it is also possible that a person with an assigned sex (a girl, for example) feels differently about the assigned gender identity and roles and develops into a different gender (a boy, for example). Some intersex individuals may be raised as a woman or a man but then identify with another gender or none later in life. Also, there can be a strong, core gender identity and a secondary one developing over the core identity (see Figure 10.1; United Nations for LGBT Equality, 2015).

Gender Roles

Learning about a particular gender involves understanding, evaluating, and accepting patterns of experience and behavior. They are called **gender roles**—prescriptions and expectations assigned to genders on the female–male continuum. These prescriptions and expectations

---

FIGURE 10.1   ■   An Individual's Gender Identity as a Process

Sex is assigned. Identity is acquired. It may remain the same, strengthen, or weaken. It may change. Variations? They are possible.

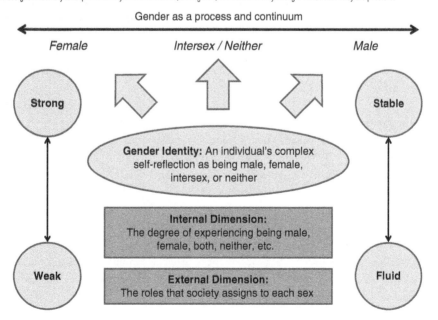

are typically embedded in cultural norms and transmitted from one generation to the next. Ideology, art, and religion play an important role preserving such expectations about gender roles and becoming embedded into the law. Popular beliefs and everyday customs are also important mediators of the knowledge about gender roles.

Across most cultural groups, two major clusters of gender roles have appeared across cultures: masculine (having the qualities attributed to males) and feminine (having the qualities attributed to females). **Masculinity**, traditionally assigned to men, is a general set of features associated with physical strength, decisiveness, and assertiveness. On the other hand, **femininity**, traditionally assigned to women, is a general set of features correlated with beauty, emotionality, and nurture. Notice how imprecise these definitions are. In fact, there is no consensus on how to define these terms. Across cultures and times there was no consistency in what was considered typically masculine and feminine in psychological characteristics, prescribed personality features, or professions. In some cultural settings, gender roles were described as opposing each other, but in others (e.g., Indian philosophies), they were presented and perceived as complementary, adding to each other. Moreover, social prescriptions related to gender roles were changing due to certain political and cultural transformations. The struggle for gender equality has involved gradually eliminating the gaps between gender roles.

Gender roles in history were about the activities the individual should have performed. In traditional cultural settings, women were supposed to be nurturing and caring, while men were supposed to be decisive and physically strong. These prescriptions referred to every area of life, including the family, work, warfare, and education. In the Korean language, a married woman is referred to as *Jip-saram*, or "home person," and a married man is referred to as *Bakkat-yangban*, or "person outside." There were also differences in how social positions and social activities (such as being a warrior or a monk) and occupations (such as being a truck driver, a firefighter, an elementary school teacher, or a nurse) associated with gender roles. You can easily provide examples from your own experiences.

Contemporary psychology considers gender roles as not exclusively limited to the dichotomous male–female categories. A view that has become increasingly common is that individuals may have many features of masculinity and femininity simultaneously. A person can be physically imposing and dominating (features assigned to masculinity) and at the same time caring and loving (features assigned to femininity). The term **transgender** refers to the roles that do not fit into the traditionally assigned gender dichotomy. Transgender individuals do not identify with distinct, traditional male and female gender roles. According to Pew Research (Brown, 2022), about 5% of young adults in the United States say their gender is different from their sex assigned at birth. This compares with 1.6% of 30- to 49-year-olds and 0.3% of those 50 and older who say they are transgender or nonbinary (gender identity that is not solely female or male).

It is critical for psychologists to understand that individuals have a choice in how they think of ourselves. This may or may not be based on the type of chromosomes we have or our external genitals or the way we were brought up. Instead, it can be based on how we see and understand the world, other people, and ourselves (Goldberg, 2014).

Sexual Orientation

Being male, female, or transgender, in terms of gender roles, does not necessarily determine our sexuality or sexual orientation. **Sexuality** is the capacity for erotic experiences and related behavioral responses. **Sexual orientation** refers to romantic or sexual attraction to people of a specific sex or gender.

Sexual orientation, in most individuals, tends to develop gradually. Although the vast majority of children have a sex assigned to them at birth, and many children have a strong sense of their gender identity, studies show they are not necessarily aware of their sexual orientation. Some children develop this orientation relatively early; some acquire it later in life. Others change it at a certain point in life. For others, sexual orientation is a "work in progress" and remains evolving or undefined throughout their life span. Some accept this uncertainty about their sexual orientation. Others struggle with it and may even emotionally suffer because of the unsettling challenge between our individual choices and societal practices (Savin-Williams, et al., 2012).

Sexual orientation is a continuum. Heterosexuality along with bisexuality and homosexuality are at least three main categories of the continuum of sexual orientation. **Heterosexuality** is an individual's romantic or sexual attraction to people of the opposite sex or gender. In Greek, *heteros* means "different" or "other." **Homosexuality** is romantic or sexual attraction between people of the same sex or gender. Bisexuality is romantic or sexual attraction toward both males and females.

In the United States, the term *homosexual* originally carried negative connotations, and it was gradually replaced by *gay* in the 1970s in academic and other publications. The terms *gay* and *lesbian* became more common by the end of the 20th century. In more recent years, the term **LGBTQ+** (lesbian/gay/bisexual/transgender/queer or questioning own sex or gender identity) gained popularity; this is an umbrella term for those who are **gender nonconforming**— people whose gender identity or gender expression does not conform to that typically associated with the sex they were assigned at birth. Some who do not identify as either male or female sometimes prefer the term *genderqueer* or *gender-variant* (American Psychological Association [APA], 2015a).

In Britain, for example, the proportion of the population aged 16 years and over identifying as heterosexual or straight was about 94% in 2020 with men and women in the same proportions (Sexual Orientation, UK, 2020). In the United States, the percentage of adults who self-identify as lesbian, gay, bisexual, transgender, or something other than heterosexual has reached 7%, which is double the percentage from 2012, when Gallup first measured the data (Jones, 2022a). Some people feel and say they are asexual. *Asexuality* is the lack of sexual attraction to another person and diminished interest in sexual activity. This lack of interest may be based on several factors involving genetic predispositions, medical conditions, religious beliefs, or aging. Asexuality may also be viewed as the person's lack of a sexual orientation, although not every specialist agrees. Yet most scholars agree that asexuality is somewhat rare, involving about 1% or less of the population (Etaugh & Bridges, 2017).

The way we identify ourselves in terms of sex, gender, or sexual orientation influences almost every part of our lives. Society always has paid attention to how individuals acquired sexual identity and expressed their sexual orientation. In a society where gender roles are strictly defined and enforced, people whose behavior differs from such norms have been targeted, isolated, and often prosecuted. These sanctioned sexual orientations were embedded in informal customs, formal legal rules, and even in politics. There were, of course, communities in which sexual identity and sexual orientation were not strictly defined.

CHECK AND APPLY YOUR KNOWLEDGE

1. Define *sex* and *intersex* as categories.
2. What is gender identity? How is a person's gender identity established?
3. What are gender roles?
4. Explain the term gender nonconforming.
5. Are you personally gender-conforming or not? Can it be somewhere in the middle of the spectrum?

KEY APPROACHES TO STUDYING GENDER

Traditional Views of the Sexes

A key question for personality psychology is how gender issues influence our knowledge about the individual. Which biological and physiological factors help us understand personality features of men, women, and intersex individuals?

For centuries, religion has been a major source of knowledge and prescriptions (authoritative recommendations) about what men and women were supposed to do. Religious prescriptions suggested how men and women were supposed to be treated as members of society. In theory, both sexes were born equal. Judaism, Christianity, and Islam, for example, share the belief that Adam and Eve were the original man and the woman created by God. Eve was created from one of Adam's sides of his ribs so that all people today are descendants from this pair. However, equality wasn't the case in reality.

Science has emphasized for centuries that women and men were born with different natural anatomical features and therefore should be different in their behavior, feelings, outlooks, and personalities. Up until the 20th century, most scientists emphasized the **natural dominance** of men, which was a general wrong assumption about men's biological superiority over women. The natural dominance paradigm focused on men's natural physical strength, firm character, stamina, willpower, intellectual strength, and creativity. As an illustration, the French physician and philosopher La Mettrie wrote that men have solid brains and nerves; therefore, they have stronger personality features and more vigorous minds than women. He wrote that in women, passion is stronger than reason; therefore, women are prone to tenderness, affection, and passing feelings. And, La Mettrie continued, because women generally lack education, men have better opportunities to demonstrate strength of mind and body. Despite men's toughness, they can be very grateful, generous, and constant in friendship. As if attempting to bring some balance to the description of men and women, La Mettrie mentioned women's beauty as their superior feature (La Mettrie, 1748/1994). Similar views were very common in the past and in most cultures.

What were the traditional views of the intersex? Descriptions of *intersex* individuals appeared in religious and philosophical traditions dating back many centuries. In ancient Egypt, for example, a male god Hapi represented fertility but had distinct male and female features, including breasts and a large belly, which were both symbols of fertility. In India, the god Ardhanarishvara appeared as half male and half female—like a synergy of two types of spiritual energy. The Navaho people in America believe in Ahsonnutli, a god-creator with male and female features. The ancient Greek philosopher Plato theorized that early in history there were three sexes: male, female, and the third—a union of the two. In ancient myths and Greco-Roman art, Hermaphroditus, the two-sexed child of Aphrodite and Hermes, was portrayed as a female figure with male genitals.

These were, of course, "spiritual" realities. In terms of the realities of human society, intersex individuals are traditionally perceived not only as different but also as odd. But true intersex individuals do live openly in some societies. In India, there is a large category of people known for centuries as the *Hijra*, or the third gender, according to some translations. Some Hijras, born with male sex characteristics, undergo an initiation into the cluster by surgically removing their penis, scrotum, and testicles. Estimates suggest that there are more than 10 million *Hijra* in India alone (Gettleman, 2018; Nanda, 1998). In Europe, the 19th-century literary sources contained descriptions of people whom we refer to as intersex today (Kennedy, 1981). However, the social stigma attached to the intersex has been and remains strong.

By the early 20th century, an increasing number of doctors and researchers argued that an individual's sex could be determined not only by the external genitalia but also by at least several other biological factors. In some cases, assigning sex to a child became a challenge because some may be born in between the male and female sexes (Dreger, 2000). Another problem was that doctors did not always agree which physical characteristics should be considered as male or female. For example, physicians across countries would agree that *testes* should be considered as male characteristics and *ovaries* as female. In other cases, disagreements were vast: British doctors, for instance, considered facial hair on women as a sign of mental illness (it was assumed that women were not supposed to have masculine features), while in France it was a sign of physical strength (Dreger, 2000).

Early in the 20th century, the developing science, medicine, and experimental psychology fields paid increasing attention to the scientifically proven differences between men and women in terms of their physical characteristics, motor reactions, sensory thresholds, behavioral patterns, and cognitive skills (Dumont, 2010). Scientists in greater numbers were challenging traditional assumptions about the typical men's superior functioning and women's naturally submissive, passive, and nurturing roles.

EVOLVING VIEWS OF THE SEXES

Modern studies focus on finding particular physiological, genetic, or evolutionary facts that help to explain sex as a biological category. Contemporary research also supports the view of sex as a continuous variable.

Genetics, Anatomy, and Neurophysiology

Modern genetics (see Chapter 2) has established that females have two of the same kind of sex chromosomes (XX), while males have two distinct sex chromosomes (XY). However, there can be other combinations. Modern science shows that intersex individuals are born with mosaic genetics—some of their cells have XX chromosomes, and some have XY. Genetics research constantly provides new evidence in support of the view that sex is a continuous variable; however, you should remember that in today's society, sex is supposed to be assigned.

Researchers have been identifying particular anatomical brain structures associated with various biological characteristics of males and females (Kruijver et al., 2000). Studies also identified certain groups of neurons in the hypothalamus that could be related to individuals of the intersex category (Zhou et al., 1995). Overall, however, studies show that the human brain can be compared to a dynamic heterogeneous mosaic of different male and female characteristics that should be placed on a continuum (Joel, 2021). According to research, what is determined as "sex" is influenced by many social and environmental factors unfolding during prenatal and postnatal periods. These "outside" factors influence the brain's structures and specific neuro-anatomical types (Joel et al., 2015).

As groups, on the average, men and women have several different physical measurements. Take height, for example, which is likely to be determined genetically (of course other factors exist). Overall, globally, men are taller than women. Yet in different parts of the world, the numbers are different. In the United States, for example, the average male is around 5 feet 9 inches, and the average female is 5 feet 4 inches. So women as a group in the United States are shorter than American men but taller than men in Indonesia, whose average height is 5 feet 2 inches. Conversely, women in the Netherlands, whose average height is 5 feet 7 inches on average, are almost as tall as men in North America.

There are differences between men and women in prevalence of certain illnesses as well. Men have higher rates of autism spectrum disorder (the incidences of autism are 7 to 10 times greater in boys than in girls), substance abuse, and AIDS. Women have higher rates of breast cancer, Alzheimer's disease, and eating disorders. Although men are stronger than women in throwing velocity and throwing distance, women, globally, on average, live longer than men by about 5 years or so, as we discuss earlier in the book.

Several studies over the last couple of decades used neuroimaging methods to demonstrate the differences in responses between men and women. Their detailed analysis is not our goal here, but just to illustrate, some studies showed that women tend to have more neurons relayed to language, hearing, and relational skills compared to men (Brizendine, 2007). Men and women, as groups, showed somewhat different types of responses in the brain related to making moral choices (Jaffee & Hyde, 2000). Females, compared to males, showed increased activity in brain regions associated with caring behavior; males, compared to females, showed increased activity in regions associated with justice-based judgments and behavior (Harenski et al., 2008). Other studies revealed mixed findings, so the discussion of these and other studies continues.

Two comments are important to make here: Some differences are mostly genetic, as in cases of autism spectrum disorder, but physical characteristics and rates for diseases vary significantly across countries and regions. Second, these and other differences are often strongly linked to socioeconomic and social conditions in which people live—chronic poor nutrition, for example, considerably affects body growth and development. Social factors and gender roles often determine what many people do, how they act, take risks, and take care of their body and mind.

Evolutionary Theories

Modern evolutionary studies (see Chapter 2) try to identify certain natural mechanisms for explaining the differences between men and women. These studies focus on comparative research and on discussion of natural selection as the main mechanism for determining major sex differences. Several conclusions have been drawn based on this research:

- Evolutionary science does not claim that all behaviors are genetically programmed, but predispositions to acquire them seem to be (Dumont, 2010).

- Evolutionary scientists maintain that sexual selection (the method of selection of a mate) is the strongest factor determining most differences between males and females. Men and women develop certain behaviors and "shape" individual features to attract the best possible partners (Geary, 2009; Rusch et al., 2015).

- Children across cultures are raised as boys and girls for a reason, evolutionary scientists claim. The prime reason is survival and preservation of humans as species (Archer, 1996).

How do these conclusions refer to the study and understanding of personality within the gender domain? Evolutionary scientists maintain that women, as a group, are more likely to be interested in a set of personality traits in men that would secure the future and safety of their children and family. Men, as a group, tend to be interested in women who display behaviors that are communal, nurturing, and socially oriented. In other words, there must be some evolutionary purpose for men and women to have somewhat different personality features. Men tend to invest more attention to new mates and activities, while women tend give more to parenting. The general difference between men and women is that women naturally tend to act altruistically to show that they can share resources. Alternately, men tend to act heroically or at times greedily to demonstrate that they can protect these resources (Miller, 2000; Rusch et al., 2015).

Societal Practices

Although the differences between males and females can be found on the biological and physiological levels, they are not necessarily significant. Human behavior cannot be explained without including psychological mechanisms with cultural and social inputs (Buss, 1996). Social practices and laws continue to influence judgments about an individual's sex.

Globally, with only few exceptions, an intersex person today has to be officially identified as either male or female simply because it is required by tradition and law. In many countries for the last several decades, hormonal treatment and sex change surgery were recommended for those who were born intersex. In Western countries (as well as in a few other non-Western countries), adults for years were able to decide to change their sex medically, which usually takes several years (Creighton, 2001). To a certain point, gender reassignment is a reversible process, and there are some who change their mind about the procedure (Dreger, 2000; Goldberg, 2014). Yet social norms require, and the laws prescribe in most countries that a "precise" sex—either male or female—should be given to every individual.

One of the first to undergo a series of sex-change procedures was George Jorgensen, a 25-year-old American artist, photographer, and Army veteran who fought in World War II. George struggled with his assigned sex and male identity for some time (he described himself as a "shy and miserable person"). He was unable to find a doctor in the United States who was willing to perform sex-reassignment surgery, so George went to Denmark for the procedure. In the early 1950s, the surgery and treatment required special permission from the Danish government. After several operations, George changed his name to Christine. She was not only among the first to undergo such surgery and postsurgical treatment, but she also became somewhat famous because of the media attention in the United States (Benjamin, 1966). She later became an advocate for the rights of transgender and intersex individuals.

Questions

On the companion website, find the links providing additional information about Christine Jorgensen, then search the web to find stories about other individuals who underwent a sex change.

What kind of problems do these individuals share?

Why were they unhappy before they insisted on the procedure?

Were they happy after the surgery?

What was the public reaction to their reassignment?

Most studies in psychology so far have focused on similarities and differences among men and women. A few studies of intersex individuals showed the evidence, based on self-assessments of people who identified themselves as intersex, of elevated levels of health problems and psychological problems including anxiety and depression (Rosenwohl-Mack et al., 2020). Psychological research involving intersex individuals is still developing.

TRADITIONAL VIEWS OF GENDER

Religion was for centuries a major source of human values related to gender. Traditional religions maintained, in general, a contradictory view on gender and gender roles. In theory, men and women were supposed to be equal in the eyes of God, but in reality, they were treated differently. Customs in most countries prescribed women only limited educational choices: elementary education or simple reading-and-writing skills. Women were also expected to play the traditional home-based role of mother and wife. Just 120 years ago, women were still being strongly cautioned in their families against becoming scientists, artists, engineers, or doctors! Although art schools were opening for women, yet practicing art as a woman to earn a living was viewed as unacceptable. In the Netherlands, until 1957, married women were required by law to be dismissed as civil servants when they became married (Netherlands Review Report, 2019).

Theoretically, according to moral prescriptions, men and women should practice moderation, self-control, modesty, and chastity. In real life today (and for centuries past), however, women more than men face more serious restrictions and regulations affecting their behavior and individual traits in terms of their prescribed clothes, specific behaviors, manners, emotional expressions, or leadership opportunities. According to Pew Research, almost two thirds of people surveyed in India said that a wife always is obligated to obey her husband (Evans et al., 2022).

In visual arts and literature, **androcentrism**, or placing males or the masculine point of view at the center of a theory or narrative, has always been common. However, written religious traditions contained female images and narratives about women, and there are female saints and sacred figures in Christianity, Islam, and Judaism, as well as female goddesses in Hinduism (Kinsley, 1986). Science history shows that for centuries scholars generally believed that prescribed gender roles should exist because they were convenient, customary, and seemingly guaranteed societal stability (Eagly, 1997).

However, during the past 2 to 3 centuries, more philosophers, scientists, and physicians began to explain gender as a social construct. By the 19th century, many believed that although there were some natural differences between men and women, these differences were rooted in societal norms. Furthermore, these norms could change. The popular English philosopher John Stuart Mill (1806–1873) was particularly admired among progressive-minded scholars. Mill's (1869/2010) historic essay *On the Subjection of Women* advocated gender equality, claiming that the differences between men and women were largely the product of social customs and should be overcome.

Ambivalent Prejudice

Many influential scientists, psychologists, and psychiatrists early in the 20th century accepted the view that women should be equal to men. Eighty and 90 years ago, anthropologists such as Margaret Mead, psychologists such as Lev Vygotsky, and behaviorists such as John Watson all claimed that the socialization practices that prescribed particular roles to boys and girls to follow were erroneous. They wrote that assumptions about fundamental differences between boys and girls were wrong. The American psychologist Leta Hollingworth (1886–1939) was among the first to find research evidence that women's performance on cognitive, perceptual, and motor tasks was consistently similar to that of males (Shiraev, 2015).

However, women were still viewed as lesser than men. Sigmund Freud, for example, emphasized women's anatomical and psychological inferiority compared to men. Alfred Adler wrote about women's **masculine protest**—a psychological reaction of opposing male dominance. He supported gender equality but was skeptical of the masculine protest because it challenged women's natural, in his view, roles as mothers and caregivers (Dumont, 2010). The Austrian American psychologist and therapist Helene Deutsch believed that women should abandon the traditional roles of mothers and wives, yet she also wrote that many women were not ready for this because they would encounter significant psychological difficulties in the process (Deutsch, 1944, 1945).

Gender Discrimination in Psychology

Early in the 20th century, many experimental psychologists in the United States shared the view that only a specially selected and trained group of highly skilled observers could perform the collection and compilation of scientific data in psychological labs—in other words, only trained professionals could conduct scientific observations in strictly controlled conditions of an experiment. Who could argue about the necessity of professional training? The problem was that these trained professionals were expected to be men. What was the logic behind this assumption? Successful researchers were expected to be scrupulous and careful observers, and they were not supposed to show any emotion while conducting research. Women in general were considered unfit as researchers because at that time many thought they were emotionally unstable and overly sentimental (Keller, 1985). Some male experimental psychologists even stated that women should play only secondary, subsidiary roles in psychological research because of their involvement in relationships and their commitment to their families and children. A better role for a woman was research assistant, not principal investigator (Noon, 2004). As a result of these beliefs, scores of skilled women were underestimated, overlooked for promotion, or simply ignored.

Functional Inequality

In the first half of the 20th century, many social scientists described gender inequality as **functional inequality**. According to this concept, a person was predisposed to perform a certain function in society. Men were expected to perform mostly instrumental functions, which involved physical work, protection, hunting, and construction. Society assigned expressive functions to women, which involved managing interpersonal conflicts, providing care, educating the young, and so forth. These role differences have created different expectations about what women and men should do. Different expectations placed men and women in different educational and economic sectors and even prescribed behaviors and skills to men and women (Parsons & Bales, 1956).

After the late 1950s, more studies focused on gender similarities. They showed the complex interaction between biological and social factors that shape male and female behavior and experience.

EVOLVING VIEWS OF GENDER

Gender Studies

Contemporary **gender studies** is a multidisciplinary field dedicated to studying gender and a wide range of gender-related issues. This field has made a major contribution to personality psychology as a great discussion is taking place about the mechanisms and consequences of social construction of gender. Gender is now commonly perceived as a continuum—there is no absolute, invariable "maleness" or masculinity and "femaleness" or femininity in individuals (Rothblatt, 2011a). If gender is a social construct, it is clear that men and women may be different due to different socialization practices and social norms. How significant are such differences? Are there "male" and "female" personalities?

Feminism

One of the most influential sources of gender studies has been feminism, which originated in political and social sciences. **Feminism** is the view that women should have equal rights and opportunities with men, and global changes are needed to achieve social justice (Hirschman, 2010). At least three points are relevant to personality psychology.

First, feminists reject the notion of a "female brain," or significant inborn and physiological changes that distinguish women from men. Second, there are gender differences because, historically, most important positions of power have gone to men, and through them men created customs, laws, and policies that systematically discriminated against women and thus satisfied men's needs to dominate and possess. Indeed, even still today, more than 90% of the world's heads of government are men (although women are gaining more important roles these days in the positions of power). Third, feminists say, most customs of today's society are rooted in a masculine culture that accepted domination, violence, and war rather than consensus and peace (Cohn, 1987). For centuries, male-dominated societies considered wars essential for conquering, achieving glory, testing patriotism, and dominating the weak. Femininity was little more than "ritualized submission" (Goldberg, 2014), and women's propensity for peace and constructive cooperation were not fully taken into consideration (Ayman & Korabik, 2010). Feminist scholars for years maintained that women should have the freedom and more opportunities to make their own choices in everyday life (Snyder-Hall, 2010).

In modern society, women have gained more power. In 2013, 23% of married American women with children "outearned" their husbands, up from 4% in 1960 (Carbone & Cahn, 2013). In 2021, this number was already 30% (Italiano, 2021). Three quarters of married women with husbands' income between $50,000 and $75,000 are in the labor force in the United States (VerBruggen, 2019). Fewer women in developed countries now need a man's support to raise a family.

Comparative Research

In the past 20 years, a significant number of studies examined similarities and differences between men and women and found noteworthy as well as many inconsistent or statistically insignificant variations. For example, studies of violent behavior show that violent behavior across the globe is more prevalent in men than it is in women: Young boys are referred to social workers for psychological help more often than girls (Hyde, 2005); globally, men are almost 4 times more likely to be murder victims than women. We already discussed in Chapter 9 that in the United States, the suicide rates among males are approximately 4 times higher than the rate among females. Most telling, in America in the 21st century, men have committed approximately 90% of murders and comprise almost 90% of the prison population.

To offer contrast, in terms of higher education, women outnumber men as university students in every region except South Asia and sub-Saharan Africa. In the most economically developed countries (such as the United States, Canada, France, or Germany), women earn 58% of college degrees, and this number is on the rise. In the United States, four women graduated from college for every three men (Birger, 2015), and this gender gap is increasing. At school, boys read somewhat less and do less homework than girls (Organisation for Economic Cooperation and Development [OECD], 2011). Teenage boys in developed countries are 50% more likely than girls to fail in three basic school subjects, such as math, reading, and science. Globally among lower achievers in reading, math, and science, boys consistently outnumber girls (OECD, 2020). More boys than girls are failing at school. However, considered as groups, girls are somewhat better in verbal reasoning, while boys, as a group, tend to be better in math. Comprehensive cross-national studies show that most people with symptoms of depression are female, approximately two thirds of the studied samples. However, there is no simple explanation, like genetics, of this phenomenon. One of the strong factors is the way men and women tend to communicate their symptoms and seek psychological help: Men, culturally, tend to be more reluctant to discuss their emotional problems, viewing them as a sign of weakness and even failure (Armstrong, 2019).

Personality research has systematically found gender differences in two of the three dimensions of the Eysenck model (see Chapter 6): neuroticism and psychoticism (Escorial, 2007). Studies also consistently show that in the context of the Big Five theory, women tended to produce higher scores than men on extroversion, agreeableness, and neuroticism (Weisberg et al., 2011).

Cross-cultural research obtained on samples from more than 25 countries reveals an important finding: The differences between male groups and female groups across the studied countries were small; however, the variations within both groups were significant and consistent with gender perceptions. Women's scores, compared to men's scores, were somewhat higher in neuroticism, agreeableness, warmth, and openness to feelings, whereas men were higher in assertiveness and openness to ideas (see Table 10.2; Costa et al., 2001).

How can we explain some gender differences obtained in psychological studies? Consider two types of answers discussed by researchers.

The Variability Hypothesis

The *variability hypothesis* is a view that men and women are likely to be similar on many behavioral and psychological measures; nevertheless, men's scores tend to group around the opposite ends of the spectrum. For example, at school there are more boys than girls with very high and very low grades and test scores (Hyde, 2005). In other words, men are supposed to have a wider

TABLE 10.2 ■ A Comparative Summary of Gender Differences in Personality Traits		
Dimensions	*Women Compared to Men*	*Men Compared to Women*
Extroversion	Higher scores	Lower scores
Agreeableness	Higher scores	Lower scores
Neuroticism	Higher scores	Lower scores
Conscientiousness	Lower scores	Higher scores
Openness	No differences	No differences
Neuroticism	Higher scores	Lower scores
Psychoticism	Lower scores	Higher scores

range of achievements as well as weaknesses and failures than women. Although this hypothesis was tested, the outcomes were inconclusive. To complicate the results, not all gender differences appear equal—some of them are significant and others are not (Hyde & Plant, 1995). In general, again, behavioral and psychological differences within the gender are in most cases far greater than differences between the gender groups (Hyde & Mertz, 2009).

The Gender Similarities Hypothesis

From the viewpoint of the gender similarities hypothesis, males and females are alike on most—but not all—psychological variables. The early research comes in publications of Eleanor Maccoby and Carol Jacklin (1974). Their most influential work, *The Psychology of Sex Differences*, is based on the review of more than 2,000 studies of gender differences, including memory, aptitudes, personality features, and social behavior. They found that there were differences between men and women on verbal skills, visual spatial ability, math skills, and aggressive behavior. However, the book challenged several common assumptions related to personality, such as girls have lower self-esteem compared to boys; men are less suggestible than women; men do better on difficult cognitive tasks, while women do fine on simple ones; and women have lower achievement motivation than men (Maccoby & Jacklin, 1974). These assumptions were criticized and even dismissed, but the debates about low self-esteem in girls compared to boys has continued for decades (Hyde, 2005; Pipher, 1994).

Research, however, including meta-analysis, gives more support for the gender similarities hypothesis (Hyde & Mertz, 2009). Men and women as groups may be slightly different in motor skills or aggression. However, other gender differences vary substantially in magnitude at different ages and are based on the context in which measurements occur. For example, there are small gender differences in computational skills (favoring girls) in elementary and middle school, but there are no gender differences in computation in higher grades. Also, there were small gender differences favoring males in complex solving problems, yet this difference surfaces in high school and does not show up in earlier years (Hyde, 2005). Testing conditions matter, too. When they believe that a math test is designed to show gender differences, women underperform (Spencer et al., 1999). Many parents as well as teachers expect that boys, compared to girls, should be better at math, thus the adults often overlook many mathematically talented girls. Parents have lower expectations for their daughters' math success than for their sons' (Hyde, 2005).

In the end, men and women are not that different psychologically (Hyde, 2005; Hyde et al., 2008). In part, the beliefs about gender differences were supported by popular stereotypes about female "emotionality," male "assertiveness," and so on. Just remember that stereotypes change with time, and so do social realities (Armstrong, 2019). Recall the discussion earlier in the chapter about the difficulties women would have faced 100 years ago as psychology researchers? In 1950, only 15% of all doctoral degrees in psychology were awarded to women. By 1960, the number had risen to just 18%. Yet in the 1970s, the number of women earning doctorates in psychology began to steadily increase, and by the early 1980s, this number had increased dramatically: For the first time in history, the proportion of women doctoral recipients was equal to men (Stewart, 2009). If this trend continues, by 2025 women will earn more than 75% of the doctoral degrees in psychology awarded in North America.

Evolving Views on Gender Roles

Earlier in the chapter, we discussed *masculinity* and *femininity* and how imprecise the definitions of these terms are. Views on masculinity and femininity are also changing. Modern developments add more facts and scientific knowledge about the evolving gender roles and the personality and behavioral features associated with these categories. Traditionally, in the past, men were expected to embrace masculinity—that is, to be physically resilient, tough, emotionless, confident, and ambitious. Masculinity was about being heterosexual and also about avoiding femininity at all costs (Levant & Kopecky, 1995). Femininity, on the other hand, was traditionally linked to emotionality, compassion, gentleness, and nurture. It was also about being heterosexual, or attracted to men (Brownmiller, 1985). Although there were some historic and cultural variations, they were few and far between.

In which ways are views of masculinity and femininity changing? First, modern global society has become increasingly less demanding about the gender roles that boys and girls and men and women are expected to follow. The perceptions seem to be shifting from labeling human beings who do not follow the prescribed gender roles as *womanly men* or *manly women* to new perceptions that focus less on gender but more on the unique individuality of them.

Studies from some years back showed that many people maintained particular expectations about where men and women were supposed to work, according to the standard gender roles of the time (Eagly, 1997). Today, it appears that more people tend to increasingly abandon these stereotypes: They adapt, adjust, and learn new professions better than men do. More women study for and obtain degrees and work in professions that were stereotypically "male." Men, on the other hand, have not embraced yet so-called "female professions" as eagerly. Women also appear to better embrace new job opportunities. Of the 30 occupations that were expected to grow fastest in America in the coming years, women dominated 20 of them, including nursing, accounting, childcare, and food preparation (Rosin, 2013).

Second, gender roles themselves became more fluid. The term **metrosexual** appeared in popular literature and then in sociological and psychological research (Hall, 2015). It means a style of thinking and behavior in men who, contrary to the prescriptions of traditional gender roles, tend to develop and display some feminine features and habits, especially related to appearance, clothes, and grooming (Bais, 2012). Only a few studies have been done; for example, a study in Thailand of urban men who identified themselves as metrosexual showed that they scored higher than average men on traditional femininity and also had high scores for appearance-related variables, such as watching the quality of their body and everyday appearance (Lertwannawit & Gulid, 2010). Metrosexual men can be heterosexual, bisexual, or gay (although most use the term *metrosexual* in reference to heterosexual men). There is a debate in popular sources about whether women can be metrosexual, too, by adopting some traditional masculine features and still paying attention to appearance and romance. In some ways, *metrosexuality* is about avoiding strict standards of gender roles (Simpson & Hagood, 2010).

Third, in the era of global cultural changes, there is an inevitable resistance coming from the supporters of traditional values and gender roles. The rejection of nontraditional roles and bias and discrimination against individuals who do not fit into the traditional standards (under the motto "Men should be men, and women should be women") are likely to continue in many parts of the world and under the influence of traditional cultural beliefs about masculinity (Kaur & Bawa, 2016).

CHECK AND APPLY YOUR KNOWLEDGE

1. Explain the natural dominance of the male paradigm.
2. What are the key differences between the traditional and evolving views of the sexes?
3. What is androcentrism?
4. Explain ambivalent prejudice.
5. What are the main assumptions of feminism?
6. Explain the variability hypothesis.
7. Explain the gender similarities hypothesis.
8. Give examples of metrosexuality.

©iStockphoto.com / Bastiaan Slabbers

PHOTO 10.2 Despite significant changes in attitudes, the LGBTQ+ community faces significant prejudice against them around the world. Homosexuality remains criminalized in many countries. What do you think motivates some people to maintain such strict views of gender or sexual orientation?

TRADITIONAL VIEWS OF SEXUAL ORIENTATION

As in the case of gender, religion throughout the ages has remained a key source of human values (see Chapter 1) about an individual's sexual orientation. Over the past few centuries, most major world religions maintained a strict moral position on what type of sexual orientation individuals should have. With only a few exceptions, religion portrayed a heterosexual person as a norm. Any deviation from heterosexuality was considered immoral and thus punishable. Women customarily faced more restrictions related to sexuality and sexual orientation than men. Social customs and laws prosecuted individuals who were accused of homosexual behavior (see Table 10.3).

Traditional views on sexual orientation influence scientists. Consider an example. German psychiatrist Richard von Krafft-Ebbing (1840–1902) provided one of the earliest and most detailed scientific analyses of individual sexuality in his famous book *Psychopathia Sexualis* (1886). He maintained a traditional view, according to which heterosexuality was normal, and homosexuality was pathological.

In medical research and psychiatric practice, people who had homosexual feelings were assumed to be ill and, therefore, in need of treatment or even punishment (Laqueur, 2004). Most early psychologists until the middle of the 20th century maintained a generally negative view of homosexuality and bisexuality and considered it a form of pathology or even disability. Individuals prone to homosexual and bisexual behavior were expected to receive medical treatment until they "recovered." In the Soviet Union until the early 1990s, homosexuality was considered a crime punishable by a lengthy prison term. Today, in some countries such as Iran, openly gay and lesbian individuals can be sentenced to death because homosexuality is considered a major offense against state religion.

An Evolution of Legal Knowledge

The evolution of views of homosexuality and gays and lesbians is a powerful example of how popular beliefs, science, legal rulings, and ideology have been evolving in the United States over the past 7 decades. Most people's views of gays and lesbians and of LGBTQ+ community in general changed along with changing scientific views and legal rulings. There have been generational cultural changes. Eight decades ago, New York had laws against cross-dressing, onstage depictions of gays, and gatherings of gays in clubs. In the 1930s, the Motion Picture Production Code banned any discussion of or allusion to homosexual behavior. Leading psychiatrists commonly labeled homosexuals as *sexual psychopaths*. President Dwight Eisenhower signed Executive Order 10450, which banned, among other things, "sexual perversion" in government and banned lesbians and gays from working in the federal government. About 50 years ago, homosexual acts were illegal in every state but Illinois. There were no openly gay political candidates or public officials. Even in the liberal press, homosexuality was attacked (Ross, 2012). The popular 1969 bestseller *Everything You Always Wanted to Know About Sex (But Were Afraid to Ask)* said that homosexuality was fixable and curable as long as people asked a psychiatrist to help.

TABLE 10.3 ■ Traditional Cultural and Legal Views of Sexual Orientation				
Sexual Orientation	*Legal Status*	*Moral Status*	*Medical Status*	*Social View*
Heterosexual	Legal	Acceptable within marriage	Normal	Normal
Nonheterosexual (homosexual or bisexual)	Illegal, criminal	Unacceptable	Abnormal	Prejudiced, discriminated against

Yet the clinical perceptions and legal ruling were changing. The classification of homosexuality as a mental disorder was scrapped in 1973 from psychiatric manuals in the United States, and by the early 1980s, most states had dropped anti-gay laws. Some public figures, including politicians and celebrities, began openly discussing their sexual identity. Other countries were making changes, too—Russia officially stopped imprisoning gays in the late 1980s. In the 21st century, scores of countries, including the United States, recognized same-sex marriages.

Around the world, many people tend to view homosexuality as a problem or a moral transgression. Despite many changes in laws and norms related to same-sex marriage and the rights of LGBTQ+ people, acceptance of homosexuality remains sharply divided by country, region, and economic development of each community. While in the United States, the United Kingdom, or Sweden, 70 to 80% of people think that society should accept homosexuality; in South Africa this number is 54%; and in Russia and Kenya the number was 14% (Poushter & Kent, 2020). The changes in attitudes are slow. Besides, in most African states, homosexuality is still illegal. Russia, for example, has passed a harsh anti-gay law that limits printed and online discussion of LGBTQ+ issues. Remember, in some countries, being openly gay and lesbian is still punishable by death.

EVOLVING VIEWS OF SEXUAL ORIENTATION

Several major developments took place in the 20th century that significantly changed scientific views of sexual orientation. Empirical research was one such development. In the first half of the 20th century, most studies of sexual orientation were conducted within psychiatry and primarily focused on psychopathology. The research samples involved a few individuals, usually patients. The publication of Alfred Kinsey's (1894–1956) *Sexual Behavior in the Human Male* (1948/1998b) and later *Sexual Behavior in the Human Female* (1953/1998a) were significant developments partly because they were based on large samples. Kinsey, an American physician, and his colleagues believed that humans were not strictly "heterosexual" and "homosexual." Based on the interviews, Kinsey described several types of sexual orientation: those who identified themselves as exclusively heterosexual with no experience with or desire for sexual activity with people of the same sex; those who identified themselves as exclusively homosexual; and those who would identify themselves as bisexual, with varying levels of desire for sexual activity with either sex (Kinsey, 1948/1998b). More studies showed that sexual orientation is a continuum with several orientations that may be present in one individual, evolving over time (Sell, 1997). Research also showed that people are not necessarily "stuck" in either of the described groups or categories—although most people do not change their sexual orientation, some evolve during their lives (Savin-Williams et al., 2012). In other words, some individuals are sexually "fluid," and sexual fluidity can be recognized as a kind of sexual orientation (see Figure 10.2; Diamond, 2008, 2009).

Debates continue about the most significant factors that influence an individual's sexual orientation. Many studies maintain that sexual orientation, at least to some degree, has biological causes, as pioneering studies of the British-born neuroscientist Simon LeVay showed (1991, 1993). His research found that a particular region of the brain's hypothalamus in gay men was similar structurally to that found in straight women. This was one of the first scientific studies to connect biological factors and an individual's sexual orientation (Le Vay, 2016).

FIGURE 10.2 ■ A Spectrum of the Individual Sexual Orientations

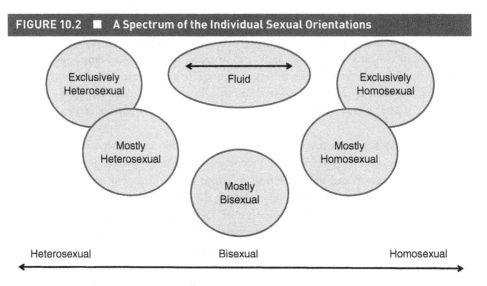

The degree of this connection was further discussed in various studies. Researchers, for example, found that if an identical twin is gay, there is about a 20% chance that the sibling will have the same sexual orientation. That percentage is more than random, but it is lower than expected for two people with the same genetic code (Kremer, 2014). Gay men tend to have more gay brothers, and lesbians tend to have more lesbian sisters than their heterosexual counterparts (Wilson & Rahman, 2008).

Science, however, does not confirm that homosexuality is exclusively or predominantly genetic. Moreover, it is still unclear whether or not the genetic factors and other biological mechanisms for determining male and female sexual orientation are similar (Jeffreys, 2003; Kremer, 2014). Overall, studies have not revealed a clear genetic cause for being gay, lesbian, bisexual, or fluid. Sexuality and sexual behavior are under the control of a complex set of centers in the brain and are certainly shaped by a person's social experiences (LeVay, 2010).

Studies over several years identified several links between sexual orientation and personality traits. Bisexual individuals reported higher levels of openness to experience than homosexual individuals. They, in turn, reported higher levels of openness compared to heterosexual individuals. Bisexual individuals also report lower levels of conscientiousness than both heterosexual and homosexual individuals. Gay men also scored higher than heterosexual men on neuroticism, agreeableness, and conscientiousness, whereas gay women scored lower than heterosexual women on extroversion, agreeableness, and conscientiousness. Personality differences between different sexual orientation categories tend to decline with age (Allen & Robson, 2020).

Gay men, as a group, tend to be later-born children in respect to their older brothers (Balthazart 2018). A similar, yet less strong pattern was found for women (Jones & Blanchard, 1998). Socialization experiences and societal customs play a role, too. Studies show that male participants report more sexual behavior (masturbation, pornography use, and casual sex) and more permissive attitudes (for example, about casual sex) compared to female participants. The gender difference in reported sexual satisfaction is insignificant (Hyde, 2005). Contemporary comparative studies show that, consistent with the gender similarities hypothesis (see earlier in this chapter), most gender differences related to attitudes about sex and sexual behavior are small, and gender differences related to sexuality change over time (Petersen & Hyde, 2010).

Transvestism, Cross-Dressing, or . . . ?

This short case should illustrate the evolution of the individual's sexual orientation and behavior. Magnus Hirschfeld, a German physician, published the first academic study of transvestism in 1910. In the book *Die Transvestiten*, he described the desire and the practice of some individuals (men more often than women) to dress in the clothes of the opposite sex (Hirschfeld, 1910/1991). At the time of the publication, European countries condemned and outlawed cross-dressing. In Germany, for example, people who wanted to cross-dress (mostly men wanting to wear women's clothes) had to apply to the police departments for special permissions (Benjamin, 1966). Doctors considered transvestism as a type of pathological, attention-seeking kind of homosexuality, which was viewed as mental illness. Hirschfeld rejected these views more than 100 years ago. He showed that not only gays and lesbians, but also straight individuals could choose transvestism. And it was not a flamboyant act of a capricious individual. For many, cross-dressing was a normal expression of their true personality and individuality. In his publications and lectures, Hirschfeld appeared as an active advocate for equality for gays and lesbians; he fought widespread prejudice and discrimination against them (1910/1991).

More than a century after Hirschfeld's initial publication, prejudice toward cross-dressing still was there. Some people continue to use the label *cross-dresser* and attach it to individuals as if cross-dressing was a personality type (the same way some people use the labels *criminal* or *mentally ill* to describe someone's entire personality). Cross-dressing has many underlying causes. To some who do it, cross-dressing is an expression of their gender identity. To others, cross-dressing is rooted in their histrionic tendencies (see Chapter 11) and the desire to impress, surprise, and even to shock. Some males cross-dress because they have erotic feelings at the thought of oneself as female, which is called *autogynephilia* (Blanchard, 1989; Goldberg, 2014). Yet to others, the desire to wear particular clothes is not necessarily sexual—they simply admire the opposite sex and want to imitate their behavior. It is important to stress that clinical psychologists and psychiatrists today recognize the term **transvestic fetishism** as a disorder: a condition in which an individual's sexual fantasies, urges, or behaviors involving cross-dressing also cause clinically significant distress or impairment in social, occupational, or other important areas of functioning.

CHECK AND APPLY YOUR KNOWLEDGE

1. Behavior considered normal, abnormal, illegal, or acceptable has changed throughout history. This probably means that some of today's definitions of *normal* and *abnormal* in our behavior may no longer be valid a few years from now. Which types of behavior (if any) that we consider abnormal (or pathological) today do you think future generations will consider acceptable or even normal? Explain your view.
2. Consider a woman wearing her brother's T-shirt for a workout and a man wearing his sister's leggings for the same workout. What kind of comments can they both expect behind their backs at the gym? How would you respond to these comments if you heard them?

APPLYING THE GENDER DOMAIN

LGBTQ+ Psychology

A modern branch of psychology that studies and assists individuals whose orientation is transgender or gender-variant, LGBTQ+ psychology is a theoretical and applied field that is gaining support and recognition globally. People who identify with LGBTQ+ may have many concerns and challenges for which they seek advice and help.

Many people who identify as transgender have to deal with significant psychological challenges. The San Francisco Unified School District, for example, surveyed middle school children and discovered that 50% of transgender kids had contemplated suicide (for a wide range of psychological reasons), compared to 6% of straight youth (Wilson, 2014). A 2020 U.S. study indicated the number of transgender youths considering suicide at 40% (Austin et al., 2020). In China the numbers were even higher than in North America: In this transgender population, the lifetime prevalence of suicidal ideation was 56% (Chen et al., 2019). Studies also showed that transsexual youth had a twofold to threefold increased risk of psychological problems, including mood and anxiety disorders, as well as suicide attempts (Reisner et al., 2015).

Another problem that needs recognition and action is the ongoing stigmatization, discrimination, and even open hostility against individuals who are gay, lesbian, transgender, or gender-variant. **Homophobia** is aversion to homosexuality and LGBTQ+ individuals. **Biphobia** is aversion toward bisexuality and bisexual people as a social group or as individuals. People of any sexual orientation can experience such feelings of aversion. Biphobia and homophobia

©iStockphoto.com / Rcarner

PHOTO 10.3 Many people still have stereotypical expectations about "male" and "female" professions. Name some of these stereotypes. What could be done to reduce them?

are often based on negative stereotypes against people who may appear different or irrational fear of something new. In many countries, as we know, homophobia and biphobia are incorporated into the law. People can face significant prison terms for speaking openly on behalf of the LGBTQ+ community, defending their rights, or just discussing intersex or transgender issues.

True, there are plenty of legal and political issues around the globe related to sex and gender, but public awareness, which can lead to significant social action, is necessary to induce political and social change.

Reducing Gender Stereotypes

Do human names have anything to do with the destructive power of hurricanes? Apparently, they do. The World Meteorological Organization assigns a name to every hurricane: Katrina, Marco, Sandy, Omar, and so on. A study published in the *Proceedings of the National Academy of Sciences* examined 92 most recent hurricanes that made landfall in the United States; it showed that hurricanes with women's names seem to have killed more people than did those with men's names. Why is that? The researchers concluded that some people do not take hurricanes with women's names as seriously as they take those with men's names. As a result of this biased perception, some people tend to act carelessly. They assume that a hurricane named after a woman is not supposed to be that destructive (Jung et al, 2014).

Such biased assumptions are called *stereotypes*. They are categorical expectations that all members of a given group have particular traits or features. Stereotypes tend to be resistant to change—even when they are fraught with errors. People tend to overlook or reject valid information when it is not consistent with our stereotypes. Propensity to stereotype is one of the most fundamental and pervasive of all human psychological activities. Stereotypes are a form of biased thinking and result in us anticipating what another person will do because we expect this behavior.

In your daily encounters, you can apply the three following strategies to help in overcoming gender stereotypes:

- **Be aware**. Try to monitor the extent to which your gender stereotypes (based on prior beliefs, knowledge, and expectancies) can affect your current experience, impressions, and perceptions. Try to become aware of your own and other people's stereotypes. Awareness of them will be the first step to increase your ability to modify them.

- **Look for multiple causes**. When you explain gender differences, look for multiple factors that may either explain the differences or show that they are not that significant. Why do girls on average tend to earn better grades in school than boys? Why are men still far more likely than women to earn degrees in the fields of science, technology, engineering, and mathematics? And why are men on average more likely to be injured in accidents and physical fights than women?

- **Promote new perceptions**. Reducing gender stereotypes is only a first step in applying your knowledge. The task is to form more accurate perceptions based on facts, including sound psychological research. It is true that in North America more men than women earn doctorate degrees in physics. Does this mean that women are not so great in advanced studies? No. At least half of doctorate degrees in molecular biology and neuroscience were awarded to women. True, there are more men getting graduate degrees in economics and philosophy, but women tend to get more doctorate degrees in history and psychology (Leslie et al., 2015).

Overcoming Sexism

A vivid case in point of sexism is provided by Dawes (1994), who tells of an incident involving flagrant gender bias in decision-making. The dean of a major medical school, perplexed as to why his institution was unsuccessful in its attempts to recruit female students, asked a colleague of Dawes to investigate the problem. What emerged was striking: One of the interviewers had been rating applicants with respect to their "emotional maturity," "seriousness of interest in medicine," and "neuroticism"; as it turned out, the vast majority of females did not receive positive evaluations on any of his criteria. Specifically, whenever the woman was not married, he judged her to be "immature." When she was married, he concluded that she was "not sufficiently interested in medicine." And when she was divorced? "Neurotic," of course. On the bright side, this example was shared more than 20 years ago, and norms and practices have changed since then. Or have they?

Sexism is prejudice resulting in discrimination based on the views of sex or gender, especially against women and girls. Sexism is often associated with the belief that one sex is superior to or more valuable than another one. Sexism imposes limits on what men and women can and should do. For years, psychologists drew attention to sexism to raise awareness about the oppression of girls and women. Later, sexism as a concept was expanded to include awareness of the discrimination of *any* sex, including men/boys and intersexual/transgender individuals.

Learning about sexism is about gaining professional knowledge and good citizenship skills. Sexism has many forms. It can be open or hostile—think of a person who states that women are incompetent and inferior to men to justify a certain decision, such as hiring or firing a woman (Glick & Fiske, 1997). Sexism can also be hidden and disguised. For example, someone in a casual conversation may state that "I think women are not inferior to men, but they are weak and unprotected; therefore, they need additional help." Sexism incorporates stereotypical statements that explain or prescribe particular behaviors to the entire group.

SUMMARY

- The term *sex* refers to anatomical and physiological characteristics or features of males and females, the two typically assigned sexes. These features include at least four commonly recognized clusters, such as external genitalia (the body's reproductive organs), glands, hormones, and chromosomes. The intersex category is based on the features that are between distinct male and female characteristics.

- Gender is a complex set of behavioral, cultural, or psychological features associated with an individual's sex. Gender identity is an individual's self-determination (or a complex self-reflection) as being male, female, intersex (between male and female), or neither.

- Gender roles are prescriptions and expectations assigned to genders on the female–male continuum. These prescriptions and expectations are typically embedded in cultural norms and transmitted from one generation to the next. Ideology, art, and religion play an important role in preserving such expectations about gender roles. Masculinity, traditionally assigned to men, is a general set of features associated with physical strength, decisiveness, and assertiveness. Femininity, traditionally assigned to women, is a general set of features correlated with beauty, emotionality, and nurture.

- Sexual orientation, in most individuals, tends to develop gradually. Although the vast majority of children have a sex assigned to them at birth and many children have a strong sense of their gender identity, they are, as studies show, not necessarily always aware of their sexual orientation. Some children develop this orientation relatively early; some acquire it later in life.

- LGBTQ+ stands for lesbian, gay, bisexual, transgender, and queer or questioning their sex or gender identity. This is an umbrella term for people who can be called *gender nonconforming*— that is, those whose gender identity or gender expression does not conform to the one typically associated with the sex to which they were assigned at birth. Some who do not identify as either *male* or *female* sometimes prefer the term *genderqueer* or *gender-variant*.

- For centuries, science emphasized that women and men were born with different natural anatomical features and therefore should be different in their behavior, feelings, outlooks, and personalities. Modern studies focus on finding particular physiological, genetic, or evolutionary facts that help explain sex as a biological category. Contemporary research also supports the view that sex is a continuous variable.

- Human behavior cannot be explained by biological factors alone without including psychological mechanisms with cultural and social inputs. Social practices continue to influence judgments about an individual's sex.

- Religion was a major source of value-based knowledge about gender. Traditional religions maintained, in general, a contradictory view of gender and gender roles. In theory, men and women were supposed to be equal in the eyes of God. In reality, they were treated differently. Traditionally, many influential scientists, psychologists, and psychiatrists early in the 20th century accepted the ambivalent view that (1) women *should* be equal to men; (2) but they are not, and there is a justifiable reason for that.

- Contemporary gender studies is a multidisciplinary field dedicated to the study of gender and a wide range of gender-related issues. Gender studies have many roots and sources. One of the most influential has been feminism, originated in political and social sciences.

- In the past 20 years, a significant number of studies examined similarities and differences between men and women and found both major and insignificant differences, as well as inconsistencies.

- The variability hypothesis and the gender similarities hypothesis attract significant research and discussion.

- Over the past few centuries, most major world religions maintained a strict moral position on what type of sexual orientation individuals should have. With only a few exceptions, religion as well as traditional science portrayed a heterosexual person as a norm. From the beginning of the 20th century, scientific knowledge related to sexual orientation has been changing.

- Gender stereotypes are categorical expectations that all members of a given group have particular traits or features. Sexism is prejudice and results in discrimination based on the views of sex or gender.

- LGBTQ+ psychology is a theoretical and applied field that is gaining support and recognition globally.

VISUAL REVIEW

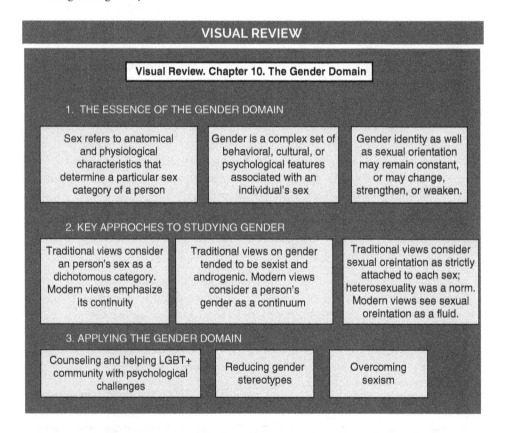

Visual Review. Chapter 10. The Gender Domain

1. THE ESSENCE OF THE GENDER DOMAIN

Sex refers to anatomical and physiological characteristics that determine a particular sex category of a person	Gender is a complex set of behavioral, cultural, or psychological features associated with an individual's sex	Gender identity as well as sexual orientation may remain constant, or may change, strengthen, or weaken.

2. KEY APPROCHES TO STUDYING GENDER

Traditional views consider an person's sex as a dichotomous category. Modern views emphasize its continuity	Traditional views on gender tended to be sexist and androgenic. Modern views consider a person's gender as a continuum	Traditional views consider sexual oreintation as strictly attached to each sex; heterosexuality was a norm. Modern views see sexual oreintation as a fluid.

3. APPLYING THE GENDER DOMAIN

Counseling and helping LGBT+ community with psychological challenges	Reducing gender stereotypes	Overcoming sexism

KEY TERMS

androcentrism

androgyny

biphobia

femininity

feminism

functional inequality

gender

gender consistency

gender identity   masculinity

gender nonconforming   metrosexual

gender roles   natural dominance

gender studies   sex

heterosexuality   sexism

homophobia   sexual orientation

homosexuality   sexuality

intersex   transgender

LGBTQ+   transvestic fetishism

masculine protest

EVALUATING WHAT YOU KNOW

Describe the key points of the gender domain in personality psychology.

Explain the sexes and the intersex.

Define *gender roles* and *sexual orientation*.

What are the traditional views of the sexes?

What are the traditional views of gender?

What are the traditional views of sexual orientation?

Explain the essence of the changing views of the sexes.

Explain the essence of the changing views of gender.

Explain the essence of the changing views of sexual orientation.

Explain LGBTQ+ psychology.

Give examples of gender stereotypes and sexism.

A BRIDGE TO THE NEXT CHAPTER

Sex, gender, and sexual orientation, of course, were not the only topics that underwent significant revision within science and psychology during the past 50 years or so. In relation to personality psychology, mental illness was another important area, the views of which have significantly evolved after the apparent decline of psychoanalysis. These views continue to change. The clinical domain will be our next area to examine in the following chapter.

11 THE CLINICAL DOMAIN

Leila Mendez/Cultura/Getty Images

LEARNING OBJECTIVES

After reading this chapter, you should be able to do the following:

- Discuss the role of the clinical domain in the study of personality.

- Describe the methods for diagnosing, classifying, and describing personality disorders.

- Describe the personality disorders in the following behavioral clusters: odd and eccentric; dramatic, emotional, or erratic; anxious and fearful.

- Discuss the etiology of personality disorders.

- Explain the concept of differential diagnosis and comorbidity.

- Apply the key principles of the clinical domain to individual behavior.

Jude Le Grice grew up in a small town in southwest England. Tall and physically imposing, he had a beautiful singing voice and wanted some day to perform in the opera. However, his severe dyslexia was a serious obstacle to a successful music career. After finishing school, he got a job as a laborer and continued taking singing classes. There, he met Rebecca, an aspiring theater student. Jude quickly fell in love with her, to her surprise, and asked her to marry him. Rebecca refused, but Jude insisted. Rebecca was upset. She then told him not to bother her any longer—but Jude continued his pursuit. His affection for Rebecca turned into an obsession. For years, his relentless, stubborn pursuit of Rebecca brought him and many people around him emotional pain, anxiety, and fear. Jude, as psychologists say, became a *stalker*.

Stalkers are engaged in a persistent and unwanted pursuit of another person. A stalker pays excessive attention to a "target," a victim. Stalking is also a form of harassment, which includes repeated following of the victims, spying on them, sending them unsolicited emails or texts, posting on their social media, trolling online, making frequent unwanted calls, loitering near their home or school, leaving unwanted gifts, or destroying or damaging the objects they love. Victims feel confused, intimidated, and profoundly unsafe. They suffer emotionally. Many of them are forced to alter their daily routines, change schools and jobs, or even relocate and hide their identity.

Jude was arrested many times for stalking Rebecca. He was not violent but went through detentions, court hearings, restraining orders, violations of restraining orders, jail sentences, and probations. Yet he did not give up his obsession. At some point, he was court-ordered to take medication. The doctors believed the medication would change his obsessive thoughts, and eventually, his behavior.

One day, many years after Rebecca and Jude had met in that singing class, Jude learned Rebecca had married. Eyewitnesses said he took this news calmly and promised he would no longer pursue her. What made the difference in his behavior? Did the medication help? Or did he change as a person and finally pick reason over obsession?

We might call Jude a stalker, but the legal system considered him a felon. The mental health system labeled him *mentally ill* and maintained that the illness had caused his obsessive behavior. Still, Jude refused to believe he was a stalker; nor he believed he had an illness; instead, he explains that some time ago he simply was passionately in love with another person.

Everybody hopes that this story is over.

Questions. If one has done something wrong, why do you think we attach a negative label to this individual's personality? For example, Jude loved to sing. Why don't we just call him a singer?

Where is the line between falling deeply in love (which is excused) and being a stalker (which is rejected)? Is it wrong to love somebody? Explain.

Was Romeo a stalker? Was Don Quixote a stalker? Why or why not? Are we selectively biased judging individuals? Explain.

What type of care or treatment would you recommend for a stalker: more understanding or more punishment? Explain your answer.

Sources: Knight, 2014; Mohandie et al., 2006; Mullen et al., 2000; Schwartz-Watts, 2006.

THE ESSENCE OF THE CLINICAL DOMAIN

The **clinical domain** involves approaches to personality from the position of abnormality, illness, and health care. In the opening case, Jude developed a persistent behavioral pattern labeled *stalking*. This persistent pattern of thought and actions

PHOTO 11.1 For centuries, folk healers, sages, witch doctors, and shamans have been engaged in the process of "correcting" abnormal or undesirable personality features. What is the difference between such healers and today's professional psychologists?

is significantly different from what most people would think and do in compatible circumstances. Jude's behavior also caused significant distress in the lives of many people, including his own. As the experts studying his case maintained, his behavior was associated with an underlying mental illness. The term **illness** (which can be used interchangeably with *disease* and *disorder*) broadly refers to any condition or functional abnormality or disturbance of the body and mind (although it is debatable how exactly the mind can be "disturbed") that impairs a person's functioning. As you remember from Chapter 1, personality disorders are enduring patterns of behavior and inner experience that deviate markedly from the expectations of the individual's culture. It is not just being different. It is a persistent behavioral pattern that leads to the individual's distress and impairment in one or several important areas of functioning (Akhtar, 2002).

To identify personality disorders (PDs), clinicians study an individual's symptoms that represent a distinct departure from normal appearance, function, desire, or feeling. In this context, **clinicians** are health care practitioners working as primary caregivers to the patient. Health care usually deals with the diagnosis, treatment, and prevention of illness. Clinicians are engaged in the clinical practice and—in most countries these days—are legally qualified (licensed) to do so.

Psychiatry and Clinical Psychology

For centuries, folk healers, sages, witch doctors, and shamans have been engaged in the process of "correcting" abnormal or undesirable behaviors as well as personality features. Mental illness appeared as a special category in medical journals by the mid-1800s, and psychiatry as a medical discipline dealing with mental illness began taking shape by the end of the 1800s. Doctors working within psychiatry called themselves *psychiatrists*. Today, this is a mainstream medical profession. Psychiatrists, who are medical schools' graduates, use primarily medical methods to diagnose and treat mental illness. Psychiatrists see mental illness mostly as a medical problem, not just an unusual personality feature, deviant behavior, or moral transgression.

Clinical psychologists are not psychiatrists but work closely with them. Clinical psychology, as a field of psychology, traces its roots to university laboratories and clinics emerging approximately early in the 20th century first in industrial countries, including the United States. Since the early years of their discipline, clinical psychologists saw an individual's personality as an integrated entity of behavior and experiences that has been disrupted due to certain conditions (Hall & Lindzey, 1957). Clinical psychologists also directed their attention to an individual's experiences. Although they generally (but not always) disagree on how to interpret those experiences, they have accumulated important knowledge about abnormal symptoms and their associated conditions. Psychiatrists and clinical psychologists also believe that personality features under their observation should correspond to specific abnormalities in the brain and nervous system and unfold in particular social circumstances, which must be examined and hopefully corrected or changed with therapeutic procedures based on science (Garfield, 2009).

On "Normal" and "Abnormal" Personality

At least two issues are important to know when we study personality disorders. First, each personality disorder (PD) is characterized by excessive "presence," as compared to the norm of certain traits and behaviors. They are interconnected and can manifest, for instance, as excessive shyness, introversion, anxiety, agitation, suspiciousness, and so on. Consider a young adult who almost always avoids making independent decisions, constantly fears separation from parents, and does not initiate new relationships for fear of rejection. This pattern of stable traits, which are markedly different from what is usually expected from such a young adult, can be labeled *abnormal*. Second, a behavior pattern is called a personality disorder because it appears as significantly different from what is considered a tolerable norm in each cultural environment (cultural norms and expectations can be different from one another). Imagine a person who constantly challenges social norms, has consistent problems with adjustment, and experiences significant distress (Akhtar, 2002). According to this view, personality traits are labels, and each of them stands for a collection of behavioral acts and manifestations that should be measured against the norm (Bus & Craik, 1986).

Both these views complement each other. Personality disorders can be seen as a kind of disturbing excessiveness of certain personality traits; it also appears that abnormal symptoms taken together are considerably different from what is labeled *normal functioning* in a particular social context. In clinical practice, most symptoms diagnosed as PDs usually represent a pattern of **excessive consistency**, which is different from moderate consistency. To illustrate, moderately present tendencies of being punctual, attentive, and detailed-oriented could be successfully used in business, education, and other professional areas. However, an extreme or excessive manifestation of these traits, such as a person's adherence to useless ritualistic habits, meticulous clinging to orderliness, or constant outbursts of anger at someone who likes to improvise, may result in constant work conflicts and, ultimately, professional failure. As we will see later in the chapter, borderline personality disorder is an exception to the pattern of excessive consistency, as it is characterized by an excessive inconsistency or instability of behaviors and emotional responses and by a lack of continuity and certainty in most aspects of a person's life. The symptoms can manifest as mild, moderate, and severe (Yang et al., 2010).

An intriguing portrayal of an unusual kind of behavior is depicted in the 1987 movie *Fatal Attraction*. The main female character of the film (Alex Forrest, played by Glenn Close) depicts a wide range of psychological and behavioral flip-flops while she deals with the aftermath of an affair with a married man. Her emotional and behavioral roller coaster storms through ups and downs of seductive tenderness and violent outbursts, fascination and hatred, pitiful vulnerability and rock-solid determination, sorrow and loathing, and creativity and idleness.

Questions

What behavioral traits and emotional patterns can you identify in the behavior of Alex Forrest? Does she manifest the symptoms of a particular personality disorder?

Most symptoms included in the category *personality disorders* are likely to be observed in a person under most life circumstances. This makes the behavior of individuals with personality disorders somewhat predictable.

Clinicians also focus on the significant, abnormal changes that have taken place in an individual's personality. When an illness strikes an individual, it affects this person's functioning, work, sleep, and leisure activities; it shapes daily routines, relationships, and communications; it changes the most important patterns of thinking and acting. Such illness can have clearly identifiable organic maladies as well as causes that are difficult to establish.

Medicalization of Personality Features

In the 20th century, social scientists began to see many social ills, such as street violence, sex crimes, homelessness, or chronic drug abuse, as mostly medical and not necessarily social problems. Therefore, as these scientists reasoned, these and other social problems required the attention of medical professionals. This was the beginning of **medicalization** of abnormal and deviant behavior. This is the process by which various facets of human behavior are interpreted in medical terms and thus diagnosed and treated by medical methods.

Consider an example. Since the inception of war, military commanders have had to deal with soldiers' fears on the battlefield. Excessive fear was often labeled *cowardice*, and soldiers' complaints about their acute emotional problems were called *malingering*—an intentional falsification of symptoms to avoid certain duties. Malingering was a punishable offense, especially during wartime. Psychology, however, early in the 20th century, brought up the term *shell shock* to describe serious psychological symptoms of traumatic nature. Professionals insisted that some people who exhibited these symptoms needed medical attention, not punishment (Lerner, 2009).

The Stigma of Mental Illness

In general terms, a **stigma** concerns the negative perception and corresponding actions related to a person or group based solely on certain social characteristics they possess or are associated with. The stigma of mental illness affects the manner with which millions of people (including those with personality disorders) are viewed (i.e., prejudged, ignored, or feared) and treated (i.e., mistreated, abused, or discriminated against; Corrigan & Wassel, 2008). Today, people with mental illness are a vulnerable group for many reasons; one of them is about the way society often treats them. They are subjected to stigma and discrimination daily, and they experience extremely high rates of physical and sexual victimization (Hankir, 2022; World Health Organization [WHO], 2014).

For centuries, popular beliefs held that the label *mental illness* explained personal features and behavior that was difficult to describe by other, more understandable causes, such as an external incentive, fear, or greed. If a person was "mentally ill," then he or she must have been profoundly different from "normal" people. This individual was expected to act and think in predictable yet disturbing ways. In fact, these individuals were placed into a special category. For example, in the 19th century, clinicians applied the label *insane* to people with behavioral patterns ranging from alcoholism to fire setting to compulsive theft and to dementia (Quen, 1983). The terms *idiocy* or *degeneration* were attached to individuals with a wide range of developmental problems (Krafft-Ebbing, 1886).

Religion was also a very powerful source of deep-seated beliefs about mental illness and its impact on personality. Across times and cultures, religion taught that psychological abnormalities must have been caused by the devil or other forms of curse. It was also seen as God's payback for an individual's inappropriate violence, shameful desires, dishonesty, or perversity. Even today, many people believe that mental illness is the result of an individual's deviation from God, tradition, and family (Shiraev & Levy, 2024). Religious prescriptions today continue to identify "abnormal" behaviors and even traits.

A significant sociocultural shift in attitudes toward mental illness took place during the second half of the 20th century. A person with symptoms of mental illness was no longer labeled as an *alcoholic*, a *schizoid*, an *addict*, or an *obsessive-compulsive*, but rather as an individual who has been affected by a range of symptoms. Instead of labeling people with mental illness with catchy words or phrases or stigmatizing them, psychologists began to see them as needing professional treatment and care (Shorter, 1997).

CHECK AND APPLY YOUR KNOWLEDGE

1. What is excessive consistency? Give examples.
2. Explain medicalization of behavior. Give examples.
3. Define and explain *stigma*.

4. Does it really matter how we label people with psychological problems? Do you see the difference between calling a woman *a drug addict* compared to calling her *a person affected by a drug addiction*? Explain.

5. If you have serious avoidant tendencies in interpersonal relationships, would you prefer to be called *one with avoidant tendencies* or *an avoidant person*? Explain.

IS THERE AN ABNORMAL "CRIMINAL PERSONALITY"?

Social scientists and psychologists in the past have always attempted to make the psychological profile of a "typical" criminal. Visit the companion site to learn about some of such studies. There you also can see how clinicians associated certain types of mental illness (such as madness, neurasthenia, or hysteria) with important personality features.

DIAGNOSING PERSONALITY DISORDERS

Diagnosing personality disorders is difficult. Although many symptoms of PDs should have an underlying biological basis (Livesley & Jang, 2008; Perugula et al., 2017), clinicians do not yet have reliable genetic, biochemical, or electrophysiological methods to detect them with certainty. Behavioral observations tend to have only limited reliability and validity due to substantial variability of symptoms within each type of PD. Other disorders may be masked under the same symptoms. This is another complicating issue, which we shall examine later.

Self-report questionnaires and inventories are commonly used in clinical practice, despite their diagnostic limitations. Many personality assessments provide psychologists with important information about the magnitude of personality traits such as extroversion, anxiety,

PHOTO 11.2 In the United States, *The Diagnostic and Statistical Manual of Mental Disorders (DSM–5–TR)* is the main diagnostic source for personality disorders. Different countries have their own traditions in defining personality disorders.

H.S. Photos/Alamy Stock Photo

agreeableness, openness, conscientiousness, independence, aggression, focus on physical symptoms, denial, and some others. After a psychologist examines various traits and their combinations, then it is important to establish a clinical diagnosis of a certain type of PD. However, the **interrater reliability** of these diagnostic methods remains low. This usually means that if several professionals separately diagnose one individual, they would often come to different diagnostic conclusions (Nelson et al., 2017; Tyrer et al., 2007).

Because people with personality disorders tend to exhibit abnormal behavioral traits in a consistent way across time and situations, clinicians often use *behavioral functional analysis* (BFA) for their assessments. This method requires a systematic observation of the immediate causes of behavior, the contextual characteristics of the behavior itself, and the consequences of this behavior. Accordingly, the analysis of a PD in an individual focuses on (1) self-reported personality characteristics and (2) the duration, intensity, and frequencies of observable behaviors consistent across time and situations. This diagnostic work takes significant time.

Among common issues related to personality questionnaires are **test-taking attitudes**. Some people tend to either give positive (socially desirable) evaluations of self ("I am always honest" or "I never lose my temper"), or they exaggerate negative symptoms ("I feel completely empty" or "I cannot focus on anything"). They may do this to draw attention to themselves, claim serious illness, receive special health benefits, or influence legal action involving them. In addition, although many people want to give sincere answers, their insights into their psychological problems can often be shallow and misleading (Krueger et al., 1996; Reich et al., 1986; Trull & Sher, 1994).

Although clinicians frequently use personality questionnaires for assessment, only a few of them have specific validity scales that help professionals identify psychological distortions that stem from the test-taking attitudes. Such scales have been long used by the authors of the Minnesota Multiphasic Personality Inventory (MMPI–2) and its later versions (MMPI History, 2016). Look, for example, at just three **validity scales: L, K, F:**

L: The lie scale measures social desirability, or the extent to which a person wants to present self in a best positive light, in accordance with cultural norms.

F: The frequency scale measures the degree to which individuals have a feeling that they are different from others.

K: The correction scale is aimed at measuring the defensiveness of a person or self-protection from criticism and exposure of own shortcomings.

These scales help clinicians assess an individual better and make a more informed judgment about other answers in this personality inventory.

Factors Contributing to Diagnosis

Psychologists also pay serious attention to factors that could contribute to diagnostic practices. For instance, the use of mental health services is significantly lower among people of lower socioeconomic status (SES). Individuals with affordable health insurance are more likely to see a psychologist than individuals who must pay high premiums for a visit. If we compare people with personality disorders that receive psychological help, we are likely to find that individuals of higher SES have less pronounced symptoms of personality disorders than do individuals of lower SES (Office of Disease Prevention and Health Promotion, 2020; WHO, 2014).

Although there are international diagnostic and classification systems of mental health that are often used, such as *The ICD–10 Classification of Mental and Behavioural Disorders* (Eleventh Revision of the International Classification of Diseases [ICD-11] has come into effect), as well as a classification system used in the United States called *The Diagnostic and Statistical Manual of Mental Disorders, Text Revision* (5th ed.; *DSM–5–TR*), countries have somewhat different traditions in defining personality disorders.

CLASSIFICATION AND DESCRIPTION OF PERSONALITY DISORDERS

Clinical practice and psychological research provided important observations of many distinct abnormal features in the individual's behavior and experience. French doctor Philippe Pinel (1745–1826) described cases of impulsive rage combined with relatively normal reasoning ability and called these symptoms *manie sans delire* (mania without delirium). Chronic aggressive behavior was labeled *moral insanity, egopathy, sociopathy*, and *psychopathy*. These individuals were described as manipulative, impulsive, self-centered, lying, and joy-seeking; they were also lacking in features such as remorse, empathy, or guilt (Cleckley, 1976; Hare, 1998). Jean-Étienne Esquirol (1772–1840), another French physician, studied *erotomania* as an excessive, irrational obsession with another person. Esquirol saw it as a grossly exaggerated affection. The difference between love, which is socially acceptable, and erotomania was not in type but in degree: People with erotomania seemed as pursuing unreasonable goals, developing unrealistic fantasies, and having wrong views of themselves. What we call *stalking* today, as described in the introduction to this chapter, may well fit into this pattern of behavior and thought. Early in the 1900s, clinicians discussed cases involving individuals who were extremely arrogant and preoccupied with self-importance. Some doctors thought this phenomenon was a sexual deviation; others postulated pathological self-love; yet others talked of an extreme form of introversion (Campbell, 1999).

For years, psychoanalysts (see Chapter 4) held a monopoly on clinical understanding of PDs. Psychoanalysts used the term **neurotic character**—one basic trait or a set of traits developed in early childhood that should lead to the overt manifestation of neurosis. Traditional psychoanalytic classifications of personality-related dysfunctions included the following types: schizoid, paranoid, inadequate (avoidant), cyclothymic (narcissistic or borderline), emotionally unstable (histrionic), passive-aggressive (dependent), compulsive, and sociopathic (English & English, 1958). With the decline of psychoanalysis, the usage of the term *neurotic* became less frequent. Other psychoanalytic terms were disappearing from the professional vocabulary, and at the same time, the term *personality disorders* was gaining popularity. It obtained support from many clinicians several decades ago and signified a separation of modern psychology from the conceptual "storage" of psychoanalysis.

The Diagnostic and Statistical Manual of Mental Disorders (3rd ed.; *DSM–3*), which was released in 1980, included the category *Personality Disorders* and emphasized that attention should be given to personality traits, which are inflexible and maladaptive and cause either significant impairment in social or occupational functioning or subjective distress (American Psychiatric Association [APA], 1980). The *DSM–3-R,* released by the APA 7 years later, provided 11 officially recognized diagnoses for personality disorders (four new descriptions were added: narcissistic, borderline, schizotypal, and avoidant), and two more were included in the appendix (sadistic and self-defeating), although the latter two were deleted entirely from the *DSM–4* (APA, 1994). Instead, passive-aggressive and depressive personality disorders were added to the appendix in *DSM–4,* but they were removed from the *DSM–5.*

Our understanding and clinical classifications of PDs continue to evolve and are likely to change in the future. Even though the *DSM–5* was published in 2013, and its Text Revision came out in 2022, there are still some controversies and uncertainties over the classifications, given the imprecise boundaries between "normal" and "pathological" features. Many diagnostic criteria for one disorder overlap with the diagnostic criteria for another, and several of the symptoms are related to other emotional and cognitive abnormalities. Contemporary scientific classifications of personality disorders are still "works in progress." For review, see Table 11.1.

TABLE 11.1 ■ Summarizing the *DSM–5–TR*: Classifications and Descriptions of Personality Disorders. Three Major Clusters.

Cluster: Dramatic Behavior	*Brief Description of Symptoms**	*Cautionary Statement*
Paranoid personality disorder	A prevalent distrust and suspiciousness of others and their motives	Should not be confused with reasonable cautious behavior and doubts about other people's loyalty
Schizoid personality disorder	A pervasive pattern of detachment from social relationships and a restricted range of emotions in interpersonal settings	Should not be confused with someone's shyness, reasonable lack of interest, or social inhibitions
Schizotypal personality disorder	A persistent pattern of social and interpersonal deficits marked by cognitive or perceptual distortions and eccentricities of behavior	Should not be confused with attention-seeking behavior or other culturally appropriate responses
Cluster: Dramatic Behavior	*Brief Description of Symptoms**	*Cautionary Statement*
Histrionic personality disorder	A pervasive pattern of excessive emotionality and attention seeking	Should not be confused with socially adaptive responses
Narcissistic personality disorder	A persistent pattern of grandiosity in fantasy or behavior, need for admiration, and lack of empathy	Should not be confused with certain patterns of leadership behavior and responses in extreme situations

TABLE 11.1 ■ Summarizing the *DSM–5–TR*: Classifications and Descriptions of Personality Disorders. Three Major Clusters. *(Continued)*		
Cluster: Dramatic Behavior	*Brief Description of Symptoms**	*Cautionary Statement*
Borderline personality disorder	A prevalent pattern of instability and unpredictability of thought, emotion, and behavior	Should not be confused with responses caused by frequently changing, highly unpredictable, and confusing situations
Antisocial personality disorder	A long-standing pattern of disregard for other people's rights, often crossing the line and violating those rights	Should not be confused with adaptive responses to extraordinary, dangerous, and threatening situations
Cluster: Anxious Behavior	*Brief Description of Symptoms**	*Cautionary Statement*
Avoidant personality disorder	A long-standing pattern of feelings of inadequacy and social inhibition	Should not be confused with the lack of social skills and reasonable self-isolation
Dependent personality disorder	A pervasive pattern of dependency and fear of abandonment	Should not be confused with temporary lack of social skills
Obsessive-compulsive personality disorder	A pervasive pattern of preoccupation with orderliness, perfectionism, and mental and interpersonal control, done at the expense of flexibility, openness, and efficiency	Should not be confused with adaptive skills of discipline and perfection that may lead to eventual success

CLUSTER: ODD BEHAVIOR

Clinicians use the characteristics of this cluster to diagnose individuals who demonstrate a stable pattern of remarkably unusual behavior. In the United States, three forms of such behavior are recognized: paranoid, schizoid, and schizotypal.

Paranoid Personality Disorder

The development of paranoid personality disorder symptoms goes hand in hand with an elevated interpersonal sensitivity—individuals feel they can see and know more about potentially dangerous or dreadful developments than other people do. Because this eminent sensitivity typically manifests in suspiciousness, a central feature of this syndrome is pervasive mistrust. High self-esteem and beliefs in one's own exclusivity contribute to suspiciousness. The individual displays emotional coldness, detachment from others, and unforgiving behavior. The world seems extremely hostile to them. Unjustified doubts about the loyalty or trustworthiness of associates, friends, and family members prevail. "I have done so much for them, and what did I get in return?" is a common pattern of thinking. Interpersonal sensitivity also manifests in a great susceptibility to criticism from others. Such criticisms appear to the individual as another sign of other people's ill intentions. Individuals with these symptoms seldom seek clinical help (Harper, 2010).

Schizoid Personality Disorder

Exaggerated introversion may be considered a prime feature of schizoid personality disorder. Introverted individuals tend to display a constant pattern of reserved and withdrawn behavior, but they do not typically draw clinical attention just because of this only trait. Individuals with schizoid PD display a pervasive pattern of withdrawn behavior. They tend to choose solitary activities and do not have warm, emotional, and close relationships (Millon et al., 2014). They rarely display their feelings to others. Not only do they have limited relationships with others, but they also seem to have almost no desire for such relationships. They often seem self-absorbed and oblivious to what is going on around them and demonstrate few social skills. Most of them do not seek marriage. The person with schizoid PD can have fantasies and creative ideas. Consider Steve, a 56-year-old man living in a small studio apartment in Westwood Village (Los Angeles) for the past 25 years. The only two people with whom he communicates regularly are his landlord and a doctor. Steve reads several books a month, usually modern philosophy, and often rereads them to understand the authors' "inner world." He loves modern science fiction and mocks contemporary pop culture. He dresses up in clean but clearly outdated clothes. Steve occasionally communicates with clerks at a neighborhood grocery store, where he works part time. Steve had a girlfriend, but they broke up several years ago.

Schizoid PD should be diagnosed with caution and in the context of specific circumstances of the individual. Persistent and seemingly unreasonable avoidance of social contacts and the lack of desire to develop meaningful relationships can appear in many cases as abnormal and maladaptive features. However, being quiet, reticent, and more observing than participating can also be indicative of a person's conscientiousness. In addition, temporary social withdrawal can be a useful means to achieve a professional or educational goal, such as when studying for exams. Sometimes individuals reduce their social contact for a reason, such as health conditions, that is not obvious to an impatient observer.

Schizotypal Personality Disorder

To be diagnosed with schizotypal personality disorder, an individual should display profound peculiarities of perceiving, thinking, acting, and communicating. The ability to express thoughts is diminished, and speech contains odd and unusual words and awkward phrases. Standard words often are said in peculiar ways. One of the features of this disorder is the belief in extraordinary, even magical personal powers. Although emotions tend to be shallow, social anxiety is persistent and elevated. Most affected individuals lack social skills, seek seclusion, and avoid friendships. Clinicians try not to confuse these symptoms with those of schizoid and paranoid personality disorders (note the overlapping symptoms). Some specialists considered this disorder as a midpoint type between healthy individuals and those with symptoms of schizophrenia (McGlashan, 1986).

It seems appropriate to consider an individual's bizarre beliefs, concerns, and communication patterns that interfere with the person's professional or educational activities as abnormal symptoms. Some of them can disrupt the clinician's efforts to treat medical or other psychological problems (such as substance addition or depression) that the person with schizotypal PD may have. Nevertheless, in some cultural groups, beliefs in extraordinary and magical powers seem appropriate and even welcome. Unusual thinking and odd ideas may also be indicators of a person's creativity in certain social contexts.

CHECK AND APPLY YOUR KNOWLEDGE

1. Explain test-taking attitudes such as social desirability and malingering.
2. What does the label *neurotic character* mean?
3. Name three disorders within the odd and eccentric behavior cluster.
4. Exaggerated introversion may be considered a prime feature of which PD?
5. Which professional occupations do you think will be the least suitable for individuals with PDs from the odd and eccentric behavior cluster?
6. Clinicians have to be cautions when diagnosing paranoid PD. Persistent, unfounded, and obviously irrational suspiciousness should probably require clinical attention. The same can be said about a person's unrelenting and inflexible accusations of other people's maliciousness. However, questioning someone's loyalty can be appropriate in certain circumstances. There are also professions that require constant vigilance. What are some of them?

CLUSTER: DRAMATIC BEHAVIOR

Disorders in this cluster share problems with the individual's impulse control and emotional regulation and include histrionic, narcissistic, borderline, and antisocial personality disorders (Table 11.2).

TABLE 11.2 ■ Main Features of Personality Disorders	
Personality Disorder	*Features Snapshot*
Paranoid	Distrust of other people. Suspiciousness of people's motives. Doubts about others' loyalty or fidelity. Accusations of people's ill motives. Lack of self-disclosure. Persistent attacks on others' reputation. Constant grudges and lack of forgiving behavior.
Schizoid	Detachment from social relationships. No desire or enjoyment of close relationships. Low interest in sexual experiences with another person. Taking pleasure in few activities. Indifference to praise or criticisms. Apparent emotional coldness and detachment.
Schizotypal	Cognitive or perceptual distortions and eccentricities of behavior. Ideas of reference. Odd and culturally inappropriate beliefs in magical thinking. Odd speech. Suspiciousness and paranoid ideation. Inappropriate or constricted affect. Excessive social anxiety.
Histrionic	Profound desires to be the center of attention. Seductive or provocative behavior. Shifting and shallow expression of emotions. Impressionistic speech, lacking in detail, with theatrical exaggerations. Gullibility. Self-dramatization.

(Continued)

TABLE 11.2 ■ Main Features of Personality Disorders *(Continued)*	
Personality Disorder	*Features Snapshot*
Narcissistic	A pervasive pattern of grandiosity and a sense of self-importance. Arrogance. Fantasies of unlimited success and power. Beliefs about being special and well connected. In search for excessive admiration. Manipulative behavior and envy. Sense of entitlement. Lack of empathy.
Borderline	A pervasive pattern of instability of interpersonal relationships, self-image, and emotions. Self-damaging impulsivity. Unstable and intense interpersonal relationships. Identity disturbance. Suicidal tendencies. Chronic feeling of emptiness. Inappropriate anger.
Antisocial	A long-standing pattern of disregard for other people, their well-being, and rights. Failure to conform to social norms. Constant lying. Impulsivity. Irritability and aggressiveness. Recklessness. Lack of responsibility and remorse.
Avoidant	A pervasive pattern of social inhibition and low self-esteem. Avoidance of interpersonal contact. Fears of disapproval or rejection. Restraints within intimate relationships. Feeling socially inept and unappealing. Reluctance to take personal risks.
Dependent	A long-standing need to be taken care of and a fear of being abandoned. Reluctance to let others assume responsibility. Seeking approval from others. Difficulty expressing disagreement because of fear of disapproval. Lack of self-confidence. Feeling uncomfortable or helpless when alone. Fearing unable to care for self.
Obsessive-Compulsive	A pervasive and inflexible preoccupation with order, perfection, and control. Excessive attention to details, rules, or organization. Excessive perfectionism and devotion to work to the exclusion of leisure. Hoarding tendencies. Miserly lifestyle. Inability to delegate tasks to others. Inflexibility about morality. Rigidity and stubbornness.

Histrionic Personality Disorder

Lilia underwent a psychological evaluation as an alleged victim of sexual abuse. She told the psychologist that she became a prostitute 7 years earlier, when she was 13, after her stepfather had sexually molested her. She provided a very detailed and disturbing account of the continuous abuse that she encountered. The psychologist who examined her turned to her medical records. According to the most recent medical examination, Lilia was a virgin (she had never had sexual intercourse). Next, the psychologist learned that she never had a stepfather and had made up her entire story about being a prostitute. Why did she lie? What was her incentive?

Individuals diagnosed with histrionic PD constantly look for attention. Their personality features resemble an extreme, exaggerated form of extroversion. Lilia, as well as other people diagnosed with this disorder, tend to grossly exaggerate their experiences. Anything—weather, traffic, friends, world economy, fashion—may be described as wonderful or horrible, stunningly beautiful, or unbelievably ugly. Being egocentric, those affected wish to remain the center of attention, which is their major motivation and thrill (such individuals are often labeled *sensitizers*). Anything is used to turn people's heads, including wearing provocative or revealing clothes or lying to a therapist. They make dramatic moves just to get people's attention.

As always, do not confuse clinical symptoms and conventional behaviors. Frequent, dramatic, and mostly unwarranted emotional outbursts or other peculiar actions that affect the person's relationships, academic, or professional career and overall well-being should draw clinical attention. These symptoms easily interfere with the treatment of other disorders (panic disorder or learning disabilities) in an individual. However, histrionic traits can be appropriate in certain activities and professions, including entertainment, the arts, politics, and some areas of teaching (Millon et al., 2004)). Performing arts or politics may create conditions that attract individuals with certain personality traits because of possible and significant public exposure associated with these occupations.

Narcissistic Personality Disorder

The term *narcissistic* comes from the classical Greek myth about Narcissus, the young hunter who fell in love with his own reflection in the water. Refusing the love of others and being unable to fall in love, he suddenly discovered that only his own reflection was worth his affection. Like Narcissus, people diagnosed with narcissistic personality disorder are typically preoccupied with self-appearance. They feel self-important and expect special favors from others. They need constant approval and admiration. They also tend to think that everything they do is exceptional, and other people do not appreciate them enough. They also have a fragile self-esteem (Campbell, 1999). To compensate for the perceived lack of admiration from others, they tend to develop a grandiose but unrealistic self-image, including fantasies of unlimited success, love, and power (John & Robbins, 1994). They pursue exploitative, even "parasitic" relationships because they feel they have the right to control others. *A profound feeling of entitlement* summarizes their attitudes toward others and self.

Diagnosing narcissistic PD requires caution and patience. Clinical symptoms often overlap with seemingly conventional behaviors. A person's pattern of self-absorption, egotism, and envy that brings harmful consequences to this person's life should certainly draw clinical attention. These individuals tend to have poor recognition of their psychological problems and need help. Yet an individual's self-confidence, self-appreciation, pride for personal accomplishments, or attention to appearance should be seen as appropriate in particular social circumstances. Could you suggest in which ones?

SELF-REFLECTION

The Drama of the Gifted Child by Alice Miller (1994) put forward a controversial hypothesis: Many professional psychotherapists are likely to be narcissistic. They do not become narcissistic after they become professionals—quite the contrary, she writes. Many individuals seek degrees in psychology because of childhood experiences that make them somewhat narcissistic. Imagine, she argues, a mother who is emotionally insecure, weak, or desperate, yet who always tries to appear confident, independent, and strong. This mother has a child who is sensitive and smart and who is seemingly capable of understanding her or his mother's struggles. The child wants to help and thus develops sensitivity to the needs of the mother and other people. The child then earns a good reputation for helping others. Unlike business, such amateur "psychological practices" generate no money; however, they bring approval from others. The child, a teenager now, becomes a homegrown "therapist" and feels important. This person now seeks people's praise. That is why many of these children later choose psychology as a profession. To them, Alice Miller argues, psychological practice is about much more than money. Helping other people with their emotional issues feeds the psychologists' childhood narcissistic tendencies—the desire to maintain a good image of self and feel special.

Questions

As a high school student, were you ever asked to help other people with their emotional problems? Did you enjoy helping or guiding others? What is the difference between (1) enjoying every opportunity to help another person and (2) having narcissistic features?

Borderline Personality Disorder

The symptoms of borderline personality disorder (BPD) point to a profound inconsistency of personality traits. In contrast to other PDs, such inconsistency represents a pervasive pattern of instability in behavior, emotions, and thinking. One of the most basic features of this disorder is the feeling of emptiness, which is often associated with extreme instability and shallowness in self-perception, habits, and opinions. Relationships are highly unbalanced—a person's kindness and compassion are followed by anger and physical aggression a few hours later. A strong need for a relationship leads persons with borderline symptoms to fear abandonment and feel unreasonably angry about a possible separation. They usually demand dedication and exclusiveness from others but do not show dedication themselves. Impulsivity, or behavior with little or no forethought, is common and includes sexual promiscuity, spending sprees, or excessive drinking or eating. People with this disorder are highly manipulative. They make threats, including suicidal ones, and frequent swings in emotions are typical (Kreger, 2008).

If an individual displays behavioral and emotional instability, impulsivity, anger, and self-destructive tendencies, these symptoms should certainly receive clinical attention. It is important, however, not to perceive occasional instability and impulsivity in someone's behavior as symptoms of this disorder. Many of us routinely change our plans, depending on the circumstances. We sometimes make abrupt decisions. Many outside factors affect an occasional emotional swing. It is always important to pay attention to the duration and severity of these and other symptoms and determine how they affect an individual's functioning in a variety of circumstances.

Antisocial Personality Disorder

Individuals with symptoms of antisocial personality disorder have difficulty controlling their own impulses and have little or no regret for the harmful things they do to others. The diagnosis is usually given to people over the age of 18, yet some key symptoms of this disorder tend to occur a few years earlier. Some individuals diagnosed with this disorder say in self-reports that they regard life as a "big game" in which they use every opportunity to manipulate others. Excitement about risks and winning seems to be especially important. People with symptoms of antisocial PD have a callous lack of concern for the rights and feelings of others. They also have little insight into their own behavior and tend to blame others for "provoking" them into deviant acts. Some individuals turn to violence and recklessness, while others can appear charming and caring. They frequently lie and do not keep their promises and commitments. Symptoms of this disorder make other psychological problems more difficult to treat. Moreover, some of those affected use therapy to learn manipulation techniques: how to lie, hide emotions, and exploit other people's vulnerabilities.

Diagnosing antisocial PD should be done with caution. Persistent manipulative or violent behavior, uncontrollable anger, and lying could result in self-destruction or endangerment of other people—these are serious clinical symptoms. Under specific social conditions, however, some features of this disorder become somewhat useful coping strategies that help the individual survive in extreme conditions. Could you think and name such conditions?

CLUSTER: ANXIOUS BEHAVIOR

Personality disorders included in the anxious behavior cluster represent a range of symptoms for abnormal manifestations of apprehensive, timid, or frightened behavior. Such symptoms become significant and distressful in an individual's life and have a major impact on daily activities. The cluster includes avoidant, dependent, and obsessive-compulsive PDs.

Avoidant Personality Disorder

Y. M. is a 27-year-old graduate of the prestigious law school at Waseda University in Tokyo, Japan. A hardworking man, he spent significant time after graduation to prepare for the bar exam. Only a handful of law school graduates in Japan pass this extremely difficult exam that allows them practice law. Y. M. passed the exam with a high score, which meant he was eligible to apply for a job in a prominent firm. However, he did not apply. He feared accepting responsibility for thousands of people at his new job as a lawyer. Such avoidant tendencies started when Y. M. was a boy: He felt uncomfortable discussing things publicly; he was extremely embarrassed for being clumsy or messy at parties or social gatherings. He also developed an irrational fear about his body's odor (he believed that people knew about his odor problem but were too polite to tell him). His avoidant tendencies grew. His lengthy preparation for the bar exam had shielded him from other people for some time, but when the time came to apply for a job, his symptoms returned.

One of the major psychological features associated with avoidant personality disorder (in Japan, this phenomenon is known as *Taijin confusho*) is elevated social anxiety (Essau et al., 2012). Low self-esteem, fear of criticism, and concerns about negative evaluation are distinct characteristics of avoidant PD. Those affected have constant doubts about their own appearance, abilities, and competence; have only a few friends; and tend to evade intimacy. Individuals with these symptoms are not likely to develop personal relationships unless they become sure another person likes and appreciates them. They tend to be extremely vigilant about their ongoing relationships, while constantly anticipating the potential pain of rejection and disenchantment. They are sensitive to negative evaluation, deception, mocking, or other negative reactions from others. They exaggerate concerns about looking foolish or incompetent in social situations.

Clinicians should pay attention to serious and persistent avoidant tendencies that thwart a person's ability to function in everyday situations such as applying for a job, establishing a personal contact, asking for help, visiting the DMV office, or making a doctor's appointment. On the other hand, shyness and some other mild avoidant tendencies can be adaptive or culturally appropriate. Some avoidant tendencies, for example, may "protect" a person from making unrealistic promises or being engaged in risky enterprises.

Dependent Personality Disorder

The movie *What About Bob?* (1991) is a Hollywood comedy in which the panicky, helpless, and annoying patient called Bob, played by Bill Murray, follows his therapist everywhere he goes and keeps asking for extra therapy sessions. In exchange for therapy, Bob promises his friendship and devotion. Bob's dependent behavior is depicted as a series of irritating and intrusive acts: He does unpleasant things just to be close to the therapist, constantly craves support and assurances from others, and feels extremely uncomfortable being alone.

Symptoms of dependent personality disorder include two basic subtypes: an individual's persistent delegation of important decisions to other people and subordination of own needs to the wishes of others. Individuals with symptoms of this disorder appear overly submissive and clingy. Their elevated anxiety is related to possible abandonment by a relative or friend. Many of these individuals believe they are irrelevant, incompetent, unattractive, or ugly. They assume that there is no reason for another person to stay in a relationship with them, which further increases their anxiety and dependent tendencies. They often make themselves available or pleasing to others, expecting that this behavior will keep them close to each other (Loranger, 1996).

Contrasting clinical symptoms with conventional behaviors is an important critical-thinking method in the diagnosis of dependent PD. Certain dependent tendencies require clinical attention if they seriously thwart a person's ability to have meaningful relationships; develop a career; or decide about education, employment, housing, or medical treatment. Yet a person's commitment to a relationship or selfless tendencies should be judged with caution. Only evident frequency, degree, or intensity of such selfless manifestations in specific social and cultural contexts can explain whether an individual should be diagnosed with this personality disorder.

Obsessive-Compulsive Personality Disorder

Individuals diagnosed with obsessive-compulsive disorder (OCD) display ritualized thought patterns and behavior. They seem to be extremely self-controlling and exceptionally organized. They prefer routines and standard procedures and reject improvisation. They appear serious, moralistic, grumpy, and demanding. They do not appreciate jokes and prefer not to crack jokes themselves. As extraordinary perfectionists, they tend to focus on small details. These individuals feel disturbed when rules are not followed or when things are not where they are supposed to be at home or in the office. Although anxiety is often reported as a significant underlying feature, individuals with OCD are unlikely to engage in irrational, ritualistic, and compulsive acts.

Clinical attention is likely required when significant preoccupation with rules and routines prevent an individual from successfully coping with changing life conditions. When a person loses flexibility and abandons common sense, clinicians should help. However, there are many healthy and efficient people among us who are extremely organized and who dislike improvisation. In fact, some professions require us to be somewhat rigid and extremely organized.

CHECK AND APPLY YOUR KNOWLEDGE

1. Name four disorders within the dramatic, emotional, or erratic behavior cluster.
2. The symptoms of which disorder point at a profound inconsistency of personality traits?
3. Which occupations do you think will be least suitable for individuals with PDs from this cluster?
4. Under specific social conditions, some features of antisocial PD become somewhat useful strategies that help individuals survive in extreme conditions. Name some of these conditions.
5. Name three disorders within the anxious and fearful behavior cluster.
6. Low self-esteem, fear of criticism, and concerns about negative evaluation are distinct characteristics of which PD?
7. Which occupations or professions do you think will be least suitable for individuals with PDs from the anxious and fearful behavior cluster?

SELF-REFLECTION

Imagine that you are a licensed psychologist who treats personality disorders (in fact, you may be one now or be a few years away from it). Which one of the previously discussed disorders appears most interesting and intriguing to you? Why?

ETIOLOGY OF PERSONALITY DISORDERS

Which factors cause and contribute to the symptoms of personality disorders? How do science, social sciences, and psychology explain personality disorders?

The Biomedical Perspective

For centuries, scientists assumed that bodily humors were foundations of four classical types of personality: the sanguine, the phlegmatic, the choleric, and the melancholic. A misbalance in bodily humors caused the person to be either persistently and unreasonably elated or constantly withdrawn and grumpy, or stubbornly belligerent and unpredictable or consistently sad or easily disturbed. Although science no longer uses the concept of body humors, it is accepted that PDs have underlying biological and physiological causes, including genetic predispositions.

Twin studies showed a genetic contribution to borderline PD (Lehman, 2003). First-degree relatives of patients with schizophrenia are more likely than people in the general population to develop schizotypal PD (Battaglia & Torgensen, 1996). Presence of mood disorders in the family also increases probability of schizotypal symptoms in close relatives (Erlenmeyer-Kimlig et al., 1995). Persistent and unreasonable suspiciousness, a key symptom of paranoid PD, runs in the family as well (Costello, 1995). Studies also showed the links between hereditary factors and antisocial behavior (Baker et al., 2006; Lykken, 1995). Impulsive physical violence and aggression—often associated with antisocial PD—have long been linked to neurotransmitter serotonin (Aluja et al., 2009; Virkkunen, 1983). Having a biological parent with antisocial features increases the child's chances of developing antisocial PD as well (Langbehn & Cadoret, 2001). Physiological factors also affect an individual's heightened or lowered anxiety levels. Low anxiety, for example, is a common condition for antisocial tendencies that include persistent reckless behavior and impulsivity and are associated with an individual's failing to predict the consequences of personal actions (Hare, 1983; Patrick, 1994). Slow alpha waves in the brain and several features of antisocial behavior were shown to be correlated (Volavka et al., 1990), which again may suggest that people with antisocial symptoms have a low measure of arousal level (in normal individuals, slower alpha waves indicate nonanxiety states).

Hereditary and environmental factors both contribute to the symptoms of PDs. To illustrate, Cadoret et al. (1995) studied people who were separated at birth from biological parents who both had antisocial PD. The children who grew up in unfavorable, difficult, and stressful environments had more antisocial symptoms than their counterparts raised in more favorable social environments. Perhaps an interplay of genetic and social factors explains these differences. High testosterone levels (which may be caused by genetic factors) can cause persistently aggressive behavior; however, testosterone levels can also increase due to the impact of constantly stressful situations, such as difficult social or living environments. In contrast, there are many individuals with high testosterone scores who choose prosocial forms of behavior and exercise moderation and self-control. Instead, it is likely that people have certain genetic **overarching liabilities**. They affect behavior and traits under unfavorable conditions; for example, internalizing liabilities are linked to emotional problems, while externalizing liabilities refer to behavioral conduct such as lack of inhibition or aggressiveness (see Table 11.3; Krueger & Markon, 2006).

The Psychoanalytic Tradition

Traditional psychoanalytic models focus on unconscious psychological mechanisms usually rooted in early childhood and heavily influenced by early experiences (English & English, 1958). A child's oversensitivity or resistance, selfishness or alienation from reality, instability or playfulness, maliciousness, or clinging behavior all may contribute to this child's behavioral and psychological problems later in life. Psychoanalysts generally believe that personality disorders refer to a person's social maladjustments. See several examples of psychoanalytic interpretations in Table 11.4. Although they may appear intriguing, they do not find significant empirical

TABLE 11.3 ■ The Biomedical Perspective: A Summary	
Personality Disorder Clusters	*Descriptions*
Odd behavior	Genetic and other biological factors determine some people's hypersensitivity, which can lead to paranoid tendencies; natural inclinations for reclusive behavior and solitary activities are commonly labeled as *schizoid* characteristics.
Dramatic behavior	Genetic and other biological factors contribute to excessive anxiety, instability in coping mechanisms, impulsivity, and other psychological responses—which manifest in various forms described as antisocial, histrionic, borderline, or narcissistic behaviors.
Anxious behavior	All of these disorders involve behavioral traits that may be related to a heightened susceptibility (liability) to anxiety and a common category of behavioral and psychological efforts to ward off anxiety.

TABLE 11.4 ■ Selected Psychoanalytic Interpretations of Personality Disorders	
Personality Disorder	*Interpretations of Causes*
Narcissistic	A redirection of a person's love inward takes place because a child does not get enough love from his or her parents. The child also has to suppress anger for the perceived abandonment. Shame formed in early childhood can also be a powerful cause of narcissistic symptoms.
Antisocial	The individual lacks the authoritative power of the super-ego as a moral guide or censor. A lack of trust toward parents in early childhood may also weaken the desire to respect any authority in the future.
Borderline	Aggressive impulses toward parents are directed inward. The weak ego allows infantile impulses pushing for the immediate satisfaction of desires.
Paranoid	Angry, threatening, and demanding parents launch the child's unconscious defenses, which later results in deep suspiciousness toward other people.
Dependent	Overprotective parents stimulate defense mechanisms that later contribute to dependent tendencies.

Sources: Broucek, 1991; Freud, 1914/1957; Gabbard, 1990; Kernberg, 1992; Kohut, 1977; Loranger, 1996; Morrison, 1989.

support in contemporary research. Psychoanalytic theories deserve credit, nevertheless, for directing attention to family-related psychological problems and early childhood experiences and their impact on personality disorders.

The Behavioral-Learning Tradition

Personality disorders are also formed in individual daily interactions and learning. People learn by means of reinforcement or example. Facing challenging life situations, some individuals learns successful strategies, but others learn poor strategies, which, if they become persistent, can appear as symptoms of PDs.

For example, a boy learns that friendship and intimacy bring no benefits, and at the same time, his parents constantly tell him that he is better than everybody else. The boy learns to diminish others to benefit himself. Such behavioral patterns could lead to narcissistic PD (Watson et al., 1984). Some people learn how to excel in life through hard work and perseverance, while others learn about drawing unwarranted attention to self and being manipulative in romantic relationships to build narcissistic features (Campbell, 1999).

Studies gave psychologists supportive evidence about the impact of interpersonal relationships on PDs. For instance, overly demanding and constantly angry parents tend to contribute to a child's fearful and even paranoid symptoms (Manschreck, 1996). Parental abuse, neglect, separation, threats of separation, and excessive violence during childhood or adolescence contribute to the symptoms of borderline PD (Gunderson & Lyoo, 1997). Schizoid personality features are rooted in the child's profound dissatisfaction with interpersonal relationships: Lacking positive reinforcement in the family, the person learns that human relationships bring nothing but trouble. Therefore, avoiding interpersonal contacts and focusing on solitary activities becomes rewarding (Horner, 1991).

It is still unclear why, under similar circumstances, some people develop distinct symptoms of a PD while others do not. Troubled learning experiences can contribute to specific personality features. Nevertheless, in many cases such personality traits do not develop into a personality disorder.

The Cognitive Tradition

The cognitive tradition focuses primarily on how people process information related to self and how they use this information in relation to their experience and behavior. Psychologists have long established a connection between self-focused cognitions and emotional responses and actions. An example helps illustrate this point:

Imagine a girl develops the belief that she is unattractive, and therefore, nobody is paying attention to her. She further concludes that she is unlovable, assuming that attention from somebody is a path to love. However, she wants to be lovable, so she looks for a way to get attention from others. One way is to appear extremely provocative, exaggerate emotions, and behave in unpredictable ways. If this pattern persists for years, it may be associated with histrionic PD. The cognitive tradition suggests that relatively stable cognitive constructs, such as expectations of outcomes, regulate our behavior in a wide range of social situations (Gramzow & Tangney, 1992).

Various cognitive variables have been linked with narcissistic PD (Emmons, 1987). These variables include exaggerated self-focus in conversations, such as the pervasive use of the pronoun *I* in spontaneous speech (Raskin & Shaw, 1988). Another variable is the exaggerated belief in personal uniqueness (Emmons, 1984), exceptional importance (Raskin et al., 1991), or the belief in superior personal features compared to other people (Gabriel et al., 1994).

Individuals diagnosed with antisocial PD have cognitive difficulty recognizing nonconfrontational or nonviolent solutions to most problems they face (Kosson & Newman, 1986). They often lack self-reflection of their own anxiety (Schalling, 1978), yet they also show a heightened responsiveness to threat (Hodgins et al., 2010). The individual's cognitive features and abnormal symptoms are interconnected. A belief that one looks ugly may contribute to this person's avoidance, and avoidance further enhances this irrational belief.

The Trait Tradition

From the trait tradition perspective, personality disorders represent "anomalous" configurations of basic, "normal" dimensions of personality. If we understand these basic dimensions well enough, then we better understand PDs. Basic research into personality, therefore, is central in the study of abnormal symptoms. One of the most popular models of personality—but not the only one—is the five-factor model (FFM) of personality (see Chapter 6). Recall that this model was originally derived from the words in the English language that describe personality traits (Lynam & Widiger, 2001). There are five broad domains of personality: extroversion (positive affectivity), neuroticism (negative affectivity), agreeableness, conscientiousness, and openness to experience. Each of these domains can be further differentiated.

If we place known PDs into the left column and arrange the five personality traits horizontally, the intersections between the rows that represent disorders and the columns representing traits become the "diagnostic cells" in reference to which specific observations and measurements can be made (see Table 11.5). For example, an individual can be assessed along

TABLE 11.5 ■ Understanding Personality Disorders From the Trait Approach					
Personality Disorders	*Personality Traits*				
	Neuroticism	*Extroversion*	*Openness*	*Agreeableness*	*Conscientiousness*
Paranoid	High	Low	Low	Low	Low
Schizoid	Mixed	Low	Low	Mixed	High
Schizotypal	High	Low	High	Low	Low
Borderline	High	High	High	Low	Low
Narcissistic	High	High	Low	Low	High
Histrionic	High	High	High	High	Low
Antisocial	High	Mixed	Mixed	Low	Low
Dependent	High	High	High	High	Low
Avoidant	High	Low	Low	Low	High
Obsessive-Compulsive	Mixed	Low	Low	Low	High

the personality dimensions first, and then an attempt can be made to associate these assessments with specific personality symptoms. Some features have been established empirically, such as a negative correlation of narcissism with agreeableness (Rhodewalt & Morf, 1995; Watson, 2012). Others are results of assumptions about how things "should be." Feel free to make your own opinion about such assumptions.

Many uncertainties in research conclusions require discussion and further studies. For example, psychologists often agree on how to describe a specific individual along the personality dimensions, but they tend to disagree about which combinations of traits represent a specific PD. One of the arguments is that any diagnostic method in psychology should take into consideration the cultural conditions in which the individual grows up and functions. Not only do we as individuals think, feel, and act according to cultural norms, but we also judge other people based on such norms.

The Cross-Cultural Approach

Some cross-cultural studies suggest that if human beings think, act, and feel according to particular cultural prescriptions, then people who are brought up in diverse cultural settings should understand what is "normal" and "abnormal" differently. This view is called the **relativist perspective of abnormal behavior** because it puts this behavior in a relative, comparative perspective (Shiraev & Levy, 2024). What is considered pathological in one culture could be regarded as simply different in another—for example, pinching somebody in one cultural environment can be seen as a friendly sign, whereas in another environment it is recognized as an inappropriate, demeaning, and even violent act.

Other cross-cultural psychologists showed that despite cultural differences, people share a great number of features, including common social norms, values, and behavioral responses (Beardsley & Pedersen, 1997). Therefore, the overall understanding of normal and abnormal individual features ought to be universal. This view is called the **universalist perspective of abnormal behavior** because it suggests the existence of some universal psychological and behavioral features shared in individuals. Deviant and abnormal phenomena across countries and cultures tend to be universal in terms of their origin and expression. Almost everywhere, people disapprove of unprovoked hostility, reject excessive suspiciousness, or condemn persistent lying (Penny et al., 2009). In a unique comparative study sponsored by the WHO, 58 psychiatrists interviewed 716 patients in 11 countries in North America, Europe, Africa, and Asia and found that personality disorders have relatively similar features (Loranger et al., 1994). They can be assessed with a reasonably high degree of reliability across different nations, languages, and cultures. Additional studies supported this point of view (Fountoulakis et al., 2002).

Which view—universalist or relativist—better describes personality disorders? We can accept both (1) the relative cultural uniqueness and (2) the universal nature of psychological symptoms. Each PD, therefore, can manifest as follows:

- A set of central symptoms that are abnormal, maladaptive, and distressful that can be observed in practically all world populations

- A set of peripheral symptoms that are culturally specific

For example, central symptoms for a case of a histrionic PD can be an individual's profound desire to be in the center of attention, a propensity for dramatic acts, and emotional exaggerations. Peripheral symptoms can include the preferred style of clothes (every region has its own requirements) or seductiveness in behavior (judged differently in various cultures). In other words, our judgments about "appropriate" and "excessive" behaviors and traits vary across cultures. Psychologists should decide whether the diagnosis is applicable to the individual given the cultural (and sometimes political) context in which this person lives. Someone's flashy and provocative clothes may cause negative comments from people in one community but not in another. What is labeled *provocative* or *promiscuous* behavior differs, too. The term *tolerance threshold*, again, is applicable here (Chapter 1). Low thresholds indicate relative societal intolerance against specific behaviors and underlying personality traits, while high thresholds designate relative tolerance. If a society accepts the diversity of behaviors, then tolerance thresholds should be relatively high.

Specific social and cultural circumstances serve as "filters" for evaluations of personality traits and disorders. Some traits can be seen as common and standard from a particular national or cultural standpoint, while they can be seen as excessive and even abnormal (if they fit specific criteria) from another cultural point of view. For instance, if a woman from a traditional culture stays away from public places, prefers solitary activities at home, does not have close relationships with anyone outside her family, and appears "cold" or unemotional in conversations with strangers (such as a Western psychologist who interviews her), these characteristics should not be considered indicative of schizoid PD. Her behavior should be judged from a broader cultural context that contains specific gender scripts or rules of behavior for men and women.

Now take, for example, discussions about obsessive-compulsive personality traits in Japan. As one Japanese educator put it, in Japanese society many people were brought up to model themselves faithfully on "role models" or general behavioral standards. This environment creates conditions that stimulate people's preoccupation with discipline, formal rules, and procedures (Esaki, 2001). If these behavioral traits are taken out of cultural context, there could be a temptation to view them as symptoms of OCD. However, within the Japanese context, to a degree, these personality traits are likely to be considered normal.

Certain personality traits may "flourish" in particular circumstances and be "blocked" in others. Some personality types can contribute to successful coping in a set of cultural conditions—take, for example, avoidant traits. In China, traditionally, interpersonal relationships have been largely based on a deep cultural tradition of exchange of favors, or, in Western language, reciprocal relationships guided by moral norms. If people believe that under specific circumstances, they are not capable of exchanging favor with others, this could be an embarrassing blow to their reputations. Therefore, to save face, it is generally appropriate for such individuals to develop avoidant tendencies because avoidance is perceived as less embarrassing than the inability to exercise appropriate social acts. Foreign observers may be inclined to perceive these persistent behaviors as symptoms of avoidant PD. Similarly, one study showed it is common for young adults from Greece to seek support (both emotional and financial) from their parents until the age of 30. However, a foreign observer may construe this as a form of dependent behavior (Fountoulakis et al., 2002).

To summarize, some symptoms of PDs in the *DSM–5–TR* could be valued as nonexcessive, nonpathological, and even normal in certain cultural settings. Cultural knowledge is essential when attempting to apply *DSM*-based diagnoses to individuals from different cultural environments.

CHECK AND APPLY YOUR KNOWLEDGE

1. What is the essence of the biomedical perspective of PDs?
2. What is the key difference between the behavioral-learning and cognitive perspectives of PDs?
3. Compare the universalist and relativist perspectives of abnormal behavior.
4. *Hikikomori* is a complex form of withdrawal behavior common in Japan. It has been the topic of numerous television documentaries and newspaper and magazine articles (Rees, 2002; Saitō, 2012). Hikikimori is found mostly in men who shut themselves in the homes of their parents and have very limited face-to-face contact with other people (according to estimates, there are over 1 million of them). They spend their days browsing the web or chatting online and only occasionally see their parents, who help them financially. These young individuals claim they lost the incentive for hard work and abandoned their ambitions, but their lives are comfortable, and the web gives them a chance to interact with others without face-to-face contact. They do not have a prevalence of any psychological disorder, compared to the general population, and studies in other countries suggest that this is not exclusively a Japanese phenomenon (Sax, 2007).
   a. Do you see Hikikomori a kind of schizoid personality disorder? Why or why not?
   b. Do you think these individuals are suffering psychologically? Have they failed as society members?
   c. How would the society in which you live change if most people in it chose Hikikomori as their lifestyle? Explain your opinions.

DIFFERENTIAL DIAGNOSIS AND COMORBIDITY

Comorbidity is the presence of one or several additional disorders in an individual. These disorders can be somewhat independent or quite related to one another. Comorbidity makes diagnostic procedures more difficult. Therefore, clinicians us a **differential diagnosis**, which is a method to identify and separate one disorder from others. This method also allows possible alternatives to an initial diagnosis.

Comorbidity of personality disorders is the norm rather than the exception. Despite the diagnostic guidelines that prescribe that only one PD diagnosis should be given, people who meet diagnostic criteria for one PD will likely meet the criteria for another or several other PDs (Lenzenweger et al., 2007; Widiger and Spitzer, 1991). For example, many symptoms of antisocial PD, including manipulativeness, grandiosity, and a lack of empathy, are found in individuals with symptoms of narcissistic PD (Hare, 1991; Hörz-Sagstetter et al., 2018). Personality disorders are comorbid with other psychological problems—there is evidence of connections between antisocial PD and pathological gambling (Slutske et al., 2001) and between alcohol use disorder and borderline PD as well as antisocial PD (Helle et al., 2019). In addition, avoidant PD and a range of mood and anxiety disorders, such as social phobia, tend to be comorbid (Brieger et al., 2003).

A person diagnosed with a PD should have a history of inflexible, maladaptive, and distressful behavioral patterns. However, it is usually a challenge for clinicians to establish such a history. The person under evaluation is likely to regard these behavioral patterns as normal; such individuals often do not understand or refuse to acknowledge their problem. Another potential diagnostic problem relates to a degree of the problem, or the scope of the observable behaviors—for instance, an individual may exhibit only one trait that requires clinical attention (such as excessive punctuality) or a couple of traits of different PDs, such as excessive fascination with one's own self-appearance put together with an inability to delegate tasks to others. And although many symptoms of PDs tend to appear early in life, they are typically not diagnosed in children (Chanen & Thompson, 2019). Late onset of PDs can take place under specific circumstances, such as the occurrence of other major psychological or physical disorders like Alzheimer's disease or substance-related disorders.

Personality disorders are especially difficult to differentiate from anxiety-related disorders. It is expected that individuals who develop symptoms of an anxiety disorder typically regard their anxiety and subsequent behavior as unusual and different from their "normal" behavior. They may exaggerate their problems that might appear as symptoms of a PD (Jansen et al., 1994). In contrast, individuals who exhibit several symptoms of a PD tend to disregard them and explain their behavior as generally normal. A person with obsessive-compulsive disorder may constantly complain that too many people are late for their appointments, disregard traffic rules, or do not plan their lives in advance.

Now consider key distinctions between several pairs of PDs. Using the examples in Table 11.6, try to establish differences for the following pairs of disorders: avoidant and schizoid, narcissistic and histrionic, and paranoid and obsessive-compulsive.

A cautionary statement is necessary here. Studying personality from the position of illness is a work in progress. Looking for a clear-cut set of symptoms that describe an "abnormal" personality to distinguish it from a "normal" one is often unproductive. The methods used by clinicians, psychiatrists, psychologists, and social workers are not necessarily precise or particularly reliable. Psychologists are still learning about the impact of cultural factors on key symptoms of PDs. Experiments in this area are very difficult to conduct, and many research hypotheses remain untestable. To summarize, there is neither a quick blood test, a real-time MRI, nor an express questionnaire to recognize a personality disorder. Not yet.

TABLE 11.6 ■ Key Distinctions Between Several Pairs of Personality Disorders

Overlapping and Common Symptoms	*Some Differences*
Dependent and Borderline: Individuals demonstrate "clinging" behavior, suffer from separation anxiety, and report fear of abandonment.	In borderline cases, individuals are likely to be angry and move from being caring to being demanding and manipulative; in dependent cases, they tend to be agreeable, trusting, and submissive.
Avoidant and Schizoid: Introversion is a common underlying personality trait; self-isolation is a significant behavioral symptom.	Avoidant symptoms are accompanied by anxiety-related symptoms—individuals are afraid to make a mistake; individuals with schizoid symptoms tend to display low neuroticism and a lack of social motivation.
Schizotypal and Borderline: Common features include bizarre behavioral manifestations, inappropriate emotional displays, and general unpredictability.	Borderline symptoms are likely to be associated with impulsivity, aggression, and reckless behavior, all of which are almost uncommon in schizotypal symptoms.
Histrionic and Antisocial: Common features include seemingly flamboyant, shocking, provocative, and inappropriate behavior.	Histrionic behavior is likely to take place within the established social norms and may be judged as eccentric; symptoms can be seen as attention-seeking behavior. Antisocial behavior is a more blatant challenge to norms, and symptoms are related to pragmatic or egotistic motives.
Paranoid and Narcissistic: Both have common features associated with lack of trust in other people, anger, inadequate self-esteem, and beliefs in self-exclusivity.	Paranoid symptoms are likely to be connected to withdrawal tendencies and elevated anxiety, as well as low self-esteem. Narcissistic tendencies are likely to be connected with attention-seeking behavior, envy, and the feeling of entitlement.
Complete the columns by comparing the following disorders. For discussion, visit the companion website.	
Avoidant and Dependent	
Narcissistic and Histrionic	
Paranoid and Obsessive-Compulsive	

CHECK AND APPLY YOUR KNOWLEDGE

1. Explain comorbidity in psychology.
2. Explain differential diagnosis in the context of PDs. Why is this method important?

APPLYING KNOWLEDGE TO THE CLINICAL DOMAIN

Treatment of Personality Disorders

There is no "magic pill" to treat personality disorders. While understanding the complexity of this type of illness and the inability of most individuals to recognize their problems, clinicians try to find the most effective, often a "tailor-made" therapeutic approach to each patient. Some individuals need lengthy therapy, while others need it for just a short period. Some individuals thrive on strong support from their families, yet others do not. As we have learned, PDs usually appear in conjunction with other illnesses.

Personality disorders are likely to have a major impact on other psychological disorders and the outcomes of their treatment (Lenzenweger et al., 2007). Patients with bipolar disorder who are also diagnosed with PDs have poorer treatment outcomes than those diag-

PHOTO 11.3 Some personality disorders, especially borderline and histrionic, are risk factors that contribute to self-destructive behavior. Discuss the ways that we can attempt to help such individuals without violating their privacy.

©iStockphoto.com / Murika

nosed as only bipolar. Clinical trials showed that a key to successful treatment can be an emphasis on educating patients about their behavior and emotions (Colom et al., 2004).

Some clinicians advance the traditional psychoanalytic methods of treatment whereas others turn to new forms of treatment such as *schema therapy*, which is a creative combination of several therapeutic techniques (Young et al., 2006). Even though PDs are very difficult to treat, there is evidence that many people diagnosed with them can improve over time (Zanarini et al., 2005). Moreover, according to clinical studies, significantly greater proportion of individuals recovered in schema therapy compared with other, more conventional forms of psychotherapy (Lotte et al., 2014).

Suicide Prevention

Some personality disorders, especially borderline and histrionic, are risk factors that contribute to suicide and self-destructive behavior (Lineham et al., 2000; Paris, 2019). Early recognition of symptoms and clinical attention to such individuals can save lives. Some assume that individuals with PDs make suicidal threats simply because they need attention and that they aren't serious about taking their own lives. This assumption should be dismissed. Suicide may take place even though it might have initially been planned as a theatrical gesture. Any suicidal threats, talk about death, or comments about "ending it all" should be taken with extreme seriousness. The most at-risk categories are the younger individuals diagnosed with a PD and those who undergo a long but unsuccessful treatment. Many individuals with PDs will respond to the arguments of clinicians and friends that persuade them to avoid any harm to themselves or others. Such arguments can be designed according to the specific patient's situation and can be used in preventive therapies (McGirr et al., 2007). Especially effective preventive methods of treatment can be provided in outpatient settings to help patients in their pursuit of their life goals and better engagement with career and social groups (Zanarini, 2009).

Criminal Justice

By studying personality disorders and associating them with behavior, specialists in criminal justice (with the help from clinicians) gather information to identify, recognize, and deal with antisocial, deviant, and criminal behavior. Let's return to the chapter's opening example to illustrate: Reports suggest that about 13 million people are stalked in the United States every year. Nearly 1 in 3 women and 1 in 6 men have experienced stalking victimization at some point in their life, according to a survey. Most victims are stalked by someone they know (Smith et al., 2017). Many factors and circumstances cause stalking, so which cases should be addressed by the criminal justice system alone, and which cases also require clinical intervention?

First, experts draw a "profile" of the stalker. On average, stalkers are single males. About half of the victims were in a relationship with the stalker, about 15% are just acquaintances, and only 10% of cases involve people who they have never met. Basic indicators, such as the stalker's age (under 30), the number of threats made, the presence of substance abuse, and the tendency to produce high levels of fear in the victim, are accurate predictors of violence in stalking cases and assist the law enforcement and criminal justice systems in creating a profile.

What about the psychological factors affecting a stalker's behavior and mind? There are at least five types of key stalking types or mindsets (Figure 11.1). The *rejected* cannot accept their rejection or loss and try to achieve their goal by receiving acceptance. *Intimacy chasers* tend to ache from unrequited love and try to reduce their suffering. *Incompetent suitors* typically lack many important social and communication skills. The *resentful* believe they have been mistreated and hope to restore "justice." Finally, the *predatory* tend to behave as seekers and hunters (Mohandie et al., 2006). Which personality disorders, in your view, could be connected to the five types described here?

Perhaps there are certain personality traits that contribute to stalkers' behavior, such as narcissistic tendencies, high or low self-esteem, compulsive habits, or impulsivity. Some stalkers realize their behavior is wrong and soon enough stop pursuing their victim, but others do not stop and calculate their next step. Unfortunately, almost every third stalking case results in physical or sexual assault.

Those who stalk strangers and acquaintances often have underlying psychological problems, and psychopathology is associated with more persistent and recurrent stalking behavior. These findings strongly support the argument for routine mental health assessment of stranger and acquaintance stalkers who become involved with the criminal justice system (McEwan & Strand, 2013).

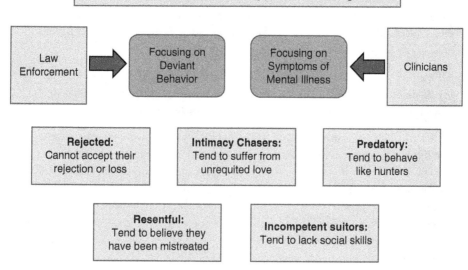

FIGURE 11.1 ■ Behavioral Profiles of Stalking Behavior

Individual features and social circumstances that contribute to the following behavioral and thinking patterns of stalking behavior

Law Enforcement → Focusing on Deviant Behavior

Focusing on Symptoms of Mental Illness ← Clinicians

Rejected: Cannot accept their rejection or loss

Intimacy Chasers: Tend to suffer from unrequited love

Predatory: Tend to behave like hunters

Resentful: Tend to believe they have been mistreated

Incompetent suitors: Tend to lack social skills

SUMMARY

- The clinical domain involves approaches to personality from the position of abnormality, illness, and health care. The term *illness* can be used interchangeably with the terms *disease* and *disorder* and broadly refers to any *condition* or a functional abnormality or disturbance of the body and mind. Psychiatry and clinical psychology, together with other disciplines, contributed to this approach.

- Personality disorders are enduring patterns of behavior and inner experience that deviate markedly from the expectations of the individual's culture. In clinical practice, most symptoms diagnosed as PDs usually represent a pattern of excessive consistency.

- Medicalization is the process by which various aspects of human behavior are interpreted in medical terms and thus diagnosed and treated by medical methods. Stigma is marked by the negative perception and corresponding actions related to a person or group solely on certain social characteristics they possess or are associated with.

- Psychologists use various methods to diagnose PDs. Clinicians are aware of the many unresolved issues with these methods and constantly improve them.

- Clinicians use the following classification of PDs based on *The Diagnostic and Statistical Manual* (*DSM–5–TR*). There are three major clusters.

- The first cluster is odd behavior. Disorders of this cluster deal with stable patterns of remarkably unusual behavior. Clinicians in the United States recognize three PDs related to this cluster: paranoid, schizoid, and schizotypal.

- The second cluster is dramatic behavior. Disorders in this cluster share problems with the individual's impulse control and emotional regulation. Named disorders include histrionic, narcissistic, borderline, and antisocial PDs.

- The third cluster is anxious behavior. Personality disorders here represent a range of symptoms for abnormal manifestations of apprehensive, timid, or frightened behavior. The disorders include avoidant, dependent, and obsessive-compulsive PDs.

- Different philosophical, sociological, and other models explained the etiology of PDs. Traditional psychoanalytic models focus on unconscious psychological mechanisms usually rooted in early childhood and heavily influenced by early experiences. According to the biomedical perspective, PDs should have underlying biological causes such as genetic or other natural predispositions that impact specific individual functions and subsequent thought, behavior, and emotion. The learning perspective states there should be social factors and corresponding learning experiences that impact PDs. The cognitive perspective focuses primarily on how people process information related to self and how they use this information to regulate their emotions and behavior. From the trait perspective, PDs represent abnormal configurations of basic, "normal" dimensions of personality. The cross-cultural approach investigates PDs from the standpoint of common, universal, and culture-specific factors.

- To better understand personality disorders, we should apply two key perspectives: the relativist perspective on abnormal behavior that puts psychological phenomena in a relative, cultural perspective; and the universalist perspective on abnormal behavior, which suggests the existence of some universal psychological and behavioral features within individuals. Judgments about appropriate and inappropriate traits vary across cultures. In the context of culture, tolerance threshold indicates a measure of tolerance or intolerance toward specific personality traits in a cultural environment.

- Personality disorders are comorbid and require differential diagnoses. Comorbidity is the presence of one or several additional disorders in an individual. These disorders can be independent or related to one another. A differential diagnosis is a method to identify and separate one disorder from others that appear with similar symptoms.

- Scientific knowledge about PDs is used—among other areas—in treatment of mental illness, in suicide prevention, and in the criminal justice system.

VISUAL REVIEW

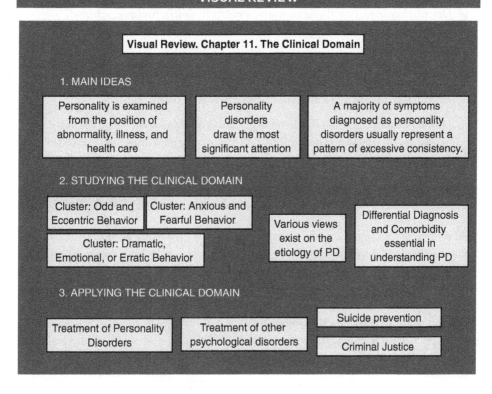

Visual Review. Chapter 11. The Clinical Domain

1. MAIN IDEAS

Personality is examined from the position of abnormality, illness, and health care	Personality disorders draw the most significant attention	A majority of symptoms diagnosed as personality disorders usually represent a pattern of excessive consistency.

2. STUDYING THE CLINICAL DOMAIN

Cluster: Odd and Eccentric Behavior

Cluster: Anxious and Fearful Behavior

Cluster: Dramatic, Emotional, or Erratic Behavior

Various views exist on the etiology of PD

Differential Diagnosis and Comorbidity essential in understanding PD

3. APPLYING THE CLINICAL DOMAIN

Treatment of Personality Disorders

Treatment of other psychological disorders

Suicide prevention

Criminal Justice

KEY TERMS

clinical domain
clinical psychologists
clinicians
comorbidity
differential diagnosis
excessive consistency
illness
interrater reliability

L, F, and *K* validity scales
medicalization
neurotic character
overarching liabilities
relativist perspective of abnormal behavior
stigma
test-taking attitudes
universalist perspective of abnormal behavior

EVALUATING WHAT YOU KNOW

Explain the essence of the clinical domain.

Explain the features of the "normal" and "abnormal" personality.

Explain excessive consistency referring to personality.

Describe key features of the following personality disorders: paranoid, schizoid, schizotypal, histrionic, narcissistic, borderline, antisocial, avoidant, dependent, and obsessive-compulsive.

Explain the relationship between differential diagnosis and comorbidity.

Explain the relativist and universalist perspectives on abnormal behavior.

How do we apply the clinical domain in personality psychology? Explain the use of knowledge in treatment of personality disorders, suicide prevention, and in criminal justice.

A BRIDGE TO THE NEXT CHAPTER

Most symptoms that appear together and are diagnosed as personality disorders usually represent a pattern of excessive consistency. We now better understand what it means: The individual experiences serious and constant problems with either a relentlessly changing environment or particular social norms that require these individuals to have behavioral corrections and emotional adjustments. When a new challenge occurs, we take valuable lessons from our experience and adjust to these new demands. Our ability or inability to adjust to new conditions plays a significant role in how we live our lives, how we feel, and who we become. This is the subject of the next chapter.

12 PERSONALITY: THE ADJUSTMENT DOMAIN

Thomas Barwick / Iconica / Getty Images

LEARNING OBJECTIVES

After reading this chapter, you should be able to do the following:

- Identify the essence of the adjustment domain and the areas of change that require adjustment and coping.

- Describe the various types of adjustment and coping and their outcomes.

- Compare "helpful" personality traits with traits that are unhelpful in the coping process as well as compare adaptive and maladaptive coping strategies.

- Identify ways to apply knowledge about personality psychology in the adjustment domain.

Her life was full of hardship. Yet through all her tragedies and challenges, Christina persevered, learned, and found renewed will and strength. She was the oldest of 15 siblings, five of whom died very young because of illness and hardship. She took care of her surviving brothers and sisters, and her first full-time job was when she was just 11 years old. She quit school so she could work. While still a young girl, she witnessed a bloody revolution and civil war in her country. She then lived through many years of poverty and political repression. She survived World War II and coped with the loss of her brothers and a husband who died on the battlefield. As a widow with two small children, she migrated from one war-torn town to another, looking for any opportunity that would help her carry on and survive. She found a stable job. She sent both her children to college. She continued working until retirement. She never complained. She maintained an active lifestyle, constantly surrounded by the younger members of her family, until well into her 90s when Alzheimer's finally took away her memories and her relentless energy.

Today, some people facing just a smidgen of Christina's problems would give up and fall apart. She did not.

She adjusted to every challenge and resolved the problems she faced.

She was resilient. She never gave up, and she remained hardy and tough on every difficult curve of her life and in every tragic situation.

iStockphoto.com/DieterMeyrl

PHOTO 12.1 Hibernation is a state of inactivity and metabolic depression as a response to cold temperatures or when sufficient food is unavailable. Do some humans have a somewhat similar response of passivity to harsh conditions? Suggest examples.

She was proactive. She disliked procrastination, and she chose preventive actions instead of late reactions.

She was optimistic. She always saw a positive side of life, and she believed that tomorrow definitely would be better than today. She always had a reason to look forward to every day.

She was my grandmother.

Questions. Who in your family has or had the great ability to overcome difficulties and challenges better than others? What specific traits does this person have?

THE ESSENCE OF ADJUSTMENT AND COPING

Life is about change. Everything evolves. Some changes are slow, and we prepare for them. Other changes strike like lightening. Who would have predicted the global outbreak of the pandemic in 2020? Some changes are exciting and enjoyable. Others bring uncertainty. Yet others are unpleasant and painful. How do we deal with significant challenges and changes? Most probably, we try to adjust to them.

Imagine you are driving and suddenly see a traffic jam ahead of you. What do you usually do in such cases? Do you immediately seek a detour? Or do you prefer moving slowly through the traffic? In general terms, adjustment is an alteration to achieve a desired result or condition. Such alteration takes place to reduce a discrepancy between (a) what is expected or desired and (b) the reality of it. Adjustments can be small, such as a slight modification or fine-tuning—for example, we sometimes alter our clothes. Adjustment could be substantial, even global, like in April 2020, most schools, businesses, and governments all over the world were shut down and turned to Zoom and other forms of distant communications. Most people on the planet adjusted to the masks on our faces. Sometimes we do not have a choice.

Many of our adjustments seem almost automatic. Moving to a different country as a volunteer or tourist you adjust to that country's climate and food. Every day when we communicate with others, we tend to automatically match these people's language style. Research shows that almost immediately after we establish contact with another person, verbal and nonverbal behaviors become—to some degree—more synchronized than they were prior to the contact (Ireland & Pennebaker, 2010; Shaw et al., 2019). We tend to slightly modify the rhythm, speed, and the use of certain words when we talk. Other adjustments can be significant. For instance, to many people, a transition from high school to college requires a major effort—they have to adjust to a new place away from home, to new friends, and to the new anxieties of college life. In the context of personality, this type of adjustment should probably interest us the most.

In personality psychology, **adjustment** refers to relatively significant changes in an individual's behavior and experiences in response to external and internal challenges. Adjustment is somewhat different from **coping**, which is a deliberate and conscious effort to adjust to challenges, changing situations, and new conditions (adjustment is not necessarily conscious and deliberate).

Why Individuals Cope

Why do species adjust? Because adjustment is essential for their survival. For example, some birds fly to warmer places in the fall and some mammals, like bears, hibernate during winters to avoid the harmful impact of cold temperatures. Humans also tend to avoid dangerous environments, physical threats, and escape from anything that causes or may cause physical harm, pain, or discomfort. People tend to perceive and recognize the discrepancy between (a) how things are now and (b) how they should be or could have been. This discrepancy is based on a subjective experience and is influenced by many underlying physical and psychological conditions and contexts. Subjectively, this discrepancy is unpleasant and occurs in many forms, ranging from a mild psychological discomfort or distress to significant suffering. Challenges that disturb the individual's physical or mental equilibrium are called stressors. The reaction to a condition that disturbs an individual's physical or mental balance is called **stress**. Almost one third of adults in the United States report that stress has a strong impact on their physical and mental health. According to a national survey, 63% of Americans said their lives have been forever changed by the COVID-19 pandemic (see Table 12.1; American Psychological Association [APA], 2022).

AREAS OF CHANGE REQUIRING COPING AND ADJUSTMENT

To study the process of coping, you have to identify the stressors the individual has to face. A stressor can be a single event in one area of life; it also can be a continuous development, involving many areas of an individual's activities. In the United States, the top three stressors in 2015 have been problems with money, problems with work, and family responsibilities (APA, 2015b). Five years later, the top stressors were high inflation, global uncertainty, and Russia's invasion of Ukraine. More than 60% of working Americans said they have not been able to see their loved ones in person in the past 2 years because of the COVID-19 pandemic. The biggest parental concerns were children's academic development and their emotional health after the pandemic. More than two thirds of parents reported concern about the pandemic's negative impact on their child's physical health and cognitive development. Overall, younger people, Latino adults, and parents have consistently reported more stress than others.

(APA, 2022).

Stress—especially continuous stress—negatively contributes to individual problems that might trigger or exacerbate various disorders, including mental illness (see Chapter 11). Many areas of life and its activities generate stressors, and they require us to cope with them. Let's mention just a few of such areas and activities. Feel free to suggest other areas not mentioned here.

Aging

Regardless of how old you are now, remember how much you enjoyed getting older when you were a child? Conversely, once we become adults, aging is sometimes unpleasant, stressful, and even traumatic. Simply ask around and listen to what people say about how they feel about getting older. Every age has some unpleasant realizations that are fairly typical but can still be stressful. A few important physical and psychological changes are associated with aging that require coping (Lazarus & Lazarus, 2006). One feature of aging is that many people never feel

TABLE 12.1 ■ Types of Challenges That Require Adjustment and Coping	
Type	*Range*
Occurrence	Sudden, unexpected to expected, planned
Duration	Fast emerging, quick to slowly developing, prolonged
Origin	Avoidable to inevitable
Significance	Major, significant to minor, insignificant

their age—they feel younger. In a 2009 survey, people over 50 in the United States claimed to feel about 10 years younger than their chronological age; those over 65 said they felt up to 20 years younger (Segal, 2013). More comprehensive studies in the United States showed that the gap between the perceived and actual age was 8 years (Robson, 2018). Why does this gap between actual age and perceived age have to be stressful? It does not. Yet in some people their physical decline and other negative changes associated with aging often do not match these individuals' perception of their age.

Physical Illness

Some health maladies, such as heart attacks, strokes, and accidents, are sudden and devastating. Such serious life-threatening events immediately alter the lives of the patient and their loved ones. To recover from an acute illness and get back to day-to-day life requires considerable effort. It is about making adjustments and coping in several areas of life. The uncertainty that is associated with the illness (some injuries may remain life-threatening for a long time) adds to the stress.

Other illnesses develop slowly and remain chronic. In fact, 6 in 10 adults in the United Stats report having at least one chronic illness (Centers for Disease Control, 2022). Suffering from these illnesses also demands from the individual significant behavioral and psychological adjustments. Serious illnesses are frequently connected with **disabilities**, which involve impairments (serious problem with a physical or psychological functioning), activity limitations (inability to perform certain tasks), and participation restrictions (problems with particular social activities). Of course, not every illness becomes a disability (see Table 12.2).

Changes in the Family

Important changes in family life may become major stressors that require adjustment and coping. Not all of these changes, whether sudden or continuing, are catastrophic; many major life events are supposed to be easy to deal with—take marriage as an example. It can be stress-free,

TABLE 12.2 ■ Areas of Change That May Require Adjustment and Coping	
Area of Change	*Types of Challenges*
Aging	Physical decline, cognitive decline, stigma of aging
Physical illness	Physical decline, uncertainty of the outcome
Disability	Physical decline, stigma of disability
Family changes	Marriage, divorce, moving in or out, new or lost members
Professional changes	Getting a new job or promotion, losing a job, retirement
Relationships	Breakup, loss of an attachment figure, chronic or acute conflicts
Social changes	War and violence, hardship, migration and immigration
Other	What other challenges not mentioned here could an individual face?

but it can also be a significant stressor, sometimes requiring big adjustments in habits and even personality traits. Now, think of divorce. Some divorces can be easy. Most others aren't. Not only does a person have to cope with moral and psychological problems associated with the divorce but also with many interpersonal, financial, and legal challenges. There are other major changes associated with the family as well. Some parents (after they have sent their grown sons and daughters off to college) experience a stressful "empty-nest syndrome"—a persistent state of sadness and loneliness. This syndrome is recognized and its stressful impact studied in many countries, such as in India (Badiani & DeSouza, 2016). Some parents cope with this new situation somewhat quickly; others do not.

Professional Changes

The process of getting a new job is as exciting as it is stressful. A new job sometimes requires adjusting to a different geographic area, a tough work schedule, additional or unfamiliar job requirements, daily commuting, and so on—all may require personal changes and significant adjustment. Individuals who are not ready to face these challenges may develop serious psychological problems, including burnout. Losing a job is also often very stressful. This event can cause negative, long-term psychological consequences in an individual. The loss of income is certainly an issue, but being out of work is also about loss of dignity, respect, and meaningful social interactions. Research suggests that an individual's unemployment is associated with social withdrawal, tension in the family, and many other stressful symptoms (Brand, 2015).

There is also noteworthy psychological research about the stressors associated with retirement. It is true that some people look forward to their retirement; yet for others, retirement can be a period they dread. Some people delay the decision to retire or never make it. They worry about financial security, fear boredom and isolation, and fret about no longer being able to do something meaningful or make a difference in other people's lives (Knoll, 2011).

Changes in Personal Relationships

Friendship and love are supposed to be fulfilling and rewarding, and for many people, they are. However, relationships often involve stress and conflict. Studies show that most individuals experience major challenges and stress during a crisis in their relationships with a significant other (Verhallen et al., 2019; Borelli & Sbarra, 2011). Such a crisis may involve separation, infidelity, dishonesty, or emotional and physical abuse, which can have a profound impact on an individual and often requires serious psychological coping. A large cross-cultural study in 96 countries (Morris et al., 2015) showed that people experience an average of three significant breakups in their relationships by age 30, and at least one of those breakups affects them strongly enough that it substantially decreases their quality of life for weeks or even months.

Immigration

Immigration (the movement of people into a country) is another source of stress, as it often requires individuals to cope and adjust to new social and cultural conditions. The process of coping with new cultural conditions is called **acculturation**. Each generation of new-comers faces the unavoidable challenge of adapting to their new country and its culture, and the process of adjustment is an extremely stressful period of their lives. They have left something significant back in their home countries. They have to learn a new language, adapt to a different value system, make friends, find new reinforcements, seek social sup-port networks, and get used to a different climate, food, and the little nuances that consti-tute culture. Individuals who fail to cope with the acculturation stressors are more likely to develop psychopathological symptoms. We will return to this subject again later in this chapter.

Significant Social Changes

There are different types of social changes. Most people—especially those who grew up in eco-nomically developed countries such as the United States, Canada, or Japan—are somewhat shielded against devastating social cataclysms. They do not have to encounter famine, political terror, violent revolutions, or a protracted civil war. Unfortunately, this is not the case for people living in many other places on the planet. Today, hundreds of millions of people remain vulner-able to serious abuse and violations of their safety and most basic rights. The wars in Syria and Ukraine have generated the most devastating refugee crises not experienced since 1940s. Today, abject poverty, social injustice, and the consequences of climate change are major and constant challenges in people's lives.

Many social changes may have a common denominator. Recall from Chapter 9 the American psychologist Rollo May's belief that individuals were caught between an epic conflict of the old world of "tradition" and the new world of "change." The old world often represented stability and certainty; the new world is about uncertainty and instability. As a result, individuals tend to lose their ability to learn and adjust to the rapidly changing surroundings (May, 1950), and their poor adjustment causes anxiety—also caused by con-sistent threats to their most fundamental values (May et al., 1958). Anxiety brings more confusion, which in turn increases the sense of powerlessness. People no longer know how to influence their lives or other people. This leads to anger, which can often lead to aggres-sion and violence (May, 1969).

Although May and his colleagues wrote about these problems about 70 years ago, their analysis tends to reflect the cultural and psychological challenges that people experienced in later decades (Huntington, 1996, 2004). The unprecedented economic and social changes that have been taken place in countries such as the former Soviet Union, China, India, Pakistan, the Middle East, Afghanistan, South Africa, the Sudan, Brazil, Colombia, and scores of others should inevitably affect billions of people's psychological well-being and their ability to cope.

CHECK AND APPLY YOUR KNOWLEDGE

1. Describe the similarities and differences between adjustment and coping.
2. Name three features of disability. Why does disability require coping?
3. How many significant breakups does an average person expect to have by age 30?
4. What is acculturation? Why does it require coping? Should immigration require coping in your view?

TYPES OF COPING AND ADJUSTMENT

Assisting people with adjustment requires a very diverse knowledge of their personalities. The **psychology of adjustment** studies problems and conditions that cause people's need for adjustment, the psychological mechanisms of adjustment, and the ways to help them in their coping process. Some people avoid dealing with challenges, while others tend to confront them. Some individuals cope by transforming their personal features, including their habits and traits, yet others remain stubborn and unchanged. Based on their age, experience, gender, and education, people choose different coping strategies (Folkman et al., 1987; Powell, 2015), and many small variables and ever-changing circumstances affect the way they adjust and cope.

What do we do when we face stressors or significant challenges in our lives? Consider several general strategies. Two of them refer to the individual, and the other two have to do with the social environment.

The Individual

Facing a stressor, we can choose—if we think logically—between two alternatives: to change something (such as our own thinking, emotional responses, and behavior) or not to change anything. The choice between these two strategies ("To change or not to change?") depends on our personality traits as well as on specific circumstances and contexts. In the first case ("change"), coping will require some personal transformation and correction. New assessments of the stressors and innovative responses should be sought and found. A change of habits and even change of some personality features may also be required.

There are some individuals who are more flexible and, thus, have a greater propensity for constant adjustments to changing environment and stressors. **Flexibility** can be viewed as a trait measured by the degree or the extent to which a person can cope in novel ways. There is evidence that flexibility can form early in life and is based on parenting style. For instance, authoritarian parents are likely to diminish psychological flexibility in their children by constantly restricting the ways their children cope with stressors in life (Williams et al., 2012). The power of psychological flexibility in the workplace is correlated with better mental health and job performance. Allowing workers more job control would likely increase work productivity as well as job satisfaction (Bond & Flaxman, 2006). Studies also show that psychological flexibility is a factor that affects long-term coping—people who are better "managers" of their emotional responses are less likely to be stressed over time (Bonanno et al., 2004). Research in Italy shows that health care workers who display psychological flexibility are more likely to show greater openness to the acceptance of setbacks in the working environment (Ramaci et al., 2019).

Individuals who choose the second alternative—not changing anything—keep most of their evaluations, responses, habits, and personality features unchanged when faced with a stressor. We may use the adjective *stubborn* to describe this pattern. Stubbornness may result in successful coping, or it may be harmful and cause intense and prolonged psychological suffering.

The Stressor

Which challenges—or stressors—do we accept, and which do we contest? The discussion has been ongoing in social sciences and the humanities for centuries. Many philosophers in the past called for the individual's active engagement in life events in attempts to transform them. Others called for more wisdom and acceptance of one's own fate (Yakunin, 2001). Both sides offered reasonable arguments in defense of their positions: On the one hand, we should be able to overcome life's challenges by standing tall against them; on the other, there are many challenges that we are incapable of overcoming, and, thus, we should not falsely believe that we can resolve every problem and negotiate every obstacle (you may recall similar arguments in Chapter 8).

Coping and adjustment can be active or passive, with many variations in between the "active" and "passive" alternatives of the imaginary spectrum. On one end of the spectrum is **approaching**, which is a type of coping that refers to deliberate attempts at changing self as well as the sources of stress. A person who is approaching is also seeking internal (self) and external (others) resources to deal with a stressor or a problem (Zeidner & Endler, 1995). Approaching involves cognitive operations, such as thinking, as well as actions. Approaching can be proactive when an individual is aware of a problem or anticipates a stressor to emerge and thus has one or more strategies to deal with them. For instance, a couple expecting a baby is proactive about understanding the challenges that new families face, such as night feeding, changing diapers, and having much less free time for a while, and they prepare for these challenges in advance. Approaching can also be reactive, as a response to the changes. Approaching might be mostly behavioral (involving actions) or mostly cognitive (involving thinking) or both.

Coping may also take a form of **avoiding**, which is keeping oneself away from addressing a challenge or a stressor. There are several types of avoidant behavior (see Table 12.3). Avoidant behavior can be rational, which means that we consciously try to discount or ignore an apparent problem for some time, even though we are aware of it. Many of us, from time to time, avoid certain unpleasant challenges because we have a realistic understanding that we have little time or opportunity to address known stressors that confront us. On the other hand, avoiding can be a way of ignoring or hiding from a problem. This often leads to a more serious problem that arises because the original stressor is not addressed. Avoiding can be behavioral (not doing anything to address the problem), cognitive (not thinking about the problem), or both. Close to half of adults said they have been less active than they wanted to be since the pandemic started in 2020. Avoiding can take a form of compensatory behavior, which may distract the individual from addressing the stressor. Such behavior is often associated with certain unhealthy activities. For example, 4 out of 10 of adults in the United States said they have overeaten or eaten unhealthy foods in the past month because of stress (APA, 2022).

PHOTO 12.2 Approaching is about changing self as well as the sources of stress. Avoiding is about keeping oneself away from addressing a challenge or a stressor. Think about your past: Have you mostly been an approaching or avoiding person? Think of some examples.

Avoiding can also be a result of our lack of knowledge and understanding, our deliberate ignorance ("I don't even want to know"), our inability to correctly assess the problem and its significance, or our specific individual psychological features, including mental illness. Recall the discussion of avoidant personality disorder in Chapter 11. It is important for psychologists to study and recognize the differences between an individual's use of avoiding as a healthy, successful way to cope and avoiding that is an unhealthy, harmful behavioral style (see Figure 12.1).

In terms of the dynamics, or speed, of coping, some people tend to adjust quickly. As soon as the stressor appears or as soon as they realize an adjustment is necessary, they think about what to do and then act. Others display a persistent pattern of behavior and thought called **procrastination**—putting off impending tasks to a later time. We procrastinate for various reasons and tend to be aware of the consequences of our procrastination. How often do you hear the phrase "I wish I had done this earlier"? It is true that for many people occasional procrastination is not a serious problem, but it may become significant when it becomes a consistent pattern. Academic procrastination is very common among college students: Approximately half of students regularly procrastinate (Hailikari et al., 2021). Chronic procrastinators have a deficiency in their self-regulation: There is a gap between their

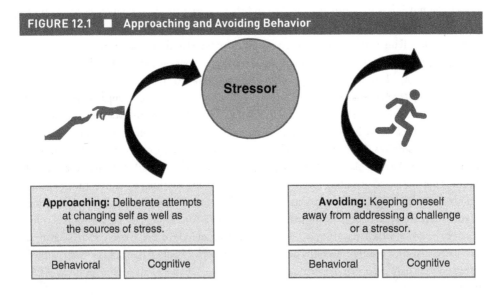

FIGURE 12.1 ■   Approaching and Avoiding Behavior

Stressor

Approaching: Deliberate attempts at changing self as well as the sources of stress.

Behavioral   Cognitive

Avoiding: Keeping oneself away from addressing a challenge or a stressor.

Behavioral   Cognitive

intentions and actions, as studies showed (Pychyl et al., 2000). Procrastinators often fail to correct their behavior and face the same problem in new situations and create a false excuse that turning to their problem later is a better choice (Pychyl et al., 2000). Research finds that procrastinators tend to carry accompanying feelings of guilt, shame, or anxiety associated with their constant choice to delay (Jaffe, 2013; Sirois & Pychyl, 2013). Some procrastinators act more efficiently when they work under time pressure; some have fine organizational and time management skills (Hailikari et al., 2021). However, many of them use this argument, as studies show, to justify their chronic inaction now and in the future (Sirois & Pychyl, 2013).

Passive adjustment, or passive coping, is a general pattern of relying on others to address or resolve stressful events or life situations. This pattern of dependency is rooted in an individual's feeling of helplessness and the inability to deal with the stressor (recall dependent personality disorder from Chapter 11). Those who engage in passive coping tend to relinquish control of the stressful situation to others. These individuals often want others to help them find the best way of coping (Carroll, 2013).

Although there are several ways we can classify different kinds of adjustment and coping, our behavior doesn't always fall into the same category from stressor to stressor. While some individuals tend to maintain a particular adjustment style, others do not. Sometimes we may use an approaching style, other times we may use an avoiding style, or we may use a combination of the two, depending on the situation.

OUTCOMES OF COPING AND ADJUSTMENT

Coping has a continuum of outcomes, ranging from successful to unsuccessful. On one end of the spectrum, successful coping responses allow an individual to maintain a happy and productive life, score high on the measures of subjective well-being (see Chapter 8), and be free of distressful symptoms. In a famous pioneering study in this area, the psychologist Shelly Taylor (1983) was looking for successful coping strategies in women treated for breast cancer. She wanted to identify the inner resources that help women return to their previous, "normal" level of functioning after going through traumatic experiences associated with their illness. The interviews conducted with the women revealed that rather than simply "getting back" to what their healthy life used to be, most of the women reported that their lives had changed for the better in many ways. Some noted that they had a new sense of themselves as being strong and resilient; others talked about their ability to stop procrastinating, reestablish priorities, and make time for the activities that were most important (Taylor et al., 2004).

On the other end of the outcomes scale is unsuccessful adjustment and coping associated with the inability to adjust to a stressor and continuous emotional distress. One of the most severe forms of such distress is adjustment disorder (see Figure 12.2).

Adjustment disorder refers to a cluster of symptoms associated with significant distress that occurs in someone who is unable to cope with a major life stressor. This stressor is associated with an individual's immediate social network (for example, separation from a significant other) or broader network (for example, being forced to become a refugee and escaping to a foreign country), or it is caused by a life transition or crisis (for example, becoming a parent or being diagnosed with a serious illness). The manifestations include persistent depressed mood,

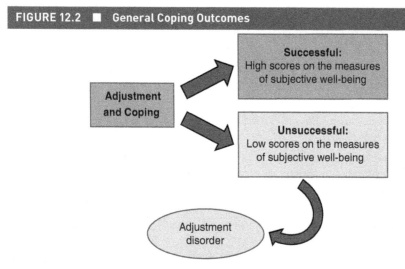

FIGURE 12.2 ■ General Coping Outcomes

Adjustment and Coping

Successful:
High scores on the measures of subjective well-being

Unsuccessful:
Low scores on the measures of subjective well-being

Adjustment disorder

anxiety, irritability, sleep problems, and feelings of helplessness. Individual personality features and circumstances may worsen the manifestation of the symptoms. Once the individual is able to cope with the stressor, the harmful symptoms diminish and can disappear. The challenge is in finding the right path to an individual's coping strategies (Powell, 2015).

One of the negative outcomes of coping is **burnout**—a state of a constant exhaustion and disappointment brought about by devotion to an activity (often work-related) that failed to produce the expected result or reward. Burnout is a problem usually born out of the individual's attempts to achieve unrealistic goals or take on undeliverable promises. Those who experience burnout feel extremely fatigued, distrustful, pessimistic, and tend to be increasingly inefficient despite their efforts (Maslach et al., 1996). They also tend to maintain a negative attitude toward work and are at risk of developing serious health problems (Bakker et al., 2014). One who once was enthusiastic and full of energy becomes irritable, frustrated, and bitter. Burnout may resemble some symptoms of depression, but one of the differences is that depression is likely to impact an individual's whole life, while burnout relates mostly to the job context (Plieger et al., 2015).

According to the Association of American Medical Colleges, burnout occurs more often among lesbian, gay, and bisexual medical students than heterosexual students (based on their self-identification): 17% versus 11% (Berman, 2021). Although earlier research showed that gender differences in how people handle general coping were relatively small (Billings & Moos, 1981), psychologists were often looking at specific stressors and situations. Some earlier studies also suggested that women tend to have a harder time coping with a breakup (Davis et al., 1999). However, more recent cross-cultural research shows that this is not the case. Researchers measured the subjective rate of the emotional and physical pain in the immediate aftermath of the breakup on a sample of more than 5,700 people in 96 countries. While breakups affect women the hardest emotionally and physically, this is true only immediately after the breakup. Men tend to have more emotional issues in the long term. In other words, women tend to recover more fully and come out emotionally stronger after a breakup than men (Morris et al., 2015).

There are different explanations for these results. Evolutionary psychologists suggest that women on average tend to cope better in the long term because they have better skills in seeking and finding new relationships (Morris et al., 2015). Men also tend to reevaluate their losses, and once they have a new partner, they realize their new partner may be not as great as the one they lost. Other research suggests that men tend to cope by either confronting the stressor or avoiding it; women, on the other hand, when their relationship becomes a source of stress tend to be better "negotiators" than men (Wang et al., 2007).

CHECK AND APPLY YOUR KNOWLEDGE

1. Define and explain *flexibility*.
2. Explain proactive approaching.
3. Ferrari (2010), in *Still Procrastinating? The No Regrets Guide to Getting It Done*, would like to see a general cultural shift from punishing procrastination to rewarding the "early bird." The author proposed, among other things, that the federal government and other agencies give financial incentives to those who do things (such as paying taxes) early, long before the deadlines. Discuss if this strategy could reduce procrastination or would just reward the people who are too anxious and do everything very early.
4. In one of the most famous plays by Shakespeare, the main character Hamlet posed probably the most frequently quoted question: "To be or not to be?" In the monologue that followed, he complained about life's pains and unfairness yet was also afraid that the alternative, which is suicide, might be worse. What kind of coping was Hamlet choosing from?
5. Define adjustment disorder.
6. Explain burnout.
7. Have you ever experienced burnout? How did you cope with it?

IDENTIFYING "HELPFUL" PERSONALITY TRAITS

Psychologists have identified a stable pattern of behavior and experience that appears helpful in the process of coping with significant stressors (Block & Block, 2012). This pattern has different names, but we can call it **stress tolerance**. At least three specific traits have been identified as contributing to stress tolerance: openness to experience, hardiness, and individual impulse control (Weiten et al., 2011). We studied openness to experience and impulse control in earlier chapters (remember, for instance, instant gratification in Chapter 2). Psychological research also provides interesting data about **hardiness**—the individual's general ability to withstand difficult conditions. Hardiness may resemble stubbornness, which was described earlier in this chapter. Hardiness and stubbornness share some common psychological features, yet stubbornness is usually a pattern of resistance to change by all costs. Hardiness has three specific characteristics (Kobasa, 1979). It involves these actions:

- Changes in strategies and behavior, as well as a commitment or sustained effort to achieve a goal

- Control, or the belief and the ability to rely on your own efforts, to solve a problem

- A challenge, or a commitment to test self and confront difficulties

These features help the individual to launch effective coping and actively seek solutions, seek and receive social support, and engage in effective self-care (Maddi, 2006). Hardiness is a continuous variable. Research showed that it is likely to be correlated with internal locus of control and self-efficacy (Bandura, 1997), which we studied in Chapter 5.

Another feature that tends to be helpful in successful coping is **optimism**—the general belief in positive or successful outcomes. Optimism involves an act of cognitive assessment of the present and the future. We call people *optimists* if they tend to believe things that belong to them and around them are (a) better than they seem or (b) they will be better in the future. These beliefs refer to material things and developments (such as the stock market or weather) as well as social and psychological phenomena (such as personal health and professional career). When facing challenges, optimists tend to think they will overcome the difficulties, or the challenges will just go away. Leonel Tiger, in *Optimism: The Biology of Hope* (1979), argued that optimism is an evolutionary useful feature, mostly because of its role in coping: It allows human beings to counteract their fears, manage their anxiety, and cope with significant problems and crises. Early research of optimism showed that *optimistic views of self are connected to the person's views of others:* Individuals who scored high on self-coherence also perceive life as comprehensible, cognitively meaningful, and manageable (Antonovsky, 1987). Optimism has also been tied to active and preventive coping efforts, which enable people to guard against undesirable life changes caused by significant stressors (Aspinwall & Taylor, 1997). Optimism is also associated with exploratory behavior, such as finding alternative solutions and experiences. *For example, a person's exploratory activities affect* building more new neurons in the hippocampus (a process called *neurogenesis*), which is the brain's center for learning and memory (Bergmann & Frisén, 2013).

Optimism can be a situational, short-lived phenomenon or a stable personality feature or trait. Scheier and Carver (1992) were among the first to study **dispositional optimism**—a general and stable belief that good things and positive outcomes will happen. People who possess this trait tend to expect that in most life situations, the balance between good and bad things will be in favor of good things. "Even in uncertain times, I still think positive," says an optimist. Dispositional optimism is likely to affect behavior since optimists tend to sustain their efforts to pursue their goals, while pessimists tend to give up (Peterson, 2000). Because optimism is associated with effective social relationships and interpersonal coping strategies, optimists develop a stronger sense of personal control and tend to have greater social support during times of stress. Dispositional optimism is a relatively stable trait. Research in neuroscience shows some biological correlates of it: Gray matter density in the putamen (a round structure located at the base of the forebrain) predicts dispositional optimism in late adolescents (Lai et al., 2020). Expectedly, various circumstances can also affect this trait. Optimism is more changeable during times of life transition when many outcomes become more uncertain.

Optimism and health are correlated. A large study involving 95,000 healthy Caucasian and African American women showed that optimists were less likely than pessimists to develop new cases of coronary heart disease, among many other health problems (Tindle et al., 2009). Another massive study of women revealed optimism as a factor associated with lower mortality from heart disease, cancer, stroke, respiratory disease, and even . . . infection (Kim et al., 2016). Overall, more than 30 years of research provide evidence that dispositional optimism and good health are linked (Scheier & Carver, 2018). Of course, there are multiple behavioral, biological, and social factors that might explain this positive correlation. Besides, as we learned in Chapter 3, correlation does not mean causation. People's positive outlook on life (and probably having less stress and anxiety) may affect their good health. On the other hand, a healthy person is probably more likely to be optimistic than not.

Pessimism is the general belief in negative or unsuccessful outcomes. A pessimistic person tends to believe in the likelihood of bad outcomes and anticipates that difficulties will continue and troubles will prevail. As a famous saying goes, optimists see a glass "half full," while pessimists see the same glass "half empty."

SELF-REFLECTION

Every person has his or her own pathway to be optimistic. However, many people near you don't know how to find this path or whether it's necessary to be optimistic. Some even say that being pessimistic is better than having a rosy view about life because pessimists are . . . right in their judgment most of the time. One of psychology's main goals is to help people to gain confidence, inner strength, and happiness. Do you think cultivating optimism in people is better than cultivating pessimism? Or is it better, from your personal view, to help people lower their expectations rather than expect something great that is unlikely to happen? Try to use specific examples.

TRAITS THAT NEGATIVELY AFFECT THE COPING PROCESS

Even in ancient times, philosophers in India, China, and Greece stated that many individuals had a distorted way of looking at things, and they could not effectively cope with difficulties (Isaeva, 1999). Modern research provides supporting evidence for those philosophical assertions. As in the case of "helpful" traits, there are also features that negatively affect coping.

Consider again procrastination, which we discussed earlier in this chapter. Research shows that constant procrastination becomes particularly maladaptive in an individual's coping strategies. It becomes especially harmful if a person is measured high on impulsivity and low on self-discipline (Jaffe, 2013). People who procrastinate persistently create false excuses that turning to their problem later is a better choice (Pychyl et al., 2000).

Consistent cognitive distortions (we reviewed them in Chapter 7 and Chapter 8) also can negatively affect the coping process. These are thoughts and assumptions that cause individuals to perceive themselves and reality with a substantial measure of negative bias. This bias is rooted in negative emotions (Burns, 1989). Imagine, for a moment, you are angry that the courses you are taking this semester are too difficult and that you are failing in most of them. Instead of seeking help and making serious changes in the ways you study, you focus instead on your anger and stress, repeating to yourself that it is always you, not others, who fail. *Rumination* is a process and tendency to focus on negative emotions, and many people experience it from time to time.

Yet some people experience rumination consistently. **Catastrophic thinking** is the stable tendency to overestimate the probability of very negative outcomes. People who have propensity for catastrophic thinking tend to see threats when there are few or none of them. They tend to exaggerate minor threats. Catastrophic thinking can be situational: For some reason a person does not believe in a positive outcome of an upcoming sports game or a job interview. However, there are those who tend to be **dispositional pessimists**—people who have the general and stable belief that bad things and negative outcomes will happen.

Research suggests that pessimism is correlated with an increased risk for depression and anxiety. Pessimism has also been associated with several adverse health outcomes (Garcia, 2020). Studies also showed that people who have a tendency for catastrophic thinking have problems coping with pain (Wideman & Sullivan, 2011).

Catastrophic thinking as a thought pattern has also been linked to certain personality characteristics. Psychologists, for example, identify the **Type D personality** (D stands for *distressed* in cognitive and behavioral terms). The Type D personality is linked to the persistent tendency toward negative affectivity (being constantly irritable, anxious, and expecting failure) and social inhibition (which involves both self-restraint and a lack of self-assurance). This type is also associated with the development of burnout (Geuens et al., 2015).

Studies also demonstrated the existence of so-called **latent vulnerability traits**, which are stable behavioral and psychological features that individuals may develop at any period in life (e.g., bad eating habits, substance use or abuse, or propensity for hostile behavior). These features may later develop into stable traits that are harmful in the process of coping (Beauchaine & Marsh, 2006). American psychologist Karen Matthews shows in her research how certain habits, such as smoking and physical immobility, contribute to physical changes in the cardiovascular system and make individuals more vulnerable in coping with their health problems (Matthews, 2005; Matthews and Gallo, 2011). John Curtin and colleagues showed that an alcohol or drug habit can also become a latent vulnerability trait for some people when a difficult life situation arises, and they turn to substances to cope rather than addressing the problem (Curtin et al., 2005).

To summarize, in the context of health and mental health, do optimists and pessimists do (or not do) something consistently different that might contribute to their health status and health issues? From the standpoint of neuroscience, dispositional optimism can affect physical health through its influence on stress and the fact that stress is the factor affecting biological systems underlying health and disease. Optimists are more likely to respond to stressful and difficult events in a more psychologically beneficial way, compared to pessimists (Veally & Perritt, 2015).

From the behavioral and cognitive standpoint, the difference is likely to be that people who are optimistic usually continue trying, even when things are difficult and the chances to succeed are bleak. People who are pessimistic, because they tend to be doubtful about the future, are less likely to act. They also are more likely to engage in temporary self-distractions or simply give up (Scheier & Carver, 2018).

IDENTIFYING ADAPTIVE COPING STRATEGIES

Successful adaptive coping strategies improve the individual's functioning in everyday situations and reduce the impact of life-changing stressors. These strategies should have significant, long-term impact. There are at least three types of such strategies that are interconnected: problem-focused, appraisal-focused, and emotion-focused (see Table 12.3; Bond & Bince, 2000).

Problem-focused coping strategies center on changing or eliminating the source of an individual's problems. Here, the individuals act independently or seek advantageous social support,

TABLE 12.3 ■ Adaptive and Maladaptive Coping Strategies: A Comparison	
Adaptive Strategies	**Maladaptive Strategies**
• Problem-focused strategies center on eliminating the stressor or reducing its harmful impact.	• Denial is a belief that something is untrue. It may appear as ignoring a problem.
• Appraisal-focused strategies usually refer to internal, stable, and unavoidable causes of the individual's problems.	• Ruminative strategies refer to behaviors and thoughts that focus on the individual's negative experiences, failing strategies, and distressful psychological symptoms.
• Emotion-focused strategies center on the emotional meaning of the stressor and on reducing anxiety.	• Learned helplessness is the belief that there is no connection between actions and their outcomes.

including practical advice and guidance from another person or people. For instance, a person diagnosed with a serious illness immediately studies online several available treatment options and chooses one. If the problem persists, the individual seeks other options, like seeing different doctors or trying new medical procedures. Success of these strategies is not necessarily about the speed of the decision. These strategies can be effective in part because they are informed (an individual's knowledge is based on a range of facts) and efficient (an individual critically analyzes and chooses the best option).

Quite often, we cannot tackle our problems head on. **Appraisal-focused** strategies center on the way we see the problem (or a particular life development), its causes, its impact on us, and the expected outcome of our coping behavior. The goal here is to gain knowledge about the stressor to help better understand and discuss the anticipated outcomes. Optimistic strategies, for example, help to deal with unfortunate events in these ways:

- Explaining a misfortune or a difficult period in a circumscribed way: "This may be difficult, but it will not ruin my life. I will deal with my problems, one day at a time."

- Identifying external, unstable, and limited causes of the problem: "I am just unlucky; bad things happen. I will be better tomorrow; things always change for the better."

People can turn to **emotion-focused** strategies that center on the emotional meaning of the stressor, distraction from it, and relaxation. These strategies include actively reevaluating the psychological impact of the existing problem, gaining emotional strength, switching attention to something else, or seeking emotional support from other people and new sources (learning about spirituality, for instance). Of course, we do not choose just one strategy and reject others. We use a mixture of coping strategies and skills, which develop and change over time.

Consider distraction, for example. **Distraction** refers to avoidant coping strategies that are employed to divert attention away from a stressor and toward other thoughts or behaviors that are unrelated to the stressor. Simple distraction, such as focusing on an external object like a painting on the wall or imagining a peaceful place like a mountain lake, may ease pain and discomfort during or after serious medical procedures. Other examples of distraction include deliberate daydreaming or engaging in substitute activities to keep one's mind from several stressors related to a chronic illness (Traeger, 2013). These are called *calming behaviors* that can grow into a habit of engaging in a pleasant activity to reduce anxiety. Successful distraction often involves daily activities, such as working out, playing sports, or getting busy as a volunteer.

Empirical research has long suggested that quality of social support is linked to coping and improvement in well-being (Stanley et. al, 1998; Weissman et al., 2007). Similar findings about the importance of social support in the coping process were obtained in Indonesia during the COVID-19 pandemic (Akbar, & Aisyawati, 2021). Interpersonal psychotherapy (IPT) aims at improving the quality of relationships and usually addresses unresolved grief, social isolation, or the significant lack of social skills. We will turn to other strategies—in the context of therapies—in the section on applications.

Psychologists do not encourage people to forget about their troubles or ignore them or see all adversities in a positive light. Instead, they teach that to cope with changing circumstances, we should learn from mistakes and find a way to recover and win. The death of a friend, an illness in the family, personal setbacks—no matter how unkind and devastating their impacts can be on our lives, they should make us reexamine what happened (to see everything from a new perspective), reevaluate our strategies (to seek a way out), and mobilize our resources (and if there are none left, then seek help from others). The psychological state of helplessness causes inaction.

We all know that, unfortunately, life is full of unpleasant "surprises." We all eventually will die, and illness strikes practically everyone. How do people cope with the inevitable threat of an illness? Weinstein (1989) examined people's perception of personal risk for illnesses and various mishaps. When people were asked to provide a percentage estimate of the likelihood that they will someday experience a particular illness or injury, most respondents underestimated their risks. The average individual sees himself or herself as far below average at risk for a variety of maladies and misfortunes. These results can spark a critical argument: What if some individuals who do not foresee many dangers in life are not necessarily optimistic? What if they are somewhat careless or ignorant about illnesses? It is known, for example, that if some people were more vigilant about their health, many illnesses could have been diagnosed at earlier stages and many lives could have been saved. However, if people are not vigilant enough about their health, this does not mean they are pessimistic. On the other hand, educating people to be aware of possible health dangers is not necessarily about making them pessimists.

IDENTIFYING MALADAPTIVE STRATEGIES

While adaptive coping strategies improve functioning, maladaptive coping strategies do not. Sure, some maladaptive techniques may be effective in the short term, but they tend to be harmful for the long-term coping process. Maladaptive coping strategies often lead to increased anxiety, other emotional problems, and even many other negative consequences. During the COVID-19 pandemic, close to half of adults in the United States said they have been less active than they wanted to be since the pandemic started, and close to 3 in 5 reported experiencing undesired weight changes (APA, 2022).

Denial

Denial, in a psychological context, is the belief that something is untrue and often presents itself as ignoring an issue or a fact. Though denial has been sometimes called an adaptive strategy, there has been little evidence that it is actually helpful for long-term coping or reduces a person's stress-related anxiety.

Denial involves several interconnected strategies. Fantasy involves persistently using creative imagination in attempts to avoid facing the problem, and it becomes a substitution for the real coping strategy. **Anxious avoidance** involves a person who dodges thinking about the stressor and refuses dealing with it in all situations and by all means. Anxious avoidance often presents in cases of alcohol and other forms of substance abuse, both common maladaptive strategies (Beckers & Craske, 2017). Giving up is a form of passive coping and results when the individual stops paying attention to the problem, most likely when the bad consequences of inaction increase. In contrast to distractive strategies (focusing on pleasant activities), giving up is mostly about withdrawal and depressive thinking. This strategy is sometimes called *dismissive.*

Ruminative Strategies

In contrast to denial, **ruminative strategies** (or rumination) refer to behaviors and thoughts that focus on the individual's negative experiences, failed strategies, and distressful psychological symptoms associated with the inability to cope with a stressor (Smith & Alloy, 2009). Examples of ruminative responses include expressing how unhappy one feels, wondering why one feels unhappy, seeking evidence that the world is constantly unfair to this person, and thinking about how difficult it will be tomorrow. Individuals who use ruminative strategies are highly involved in their attachment experiences (like love or friendship) and focus on the possible negative outcomes that might negatively affect their attachment (Boardman, 2021).

Learned Helplessness

Experiencing uncontrollable aversive events or a crisis, some people become helpless passive and unresponsive presumably because they have learned during the crisis that there is nothing they can do to help themselves. This phenomenon has been called **learned helplessness** (Abramson et al., 1978; Abramson et al., 1989). People believe there is no connection between their actions and the outcomes of these actions—no matter what they do, it will be irrelevant. Therefore, during a crisis the chances of resolving it will be next to zero. This expectation becomes prevailing, affects individual activities, and interferes with subsequent learning from self and others. Individuals then become passive and withdrawn. Learned helplessness may be a result of a certain parenting style, personal negative experiences during adolescence and adulthood, unsafe social environment, unpleasant accidents, and a variety of other contributing circumstances and conditions (see Table 12.4).

TABLE 12.4 ■ Examples of Learned Hopelessness Statements and Consecutive Plans	
Statement	*Pattern of Inaction*
"I have tried two times, and still my LSAT (or MCAT or GRE) score is too low."	"There is no reason to study for the tests; I will never improve."
"I have tried several medications, but my illness does not go away."	"There is no reason to continue treatment; I am hopeless."
"I have tried to ask my friends for help many times; nobody helped me."	"People are just selfish; the whole world is unhelpful. I give up."

CHECK AND APPLY YOUR KNOWLEDGE

1. Describe the Type D personality.
2. What are latent vulnerability traits?
3. Some say, "Optimism is costly if it is unrealistic." Give examples of unrealistic and realistic optimism.
4. Describe and give an example of a problem-focused strategy.
5. Describe and give an example of an emotion-focused strategy.
6. Denial involves several interconnected strategies. Describe them.
7. Explain ruminative strategies and give an example. Do you use these strategies and how often?
8. Have you experienced learned helplessness? How did it affect your life? What is your advice on how to overcome learned helplessness?

© iStockphoto.com/FangXiaNuo

PHOTO 12.3 Sensitization is a protective coping effort to prevent negative emotions and despair. Have you ever used sensitization to help yourself and others? If yes, how?

APPLYING THE ADJUSTMENT DOMAIN

Coping With Serious Illness

When the Australian scientist Denis Wright was diagnosed in 2009 with an aggressive brain cancer, his doctors said the illness was incurable. While his health was slowly deteriorating, he started a blog called *My Unwelcome Stranger* (the title was referring to his illness) in which he shared his daily experiences. He gave his most sincere advice about how we can live fulfilling and happy lives even with a terminal illness (Wright, 2013). His blog shared a very optimistic, caring, and powerful story of coping.

The coping strategy Wright used is called **sensitization**. This is a strategy to learn about, rehearse, and anticipate fearful events in a protective coping effort to prevent negative emotions and despair. Recall from Chapter 8 that psychologist Rollo May believed people can be happy only if they confront the difficult circumstances of their lives, especially those that are manageable (May, 1967). Yet how can we manage the fear of an outcome as frightening as our own death? One strategy is to focus on acceptance—we cannot deny death. It is better to accept the existential inevitability of death rather than being afraid of it (Fernandez et al., 2010). Recall again from Chapter 8 that the humanistic tradition in personality psychology considers the issue of acceptance as important in an individual's life.

From their research, Shelly Taylor and her colleagues (1983) formulated and applied the **cognitive adaptation theory** (her research was described earlier in this chapter). Their theory evolved from a psychological study of breast cancer patients. Psychologists showed that human perception tends to be marked by three *positive illusions*, which are mild and positive distortions of reality: self-enhancement, unrealistic optimism, and an exaggerated perception of personal control (Taylor, 2000). They are called illusions because they may contradict, to some degree, the facts. Self-enhancement is a tendency to think better of yourself. Unrealistic optimism is a tendency to believe mostly in positive outcomes (even when the facts do not suggest the same). And finally, personal control is the belief that the individual can exercise control over many events in their lives.

Studies showed that positive illusions tend to promote healthy behaviors. People who develop (1) a positive sense of self-worth, (2) beliefs in their own control, and (3) optimism are more likely to practice conscientious health habits, including healthy dieting and exercising. Positive illusions appear to have protective psychological effects and become especially important in the context of predicaments and threatening events. Positive beliefs, such as those that form the core of positive illusions, might influence the course of various illnesses, including depression (Taylor, 1989). While finding evidence of several behavioral and emotional benefits of positive illusions, there is evidence of their potential negative impact, especially in the fields such as gambling, financial investments, start-up businesses, preventive medicine, and wars (Makridakis & Moleskis, 2015).

Fighting Alcoholism

One of the most harmful coping strategies is substance abuse. Some people use substances as a distraction. They turn to alcohol to relax and "forget" for a short period about their problems or stressors. A short-term effect of substance use may seem positive since alcohol, as a depressant, may temporarily reduce an individual's pain, anxiety, stress, and physical tension. However, drinking (and other substance use) does not address the stressor itself, and it does not produce adaptive coping strategies. On the contrary, many individuals end up turning to substances again and again, which can lead to dependency and addiction. Psychologists have a professional responsibility to spread awareness about the harmful effects of drinking, especially as a coping strategy. This "strategy" quickly becomes a habit, the consumption of alcohol increases, and the dependency grows.

Many interventions related to alcoholism require face-to-face interaction between a professional therapist and a person who seeks help. Support groups gained popularity as well. During the past 2 decades, research has provided evidence about the effectiveness of online groups (connected via emails, social networks, or video chats) in providing help to find social support, distributing new facts about coping strategies with alcoholism, and encouraging members to share personal experiences and success stories with others (Das & Rae, 1999; Griffiths et al., 2012). Studies suggest that online support groups for people with alcohol-related problems could strengthen a person's "circle of support" in almost the same way as face-to-face groups (National Council on Alcoholism and Drug Dependence, 2016). There are encouraging data collected during the COVID-19 pandemic about the effectiveness of online group meetings for individuals with substance use disorder (Bergman et al., 2021).

Relaxation Techniques

Close your eyes, and relax . . .

Millions of people over the years have heard this phrase in the beginning of their sessions of relaxation therapies. **Relaxation training** is a technique or method to cope with stress. This method has been used in developing effective skills of self-control—the skills that can be an asset in coping with serious life problems (Davis et al., 2008). In the 1920s, German physician Johannes Shultz suggested the method of **autogenic training** (AT), which is a self-administered technique for physical and emotional relaxation. For many years, it has been used as a stress management procedure to build and improve self-control skills (Sadigh, 2012). The main technique is autosuggestion. In a relaxed sitting position, the person who learns AT concentrates on heaviness in the arms and legs, warmth in the body, respiratory and cardiac regularity, abdominal warmth and comfort, coolness of the forehead, and overall feelings of harmony and peace. Each of these experiences is learned and practiced with a professional and then alone at home for several weeks until the intended effects are achieved (Krampen, 1999). Once learned, autogenic exercises may provide relief for psychological and somatic symptoms associated with stressors. Individuals reduce their anxiety and improve their memory and cognitive skills as well as report greater levels of self-control (Stetter & Kupper, 2002).

With a measure of imagination, we can find many similarities between AT and several techniques in Chinese and Japanese holistic treatments, which emphasize the balanced interaction of the body and the mind (Sutton, 1998). These techniques have been very popular among millions of people around the world. For example, according to academic research, the methods of tai chi, which originated in China, have been found to be beneficial for individual physical and emotional health from other countries (Lee & Ernst, 2011). Health psychology has accumulated evidence that regular relaxation can be more beneficial if it is combined with proper diet and physical exercises (Lewis, 2001; McCarthy, 2013). A combination of physical and talk therapy is welcome if it helps the client overcome persistent anxiety or chronic pain (Clay, 2002). Some forms of physical therapy can reduce a client's constant anxiety, thus easing a therapeutic dialogue with a psychologist.

To achieve deep relaxation or concentration, therapists can teach their clients various forms of meditation. In fact, during the 1960s, various relaxation methods rooted in Eastern philosophies and religious traditions, including Hinduism and Buddhism, gained significant popularity (Aanstoos et al., 2000). These methods remain very popular today, gaining acceptance because they placed self-awareness, forgiveness, and growth-seeking experiences at the center of therapeutic treatment. Interest in mindfulness (internal and external experiences occurring in the present moment) and the practice of meditation is growing (Kabat-Zinn, 2012). Richard Davidson at the University of Wisconsin, who founded the Center for Investigating Healthy Minds, has developed a serious research base to support and further develop many traditional methods of therapy (Davidson & Begley, 2012; Goleman & Davidson, 2017). There is evidence that even brief mindfulness practices (on breath awareness, on kindness, and on gratitude) could positively impact individuals suffering from acute stress (Goldberg et al., 2021)

Along the way, the implementation of key principles of the humanistic tradition (see Chapter 8) inadvertently invited psychologists and their clients to discover the incredible world of Indian and Asian philosophy and mythology.

Overcoming Acculturative Stress

Acculturative stress (sometimes called *culture shock*) is a distressful psychological reaction to an unfamiliar cultural environment. The symptoms include significant psychological changes in individuals who undergo major cultural transitions usually associated with immigration and might manifest as persistent anxiety, sadness, pessimistic thoughts, and low self-esteem (see Table 12.5).

Acculturative stress can be short-term and continuous, as earlier studies have shown (Tsytsarev & Krichmar, 2000). Significant language barriers, lack of knowledge about local norms, detachment from familiar environments, and the challenges of a new country can be very stressful (Shiraev & Levy, 2024). Individuals who cope with the negative consequences of their life as immigrants often need the acquisition and development of the skills and habits required in the new cultural settings. Several steps are necessary to help individuals cope with acculturative stress:

TABLE 12.5 ■ Symptoms of Acculturative Stress ("Culture Shock")	
Symptoms	*Description*
Nostalgic feelings	Longing for relatives, friends, familiar scenes, foods, and other precious experiences
Disorientation and loss of control	Inability to solve simple problems, lack of power, anxiety, and depressive symptoms
Dissatisfaction over communication barriers	Lack of spoken and written language skills create frustration and affective symptoms
Loss of habits and lifestyle	Inability to do many previously enjoyed activities, which causes negative affective symptoms
Dissatisfaction over perceived differences	Differences between the new and old cultures are exaggerated and seem difficult to accept
Dissatisfaction over perceived value gap	Differences in values typically exaggerated, new values seem difficult to accept

Source: Maldonado et al., 2018; Shiraev and Boyd, 2008

1. *Gaining knowledge.* The person should be aware of the symptoms of acculturative stress.

2. *Overcoming stigma.* Many individuals do not want to accept that they have developed a psychological disorder. The phrase *mental illness* terrifies them. The less educated a person is, the stronger the stigma (or negative perception) of mental illness in this person's mind (Wood & Wahl, 2006). It takes a significant effort to explain that suffering from the symptoms of acculturative stress should not be embarrassing, and it is not a sign of personal failure—it is a treatable problem that social workers or psychologists can help with.

3. *Commitment.* Several forms of cognitive and behavioral intervention can be used to reduce the harmful impact of acculturative stress. However, the key to successfully coping with this problem is the person's commitment and perseverance where treatment is concerned.

SUMMARY

- Adjustment refers to relatively significant changes in an individual's behavior and experiences in response to external and internal challenges. Adjustment is somewhat similar to coping, which is a deliberate and conscious effort to adjust to challenges, changing situations, and new conditions.

- Many areas of life and activities produce stressors and thus require adjustment. Among them are aging, illness, changes in the family, professional changes, migration, and many others.

- Psychology of adjustment studies problems and conditions that cause the individual's need for adjustment, the psychological mechanisms of adjustment, and the ways to help individuals in their coping process.

- Different types of adjustment have been identified. They can relate to the individual or to the stressor.

- Coping and adjustment can be active or passive, with many variations in between the "active" and "passive" alternatives. One style is approaching, which is a type of coping that refers to deliberate attempts at changing self as well as the sources of stress. Another is avoiding; contrary to approaching, it is keeping self away from addressing a challenge or a stressor.

- In terms of the dynamics, or speed of coping, some people tend to adjust quickly. As soon as the stressor appears or as soon as they realize that an adjustment is necessary, they think about what to do and then act. Others display a persistent pattern of behavior and thought called *procrastination*—putting off impending tasks to a later time.

- Successful coping responses that allow the individual to maintain a happy and productive life score high on the measures of subjective well-being. Unsuccessful coping is associated with the inability to adjust to a stressor or continuous problem and includes emotional distress—the most severe version of which is adjustment disorder.

- Another feature that tends to be helpful in successful coping is optimism—the general belief in positive or successful outcomes. Optimism involves an act of cognitive assessment of the present and future.

- As in the case of "helpful" traits, there should be individual features that negatively affect coping.

- Adaptive, successful coping strategies improve the individual's functioning in everyday situations and reduce the impact of life-changing stressors. These strategies should have significant, long-term impact. On the other hand, maladaptive coping strategies often lead to increased anxiety, other emotional problems, and even substance abuse.

- Scientific knowledge of adaptive strategies can be applied to a wide variety of problems that people face in their daily lives. These problems range from coping with illness to alcoholism to stress-reduction techniques.

VISUAL REVIEW

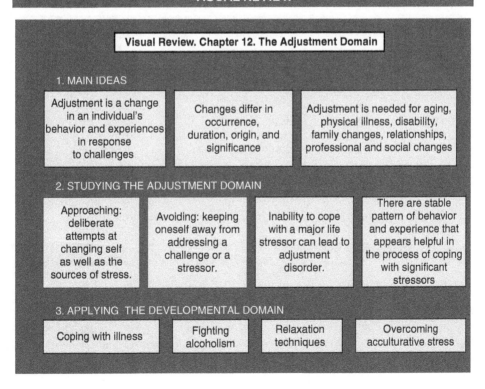

Visual Review. Chapter 12. The Adjustment Domain

1. MAIN IDEAS

Adjustment is a change in an individual's behavior and experiences in response to challenges	Changes differ in occurrence, duration, origin, and significance	Adjustment is needed for aging, physical illness, disability, family changes, relationships, professional and social changes

2. STUDYING THE ADJUSTMENT DOMAIN

Approaching: deliberate attempts at changing self as well as the sources of stress.	Avoiding: keeping oneself away from addressing a challenge or a stressor.	Inability to cope with a major life stressor can lead to adjustment disorder.	There are stable pattern of behavior and experience that appears helpful in the process of coping with significant stressors

3. APPLYING THE DEVELOPMENTAL DOMAIN

Coping with illness	Fighting alcoholism	Relaxation techniques	Overcoming acculturative stress

acculturation

acculturative stress

adjustment

adjustment disorder

anxious avoidance

appraisal-focused

approaching

autogenic training

avoiding

burnout

catastrophic thinking

cognitive adaptation theory

coping

denial

disabilities

dispositional optimism

dispositional pessimists

distraction

emotion-focused

flexibility

hardiness

latent vulnerability traits

learned helplessness

optimism

passive adjustment

pessimism

problem-focused

procrastination

psychology of adjustment

relaxation training

ruminative strategies

sensitization

stress

stress tolerance

Type D personality

EVALUATING WHAT YOU KNOW

What is the focus of the adjustment domain?

What are the areas of changes requiring adjustment?

Describe the types of coping and adjustment.

What are key outcomes of coping and adjustment?

Describe traits that affect coping and adjustment.

Provide an example for each of the areas of application: coping with serious illness, fighting alcoholism, relaxation techniques, and overcoming acculturative stress.

A BRIDGE TO THE NEXT CHAPTER

Each technological breakthrough is a trade-off if we consider its consequences. The wheel expedited travel but also helped the armies of conquerors move their weapons and provisions more efficiently. Engineering inventions allowed the creation of new types of ships to encourage global trade. Yet those frigates and galleons were also used for conquest and colonization. The dynamite was initially planned for mining. In war, countless lives were lost because dynamite was weaponized. A critical thinker can easily argue that dynamite didn't kill: The people who used it did. This is a valid argument. But does this mean that humans are trapped in this perpetual "good-evil" tradeoff related to technological discoveries and innovations? For example, what consequences do we see and expect from digital technologies? How will they affect us, as individuals, our emotions, behavior, personality traits, or identity? Research in this field is taking its first baby steps. Let's discuss them in the next chapter.

THE DIGITAL DOMAIN

LEARNING OBJECTIVES

After reading this chapter, you should be able to do the following:

- Critically discuss the essential features of the digital domain of the individual's personality.

- Explain the many meanings of digital personality footprints.

- Competently discuss the impact of the Internet on the individual's personality.

- Critically evaluate the meaning of the individual's reputation in the digital age.

- Learn about the key principles and areas of application of the research into the digital domain of personality.

Fake Famous is a documentary to explore the meaning of fame and influence in the digital world. It was also a shrewd social experiment: The creators of this documentary hired several young, aspiring—yet unknown—people and tried to transform them into social media influencers by constructing their new "fake" online personalities. An influencer, as you know, is a person who has acquired the capability to affect the thoughts and actions of many people. Most influencers achieve their prominent status because they do something important or produce something noticeable: Most of them are athletes, designers, actresses, or journalists. The *Fake Famous* director Nick Bilton was not interested in working with already established influencers. He hoped to create a new brand of famous people by simply . . . making them famous during the filming. But how could you make anybody famous if this person has not done anything important? To demonstrate their version of fame-creation, the filmmakers first advertised ("Do you want to be famous?") their project, then screened 4,000 applicants, interviewed a few, and finally contracted three of them—Dominique, Chris, and Wylie—all from Los Angeles.

How "many" followers are enough to make one famous? If you have 100 followers on Instagram, this is quite an average score. But what if you have 100,000, this is a different story. This means you are better recognized than others. Like houses in which we live, cars we drive, and clothes we wear often hint to other people about our social and financial status, the same way the very high number of likes and comments can indicate how famous this person is online. This is exactly what the filmmakers had in mind: They wanted to fabricate Dominique, Chris, and Wylie's profiles and create a big number of fake Instagram followers and commentators. To begin, there are services that can help you boost the number of likes on your page, or subscriber count on your channel, or view count on your videos. Pay a few hundred dollars for this service, and you get a few hundred likes. Pay a few hundred dollars more, and you will get plenty of bot generated, "I love it, man!" or, "You go, girl!" and similar types of online comments.

Second, besides fake "thumbs up," there also are companies, photographers, and designers willing for a fee to make anyone appear younger, more beautiful, glamorous, rich, and even powerful. Using these services, the filmmakers started to build fake new images of glamour and power for the three participants. Expensive mansions and fake decorations resembling a private jet were leased for brief photo sessions. Mock vacations were staged for the three participants to create the impression on their Instagram pages that these individuals were "living large" in the world of incredible influence, luxury, expensive Champagne, and *haute couture*. The filmmakers then purchased computer-generated online followers for the young trio—an aspiring actress Dominique, fashion designer Chris, and real estate assistant Wylie—who saw their fake fans grow by the thousands each day. In fact, the trio were witnessing the creation of three new digital personality profiles—all with "enhanced" features. But soon enough the number of "real" followers also grew. People tend to follow those who already have . . . a bunch of followers. Indeed, if one unknown blogger or podcaster has 60 subscribers, and the other one has 60,000, which one in all probability is more likely to catch our interest?

The conclusion of the experiment was a bit disappointing to the filmmakers, and not because of the COVID outbreak that year. The idea of digital fake-empowering increasingly bothered two participants: Chris and Wylie. They grew uncomfortable witnessing the creation of their bogus identities online. They wanted to become recognized for who they were, by doing things they wanted and liked to do. They quit the project. Dominique, on the other hand, did not mind becoming fake-famous. Although the roots of her online fame were clearly forged, she was developing into a well-known person. With thousands of new real followers attracted by her initial fake fame, she was transforming into an asset for several retailers who were now paying her for her role of an influencer: to serve as an access to tens of thousands of potential buyers. Dominique's "fake" personality gave a boost to her "real" self. Her two identities grew into each other.

THE ESSENCE OF THE DIGITAL DOMAIN

The word *digital* is relatively new in the English language. Scientists first began using it about a hundred years ago—thanks to those brilliant mathematicians and engineers working on new computing devices (Oxford English Dictionary, 2021). For several decades after, the term mostly indicated the use of digits, specifically applied to computing machines. By the end of the 20th century, *digital* as adjective was already semantically attached to almost all products and services containing a digital equivalent: an audio CD, a video camera, or a musical instrument, and so on. Soon this term came to be used for satellite radio and digital television, the Internet, websites, blogs, and social networks. Today the word **digital**, according to linguists, broadly refers to the use of computer technology, especially the Internet. The meaning of the word is evolving.

Sociologists and economists already discuss **digital divide**, or the gap between the well-to-do and the poor in terms of their access to digital technology. Digital divide is mostly about the socioeconomic gap between those who get many benefits from digital technologies and services, on the one hand, and those who get little, on the other. There is also age-related digital divide. We know, for starters, that age in education can be among such factors: Across the world, the older and the less educated tend to use social networks less and depend on them much less than those individuals who are more educated and younger.

The meaning of "digital" in the context of personality is far from being settled either, which is not surprising. In a general sense, "digital" is about the many interactions between the individual and information technologies. But psychological research about such interactions is only developing, and there is open field for new interpretations, theories, studies, and, of course, discussions. At least four initial questions should help facilitate this chapter's discussion.

First. Do our personality features, such as individual traits, influence the ways we function online: such as making decisions in front of our smartphones, presenting ourselves in social networks, or interacting with other people in the digital dimension?

It is easy to suppose immediately that our personality traits should influence somehow our choices of online content, the intensity of the use of certain online services, or a general preference of certain forms of online communication when compared to face-to-face communication. But what are those specific personality features that explain individual differences in the use of digital technologies? For instance, are some people including children—because of their personality traits—better prepared to function in the digital world compared to other people? Could we find specific individual characteristics that can be particularly beneficial or detrimental in the use of social media, for example?

Second. In which ways does the digital world change us as individuals in the context of our individual personalities?

What are those cognitive and behavioral changes that take place in us when we are texting, emailing, surfing, posting, commenting, etc.? Obviously, our individual daily schedules have changed in some ways. Think about the early 1990s when most people did not have personal computers in their homes, and nobody had a smartphone: How many hours a day did people during those days spend checking their mobile devices? Zero. And what did they do on the subway, for example? Obviously, they were not checking their smartphones. Another obvious change refers to people's attention span: When many learn to multitask online, select priorities, and better focus on a task, many others experience serious attention problems under the constant barrage of information. Sleep hours probably shifted as well affecting somehow our emotional stability, work efficiency, or stress thresholds. But did people in the 2020s become friendlier and develop better communication skills compared to their parents from the 1990s and earlier? Human society constantly acquires new technologies, yet scientists are not certain about specific psychological qualities that can be associated with the use of new technologies.

iStockphoto.com /atlantic–kid

PHOTO 13.1 Technology has always been responsible for a host of changes in people's daily habits. Just 20 years ago people didn't have smartphones. Can you imagine yourself back 20 or 30 years ago? What would you actually do being on a subway train?

Third. What do our online activities (we will define them a bit later as digital footprints) reveal about our individual personalities?

We know that employers can learn about their prospective employees by administering to them various personality tests. Matchmaking services ask their clients to fill out forms with many personal questions. People can judge about our individual features by studying our personality tests scores or by observing what we do, write, or say. In the digital world, deliberately or unwillingly, people leave their digital footprints, too. Besides our posted email addresses, phone numbers, and birthdays, most of us have already left other substantial information referring to ourselves, our hobbies, friends, travel, emotional attachments, and political views. We can be increasingly judged by others by our digital footprint. It is available to basically anybody. Friends will find online many good things about us. Critics and ill-wishers are likely to find something different. Reputation matters.

Fourth. Does a separate and distinct "digital" dimension of personality exist?

In short, is there another "you" in the digital space that is different from you reading these pages? The world of creative fantasy, where children become somebody else in their minds, is not exclusive to kids. Creative imagination is part of most people's adult life. This inner world is mostly private, which means that others have no access to it. However, digital technology these days allows people under assumed names and profiles to reveal their private world to thousands and millions of strangers. There are plenty unexplored possibilities about an individual's assumed personality online: from having just a different name on a social network to creating a completely different personality profile. Different motivations seat behind these "extra" or "spare" personalities of ours. We know that some people become somebody else clearly for some questionable or even criminal gain. Others work for law enforcement or intelligence and must hide their real identities. Yet in other cases, people are driven by psychological reasons, including curiosity, jealousy, envy, shyness, or anger. Pranksters and trolls, unless pranking and trolling is their source of income, should have their own psychological reasons as to why they are pranking and trolling. How about just having fun?

Many new questions continue to come. Let's address them by first exploring the meaning of digital footprints and then turning to the digital personality continuum.

DIGITAL PERSONALITY FOOTPRINTS

Throughout centuries, humans were leaving their physical footprints. Understood literally, a footprint is an impression left by a person standing or moving. In a broader anthropological sense, **footprints** refer to physical markings that reflect human activities. Intentionally or not, our ancestors left their "physical markings," ranging from Egyptian pyramids and Mayan temples to private handwritten letters, unpublished manuscripts, or published books. Many families today keep framed photographs of relatives who lived many decades ago. Yet if a person has no physical "footprints" left, no written records preserved, or if this person's name is not attached to a building or street, then all knowledge about this individual inevitably disappears from the memory of coming generations. Do you know, for example, the name of your great grandmother? Who was she? There are modern digital databases, but they are available only in a few countries. Sure, there are cultural traditions embedded in folklore that maintains written memories of significant events and certain individuals. These examples, however, are rather exceptions from the rule: no footprints, no memory of an individual's existence.

The digital domain's rapid growth has changed the ways in which people now leave their footprints. Still, there are bridges, airports, university halls, and entire cities named after former politicians or wealthy sponsors. A major airport in India is named after Indira Gandhi, the late prime minister. Some famous writers, scientists, and composers have their share of airports and public squares named after them, too. An airport in Salzburg, Austria, is branded after Wolfgang Mozart, the famous composer. Many physical footprints will likely remain part of people's anthropological space. However, some of our digital footprints have already been planted regardless of our knowledge, expressed consent, or historical significance of our actions: These are our names, pictures, opinions, tweets, "likes," purchases, and many more that are stored on the web. No matter if we like this or not, most people today see you by simply how you appear to them through your digital footprints.

To a college admission office, an applicant typically appears (sorry about this) as a digital footprint, as digital information about this person. Moreover, a particular "score" is likely to be attached to each applicant's digital footprint. To most businesses, we are consumers with "footprint profiles" because we buy certain products online, fly to specific places, "like" some musical videos, or make comments on social networks. You are a paying consumer to them, and they try to obtain as many of your shopping footprints as possible. On a dating site (see the chapter on traits), you "exist" in the minds of this sight's subscribers as an individual of a certain reported height (often a bit increased by applicants to appear taller); weight (often a bit decreased by applicants to appear thinner); and a digital lineup of your preferences, "likes," and "thumb downs." For political campaigns, you are a potential voter with a certain history or participation, influence, comments, and, importantly, financial donations. Studies conducted a few years ago already showed many possibilities for an intelligent Internet service system that by analyzing an individual's digital footprints can detect a few characteristics of this individual and then make recommendations related to consumption patterns and consequently predicting how to pitch certain products and services to this individual (Adeyemi et al., 2016).

The arrival of the Internet a few decades ago allowed people to accomplish a range of goals related to their footprints that were essentially impossible for all previous generations. Two tendencies have emerged. The first one refers to **footprint accessibility**. Practically anyone can become noticeable to thousands and millions of people by just establishing their profiles on the web. What chance had a teenage girl in a small Siberian village 50 years ago to be noticed by a global audience? It was almost zero. Today, she can display her profile on Instagram (as an example) and thus she can be noticed. How many people would be aware of her existence? It depends on the quality of information that is posted, the impact it makes, and by whom and how it is promoted, as we could see in the introduction to this chapter.

The second is **digital separation**. Digital platforms allow people to create a "separate," digital identity for themselves. Perhaps most people do not realize this, but by posting their "likes," photos, and selfies, or leaving comments, they can establish—willingly or not—their separate "digital footprint portfolio" or a separate personality profile. A quiet and seemingly nice person to most people who personally know him or her, can appear digitally as an angry, tense, and seemingly unsettled individual posting under an assumed name. Our "meanness" often surfaces under fake accounts, as we can see later in this chapter.

CHECK AND APPLY YOUR KNOWLEDGE

1. Explain the concept of digital divide.
2. What do our online activities reveal about our individual personalities?
3. Give an example of your own digital footprint.
4. Explain footprint accessibility.

The Digital Personality Continuum

In which ways does the world of interactive digital technology, including emails, Instagram postings, Tweets, and comments, differ from the means the humans traditionally use to learn, make statements, and interact with one another?

At least four views or approaches about the Digital Domain can be identified. In these contexts, the Digital Domain can be discussed, for convenience, as either or mostly as a *reflector*, an *enhancer*, a *transformer*, or a *separator* of the individual's personality. Let's decipher these categories or, if you chose to call them this way, metaphors.

The Reflector. The digital world is just another means of communication reflecting our behavior and mirroring our "selves" as individuals. Like a team of engineers and workers who build a bridge to help people cross the river, a team of programmers and designers creates online tools for us to use. In a way, the digital domain is—nothing more, nothing less—just another space to communicate, express ourselves, and learn from others.

The Enhancer. The digital platform is not only a reflection of who we are. It provides individuals with opportunities for enhancement of their cognitive, emotional, and behavioral features. For example, a shy person in most social situations who is eager to express self, can find a social network as a great opportunity, which is difficult to find otherwise, to communicate this person's thoughts and emotions. An individual who finds it difficult to seek friendship in real life can explore new and easy possibilities of online dating.

The Transformer. The digital platform indeed provides for us the venues for reflection and enhancement. But it also, and this is most important, has changed most of us as individuals and in different ways. Like in space, according to physics, light rays passing near very massive objects—such as stars—are seen to travel in curves. The digital world, as an analogy, is something that "curves" in our personality characteristics and transforms our behavior in both consistent and unpredictable ways.

The Separator. The digital world, in addition to the three other functions, has created a new "reality" for most humans. Our postings, our thoughts, or our "likes" are not just reflecting on our emotions and indicating our decisions. These digital footprints are our new personality's footprints. They essentially stand for who we are in the digital dimension. People do not know who you are unless they access your digital footprints. To dozens, hundreds, and thousands of people, we appear and we exist as if our digital footprints exist. Moreover, when we die, we continue to exist in the digital world.

These are just four brief descriptions of each approach or category. Let's discuss them in some detail.

The Reflector

To repeat an argument presented here earlier, skeptics maintain that our digital footprints, despite their multiplicity and complexity, are just reflections, or "shadows," of us as individuals. In other words, the digital world is simply another platform for interpersonal communication.

As far as the argument goes, an honest person in daily face-to-face interactions is very likely to be honest online. A person with aggressive and violent tendencies is likely to express his or her aggressive tendencies online. Like in the "physical" world, where crime can occur, criminal acts take place online as well. Like thieves who still valuable items from people's homes and business offices, online crooks steal other people's valuable information, ideas, and assets. The way we sign our email letters, the way we introduce ourselves in them, and even the length of our emails resembles the way we write and sign letters on paper. Personality tests allow psychologists to understand better a person's individual features revealed by these tests. People's online footprints—as if they were personality tests—also could tell a lot about these people.

Some empirical data support these assumptions. A classical study by Leary (2005) using 58,000 Facebook volunteers who agreed to have their "likes" and "dislikes" analyzed, showed that the researchers in this study could accurately predict a range of highly sensitive personal attributes of the volunteers including their sexual orientation, ethnicity, religious and political views, personality traits (such as openness to experience), intelligence, happiness, use of addictive substances, parental separation, age, and gender. Other studies of online behavior showed, for example, that conscientiousness, as a personality trait, can clearly be detected in our online communications (Adeyemi et al., 2016).

Let's Discuss. Do you think that the digital database of selfies and postings on Instagram or X/Twitter is something fundamentally new in an anthropological sense? Perhaps, not. People always tried to preserve their images and make them accessible to other people. Consider a description of a real collection of printed photographs from the distant past (Delson, 2021). On them, a young man with a watering container pretends to jokingly splash his friends. Another photo features women wearing men's hats while smoking, drinking, and playing cards. On the next photo, a woman is pretending to be in a dramatic theatrical posture to express extreme worry. And here, a man in fancy women's clothes glances upward with a slight trace of flirtation. Yet another picture shows a smiling girl taking aim with a toy pop gun.

These pics today may appear as typical Instagram material (well, maybe not the one with a toy gun)—except for the fact that the images are more than 130 years old. This is our anthropological reality: Even in the late 1800s, people enjoyed entertaining the camera with a purpose of letting other people see the photos (Delson, 2021). These pictures were a part of so-called "cabinet cards" culture, a new style of entertainment that peaked in popularity at the end of the 19th century. Rapidly developing technologies allowed retouching—a new skill to modify the images and enhance them with some spectacular visual effects. This investment of money and time was worth it: Friends and family members would exchange cabinet cards, collect them, and display some of them in albums and in living rooms. Performers like dancers and singers would sell their cards in theater lobbies before and after performances.

As you can see, people many years ago already had their "space" in dining rooms and bedrooms to display the images of themselves, and for a variety of reasons. They did not have the Internet. But they had all the means and ways to "post" their images in their homes and offices.

What is the moral of this story about cabinet cards? Perhaps this is about the old axiom that "there is nothing new under the sun": new technologies of the coming centuries, like new powerful electric lighting and faster chemical emulsions, changed the art and culture of photography. Digital photography changed the world of printed photography. Yet the people's desire to express themselves and to claim their psychological presence in other people's lives remains timeless.

People used different forms of communication throughout history, and each historical period had its own prevalent domain. Our ancestors hundreds of years ago used human messengers who would walk through the woods and prairies to deliver to other people important news or warnings. Later in history, postal services would deliver handwritten letters. Then came printed pamphlets, books, and daily newspapers as new forms of self-expression and interaction. The 19th century brought telegraph. The 20th century brought radio and television. Fax machines were a technological culmination of a pre-computer world of the 1980s. Those technologies and venues allowed people to broadcast facts, share opinions, or even convey their emotions. The digital media today—although they are faster, bigger, and mightier than all other media in history—remain just another platform for people to communicate, express self, and learn from other people. Years from now, new communication technologies, as far as this argument goes, will likely make the Internet of today an antiquated platform of yesterday.

The Amplifier

According to this view, the digital platform is not merely a reflection of who we are. As a magnified glass or a chemical catalyst, it enhances and boosts thoughts, ideas, and emotional states. For example, an introverted and isolated person can find a social network as a great opportunity to express his or her thoughts and emotions, which otherwise, without social networks, would have been kept in private. An individual who finds it difficult to seek friendship in real-life situations (like in school or at work) can explore new possibilities of online chatting and even dating. People going online now discuss things that they would never mention in face-to-face meetings. Individuals who keep their anger under control can now use the web for bullying others or for relentless emotional ranting and raving. The web can be a convenient platform for a person with a propensity for anxiety or obsessive-compulsive tendencies: Keeping oneself busy by constantly checking the news and posting messages can address some anxiety symptoms or satisfy certain addictive cravings. In short, the digital platform can be seen as a digital enhance-ment or "amplification" of the individual's characteristics. According to research, online politi-cal discussions (often involving anonymous people) are evaluated as angrier and less civil than those in real life; networks of online partisans create worldviews that appear to become way too extreme; online disinformation campaigns appear more intense than ever before (Haidt & Rose-Stockwell, 2019).

The Internet provides people with knowledge, which they, in theory, could have obtained elsewhere (for example, from books, friends, or teachers). The difference today is the speed with which we obtain information and accessibility of such information. A hundred years ago, most educated people didn't know as much about mental illness, compared to what we know today. In those days, educated people called their persistent and elevated state of anxiety "a neurosis." Today, similarly, instead of saying, "I am sad, tired, and bored," a person learns about clinical symptoms of depression. Results? The appearance of the reportedly increasing incidences of depression compared to the pre-Internet era.

The social psychologist Mark Leary (2005, 2012) coined the term *sociometer* to describe the inner mental device that tells us, moment by moment, how we are doing in the eyes of others. According to the sociometer theory, when people do things that appear intended to protect or increase their self-esteem, their goal is usually to protect and enhance the likelihood of inter-personal acceptance. The Internet and social networks, in fact, provide us with the ability to protect and enhance our relational value.

To further illustrate the argument, one of such amplifications refers to the syndrome of grandstanding. This is the action of behaving in a showy manner to attract favorable attention from the audience regarding a certain issue or a problem (Tosi & Warmke, 2016). Psychologists also report an increased need of individuals to be on the web just to make themselves noticeable by others (Haidt & Rose-Stockwell, 2019). Like a chain of speakers in a public forum, trying to outperform previous speakers, people in social networks are increas-ingly moving toward grandstanding. **Personality grandstanding** refers to the tendency of individuals to present themselves in an exaggerated, flamboyant way with an intention to impress. Personality grandstanding is not always and necessarily deliberate. A person may be passionately advocating an issue or pleading for a solution to a problem without having a desire to impress. Grandstanding can also be associated with a somewhat protracted emo-tional and cognitive state over a certain period. Yet grandstanding can be a trait, a common and stable pattern of action and self-expression. Individuals with such a trait tend to launch moral attacks, attach offensive labels on others, initiate public shaming, claim that anyone who disagrees with them is wrong, or repeatedly exaggerate their own emotional display (Haidt & Rose-Stockwell, 2019). The Internet offers a generous opportunity for individuals with hidden or mild grandstanding tendencies to unleash them online with little restrictions. TikTok, as an example, attracts people's attention related to performance: Most unusual and flamboyant behaviors are likely to attract viewers. TikTok is a magnet for individuals grand-standing in this way. Instagram, on the other hand, focused so far heavily on the body and lifestyle. Grandstanding on Instagram thus can reflect the individual's tendency to share only the best moments, a pressure to look perfect (Hobbs et al., 2021).

SELF-REFLECTION

Can you deep work? Deep work is the ability to focus on a cognitively demanding task without being constantly distracted (Newport, 2016). For example, you are working on an important project, but you are periodically sidetracked: You can be checking the news every 5 minutes, then browsing YouTube, then posting on X/Twitter, and then getting back to your work while realizing you have already wasted some valuable time. Studies showed that most people want to spend less time online but lacked the self-control to do so (Haidt & Rose-Stockwell, 2019). This constant inability to stay focused and avoid—irrelevant to the task in hand—online activities is negatively related to life satisfaction (Blachnio et al., 2016). For starters, begin paying attention to the style of your work online. How often are you distracted within one hour? Can you resist the temptation to browse the web for the latest news while working? Try to focus and stay focused for an extended period. Impulse control related to deep work is a learned skill that allows you to master complicated information and produce better results in less time. So can you deep work?

The Transformer

According to this view, the digital domain is not only a reflector and enhancer of our personality traits. The digital platform has changed and transformed many aspects of our behavior, cognition, and emotional experience. It continues to change us as individuals. Like in the world of physics, out in space, light rays passing near very massive objects—such as stars—are seen to travel in curves. This is called "gravitational lensing." The digital domain is like "gravitational lenses" in astrophysics: Modern technologies can be associated with **personality lensing** that stands for change—both small and substantial—in the ways we feel, think, and act when functioning online, compared to how we function in the physical or social world. For example, students who took part in a lab experiment involving risky behavior (such as pumping up air balloons and receiving a small monetary reward for each pump and financial penalties for making them explode) were aware about the presence of a robot, which would comment on each student's performance. Students knew that the robot was just a talking machine. Yet it was able to exert influence on risk-taking behavior through positive and negative verbal reinforcement in the same way a human might (Ward, 2021). The digital domain changes the individual's personality in terms of short-living manifestations as well as long-term traits. It also changes the ways other people see, understand, and react to our digital footprints, compared to how they would have responded in the physical and social world unmediated by the Internet.

Consider just a sample of research suggesting emotional, cognitive, and behavioral changes in people—all associated with the use of the Internet (see Table 13.1).

Linguistic patterns in communications are changing, too. An example of Iceland is telling. Researchers and educators in this small Scandinavian nation talk about English becoming a main language of online communication especially among the very young who began using smartphones at a very young age and begin to read and write in English very early (Bjarnason, 2021). In their world of computer games, Netflix, voice-activated online assistants, and viral

TABLE 13.1 ■ Research on Psychological and Behavioral Changes Linked to the Use of the Web	
Areas of experience and behavior	*Empirical Facts*
Emotional stability	Pioneering studies showed some changes in emotional stability and some other personality traits in people working on the web, compared to them being online (Blumer & Döring, 2012).
Mental health problems	Studies involving more than 500,000 middle school and high school students found more time on new media (cells or social media) was correlated with more mental health problems (Twenge et al., 2017).
Body image	Thirty-two percent of teen girls said that when they felt bad about their bodies, Instagram made them feel worse (Wells et al., 2021).
Depressive symptoms	More time spent on Facebook, more depressive symptoms (Steers, et al., 2014). Survey respondents who had minimal symptoms of depression early on were more likely to report an increase in symptoms in later surveys if they used social media (Perlis et al., 2021).
Positive emotions	A 1-week experiment of 1,095 subjects found that taking a break from Facebook increased life satisfaction and positive emotions (Tromholt, 2016).
Interpersonal bonding	In-person communications in experiments produced more bonding between individuals then online communication via texts or videos (Sherman et al., 2013).
Positive mood	The more constantly one checks social media daily, the less positive one's mood (Wang et al, 2015).
Memory and learning	Constant cellphone ringing compared to other irrelevant sounds decreases memory and learning (Shelton et al., 2009).
Changes in personality traits	Digital psychological intervention can be associated with changes in personality traits in people who were influenced (Stieger et al., 2021).

videos—almost everything is in English. On the one hand, kids quickly learn the second language in the most interactive way. On the other hand, the native, Icelandic, language becomes increasingly irrelevant.

The Internet has already initiated a range of behavioral, cognitive, and emotional changes in billions of human beings. Consider the transformations in individual time allocation over the past 3 decades. Today most of us spend many hours a day looking at and touching our digital screens. Thirty years or so ago for people who lived then—this time was almost zero. In the 1990s, a student would visit a campus library to learn about the average yearly temperature in Bolivia in January. Today we literally dictate our questions to our mobile devices and receive immediate answers while walking. Thirty years ago, unless you are not in a telephone-based business, a busy professional would receive a dozen, maybe two dozen phone calls a day. Today many of us daily go through hundreds of emails, texts, tweets, and other digital messages. A quarter of a century ago you could literally "disappear" for a few days so that nobody could get in touch with you even if you wanted it. Today people can connect with you at any place and anytime—unless you explicitly turn off all your mobile devices—and not many of us would do this.

The Separator

My academic mentor passed away a few years ago. He was a distinguished professor in his late 90s. As a tribute to his legacy and life, my friend historian and I decided to write this professor's biography. When we asked his family—and they were eager to help us—to share with us his written archives such as diaries, handwritten notes, and letters, we were told that, regretfully, there were none of those. The professor deliberately left nothing except his already published works and posted essays. We quicky rushed and saved a few remaining emails from the professor that were kept in our inboxes from a few years ago. What was left of his legacy were the memories of his relatives and friends plus the professor's printed books and articles. His digital reality that could reflect on his individual personality . . . was nearly empty.

There is a view that the digital domain represents an "enhanced" but also a new dimension of our personality. Our actions, thoughts, and emotions become digital footprints and thus they form a new, extended reality of us as individuals. Other people perceive us and make evaluations of our behavior and our personality traits from at least two different platforms: One is the "physical" world of interpersonal interactions, the other is the digital. We appear in our digital footprints differently, compared to how people perceive us face-to-face.

However, this is not the case for most people these days. The digital world has created for human beings a new and distinct psychological reality. The digital footprints that we constantly leave when we log on, sign up, and sign on stand for our separate identities. Our postings, our thoughts, and our "likes" are not just digital footprints. They are not our "reflections" either . . . . They, essentially, stand for how we appear in the eyes and ears and perhaps other senses of others. People do not know who you are unless they access your digital footprints. To dozens, hundreds, and thousands of people, we appear and we exist if our digital footprints exist. When we pass on, we continue to exist in the minds of other people because of the digital footprints that we left.

There are individuals and companies who create "fake personalities" who perform specific online tasks as commentators and organizers. They act according to a business plan designed to achieve a commercial or political goal, like to advertise a product or to sway votes. Such "fakes" tend to use individual profiles and photos generated by machine learning techniques like generative adversarial networks (GAN). For example, a GAN using artificial intelligence can generate new human photographs that have many realistic characteristics that look authentic to most human observers. To make the images unique and thus more difficult to find using a reverse image search, some of the more active profiles cropped the images and flipped them horizontally. The images had also been manipulated to change certain colors without looking overly edited (Knight, 2021). To make the images unique and thus more difficult to find using a reverse image search, some of the more active profiles cropped the images and flipped them horizontally. The images had also been manipulated to change certain colors without looking overly edited. The DFRLab tried to recreate these edits using image editing software and found it required multiple subtle changes. Most notable, the different images required different edits; in one example, a T-shirt was changed from red to orange, while in another example a long-sleeved shirt was changed from blue to purple (Knight, 2021).

Early in this book, you read about the work of Turing. His work gave a significant boost to the field of studies of **artificial intelligence** (AI), which is the study and design of intelligent machines. In the context of cognitive neuroscience, artificial intelligence is the study and creation of systems that perceive their environment and make decisions to maximize success. In the 1950s after Turing proposed his ideas, AI became a reasonable possibility, and even skeptics had to lower their critical voices. Chess was one of several areas in which computers began to gain both strength and public attention. Digital computers provided both mathematical and sophisticated technical solutions for the game. Soon enough, chess computers began to compete with humans. Some computers already competed early in the 21st century on the highest level of the game, repeatedly winning against world chess champions (Hsu, 2002). Creative or academic writing was another field that AI tried to infiltrate. The massive and diverse abilities of ChatGPT became well-known in 2023. Some also assumed that poetry would become a routine procedure for machines as soon as mathematicians wrote clever programs for metaphors and rhyming. It did not happen, however. Not yet. Computer-produced poetry was sophisticated grammatically but remained awful as an art for years (Funkhouser, 2012).

Optimists, however, suggest that artistic creativity can be programmed and advanced. Technology guru and futurist Ray Kurzweil suggested that by 2045 humans would have achieved digital immortality by uploading their minds to computers, allowing humans to overcome the need for a biological body for survival. According to Kurzweil (2005), advances in neural engineering and modeling of brain function will make it possible to reproduce human minds in a digital medium in the future. Kurzweil claims that even if a biological part dissolves and dies, it won't make any difference—people will be able to create virtual bodies and virtual reality that will be as realistic as the actual reality. There is also the concept of **mindclones**—digital versions of human individuals that live forever. A "mindclone" can be created from a "mindfile"—an online repository of an individual's personality that many believe is already taking shape in the form of social media, such as Facebook (Rothblatt, 2009). A mindclone is a software version of your mind run by AI: It is all your thoughts, recollections, feelings, beliefs, attitudes, and values, and it allows a person to experience reality from the standpoint of whatever machine their mindware is running on (Rothblatt, 2011b). We tend to think of our personal identity as being "installed" into our body; the new idea is that it can be reinstalled and uploaded to a different hardware!

Even if mindcloning is scientifically and technologically possible, many puzzling philosophical and psychological questions arise. In popular culture, scores of authors long entertained the literary idea that "thinking" machines would eventually compete with humans in all intellectual and practical fields. Yet what if these clever computers and machines went out of control and rebelled against humans? One such example is in the movie *The Terminator* (1984). If we allow machines to think and give them the ability to develop their practical thinking, what will happen to us? What if mindclones inherit software glitches and catch viruses and bugs? Moreover, can we teach moral values to machines? And will mindclones have to pay taxes?

Since the 1950s, researchers have judged the progress of AI by establishing certain goals or benchmarks for computers, such as their ability to recognize images, create meaningful sentences, and play games like checkers or chess (Snow, 2021). For today's researchers, the task now is to create new benchmarks that could capture the more complicated aspects of intelligence, such as reasoning, creativity, and the ability to learn and especially—the ability to feel. You can ask an AI system which team won the last FIFA World Cup in soccer, and you will get the correct answer. But when you ask whether this team deserved winning the championship, the system is likely to be puzzled. It will likely fail in the process of the emotional understanding that is needed to sufficiently answer (Snow, 2021). A soccer fan is likely to answer this question with passion.

More than 150 years ago, a book of fiction by the theologian Edwin Abbott described people living in different dimensions: Pointland, Lineland, Flatland, and Spaceland. People living in the "point" did not understand those who lived in the "line." These people could not comprehend people living in a two-dimensional flat surface. And, as you expect, people living in the flat world, could not comprehend anything happening in a tree-dimensional universe (Abbott, 1884/2019). Every aspect of human life these days is fueled by data. Our social selves, our social roles, our strengths, and vulnerabilities, are all shaped by data we create and exchange. No longer is your own self belonging to you. It is shared among hundreds, thousands, and millions (Smith & Browne, 2019). The fallout of our ability to generate digital footprints can be sad.

CHECK AND APPLY YOUR KNOWLEDGE

1. Explain personality lensing in the digital context.
2. What are the key psychological and behavioral changes linked to the use of the web?
3. Who are (or what are) mindclones? Do you think you have your own mindclone? If yes, what is it?

We now examine these four assumptions while discussing four complex and very intriguing phenomena related to our life as well as to the digital world: privacy, reputation, and trolling. Why these three? Privacy refers to our ability and right to select knowledge that we wish not to share with others. Reputation, on the other hand, is what other people know about us and how they evaluate this information. And trolling refers to a deliberate act of some people to violate the privacy of others as well as damage their reputation.

PRIVACY

In college sports, taunting of the opposite team is almost unavoidable and has been part of competitive sports for generations. Modern taunting involves the use of private digital footprints. Before the game, home team fans learn online about many details of the opposite team players' personal life from Instagram or other networks, and then during the game heckle these players about their pets, visiting relatives, or even recent breakups (Kessler, 2022). More data and facts about us become known to the public. What is happening to our privacy today?

We have already discussed in this book about the necessity for us, as individuals, to keep certain information about ourselves private, not easily accessible to other people. In a general sense, what does it mean to keep things private? What is privacy anyway?

Law experts describe privacy as someone's legal "right to be let alone." Communication professionals understand privacy as the extent of the individual to send and receive information selectively. For psychologists, **privacy** is the ability of individuals to withdraw themselves from the presence of other people or remove this information from public knowledge. When something is private to you, you try to keep it for yourself. If somebody is aware of your thoughts and emotions, they no longer are private. There are exceptions, of course. Attorney-client privilege as well as doctor-patient confidentiality are two examples. In most other cases, people exercise selective control over transactions of information between self and others, and the purpose of this control is to protect personal autonomy (Margulis, 2003).

iStockphoto.com/Dima Berlin

PHOTO 13.2 Goes About here. A picture of a person checking his or her smartphone. Caption: Privacy, among many other things, means your ability to control information about yourself. This is not only about your financial records. Privacy is also about your features as person. Are you a person who wants the whole world know about you, or do you rather limit people's access to you?

One of the most important aspects of privacy is the desire and ability to keep material objects and ideas that we consider essential parts of who we are. They include, among others, our body and some personal possessions, such as clothes, toys, amulets, or artifacts. They also include some behaviors, thoughts, feelings, and even knowledge we qualify as private. Our awareness about privacy gives us the ability to choose which elements of our material and psychological world can be accessed by others, and to control the extent, manner, and timing of the use of those parts we choose to disclose (Onn et al., 2003). Privacy is a continuous variable. Some of us tend to be more "private" than others because we tend to share less information about ourselves, compared to others. Some of us choose sharing more information and accept more public exposure. Overall, privacy is not necessarily an absence of information about us in the minds of other people. It is also about our ability to control this information.

Are digital technologies fundamentally limiting or changing our privacy? Many cultural norms related to privacy were changing throughout history along with cultural, ethical, and legal barriers that protected privacy. In predominantly collectivist cultures, privacy tended to be limited; individualist cultures are likely to boost privacy norms (Shiraev & Levy, 2024). Therefore, one can argue—defending the Reflector argument—that the Internet and social networks have not principally changed the meaning of privacy: True, some rules regulating privacy have evolved, but people still can withdraw themselves and the information related to them from other people. This means they can exercise their online privacy the same way they exercised it 50 or 100 years ago. This argument sounds reasonable. Yet it has flaws because privacy barriers in online communications today are rapidly weakening compared to the pre-Internet era. For example, our personal information which is subsequently stolen or misused tends to lead to **identity theft,** which is significantly easier to commit in the digital space, compared to a physical one.

Kirsty Hughes (2012) identified three kinds of privacy barriers of individuals: physical, behavioral, and normative. Physical barriers, such as walls and doors, prevent others from accessing and experiencing the individual. (In this sense, "accessing" an individual includes accessing personal information about them.) Behavioral barriers communicate to others—verbally, through language, or non-verbally, through personal space, body language, or clothing—that an individual does not want them to access or experience him or her. Lastly, normative barriers, such as laws and social norms, restrain others from attempting to access or experience an individual. It appears that all three types of barriers have significantly weakened in the Internet age (See Diagram 13.1).

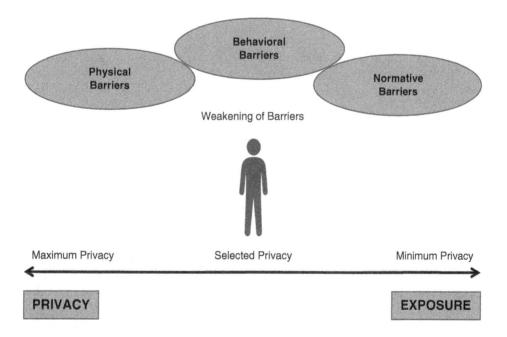

Behavioral Barriers

Physical Barriers

Normative Barriers

Weakening of Barriers

Maximum Privacy   Selected Privacy   Minimum Privacy

PRIVACY   **EXPOSURE**

Most recent technological and social developments increasingly challenge our capacity to build such barriers and exercise privacy (Smith et al., 2011; Stuart et al., 2019). In the 2020s, the ability of any random person to make online inquiries about you, to learn many personal details, such as your age, addresses, your phones, financial transactions, travels, purchases, and meetings, has expanded dramatically. Importantly, many forms of directly observed behavior, such as browsing logs, search queries, or contents of a public X/Twitter, Facebook, or Instagram profile, can be processed to infer secondary information about you, such as your sexual orientation, political and religious views, occupation, hobbies, race, substance use, decision-making, and a range of personality features (Kosinski et al., 2013). The introduction of vaccination "passports" and QR codes during the COVID pandemic potentially exposed personal and medical information of hundreds of millions of people around the globe (Economist, 2021).

Invasion of privacy is an attack on or weakening of the right of individuals to keep some personal information private. Studies showed that whether intentional or not, intended to be public or not, invasion of privacy tends to produce a negative emotional impact on the person whose privacy is invaded (Solove, 2010). Over the years, scholars created a list of activities which can be remedied with privacy protection (Prosser, 1960; Solove, 2010). They include intrusion into a person's private space, personal affairs, or desire for solitude; public disclosure of personal information about a person which could be embarrassing for them to have revealed; and promoting access to information about a person which could lead the public to have wrong beliefs about them. Of course, there may be individual differences in the measures of the concern for privacy (CFP), which acts as a generalized predictor of privacy behavior across domains and technologies (Smith et al., 2011). Some gender differences exist. Researchers found that among users posting selfies on social media, women generally have greater concerns over privacy than men, and that users' privacy concerns inversely predict their behavior and activity (Dhir et al., 2017).

In sum, individual privacy has diminished significantly during the Internet age, and the consequences of this decline should significantly affect behavior of billions: More of them will be aware of their diminished ability to protect their private information. This fundamental change will likely and increasingly affect most people's reputation.

REPUTATION

While the term *character* in psychology mostly refers to a moral side of an individual, which we briefly discussed in Chapter 7, **reputation** is a broader category. It is a result of a complex evaluation of an individual's character and behavior. Reputation is mostly about how we appear to others. Three key points are necessary to underline in our discussion.

First, reputation is concerned with how other people perceive, evaluate, and then judge an individual. In a way, reputation is a "sum of the images" and a complex social assessment of an individual's personality and behavior (Fombrun, 1996). Reputation is not what we think of ourselves; it is about what other people think of us based on available information (and disinformation as well) including, of course, digital footprints.

Second, this act of judgment is based on social standards, which can be different in unlike historical or cultural settings. The individual's social position, age, and gender have always played a role in reputational standards. To take an illustration from history, a male member of the aristocracy in the 18th or 19th century's France, Ottoman Empire, or Russia had to uphold certain standards to maintain a good reputation, i.e., they had to show respect of their fellow aristocrats and display refined manners, eloquent speech, bravery on the battlefield, and devotion to military glory. A female member of aristocracy (notice the gendered similarities and differences here) was supposed to maintain her good reputation based on erudition, polite manners, restraint, and dedication to her family (Shiraev et al., 2022).

Third, at least two general types of reputation can be identified: *positive reputation* (a measure of how others like you and what you do) and *negative reputation* (a measure of how others dislike you). These two types are not mutually exclusive: It is possible to be both much liked and much disliked by different groups at the same time (Sandman, 2010). It is also possible to have an ambivalent reputation—a combination of positive and negative evaluations.

Reputation plays a great role in our lives, and most people during their lifetime care about what other people think of them. In today's professional world, for a business owner, manager, teacher, nurse, or doctor, their good reputation is obviously a must. A good reputation of an applicant is important for them to be admitted to graduate school or to get a good job. People who occupy important positions of power or influence, such as holding an elected political office, always try very hard (often unsuccessfully) to maintain a good reputation in the eyes of the public, or at least in the eyes of voters. There is no need to remind ourselves that our personal reputation matters in our personal relationships. Bad reputation, obviously, damages an individual's educational and professional opportunities, as well as personal relationships.

Yet do digital technologies change the ways we tend to see reputation these days? **Digital reputation** is a summary outcome of the evaluation of an individual's digital footprints. Digital footprints, as we already discussed, accumulate through various contents created online. Time passes, the footprints remain. A television producer Mike Richards, who also became a host of *Jeopardy*, one of the most recognized television shows in the United States, was fired from his lucrative job in 2021 due to allegations about his inappropriate comments and actions from years ago. Apparently, the producer maintained a good reputation for many years, but it was damaged and became negative almost overnight in the eyes of his bosses who though that his negative reputation would affect the image of the company (Aquilina, 2021). In a different real-life story, another person named Donny Wiseman showed remarkable bravery and saved the life of a zoo worker who was suddenly attacked by an alligator. The video of this remarkable rescue went viral (Summers, 2021). The reputation of the rescuer—who was unknown to the public before the incident—skyrocketed within hours.

Yet is it necessary to separate an individual's "reputation" from his or her "digital reputation"? If we agree with the Reflector hypothesis presented earlier in the chapter, the digital dimension does not create a unique space for our individual features to unfold. In short, our digital reputation is just an aspect of our reputation: It does not matter how a person's words and actions appears to others. Eyewitness accounts, our own postings, or Instagram videos posted by somebody else—they all contribute to our reputation.

There is a difference, however, between how people's reputation was formed 50 years ago compared to the world of news feeds and social media today. The Amplifier hypothesis, as you remember, suggests that the digital platform is not a simple reflection or an extension of who we are. It provides an individual with new opportunities for new cognitive activities and new behaviors. More people have additional opportunities to judge us based on more facts and opinions available to them today, compared to 30 years ago. Such facts and opinions can be based on reality, or often be "fake."

According to the **bank account theory** of reputation (Coombs, 2019; Sandman, 2010), most events that improve or damage an individual's reputation can be compared to bank deposits and withdrawals. This is how we build our "reputational capital." A person with abundant reputational capital can spend or lose some investment and still maintain a mostly good reputation (Alsop, 2004). Instead, individuals with a bad reputation could repair it by engaging in socially appropriate, moral acts. Many celebrities are known for their overdramatic and often inappropriate social behavior. Yet their professional accomplishments on the soccer field or on screen give them a reputational safety "cushion." Think about the legendary Diego Maradona (1960–2020), an Argentine soccer superstar, whose exceptional athletic skills and most prestigious trophies helped him maintain a hero status among tens of millions of his fans for years despite constant media reports about his embarrassing problems with alcohol abuse.

iStockphoto.com/Dima Berlin

PHOTO 13.3 In most situations today, people judge other people by what the media or social networks display about them. Are you taking care of your digital reputation today? Think about it and give examples of what you specifically do regarding your reputation.

The second, opposing view, is the **halo effect theory** (Sandman, 2010). According to this theory, human beings tend to "balance" their views about other people by holding onto a general expectation: A good person is supposed to do good things; a bad person is supposed to do bad things. *Halo* in these cases refers to the metaphorical aura of positivity, regard, and respect associated with an individual. The halo effect theory is rooted in the assumptions of cognitive dissonance theory in social psychology (Festinger, 1957). Following this theory, public opinion can turn in support or against a person and determine who is "good" or "bad" very quickly—all based on this halo effect. The bicyclist Lance Armstrong (b. 1971) was for some time one of the most famous athletes in the world. Winner of many prestigious tournaments, a cancer survivor, and a global social influencer, he was actively engaged in many successful charitable projects. However, after he was forced to reveal in 2013 that he had used illegal performance-enhancing drugs before 2005, Armstrong's reputation took a major dive—the facts of cheating were enough to overshadow all his charitable work. He disappeared from the media. You can ask a question: Can a cheater still do good charitable work? They may, but the public, according to the halo effect hypothesis, is likely to disagree with any positive assessment of a cheater. Unlike most physical footprints, digital footprints tend to be instantly accessible to others.

SELF-REFLECTION

An individual's personality traits are a gateway to this person's reputation, yet they are not identical. Consider the following example. We all have our personality traits, but we also can have, at least in theory, zero reputation: If nobody knows about your existence, how could you establish your reputation? Moreover, one person can have two or more reputations. Imagine for a second that you joined a witness protection program (which exists in the United States and some other countries), according to which, the government provided you with a completely new identity. You have been an honest, resilient, and open-minded individual. Now, as part of the program, you, under a new name, move to a new area of the country where nobody knows you personally. They have no idea that you have been open-minded or resilient. Then you open a personal account on two social networks and create two new profiles. Of course, because of you are under witness protection, you may not publish any identifiable pictures and selfies from your past. You upload the photos that bear no resemblance of you. After your new profiles are created, you request new friends and join a few groups or ongoing discussions. The fact that you have been honest, resilient, and open-minded in the past is mostly irrelevant today. What people know about you is what they take from your new profile, your new posts, and latest comments. Sooner or later, you will develop your new reputation or reputations. What it will be depends on what you have posted on these social networks, what you have commented on, and on several other circumstances.

Not only can people build their reputations over years, they also can ruin them in minutes. In the world of daily face-to-face interactions, most people learn about us by observing and analyzing our behavior. Based on those assessments, people make judgments—the foundation of reputation. Within the digital domain, however, a person can appear as completely different from the one he or she can be in "non-digital" life of physical presence. We have seen an example of this in the opening vignette in this chapter where three individuals have been deliberately given their new, refined reputations.

Good reputation can be built or ruined instantly by a single Instagram post or a Tweet. But usually, a reputation takes some time to construct and maintain. It is true that if someone has earned a bad online reputation, they can easily create new accounts. However, new accounts on most sites, such as eBay or Amazon, are increasingly distrusted: People tend to judge others based on their long history of digital footprints.

Our digital footprints reflect not only our postings. Like in real life, most adults in the United States have a credit score, which is a numerical expression based on a level analysis of a person's credit files and financial records, to represent the credit capacity and risk of an individual. A long record of financial solvency indicates a "good" reputation. Similarly, a seller on *eBay* has generally a high reputation if they have a high feedback score and a high percentage of positive feedback shown for an extended period. The *Uber* platform allows drivers and riders to give each other ratings based on their trip experience. A driver rating is an average of the last 500 ratings from riders.

The Troll

Not long ago, while making a dinner reservation in a Stockholm restaurant, my colleague decided to go by a different name. He went by the name *Olaf*, the first name that popped in his mind when he was on the phone with a scheduler. "Why not?", he responded to his friends, who were slightly surprised about him giving a fake name. "Why couldn't I use a bogus name? Nobody is harmed!" In similar situations, like at department stores, when a clerk asks for our phone, some people deliberately give wrong information about themselves. Among several reasons for doing this (except deliberate fraud, of course) is people's concern for their privacy, which we already discussed. Online, browsers' private and incognito windows can somehow provide a measure of privacy for us by preventing your cookies and browsing history from being saved. Again, this is done to prevent potential harm.

Yet some individuals pursue different goals by hiding their online identity. One of them is "trolling." An **Internet troll** is someone who enters an online discussion or posts comments almost exclusively to upset the discussants, disrupt the conversation, or achieve other destructive goals while remaining anonymous. Trolls deliberately protect their privacy! Some trolls seek profit through their fraudulent actions: They purposely seek other people's vulnerabilities to commit financial or other type of fraud online. Others are employed by private companies, politicians, or government agencies. Such trolls create fake accounts and act according to a plan to either weaken a political opponent, promote a candidate or a political idea, or provoke confusion among audiences (Buckels, 2019). Psychologists are interested in a different kind of Internet troll. For psychologists studying online interactions, **trolling** is a pattern of repetitive behavior in which a person purposefully provokes, angers, humiliates, or upsets people online. Financial gain or material rewards are typically not essential in this type of trolling.

Are modern trolls different from the individuals who were engaged in such activities in the past? One can easily suggest that today trolls are like those mythological creatures from Scandinavian folklore: They appear ugly and nasty to humans. Other critics refer to "bad" or "evil" clowns" known in national folklore or from popular films. Remember Joker, an infamous supervillain from several Hollywood blockbusters about *Batman*? Evil clowns tend to hide their identity and may or may not dress up as traditional clowns. However, their major goal is not to appear in public to tease and exploit other people's perceived shortcomings to notice them, exaggerate them, and—most importantly—to offend people and to gain a reaction from them (Radford, 2016). Traditional clowns, those who appear in variety shows and in circus performances, are supposed to exaggerate and lie. But their main task is to entertain. On the contrary, evil clowns mostly destroy, insult, and offend. A few studies have shown similar personality characteristics attributed to evil clowns and Internet trolls (Buckels et al., 2014).

Pranksters and tricksters, as researchers show, existed in all cultures and throughout history (Hyde, 1998). Although many individual characteristics of people who are prone to insulting others tend to show little variation across cultures and times, it is quite plausible that today's trolling within the Digital Domain is different from seemingly similar patterns of behavior in the past. Clowns and Scaramouches hundreds of years ago were actors who entertained people for money. Internet trolls today disrupt and scorn mostly for their own enjoyment or for gratification of other desires. Researchers identified at

Public Domain

PHOTO 13.4 *Aggravation* by Briton Rivière (1896). Researchers suggest that many online trolls tend to perceive themselves as "bad clowns" disturbing their targets from relative safety of their anonymity and perceived safety.

least two personal factors such as sadistic pleasure and harm rationalization that can explain some individual's motivation behind trolling (Buckles et al., 2019).

If there is no identifiable financial reward for being engaged in trolling, then it is logical to assume that trolls tend to fulfill certain cravings or desires that they could not achieve in their daily world of interpersonal conversations and interactions. Quite often, trolling allows already existing behavioral and emotional patterns to continue. Studies have shown that people who enjoy trolling online tend to also enjoy hurting other people in everyday life, therefore corroborating a persistent pattern of sadism (Buckles, 2019). Trolls tend to dislike successful people. They are most likely to be angry, antisocial, narcissistic, and expressing little remorse. They tend to have a high expectation of themselves and enjoy what they consider "power" (which, in their cases, is their ability to disrupt conversations and cause harm to others with their words). A study in Australia (Sest & March, 2017) showed that those who identified themselves as "trolls" scored differently than others on several measures of personality traits. Among them were psychopathy, empathy, and sadistic tendencies. Psychopathy, among other features, as you remember, stands for a lack of care for others' feelings. The lack of empathy means that the person does not internalize the emotional experience of others. Sadistic tendencies stand for the desire to inflict pain, suffering, or humiliation on others. Trolls vent their negative emotions and antisocial impulses on strangers because they can remain anonymous and unpunished. The Digital Domain allows more people to exercise their behaviors associated with katagelasticism.

Some trolls too are likely to expose patterns of **katagelasticism**, a psychological condition in which a person excessively enjoys laughing at others. People who are prone to katagelasticism actively seek and establish situations in which they can make fools of others and joke at their actions, appearance, and thoughts (Andjelovic et al., 2019). People with tendencies toward katagelasticism were found to be mostly younger males, with higher scores related to cynicism, which is a general and scornful distrust in people's motives, and vengefulness, a strong desire to retaliate against someone for something they did to you (Ruch et al., 2013).

Trolls openly admit to receiving pleasure from trolling. Moreover, of all the personality variables, it was everyday sadism—the tendency to enjoy hurting other people—that was the best predictor of trolling. In other words, people who enjoy trolling online tend to also enjoy hurting others in everyday life. These studies support a commonsense assumption that online trolling is often motivated by sadistic enjoyment. The results also hint at the rationalization process, which is a form of moral disengagement that allows people to hurt others without experiencing guilt. Of course, the relative anonymity of the Internet contributes to trolling. By downplaying the consequences of their actions, trolling often becomes a fun game that is often perceived as not really hurting anyone. Even if someone does get hurt, trolls can minimize their guilt, if admit it at all (Buckles et al., 2019).

Social media would immediately become far less toxic if the major platforms required basic identity verification before anyone could open an account—or at least an account type that allowed the owner to reach large audiences (Haidt & Rose-Stockwell, 2019).

SELF-REFLECTION

Let's punish trolls! Imagine the following hypothetical scenario. Researchers from Stanford University—in cooperation with Meta, X/Twitter, Google, and several other companies—will conduct a 1-year study that examines posting patterns and personality profiles of 100 million people around the globe. Inspired by studies of trolling conducted a decade earlier, psychologists and computer scientists conducting this study will be able, using AI, to identify trolls' most significant and stable personality traits by looking at their postings, comments, and pictures over the course of just 1 week. Researchers will also examine billions of private messages (assuring that people's privacy will be protected) and incorporate their findings into the main study's results. As a result of this project, all users of major social networks will be able to install an app called *PersonApp* that will instantly reveal the personality profiles of every person who is communicating with them via these social networks. Users will have their most salient personality traits appear as multicolored emojis next to their online profiles.

Critics say that *PersonApp* will be a significant violation of personal privacy. Imagine that you are posting a message and your personality features (for example, kind, disorganized, open to experience, overanxious, or masculine) are immediately revealed to other users. Proponents, however, insist that the presence of *PersonApp* will encourage millions of people to communicate in a more responsible, kind, and considerate way.

According to one of the principal investigators of this [hypothetical] study, "This feature will essentially reduce and even eliminate trolling on the web. Who wants to appear online as a mean and angry person?" Another researcher added, "In real life, most of us smile and say hello to each other. Why should this be different online?"

Questions

Do you think this type of study with this type of results is (a) very likely, (b) somewhat likely, or (c) very much unlikely to take place in 2026?

Would you support the idea that users of social networks should have several emojis attached to their profiles based on the scientific analysis of these users' postings?

If you are using these emojis, will it somehow change your online behavior? Will it make you at least "kinder"?

In real life, you normally don't want to talk to people who are visibly angry or agitated. Why would you do this online? This should be different online?"

CHECK AND APPLY YOUR KNOWLEDGE

1. Explain digital reputation.
2. In your opinion, are modern online trolls different from the individuals who were engaged in such activities in the past?
3. Explain katagelasticism and why it has an important role in today's digital world of social networks.

APPLYING THE DIGITAL DOMAIN

Digital Defenses: Managing Privacy and Reputation

How much does the world need to know about you? How much do your friends on social networks have to know about what you are up to today? Of course, certain information about us becomes public no matter if we like this disclosure or not: This information is either legally required or allowed. For example, in the United States, most records kept by any government agency are treated as public. Thus, information about our legal problems, including traffic violations, usually is available to anyone who wants to see it. Prices of apartments and homes in which we live, as well as salaries of most state and federal employees are available online, too. Besides having our names attached to public records, we leave numerous digital footprints. However, we still can take better care of our individual privacy and personal reputation.

Psychological research into managing privacy and reputation in the digital age is only developing (De Ridder, 2021). Some suggest that privacy protection can be compared to actual physical barriers or fences that protect our privacy in the physical world (Fontaine & Frederick,

2021). Other practitioners come up with a list of general suggestions for people who care about their reputation about what to do and what not to do online (Nierman, 2021). Several behavioral and cognitive habits are worth considering and practicing. Let's discuss some of them.

Taking a pause. Heated debates or even small confrontations can create certain conditions when people do not control their emotions and thus say inappropriate things. In the world of verbal communications, people often regret the words they said to other people. In the world of online communications, such words stay. Like in psychological exercises about anger control, when the psychologists suggests the client to "count to 10" before saying or doing something under the influence of anger (Osgood & Muraven, 2016), a fine online habit can be "taking a pause" before sending or posting something under the influence of an emotion. A few extra seconds or even minutes would allow you to ask a few questions. For example: Do I have a good reason for posting it, or am I acting on impulse? What is the purpose of my posting, what do I want to convey in it? Is it possible that I will later regret posting this?

Like a good habit, pause for a minute before sending an email or writing a comment online; consider possible consequences, because once you release your words or images, you cannot erase them in many cases. Adding some friction back in has been shown to improve the quality of content of our messages and postings (Haidt & Rose-Stockwell, 2019).

Self-reflecting. As we have already discussed in this chapter, most people's privacy has diminished due to global proliferation of digital footprints. However, certain steps can be taken to protect your privacy. There is a view that an individual's behavior related to digital defenses can be seen as—in the physical world—actual physical or behavioral barriers or fences (Fontaine & Frederick, 2021). This analogy can be useful. Find a moment to think how high this imaginary wall should be between you and the curious world. How much does the world need to know about your hobbies, pet peeves, interests, or planned travels? What is good for your reputation and what is not? The answer of course is based on personal preferences, legal rules, and a historic cultural perspective. Research is certainly needed. Yet some interesting results have emerged. A study in Belgium showed that young people participating in the study overwhelmingly agreed that practices such as sexting, sharing nude pictures of self, glorifying being a "stripper," glorifying teen pregnancy, having a "romantic sponsor," and participating in reality-TV shows such as *Temptation Island* are all not good for a person's reputation (De Ridder, 2021).

Self-reflecting is not about shutting down your communications; it is about limiting them. It is about protecting your identity and privacy (Haidt & Rose-Stockwell, 2019). Some people start employing "data pollution" to flood their digital records with random activities, thus frustrating attempts to draw out a consistent pattern in their Internet browsing history that is regularly collected by many apps, including our location, contacts, buying patterns, and travel habits (Fontaine & Frederick, 2021).

Thinking about others. In a free society, people should be free to express themselves within the limits of the law. Freedom of expression also means freedom of judgment: Other people have a right to form and express an opinion about us and share it with others. However, there is a limit on this right: Most of us do not like rudeness and bullying. An empirical study in Belgium showed there is a shared agreement among its participants that they overwhelmingly condemned online trolling and shaming, which is often labeled as "reputation warfare" (De Ridder, 2021). In our communications, unless we carefully limit the number of people who have access to our tweets, comments, and pics, our audience includes people from many different backgrounds. Take humor, for example. Treat carefully and cautiously when it comes to what you think is funny. What appears amusing for you now, may appear offensive to another person due to this person's cultural background and personal experience (Nierman, 2021). People of different ages and social groups sometimes define funny things differently. Our intention not to offend others does not mean that other people will not be offended. Therefore, let's remain on the side of thoughtfulness.

Thinking about your career. Employers increasingly often study online reputations of job applicants to help with the employers' hiring choices. By checking a candidate's social networking profiles, employers gain insight into a candidate's personality traits and suitability for a job. Before posting a photo of yourself (again, take a pause!), imagine this pic being viewed in the future by a hiring committee or a graduate admissions office. Remember, you have the right to post a picture, but other people have the right to pass a judgment—often silent—about you. Showing yourself online in an embarrassing situation may entertain a few of your friends today, but tomorrow there will be different judges, colleagues, and supervisors for whom our, "Sorry, I didn't think it over before posting" is not a good answer.

Digital Footprints and Social Behavior

In China, the *Social Credit System* is a massive attempt to create and maintain a unified digital record system for individuals and businesses to be traced and evaluated for their trustworthiness and "good behavior" (Stevenson & Mozur, 2019). How does this system work? For example, for playing loud music in public places, jaywalking or speeding, failing to appear after making a restaurant reservation, smoking outside designated places—for these and other infractions, your social score is lowered, and the reputation goes down. If you volunteer in community services, donate blood, or regularly visit your elderly parents, your score goes up. The score also goes up if a person makes a formal public apology for offending another person or if an individual praises the government's work in social media (Ahmed, 2019). Most importantly, reputation scores can affect many aspects of an individual's life: their ability to travel by air, waiting time for a medical appointment, the ability to attend college, or to be promoted at work. Moreover, the digital score should reveal to the public every person's "social value" including the list of rewards. For example, if you are looking for a spouse online using the help of a matchmaking service, you should publish your social score. The higher your "social value" the more candidates would appear.

Many people in China support a further idea of revealing every person's digital reputation by posting everyone's social record online. This measure, as it is argued, would allow the public to identify *laolai* or "discredited individuals," those who cheat on taxes, shoplift, constantly jaywalk, and so on. The goal of such "outing" is to be shaming people into changing their behavior (Ahmed, 2019). Critics, obviously, see this system as intrusive, inhumane, and unjust. First, the system violates people's privacy. Second, the system becomes a means to control virtually every facet of human life. Third, the system can empower government bureaucrats on all levels, who would treat other individuals as high, medium, and low scores (Kostka, 2019). The digital score thus becomes under the Social Credit System an important personality feature, a measure of an individual's identity.

What is your personal view of such surveillance and digital score systems? In a way, in democratic societies, we know most of us are constantly evaluated: Take for example, our grade point averages and credit scores, these are measures to assess people's credit risks. The resemblance with a radical Behaviorist model from the early 20th century is obvious (see the chapter on Behavioral Learning Tradition): If you behave properly, you should get your social benefits; if you slip up, then go back to the end of the line. Psychologists, supporters of this system of actions and rewards, praised it as a future social model of an ideal society that is stable, predictable, manageable, and where most people practice moral behavior. Trained psychologists would replace government officials and manage society by the system of reward and punishment.

True, that in the age of street cameras, tags, and massive digital footprints there always will be a temptation from the powerful to use all this information to increase their power and influence in all spheres of human life. Yet as a hundred years ago, when the ideas of radical behaviorism were soundly rejected, there is hope that people these days would find better and more dignified ways in which their digital footprints are used.

Digital Companionship

Despite all the super-connectivity of the modern world, social and psychological isolation remains a serious challenge. Demographics play a role here. Falling fertility rates, and as a result, smaller families in most countries in the 21st century, have left increasing numbers of older people living alone. Changing socioeconomic and cultural conditions is another factor: Many among the young believe they no longer need to live with their aging parents, who can afford to live alone. Pandemics and mandatory social isolation can play a role, too. Research shows that social isolation adds nearly 7 billion dollars a year to the total cost of Medicare (a federal health insurance program), in the United States, in part because people who live alone show up to the hospital sicker and tend to stay longer (Engelhart, 2021). One of the results of prolonged social isolation is loneliness.

Loneliness intervention is not a new subject in clinical and developmental psychology. Yet the digital world is creating a new kind of therapeutic intervention: digital companionship. This is different from digital assistantship provided by Google, Siri, Alexa, and similar devices to help us with quick information, shortcuts, and tips. **Digital companionship** is the use of digital technologies to assist an individual in numeral tasks as well as provide a personalized form of emotional support and companionship. One of the goals of digital companionship is providing behavioral and cognitive assistance plus emotional comfort to people who need it.

There is psychological research on the use of computer technologies, gadgets, and toys in helping children and adults cope with symptoms of Autism Spectrum Disorder (Giansanti, 2021). A study found that elderly users who interacted with pets for 60 days reported greater optimism and "sense of purpose," and were sometimes less lonely. The use of digital companionship among the lonely—most of whom are the elderly—is a relatively new line of research into therapeutic methods and psychological support (Intuition Robotics, 2020).

Digital companionship is linked to the use of so-called *social robots* or robots-companions, which are collaborative devices specialized in social interaction. They can be physical devices looking like toys of various shapes (like animals, robots, or funny creatures) or just apps. They offer customizable interaction that responds to the user's personality and learn from such interactions. Recent advances in AI have made conversational and interactive technology better and less expensive than a few years ago. Robots-companions now can interact more fluidly and with more sophistication. They communicate via smartphones or special audio-visual devices such as headsets. Some users can scan pictures of another person, which are then used to create an AI partner resembling that individual. Further, some internal properties of a social robot can be created: In fact, it can acquire a specific "digital personality" type, which can be changed in the future, if the user wants it. It can be empathetic, enigmatic, or confident. They can remind the user about lunch, medications to be taken, and routine house chores. But this is not all that they can do. Social robots can do poetry reading, discuss latest news, and keep attention to things relevant to the user. Some robots can track the progression of dementia in elderly clients by monitoring changes in vocal patterns in conversations (Engelhart, 2021). As it is mentioned earlier, many of these robots look like small monitors. Other can resemble kitchen lamps, small gadgets, or even small animals. Some owners decorate these devices with funny eyes, smileys, and eyelashes—to make the robots look more human.

Digital companions do not simply wait around to carry out the user's commands. They can use various sensory inputs to be proactive, to check if the person needs assistance, if this individual is in a good mood to chat, and if this is the case, to figure out the suitable topic for a conversation. When digital assistants use the same approach to every user, companions learn how to personalize their interactions and may use creativity and humor, when necessary. Table 13.2 displays a list of differences between digital assistants and digital companions.

iStockphoto.com/demaerre

PHOTO 13.5 Do you think that digital companions and their modified versions will soon help many people of all ages to evade loneliness or boredom?

TABLE 13.2 ■ Several Comparisons Between Digital Assistants and Companions	
Digital Assistants	**Digital Companions**
Mostly reactive	Reactive and proactive
Use short exchanges with the user	Use interactive exchanges with the user
Tend not to display a distinct personality	Tend to display features of a personality
Tend to provide uniform experience for all users	Tend to provide varied and personalized experience for the user
Incorporate some experience about the user	Incorporate significant and evolving experience about the user
Do not incorporate contexts into responses and suggestions to the user	Incorporate contexts into responses and suggestions to the user

Adopted from: (Intuition Robotics, 2020).

Social robots are expected to be instruments of competence, companionship, and independence. They can play a therapeutic role. How successful are they so far? Is digital companionship effective and in which areas? Long-term studies are planned or already underway. However, some nursing homes and organizations have started studying the effects of the use of social robots in alleviating loneliness and easing negative emotions (Sheridan, 2020). Among preliminary results, several are encouraging. Social robots, for example, can assist in certain motor activities and act as interactive timekeepers for the elderly. Digital companions serve as cognitive stimulators by offering interactive games, trivia, or maintaining a conversation (Giansanti, 2021). Not long ago, New York State's Office for the Aging launched an experimental project, distributing a kind of therapeutic robot to 60 state residents and then tracking these people's self-assessments over time. Researchers found that 70% of participants felt less lonely after 1 year of digital companionship (Engelhart, 2021).

In history, every new communication technology brings a range of unknown effects, and over time, ways are found to improve the balance between positive and negative consequences (Haidt & Rose-Stockwell, 2019).

CHECK AND APPLY YOUR KNOWLEDGE

1. Why is "taking a pause" important in our digital communications?
2. What is your opinion of the Digital Credit System? Should it be implemented in your country?
3. What are the differences between digital companions and digital assistants?

SUMMARY

- The term digital, according to linguists, broadly refers to the use of computer technology, especially the Internet. The meaning of the word is constantly evolving.

- Digital footprints refer to digital markings that individuals leave online. These are our names, pictures, opinion, tweets, "likes," purchases, and many more that are stored on the web.

- At least four views or approaches about the digital domain can be identified. In these contexts, the digital domain can be discussed, for convenience, as either or mostly as a *reflector*, an *enhancer*, a *transformer*, or a *separator* of the individual's personality.

- Personality grandstanding refers to the tendency of individuals to present themselves in an exaggerated, flamboyant way with an intention to impress. Personality lensing that stands for change—both small and substantial—in the ways we feel, think, and act when functioning online, compared to how we function in the physical or social world.

- For psychologists, privacy is the ability of individuals to withdraw themselves from the presence of other people or remove this information from public knowledge. Digital technologies fundamentally limit our privacy. Many cultural norms related to privacy were changing throughout history along with cultural, ethical, and legal barriers that protected privacy.

- Individual privacy has diminished significantly during the Internet age, and the consequences of this decline should significantly affect behavior of billions.

- Invasion of privacy is an attack on or weakening of the right of individuals to keep some personal information private.

- Reputation is concerned with how other people perceive, evaluate, and then judge an individual. Reputation is about what other people think of us based on information that is available to them including, of course, digital footprints. This act of judgment is based on social standards, which can be different in unlike historical or cultural settings.

- At least two general types of reputation can be identified: *positive reputation* (a measure of how others like you and what you do) and *negative reputation* (a measure of how others dislike you). Digital reputation is a summary outcome of the evaluation of an individual's digital footprints.

- An Internet troll is someone who enters an online discussion or posts comments almost exclusively to upset the discussants, disrupt the conversation, or achieve other destructive goals while remaining anonymous. For psychologists studying online interactions, trolling is a pattern of repetitive behavior in which a person purposefully provokes, angers, humiliates, or upsets people online.

- Some trolls are likely to expose patterns of katagelasticism, a psychological condition in which a person excessively enjoys laughing at others. People who are prone to katagelasticism actively seek and establish situations in which they can make fools of others, joke at their actions, appearance, and thoughts.

- Psychological research into managing privacy and reputation in the digital age is only developing. Several behavioral and cognitive habits are worth considering and practicing, such as, taking a pause, thinking of others, thinking about own career, or self-reflecting.

- Some governments are tempted to use people's digital footprints to strengthen these governments' political control over individuals.

- Loneliness intervention is not a new subject in clinical and developmental psychology. Yet the digital world is creating a new kind of therapeutic intervention: digital companionship, or the use of digital technologies to assist an individual in numeral tasks as well as provide a personalized form of emotional support and companionship.

VISUAL REVIEW

Visual Review. Chapter 13. The Digital Domain

1. MAIN IDEAS

The word *digital* broadly refers to the use of computer technology, especially the Internet	Digital footprints are digital markings individual leave online, intentionally or not	Digital platforms allow people to create accessible and "separate", digital identity for themselves

2. STUDYING THE DIGITAL DOMAIN

The Digital Domain can be discussed as either or mostly as a *reflector*, an *enhancer*, a *transformer*, or a *separator*

Privacy refers to our ability and right to select knowledge that we wish not to share with others.

Reputation is what other people know about us and how they evaluate this information

Trolling refers to a deliberate act to violate the privacy of others and damage their reputation.

3. APPLYING THE DIGITAL DOMAIN

Digital (personal) defenses	Digital footprints and social behavior	Digital companionship

KEY TERMS

artificial intelligence

bank account theory

digital

digital companionship

digital divide

digital reputation

digital separation

footprint accessibility

footprints

halo effect theory

identity theft

Internet troll

invasion of privacy

katagelasticism

mindclones

personality grandstanding

personality lensing

privacy

reputation

trolling

EVALUATING WHAT YOU KNOW

What is the focus of the digital domain?

Describe the four functions or realities of the digital domain as a reflector, an enhancer, a transformer, or a separator of the individual's personality.

How important is your digital reputation in your personal life and professional career?

Explain katagelasticism and its role in online trolling.

Do you support the idea that our government, for the sake of social stability, should have access to all citizens' digital footprints?

What is the importance of digital companionship for people of advanced age?

A BRIDGE TO THE NEXT CHAPTER

The next and final chapter of this book is likely to be studied at the very end of the semester or quarter. A pessimist would say that the odds are very high that (1) many unforeseen circumstances have arisen in the past to make this class schedule extremely packed and that (2) our time will be absolutely, indisputably scarce to study this chapter. An optimist with certainly disagree. Let's read it!

CONCLUSION

14 PERSONALITY PSYCHOLOGY IN THE 2030S

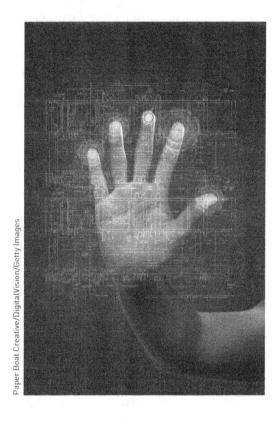

Paper Boat Creative/DigitalVision/Getty Images

In about 10 years from now, you will be conducting your own research into personality. Others will be reading and critically reviewing this research. Yet others will be applying it to various practical fields, including education, health care, counseling, business, conflict resolution, political campaigns, and many more. How will personality psychology evolve in the coming 10 years? On what type of research will personality psychologists focus? What will they discover, and where will they apply their findings? In the past, social scientists have not been very accurate in predicting social trends. In fact, they have been awful in this. Forecasting the future and what our society will look like is difficult for at least three reasons. First, there are too many variables that require researchers' attention and deep knowledge. Second, these variables tend to be too complex and interconnected in too many unpredictable ways. Third, there are even more variables that remain unknown to the researcher. Scientists can predict the movement of comets and space objects, and yet do you know what we are going to be doing exactly 2 years from now? How many people in 2018 could have predicted the COVID-19 outbreak? For these and other reasons, it is particularly difficult to forecast the specific research developments of psychology and personality psychology. That is why we only can humbly suggest something about the general direction of this research. At least three trends ought to emerge.

First, psychologists studying personality will receive major feedback from neuroscience. Studies of the brain and its functioning should be making almost revolutionary changes in science and in the ways we understand individual behavior, experience, and personality. Second, personality psychology will also receive a significant boost from cognitive psychology and computer science. And third, psychologists will make a quantum leap in applying their research to practice.

Let's suggest some hypothetical examples of these research trends. On these next pages, you will find several imaginary scenarios involving research into personality. There will be several cases based on studies conducted in the recent past or being conducted these days. Each case is then followed by hypothetical development about specific follow-up research that might be conducted about 10 years from now. As you read about the possible future developments, consider whether you agree or disagree and answer the questions that follow.

CASE 1: "HACKING" LIVING CELLS FOR A GOOD CAUSE

Scientists at MIT have conducted successful experiments that allow them to "hack" living cells and give them special programs to perform new tasks. In other words, cells are now able to directly receive new information and act accordingly. Biologists have used single-celled organisms in this way to produce drugs, biological sensors that include cells or antibodies, enzymes, and more (Nielsen et al., 2015; Nowogrodski, 2018). Scientists have put together a new programming language for various cells, including bacteria. This is a text-based language, like what computer scientists use to create software or a computer program. Cells, like students, learn in several steps, and each step involves the performance of a more complex task. First, they learn to act differently in various environmental conditions, such as in changing levels of oxygen. Then cells learn new tasks about carrying and delivering information. One of the goals of this research is to teach human cells to transport and then release cancer drugs upon encountering a tumor in the body or teach cells in plants to discharge natural insecticide to fight insects. In the future, researchers hope they will be able to find significant breakthroughs in the treatment of most diseases by creating special informational programs for the living cells. These programs are likely to replace many medications or be significantly more effective than most of them.

Fiction, Reality, or Something in Between? Possible Research 10 Years From Now: "Hacking" Living Cells to Change Personality Traits

Based on the series of studies initiated by MIT researchers, a team of behavioral psychologists and neuroscientists from several cooperating universities in the United States, India, and China are looking for a way to install special "educational codes" into the living cells of the human brain cells. First, the educational "cell software" needs to be completed. After several educational "sessions," the cells will then learn to create specific physiological conditions and change the function of several brain structures, such as the amygdala and the prefrontal cortex, so that the individual begins to respond differently to various environmental conditions. Cells continue to learn, and the changes in an individual's behavior and emotions become somewhat permanent.

To test their technique, the researchers conducted a series of preliminary experiments on anger management. The subjects who volunteer for these experiments (in China, they have been appointed by the government through the court system) had documented anger-related behavioral troubles in the past; some of them had problems with the law as the result of their anger and resulted violence. After several learning sessions involving the subjects' "hacked" brain cells, more than 57% of the subjects have demonstrated a significant reduction in the number of angry and violent reactions during 1 year of postexperimental, drone-monitored observations. Many of these individuals' personality traits have been affected as well. For example, about 60% of the subjects who displayed high scores on the measure of neuroticism showed significantly lower scores on this measure 1 year later, after the cell modification procedure. Researchers believe that in 3 years, they will be able to design special cell programs to reduce the number of angry responses in an individual by more than 75% and replace them with joyful responses. Will this be the end of anger as we know it?

Questions

- Do you think this type of study with these types of results is (a) very likely, (b) somewhat likely, or (c) very much unlikely to take place in 10 years?

- Assume this research has taken place. What ethical limitations do you see in these research applications?

- Would you personally support the idea that human beings be able to change their personality features and even traits at will via computerized methods of cell modification? What is wrong (if anything) with the idea that under the influence of the "hacked cells" most of us, if not all, would feel happier, less angry, and more optimistic then we felt yesterday?

CASE 2: UNDERSTANDING MULTIMORBIDITY

Do you want to live a long life? But what if your life expectancy is genetically programed? If our longevity is not completely determined by our genes, then what do you have to do to live as long as possible?

For many years, scientists studied individual cases of healthy men and women, especially those who remained healthy through old age. There were also several studies using very large and diverse samples. Scientists in the United Kingdom turned to a massive research database involving 1,200,000 people who were tracked and studied for years (Danesh, 2015). The researchers were interested in multimorbidity, which is the co-occurrence of two or more chronic medical conditions in one person (Glynn, 2009). They found a relatively simple formula for the unhealthiest lifestyle—specifically, it involves three things:

- little exercise,

- poor diet,

- and smoking.

The researchers' forecast was staggering. People who maintain these habits were likely to cut their life span by 23 years. It is estimated that around 80% of premature deaths could be prevented by keeping weight under control, exercising more, eating a healthy diet, and not smoking. Researchers did not suggest that medications could or should be abandoned. The main conclusion of this massive study was that people should learn about, agree on, and sustain a healthier lifestyle (Danesh, 2015). However, to change one's lifestyle may take a serious personality change. This is a daunting task.

Fiction, Reality, or Something in Between? Possible Research 10 Years From Now: Understanding Psychological Multimorbidity

Inspired by the multimorbidity study conducted by British doctors back in 2015, an international group of researchers (sponsored by the United Nations) from 11 universities have collected data from 59 countries in a variety of world regions over an extended period. The key idea of the research was to establish the most significant personality factors involved in multimorbidity. The researchers have formulated a hypothesis: If there is a particular lifestyle (described in the 2015 study) that negatively affects the individual's longevity, then there should be a particular personality trait or a combination of traits or other individual features that negatively affect the person's life expectancy. Other studies mentioned as risk factors reducing longevity include the following: sociodemographic and physical characteristics, self-rated health, quality of life, and loneliness (de Souza et al., 2021). Earlier studies also described healthy traits affecting longevity, such as conscientiousness, optimism, and social connectedness (Kern & Friedman, 2008). Yet most earlier studies were conducted on relatively small samples.

The new study is different. Online surveys were combined with face-to-face and Zoom interviews to collect a massive set of data. Using factor analysis and AI, researchers established several important personality and behavioral features related to longevity and that are multimorbid. Among them, three have turned out to be most significant: (1) high-level neuroticism, (2) high frequency of lying, and (3) low measures on the sense of humor (in particular, understanding sarcasm and irony). People who score high on neuroticism and lying and who scored very low on sense of humor displayed a great number of physical symptoms to suggest a reduction of their life expectancy up to 10 years. One of the study's applications will be discussed with educational ministries of all the countries, which citizens participated in the survey. A proposal will circulate about the establishment of a mandatory training program for schoolchildren on how to manage stress and anxiety, how to be honest and avoid lying in most circumstances, and how to better understand irony and sarcasm in interpersonal communications.

Questions

- Do you think this type of study with these types of results is (a) very likely, (b) somewhat likely, or (c) very much unlikely to take place in 10 years? Research online to see if similar studies of longevity factors have been conducted. What were their results?

- Suppose this research on multimorbidity of personality traits has taken place. What moral or legal limitations do you see in this research's applications? Would you personally support the idea that all schoolchildren should undergo special training to develop certain personality traits that could increase their longevity? What is wrong with that idea that some of us (maybe even most of us) would live longer if we changed our behavior because of special educational training?

CASE 3: HEIGHT, MIND, AND SELF-ESTEEM

In 2014, researchers at Oxford University in the United Kingdom used virtual reality technology to "reduce" the perceived height of female volunteers traveling on a computer-simulated subway train by 10 inches (25 cm). In a series of experiments, scientists found out that when people feel smaller than they really are, they are more frustrated, scared, and less trustful of others Feeling shorter than normal makes people think others are staring or talking about them. Reducing a person's perceived height also results in more negative views of the self (Freeman et al., 2014).

At about the same time, researchers at the Federal Centers for Disease Control in Atlanta, Georgia, studied "male discrepancy stress"—an unpleasant feeling of falling short of traditional masculine gender norms that emphasize physical strength and decisiveness (Reidy et al., 2015). The men who considered themselves less masculine than average and who experienced male discrepancy stress were nearly 3 times more likely to have committed violent assaults than those who didn't worry about such "male discrepancy." Both studies indicate a discrepancy between how we want to appear and the way we are (as seen by ourselves or others) can cause significant emotional and behavioral challenges and problems.

Fiction, Reality, or Something in Between? Possible Research 10 Years From Now: Matching Self-Esteem and Social Perception

Following years of research on self-perception and self-esteem, psychologists in Japan, with the cooperation of their friendly colleagues in Iran, Russia, and the United States, created a battery of tests to allow researchers to instantly measure not only major personality traits of individuals but also their undisclosed expectations about which traits and characteristics they would love to have or develop in themselves. Such tests involved online self-assessment questionnaires, as well as assessments based on brain imaging and several scanning techniques, allowing the instant detection of unconscious impulses, thoughts, and desires. This research provided some explanations regarding the function of defense mechanisms introduced by psychoanalysts in the 20th century. The results of these tests allowed the researchers to create a new model for an individual's personality, which took into consideration the discrepancy between a person's ideal self and real self. A 1-hour online interview with simultaneous brain scanning and instantaneous data analysis produced a detailed description of participants' individual traits, as well as their level of aspirations, propensity for envy and forgiveness, ability to love and be loved, their sexual orientation, and preferred gender role (with varying degrees of masculinity and femininity).

Eventually, this method will be available commercially. Not only will people who pay for the services be able to examine their individual profiles, but they also will be able to obtain a list of individuals (upon their agreement) with similar psychological profiles for matchmaking. This method will be free for parents on a limited basis (after they sign up for a corresponding online service) who want to test their children for their actual or potential personality conflicts and discrepancies.

Questions

- Do you think that type of a study with these types of results is (a) very likely, (b) somewhat likely, or (c) very much unlikely to take place in 10 years? Research online to see if similar studies have been conducted. What were their results?

- Would you personally want to study your own relational and unconscious discrepancies? Why or why not?

- What are the advantages and disadvantages of knowing about such discrepancies or problems?

SUMMING UP

In the classic 1989 movie *Dead Poets Society*, the late actor Robin Williams played an eccentric teacher, Mr. Keating, at an elite, private high school. At one point in the movie, Mr. Keating angrily declared, "No one can measure poetry!" He lashed out at a textbook's author, whose method quantified the creative verses of the poet's mind. Mr. Keating touched upon a centuries-old scientific debate about whether it is proper to use gadgets, numbers, and formulas to measure the complexity of human experience and behavior. Of course, scientists do not use yardsticks and barometers to study personality, but to better understand human beings, we need to have some reliable ways to understand, assess, and then critically evaluate individual personalities.

Today, the argument is not *if* we can scientifically examine and measure personality features—we know that we *can* do it better than yesterday. A more intriguing question is whether we can correctly explain the results of these research procedures. Next, can we interpret scientific knowledge in the most unbiased way? And then, how can we as psychologists use this knowledge to effectively help people develop particular personality traits, feel happier, recover from a mental malady, or avoid a potentially harmful relationship? Will we be able to, for example, design a questionnaire and a corresponding brain imaging technique to predict a person's successful professional career or a happy marriage? Or are we on the wrong path? Should understanding individual personalities involve something dramatically different than is done today? The psychological jury is still out on this.

GLOSSARY

16PF: The Sixteen Personality Factor Questionnaire was developed by Raymond Cattell.

Absentmindedness: In behavioral terms, absentmindedness can be called lack of practical skills, common sense, or, simply, attention.

Academic traditions: These traditions bring together scholars that share similar views on a particular scientific approach, subject, or method.

Accommodation: In Piaget's system, accommodation is modifying one's mental structures to fit the new demands of the environment.

Acculturation: The individual's process of coping with the new cultural conditions is acculturation.

Acculturative stress: Sometimes called *culture shock*, acculturative stress is a distressful psychological reaction to an unfamiliar cultural environment.

Adjustment: Relatively significant changes in an individual's behavior and experiences in response to external and internal challenges are known as adjustment.

Adjustment disorder: Someone unable to cope with a major life stressor experiences a cluster of symptoms associated with significant distress and is diagnosed with adjustment disorder.

Agility of the nervous system: The quickness of the activation of excitement or the quickness of change between inhibition and excitement.

Aircrib: Designed by Skinner to form good habits in children, an Aircrib is a thermostatically controlled crib with a safety-glass front and a stretched-canvas floor.

Alpha males: They are the strongest and most aggressive males and are able to reproduce better than other, weaker males.

Amygdala: The amygdala is the almond-shaped part of the brain crucial for processing emotions and is also apparently correlated with violent traits.

Analysis: Analysis occurs with the breaking of something complex into smaller parts to understand their essential features and relations.

Analytical psychology: Jung used the term *analytical psychology* to distinguish his views from Freud's.

Androcentrism: Placing males or the masculine point of view at the center of a theory or narrative is androcentrism.

Androgyny: A combination and a coexistence of both male and female behavioral characteristics, features, and reflections is known as androgyny.

Anthropomorphism: Anthropomorphism is portraying animal behavior in human terms.

Anxious avoidance: Behavior that involves a person who dodges thinking about the stressor and refuses dealing with it in all situations and by most means.

Appraisal-focused strategies: Appraisal-focused strategies are methods that center on the way we see the problem (or a particular life development), its causes, its impact on us, and the expected outcome of our coping behavior.

Approaching: Some patients use approaching, or type of coping that refers to deliberate attempts at changing self as well as the sources of stress.

Archetypes: According to Jung, archetypes are the content of the collective unconscious that consist of images of the primordial (elemental, ancient) character. These archetypes manifest in three universal ways: dreams, fantasies, and delusions.

Art: Art is the expression of human imagination through creativity.

Artificial intelligence (AI): Artificial intelligence, or AI, is the study and design of intelligent machines.

Assimilation: In Piaget's system, assimilation is adopting operations with new objects into old mind patterns.

Atavism: Atavism is the reversion of behavior to some earlier developmental stages.

Attitudes: The cognitive representations and evaluations of various features of the social and physical world are present in attitudes.

Attribution: The process by which individuals explain the causes of behavior and events.

Authoritarian personality: An authoritarian personality is exhibited in a complex pattern of behavior and thought based on the individual's faithful acceptance of the power of authority, order, and subordination.

Autogenic training (AT): Autogenic training, or AT, is a self-administered technique for physical and emotional relaxation.

Autotelic personality: Autotelic describes the personality of a person who tends to be engaged in activities that are naturally rewarding and not necessarily associated with material goals such as money, fame, or high social status (*auto* in Greek means "self" and *telos* means "goal").

Avoiding: Keeping oneself away from addressing a challenge or a stressor is also called avoiding.

B-values: Examples of "being-values," or B-values, are truthfulness, goodness, beauty, wholeness, justice, and meaningfulness.

Balance of the nervous system: The equilibrium between excitement and inhibition within the nervous system is known as the balance of the nervous system.

Bank account theory: The theory referring to reputation, according to which most events that improve or damage an individual's reputation can be compared to bank deposits and withdrawals. This is how people build their "reputational capital."

Behavioral economics: The study of the effects of individual factors on personal economic decisions is behavioral economics.

Behaviorism: The rich and diverse interdisciplinary tradition that focuses on observable behavior is called behaviorism.

Big Five: The Big Five personality theory states that individual traits are likely to fall into these five categories: openness, conscientiousness, extraversion, agreeableness, and neuroticism.

Biphobia: The aversion toward bisexuality and bisexual people as a social group or as individuals is biphobia.

Burnout: Often a work-related term, *burnout* is a state of a significant exhaustion and disappointment brought about by a devotion to an activity that failed to produce the expected result or reward.

Catastrophic thinking: The stable tendency to overestimate the probability of very negative outcomes is catastrophic thinking.

Categorization: The process of categorization entails a variety of mental shortcuts, or heuristics, that tend to reduce complex and time-consuming tasks of describing and analyzing to seemingly more simple, manageable, practical, and efficient labeling strategies.

Censorship: Censorship is practicing the dissemination or restriction of what is deemed "appropriate" or "inappropriate" knowledge.

Central: Central personality features tend to be somewhat wide-ranging and present—to various degrees—in most people, most of the time.

Class consciousness: Members of social classes possess a set of core beliefs and perceptions about their life and the world around them based on their position in society.

Client-centered therapy: In Rogers's system, client-centered therapy is a therapeutic method in which therapists show their clients genuineness, empathy, and unconditional positive regard and create a supportive, non judgmental environment that encourages clients to think about their own problems, discuss them, prepare a course of action, and reach their full potential.

Clinical domain: In studies of personality, the clinical domain involves approaches to personality from the position of abnormality, illness, and health care.

Clinical–pathological method: Using the clinical–pathological method, clinical observations of a patient's abnormal symptoms are compared with reliable data of brain pathology, most likely obtained during an autopsy.

Clinical psychologists: Researchers and practitioners who integrate scientific knowledge for the purpose of understanding, preventing, and relieving psychological problems and promote subjective well-being and personal development.

Clinicians: Health care practitioners who work as primary caregivers of the patient are clinicians.

Cognitive adaptation theory: The cognitive adaptation theory is rooted in a set of ideas suggesting that adjustment depends on personal ability to sustain and modify positive illusions.

Cognitive dissonance: Individuals experience the unpleasant psychological state known as cognitive dissonance when they perform an action that is contradictory to their beliefs and ideas or when they are confronted by new information that conflicts with their beliefs or ideas.

Cognitive map: In Tolman's system, a cognitive map results from the internal processing by which individuals code, store, recall, and decode information about particular elements of their experience.

Cognitive neuroscience: The study of cognitive neuroscience examines the brain mechanisms that support the individual's mental functions and subsequent behaviors.

Cognitive revolution: The cognitive revolution refers to the gradual yet significant shift of focus within university psychology from being primarily behavioral (studying actions) to being increasingly cognitive (studying the work of the mind).

Cognitive science: The field of cognitive science includes cognitive neuroscience, computer science, philosophy, and linguistics, among others.

Collaborative empiricism: When a therapist and a client engage in collaborative empiricism, they form a therapeutic alliance in which they become coinvestigators and together examine the evidence to accept, support, reevaluate, or reject the client's thoughts, assumptions, intentions, and beliefs.

Collective unconscious: In Jung's theory, the collective unconscious is an impersonal layer in the human psyche that is different from the individual unconscious, as well as inherited and shared with other members of the species.

Collectivism: Collectivism is complex behavior based on concerns for other individuals and care for shared traditions and values.

Comorbidity: The presence of one or several additional disorders in an individual.

Compensation: In Adler's vocabulary, compensation refers to attempts to overcome the discomfort and negative experiences caused by a person's feelings of inferiority.

Conditioned reflexes: In Pavlov's theory, conditioned reflexes appear only under certain conditions.

Confident arrogance: The behavior and thinking to support people's belief that their ability to do something outweighs their actual ability to do it is called confident arrogance.

Consistency model: The consistency model states that most adults acquire (or learn) behaviors and develop stable traits early in life and tend not to change them later.

Constructs: In Kelly's system, constructs are stable assumptions that the individual develops about other people, the self, and the world in general.

Continuous variables: Continuous variables consist of a theoretically infinite number of points lying between two polar opposites.

Coping: The process of coping includes deliberate and conscious efforts to adjust to challenges, changing situations, and new conditions.

Correlation: A correlation is a statement about the relationship or association between two (or more) variables.

Critical thinking: The process of critical thinking is an active and systematic strategy for understanding knowledge on the basis of sound reasoning and evidence.

Cross-cultural psychology: The critical and comparative study of cultural effects on human psychology is cross-cultural psychology.

Culture: A large group of people share a culture, or a

set of beliefs, behaviors, and symbols that is usually communicated from one generation to the next.

Cynicism: The persistent distrust of other people's motives is shown in cynicism.

D-needs: "Deficit needs," or D-needs, are rooted in a scarcity of something, such as food or esteem from others.

Death wish: Often called a *death instinct* or *death drive*, a death wish is the repressed instinctual tendencies that lead toward destruction.

Defense mechanisms: The specific unconscious structures that enable individuals to avoid awareness of unpleasant, anxiety-arousing issues are called defense mechanisms.

Degeneration: Coined in the 1800s, the term *degeneration* refers to the generational regress in physical and psychological traits.

Deindividuation: After joining a group, an individual may go through deindividuation, or the weakening of the awareness of self.

Denial: In a psychological context, denial is the belief that something is untrue.

Determinism: Determinism is the view that psychological phenomena are causally determined by preceding events or some identifiable factors.

Developmental stages: The definite periods in an individual's life that are characterized by certain physical, psychological, behavioral, and social characteristics are called developmental stages.

Dichotomous variables: Dichotomous variables are phenomena that may be divided into two mutually exclusive or contradictory categories.

Differential diagnosis: A differential diagnosis is a method to identify and separate one disorder from others. This method also might identify possible alternatives to an initial diagnosis.

Digital: According to linguists, this term broadly refers to the use of computer technology, especially the Internet. The meaning of the word is evolving.

Digital companionship: This is the use of digital technologies to assist an individual in numeral tasks as well as provide a personalized form of emotional support and companionship.

Digital divide: The gap between the well-to-do and the poor in terms of their access to digital technology.

Digital reputation: This is a summary outcome of the evaluation of an individual's digital footprints.

Digital separation: The opportunity for individuals to create a "separate," digital identity for themselves on digital platforms.

Disabilities: Disabilities take the form of impairments (significant problems with physical or psychological functioning), activity limitations (inability to perform certain tasks), and participation restrictions (problems with particular social activities).

Dispositional optimism: An individual's general and stable belief that good things and positive outcomes will happen is displayed as dispositional optimism.

Dispositional pessimists: People who have the general and stable belief that bad things and negative outcomes will happen.

Distraction: Distraction is an avoidant coping strategy that diverts attention away from a stressor and toward other thoughts or behaviors that are unrelated to the stressor.

Dual-evaluation attitudes: Dual-evaluation attitudes contain an ambivalent emotional component.

Ego: In psychoanalysis, the ego is the component of the psyche that is guided by the reality principle and makes compromises between the id and the environment. Ego is the aspect of the human psyche that is conscious and mostly in touch with reality.

Emerging adulthood: One of Erikson's developmental stages, emerging adulthood extends from the late teens to the mid-20s (and even later) and is characterized by self-focused exploration of possibilities in work, relationships, interests, and values.

Emotion-focused strategies: Methods that center on the emotional meaning of the stressor, on distraction, and on relaxation are called emotion-focused strategies.

Enlightenment: Enlightenment is the view of validating knowledge and education based on science and reason rather than on religious dogmas.

Eros: In psychoanalysis, eros refers to all the tendencies that strive toward the integration of a living substance.

Ethnic disidentification: Detaching an individual's self from the ethnic group with which they've been previously or currently associated.

Ethnocentrism: Ethnocentrism is the view that supports judgment about other ethnic, national, and cultural groups and events from the observer's own ethnic, national, or cultural group's outlook.

Evolutionary psychology: The study of evolutionary psychology combines the knowledge of evolutionary science and psychology and explores the ways in which complex evolutionary factors affect human behavior, experience, and personality features.

Evolutionary science: The study of evolutionary science explains how large populations of organisms—plants, animals, and human beings—evolve over time.

Excessive consistency: An individual who exhibits excessive consistency has the condition of feeling and behaving in the same way regardless of changing circumstances and contexts, although a change in such behavior and feelings is generally expected.

Existential crisis: An existential crisis is a period in which an individual questions the very foundations of life and asks whether his or her life has any meaning, purpose, or value.

Existential psychology: An eclectic and diverse field of study, existential psychology embraces the idea of the exceptionality of human existence, the importance of individual free choice and independent will, and the necessity to consider each person as a unique entity.

Existential therapy: A method of psychotherapy based on the assumption that we, as human beings, make our own choices and should assume full responsibility for the outcomes of our behavior, experiences, and feelings.

Existentialism: An intellectual tradition, existentialism focuses on individual existence, its uniqueness, free will, and responsibility.

Experimental introspection: Experimental introspection is the method according to which the researcher had to carefully observe his or her own experience as a response to a physical stimulus delivered in laboratory surroundings.

External locus of control: An external locus of control is an individual tendency to explain events as influenced by uncontrollable external factors, such as powerful others, luck, the great complexity of the "outside" forces, and so on.

Extinction: The process of extinction is the act of abandoning a bad habit or decreasing a fearful reaction.

Extroversion (E): In Eysenck's system, extroversion (E) is characterized by talkativeness, positive emotions, and the need to seek external sources of stimulation. In Jung's view, extroversion is the attachment by a person with hysteric symptoms of his or her energy to other people.

Eysenck's E and N: Hans Eysenck studied two personality dimensions, extraversion (E) and neuroticism (N).

Factor analysis: Factor analysis is a method to deal with large numbers of observed variables that are thought to reflect a smaller number of underlying variables.

Fatalism: The view that humans are not in control of their lives because something or somebody else predetermines or "programs" them is called fatalism.

Femininity: Traditionally assigned to women, femininity is a general set of features correlated with beauty, emotionality, and nurture.

Feminism: Feminism is the view that women do not have equal rights and opportunities with men, and global changes are needed to achieve social justice.

Field theory: Lewin's approach to combining the main principles of Gestalt psychology and topology is called field theory. According to this approach, the acting and thinking individual is part of a dynamic field of interdependent forces.

Fixed-role therapy: In Kelly's system, fixed-role therapy is a method to change the individual's perception of self during a relatively short period.

Flexibility: Flexibility is a trait measured by the degree (scope and depth) or the extent to which a person can cope in novel ways.

Flow: Flow indicates a state of complete concentration and joyful immersion in the situation or activity.

Footprint accessibility: In terms of human activities on the web, the term stands for people's ability to become noticeable by just establishing their own profiles on the web.

Footprints: This term refers to physical markings that reflect human activities.

Four Noble Truths: In Buddhism, these are four major teachings about the origins of suffering and the path that leads to the end of suffering.

Functional inequality: Functional inequality refers to a concept according to which men and women have to perform a certain function in society. Men were expected to perform mostly instrumental functions, but society assigned expressive functions to women. These role differences have created different expectations about what women and men should do.

Fundamental attribution error: A common cognitive error based on the assumption the behavior of others is resulting predominantly from their personality, while our behavior moistly caused by the situation.

Gender: The complex set of behavioral, cultural, or psychological features associated with an individual's sex is a person's gender.

Gender consistency: The understanding that maleness or femaleness is fixed across situations, regardless of superficial changes in appearance or activities.

Gender identity: An individual's self-determination (or a complex self-reflection) as being male, female, intersex (between male and female), or neither is called gender identity.

Gender nonconforming: Individuals whose gender identity or gender expression does not conform to that typically associated with the sex to which they were assigned at birth are referred to as gender nonconforming.

Gender roles: Prescriptions and expectations assigned to genders on the female–male continuum constitute gender roles.

Gender studies: The term *gender studies* encompasses the multidisciplinary field dedicated to studying gender and a wide range of gender-related issues.

Gene: A gene is a segment or portion of the DNA (a complex molecule) that contains codes or "instructions" as biological information about how to build new protein structures.

Genetics: Genetics is the study of heredity through genetic transmission and genetic variations.

Genius: In Adler's vocabulary, a genius is the type of individual who overcomes the old inferiority problems and achieves success and happiness.

Genotypes: In Allport's theory, genotypes are individual forces that relate to how we keep information and use it to interact with the social and physical world around us.

Gestalt therapy: The Gestalt therapy uses ideas about the holistic nature of human experience, the disruption of its structure, and the emphasis on the actuality of the moment.

Habit disturbance: In Watson's system, the habit disturbance is the cause of mental illness.

Habit formation: The process by which new behaviors become automatic is habit formation.

Halo effect theory: According to this theory, human beings tend to "balance" their views about other people by holding onto a general expectation: A good person is supposed to do good things; a bad person is supposed to do bad things.

Hardiness: An individual's general ability to withstand difficult conditions is called hardiness.

Heterosexuality: Heterosexuality is an individual's romantic or sexual attraction to people of the opposite sex or gender. In Greek, *heteros* stands for "different" or "other."

Holistic: *Holistic* is a term that refers to the study of systems with multiple interconnected elements.

Holistic health movement: A multidisciplinary applied field, the holistic health movement is focused on the fundamental assumption that physical, mental, and spiritual factors contributing to an individual's illness are interconnected and equally important in treatment.

Homophobia: Homophobia is an aversion to homosexuality and gays, lesbians, bisexuals, and gender-variant individuals.

Homosexuality: Romantic or sexual attraction between people of the same sex or gender is homosexuality.

Hospice care: Hospice care refers to the complex medical and psychological system of help focusing on palliative and other humane principles of medical care.

Human development: The changes in physical, psychological, and social behavior that individuals experience across the life span, from conception to their last days, are called human development.

Humanist tradition: Also called humanism, the humanist tradition in science emphasizes the subjective side of the individual—the sense of freedom, beauty, creativity, and moral responsibility.

Humanistic psychologists: Humanistic psychologists encourage efforts to study the phenomena that distinguish human beings—love, happiness, and self-growth.

Humanistic psychology: Humanistic psychology refers to a tradition or a value orientation in psychology that holds a hopeful and constructive view of people and of their substantial capacity to be self-determining.

Humanities: In general terms, the field of humanities studies human culture.

Hypotheses: Expectations or proposed explanations for something that you study are called hypotheses.

Id: In psychoanalysis, the id is the component of the psyche that contains inborn biological drives (the death wish and the life instinct); the id seeks immediate gratification of its impulses.

Identity theft: The theft and misuse of personal information.

Idiographic: The idiographic approach is person-centered and focuses on many characteristics integrated in a unique person. It refers to specific features within an individual and uses various assessments and measurements.

Illness: An illness refers to any condition, or a functional abnormality or disturbance, of the body and mind (although it is debatable how exactly the mind can be "disturbed"), which impairs functioning.

Independent variable: In an experiment, an independent variable is a condition that is controlled—that is, it can be changed by you, an experimenter.

Individualism: Complex behavior based on concern for oneself and one's immediate family or primary group (as opposed to concern for other groups or society to which one belongs) is called individualism.

Individuation: In Jung's view, individuation is the process

of fulfilling an individual's potential by integrating opposites into a harmonious whole, by getting away from the aimlessness of life (a condition most of his patients were suffering from).

Inheritance: The term *inheritance* refers to how certain traits in living organisms were handed down from parents to offspring.

Inkblot test: An inkblock personality test involves the evaluation of a subject's response to ambiguous inkblots.

Instinct: A person's instinct is an inherent pattern or a complex behavior.

Inter-rater reliability: The inter-rater reliability is the degree of agreement among several professionals when they separately diagnose an individual.

Internal locus of control: A person's internal locus of control is the individual tendency to explain events as influenced by somewhat controllable, internal, relatively permanent characteristics such as skill, preparedness, will, and the like.

Internet troll: It is someone who enters an online discussion or posts comments almost exclusively to upset the discussants, disrupt the conversation, or achieve other destructive goals while remaining anonymous.

Intersex: The features that are between distinct male and female characteristics are referred to as intersex.

Introversion: In Jung's view, introversion happens when a person with schizophrenic symptoms attaches his or her energy back to self.

Invasion of privacy: An attack on or weakening of the right of individuals to keep some personal information private is an invasion of privacy.

Katagelasticism: A psychological condition in which a person excessively enjoys laughing at others. People who prone to katagelasticism actively seek and establish situations in which they can make fools of others, joke at their actions, appearance, and thoughts.

Knowledge: Information that has a purpose or use is also called knowledge.

Lack of control: Behavior that is supposed to be directed to achieve an important goal but distracted for some other unimportant activity instead.

L, K, and F validity scales: Special scales to help professionals identify psychological distortions that stem from the test-taking attitudes.

Latent vulnerability traits: Specific behavioral and psychological features that individuals may develop at any period in life that are harmful in the process of coping are latent vulnerability traits.

Laws of learning: In Thorndike's system, the laws of learning are the most essential principles on which learning is based.

Learned helplessness: When they experience uncontrollable, aversive events or a crisis, some people exhibit learned helplessness—become passive and unresponsive presumably because they have

learned during the crisis that there is nothing they can do to help themselves.

Learning curve: In Thorndike's theory, the learning curve is a concept that describes the dynamic of learning a habit; it also indicates the connection between learning and the time it takes to learn.

Least-effort principle: The least-effort principle is the tendency to minimize the number of cognitive operations to reach a goal.

Legal knowledge: Legal knowledge emerges in official, legal prescriptions by authorities (ranging from tribal leaders to countries' governments).

Level of aspiration: The degree of difficulty of the goal toward which a person is striving is the level of aspiration.

LGBTQ+: An acronym for lesbian/gay/bisexual/transgender/queer or questioning own sex or gender identity.

Libido: In psychoanalysis, libido is the energy of the sexual drive or an erotic desire common in women and men.

Marshmallow experiments: The psychologist Walter Mischel conducted the marshmallow experiments, a series of studies of delayed gratification in children.

Masculine protest: A masculine protest is a psychological reaction of opposing male dominance.

Masculinity: Traditionally assigned to men, masculinity is a general set of features associated with physical

strength, decisiveness, and assertiveness.

Medicalization: The process by which various facets of human behavior are interpreted in medical terms and thus diagnosed and treated by medical methods is called medicalization.

Meta-analysis: Meta-analysis is the analysis of analyses (usually termed *combined tests*) of a large collection of individual results in an attempt to make sense of a diverse selection of data.

Metrosexual: Metrosexual refers to the style of thinking and behavior in men who, contrary to the prescriptions of traditional gender roles, tend to develop and display some feminine features and habits, especially related to appearance, clothes, and grooming.

Mindclones: Mindclones are digital versions of human individuals that live forever.

Molar responses: In Holt's system, a molar response is the reaction that has something to do with the meaning of the situation—that is, the way an animal or human interprets the situation.

Morality: This term is commonly defined as a complex cognitive, emotional, and behavioral construct associated with the person's understanding of right and wrong based on societal norms.

Naïve scientists: Naïve scientists are individuals who seek rational and reasonable answers yet lack scientific knowledge and critical judgment.

Narrative medicine: A clinical field that helps medical professionals recognize, absorb, interpret, and be moved by the stories of illness is narrative medicine.

Narrative psychology: Narrative psychology focuses on how published stories and essays shape lives.

Natural dominance of men: A general assumption about men's physical, biological superiority over women is referred to as the natural dominance of men.

Natural science: Natural science is concerned with the description, prediction, and understanding of natural phenomena.

Nature–nurture debate: The general discussion about biological and social factors that affect human development, behavior, and experience is known as the nature–nurture debate.

Neuropsychoanalysis: Neuropsychoanalysis is a discipline that provides a link between psychoanalysis and the neurosciences.

Neuroscience: The scientific study of the nervous system is called neuroscience.

Neurotic character: In psychoanalysis, a neurotic character is a basic trait or a set of traits developed in early childhood that lead to the overt manifestation of neurosis.

Neuroticism (N): In Eysenck's system, neuroticism (N) refers to an individual's level of emotionality. People who measure high in neuroticism have the tendency to see danger in many people, events, and developments around them.

Neurotransmitters: Neurotransmitters are endogenous chemicals that enable neurotransmission between two cells. They are associated with a variety of behavioral and psychological functions, including propensity to depression, anxiety, and even social delinquency.

Nomothetic: A nomothetic strategy, or approach, uses the same method to compare many people or subjects to a certain average, standard, or norm. This approach focuses on comparisons and generalizations.

Nudging: Nudging is the influencing of behavior without coercion.

Observation: Observation is the acquisition of information about identifiable variables from a primary source.

Observer ratings: Observer ratings are structured observations of behaviors or features that require assessment of these actions and features.

Openness model: The openness model states that most people do constantly change their behaviors and adjust their traits to changing life situations.

Operant conditioning: In Skinner's system, operant conditioning is based using activities to produce effects.

Optimism: The general belief in the positive or successful outcomes is referred to as optimism.

Organ inferiority: In Adler's view, organ inferiority refers to a wide range of physical problems that become psychological impediments.

Overarching liabilities: An individual with overarching liabilities has a genetic predisposition that affects his or her behavior and traits under particular, unfavorable, conditions.

Palliative care: Palliative care is used to prevent and relieve the suffering and distress of individuals affected by a serious illness and to improve their well-being when it is possible.

Parsimony: Parsimony is the scientific principle that refers to the necessity to seek the simplest explanations available to explain complex phenomena.

Passive adjustment: Passive adjustment is a general pattern of relying on others to address or resolve stressful events or life situations.

Peace psychology: Peace psychology is a theoretical and applied branch of psychology that studies ideological and psychological causes of war and develops educational programs to reduce the threat of violence in international relations and domestic policies of some countries.

Peak experiences: Peak experiences are periodic and profound episodes of happiness, optimism, inner harmony, and creativity.

Peripheral: Peripheral personality features tend to be more specific and also tend to appear in specific individual or cultural circumstances.

Personality: A personality is a stable set of behavioral and experiential characteristics of an individual.

Personality disorders: Personality disorders are enduring patterns of behavior and inner experience that deviate markedly from the expectations of the individual's culture.

Personality grandstanding: The term refers to the tendency of individuals to present themselves in an exaggerated, flamboyant way with an intention to impress.

Personality lensing: The concept that stands for change—both small and substantial—in the ways we act, we feel, we think, and act when functioning online, compared to how we function in the physical or social world.

Personality psychology: Personality psychology is a branch of psychology that studies personality.

Pessimism: Pessimism refers to a persistent, broad-spectrum belief in and anticipation of undesirable, negative, or damaging outcomes.

Phenotypes: In Allport's theory, phenotypes are internal and external forces that reflect the way individuals accept their environments and how others influence their behavior.

Philosophy: Philosophy is the study of the most general and basic problems of nature, human existence, mind, and society.

Plasticity: Plasticity is the capacity for new habit formation or change of old habits.

Pleasure principle: The pleasure principle is a demand that an instinctual need be immediately gratified.

Political psychology: Political psychology is the field of study that examines psychological factors in politics as well as an individual's political behavior.

Pop psychology: Pop psychology is a type of knowledge related to personality and designed for mass consumption; it reaches people primarily through the media—television, radio, popular books, magazines, and the Internet.

Popular (or folk) beliefs: Observations and assumptions that represent a form of "everyday psychology" created by the people and for the people are referred to as popular (or folk) beliefs (*folk* is an old Germanic word meaning "people").

Positive psychology: Positive psychology studies the strengths and virtues that enable individuals and communities to thrive.

Positive psychotherapy: Positive psychotherapy is a therapeutic procedure based on the scientific premise that the human mind is capable of changing itself through behavior.

Positive self-regard: A positive self-regard refers to high self-esteem and positive emotions toward the self.

Post hoc error: With post hoc error, there is mistaken logic that because Event B follows Event A, then B must have

been caused by A. This error is also known as parataxic reasoning.

Power distance: Power distance is the extent to which the members of a society accept that power in institutions and organizations is distributed unequally.

Prenatal period: The time between conception and birth, which is 38 weeks for humans on average, is known as the prenatal period.

Privacy: This is the ability of individuals to withdraw themselves from the presence of other people or remove this information from public knowledge.

Problem-focused strategies: Problem-focused strategies are methods that center on changing or eliminating the source of an individual's problems.

Procrastination: Putting off impending tasks to a later time is called procrastination.

Progressivism: Progressivism is a general way of thinking and a social movement based on the deep belief that human beings and their society can be improved through social reform, education, and opportunity available to all people.

Projective methods: In personality psychology, projective methods require the respondent to ask questions or perform particular tasks—the results of which are expected to reveal certain meanings that are typically concealed from a direct observation.

Psychoanalysis: Psychoanalysis is a broad term that

encompasses the psychological views and the psychotherapeutic methods attributed to Sigmund Freud and his followers.

Psychobiography: Psychobiography is the genre of historical biography based on psychoanalysis.

Psychology of adjustment: The psychology of adjustment is the study of problems and conditions that cause the individual's need for adjustment, the psychological mechanisms of adjustment, and the ways to help individuals in their coping process.

Psychoticism: A personality pattern that manifests in persistent aggressiveness and hostility to others.

Public diplomacy: Public diplomacy refers to the organized interaction among citizens of different countries to establish a dialogue intended to find solutions to international disputes or other issues.

Purposive or operational behaviorism: In Tolman's system, purposive or operational behaviorism involves the idea of purpose or a goal.

Qualitative research: Qualitative research does not involve measurement or statistical procedures.

Quality of life: An individual's quality of life refers to her or his general well-being measured by the availability of resources, physical and financial security, type of living conditions, quality of education and health care, presence or absence of violence, and a number of other factors—all of which significantly affect the individual's development and socialization.

Quantitative research: Quantitative research uses systematic investigation of behavioral or psychological phenomena by means of statistical or mathematical data and various computational techniques.

Reality principle: The reality principle involves the realization of the demands of the environment (which is, mostly, the social world) and the adjustment of behavior to these demands.

Reciprocal determinism: Reciprocal determinism offers the suggestion that individuals influence their environment and vice versa.

Reflexology: In Bekhterev's system, reflexology is a unifying science to study reflexes.

Relativist perspective of abnormal behavior: Using a relativist perspective of abnormal behavior puts it in a relative, comparative perspective. What is considered pathological in one culture could be regarded as simply different in another.

Relaxation training: A technique or method to cope with stress. This method has been used in developing effective skills of self-control—the skills that can be an asset in coping with serious life problems.

Reliability: The extent to which a particular method gives consistent results is its reliability.

Religion: The beliefs, practices, and prescriptions relevant to the supernatural and the relationships between the individual and the supernatural make up religion.

Representative sample: A representative sample's characteristics should accurately reflect the characteristics of the population.

Reputation: It is a result of a complex evaluation of an individual's character and behavior. Reputation is mostly about how we, as individuals, appear to others.

Retention: In behaviorism, retention is the ability of individuals to keep their habits ready to be used in a new situation.

Ruminative strategies: Ruminative strategies are behaviors and thoughts that focus on the individual's negative experiences, failing strategies, and distressful psychological symptoms associated with the inability to cope with a stressor.

Sample: By studying a sample, or a part of a larger group, the researcher can generalize the results to that larger group.

Sampling error: A sampling error indicates the extent to which the sample is different from the population it represents.

Scarcity mindset: A scarcity mindset is a reaction to a shortage of resources.

Schedules of reinforcement: In Skinner's system, schedules of reinforcement are conditions involving different rates and times of reinforcement.

Scientific knowledge: Scientific knowledge is based on

science, or systematic empirical observation, measurement, and evaluation of facts.

Scientific method: The scientific method uses careful research procedures designed to provide reliable and verifiable evidence.

Self: The term *self* refers to the representation of one's identity or the subject of experience.

Self-actualization: The highest stage of individual development, self-actualization is governed by the search for truth, goodness, beauty, wholeness, justice, and meaningfulness.

Self-awareness: Self-awareness is a reflection of a state of awareness of our own existence; it allows us to perceive our existence with a sense of consistency.

Self-control therapy: A behavioral method in dealing with emotional problems, self-control therapy contains three phases: self-monitoring, self-evaluation, and self-reinforcement.

Self-determination: Self-determination is the view that we, as individuals, generally are in control of our plans, actions, responses, minds, and personality features.

Self-efficacy: Self-efficacy is our belief in our own ability to manage our lives and to exercise control over events that affect our lives.

Self-enhance: The tendency to deem our self as superior to peers is self-enhancement; in other words, we tend to believe that we are somewhat

better, smarter, and more reasonable than others.

Self-esteem: Self-esteem is a person's general subjective evaluation, both emotional and rational, of his or her own worth.

Self-fulfilling prophecy: A perceiver's assumptions about another person that may lead that person to adopt those expected attributes is known as self-fulfilling prophecy.

Self-serving bias: The tendency to assess our own features as better or more advanced than those of the "average" person is known as self-serving bias.

Sensation seeking: Sensation seeking is the constant tendency to search for new experiences and feelings.

Sensitization: Sensitization is a strategy to learn about, rehearse, and anticipate fearful events in a protective coping effort to prevent negative emotions and despair.

Sex: Sex refers to the anatomical and physiological characteristics or features of males and females, the two typically assigned sexes.

Sexism: The prejudice and resulting discrimination based on the views of sex or gender, especially against women and girls, is known as sexism.

Sexual orientation: A sexual orientation refers to romantic or sexual attraction to people of a specific sex or gender.

Sexuality: Sexuality is the capacity for erotic experiences and related behavioral responses.

Single-evaluation attitudes: Single-evaluation attitudes have a single composition of the affective component.

Social desirability bias: The tendency of respondents to give answers that are supposed to be received favorably by others is the social desirability bias.

Social identity: People's perceived membership in one or several social groups is their social identity.

Social interest: In Adler's view, social interest is the desire to be connected with other people and to adapt positively to the perceived social environment.

Social learning theory: A general term, *social learning theory* states, among other things, that learning does not necessarily need reinforcement and conditioning.

Social science: The study of social science is concerned with society and the relationships among individuals within it.

Social status: A social status is a position within the society. Social status can be a measure of an individual's access to resources and power.

Socialization: Socialization is the process by which an individual becomes a member of a society and takes on its ideas and behaviors.

Sociology: Sociology is the study of society and the social action of humans.

Stereotyping: Stereotyping is a generalization of others' behaviors and traits based on their social status or membership in a particular gender, age, ethnic, or professional group.

Stigma: A stigma is the negative perception and corresponding actions related to a person or group based solely on certain social characteristics they possess or are associated with.

Strength of the nervous system: The strength of the nervous system is a reflection of the functional ability of the neurons to maintain the state of activation or excitement without developing self-protecting inhibition.

Stress: Stress is the reaction to a condition that disturbs an individual's physical or mental balance.

Stress tolerance: Stress tolerance is a stable pattern of behavior and experience that appears helpful in the process of coping with significant stressors.

Striving toward superiority: In Adler's view, striving toward superiority is an individual's vigorous exertion or effort to achieve security, improvement, control, and conquest.

Style of life: In Adler's view, the style of life is a technique for dealing with one's inadequacies and inferiorities and for gaining social status.

Superego: In psychoanalysis, superego is the moral guide that passes on imperatives regarding appropriate or inappropriate actions and thoughts.

Taxonomies: Taxonomies are descriptive models or classifications based on similarity, function, structure, size, origin, and the like.

Test-taking attitude: An individual's view about taking tests in general or taking a particular test is referred to as test-taking attitude.

Thanatos: According to Freud, thanatos ("death" in ancient Greek) means striving for destruction, humiliation, pain, and death.

Thematic Apperception Test: This projective test was (TAT) was developed by Henry Murray's and Christina Morgan. In its original form TAT contained 19 pictures creatively selected from popular magazines. A person undergoing testing was asked to tell a story about each of these pictures.

Theory: Applied to personality, theory is a type of comprehensive, scientific explanation about what personality is, how it develops, and how it functions.

Tolerance threshold: An individual's tolerance threshold is a measure of tolerance or intolerance toward specific personality traits in a society or within a cultural group.

Traits: Traits are distinguishable and stable patterns of behavior and experience.

Transcendental: Transcendental refers to the spiritual, nonphysical side of human experience.

Transgender: The term *transgender* refers to roles that do not fit into the traditionally assigned gender dichotomy, such as male or female.

Transpersonal psychology: Transpersonal psychology is a theoretical and applied field that focuses on spiritual and transcendent states of consciousness.

Transvestic fetishism: A condition in which an individual's sexual fantasies, urges, or behaviors involve crossdressing, transvestic fetishism also causes clinically significant distress or impairment in social, occupational, or other important areas of function.

Trolley dilemma: A thought exercise, the trolley dilemma involves rational reasoning and moral choices related to saving a human life by sacrificing another.

Trolling: This is a pattern of repetitive behavior in which a person purposefully provokes, angers, humiliates, or upsets people online. Financial gain or material rewards are not essential in this type of trolling.

Type: A type refers to a kind or category of elements or features sharing similar characteristics or qualities.

Type D personality: A Type D personality has the persistent tendency toward (a) negative affectivity (being constantly irritable, anxious, and expecting failure) and (b) social inhibition (involving both self-restraint and a lack of self-assurance).

Uncertainty orientation: Uncertainty orientation refers to common ways used by people to handle uncertainty in their daily situations and lives in general.

Unconscious: The unconscious refers to the psychological activities not open to direct rational scrutiny but that influence individual experience and behavior.

Universalist perspective on abnormal behavior: The universalist perspective on abnormal behavior suggests the existence of some universal psychological and behavioral

features shared in individuals. Deviant and abnormal phenomena across countries and cultures tend to be universal in terms of their origin and expression.

Validity: The degree to which an assessment measures what it is supposed to measure and not other variables is its validity.

Values: Stable perceptions about the individual's place and his or her role in the world are represented by values.

Witchcraft: Witchcraft is the alleged practice or art of witches.

Yoga: Yoga is a system of beliefs and practices to facilitate the transformation of body and consciousness.

Zone of proximal development: The zone of proximal development indicates the difference between a child's learning progress with help or guidance and another child's learning achievement without the guidance of an adult.

REFERENCES

Aanstoos, C., Serlin, I., & Greening, T. (2000). History of division 32 (humanistic psychology) of the American Psychological Association. In D. Dewsbury (Ed.), *Unification through division: Histories of the divisions of the American Psychological Association* (Vol. 5, pp. 85–112). American Psychological Association. http://www.apa.org/pubs/books/431640A.aspx

Abbott, E. (2019). *Flatland: A romance of many dimensions (Dover thrift editions)*. Dover Publications. (Originally published in 1884)

Abramson, L. Y., Seligman, M. E. P., & Teasdale, J. D. (1978). Learned helplessness in humans: Critique and reformulation. *Journal of Abnormal Psychology, 87*, 49–74.

Abramson, L., Metalsky, G., & Alloy, L. (1989). Hopelessness depression: A theory-based subtype of depression. *Psychological Review, 96*, 358–372.

Aczel, B., Palfi, B., & Kekecs, Z. (2015). What is stupid? People's conception of unintelligent behavior. *Intelligence, 53*, 51–58.

Adeyemi, I. R., Razak, S. A., & Salleh, M. (2016, May 31). Understanding online behavior: Exploring the probability of online personality trait using supervised machine-learning approach. *Frontiers*

in ICT. https://doi.org/10.3389/fict.2016.00008

Adler, A. (1930). *Problems of neurosis*. Cosmopolitan.

Adorno, T. W., Frenkel-Brunswik, E., Levinson, D. J., & Sanford, R. N. (1950). *The authoritarian personality*. Harper & Row.

Ahmed, A., & Simmons, Z. (2013). Pseudobulbar affect; Prevalence and management. *Therapeutic and Clinical Risk Management, 9*(1), 483–489.

Ahmed, S. (2019, May 1). The messy truth about social credit. *Logic*. https://logicmag.io/china/the-messy-truth-about-social-credit/

Akbar, Z., & Aisyawati, M. S. (2021). Coping strategy, social support, and psychological distress among university students in Jakarta, Indonesia during the covid-19 pandemic. *Frontiers of Psychology, 12*. https://doi.org/10.3389/fpsyg.2021.694122

Akerlund, D., Gronqvist, H., & Lindhal, L. (2014, May). Time preferences in criminal behavior. IZA Discussion Paper Series. N. 8168. http://ftp.iza.org/dp8168.pdf

Akhtar, S. (2002). *Broken structures: Severe personality disorders and their treatment*. Aronson.

Alexander, M. G., & Fisher, T. D. (2003). Truth and

consequences: Using the bogus pipeline to examine sex differences in self-reported sexuality. *Journal of Sex Research, 40*, 27–35.

Alivernini, F., Manganelli, S., Girelli, L., Cozzolino, M., Lucidi, F., & Cavicchiolo, E. (2020). Physical distancing behavior: The role of emotions, personality, motivations, and moral decision-making. *Journal of Pediatric Psychology, 46*(1), 15–26.

Allen, M., & Robson, D. (2020). Personality and sexual orientation: New data and meta-analysis. *The Journal of Sex Research, 57*(8), 953–965.

Allen, D., & Price, J. (2019). Stability rates of same-sex couples: With and without children. *Marriage and Family Review, 56*(1), 51–71. https://doi.org/10.1080/01494929.2019.1630048

Allen, J. (2004). Methodological issues in cross-cultural and multicultural rorschach research. *Journal of Personality Assessment, 82*(2), 189–208.

Allport, F. (1924). *Social psychology*. Houghton-Mifflin.

Allport, G. (1937). *Personality: A psychological interpretation*. Henry Holt.

Allport, G. W. (1935). Attitudes. In C. Murchinson (Ed.), *A handbook of social psychology* (pp. 798–844). Clark University Press.

Allport, G. W., & Odbert, H. S. (1936). *Trait-names: A psycho-lexical study*. Psychological Review.

Alper, S., Bayrak, F., & Yilmaz, O. (2021). Psychological correlates of COVID-19 conspiracy beliefs and preventive measures: Evidence from Turkey. *Current Psychology, 40*(11), 5708–5717.

Alsop, R. J. (2004). *The 18 immutable laws of corporate reputation: Creating, protecting, and repairing your most valuable asset*. Free Press.

Aluja, A., Garcia, L., Blanch, A., De Lorenzo, D., & Fibla, J. (2009). Impulsive-disinhibited personality and serotonin transporter gene polymorphisms: Association study in an inmate's sample. *Journal of Psychiatric Research, 43*(10), 906–914.

Alvarez, P. (2022). Charted: The global decline of fertility rates. *Visual Capitalist*. https://www.visualcapitalist.com/cp/charted-the-global-decline-of-fertility-rates/

American Medical Association. (2022). Physician assisted suicide. https://www.ama-assn.org/delivering-care/ethics/physician-assisted-suicide

American Pet Products Association. (2022). The 2021-2022 APPA national pet owners survey. *Journal of Sex*. https://www.americanpetproducts.org/pubs_survey.asp

American Psychological Association. (1980). *The diagnostic and statistical manual of mental disorders* (3rd ed.). Author.

American Psychological Association. (1994). *The diagnostic and statistical manual of mental disorders* (4th ed.; text revision). Author.

American Psychological Association. (2013). *The diagnostic and statistical manual of mental disorders* (5th ed.). Author.

American Psychological Association. (2022). DSM-5-TR. *The diagnostic and statistical manual of mental disorders* (5th ed., text rev.). https://doi.org/10.1176/appi.books.9780890425787

American Psychological Association. (2015a). Psychology topics: Lesbian, gay, bisexual, transgender. http://www.apa.org/topics/lgbt/index.aspx

American Psychological Association. (2015b). Stress in America. http://www.apa.org/news/press/releases/stress/index.aspx?tab=1

American Psychological Association. (2022). Stress in America. https://www.apa.org/news/press/releases/stress

American Psychological Association Dictionary of Psychology. (2022a). Personality. https://www.apa.org/topics/personality

American Psychological Association Dictionary of Psychology. (2022b). *Structured observation*. https://dictionary.apa.org/structured-observation

American Psychological Association Dictionary of Psychology. (2022c). Gender consistency. https://dictionary.apa.org/gender-consistency

American Veterinary Medical Association. (2016). U.S. pet ownership statistics. https://www.avma.org/KB/Resources/Statistics/Pages/Market-research-statistics-US-pet-ownership.aspx

Anderson, C. (1987). Temperature and aggression: Effects on quarterly, yearly, and city rates of violent and nonviolent crime. *Journal of Personality and Social Psychology, 52*, 1161–1173.

Andjelovic, T., Buckels, E., Paulhus, D., & Trapnell, P. (2019). Internet trolling and everyday sadism: Parallel effects on pain perception and moral judgment. *Journal of Personality, 87*(2), 328–340.

Andreason, N. J. C., & Canter, A. (1974). The creative writer: Psychiatric symptoms and family history. *Comprehensive Psychiatry, 15*(2), 123–131.

Andreason, N. J. C., & Powers, P. S. (1975). Creativity and psychosis: An examination of conceptual style. *Archives of General Psychiatry, 32*, 70–73.

Antonovsky, A. (1987). *Unraveling the mystery of health: How people manage stress and stay well*. Jossey-Bass.

Anusic, I., Lucas, R. E., & Donnellan, M. B. (2012). Cross-sectional age differences in personality: Evidence from nationally representative samples from Switzerland and the United States. *Journal of Research in Personality, 46*, 116–120.

Aquilina, T. (2021). Past discrimination allegations against reported *Jeopardy* host frontrunner Mike Richards resurface. *Entertainment*. https://ew.com/tv/mike-richards-jeopardy-past-discrimination-allegations-resurface/

Archer, J. (1996). Sex differences in social behavior. Are

the social role and evolutionary explanations compatible? *American Psychologist, 51*(9), 909–917.

Archer, R., & Smith, S. (2014). *Personality assessment.* Routledge.

Armstrong, K. (2014). *Fields of blood: Religion and the history of violence.* Knopf.

Armstrong, K. (2019). Janet Shibley Hyde sinks stereotypes with data. *Association for Psychological Science.* https://www.psychologicalscience.org/observer/janet-shibley-hyde-sinks-stereotypes-with-data

Arnett, J. J. (2002). The psychology of globalization. *American Psychologist, 57*(10), 774–783.

Arnett, J. J. (2008). The neglected 95%: Why American psychology needs to become less American. *American Psychologist, 63*, 602–614.

Arnold, K. (2014). Behind the mirror: Reflective listening and its tain in the work of Carl Rogers. *The Humanistic Psychologist, 42*(4), *354–369.*

Aschwanden, K. (2018, July). Psychologists looked in the mirror and saw a bunch of liberals. *FiveThurtyEight.* https://fivethirtyeight.com/features/psychologists-looked-in-the-mirror-and-saw-a-bunch-of-liberals/

Aspinwall, L. G., & Taylor, S. E. (1997). A stitch in time: Self-regulation and proactive coping. *Psychological Bulletin, 121*(3), 417–436.

Asselmann, E., & Specht, J. (2021). Testing the social investment principle around childbirth: Little evidence for personality maturation before and after becoming a parent. *European Journal of Personality, 35*(1), 85–102.

Association for Humanistic Psychology. (2023). Humanistic psychology overview. https://ahpweb.org/

Astuti, R., & Bloch, M. (2010). Why a theory of human nature cannot be based on the distinction between universality and variability: Lessons from anthropology. *Behavioral and Brain Sciences, 33*(2/3), 23–24.

Auden, W. H. (1949). *The age of anxiety.* Faber & Faber.

Austin, A., Craig, S., D'Souza, S., & McInroy, L. (2020, March). Suicidality among transgender youth: Elucidating the role of interpersonal risk factors. *Journal of Interpersonal Violence, 37*(5–6).

Ayman, R., & Korabik, K. (2010). Why gender and culture matter. *American Psychologist, 65*(3), 157–170.

Badiani, F., & DeSouza, A. (2016). The empty nest syndrome: Critical clinical considerations. *Indian Journal of Mental Health, 3*(2), 135–142.

Bailey, J., & Burch, M. (2017). *Research methods in applied behavior analysis.* Routledge.

Bais, A. (2012). Relevance of metrosexuality in the post modern society. *Research Journal of Humanities and Social Sciences, 3*(1), 154–157.

Baker, D. S., & Carson, K. (2012). The two faces of uncertainty avoidance: Attachment and adaptation. *The Journal of Behavioral and Applied Management, 12*(2), 128–141.

Baker, L., Bezdjian, S., & Raine, A. (2006). Behavioral genetics: The science of antisocial behavior. *Law and Contemporary Problems, 69*(1–2), 7–46.

Bakker, A. B., Demerouti, E., & Sanz-Vergel, A. I. (2014). Burnout and work engagement: The JD–R approach. *Annual Review of Organizational Psychology and Organizational Behavior, 1*, 389–411.

Balthazart, J. (2018). Fraternal birth order effect on sexual orientation explained. *Proceedings of the National Academy of Sciences of the United States of America, 115*(2), *234–236.*

Bandura, A. (1963). *Social learning and personality development.* Holt, Rinehart, & Winston.

Bandura, A. (1977). *Social learning theory.* Prentice-Hall.

Bandura, A. (1986). *Social foundations of thought and action: A social cognitive theory.* Prentice-Hall.

Bandura, A. (1997). *Self-efficacy: The exercise of control.* Freeman.

Bandura, A. (2001). Social cognitive theory: An agentic perspective. *Annual Review of Psychology, 52*, 1–26.

Bandura, A., Ross, D., & Ross, S. A. (1961). Transmission of aggression through the imitation of aggressive models. *Journal of Abnormal and Social Psychology, 63*(3), 575–582.

Bandura, A., Ross, D., & Ross, S. A. (1963). Imitation of film-mediated aggressive models. *Journal of Abnormal and Social Psychology, 66*(1), 3–11.

Banerjee, A., & Duflo, E. (2011). *Poor economics: A radical rethinking of the way to fight global poverty*. Public Affairs.

Banerjee, A., & Duflo, E. (2019). *Good economics for hard times*. Public Affairs.

Banks, D., & Rose, D. (2010). Diversity in representations, uniformity in learning. *Behavioral and Brain Sciences*, *33*(2/3), 30–31.

Barceló, J., & Sheen, G. (2020). Voluntary adoption of social welfare-enhancing behavior: Mask-wearing in Spain during the COVID-19 outbreak. Preprint at *OSF*. https://osf.io/preprints/socarxiv/6m85q/

Barrash, J., Stuss, D., Aksan, N., Anderson, S., Jones, R., Manzel, K., & Tranel, D. (2018, September). Frontal lobe syndrome"? Subtypes of acquired personality disturbances in patients with focal brain damage. *Cortex*, *106*, 65–80.

Barrett, P., & Eysenck, S. B. G. (1984). The assessment of personality factors across 25 countries. *Personality and Individual Differences*, *5*, 615–632.

Battaglia, M., & Torgensen, S. (1996). Schizotypal disorder: At crossroads of genetics and nosology. *Acta Psychiatrica Scandinavica*, *94*, 303–310.

Baumann, N. (2012). Autotelic personality. In S. Engeser (Ed.), *Advances in flow research* (pp. 165–186). Springer.

Baumeister, R. (2010). *Is there anything good about men?: How cultures flourish by exploiting men*. Oxford University Press.

Baumeister, R., & Tierney, J. (2012). *Willpower*. Penguin Books.

Beard, M. (2014). *Laughter in ancient Rome: On joking, tickling, and cracking up*. University of California Press.

Beardsley, L., & Pedersen, P. (1997). Health and culture-centered intervention. In J. Berry & C. Kagitcibasi (Eds.), *Handbook of cross-cultural psychology: Social behavior and applications* (Vol. 3, pp. 413–448). Allyn & Bacon.

Beauchaine, T. P., & Marsh, P. (2006). Taxometric methods: Enhancing early detection and prevention of psychopathology by identifying latent vulnerability traits. In D. Cicchetti & D. Cohen (Eds.), *Developmental psychopathology* (2nd ed., pp. 931–967). Wiley.

Beaudry, G., Yu, R., Perry, A. E., & Fazel, S. (2021). Effectiveness of psychological interventions in prison to reduce recidivism: A systematic review and meta-analysis of randomised controlled trials. *The lancet Psychiatry*, *8*(9), 759–773. https://www.thelancet.com/journals/lanpsy/article/PIIS2215-0366(21)00170-X/fulltext

Beck, A. T. (1964). Thinking and depression: II. Theory and therapy. *Archives of General Psychiatry*, *10*, 561–571.

Beck, A. T. (1991). Cognitive therapy: A 30-year retrospective. *American Psychologist*, *46*(4), 368–375.

Beck, A. T., & Weishaar, M. (2005). Cognitive therapy. In R. J. Corsini & D. Wedding (Eds.), *Current psychotherapies* (pp. 238–268). Thomson Brooks/Cole Publishing Co.

Beck, A. T., & Weishaar, M. (2013). Cognitive therapy. In D.

Wedding & R. J. Corsini (Eds.), *Current psychotherapies* (10th ed., pp. 231–264). Brooks/Cole, Cengage Learning.

Becker, G. (1968). Crime and punishment: An economic approach. *Journal of Political Economy*, *76*, 169–217.

Beckers, T., & Craske, M. (2017, September). Avoidance and decision making in anxiety: An introduction to the special issue. *Behavioral Research and Therapy*, *96*, 1–2.

Bekhterev, V. (2017). *Suggestion and its role in social life*. Routledge. (Original work published 1908)

Bekhterev, V. M. (1904). *Psikhicheskaia deiatelnost i Zhizn* [Psychological activity and life]. St. Military Medical Academy.

Bekhterev, V. M. (1933). *General principles of human reflexology: An introduction to the objective study of personality* (Translation of the 4th Russian ed.). Jarrolds. (Original work published 1918)

Bekhterev, V. M. (2001a). *Collective reflexology: The complete edition* (E. Lockwood & A. Lockwood, Trans.). Transaction. (Original work published 1921)

Bekhterev, V. M. (2001b). Immortality from a scientific point of view. *Journal of Russian and East European Psychology*, *39*(5), 34–70. (Original work published 1916)

Bélanger, J. J., Caouette, J., Sharvit, K., & Dugas, M. (2014). The psychology of martyrdom: Making the ultimate sacrifice in the name of a cause. *Journal of Personality and Social Psychology*, *107*(3), 494–515.

Bemak, F., & Chung, R. C.-Y. (2004). Culturally oriented psychotherapy with refugees. In U. Gielen, J. Fish, & J. Draguns (Eds.), *Culture, therapy and healing* (pp. 121–132). Lawrence Erlbaum.

Bendi, H., & Garcia, A. (2015). TEMAS (tell-me-a-story) multicultural thematic apperception test. *Encyclopedia of Cross-Cultural School Psychology*. https://doi.org/10.1007/978-0-387-71799-9_424

Benedict, R. (1946). *The chrysanthemum and the sword: Patterns of Japanese culture*. Houghton Mifflin.

Bengson, J., Kelley, T., Zhang, X., Wang, J.-L., & Mangun, G. (2014). Spontaneous neural fluctuations predict decisions to attend. *Journal of Cognitive Neuroscience, 26*(11), 2578–2584.

Benight, C. C., & Bandura, A. (2004). Social cognitive theory of post-traumatic recovery: The role of perceived self-efficacy. *Behaviour Research and Therapy, 42*(10), 1129–1148.

Benjamin, H. (1966). *The transsexual phenomenon*. Julian Press.

Berdyaev, N. (2009). *The destiny of man*. Semantron Press. (Original work published 1931)

Berger, A., & O'Neal, J. (2021). *Principles and practice of palliative care and support oncology* (5th ed.). Wolters Kluwer Health.

Bergman, B., Kelly, J., Fava, M., & Evins, A. E. (2021, February). Online recovery support meetings can help mitigate the public health consequences of COVID-19 for individuals with substance use disorder. *Addictive Behavior, 113,* 106661. https://doi.org/10.1016/j.addbeh.2020.106661

Bergmann, O., & Frisén, J. (2013). Why adults need new brain cells. *Science, 340*(6133), 695–696.

Berman, P. (2004). *Terror and liberalism*. Norton.

Berman, R. (2021). Burnout is more frequent among lesbian, gay, and bisexual med students. *Medical News Today.* https://www.medicalnewstoday.com/articles/burnout-is-more-frequent-among-lesbian-gay-and-bisexual-med-students

Best, D. (2018). Off to great places! Celebrating 50 years of the journal of cross-cultural psychology. *Journal of Cross-Cultural Psychology, 50*(1), 3–4.

Bhikkhu, T. (2002). *The karma of questions*. Metta Forest Monastery.

Bilger, B. (2004, April 5). The height gap. *The New Yorker.* http://www.newyorker.com/magazine/2004/04/05/the-height-gap

Billings, A. G., & Moos, R. H. (1981). The role of coping responses and social resources in attenuating the stress of life events. *Journal of Behavioral Medicine, 4*(2), 139–157.

Binswanger, L. (1963). *Being-in-the-world: Selected papers of Ludwig Binswanger* (J. Needleman, Trans.). Basic Books.

Birger, J. (2015). *Date-onomics: How dating became a lopsided numbers game*. Workman.

Birkhaug, K. (2022). Better things than happiness. *Law and Liberty.* https://lawliberty.org/better-things-than-happines/

Biswas, T., Scott, J., Munir, K., Renzano, A. M. N., Rawal, L., Baxter, J., & Mamun, A. (2020). Global variation in the prevalence of suicidal ideation, anxiety and their correlates among adolescents: A population based study of 82 countries. *EClinicalMedicine, 24,* 100395.

Biswas, U. N., & Pandey, J. (1996). Mobility and perception of socioeconomic status among tribal and caste group. *Journal of Cross-Cultural Psychology, 27*(2), 200–215.

Bizer, G., & Krosnick, J. (2001). Exploring the structure of strength-related attitude features: The relation between attitude importance and attitude accessibility. *Journal of Personality and Social Psychology, 81*(4), 566–586.

Bjarnason, E. (2021). Computers speaking icelandic could save the language from 'Stafrænn Dauði' (That's icelandic for 'digital death'). *The Wall Street Journal.* https://www.wsj.com/articles/computers-speaking-icelandic-could-save-the-language-from-stafrnn-daui-thats-icelandic-for-digital-death-11621533891

Bjarnason, E. (2021, May 21). A digital future for icelandic. *The Wall Street Journal.*

Blachnio, A., Przepiorka, A., & Pantic, I. (2016). Association between Facebook addiction, self-esteem and life satisfaction: A cross-sectional study. *Computers in Human Behavior, 55,* 701–705.

Blanchard, R. (1989). The concept of autogynephilia and the typology of male gender dysphoria. *Journal of Nervous and Mental Disease, 177*(10), 616–623.

Block, J. (2001). Millennial contrarianism: The five-factor approach to personality description 5 years later. *Journal of Research in Personality, 35*, 98–107.

Block, S., & Block, C. (2012). *Mind-body workbook for stress: Effective tools for lifelong stress reduction and crisis management.* New Harbinger.

Blumer, T., & Döring, N. (2012). Are we the same online? The expression of the five factor personality traits on the computer and the Internet. *Cyberpsychology: Journal of Psychosocial Research on Cyberspace, 6*(3), Article 5. https://doi.org/10.5817/CP2012-3-5

Boardman, S. (2021). *Everyday vitality: Turning stress into strength.* Penguin.

Boeree, C. G. (2006). Carl Rogers. http://webspace.ship.edu/cgboer/rogers.html

Bonanno, G. A., Papa, A., Lalande, K., Westphal, M., & Coifman, K. (2004). The importance of being flexible: The ability to both enhance and suppress emotional expression predicts long-term adjustment. *Psychological Science, 15*(7), 482–487.

Bond, F. W., & Bince, D. (2000). Mediators of change in emotion-focused and problem-focused Woodside Stress Management Interventions. *Journal of Occupational Health Psychology, 5*(1), 156–163.

Bond, F. W., & Flaxman, P. E. (2006). The ability of psychological flexibility and job control to predict learning, job performance, and mental health. *Journal of Organizational Behavior Management, 26*(1–2), 113–130.

Boninger, G. F., Boninger, D. S., Strathman, A., Armor, D., Hetts, J., & Ahn, M. (1995). With an eye toward the future: The impact of counterfactual thinking on affect, attitudes, and behavior. In N. Roese & J. Olson (Eds.), *What might have been: The social psychology of counterfactual thinking* (pp. 283–304). Lawrence Erlbaum.

Borelli, J. L., & Sbarra, D. A. (2011). Trauma history and linguistic self-focus moderate the course of psychological adjustment to divorce. *Journal of Social and Clinical Psychology, 30*, 667–698.

Borge, J. (2020). How being a first-generation American affected my mental health. *Health.* https://www.health.com/mind-body/first-generation-american-mental-health-immigrant-parado

Boring, E. G. (1950). *A history of experimental psychology* (2nd ed.). Century. (Original work published 1929)

Bornstein, R. F. (2001). The impending death of psychoanalysis. *Psychoanalytic Psychology, 18*, 3–20.

Boster, J. (1985). Selection for perceptual distinctiveness: Evidence from Aguaruna Cultivars of Manihot Esculenta. *Economic Botany, 39*(3), 310–325.

Bouchard, T. J., & McGue, M. (2003). Genetic and environmental influences on human psychological differences. *Journal of Neurobiology, 54*(1), 4–45.

Bouchard, T., Lykken, D., McGue, M., Segal, N. L., & Tellegen, A. (1990). Sources of human psychological differences: The Minnesota study of twins reared apart. *Science, 250*, 223–228.

Boucher, H. C., Peng, K., Shi, J., & Wang, L. (2009). Culture and implicit self-esteem: Chinese are "good" and "bad" at the same time. *Journal of Cross-Cultural Psychology, 40*(1), 24–45.

Boyle, G., & Helmes, E. (2009). Methods of personality assessment. In P. Corr & G. Matthews (Eds.), *The Cambridge handbook of personality psychology* (pp. 110–126). Cambridge University Press.

Brand, J. (2015). The far-reaching impact of job loss and unemployment. *Annual Review of Sociology, 41*, 359–375.

Bray, J. (2010). The future of psychology practice and science. *American Psychologist, 65*(5), 355–369.

Brewer, M. B. (1991). The social self: On being the same and different at the same time. *Personality and Social Psychology Bulletin, 17*(5), 475–482. https://doi.org/10.1177/0146167291175001

Brewer, M. B., & Pierce, K. P. (2005). Social identity complexity and outgroup tolerance. *Personality and Social Psychology Bulletin, 31*, 428–437. A Brief History of the MMPI Instruments. (2016). University of Minnesota Press. https://www.upress.umn.edu/testdivision/bibliography/mmpi-history

Brieger, P., Ehrt, U., & Marneros, A. (2003). Frequency of comorbid personality disorders in bipolar and unipolar affective disorders. *Comprehensive Psychiatry, 44*(1), 28–34.

Brieger, P., Ehrt, U., & Marneros, A. (2003). Frequency of comorbid personality disorders in bipolar and unipolar affective disorders. *Comparative Psychiatry, 44*(1), 28–34.

Brinol, P., Petty, R., & Stavraki, M. (2019). Structure and function of attitudes. *Oxford Research Encyclopedia. Psychology.* https://bit.ly/3R6o8Q9

Brizendine, L. (2007). *The female brain.* Harmony.

Broad, W. (2012). *The science of yoga: The risks and the rewards.* Simon & Schuster.

Bronfenbrenner, U. (1979). *The ecology of human development: Experiments by nature and design.* Harvard university press.

Broucek, F. (1991). *Shame and the self.* Guilford.

Browder, L. (2000). *Slippery characters: Ethnic impersonators and American identities.* University of North Carolina Press.

Brown, A. (2022). About 5% of young adults in the U.S. Say their gender is different from their sex assigned at birth. *Pew Research Center.* https://www.pewresearch.org/fact-tank/2022/06/07/about-5-of-young-adults-in-the-u-s-say-their-gender-is-different-from-their-sex-assigned-at-birth/

Brown, J. D., & Cai, H. (2010). Self-esteem and trait importance moderate cultural differences in self-evaluations. *Journal of Cross-Cultural Psychology, 41*(1), 116–123.

Brownmiller, S. (1985). *Femininity.* Ballantine Books.

Brubaker, P., Montez, D., & Church, S. (2021, April). The power of schadenfreude: Predicting behaviors and perceptions of trolling among reddit users. *Social Media Society.* https://journals.sagepub.com/doi/full/10.1177/20563051211021382

Bruehl, E. (1990). *Anna Freud: A biography.* Pocket Books.

Bruner, J. (1960). *The process of education.* Harvard University Press.

Bruner, J. (1990). *Acts of meaning.* Harvard University Press.

Bruner, J., & Goodman, C. (1947). Value and need as organizing factors in perception. *Journal of Abnormal and Social Psychology, 42*, 33–44.

Bryan, A., Aiken, L. S., & West, S. G. (2004). HIV/STD risk among incarcerated adolescents: Optimism about the future and self-esteem as predictors of condom use self-efficacy. *Journal of Applied Social Psychology, 34*, 912–936.

Bryan, C. (2021). The pandemic didn't increase suicides. That shouldn't be a surprise. *Stat.* https://www.statnews.com/2021/11/16/the-pandemic-didnt-increase-suicides-that-shouldnt-be-a-surprise/

Buckels, E. (2019). Probing the sadistic minds of internet trolls. *The Society for Personality and Social Psychology.* https://www.spsp.org/news-center/blog/buckels-internet-trolls

Buckels, E. E., Trapnell, P. D. Andjelovic, T, & Paulhus, D. L. (2019). Internet trolling and everyday sadism: Parallel effects on pain perception and moral judgment. *Journal of Personality, 87*(2), 328–340.

Buckels, E. E., Trapnell, P. D., & Paulhus, D. L. (2014). Trolls just want to have fun. *Personality and Individual Differences, 68*, 97–102.

Buckley, K. (1989). *Mechanical man: John B. Whatson and the beginnings of behaviorism.* The Guilford Press.

Buettner, D. (2017). *The blue zones of happiness: Lessons from the world's happiest people.* National Geographic.

Bugental, J. (1964). The third force in psychology. *Journal of Humanistic Psychology, 4*(1), 19–25.

Burgess, R., & Akers, R. (1966). Differential association-reinforcement theory of criminal behavior. *Social Problems, 14*(2), 128–147.

Burns, D. D. (1989). *The feeling good handbook: Using the new mood therapy in everyday life.* W. Morrow.

Bus, D., & Craik, K. (1986). Acts, dispositions, and clinical assessment: The psychopathology of everyday conduct. *Clinical Psychology Review, 6*, 387–406.

Buss, D. (1996). Paternity uncertainty and the complex repertoire of human mating strategies. *American Psychologist, 51*(2), 161–162.

Cadoret, R., Yates, W., Troughton, E., Woodworth, G., & Stewart, M. (1995). Genetic-environmental interaction in the genes of aggressivity and conduct disorders. *Archives of General Psychiatry, 52*(11), 916–924.

Caeiro, C., Guo, K., & Mills, D. (2017). Dogs and humans respond to emotionally competent stimuli by producing different facial actions. *Sci Rep, 7*, 15525. https://doi.org/10.1038/s41598-017-15091-4

Calkins, M. W. (1906). A reconciliation between structural and functional psychology (Calkins' APA presidential address). *Psychological Review, 8*, 61–81.

Callanan, K., & Kelley, P. (1997). *Final gifts: Understanding the special awareness, needs, and communications of the dying.* Bantam Books.

Campbell, D. (2006). *Inner strength defies the skeptic: A psychological and spiritual guide from fear to freedom.* Immediex.

Campbell, W. K. (1999). Narcissism and romantic attraction. *Journal of Personality and Social Psychology, 77*(6), 1254–1270.

Campbell-Arvai, V., Arvai, J., & Kalof, L. (2014). Motivating sustainable food choices: The role of nudges, value orientation, and information provision. *Environment and Behavior, 46*(4), 453–475.

Camus, A. (1992). *The rebel.* Vintage. (Original work published 1951)

Canada World Survey. (2018). *Environics Institute.* Projects. https://www.environicsinstitute.org/projects/project-details/canada's-world-2017-survey

Canudas-Romo, V. (2018). Life expectancy and poverty. *The Lancet Global Health.* https://www.thelancet.com/journals/langlo/article/PIIS2214-109X(18)30327-9/fulltext

Caplan, E. (1998). Popularizing American psychotherapy: The Emmanuel movement, 1906–1910. *History of Psychology, 1*, 289–314.

Caprara, G., & Vecchione, M. (2009). Personality and politics. In P. Corr & G. Matthews (Eds.), *The Cambridge handbook of personality psychology* (pp. 589–607). Cambridge University Press.

Car, A. (2011). *Positive psychology. The science of happiness and human strengths.* Routledge.

Carbone, J., & Cahn, N. (2013). The end of men or the rebirth of class? Boston University Law Review, *871.* http://scholarship.law.umn.edu/facultyarticles/125

Carducci. (2017, June). Everything you ever wanted to know about shyness in an international context. *Psychology International.* https://www.apa.org/international/pi/2017/06/shyness

Carroll, L. (2013). Passive coping strategies. In M. Gellman & J. R. Turner (Eds.), *Encyclopedia of Behavioral Medicine* (p. 1442). Springer, Cham.

Carver, C. S., & Harmon-Jones, E. (2009). Anger is an approach-related affect: Evidence and implications. *Psychological Bulletin, 135*, 183–204.

Casey, B., Somerville, L., Gotlib, I., Ayduk, N., Franklin, M., Askren, J., . . . Shoda, Y. (2011).

Behavioral and neural correlates of delay of gratification 40 years later. *Proceedings of the National Academy of Sciences, 108*(36), 14998–15003.

Cashdan, M., & Steele, E. (2013). Pathogen prevalence, group bias, and collectivism in the standard cross-cultural sample. *Human Nature, 24*(1), 59–75.

Cattell, H. E. P., & Mead, A. D. (2008). *The sixteen personality factor questionnaire (16PF).* In G. J. Boyle, G. Matthews, & D. H. Saklofske (Eds.), *The SAGE handbook of personality theory and assessment: Vol. 2– Personality measurement and testing.* SAGE.

Cattell, R. B. (1946). *The description and measurement of personality.* Harcourt, Brace, & World.

Cattell, R. B. (1965). *The scientific analysis of personality.* Penguin.

Cattell, R. B. (1978). *The scientific use of factor analysis in behavioral and life sciences.* Plenum.

Cattell, R. B. (1983). *Structured personality-learning theory: A holistic multivariate research approach* (pp. 419–457). Praeger.

Centers for Disease Control. (2015). Deaths and mortality. http://www.cdc.gov/nchs/fastats/deaths.htm

Centers for Disease Control. (2022a). Chronic Diseases in America. https://www.cdc.gov/chronicdisease/resources/infographic/chronic-diseases.htm

Centers for Disease Control. (2022b). *Suicide Prevention.*

Chandler, S. (2020). 'World's first' digital human AI partner promises companionship during coronavirus era. *Forbes*. https://www.forbes.com/sites/simonchandler/2020/06/23/worlds-first-digital-human-ai-partner-promises-companionship-during-coronavirus-era/?sh=af4b6a4359be

Chanen, A., & Thompson, K. (2019). The age of onset of personality disorders. In G. de Girolamo, P. McGorry, & N. Sartorius (Eds.), *Age of onset of mental disorders* (pp. 183–201). Springer, Cham. https://doi.org/10.1007/978-3-319-72619-9_10

Charon, R. (1992). To build a case: Medical histories as traditions in conflict. *Literature and Medicine*, *11*(1), 93–105.

Charon, R. (1993). The narrative road to empathy. In H. Spiro (Ed.), *Empathy and the medical profession: Beyond pills and the scalpel* (pp. 147–159). Yale University Press.

Chaudhary, N. (2010). Review of the book *Handbook of Indian psychology*,. In K. R. Rao, A. C. Paranjpe, & A. K. Dala (Eds.), , Cambridge University Press.

Chaudhary, N., Misra, G., Bansal, P., Valsiner, J., & Singh, T. (2022). Making sense of culture for the psychological sciences. *Review of General Psychology*, *26*(4). https://doi.org/10.1177/10892680211066473

Chen, R., Zhu, X., Wright, L., Drescher, J., Gao, Y., Wu, L., Ying, X., Qi, J., Chen, C., Xi, Y., Ji, L., Zhao, H., Ou, J., & Broome, M. (2019). Suicidal ideation and attempted suicide amongst Chinese transgender persons: National population study. *Journal of Affective Disorders*, *15*(245), 1126–1134.

Cheryan, S., & Markus, H. R. (2020). Masculine defaults: Identifying and mitigating hidden cultural biases. *Psychological Review*, *127*(6), 1022–1052. https://doi.org/10.1037/rev0000209

Chiao, J. Y. (2009). Cultural neuroscience: A once and future discipline. *Progress in brain research*, *178*, 287–304.

Chiraag, M., & Griskevicius, V. (2014). Sense of control under uncertainty depends on people's childhood environment: A life history theory approach. *Journal of Personality and Social Psychology*, *107*(4), 621–663.

Chung, R., & Bemak, F. (2011). *Social justice counseling*. SAGE.

Clark, G., & Egan, S. (2015). The Socratic method in cognitive behavioral therapy: A narrative review. *Cognitive Therapy and Research*, *39*(6), 863–879.

Clay, R. A. (2002). A renaissance for humanistic psychology: The field explores new niches while building on its past. *American Psychological Association Monitor*, *33*(8), 42.

Cleckley, H. (1976). *The mask of sanity* (5th ed.). CV Mosby.

Cochran, G., & Harpending, H. (2010). *The 10,000-year explosion: How civilization accelerated human evolution*. Basic Books.

Cohen, D. (2000). *Carl Rogers: A critical biography*. Constable.

Cohn, C. (1987). Sex and death in the rational world of defense intellectuals. *Signs*, *12*(4), 687–718.

Colamonico, J., Formella, A., & Bradley, W. (2012). Pseudobulbar affect: Burden of illness in the USA. *Advances in Therapy*, *29*(9), 775–798.

Collins, F. S. (2010). *The language of life: DNA and the revolution in personalized medicine*. HarperCollins.

Collins, S. (1990). *Selfless persons: Imagery and thought in Theravada Buddhism*. Cambridge University Press.

Colom, F., Vieta, E., Sánchez-Moreno, J., Torrent, C., Reinares, M., Goikoela, J. M., . . . Comes, M. (2004). Psychoeducation in bipolar patients with comorbid personality disorders. *Bipolar Disorders*, *6*(4), 294–298.

Compton, W. C. (2004). *An introduction to positive psychology*. Wadsworth.

Computer Science. (2022). Women in computer science: Getting involved in STEM. https://www.computerscience.org/resources/women-in-computer-science/

Confer, J., & Cloud, M. (2010). Sex differences in response to imagining a partner's heterosexual or homosexual affair. *Personality and Individual Differences*, *50*(7), 11–55.

Confer, J., Easton, J., Fleischman, D., Goetz, C., Lewis, D., Perilloux, C., & Buss, D. (2010). Evolutionary psychology: Controversies, questions, prospects, and limitations. *American Psychologist*, *65*(2), 110–126.

Connelly, B., & Ones, D. (2010). Another perspective on personality: Meta-analytic integration of observers' accuracy and predictive validity.

Psychological Bulletin, 136(6), 1092–1122.

Coombs, W. T. (2019). *Ongoing crisis communication. Planning, managing, and responding* (5th ed.). SAGE.

Coonan, C. (2012, August 27). Wanted: 'Innocent' brides for China's ultra-rich. *The Independent.* http://www.independent.co.uk/news/world/asia/wanted-innocent-brides-for-chinas-ultrarich-8082065.html

Cooper, D. (2003). *World philosophies.* Blackwell.

Cooper, M., O'Hara, M., Schmid, P., & Wyatt, G (Eds.). (2013). *The handbook of person-centered psychotherapy and counselling,* 2/e. Palgrave Macmillan.

Corr, P., & Matthews, G (Eds.). (2009). *The Cambridge handbook of personality psychology* (pp. 110–126). Cambridge University Press.

Corrigan, P. W., & Wassel, A. (2008). Understanding and influencing the stigma of mental illness. *Journal of Psychosocial Nursing and Mental Health Services, 46*(1), 42–48.

Costa, P. T., & McCrae, R. R. (1995). Domains and facets: Hierarchical personality assessment using the revised NEO personality inventory. *Journal of Personality Assessment, 64*(1), 21–50. https://doi.org/10.1207/s15327752jpa6401_2

Costa, P. T., Jr., & McCrae, R. R. (1988). Personality in adulthood: A six-year longitudinal study of self-reports and spouse ratings on the NEO Personality Inventory. *Journal of Personality and Social Psychology, 54,* 853–863.

Costa, P. T., Jr., & McCrae, R. R. (1992). *NEO PIR professional manual.* Psychological Assessment Resources.

Costa, P. T., Terracciano, A., & McCrae, R. R. (2001). Gender differences in personality traits across cultures: Robust and surprising findings. *Journal of Personality and Social Psychology, 81*(2), 322–331.

Costello, C. G. (Ed.). (1995). *Personality characteristics of the personality disordered.* John Wiley & Sons.

Cowen, T., & Gross, D. (2022). *Talent: How to identify energizers, creatives, and winners around the world.* St. Martin's.

Craighead, W. E., Miklowitz, D. J., & Craighead, L. W. (Eds.). (2013). *Psychopathology: History, diagnosis, and empirical foundation* (2nd ed.). John Wiley & Sons.

Cramer, P. (1991). *The development of defense mechanisms: Theory, research, and assessment.* Springer-Verlag.

Cravens, H. (2002). *Before Head Start: The Iowa station and America's children.* University of North Carolina Press.

Creighton, S. (2001). Surgery for intersex. *Journal of the Royal Society of Medicine, 94,* 218–220.

Csíkszentmihályi, M. (1990). *Flow: The psychology of optimal experience.* Harper & Row.

Csíkszentmihályi, M. (1997). *Finding flow: The psychology of engagement with everyday life.* Basic Books.

Csíkszentmihályi, M. (2014). *Flow and the foundations of positive psychology: The collected works of Mihaly Csikszentmihalyi.* Springer.

Curtin, J. J., McCarthy, D. E., Piper, M. E., & Baker, T. B. (2005). Implicit and explicit drug motivational processes: A model of boundary conditions. In R. Reinout & A. Stacy (Eds.), *Handbook on implicit cognition and addiction* (pp. 233–250). SAGE.

Da Conceição, C. G., & De Lyra Chebabi, W. (1987). Psychoanalysis and the role of black life and culture in Brazil. *International Review of Psycho-Analysis, 14,* 185–202.

Dahlsgaard, K., Peterson, C., & Seligman, M. E. P. (2005). Shared virtue: The convergence of valued human strengths across culture and history. *Review of General Psychology, 9*(3), 203–213. https://doi.org/10.1037/1089-2680.9.3.203

Damasio, A. (2012). *Self comes to mind: Connecting the conscious brain.* Vintage Books.

Damian, R. I., Spengler, M., Sutu, A., & Roberts, B. W. (2019). Sixteen going on sixty-six: A longitudinal study of personality stability and change across 50 years. *Journal of Personality and Social Psychology, 117*(3), 674–695.

Danesh, J. (2015). Association of cardiometabolic multimorbidity with mortality. *Journal of the American Medical Association, 314*(1), 52–60.

Das, G., & Rae, A. (1999). The new face of self-help: Online support for anxiety disorders. *Dissertation Abstracts International: Section B. Sciences and Engineering, 59*(7B), 36–91.

Dasen, P. R. (1994). Culture and cognitive development from a Piagetian perspective. In W. J. Lonner & R. Malpass (Eds.), *Psychology and culture* (pp. 145–149). Allyn & Bacon.

David, E. J. R. (2013). *Brown skin, white minds: Filipino American postcolonial psychology*. Information Age.

Davison, A. R., & Thompson, E. (1980). Cross-cultural studies of attitudes and beliefs. In H. C. Triandis & W. J. Lonner (Eds.), *Handbook of cross-cultural psychology: Vol. 5. Basic Processes*, (pp. 25–35). Allyn & Bacon.

Davidson, R., & Begley, S. (2012). *The emotional life of your brain*. Plume.

Davies, J. (2014). *Life unfolding: How the human body creates itself*. Oxford University Press.

Davis, M. C., Matthews, K. A., & Twamley, E. W. (1999). Is life more difficult on Mars or Venus? A meta-analytic review of sex differences in major and minor life events. *Annals of Behavioral Medicine, 21*(1), 83–97.

Davis, M., Eshelman, E. R., & McKay, M. (2008). *The relaxation and stress reduction workbook*. New Harbinger.

Davis, M. L., Morina, N., Powers, M. B., Smits, J. A. J., & Emmelkamp, P. M. G. (2015). A meta-analysis of the efficacy of acceptance and commitment therapy for clinically relevant mental and physical health problems. *Psychotherapy and Psychosomatics, 84*(1), 30–36.

Dawes, R. M. (1994). *House of cards: Psychology and psychotherapy built on myth*. Free Press.

Dawson, A. (2011, October 26). Study says generation X is balanced and happy. *CNN.* http://www.cnn.com/2011/10/26/living/gen-x-satisfied/

Dawson, J. (1975). Socio-economic differences in size judgments of discs and coins by Chinese primary VI children in Hong Kong. *Perceptual and Motor Skills, 41*, 107–110.

De Ridder, S. (2021). The banality of digital reputation: A visual ethnography of young people, reputation, and social media. *Media and Communication (ISSN: 2183–2439), 9*(3), 218–227. https://doi.org/10.17645/mac.v9i3.4176

de Souza, D., Oliveras-Fabregas, A., Espelt, M., Cancela, M., Teixidó-Compañó, E., & Jerez-Roig, J. (2021). Multimorbidity and its associated factors among adults aged 50 and over: A cross-sectional study in 17 European countries. *PlusOne.* https://journals.plos.org/plosone/article?id=10.1371/journal.pone.0246623

Death With Dignity. (2022). *State legislation report*. States. https://deathwithdignity.org/states/

Deaton, A. (2013). *The great escape*. Princeton University Press.

Delson, S. (2021, July 31). Nineteenth-century Instagram. *The Wall Street Journal*, C14

Department of Labor. (2016). Occupational outlook handbook. https://www.bls.gov/ooh/life-physical-and-social-science/psychologists.htm

Deshpande, S., Nagendra, H., & Nagarathna, R. (2009). A randomized control trial of the effect of yoga on *gunas* (personality) and self esteem in normal healthy volunteers. *International Journal of Yoga, 2*(1), 13–21.

Deutsch, H. (1944). *The psychology of women: A psychoanalytic interpretation: Vol. 1. Girlhood*. Grune & Stratton.

Deutsch, H. (1945). *The psychology of women: A psychoanalytic interpretation: Vol. 2. Motherhood*. Grune & Stratton.

Devereux, G. (1953). Cultural factors in psychoanalytic therapy. *Journal of the American Psychoanalytic Association, 1*, 629–655.

Dewey, J. (1884). The new psychology. *Andover Review, 2*, 278–289.

Dhir, A., Torsheim, T., Pallesen, S., Andreassen, C. S. (2017). Do online privacy concerns predict selfie behavior among adolescents, young adults and adults? *Frontiers in Psychology, 8*, 815. https://doi.org/10.3389/fpsyg.2017.00815

Diamond, L. (2009). *Sexual fluidity: Understanding women's love and desire*. Harvard University Press.

Diamond, L. M. (2008). Female bisexuality from adolescence to adulthood: Results from a 10-year longitudinal study. *Developmental Psychology, 44*(1), 5–14.

DiClemente, D., & Hantula, D. (2000). John Broadus Watson, IO psychologist. http://www.siop.org/tip/backissues/TipApri l00/7Diclemente.aspx

Dijksterhuis, A. (2004). Think different: The merits of unconscious thought in preference development and decision making. *Journal of Personality and Social Psychology, 87,* 586–598.

Dijksterhuis, A., Bos, M. W., Nordgren, L. F., & van Baaren, R. B. (2006). On making the right choice: The deliberation without attention effect. *Science, 311,* 1005–1007.

Dilthey, W. (2002). *The formation of the historical world in the human sciences.* Princeton University Press. (Original work published 1910)

Djikic, M., Oatley, K., & Carland, M. (2012). Genre or artistic merit? The effect of literature on personality. *Scientific Study of Literature, 2*(1), 25–36.

Dobreva-Martinova, T., & Strickland, L. H. (Eds.). (2001, September/October). The many sides of Bekhterev [Special issue]. *Journal of Russian and East European Psychology, 39,* 5.

Docker, C. (2013). *Five last acts—The exit path: The arts and science of rational suicide in the face of unbearable, unbelievable suffering.* CreateSpace.

Doebel, S., & Munakata, Y. (2018). Group influences on engaging self-control: Children delay gratification and value it more when their in-group delays and their out-group doesn't. *Psychological Science, 29*(5), 738–748.

Dolan, M. (2014). Disgraced journalist Stephen Glass unlikely ever be a lawyer. *Los Angeles Times.* https://www.latimes.com/local/lanow/la-me-ln-stephen-glass-lawyer-ruling-20140128-story.html#axzz2rixUCEx0

Donnellan, M. B., Conger, R. D., & Burzette, R. G. (2007). Personality development from late adolescence to young adulthood: Differential stability, normative maturity, and evidence for the maturity-stability hypothesis. *Journal of Personality, 75,* 237–267.

Donnellan, M. B., & Robins, R. (2009). The development of personality across the lifespan. In P. Corr & G. Matthews (Eds.), *The Cambridge handbook of personality psychology* (pp. 191–204). United Kingdom Cambridge University Press.

Draguns, J. (2009). Personality in cross-cultural perspective. In P. Corr & G. Matthews (Eds.), *The Cambridge handbook of personality psychology* (pp. 556–576). Cambridge University Press.

Dreger, A. (2000). *Hermaphrodites and the medical invention of sex.* Harvard University Press.

Drob, S. L. (1999). Jung and the kabbalah. *History of Psychology, 2*(2), 102–118.

Dubal, D. B., Yokoyama, J. S., Zhu, L., Broestl, L., Worden, K., Wang, D., . . . Mucke, L. (2014). Life extension factor KLOTHO enhances cognition. *Cell, 7,* http://www.ncbi.nlm.nih.gov/pubmed/24813892

Dubiel, R. M. (2004). *The road to fellowship: The role of the Emmanuel movement in the development of alcoholics anonymous. iUniverse.*

Dufresne, T. (2003). *Killing Freud.* Continuum International.

Dumont, F. (2010). *A history of personality psychology.* Cambridge University Press.

Dunning, D., & Kruger, J. (1999). Unskilled and unaware of it: How difficulties in recognizing one's own incompetence lead to inflated self-assessments. *Journal of Personality and Social Psychology, 77*(6), 1121–1134.

Dutt, A., Wahl, H.-W., & Diehl, M. (2018). Awareness of aging process. *Oxford Research Encyclopedia of Psychology.* https://oxfordre.com/psychology/view/10.1093/acrefore/9780190236557.001.0001/acrefore-9780190236557-e-397

Eagly, A. H. (1997). Sex differences in social behavior: Comparing social role theory and evolutionary psychology. *American Psychologist, 52*(12), 1380–1383.

Eatwell, R., & Goodwin, M. (2018). "Chapter 1: Myths." *National populism - The revolt against liberal democracy.* Pelican Books.

Economist. (2021, October 26). Why vaccine passports are creating a chaos. *The Economist.* https://www.economist.com/.../why-vaccine.../21805939

Edwards, S. (2013). Holistic psychology: A brief primer. *Journal of Psychology in Africa, 23*(3), 531–537.

Einstein, A. (1905). On the electrodynamics of moving bodies. *Annalen der Physik, 17,* 891–921.

Eisold, K. (2002). Jung, Jungians, and psychoanalysis. *Psychoanalytic Psychology, 19,* 501–524.

Elia, I. E. (2013). A foxy view of human beauty: Implications of the farm fox experiment for understanding the origins of structural and experiential aspects of facial attractiveness. *Quarterly Review of Biology*, *88*, 3. http://www.jstor.org/stable/10.1086/671486

Ellens, J. H. (Ed.). (2011). *Explaining evil*. Praeger.

Ellis, H. H., & Symonds, J. A. (2006). *Sexual inversion*. Bibliobazaar. (Original work published 1897)

Eme, R. (2008). Male life-course persistent antisocial behavior: A review of neurodevelopmental factors. *Aggression and Violent Behavior*, *14*, 348–358.

Emergen Research. (2022). Top 10 global leading and promising companies in the assessment services industry. *Emergen Research*. https://www.emergenresearch.com/blog/top-10-global-leading-and-promising-companies-in-the-assessment-services-industry

Emmons, R. A. (1984). Factor analysis and construct validity of the narcissistic personality inventory. *Journal of Personality Assessment*, *48*, 291–300.

Emmons, R. A. (1987). Narcissism: Theory and measurement. *Journal of Personality and Social Psychology*, *52*, 11–17.

Emmons, R. A., & McCullough, M. E. (2003). Counting blessings versus burdens: Experimental studies of gratitude and subjective well-being in daily life. *Journal of Personality and Social Psychology*, *84*, 377–389.

Engelhart, K. (2021, May 31). Home and alone. *What robots can—and can't—do for the old and lonely* (pp. 24–29). The New Yorker.

English, H., & English, A. C. (1958). *A comprehensive dictionary of psychological and psychoanalytical terms*. Longmans, Green.

Epel, E. (2009). Psychological and metabolic stress: A recipe for accelerated cellular aging? *Hormones (Athens)*, *8*, 7–22.

Epel, E. (2012). How reversible is telomeric aging? *Cancer Prevention Research*, *5*(10), 1163–1168.

Erikson, E. (1950). *Childhood and society*. Norton.

Erikson, E. (1968). *Identity: Youth and crisis*. Norton.

Erlenmeyer-Kimlig, L., Squires-Wheeler, E., Adamo, U., Bassett, A., Cornblatt, B., Kestenbausm, C., . . . Gottesman, I. (1995). The New York high-risk project—Psychoses and cluster: A personality disorders in offspring of schizophrenic patients at 23 years of follow-up. *Archives of General Psychiatry*, *52*, 857–865.

Esaki, L. (2001, April 1). Connecting to the 21st century educational reform in Japan and reflections on global culture. The Daily Yomiuri, P. 6.

Esang, M., & Ahmed, S. (2018). A closer look at substance use and suicide. *The American Journal of Psychiatry*. https://doi.org/10.1176/appi.ajp-rj.2018.130603

Escorial, S. (2007). Analysis of the gender variable in the Eysenck personality questionnaire–Revised scales using differential item functioning techniques. *Educational and Psychological Measurement*, *67*(6), 990–1001.

Essau, C., Sasagawa, S., Ishikawa, S., Okajima, I., O'Callaghan, J., & Bray, D. (2012, November). A Japanese form of social anxiety (taijin kyofusho): Frequency and correlates in two generations of the same family. *International Journal of Social Psychiatry*, *58*(6), 635–642.

Esterson, A. (2002). The myth of Freud's ostracism by the medical community in 1896–1905: Jeffrey Masson's assault on truth. *History of Psychology*, *5*(2), 115–134.

Etaugh, C., & Bridges, J. (2017). *Women's lives: A psychological exploration* (4th ed.). Taylor & Francis.

Evans, J., Saghal, N., Salazar, A. M., Starr, K., & Corichi, M. (2022, March 2). Gender roles in the family. How Indians view gender roles in families and society. *Pew Research Center*. https://www.pewresearch.org/religion/2022/03/02/how-indians-view-gender-roles-in-families-and-society/

Eysenck, H. (1948). *Dimensions of personality*. Routledge & Kegan.

Eysenck, H. J. (1956). *Sense and nonsense in psychology*. Penguin Books.

Eysenck, H. J. (1993). Creativity and personality: Suggestions for a theory. *Psychological Inquiry*, *4*(3), 147–178.

Eysenck, H. J., & Eysenck, S. B. G. (1976). *Psychoticism as a dimension of personality*. Hodder & Stoughton.

Faiola, A. (2003, December 27). Japan's empire of cool: Country's culture becomes its biggest export. Washington Post, p. A01.

Fairhall, J. (2012). Nature, existential shame, and transcendence: An ecocritical approach to Ulysses. *Joyce Studies Annual*, 66–95.

Faja, S., & Dawson, G. (2013). Reduced delay of gratification and effortful control among young children with autism spectrum disorders. *Autism*. http://aut.sagepub.com/content/early/2013/12/09/1362361313512424.long

Farmer, R., & Chapman, A. (2007). *Behavioral interventions in cognitive behavior therapy: Practical guidance for putting theory into action.* American Psychological Association.

Farrington, D. P. (2002). Families and crime. In J. Q. Wilson & J. Petersilia (Eds.), *Crime: Public policies for crime control* (2nd ed., pp. 129–148). Institute for Contemporary Studies Press.

Fausto-Sterling, A. (2012). *Sex/gender: Biology in a social world.* Routledge.

Fazio, R. (1989). On the power and functionality of attitudes: The role of attitude accessibility. In A. R. Pratkanis et al. (eds.), *Attitude structure and function* (pp. 153–179). Lawrence Erbaum Associates.

Fazio, R., Williams, C., & Powell, M. (2000). Measuring associative strength: category-item associations and their activation from memory. *Political Psychology, 2*(1), 7–27.

Feldman, R., Forrest, L., & Happ, B. (2002).

Self-presentation and verbal deception: Do self-presenters lie more? *Journal of Basic and Applied Social Psychology, 24*(2), 163–170.

Felson, R., & Palmore, C. (2018). Biases in blaming victims of rape and other crime. *Psychology of Violence, 8*(3), 390–399.

Fernald, A. (2010). Getting beyond the "convenience" sample in research on early cognitive development. *Behavioral and Brain Sciences, 33*(2/3), 31–32.

Fernandez, S., Castano, E., & Singh, I. (2010). Managing death in the burning grounds of Varanasi, India: A terror management investigation. *Journal of Cross-Cultural Psychology, 41*, 182–194.

Ferrari, J. R. (2010). *Still procrastinating? The no regrets guide to getting it done.* Wiley.

Festinger, L. (1957). *A theory of cognitive dissonance.* Stanford University Press.

Festinger, L., Riecken, H. W., & Schachter, S. (1956). *When prophecy fails: A social and psychological study of a modern group that predicted the destruction of the world.* University of Minnesota Press.

Fine, C. (2006). *A mind of its own: How your brain distorts and deceives.* Icon Books.

Finkel, E. J., Eastwick, P., Karney, B., Reis, H., & Specher, S. (2012, January). Online dating: A critical analysis from the perspective of psychological science. *Psychological Science in the Public Interest, 13*, 3–66.

Finlayson, C. (2014). *The improbable primate: How

water shaped human evolution.* Oxford University Press.

Fischer, R., & Smith, P. (2003). Reward allocation and culture: A meta-analysis. *Journal of Cross-Cultural Psychology, 34*(3), 251–268.

Fisher, H. (2004). *Why we love: The nature and chemistry of romantic love.* Henry Holt.

Fiske, S. (2010). Envy up, scorn down: How comparison divides us. *American Psychologist, 65*(8), 688–706.

Fiske, S. T., Gilbert, D. T., & Lindzey, G. (2009). *Handbook of social psychology.* Wiley.

Flood, G. (2012). *An introduction to Hinduism.* Cambridge University Press.

Folkman, S., Lazarus, R. S., Pimley, S., & Novacek, J. (1987). Age differences in stress and coping processes. *Psychology and Aging, 2*(2), 171–184.

Fombrun, C. J. (1996). *Reputation: Realizing value from the corporate brand.* Harvard Business School Brand.

Fontaine, R., & Frederick, K. (2021, May 8–9). Democracy's digital defenses. *The Wall Street Journal.* P. C3.

Foschi, R., & Lombardo, G. (2006). Lewinian contribution to the study of personality as the alternative to the mainstream of personality psychology in the 20th century. In J. Trempala, A. Pepitone, & B. Raven (Eds.), *Lewinian psychology* (Vol. 1., pp. 86–98). Kazimierz Wielki University Press.

Fountoulakis, K. N., Iacovides, A., Ioannidou, C., Bascialla, F., Nimatoudis, I., Kaprinis, G., et al. (2002). Reliability and cultural applicability of the Greek version of the international personality disorders examination. *BMC Psychiatry*, *2*(1), 6.

Fowers, B. J., & Richardson, F. C. (1996). Why is multiculturalism good? *American Psychologist*, *51*, 609–621.

Frank, H., Lueger, M., & Korunka, C. (2007). The significance of personality in business start-up intentions, start-up realization and business success. *Entrepreneurship & Regional Development: An International Journal*, *19*(3), 227–251.

Frankl, V. (1959). *Man's search for meaning*. Pocket.

Freeman, D., Evans, N., Lister, R., Antley, A., Dunn, G., & Slater, M. (2014). Height, social comparison, and paranoia: An immersive virtual reality experimental study. *Psychiatry Research*, *218*(3), 348–352.

Freud, A. (1966). *The ego and the mechanisms of defense*. International Universities Press. (Original work published 1936)

Freud, S. (1957). On the history of the psychoanalytic movement. In J. Strachey (Ed. & Trans.), *The standard edition of the complete psychological works of Sigmund Freud* (Vol. 14, pp. 3–66). Hogarth. (Original work published 1914)

Freud, S. (1990). *Beyond the pleasure principle*. Norton. (Original work published 1920)

Freud, S. (2000). *Three essays on the theory of sexuality*. Basic Books. (Original work published 1905)

Freud, S. (2009a). *Beyond the pleasure principle*. Martino Fine Books. (Original work published 1920)

Freud, S. (2009b). *The psychopathology of everyday life*. General Books LLC. (Original work published 1901)

Freud, S., & Bullitt, W. (1966). *Thomas Woodrow Wilson: A psychological study*. Houghton Mifflin.

Friedman, M., & Ulmer, D. (1984). *Treating type A behavior and your heart*. Knopf.

Frost, E. P. (1912). Discussion: Can biology and physiology dispense with consciousness? *Psychological Review*, *19*(3), 246–252. https://doi.org/10.1037/h0073496

Fung, Y.-L. (1948). *A short history of Chinese philosophy*. Free Press.

Funkhouser, C. T. (2012). *New directions in digital poetry*. Continuum.

Furnham, A., & Baguma, P. (1999). A cross-cultural study from three countries of self-estimates of intelligence. *North American Journal of Psychology*, *1*, 69–77.

Furnham, A., Rakow, T., Sarmany-Schuller, I., & Fruyt, F. (1999). European differences in self-perceived multiple intelligences. *European Psychologist*, *4*(3), 131–138.

Gabbard, G. (1990). *Psychodynamic psychiatry in clinical practice*. American Psychiatric Press.

Gabriel, M. T., Critelli, J. W., & Ee, J. S. (1994). Narcissistic illusions in self-evaluations of intelligence and

attractiveness. *Journal of Personality*, *62*(1), 143–155.

Gaertner, L., Sedikides, C., Cai, H., & Brown, J. (2010). It's not weird, it's wrong: When researchers overlook underlying genotypes, they will not detect universal processes. *Behavioral and Brain Sciences*, *33*(2/3), 33–34.

Galambos, N. L., Fang, S., Krahn, H. J., Johnson, M. D., & Lachman, M. E. (2015). Up, not down: The age curve in happiness from early adulthood to midlife in two longitudinal studies. *Developmental Psychology*, *51*(11), 1664–1671.

Gallup International. (2017). Religion Prevails in the World. https://www.gallup-international.bg/en/36009/religion-prevails-in-the-world/

Gallup Polls. (2019). Americans give US world image highest ratings since 2003. *Gallup*.

Gangestad, S. W., Haselton, M. G., & Buss, D. M. (2006). Evolutionary foundations of cultural variation: Evoked culture and mate preferences. *Psychological Inquiry*, *17*, 75–95.

Gao, G. (2015). How do Americans stand out from the rest of the world? *Pew Research Center*. www.pewresearch.org/fact-tank/2015/03/12/how-do-americans-stand-out-from-the-rest-of-the-world/

Garcia, R. (2020). Pessimism. In M. Gellman (Ed.), *Encyclopedia of behavioral medicine*. Springer. https://doi.org/10.1007/978-3-030-39903-0_976

Gardiner, H., Mutter, J., & Kosmitzki. (1998). *Lives across cultures: Cross-cultural human development*. Allyn & Bacon.

Gardner, H., & Davis, K. (2013). *The app generation: How today's youth navigate identity, intimacy, and imagination in a digital world.* Yale University Press.

Garfield, S. (2009). The clinical method in personality assessment. In J. Wepman & R. Heine (Eds.), *Concepts of personality* (pp. 474–501). Transaction.

Gay, P. (1998). *Freud: A life for our time.* Norton.

Geary, D. (2009). *Male, female: The evolution of human sex differences.* American Psychological Association.

Gensler, H. (2013). *Ethics and the golden rule.* Routledge.

Gerber, A., Huber, G., Doherty, D., Dowling, C., & Ha, S. (2010). Personality and political attitudes: Relationships across issue domains and political contexts. *American Political Science Review, 104*(1), 111–133.

Gerber, A., Kocsis, J., Milrod, B., Roose, S., Barber, J., Thase, M., Perkins, P., & Leon, A. (2011). A quality-based review of randomized controlled trials of psychodynamic psychotherapy. *American Journal of Psychiatry, 168*(1), 19–28.

Gergen, K. (2001). Psychological science in a postmodern context. *American Psychologist, 56*, 803–813.

Gethin, R. (1998). *Foundations of Buddhism.* Oxford University Press.

Gettleman, J. (2018). The peculiar position of India's third gender. *The New York Times.* https://www.nytimes.com/2018/02/17/style/india-third-gender-hijras-transgender.html

Geuens, N., Braspenning, M., Van Bogaert, P., & Franck, E. (2015). Individual vulnerability to burnout in nurses: The role of type D personality within different nursing specialty areas. *Burnout Research, 2*(2/3), 80–86.

Giansanti, D. (2021, March). The social robot in rehabilitation and assistance: What is the future? *Healthcare, 9*(3), 244. https://doi.org/10.3390/healthcare9030244

Gibson, C. (2013, May 2). Connie Picciotto has kept vigil near the White House for 32 years. Why, and at what cost? *The Washington Post.* http://www.washingtonpost.com/sf/feature/wp/2013/05/02/conniepicciottohaskeptvigilnearthewhitehousefor32yearswhyandatwhatcost/

Gibson, M. (2002). *Born to crime: Cesare Lombroso and the origins of biological criminology.* Praeger.

Glass, S. (2003). *The fabulist.* Simon & Schuster.

Glick, P., & Fiske, S. T. (1997). Hostile and benevolent sexism. *Psychology of Women Quarterly, 21*, 119–135.

Glynn, I. (1999). *An anatomy of thought.* Oxford University Press.

Glynn, L. G. (2009). Multimorbidity: Another key issue for cardiovascular medicine. *Lancet, 374*(9699), 1421–1422.

Gold, E., & Zahn, S. (2018). *Buddhist psychology & gestalt therapy integrated: Psychotherapy for the 21st century.* Metta Press.

Goldberg, L. R. (1993). The structure of phenotypic personality traits. *American Psychologist, 48*, 26–34.

Goldberg, M. (2014, August 4). What is a woman? *The New Yorker,* 24–28.

Goldberg, S., Flook, L., Hirshberg, M., Davidson, R., & Schaefer, S. (2021). Brief breath awareness training yields poorer working memory performance in the context of acute stress. *Cognitive Emotions, 35*(5), 1009–1017.

Goldman. (2010). Man's new best friend? A forgotten Russian experiment in fox domestication. *Scientific American.* https://blogs.scientificamerican.com/guest-blog/mans-new-best-friend-a-forgotten-russian-experiment-in-fox-domestication/

Goldston, D., Molock, S., Whitbeck, L., Murakami, J., Zayas, L., & Hall, G. C. N. (2008). Cultural considerations in adolescent suicide prevention and psychosocial treatment. *American Psychologist, 63*(1), 14–31.

Goleman, D., & Davidson, R. (2017). *Altered traits: Science reveals how meditation changes your mind, brain, and body.* Avery.

Gollob, H., & Levine, J. (1967). Distraction as a factor in the enjoyment of aggressive humor. *Journal of Personality and Social Psychology, 5*(3), 368–372.

Gordon, D. (2012). A flood of emotions: Treating the uncontrollable crying and laughing of pseudobulbar affect. *Neurology Now, 8*(1), 26–29.

Gottfredson, M. R. (2007). Self-control theory and criminal violence. In D. J. Flannery,

A. T. Vazsonyi, & I. Waldman (Eds.), *The Cambridge handbook of violent behavior and aggression* (pp. 533–544). Cambridge University Press.

Graham, J., & Haidt, J. (2010). Beyond beliefs: Religions bind individual into moral communities. *Personality and Social Psychology Review, 14*, 140–150.

Gralmich, J., & Devlin, K. (2019). More people around the world see U.S. power and influence as a 'major threat' to their country. *Pew Research Center*. https://www.pewresearch.org/fact-tank/2019/02/14/more-people-around-the-world-see-u-s-power-and-influence-as-a-major-threat-to-their-country/

Gramzow, R., & Tangney, J. P. (1992). Proneness to shame and the narcissistic personality. *Personality and Social Psychology Bulletin, 18*, 369–376.

Grant, A. (2021). *Think again: The power of knowing what you don't know*. Penguin.

Gravert, C., & Collentine, L. (2021). When nudges aren't enough: Norms, incentives, and habit formation in public transport usage. *Journal of Economic Behavior and Organization, 190*, 1–14.

Greening, T. (1971). *Existential humanistic psychology*. Brooks/Cole.

Greening, T. (1986). Passion bearers and peace psychology. *Journal of Humanistic Psychology, 26*(4), 98–105.

Greening, T. (2011). An interview. *Journal of Humanistic Psychology, 51*(4), 396–399.

Griffiths, K., Mackinnon, A., Crisp, D., Christensen, H., Bennett, K., & Farrer, L. (2012). The effectiveness of an online support group for members of the community with depression: A randomized controlled trial. *PLOS Online*. http://dx.doi.org/10.1371/journal.pone.0053244

Grossmann, I. (2017). Wisdom in context. *Perspectives on Psychological Science, 12*(2), 233–257.

Gunderson, J., & Lyoo, K. (1997). Family problems and relationships for adults with borderline personality disorder. *Harvard Review of Psychiatry, 4*, 272–278.

Gurven, M., Von Rueden, C., Massenkoff, M., Kaplan, H., & Lero Vie, M. (2013). How universal is the big five? Testing the five-factor model of personality variation among forager–farmers in the Bolivian Amazon. *Journal of Personality and Social Psychology, 104*(2), 354.

Hafenbrack, A., LaPalme, M., & Solal, I. (2022). Mindfulness meditation reduces guilt and prosocial reparation. *Journal of Personality and Social Psychology, 123*(1), 28–54.

Haidt, J., & Rose-Stockwell, T. (2019, December). The dark psychology of social networks. *The Atlantic*. https://www.theatlantic.com/magazine/archive/2019/12/social-media-democracy/600763/

Hailikari, T., Katajavuori, N., & Asikainen, H. (2021). Understanding procrastination: A case of a study skills course. *Social Psychological Education, 24*(2), 589–606.

Hall, C., & Lindzey, G. (1957). *Theories of personality*. Wiley.

Hall, G. S. (1904). *Adolescence: Its psychology and its relations to physiology, anthropology, sociology, sex, crime, religion and education* (2 Vols.). Appleton.

Hall, H. (2020). Progeria. Science-based medicine. https://sciencebasedmedicine.org/progeria/

Hall, M. (2015). *Metrosexual masculinity*. Macmillan.

Halperin, D. (2012). *How to be gay*. Belknap Press.

Hamamura, T. (2017). Cultural differences in self-esteem. In V. Zeigler-Hill & T. Shackelford (Eds.), *Encyclopedia of personality and individual differences*. Springer, Cham. https://doi.org/10.1007/978-3-319-28099-8_1126-1

Hampson, S. E., Edmonds, G. W., Goldberg, L. R., Dubanoski, J. P., & Hillier, T. A. (2015). A life-span behavioral mechanism relating childhood conscientiousness to adult clinical health. *Health Psychology, 34*(9), 887–895.

Hankir, A. (2022). Fighting mental health stigma. *Bulletin of the World Health Organization, 100*(8), 472–473. https://doi.org/10.2471/BLT.22.030822

Harari, Y. N. (2014, September 5). Were we happier in the stone age? *The Guardian*.

Harden, K. (2021). *The genetic lottery: Why DNA matters for social equality*. Princeton University Press.

Hare, R. D. (1983). Diagnosis of antisocial personality disorder in two prison populations.

American Journal of Psychiatry, 140, 887–890.

Hare, R. D. (1991). *The Hare psychopathy checklist—revised*. Multi-Health Systems.

Hare, R. D. (1998). The PCL-R assessment of psychopathy: Some issues and concerns. *Legal and Criminological Psychology, 3*, 101–122.

Harenski, C., Antonenko, O., Shane, M., & Kiehl, K. (2008). Gender differences in neural mechanisms underlying moral sensitivity. *Social Cognitive and Affective Neuroscience, 3*(4), 313–321.

Harkness, S. (1992). Human development in psychological anthropology. In T. Schwartz, G. M. White, & C. A. Lutz (Eds.), *New directions in psychological anthropology* (pp. 102–121). Cambridge University Press.

Harley, N. (April 3). Progeria sufferer Hayley Okines dies, aged 17. *The Telegraph*. 2015 http://www.telegraph.co.uk/news/health/children/11513990/Hayley-Okines-who-had-the-body-of-a-104-year-old-has-died-aged-17.html

Harper, R. (2010). Paranoid personality disorder. *Corsini Encyclopedia of Psychology*. http://onlinelibrary.wiley.com/doi/10.1002/9780470479216.corpsy0637/full

Harrington, A. (1996). *Reenchanted science: Holism in German culture from Wilhelm II to Hitler*. Princeton University Press.

Harris, M., Brett, C., Johnson, W., & Deary, I. (2016). Personality stability from age 14 to age 77 years. *Psychology of Aging, 31*(8), 862–874.

Hart, J. (2013). *Empire of ideas: The origins of public diplomacy and the transformation of US foreign policy*. Oxford University Press.

Hart, J., Nailling, E., Bizer, G. Y., & Collins, C. K. (2015). Attachment theory as a framework for explaining engagement with Facebook. *Personality and Individual Differences, 77*, 33–40.

Hartmann, H. (1958). *Ego psychology and the problem of adaptation*. International Universities Press.

Haun, D. B. M., Call, J., Janzen, G., & Levinson, S. (2006). Evolutionary psychology of special representations in the Hominade. *Current Biology, 16*(17), 1736–1740.

Hawley, J. (Ed.). (1987). *Saints and virtues*. University of California Press.

Hayward, R. D., & Kemmelmeier, M. (2011). Weber revisited: A cross-national analysis of religiosity, religious culture, and economic attitudes. *Journal of Cross-Cultural Psychology, 42*, 1406–1420.

Healthy People. (2020). Access to health services. https://www.healthypeople.gov/2020/topics-objectives/topic/social-determinants-health/interventions-resources/access-to-health

Heider, F. (1944). Social perception and phenomenal causality. *Psychological Review, 51*, 358–374.

Heider, F. (1958). *The psychology of interpersonal relations*. Wiley.

Heiman, G. (1996). *Basic statistics for the behavioral sciences*. Houghton Mifflin.

Heine, S. J. (2008). *Cultural psychology*. W. W. Norton.

Heine, S., Lehman, D., Markus, H., & Kitayama, S. (1999). Is there a universal need for positive self-regard? *Psychological Review, 106*(4), 766–794.

Heine, S., Lehman, D., Peng, K., & Greenholtz, J. (2002). What's wrong with cross-cultural comparisons of subjective Likert scales? The reference group effect. *Journal of Personality and Social Psychology, 82*(6), 903–918.

Helle, A., Watts, A., Trull, T., & Sher, K. (2019). Alcohol use disorder and antisocial and borderline personality disorders. *Alcohol Research: Current Reviews, 40*(1), 35–50.

Henrich, J., Heine, S., & Norenzayan, A. (2010a). The weirdest people in the world? *Behavioral and Brain Sciences, 33*(2/3), 123.

Hesse, M. (2014, September 20). When no gender fits: A quest to be seen as just a person. *The Washington Post*, A1,14–15,

Heydari, M., Masafi, S., Jafari, M., Saadat, S. H., & Shahyad, S. (2018). Effectiveness of acceptance and commitment therapy on anxiety and depression of Razi psychiatric center staff. *Open Access Macedonian Journal of Medical Science, 6*(2), 410–415.

Hilger, K., & Markett, S. (2021). Personality network neuroscience: Promises and challenges on the way toward a unifying framework of individual variability. *Network*

Neuroscience, 5(3), 631–645. https://doi.org/10.1162/netn_a_00198

Hilsenroth, M. J. (2007). A programmatic study of short-term psychodynamic psychotherapy: Assessment, process, outcome, and training. *Psychotherapy Research, 17*(1), 31–45.

Hilton, D., & Liu, J. H. (2017). History as the narrative of a people: From function to structure and content. *Memory Studies, 10*(3), 297–309.

Hintze, J. M., Volpe, R. J., & Shapiro, E. S. (2002). Best practices in the systematic direct observation of student behavior. In A. Thomas & J. Grimes (Eds.), *Best practices in school psychology IV* (pp. 993–1006). National Association of School Psychologists.

Hirschfeld, M. (1991). *The transvestites: The erotic drive to cross-dress.* Prometheus Books. (Original work published in German 1910)

Hirschman, N. (2010). Choosing betrayal. *Perspectives on Politics, 8*(1), 271–278.

Ho, D. (1998). Indigenous psychologies: Asian perspectives. *Journal of Cross-Cultural Psychology, 29*(1), 88–103.

Hobbs, T., Barry, R., & Koh, Y. (2021, December). How TikTok inundates teens with eating disorder videos. *The Wall Street Journal,* 18–19, A 1, 15.

Hock, R. (2013). Personality. In C. Campanella, J. Mosher, S. Frail, & M. Schricker (Eds.), *Forty studies that changed psychology* (pp. 190–197). Pearson Education.

Hodges, A. (1983). *Alan Turing: The enigma.* Burnett.

Hodgins, S., De Brit, S., Chhabra, P., & Côté, G. (2010). Anxiety disorders among offenders with antisocial personality disorders: A distinct subtype? *Canadian Journal of Psychiatry, 55*(12), 784–791.

Hoffman, E., & Compton, W. (2022, March). The dao of Maslow: A new direction for mentorship. *Journal of Humanistic Psychology.* https://doi.org/10.1177/00221678221076574

Hoffman, L., Granger, N., Vallejos, L., & Moats, M. (2016). An existential–humanistic perspective on black lives matter and contemporary protest movements. *Journal of Humanistic Psychology, 56*(6), 595–611.

Hofstede, G. (1980). *Culture's consequences: International differences in work-related values.* SAGE.

Hogan, R., & Bond, H. (2009). Culture and personality. In P. Corr & G. Matthews (Eds.), *The Cambridge handbook of personality psychology* (pp. 577–588). Cambridge University Press.

Hooker, R. (1982). *The complete works of Richard Hooker.* Harvard University Press.

Hopwood, C., Donnellan, B., Blonigen, D., Krueger, R., McGue, M., Iacono, W. G., & Burt, A. (2011). Genetic and environmental influences on personality trait stability and growth during the transition to adulthood: A three-wave longitudinal study. *Journal of Personality and Social Psychology, 100*(3), 545–556.

Horner, A. J. (1991). *Psychoanalytic object relations therapy.* Jason Aronson.

Hornstein, G. (1992). The return of the repressed: Psychology's problematic relations with psychoanalysis, 1909–1960. *American Psychologist, 47,* 254–263.

Hörz-Sagstetter, S., Diamond, D., Clarkin, J., Levy, K., Rentrop, M., Fischer-Kern, M., Cain, N., & Doering, S. (2018). Clinical characteristics of comorbid narcissistic personality disorder in patients with borderline personality disorder. *Journal of Personality Disorders, 32*(4), 562–575.

Hovenkamp-Hermelink, J. H. M., Jeronimus, B., van der Veen, D., Spinhoven, P., Penninx, B. W., Schoevers, R., & Riese, H. (2019). Differential associations of locus of control with anxiety, depression, and life-events: A five-wave, nine-year study to test stability and change. *Journal of Affective Disorders, 253*(6), 26–34. https://doi.org/10.1016/j.jad.2019.04.005

Ho-Ying Fu, J., & Chiu, C-Y. (2007). Local culture's responses to globalization: Exemplary persons and their attendant values. *Journal of Cross-Cultural Psychology, 38*(5), 636–653.

Hsu, F.-H. (2002). *Behind deep blue: Building the computer that defeated the world chess champion.* Princeton University Press.

Hughes, K. (2012). A behavioral understanding of privacy and its implications for privacy law. *The Modern Law Review, 75*(5), *806–836.*

Huizinga, J. (2013). *The waning of the middle ages*. Dover. (Original work published 1924)

Hume, D. (1987). *Essays: Moral, political, and literary*. Liberty Classics. (Original work published 1777)

Huntington, S. (1993). Clash of civilizations. *Foreign Affairs, 72*, 22–49.

Huntington, S. (1996). *The clash of civilizations and the remaking of world order*. Simon and Schuster.

Huntington, S. (2004). *Who are we? The challenges to America's national identity*. Simon and Schuster.

Hurlburt, R. T., & Knapp, T. J. (2006). Münsterberg in 1898, not Allport in 1937, introduced the terms idiographic and nomothetic to American psychology. *Theory & Psychology, 16*(2), 287–293.

Hyde, J. (2005). The gender similarities hypothesis. *American Psychologist, 60*(6), 581–592.

Hyde, J., & Plant, E. (1995). Magnitude of psychological gender differences: Another side to the story. *American Psychologist, 50*, 159–161.

Hyde, J. S., Lindberg, S. M., Linn, M. C., Ellis, A., & Williams, C. (2008). Gender similarities characterize math performance. *Science, 321*, 494–495.

Hyde, J. S., & Mertz, J. (2009). Gender, culture, and math. *Proceedings of the National Academy of Sciences, 106*(22), 8801–8807.

Hyde, L. (1998). *Trickster makes this world: Mischief, myth, and art*. Farrar, Straus and Giroux.

Intuition Robotics. (2020). Digital assistants vs digital companions: What's the difference? *Intuition Robotics*. https://blog.intuitionrobotics.com/digital-assistants-vs-digital-companions-whats-the-difference

Ireland, M., & Pennebaker, J. (2010). Language style matching in writing: Synchrony in essays, correspondence, and poetry. *Journal of Personality and Social Psychology, 99*(3), 549–571.

Isaeva, N. (1999). *From early Vedanta to Kashmir Shaivism*. State University of New York Press.

Italiano, L. (2021). Only 30 percent of US wives earn more than their husbands, data shows. *The New York Post*. https://nypost.com/2021/02/04/only-30-percent-of-us-wives-earn-more-than-their-husbands-data/

Iusitini, L., Gao, W., Sundborn, G., & Paterson, J. (2011). Parenting practices among fathers of a cohort of Pacific infants in New Zealand. *Journal of Cross-Cultural Psychology, 42*(1), 39–55.

Jabr, F. (2015). Life's big leaps: Critical moments in evolution. *Quanta Magazine*. https://www.quantamagazine.org/20151110-evolution-of-big-brains/

Jackson, T. (2019). *The history of black psychology and humanistic psychology*. Routledge.

Jaffe, E. (2013). Why wait? The science behind procrastination. *The Observer*. http://www.psychologicalscience.org/index.php/publications/observer/2013/april-13/why-wait-the-science-behind-procrastination.html

Jaffee, S., & Hyde, J. S. (2000). Gender differences in moral orientation: A meta-analysis. *Psychological Bulletin, 126*, 703–726.

Jamison, K. R. (1993). *Touched with fire: Manic-depressive illness and the artistic temperament*. Free Press.

Jang, K., Livesley, W. J., & Vemon, P. A. (1996). Heritability of the Big Five personality dimensions and their facets: A twin study. *Journal of Personality, 64*(3), 577–591.

Jansen, M., Arntz, A., Merckelbach, H., & Mersch, P. P. (1994). Personality disorders and features in social phobia and panic disorder. *Journal of Abnormal Psychology, 103*(2), 391–395.

Jasielska, D., Stolarski, M., & Bilewicz, M. (2018). Biased, therefore unhappy: Disentangling the collectivism-happiness relationship globally. *Journal of Cross-Cultural Psychology, 49*(8), 1227–1246.

Jeffreys, S. (2003). *Unpacking queer politics*. Polity.

Jenkins, A. (1995). *Psychology and African Americans* (2nd ed.). Allyn & Bacon.

Jeronimus, B. F., Riese, H., Sanderman, R., & Ormel, J. (2014). Mutual reinforcement between neuroticism and life experiences: A five-wave, 16-year study to test reciprocal causation. *Journal of Personality and Social Psychology, 107*(4), 751–764.

Jessup, J. (1948, June 28). The newest utopia. *Life, 38*.

Joel, D. (2021). Beyond the binary: Rethinking sex and the brain. *Neuroscience and Behavioral Reviews, 122*(11), 165–175.

Joel, D., Berman, Z., Tavor, I., Wexler, N., Gaber, O., Stein, Y., Shefi, N., Pool, J., Urchs, S., Margulies, D., Liem, F., Hänggi, J., Jäncke, L., & Assaf, Y. (2015). Sex beyond the genitalia: The human brain mosaic. *Proceedings of the National Academy of Sciences USA, 112*(50), 15468–15473.

John, O. P., & Robbins, R. W. (1994). Accuracy and bias in self-perception: Individual differences in self-enhancement and the role of narcissism. *Journal of Personality and Social Psychology, 66*(1), 206–219.

John, O., & Srivastava, S. (2001). The big-five trait taxonomy: History, measurement, and theoretical perspectives. In L. Pervin & O. John (Eds.), *Handbook of personality: Theory and research* (2nd ed.). Guilford Press.

Johnson, J. (2001). Personality psychology: Methods. In N. Smelser & P. Baltes (Eds.), *International encyclopedia of the social and behavioral sciences*. Pergamon.

Johnson, W., & Krueger, R. F. (2005). Higher perceived life control decreases genetic variance in physical health: Evidence from a national twin study. *Journal of Personality and Social Psychology, 88*, 165–173.

Johnston, T. D. (2002). An early manuscript in the history of American comparative psychology Lewis Henry Morgan's "Animal Psychology" (1857). *History of Psychology, 5*, 323–355.

Jones, H. E. (2008). Scientific evidence and practical experience with methadone-assisted withdrawal of heroin-dependent pregnant patients. *Heroin Addiction and Related Clinical Problems, 10*, 33–38.

Jones, J. (2022a). Belief in god in U.S. dips to 81%, a new low. *Gallup News*. https://news.gallup.com/poll/393737/belief-god-dips-new-low.aspx

Jones, M. B., & Blanchard, R. (1998). Birth order and male homosexuality: Extension of Slater's index. *Human Biology, 70*, 775–787.

Jung, C. G. (1924). *Psychological types or the psychology of individuation*. Random House.

Jung, C. G. (1961). Recorded & edited by A. Jaffe. *Memories, dreams, reflections*. Random House.

Jung, C. G. (1967). *C. G. Jung collected works: Alchemical studies*. Princeton University Press. (Original work published 1929)

Jung, C. G., & Hinkle, B. M. (1912). *Psychology of the unconscious: A study of the transformations and symbolisms of the libido, a contribution to the history of the evolution of thought*. Kegan Paul.

Jung, K., Shavitt, S., Viswanathan, M., & Hilbe, J. (2014). Female hurricanes are deadlier than male hurricanes. *Proceedings of the National Academy of Sciences, 111*(24), 8782–8787.

Kabat-Zinn, Jon. (2012). *Mindfulness for beginners: Reclaiming the present moment—And Your Life*. Sounds True.

Kagan, J., & Herschkowitz, N. (2005). *Young mind in a growing brain*. Psychology Press.

Kagan, J., & Snidman, N. (1991). Temperamental factors in human development. *American Psychologist, 46*, 856–862.

Kahan, D. (2012). Ideology, motivated reasoning, and cognitive reflection: An experimental study. *Judgment and Decision Making, 8*, 407–424.

Kakar, S. (1995). Clinical work and cultural imagination. *Psychoanalytic Quarterly, 64*, 265–281.

Kallgren, C. A., & Wood, W. (1986). Access to attitude-relevant information in memory as determinant of attitude-behavior consistency. *Journal of Experimental Social Psychology, 22*, 328–338.

Kandel, E. (2012). *The age of insight*. Random House.

Kang, C. (2015, January 4). The "halo" effect. *The Washington Post Magazine*, 12–17.

Kaniel, R., Massey, C., & Robinson, D. (2010, September). The importance of being an optimist: Evidence from labor markets. *NBER Working Paper No. 16328*.

Kant, I. (1956). *Groundwork for a metaphysics of morals*. Harper & Row. (Original work published 1785)

Kaplan, R. (2012). *The revenge of geography: What the map tells us about coming conflicts and the battle against fate*. Random House.

Kaplan, R. M., & Saccuzzo, D. P. (2013). *Psychological testing: Principles, applications, and issues* (8th ed.). Wadsworth.

Kaplan-Solms, K., & Solms, M. (2000). *Clinical studies in neuro-psychoanalysis: Introduction to a depth neuropsychology.* Karnac.

Karimi, R., Bakhtiyari, M., & Masjedi, A. (2019). Protective factors of marital stability in long-term marriage globally: A systematic review. *Epidemiology and Health.* https://www.ncbi.nlm.nih.gov/pmc/articles/PMC6702121/

Karlsson, G. (2010). *Psychoanalysis in a new light.* Cambridge University Press.

Karon, B. P., & Widener, A. J. (2001). Repressed memories: Avoiding the obvious. *Psychoanalytic Psychology, 18,* 161–164.

Kasule, O. (2000). *Personality development in Islam.* Paper presented at the Leadership Training Programme, Islamic College of South Africa 1922 June. http://omarkasule02.tripod.com/id611.html

Kaur, J., & Bawa, J. (2016). Males, media and metrosexuality: An exploratory study of persuasion. *International Journal of Latest Technology in Engineering, Management & Applied Science, 5*(10). https://bit.ly/3cZWQfq

Kaur, V., & Lindinger-Sternart, S. (2020). Masturbation: Gender stigmatized sexual behavior affecting women's sexual wellness. *Journal of Counseling Sexology & Sexual Wellness Research Practice and Education.* https://digitalcommons.unf.edu/jcssw/

Keller, E. F. (1985). *Reflections on gender and science.* Yale University Press.

Kelley, H. H. (1967). Attribution theory in social psychology. In D. Levine (Ed.), *Nebraska Symposium of Motivation* (Vol. 15, pp. 192–240). University of Nebraska Press.

Kelley, H. H. (1979). *Personal relationships: Their structures and processes.* Erlbaum.

Kelly, G. A. (1955). *The psychology of personal constructs:* Vol. 1–2. W. W. Norton.

Kelly, G. A. (1963). *A theory of personality: The psychology of personal constructs.* W. W. Norton.

Kendler, H. H. (1999). The role of value in the world of psychology. *American Psychologist, 54,* 828–835.

Kennedy, H. (1981). The "third sex" theory of Karl Heinrich Ulrichs. *Journal of Homosexuality, 6*(1–2), 103–111.

Kenny, D. (2015). Stairway to hell: Life and death in the pop music industry. *The Conversation.* https://theconversation.com/stairway-to-hell-life-and-death-in-the-pop-music-industry-32735

Kenrick, D., & Funder, D. (1988). Profiting from controversy: Lessons from the person-situation debate. *American Psychologist, 43,* 23–34.

Kenrick, D. T., Li, N. P., & Butner, J. (2003). Dynamical evolutionary psychology: Individual decision rules and emergent social norms. *Psychological Review, 110,* 3–28.

Kern, M. L., & Friedman, H. S. (2008). Do conscientious individuals live longer? A quantitative review. *Health Psychology, 27*(5), 505–512.

Kernberg, O. (1992). *Aggression in personality disorders and perversions.* Yale University Press.

Kessler, A. (2022, January 2). Can social media alter a war? *The Wall Street Journal.* https://www.wsj.com/articles/can-social-media-alter-a-war-nato-russian-bots-colonial-pipline-national-security-ukraine-cyberwarfare-hack-invasion-11641130267

Kierkegaard, S. (1992). *Either/or: A fragment of life.* Penguin. (Original work published 1843)

Kim, E., Hagan, K., Grodstein, F., DeMeo, D., Vivo, I., & Kubzansky, L. (2016). Optimism and cause-specific mortality: A prospective study. *American Journal of Epidemiology, 185*(1), 21–29.

Kim, H., Schimmack, U., Cheng, C., Webster, G., & Spectre, A. (2016). The role of positive self-evaluation on cross-cultural differences in well-being. *Cross-Cultural Research, 50*(1), 85–99.

Kim, Y., O'Brien, K., & Kim, H. (2016). Measuring career aspirations across cultures: Using the career aspiration scale with young Korean women. *Journal of Career Assessment, 24*(3), 573–585.

Kinsey, A. (1998a). *Sexual behavior in the human female.* Indiana University Press. (Original work published 1953)

Kinsey, A. (1998b). *Sexual behavior in the human male.* Indiana University Press. (Original work published 1948)

Kinsley, D. (1986). *Hindu goddesses: Visions of the feminine in the Hindu religious tradition.* University of California Press.

Kitayama, S., Ishii, K., Imada, T., Takemura, K., & Ramaswamy, J. (2006). Voluntary settlement and the spirit of independence: Evidence from Japan's "northern frontier." *Journal of Personality and Social Psychology, 91,* 369–384.

Klages, L. (1929). *The science of character.* George Allen & Unwin.

Kleinman, A., & Kleinman, J. (1991). Suffering and its professional transformation: Toward an ethnography of interpersonal experience. *Culture, Medicine, and Psychiatry, 15,* 275–301.

Knight, S. (2014, February). A God more powerful than I. *Harper's,* 53–62.

Knight, T. (2021). Inauthentic Facebook assets promoted Russian interests in Sudan. *The Atlantic Council's Digital Forensic Research Lab.* https://medium.com/dfrlab/inauthentic-facebook-assets-promoted-russian-interests-in-sudan-2623c58b1f7f

Knoll, M. (2011). Behavioral and psychological aspects of the retirement decision. *Social Security Bulletin, 71*(4), 15–32. http://www.ssa.gov/policy/docs/ssb/v71n4/v71n4p15.html

Kobasa, S. C. (1979). Stressful life events, personality, and health— Inquiry into hardiness. *Journal of Personality and Social Psychology, 37*(1), 1–11.

Koenigsberg, R. (2014). The delusion of rationality. http://blog.libraryofsocialscience.com/the-delusion-of-rationality/

Kohlberg, L. (1981). *The philosophy of moral development: Moral states and the idea of justice.* Harper & Row.

Köhler, W. (1959). Gestalt psychology today. *American Psychologist, 14,* 727–734.

Kohut, H. (1977). *The restoration of the self.* International Universities Press.

Konnikova, M. (2014, April 30). I want you to know that I'm Tyrion Lannister. *The New Yorker.* http://www.newyorker.com/science/maria-konnikova/i-want-you-to-know-that-im-tyrion-lannister

Koriat, A., & Ackerman, R. (2010). Metacognition and mindreading: Judgments of learning for self and other during self-paced study. *Consciousness and Cognition: An International Journal, 19*(1), 251–264.

Kosinski, M., Stillwell, D., & Graepel, T. (2013). Private traits and attributes are predictable from digital records of human behavior. *Proceedings of the National Academy of Sciences, 110*(15), *5802–5805.*

Kosson, D. S., & Newman, J. P. (1986). Psychopathy and allocation of attentional capacity in a divided-attention situation. *Journal of Abnormal Psychology, 95*(3), 257–263.

Kostka, G. (2019, February 13). China's social credit systems and public opinion: Explaining high levels of approval. *New Media & Society, 21*(7), 1565–1593.

Kouzes, E., Thompson, C., Herington, C., & Helzer, L. (2017, November 30). Sun smart schools Nevada: Increasing knowledge among school children about ultraviolet radiation. *Preventing Chronic Disease, 14.* https://www.cdc.gov/pcd/issues/2017/17_0202.htm

Krafft-Ebbing, R. (1886). *Psychopathia sexualis.* Verlag von Ferdinand Enke.

Krampen, G. (1999). Longterm evaluation of the effectiveness of additional autogenic training in the psychotherapy of depressive disorders. *European Psychologist, 4*(1), 11–18.

Krantz, D. L., & Wiggins, L. (1973). Personal and impersonal channels of recruitment in the growth of theory. *Human Development, 16*(3), 133–156.

Krauss, D., & Lieberman, J. (2016). *Psychological expertise in court: Psychology in the courtroom, Volume II (Psychology, Crime and Law).* Routledge.

Kreger, R. (2008). *The essential family guide to borderline personality disorder: New tools and techniques to stop walking on eggshells.* Hazeldenc.

Kremer, W. (2014). The evolutionary puzzle of homosexuality. *BBC News Magazine.* http://www.bbc.com/news/magazine-26089486

Krueger, R., Caspi, A., Moffitt, T., & Silva, P. (1996). Personality traits are differentially linked to mental disorders: A multitrait multidiagnosis study of an adolescent birth cohort. *Journal of Abnormal Psychology, 105*(3), 299–312.

Krueger, R. F., & Markon, K. E. (2006). Reinterpreting comorbidity: A model based approach to understanding and classifying psychopathology. *Annual Review of Clinical Psychology, 2,* 111–133.

Kruijver, F. P., Zhou, J. N., Pool, C. W., Hofman, M. A., Gooren, L. J., & Swaab, D. F. (2000). Male-to-female transsexuals have female neuron numbers in a limbic nucleus. *Journal of Clinical Endocrinology and Metabolism, 85,* 2034–2041.

Kumpulainen, K., & Rajala, A. (2017). Dialogic teaching and students' discursive identity negotiation in the learning of science. *Learning and Instruction, 28,* 23–31.

Kumpulainen, K., & Wray, D. (2002). *Classroom interaction and social learning: From theory to practice.* Routledge Falmer.

Kuntz, K. (2019). The billion-dollar business of matchmaking China's 200m singles. *Financial Review.* https://www.afr.com/world/asia/the-billiondollar-business-of-matchmaking-chinas-200m-singles-20180907-h153bj

Kurman, J., & Sriram, N. (2002). Interrelationships among vertical and horizontal collectivism, modesty, and self-enhancement. *Journal of Cross-Cultural Psychology, 33*(1), 71–86. https://doi.org/10.1177/0022022102033001005

Kurtz, S. N. (1992). *All the mothers are one: Hindu India and the cultural reshaping of psychoanalysis.* Columbia University Press.

Kurzweil, D. (2012). *How to create a mind: The secret of human thought revealed.* Viking Press.

Kurzweil, R. (2005). *The singularity is near.* Viking.

Kurzweil, R. (2013). *How to create a mind.* Penguin Books.

Kusch, M. (1999). *Psychological knowledge: A social history and philosophy.* Routledge.

La Mettrie, J. O. (1994). *Man a machine, man a plant* (R. A. Watson & M. Rybalka, Trans.). Hackett. (Original work published 1748)

Lai, H., Wang, S., Zhao, Y., Qiu, C., & Gong, Q. (2020). Neurostructural correlates of optimism: Gray matter density in the putamen predicts dispositional optimism in late adolescence. *Human Brain Mapping, 41*(6), 1459–1471.

Laney, M. O. (2002). *The introvert advantage.* Thomas Allen & Son.

Lang, F., Weiss, D., Gerstrof, D., & Wagner, G. (2013). Forecasting life satisfaction across adulthood: Benefits of seeing a dark future? *Psychology and Aging, 28*(1), 249–261.

Langbehn, D. R., & Cadoret, R. J. (2001). The adult antisocial syndrome with and without antecedent conduct disorder: Comparisons from an adoption study. *Comprehensive Psychiatry, 42*(4), 272–282.

Laqueur, T. (2004). *Solitary sex: A cultural history of masturbation.* Zone Books.

Lavine, H., Bordiga, E., & Sullivan, J. (2000). On the relationship between attitude involvement and attitude accessibility: Toward a cognitive-motivational model of political information-processing. *Political Psychology, 21*(1), 81–107.

Lazarus, R., & Lazarus, B. (2006). *Coping with aging.* Oxford University Press.

Le Bon, G. (1896). *The crowd: A study of the popular mind.* Ernest Benn.

Lea, M., & Spears, R. (1991). Computer-mediated communication, de-individuation and group decision-making. *International Journal of Man-Machine Studies, 34,* 283–301.

Leary, M. R. (2005). Sociometer theory and the pursuit of relational value: Getting to the root of self-esteem". *European Review of Social Psychology, 16,* 75–111.

Leary, M. R. (2012). Sociometer theory. In P. A. M. Van Lange, A. W. Kruglanski, & E. T. Higgins (Eds.), *Handbook of theories of social psychology* (pp. 151–159). SAGE. https://doi.org/10.4135/9781446249222.n33

LeCroy, K., & Milligan-LeCroy, S. (2020). Public perceptions of child maltreatment: A national convenience sample. *Children and Youth Services Review, 119.* https://www.sciencedirect.com/science/article/pii/S0190740920321009

Lee, M. S., & Ernst, E. (2011). Systematic reviews of tai chi: An overview. *British Journal of Sports Medicine, 46*(10), 713–718.

Leenen, I., Givaudan, M., Pick, S., Venguer, T., Vera, J., & Poortinga, Y. H. (2008). Effectiveness of a Mexican health education program in a poverty-stricken rural area of Guatemala. *Journal of Cross-Cultural Psychology, 39*(1), 198–214.

Lehman, C. (2003). Genes may play key role in impulsive aggression in BPD. *Psychiatric News, 38*(2), 20.

Lehrer, J. (2012, January 30). Groupthink: The brainstorming myth. *The New Yorker,* 22–27.

Leichsenring, F., Biskup, J., Kreische, R., & Staats, H. (2005). The Gottingen study of psychoanalytic therapy: First results. *International Journal of Psychoanalysis, 86,* 433–455.

Lemov, D. (2014). *Teach like a champion 2.0: 62 techniques that put students on the path to college.* Jossey-Bass.

Lenzenweger, M., Lane, M., Loranger, A., & Kessler, R. (2007). *DSM-IV personality disorders in the national comorbidity survey replication. Biological Psychiatry, 62*(6), 553–564.

Lepore, J. (2009, November 30). The politics of death. *The New Yorker,* 60–67.

Lerner, P. (2009). *Hysterical men: War, psychiatry, and the politics of trauma in Germany, 1890–1930.* Cornell University Press.

Lertwannawit, A., & Gulid, N. (2010). Metrosexual identification: Gender identity and beauty-related behaviors. *International Business & Economics Research Journal, 9*(11), 85.

Leslie, S. J., Cimpian, A., Meyer, M., & Freeland, E. (2015). Expectations of brilliance underlie gender distributions across academic disciplines. *Science, 347,* 262–265.

Levant, R. F., & Kopecky, G. (1995). *Masculinity reconstructed: Changing the rules of manhood—At work, in relationships, and in family life.* Dutton.

LeVay, S. (1991). A difference in hypothalamic structure between homosexual and heterosexual men. *Science, 253,* 1034–1037.

LeVay, S. (1993). *The sexual brain.* MIT Press.

LeVay, S. (2010). *Gay, straight, and the reason why: The science of sexual orientation.* Oxford University Press.

LeVay, S. (2016). *Gay, straight, and the reason why: The science of sexual orientation* (2nd ed.). Oxford University Press.

Levine, M., Philpot, R., & Kovalenko, A. (2019). Rethinking the bystander effect in violence reduction training programs. *Social Issues and Policy Review, 14*(1). https://doi.org/10.1111/sipr.12063

Levine, M., Taylor, P. J., & Best, R. (2011). Third parties, violence, and conflict resolution: The role of group size and collective action in the microregulation of violence. *Psychological Science, 22*(3), 406–412.

Levine, T. B.-Y. (Ed.). (2011). *Gestalt therapy: Advances in theory and practice.* Routledge.

Levitt, S., & Dubner, S. (2009). *Freakonomics: A rogue economist explores the hidden side of everything.* Harper.

Levy, D. (1997). *Tools of critical thinking.* Allyn & Bacon.

Levy, D. (2009). *Tools of critical thinking: Meta thoughts for psychology* (2nd ed.). Waveland Press.

Lewin, K. (1942). *Field theory in social science.* University of Chicago Press.

Lewin, K. (1943). Defining the "field at a given time." *Psychological Review,* (Republished in *Resolving Social Conflicts & Field Theory in Social Science, 50,* 292–310. American Psychological Association, 1997.

Lewin, K. (1944). Constructs in psychology and psychological ecology. *University of Iowa Studies in Child Welfare,* (Republished in *Resolving Social Conflicts and Field Theory in Social Science, 20,* 1–29. American Psychological Association, 1997.

Lewinsohn, P. M., Rohde, P., Seeley, J. R., Klein, D. N., & Gotlib, I. H. (2003). Psychosocial functioning of young adults who have experienced and recovered from major depressive disorder during adolescence. *Journal of Abnormal Psychology, 112,* 353–363.

Lewis, M. (2001). *Multicultural health psychology: Special topics acknowledging diversity.* Pearson.

Li, J. (2003). The core of Confucian learning. *American Psychologist, 58*(2), 146–147.

Liebst, L., Philpot, R., Poder, P., & Lindegaard, M. (2019). The helpful bystander: Current evidence from CCTV captured public conflicts. *Discover Society.* https://archive.discoversociety.org/2019/06/05/the-helpful-bystander-current-evidence-from-cctv-captured-public-conflicts/

Linehan, M., Rizvi, L., Welch, S. S., & Page, B. (2000). Psychiatric aspects of suicidal behaviour: Personality disorders. In

K. Hawton & K. van Heeringen (Eds.), *The international handbook of suicide and attempted suicide*. West Sussex. John Wiley & Sons.

Liu, J. H., Goldstein-Hawes, R., Hilton, D. J., Huang, L. L., Gastardo-Conaco, C., Dresler-Hawke, E., & Hidaka, Y. (2005). Social representations of events and people in world history across twelve cultures. *Journal of Cross-Cultural Psychology, 36*, 171–191.

Livesley, W., & Jang, K. (2008). The behavioral genetics of personality disorder. *Annual Review of Clinical Psychology, 4*, 4247–4274.

Lock, A. (1981). Ingenious psychology and human nature: A psychological perspective. In P. Heelas & A. Lock (Eds.), *Indigenous psychologies* (pp. 183–204). Academic Press.

Lombroso, C., & Ferrero, G. (1959). *The female offender*. Appleton. (Original work published 1895)

Loranger, A. (1996). Dependent personality disorder: Age, sex, and axis I comorbidity. *Journal of Nervous and Mental Disease, 184*(1), 17–21.

Loranger, A. W., Sartorius, N., Andreoli, A., Berger, P., Buchheim, & P., Channabasavanna, S. M. et al. (1994). The international personality disorder examination. *Archives of General Psychiatry, 51*(3), 215–224.

Lotte, L., Bamelis, S., Evers, P., & Arnoud, A. (2014). Results of a multicenter randomized controlled trial of the clinical effectiveness of schema therapy for personality disorders. *American Journal of Psychiatry, 171*(3), 305–322.

Lucas, R. E., & Donnellan, M. B. (2009). Age differences in personality: Evidence from a nationally representative sample of Australians. *Developmental Psychology, 45*, 1353–1363.

Lucas, R. E., & Donnellan, M. B. (2011). Personality development across the lifespan: Longitudinal analyses with a national sample from Germany. *Journal of Personality and Social Psychology, 101*, 847–861.

Lustgarten, S., Garrison, Y., Sinnard, M., & Flynn, A. (2020). Digital privacy in mental healthcare: Current issues and recommendations for technology use. *Current Opinions in Psychology*. https://www.ncbi.nlm.nih.gov/pmc/articles/PMC7195295/

Lykken, D. (1995). *The antisocial personalities*. Lawrence Erlbaum.

Lynam, D., & Widiger, T. (2001). Using the five-factor model to represent the *DSM—IV* personality disorders: An expert consensus approach. *Journal of Abnormal Psychology, 110*(3), 401–412.

Lyubomirsky, S. (2007). *The how of happiness: A scientific approach to getting the life you want*. Penguin Press.

Lyubomirsky, S. (2014). *The myths of happiness: What should make you happy, but doesn't, what shouldn't make you happy, but does*. Penguin.

Ma, F., Zeng, D., Xu, F., Compton, B., & Heyman, G. (2020). Delay of gratification as reputation management. *Psychological Science, 31*(9), 1174–1182.

Maccoby, E., & Jacklin, C. (1974). *The psychology of sex differences*. Stanford University Press.

Macmillan, M. (2014). *The war that ended peace: The road to 1914*. Random House.

Maddi, S. R. (2006). Hardiness: The courage to grow from stresses. *Journal of Positive Psychology, 1*(3), 160–168.

Mahbubani, K. (1999). *Can Asians think?* Times Books International.

Makridakis, S., & Moleskis, A. (2015). The costs and benefits of positive illusions. *Frontiers of Psychology*. https://doi.org/10.3389/fpsyg.2015.00859

Maldona, A., Preciado, A., Buchanan, M., Pulvers, K., Romero, D., & D'Anna-Hernandez, K. (2018). Acculturative stress, mental health symptoms, and the role of salivary inflammatory markers among a Latino sample. *Cultural Diversity & Ethnic Minority Psychology, 24*(2), 277–283.

Malouf, E., Stuewing, J., & Tangney, J. (2012). Self-control and jail inmates' substance misuse post-release: Mediation by friends' substance use and moderation by age. *Addictive Behaviors, 37*(11), 1198–1204.

Maltby, J., Day, L., & Macaskill, A. (2013). *Personality, individual differences and intelligence*. Pearson Education Limited.

Mandler, G. (2007). *A history of modern experimental psychology: From James and Wundt to cognitive science*. MIT Press.

Manschreck, T. C. (1996). Delusional disorder: The recognition and management of paranoia. *Journal of Clinical Psychiatry, 57*(3), 32–38.

Margulis, S. T. (2003). Privacy as a social issue and behavioral concept. *Journal of Social Issues, 59*(2), 243–261.

Martínez-Tejada, L., Maruyama, Y., Yoshimura, N., & Koike, Y. (2020). Analysis of personality and EEG features in emotion recognition using machine learning techniques to classify arousal and valance labels. *Machine Learning and Knowledge Extraction, 2*(2), 99–124.

Maslach, C., Jackson, S. E., & Leiter, M. P. (1996). *MBI: The Maslach burnout inventory—Manual.* Consulting Psychologists Press.

Maslow, A. (1962). *Toward a psychology of being.* Van Nostrand.

Maslow, A. (1970). *Motivation and personality* (2nd ed.). Harper & Row.

Mathers, D., Miller, M., & Ando, O. (Eds.). (2009). *Self and no-self: Continuing the dialogue between Buddhism and psychotherapy.* Routledge.

Matsumoto, D. (1992). American-Japanese cultural differences in the recognition of universal expressions. *Journal of Cross-Cultural Psychology, 23*(1), 72–85.

Matsumoto, D. (1994). *People: Psychology from a cultural perspective.* Brooks/Cole.

Matsumoto, D. (2007). Individual and cultural differences on status differentiation: The status differentiation scale. *Journal of Cross-Cultural Psychology, 38*(4), 413–431.

Matthews, K. (2005). Psychological perspectives on the development of coronary heart disease. *American Psychologist, 60*, 783–796.

Matthews, K., & Gallo, L. (2011). Psychological perspectives on pathways linking socioeconomic status and physical health. *Annual Review of Psychology, 62*, 501–530.

May, R. (1950). *The meaning of anxiety.* Ronald Press.

May, R. (1967). *Psychology and the human dilemma.* Van Nostrand.

May, R. (1969). *Love and will.* Norton.

May, R. (1994). *The courage to create.* W. W. Norton.

May, R., Angel, E., & Ellenberger, H. F. (Eds.). (1958). *Existence.* Basic Books.

McCarthy, J. (2013). The psychology of spas and wellbeing. *CreateSpace.* http://psychologyofwellbeing.com/psychology-of-spa

McCrae, R., & Costa, P. (1990). *Personality in adulthood.* Guilford Press.

McCrae, R., & Costa, P. (1999). A five-factor theory of personality. In L. A. Pervin & O. P. John (Eds.), *Handbook of personality* (pp. 139–153). Guilford.

McCrae, R. R., & Costa, P. T. (1987). Validation of the five-factor model of personality across instruments and observers. *Journal of Personality and Social Psychology, 52*(1), 81–90.

McCrae, R. R., & Costa, P. T., Jr. (1997). Personality trait structure as a human universal. *American Psychologist, 52*, 509–516.

McDougall, W. (1908). *An introduction to social psychology.* Methuen.

McDowell, N. (1988). A note on cargo cults and cultural construction of change. *Pacific Studies, 11*(2), 121–134.

McEwan, T., & Strand, S. (2013). The role of psychopathology in stalking by adult strangers and acquaintances. *Australian and New Zealand Journal of Psychiatry, 47*(6), 546–555.

McFadden, R. (2013, August 16). Jacques Vergès, defender of terrorists and war criminals, is dead at 88. *The New York Times.* http://www.nytimes.com/2013/08/17/world/europe/jacques-verges-88-defender-of-war-criminals-and-terrorists.html?pagewanted=all&r=1&

McGirr, A., Paris, J., Lesage, A., Renaud, J., & Turecki, G. (2007). Risk factors for suicide completion in borderline personality disorder: A case-control study of cluster B comorbidity and impulsive aggression. *Journal of Clinical Psychiatry, 68*, 721–729.

McGlashan, T. (1986). Schizotypal personality disorder. *Archives of General Psychiatry, 43*, 329–334.

Mehrabian, A., & Bloom, J. (1997). Physical appearance, attractiveness, and the mediating role of emotions. *Current Psychology, 16*(1), 20–42.

Meinert, D. (2015). What do personality tests really reveal? *SHRM Online.* https://www.shrm.org/publications/hrmagazine/editorialcontent/20

15/0615/pages/0615-personality-tests.aspx

Meissner, S. J. W. W. (2006). Prospects for psychoanalysis in the 21st century. *Psychoanalytic Psychology, 23*, 239–256.

Menand, L. (2009, December). Road warrior: Arthur Koestler and his century. *The New Yorker.* http://www.newyorker.com/arts/critics/atlarge/2009/12/21/091221cratatlargemenand? printable=true#ixzz27jCrWmP7

Menand, L. (2010, January 11). Top of the pops: Did Andy Warhol change everything? *The New Yorker*, 57–65.

Menand, L. (2014, January 27). The prisoner of stress. *The New Yorker*, 64–68.

Metzl, J. (2005). *Prozac on the couch*. Duke University Press.

Mill, J. S. (2010). *On the subjection of women*. Nabu Press. (Original work published 1869)

Miller, G. (2000). *The mating mind: How sexual choice shaped the evolution of human nature*. Heineman.

Miller, G., Galanter, E., & Pribram, K. (1960). *Plans and the structure of behavior*. Holt.

Miller, J. (2019). *Virtue signaling: Essays on Darwinian politics & free speech*. Cambrian Moon.

Miller, J. D., & Lynam, D. (2001). Structural models of personality and their relation to antisocial behavior: A meta-analytic review. *Criminology, 39*, 765–798.

Miller, K. (2021). Pseudobulbar affect (PBA). Medically reviewed by C. Melinoski, M.D. *WebMD.* https://www.webmd.com/brain/pseudobulbar-affect

Millon, T., Millon, C., Meagher, S., Grossman, S., & Ramnath, R. (2004). *Personality disorders in modern life*. Wiley.

Mills, E., & Singh, S. (2007). Health, human rights, and the conduct of clinical research within oppressed populations. *Globalization and Health, 3*(10). http://www.globalizationandhealth.com/content/pdf/1744-8603-3-10.pdf

Mills, J. (2001). Reexamining the psychoanalytic corpse from scientific psychology to philosophy. *Psychoanalytic Psychology, 19*, 552–558.

Miranda, R., & Jeglic, E. (2022). *Handbook of youth suicide prevention: Integrating research into practice*. Springer Nature.

Mischel, W. (1993). Behavioral conceptions. In W. Mischel (Ed.), *Introduction to personality* (pp. 295–316). Harcourt Brace.

Mischel, W. (2014). *The marshmallow test: Mastering self-control*. Little, Brown.

Mischel, W., Ebbesen, E., & Raskoff, Z. (1972). Cognitive and attentional mechanisms in delay of gratification. *Journal of Personality and Social Psychology, 21*(2), 204–218.

MMPI History. (2016). https://www.upress.umn.edu/test-division/bibliography/mmpi-history

Moffitt, T. E. (1990). The neuropsychology of juvenile delinquency: A critical review. In M. Tonry & N. Morris (Eds.), *Crime and Justice* (Vol. 12, pp. 99–169). University of Chicago Press.

Moghaddam, F. (1998). *Social psychology*. Freeman.

Moghaddam, F. M. (2019). Threat to democracy: *The appeal of authoritarianism in an age of uncertainty*. American Psychological Association Press.

Mohandie, K., Meloy, J. R., McGowan, M. G., & Williams, J. (2006). The RECON typology of stalking: Reliability and validity based upon a large sample of North American stalkers. *Journal of Forensic Science, 51*(1), 147–155.

Mondak, J., Hibbing, M., Canache, D., Seligson, M., & Anderson, M. (2010). Personality and civic engagement: An integrative framework for the study of trait effects on political behavior. *American Political Science Review, 104*(1), 85–110.

Moore, M. (2015). Throwback thursday: Matchmaking China's millionaires. *That's Shanghai.* https://www.thatsmags.com/shanghai/post/10482/how-to-marry-a-millionaire

Morel, B. A. (1976). *Traite des degenerescence physique, et intellectuelles et morales de l'espece humaine* [Degenerative physical, intellectual and moral traits in human beings]. Arno. (Original work published 1857)

Morris, C. E., Reiber, C., & Roman, E. (2015). Quantitative sex differences in response to the dissolution of a romantic relationship. *Evolutionary Behavioral Sciences*. Advance online publication. http://dx.doi.org/10.1037/ebs0000054

Morrison, A. P. (1989). *Shame: The underside of narcissism*. Analytic Press.

Mosing, M., Madiason, G., Pedersen, N., Kuja-HAlkola, R., & Illen, F. (2014, July 30). Practice does not make perfect: No causal effect of music practice on music ability. *Psychological Science*. doi:10.1177/09567976 14541990

Mullainathan, S., & Shafir, E. (2013). *Scarcity: Why having too little means so much*. Times Books.

Mullen, P. E., Pathé, M., & Purcell, R. (2000). *Stalkers and their victims*. Cambridge University Press.

Münsterberg, H. (1915). *Psychology: General and applied*. Appleton.

Murray, H. (1943, October). Analysis of the personality of Adolf Hitler. http://library.law school.cornell.edu/WhatWeH ave/SpecialCollections/Donov an/Hitler/

Murray, H. A. (1938). *Explorations in personality*. Oxford University Press.

Murray, K. (1985). Life as fiction. *Journal for the Theory of Social Behaviour, 15*(2), 173–188.

Mursalieva, S. (2003, July 18). Sudba psychoanalyze v Rossii [Psychoanalysis' fate in Russia]. *Novaya Gazeta*. http://ww w.novayagazeta.ru/data/2002 /51/21.html

Mussino, E., Wilson, B., & Andersson, G. (2021). The fertility of immigrants from low-fertility settings: Adaptation in the quantum and tempo of childbearing? *Demography, 58*(6), 2169–2191.

Myers, D. (2008). *A friendly letter to skeptics and atheists: Musings on why god is good and faith isn't evil*. Jossey-Bass/ Wiley.

Myers, K. M., & Davis, M. (2002). Behavioral and neural analysis of extinction: A review. *Neuron, 36*, 567–584.

Nagasawa, M., Kawai, E., Mogi, K., & Kikusui, T. (2013). Dogs show left facial lateralization upon reunion with their owners. *Behavioural Processes, 98*, 112–116.

Nakamura, T., Kiyono, K., Yoshiuchi, K., Nakahara, R., Struzik, Z. R., & Yamamoto, Y. (2007). Universal scaling law in human behavioral organization. *Physical Review Letters, 99*(13), 138103.

Nanda, S. (1998). *Neither man nor woman: The Hijras in India*. Wadsworth.

Nanda, S., & Warms, R. L. (2009). *Cultural anthropology* (10th ed.). Cengage Learning/ Wadsworth.

Nardone, I. B., Ward, R., Fotopoulou, A., & Turnbull, O. H. (2007). Attention and emotion in anosognosia: Evidence of implicit awareness and repression? *Neurocase, 13*(5), 438–445.

National Council on Alcoholism and Drug Dependence. (2016). Self-support groups. ht tps://www.ncadd.org/people-i n-recovery/hope-help-and-he aling/self-help-recovery-sup port-groups

Nave, C. S., Sherman, R. A., Funder, D. C., Hampson, S. E., & Goldberg, R. (2010). On the contextual independence of personality: Teachers' assessments predict directly observed behavior after four decades. *Social Psychological and Personality Science, 1*(4), 327–334.

Nelson, S., Huprich, S., Shankar, S., Sohnleitner, A., & Paggeot, A. (2017). A quantitative and qualitative evaluation of trainee opinions of four methods of personality disorder diagnosis. *Personality Disorders: Theory, Research, and Treatment, 8*(3), 217–227.

Netherlands Review Report. (2019). Implementation of the Beijing Declaration and Platform for Action. https://www.u nwomen.org/sites/default/file s/Headquarters/Attachments /Sections/CSW/64/National-r eviews/Netherlands.pdf

Nevis, E. C. (1983). Cultural assumptions and productivity: The United States and China. *Sloan Management Review, 24*, 17–29.

Newport, K. (2016). *Deep work: Rules for focused success in a distracted world*. Grand Central.

Ng, Y. K. (2022). The East-Asian happiness gap: Causes and implications. In Y. K. Ng (Ed.), *Happiness: Concept, measurement, and promotion* (pp. 133–143). Springer.

Nicholson, I. A. M. (2000). "A coherent datum of perception": Gordon Allport, Floyd Allport, and the politics of "personality." *Journal of the History of Behavioral Sciences, 36*, 463–470.

Nielsen, A., Der, B. S., Shin, J., Vaidyanathan, P., Paralanov, V., Strychalski, E. A., . . . Voigt, C. A. (2015). Programming circuitry for synthetic biology. *Science, 352*, 7341.

Nierman, E. (2021, October 5). Be careful: Cancel culture is here to stay. *Forbes*.

Nierman, E., & Banyan, R. (2021). Be careful: Cancel culture is here to stay. *Forbes*. https://www.forbes.com/sites/theyec/2021/10/05/be-careful-cancel-culture-is-here-to-stay/?sh=28f28e9c2ac7

Nietzsche, F. (1968). *The will to power*. Vintage Books. (Original work published 1901)

Nindl, A. (2019). Crisis: Threat and opportunity. In S. Längle & C. Wurm (Eds.), *Living your own life*. Routledge.

Nolen-Hoeksema, S. (1991). Responses to depression and their effects on the duration of the depressive episode. *Journal of Abnormal Psychology*, *100*, 569–582.

Noon, D. H. (2004). Situating gender and professional identity in American child study, 1880–1910. *History of Psychology*, *7*, 107–129.

Nowicki, S. (2016). *Choice or chance: Understanding your locus of control and why it matters*. Prometheus Books.

Nowogrodksi, A. (2018). The automatic-design tools that are changing synthetic biology. *Nature*. https://www.nature.com/articles/d41586-018-07662-w

Nugent, W. (2009). *Progressivism: A very short introduction*. Oxford University Press.

Odajnyk, W. (2012). *Archetype and character: Power, eros, spirit, and matter personality types*. Palgrave Macmillan.

Offermann, L., & Hellmann, P. (1997). Culture's consequences for leadership behavior: National values in action. *Journal of Cross-Cultural Psychology*, *28*(3), 342–351.

Office of Disease Prevention and Health Promotion. (2020). *Access to health services. Office of Disease Prevention and Health Promotion*.

Okines, H. (2012). *Old before my time*. Accent Press.

Olson, R. (2017). *An Introduction to existentialism*. Dover.

O'Neal, A. (2019, August 23). Why Bernie Sanders is wrong about Sweden. *The Wall Street Journal*. https://www.wsj.com/articles/why-bernie-sanders-is-wrong-about-sweden-11566596536

Onn, Yael et al. (2005). *Privacy in the digital environment* (pp. 1–12). Haifa Center of Law & Technology.

Oppenheimer, S. (2003). *The real Eve: Modern man's journey out of Africa*. Basic Books.

Orbuch, T. (2015). *Five simple steps to take your marriage from good to great*. River Grove Books.

Organisation for Economic Cooperation and Development. (2011). Against the odds: Disadvantaged students who succeed in school. *OECD*. http://bit.ly/1MTXJxF

Organisation for Economic Cooperation and Development. (2020). Girls' and boys' performance in PISA. In *PISA 2018 Results (Volume II): Where all students can succeed*. OECD. https://doi.org/10.1787/f56f8c26-en

Osgood, J., & Muraven, M. (2016). Does counting to ten increase or decrease aggression? The role of state self-control (ego-depletion) and consequences. *Journal of Applied Social Psychology*, *46*(2), 105–113.

Otte, K., Ellermeyer, T., Suzuki, M., Röhling, H. M., Kuroiwa, R., Cooper, G., Mansow-Model, S., Mori, M., Zimmermann, H., Brandt, A. U., Paul, F., Hirano, S., Kuwabara, S., & Schmitz-Hübsch, T. (2021). Cultural bias in motor function patterns: Potential relevance for predictive, preventive, and personalized medicine. *EPMA Journal*, *12*(1), 91–101. https://doi.org/10.1007/s13167-021-00236-3

Oxford English Dictionary. (2021). Digital. https://public.oed.com/blog/word-stories-digital/

Palermo, D., & Jenkins, J. (1964). *Word association norms: Grade school through college* (NED-New edition). University of Minnesota Press.

Panksepp, J. (1998). *Affective neuroscience: The foundations of human and animal emotions*. Oxford University Press.

Paranjpe, A. (1998). *Self and identity in modern psychology and Indian thought*. Plenum Press.

Paris, J. (2019, May). Suicidality in borderline personality disorder. *Medicina (Kaunas Lithuania)*, *55*(6), 223.

Park, B., Cho, H. N., Choi, E., Seo, D. H., Kim, S., Park, Y. R., Choi, K. S., & Rhee, Y. (2019). Self-perceptions of body weight status according to age-groups among Korean women: A nationwide population-based survey. *PloS one*, *14*(1), e0210486. https://d

oi.org/10.1371/journal.pone. 0210486

Park, C. L. (2005). Religion and meaning. In R. F. Paloutzian & C. L. Park (Eds.), *Handbook of the psychology of religion and spirituality* (pp. 295–314). Guilford Press.

Parsons, T., & Bales, R. (1956). *Family, socialization and interaction process*. Routledge.

Parvizi, J., & Damasio, A. (2001). Consciousness and the brainstem. *Cognition, 79*(12), 135–160.

Patrick, C. J. (1994). Emotion and psychopathy: Startling new insights. *Psychophysiology, 31*, 319–330.

Paul, M. (2014, Winter). First blood test to diagnose depression in adults. *Northwestern Medicine Magazine, 2*(1). http://magazine.nm.org/winter-2014/research-briefs/blood-test-adult-depression/

Peltzman, S. (2011). Offsetting behavior, medical breakthroughs, and breakdowns. *Journal of Human Capital, 5*(3), 302–341.

Penny, E., Newton, E., & Larkin. (2009). Whispering on the water: British Pakistani families' experiences of support from an early intervention service for first-episode psychosis. *Journal of Cross-Cultural Psychology, 40*(6), 969–987.

Perez-Arce, F. (2011, March). The effects of education on time preferences. *Rand Corporation Working Papers, WR-844*. http://www.rand.org/pubs/workingpapers/WR844.html

Perlis, R. H., Green, J., Simonson, M., Ognyanova, K., Santillana, M., Lin, J., Quintana,

A., Chwe, H., Druckman, J., Lazer, D., Baum, M. A., & Volpe, J. D. (2021). Association Between Social Media Use and Self-reported Symptoms of Depression in US Adults. *JAMA Netw Open, 4*(11), e2136113. https://jamanetwork.com/journals/jamanetworkopen/fullarticle/2786464?utm_source=For_The_Media&utm_medium=referral&utm_campaign=ftm_links&utm_term=112321

Perls, F. (1968). *Gestalt therapy verbatim*. Real People Press.

Perls, F., Hefferline, R., & Goodman, P. (1951). *Gestalt therapy: Excitement and growth in the human personality*. Julian.

Perry, K. (2014, June 4). Hidden in her bedroom, a young cancer victim's secret message of hope. *Telegraph*. http://bit.ly/TgA986

Perugula, M., Narang, P., & Lippmann, S. (2017). The biological basis to personality disorders. *Prime Care Companion CNS Disorders. 19*(2). https://pubmed.ncbi.nlm.nih.gov/28407461/

Petersen, J. L., & Hyde, J. S. (2010). A meta-analytic review of research on gender differences in sexuality, 1993–2007. *Psychological Bulletin, 136*(1), 21–38.

Peterson, B., Smirles, K., & Wentworth, P. (1997). Generativity and authoritarianism: Implications for personality, political involvement, and parenting. *Journal of Personality and Social Psychology, 72*(5), 1202–1216.

Peterson, C. (2000). The future of optimism. *American Psychologist, 55*(1), 44–55.

Pethokoukis, J., & Cowen, T. (2022). How to identify and allocate talent: My long-read Q&A with Tyler Cowen. *American Enterprise Institute*. https://www.aei.org/economics/how-to-identify-and-allocate-talent-my-long-read-qa-with-tyler-cowen/

Pew. (2016a). Five facts about online dating. http://www.pewresearch.org/fact-tank/2016/02/29/5-facts-about-online-dating/

Pew. (2016b). Pew research: Japanese and Chinese hold negative views of each other. *Pew Research Center*. https://www.pewresearch.org/global/2016/09/13/hostile-neighbors-china-vs-japan/china-japan_2016_01/

Pew. (2019). About one-in-five U.S. adults know someone who goes by a gender-neutral pronoun. *Pew Research Center*. https://www.pewresearch.org/fact-tank/2019/09/05/gender-neutral-pronouns/

Pew. (2020). Most Americans point to circumstances, not work ethic, for why people are rich or poor. *Pew Research Center*. https://www.pewresearch.org/politics/2020/03/02/most-americans-point-to-circumstances-not-work-ethic-as-reasons-people-are-rich-or-poor/

Phillips, I. E. (2021). Big five personality traits and political orientation: An inquiry into political beliefs. *The Downtown Review, 7*(2). https://engagedscholarship.csuohio.edu/tdr/vol7/iss2/6/

Pickard, H. (2011, May 4). What Aristotle can teach us about personality disorder. *National Personality Disorder Website*.

Available from author by request at http://www.philosophy.ox.ac.uk/members/researchstaff/hannapickard

Piekkola, B. (2011). Traits across cultures: A neo-Allportian perspective. *Journal of Theoretical and Philosophical Psychology*, *31*, 2–24.

Pinsky, D., & Young, S. M. (2006). Narcissism and celebrity. *Journal of Research in Personality*, *40*(5), 463–471.

Pinsky, D., & Young, S. M. (2009). *The mirror effect: How celebrity narcissism is seducing America*. HarperCollins.

Pipher, M. (1994). *Reviving Ophelia: Saving the selves of adolescent girls*. Ballantine Books.

Plieger, T., Melchers, M., Montag, C., Meermann, R., & Reuter, M. (2015). Life stress as potential risk factor for depression and burnout. *Burnout Research*, *2*(1), 19–24.

Plomin, R. (2018). *Blueprint: How DNA makes us who we are*. Penguin.

Popper, K. (1992). *The logic of scientific discovery*. Routledge. (Original work published 1950)

Post, J., & George, A. (2004). *Leaders and their followers in a dangerous world: The psychology of political behavior*. Cornell University Press.

Poushter, J., & Kent, N. (2020). The global divide on homosexuality persists. *Pew Research Center*. https://www.pewresearch.org/global/2020/06/25/global-divide-on-homosexuality-persists/

Powell, A. D. (2015). Grief, bereavement, and adjustment disorders. In T. A. Stern, M. Fava, & T. E. Wilens et al.

(Eds.), *Massachusetts general hospital comprehensive clinical psychiatry* (2nd ed., pp. 428–432). Elsevier.

Powell, L. H., Shahabi, L., & Thoresen, C. E. (2003). Religion and spirituality: Linkages to physical health. *American Psychologist*, *58*, 36–52.

Power, R., Verweij, K., Zuhair, M., Montgomery, G., Henders, A., Heath, A., . . . Martin, N. (2014). Genetic predisposition to schizophrenia associated with increased use of cannabis. *Molecular Psychiatry*, *19*, 1201–1204.

Pratkanis, A. (1988). The attitude heuristic and selective fact identification. *British Journal of Social Psychology*, *27*, 257–263.

Prosser, W. (1960). Privacy. *California Law Review*, *48*(383), 389.

Pychyl, T. A., Lee, J. M., Thibodeau, R., & Blunt, A. (2000). Five days of emotion: An experience sampling study of undergraduate student procrastination. *Journal of Social Behavior and Personality*, *15*, 239–254.

Quas, J. A., Malloy, L., Goodman, G. S., Melinder, A., Schaaf, J., & D'Mello, M. (2007). Developmental differences in the effects of repeated interviews and interviewer bias on young children's false reports. *Developmental Psychology*, *43*, 823–837.

Quen, J. (1983). Psychiatry and the law: Historical relevance to today. In L. Freedman (Ed.), *By reason of insanity: Essays on the psychiatry and the law*

(pp. 153–166). Scholarly Resources.

Radford, B. (2016). *Bad clown*. University of New Mexico Press.

Raine, A. (2014). *The anatomy of violence: The biological roots of crime*. Vintage.

Ramaci, T., Bellini, D., Presti, G., & Santisi, G. (2019, June 12). Psychological flexibility and mindfulness as predictors of individual outcomes in hospital health workers. *Frontiers of Psychology*, *10*, 33–89.

Ramanujan, A. K. (1989). Is there an Indian way of thinking? *Contributions to Indian Sociology*, *23*(1), 41–58.

Rang, H. P. (2003). *Pharmacology*. Churchill Livingstone.

Rao, K. R., Paranjpe, A. C., & Dalal, A. K. (Eds.). (2008). *Handbook of Indian psychology*. Cambridge University Press.

Raskin, R. N., Novacek, J., & Hogan, R. (1991). Narcissism, self-esteem, and defensive self-enhancement. *Journal of Personality*, *59*(1), 19–38.

Raskin, R. N., & Shaw, R. (1988). Narcissism and the use of personal pronouns. *Journal of Personality*, *56*, 393–404.

Rauh, V., & Margolis, A. (2016). Research review: Environmental exposures, neurodevelopment, and child mental health - new paradigms for the study of brain and behavioral effects. *Journal of Child Psychology and Psychiatry*, *57*(7), 775–793.

Ray, O. (2004). How the mind hurts and heals the body. *American Psychologist*, *59*, 29–40.

Rees, P. (2002, October 20). Japan: The missing million. *BBC News, World Edition.* http://news.bbc.co.uk/2/hi/programmes/correspondent/2334893.stm

Reich, J., Noyes, R., Coryell, W., & O'Gorman, T. W. (1986). The effect of state anxiety on personality measurement. *American Journal of Psychiatry, 143*(6), 760–763.

Reid, J. (2011). Crime and personality: Personality theory and criminality examined. *Student Pulse, 3*(1), 1–26. http://www.studentpulse.com/articles/377/crime-and-personality-personality-theory-and-criminality-examined

Reidy, D., Berke, D., Gentile, B. C., & Zeichner, A. (2015, August). Discrepancy stress, substance use, assault, and injury in a survey of U.S. men. *Injury Prevention.* http://bit.ly/1Ua4ltG

Reilly, D., Neumann, D., & Andrews, G. (2022). Gender differences in self-estimated intelligence: Exploring the male hubris, female humility problem. *Frontiers in Psychology. 13.* https://www.frontiersin.org/article/10.3389/fpsyg.2022.812483

Reisner, S., Vetters, R., Leclerc, M., Zaslow, S., Wolfru, S., Shumer, D., & Mimiaga, M. (2015, January). Mental health of transgender youth in care at an adolescent urban community health center: A matched retrospective cohort study. *Journal of the Adolescent Health, 56*(3), 274–279.

Remen, R. N. (1996). *Kitchen table wisdom: Stories that heal.* Riverhead Books.

Renshon, S. (1989). Psychological perspectives on theories of adult development and the political socialization of leaders. In R. Sigel (Ed.), *Political learning in adulthood: A sourcebook of theory and research* (pp. 203–264). University of Chicago Press.

Rhodewalt, F., & Morf, C. C. (1995). Self and interpersonal correlates of the narcissistic personality inventory. *Journal of Research in Personality, 29,* 1–23.

Riger, S. (2002). Epistemological debates, feminist voices: Science, social values, and the study of women. In W. Pickren & D. Dewsbury (Eds.), *Evolving perspectives on the history of psychology* (pp. 21–44). American Psychological Association.

Ritvo, L. R. (1990). *Darwin's influence on Freud: A tale of two sciences.* Yale University Press.

Robbie, N. (2014). Thirteen Christian personality types. http://transforminggrace.wordpress.com/2008/06/04/13christianpersonalitytypes/Roberti, J. W. (2004). A review of behavioral and biological correlates of sensation seeking. *Journal of Research in Personality, 38*(3), 256.

Roberts, B. W., & Friend-DelVecchio, W. (2000). Consistency of personality traits from childhood to old age: A quantitative review of longitudinal studies. *Psychological Bulletin, 126,* 3–25.

Roberts, B. W., Walton, K., & Viechtbauer, W. (2006). Patterns of mean-level change in personality traits across the life course: A meta-analysis of longitudinal studies. *Psychological Bulletin, 132,* 1–25.

Robinson, D. (2022). *The expectation effect.* Canongate.

Robson, D. (2018). Most people feel younger or older than they really are – and this 'subjective age' has a big effect on their physical and mental health. *BBC Future.* https://www.bbc.com/future/article/20180712-the-age-you-feel-means-more-than-your-actual-birthdate

Roer-Strier, D., & Kurman, J. (2009). Combining qualitative and quantitative methods to study perceptions of immigrant youth. *Journal of Cross-Cultural Psychology, 40*(6), 988–995.

Roese, N. J., & Olson, J. M. (1994). Self-esteem and counterfactual thinking. *Journal of Personality and Social Psychology, 65,* 199–206.

Rogers, C. (1947). Some observations on the organization of personality. Address of the retiring president of the American Psychological Association. The 1947 Annual Meeting. *American Psychologist, 2,* 358–368.

Rogers, C. (1951). *Client-centered therapy: Its current practice, implications and theory.* Constable.

Rogers, C. (1959). The essence of psychotherapy: A client-centered view. *Annals of Psychotherapy, 1,* 51–57.

Rogers, C. (1961). *On becoming a person: A therapist's view of psychotherapy.* Houghton Mifflin.

Roland, A. (2006). Across civilizations: Psychoanalytic therapy with Asians and Asian

Americans. *Psychotherapy: Theory, Research, Practice, Training, 43*, 454–463.

Romanes, G. J. (1882). *Animal intelligence.* Kessinger.

Rook, S., Stephenson, N., Ortega, J., de Calvo, M., & Iyer-Eimerbrink, P. (2021). Morality development and its influence on emotion, attitudes, and decision making. *Psychology, 12*, 1722–1741.

Rosenthal, R., & Jacobson, L. (1968). *Pygmalion in the classroom: Teacher expectation and pupils' intellectual development.* Holt, Rinehart, & Winston.

Rosin, H. (2013). *The end of men.* Riverhead Books.

Rosin, H. (2014, November 10). Hello, my name is Stephen Glass, and I'm sorry. *New Republic.* http://bit.ly/1oE5hMZ

Roskies, A. (2010). How does neuroscience affect our understanding of volition? *Annual Review of Neuroscience, 33*, 109–130.

Ross, A. (2012, November 12). Love on the march: Reflections on the gay community's political progress—and its future. *The New Yorker*, 45–53.

Ross, L. (1977). The intuitive psychologist and his shortcomings: Distortions in the attribution process. In L. Berkowitz (Ed.), *Advances in experimental social psychology* (pp. 173–220). Academic Press.

Rothblatt, M. (2009, May 4). What are mindclones? *Mindflies, Mindware, and Mindclones* [Web log post]. http://ieet.org/index.php/IEET/more/rothblatt20090502

Rothblatt, M. (2011a). *From transgender to transhuman: A manifesto on the freedom of form.* Rothblatt.

Rothblatt, M. (2011b, January 27). How can a mindclone be an exact copy of a person's mind? *Mindflies, mindware, and mindclones* [Web log post]. http://ieet.org/index.php/IEET/more/rothblatt20110127

Rotter, J. (1966). Generalized expectations for internal versus external control of reinforcement. *Psychological Monographs, 80*, 1–28.

Rotter, J. (1990). Internal versus external control of reinforcement: A case history of a variable. *American Psychologist, 45*(4), 489–493.

Ruch, W., Harzer, C., & Proyer, R. (2013). Beyond being timid, witty, and cynical: Big five personality characteristics of gelotophobes, gelotophiles, and katagelasticists. *Psychology.*

Rusch, H., Leunissen, J., & Van Vugt, M. (2015). Historical and experimental evidence of sexual selection for war heroism. *Evolution and Human Behavior.* http://www.ehbonline.org/article/S1090-5138%2815%2900023-9/fulltext

Sabatier, C., Mayer, B., Friedlmeier, M., Lubiewska, K., & Trommsdorff, G. (2011). Religiosity, family orientation, and life satisfaction of adolescents in four countries. *Journal of Cross-Cultural Psychology, 42*, 1375–1393.

Sackett, P. R., & Walmsley, P. T. (2014). Which personality attributes are most important in the workplace? *Perspectives on Psychological Science, 9*(5), 538–551.

Sadigh, M. (2012). *Autogenic training: A mind-body approach to the treatment of chronic pain syndrome and stress-related disorders.* McFarland.

Sahgal, N., Evans, J., Salazar, A. M., Starr, K. J., & Corich, M. (2021). Religion in India: Tolerance and segregation. *Pew Research.* https://www.pewresearch.org/religion/wp-content/uploads/sites/7/2021/06/PF_06.29.21_India.full_.report.pdf

Saitō, T. (2012). *Social withdrawal: Adolescence without end.* University of Minnesota Press.

Sanchez, C., & Dunning, D. (2021). Jumping to conclusions: Implications for reasoning errors, false beliefs, knowledge corruption, and impeded learning. *Journal of Personality and Social Psychology, 120*(3), 789–815.

Sandman, P. M. (2010, December 3). Two kinds of reputation management. *Risk = Hazard + Outrage.* http://www.psandman.com/col/reputation.htm

Sarnobat, S. (2020). Character sketch of Gandhiji. *India Study Chanell.* https://www.indiastudychannel.com/resources/178961-character-sketch-of-gandhiji

Saroglou, V. (2011). Believing, bonding, behaving, and belonging: The big four religious dimensions and cultural variation. *Journal of Cross-Cultural Psychology, 42*, 1320–1340.

Saroglou, V. (2014). *Religion, personality, and social behavior.* Psychology Press.

Sartre, J. P. (1969). *Being and nothingness.* Washington

Square Press. (Original work published 1943)

Sasaki, J. Y., Kim, S. H., & Xu, J. (2011). Religion and well-being: The moderating role of culture and the oxytocin receptor (OXTR) gene. *Journal of Cross-Cultural Psychology, 42*, 1394–1405.

Sathyanarayanan, G., Vengadavaradan, A., & Bharadwaj, B. (2019). Role of yoga and mindfulness in severe mental illnesses: A narrative review. *International Journal of Yoga, 12*(1), 3–28.

Savin-Williams, R. C., Joyner, K., & Rieger, G. (2012). Prevalence and stability of self-reported sexual orientation identity during young adulthood. *Archives of Sexual Behaviour, 41*(1), 103–110.

Sax, L. (2007). *Boys adrift: The five factors driving the growing epidemic of unmotivated boys and underachieving young men.* Basic Books.

Schalling, D. (1978). Psychopathology-related personality variables and the psychophysiology of socialization. In R. Hare & D. Schalling (Eds.), *Psychopathic behavior: Approaches to research.* Wiley.

Scheier, M. F., & Carver, C. S. (1992). Effects of optimism on psychological and physical well-being: Theoretical overview and empirical update. *Cognitive Therapy and Research, 16*, 201–228.

Scheier, M., & Carver, C. (2018). Dispositional optimism and physical health: A long look back, a quick look forward. *American Psychologist, 73*(9), 1082–1094.

Schiae, K. W. (2012). *Developmental influences on adult intelligence: The Seattle longitudinal study.* Oxford University Press.

Schlegel, A., & Barry, H. (1991). *Adolescence: An anthropological inquiry.* Free Press.

Schmitt, D., Allik, J., McCrae, R., & Benet Martínez, V. (2007). The geographic distribution of big-five personality traits: Patterns and profiles of human self-description across 56 nations. *Journal of Cross-Cultural Psychology, 38*(2), 173–212.

Schneider, K., Pierson, J. F., & Bugental, J (Eds.). (2014). *The handbook of humanistic psychology: Theory, research, and practice* (2nd ed.). SAGE.

Schwartz-Watts, D. M. (2006). Commentary: Stalking risk profile. *Journal of the American Academy of Psychiatry the Law, 34*(4), 455–457.

Scott, S., Doolan, M., Beckett, C., Harry, S., & Cartwright, S. (2010). *How is parenting style related to child antisocial behaviour? Preliminary findings from the Helping Children Achieve Study.* UK Department of Education. http://learning.gov.wales/docs/learningwales/publications/121127parentingstylechild behaviouren.pdf

Searle, J. (1992). *The rediscovery of the mind.* MIT Press.

Searle, J. (1998). *The mystery of consciousness.* Granta.

Sears, D., & Funk, C. (1999). Evidence of long-term persistence of adults' political predispositions. *Journal of Politics, 61*, 128.

Segal, L. (2013). *Out of time: The pleasures and the perils of ageing.* Verso.

Segal, N. (2012). *Born together reared apart: The landmark Minnesota twin study.* Harvard University Press.

Segall, M. H., Dasen, P. R., Berry, J. W., & Poortinga, Y. H. (1990). *Human behavior in global perspective: An introduction to cross-cultural psychology.* Pergamon.

Seitelberger, F. (1997). Theodor Meynert (1833–1892), pioneer and visionary of brain research. *Journal of the History of the Neurosciences, 6*, 264–274.

Seligman, M. E. P., Rashid, T., & Parks, A. C. (2006). Positive psychotherapy. *American Psychologist, 61*, 774–788.

Sell, R. L. (1997). Defining and measuring sexual orientation: A review. *Archives of Sexual Behavior, 26*(6), 643–658.

Sest, N., & March, E. (2017). Constructing the cyber-troll: Psychopathy, sadism, and empathy. *Personality and Individual Differences, 119*(1), 69–72.

Settersten, R., & Ray, B. (2010). What's going on with young people today? The long and twisting path to adulthood. *The Future of Children, 20*(1). bit.ly/1V7PG77

Sexual Orientation, UK. (2020). Office for National Statistics. https://www.ons.gov.uk/peoplepopulationandcommunity/culturalidentity/sexuality/bulletins/sexualidentityuk/2020

Shalvi, S., & De Dreu, C. (2014). Oxytocin promotes group-serving dishonesty.

Proceeedings of the National Academy of Science of the USA, 111(15), 5503–5507.

Shariff, D. (Ed.). (2021). *Psychoanalysis and psychotherapy in China* (Vol. 4, p. 2). Phoenix.

Shaw, H., Taylor, P., Conchie, S., & Ellis, D. A. (2019). Language style matching: A comprehensive list of articles and tools. *PsyArXiv Reprints.* https://doi.org/10.31234/osf.io/yz4br

Shedrovitsky, P. (2009). Lev ygotsky I sovremennaja pedagogicheskaya antropologiya [Lev Vygotsky and modern pedagogical anthropology]. *Russian Archipelago.* http://www.archipelag.ru/authors/shedrovickypetr/?library=1308

Shelton, J. T., Elliott, E. M., Lynn, S. D., & Exner, A. L. (2009). The distracting effects of a ringing cell phone: An investigation of the laboratory and the classroom setting. *Journal of Environmental Psychology, 29*(4), 513–521.

Sheridan, T. B. (2020). A review of recent research in social robotics. *Current Opinion in Psychology, 36*, 7–12. https://doi.org/10.1016/j.copsyc.2020.01.003

Sherman, L. E., Michikyan, M., & Greenfield, P. M. (2013). The effects of text, audio, video, and in-person communication on bonding between friends. *Cyberpsychology: Journal of Psychosocial Research on Cyberspace, 7*(2), 2–3.

Shermer, M. (2015). *The moral arc: How science and reason lead humanity toward truth, justice, and freedom.* Holt.

Shiner, R., & Caspi, A. (2003). Personality differences in childhood and adolescence: Measurement, development, and consequences. *Journal of Child Psychology and Psychiatry, 44*(1), 2–32.

Shiraev, E. (2015). *A history of psychology: A global perspective.* SAGE.

Shiraev, E. (2021). *Russian government and politics* (3rd ed.). MacMillan/Red Globe Press.

Shiraev, E., & Boyd, G. (2008). *The accent of success.* University of Michigan Press.

Shiraev, E., & Fillipov, A. (1990). Cross-cultural social perception. *St. Petersburg University Quarterly, 13*, 53–60.

Shiraev, E., & Levy, D. (2013). *Cross-cultural psychology* (5th ed.). Pearson.

Shiraev, E., & Levy, D. (2024). *Cross-cultural psychology* (8th ed.). Taylor and Francis.

Shiraev, E., Keohane, J., Icks, M., & Samoilenko, S. (2022). *Character assassination and reputation management.* Routledge.

Shirmohammadi, M., Kohan, S., Shamsi-Gooshki, E., & Shahriari, M. (2018). Ethical considerations in sexual health research: A narrative review. *Iran Journal of Nursing and Midwifery Research, 23*(3), 157–166.

Shorter, E. (1997). *A history of psychiatry.* Wiley.

Shweder, R. (2010). Donald Campbell's doubt: Cultural difference or failure of communication? *Behavioral and Brain Sciences, 33*(2/3), 49–50.

Shweder, R., Mahapatra, M., & Miller, J. (1990). Culture and moral development. In J. Stigler, R. Shweder, & G. Herdt (Eds.), *Cultural psychology* (pp. 130–204). Cambridge University Press.

Sidanius, J., & Pratto, F. (1999). *Social dominance: An intergroup theory of social hierarchy and oppression.* Cambridge University Press.

Sigel, R. (1989). Introduction: Persistence and change. In R. Sigel (Ed.), *Political learning in adulthood: A sourcebook of theory and research.* University of Chicago Press.

Simpson, M., & Hagood, C. (2010, June 13). On wo-metrosexuality and the city. *Huffington Post.* http://www.huffingtonpost.com/carolinehagood/metrosexuality-and-the-cib535333.html

Sindhuja, S., Maciek, S., & von Hecker, U. (2017). The role of Indian caste identity and caste inconsistent norms on status representation. *Frontiers in Psychology, 8, 487.*

Sinha, J., & Verma, J. (1983). Perceptual structuring of dyadic interactions. *Journal of Cross-Cultural Psychology, 14*, 187–199.

Sirois, F. M., & Pychyl, T. A. (2013). Procrastination and the priority of short-term mood regulation: Consequences for future self. *Social and Personality Psychology Compass, 7*, 115–127.

Skinner, B. F. (1938). *The behavior of organisms.* Appleton-Century-Crofts.

Skinner, B. F. (1960). Pigeons in a pelican. *American Psychologist, 15*, 28–57.

Skinner, B. F. (1971). *Beyond freedom and dignity*. Bantam Vintage Books.

Skinner, B. F. (2005). *Walden two*. Hackett. (Original work published 1948)

Slater, M., Rovira, A., Southern, R., Swapp, D., Zhang, J. J., Campbell, C., & Levine, M. (2013). Bystander responses to a violent incident in an immersive virtual environment. *Plos One, 8*(1). http://www.plosone.org/

Slife, B. (1993). *Time and psychological explanation*. State University of New York Press.

Slutske, W., Eisen, S., Xian, H., True, W., Lyons, M., Goldberg, J., & Tsuang, M. (2001). A twin study of the association between pathological gambling and antisocial personality disorder. *Journal of Abnormal Psychology, 110*(2), 297–308.

Small, D. J. (2005). *Power interest and psychology*. PCCS Books.

Smith, B. (2019). *Positive psychology for your hero's journey: Discovering true and lasting happiness*. Independent.

Smith, B., & Browne, C. A. (2019). *Tools and weapons: The promise and the peril of the digital age*. Penguin.

Smith, H. J., Dinev, T., & Xu, H. (2011). Information privacy research: An interdisciplinary review. *MIS Q, 35*(4), 989–1016.

Smith, J. (1982). *Imagining religion, from Babylon to Jonestown*. University of Chicago Press.

Smith, J., & Alloy, L. (2009). A roadmap to rumination: a review of the definition, assessment, and conceptualization of this multifaceted construct. *Clinical Psychology Review, 29*(2), 116–128.

Smith, K. (2011). Neuroscience vs. philosophy: Taking aim at free will. *Nature, 477*(7362), 23–25.

Smith, M. B. (1978). Psychology and values. *Journal of Social Issues, 34*, 181–199.

Smith, S., Basile, K., & Kresno, M-J. (2017). The National Intimate Partner and Sexual Violence Survey: 2016/2017 Report on Stalking — Updated Release. https://www.cdc.gov/violenceprevention/pdf/nisvs/nisvsstalkingreport.pdf

Smoot, K. (2022). If you think my pronouns are optional, We can't keep being friends. *Huffington Post*. https://news.yahoo.com/think-pronouns-optional-cant-keep-130006513.html

Snarey, J. (1985). Cross-cultural universality of social-moral development: A critical review of Kohlbergian research. *Psychological Bulletin, 97*, 202–232.

Snow, J. (2021, April 7). It's time to come up with new AI benchmarks. *The Wall Street Journal*, R4.

Snyder, M., & Swann, W. B., Jr. (1978). Behavioral confirmation in social interaction: From social perception to social reality. *Journal of Experimental Social Psychology, 14*, 148–162.

Snyder-Hall, R. C. (2010). Third-wave feminism and the defense of "choice". *Perspectives on Politics, 8*(1), 255–261.

Solms, M., & Turnbull, O. (2011). What is neuropsychoanalysis? *Neuropsychoanalysis, 13*(2), 133–145.

Solomon, A. (2022). The mysterious rise of child suicide. *The New Yorker*. https://www.newyorker.com/magazine/2022/04/11/the-mystifying-rise-of-child-suicide

Solove, D. J. (2010). *Understanding privacy*. Harvard University Press.

Soon, C., He, A., Bode, S., & Haynes, J.-D. (2013). Predicting free choices for abstract intensions. *Proceedings of the National Academy of Sciences, 110*(15), 6217–6222.

Sorrentino, R. M., Nezlek, J. B., Yasunaga, S., Kouhara, S., Otsubo, Y., & Shuper, P. (2008). Uncertainty orientation and affective experiences: Individual differences within and across cultures. *Journal of Cross-Cultural Psychology, 39*(2), 129–146.

Soto, C. J. (2019). How replicable are links between personality traits and consequential life outcomes? The life outcomes of personality replication project. *Psychological Science, 30*(5), 711–727.

Span, L. (2009). *When the time comes: Families with aging parents share their struggles and solutions*. Grand Central Life & Style.

Specht, J., Egloff, B., & Schmukle, S. C. (2011). Stability and change of personality across the life course: The impact of age and major life events on mean-level and rank-order stability of the Big Five. *Journal of Personality and Social Psychology, 101*(4), 862–882. https://doi.org/10.1037/a0024950

Spencer, S. J., Steele, C. M., & Quinn, D. M. (1999). Stereotype threat and women's math performance. *Journal of Experimental Social Psychology*, *35*, 4–28.

Sperry, R. (1961). Cerebral organization and behavior. *Science*, *133*, 1749–1757.

Spiegler, M. (2016). *Contemporary behavior therapy*. Cengage Learning.

Spillett, R. (2014, June 6). Maybe it's not about the happy ending, maybe it's about the story. *Daily Mail*. http://dailym.ai/1EBXYNg

Stanley, J., Lohani, M., & Isaacowitz, D. (2014). Age-related differences in judgments of inappropriate behavior are related to humor style preferences. *Psychology and Aging*, *29*(3), 528–541.

Stanley, M., Beck, J., & Zebb, B. (1998). Psychometric properties of the MSPSS in older adults. *Aging and Mental Health*, *2*(3), 186–193.

Statista. (2022). Number of online dating users in the United States. https://www.statista.com/statistics/417654/us-online-dating-user-numbers/

Stavrova, O., & Ehlebracht, D. (2018). Education as an antidote to cynicism: A longitudinal investigation. *Social Psychological and Personality Science*, *9*(1), 59–69.

Steers, M. N., Wickham, R. E., & Acitelli, L. K. (2014). Seeing everyone else's highly reels: How Facebook usage is linked to depressive symptoms. *Journal of Social and Clinical psychology*, *33*, 701–731.

Stern, J. (2010). Mind over martyr: How to deradicalize Islamist extremists. *Foreign Affairs*, *89*(1), 95–108.

Sternberg, R. J. (2007). Who are the bright children? *The Cultural Context of Being and Acting Intelligent. Educational Researcher*, *36*(3), 148–155. https://doi.org/10.3102/0013189X07299881

Stetter, F., & Kupper, S. (2002). Autogenic training: A meta-analysis of clinical outcome studies. *Applied Psychophysiology and Biofeedback*, *27*(1), 45–98.

Stevens, S. (1946). On the theory of scales of measurement. *Science*, *103*(2684), 677–680.

Stevenson, A., & Mozur, P. (2019, September 22). China scores businesses, and low grades could be a trade-war weapon. *The New York Times*. https://www.nytimes.com/2019/09/22/business/china-social-credit-business.html

Stewart, C. (2009). *APA membership: Past, present, and possible futures*. In *Paper presented at the annual meeting of the American Psychological Association*.

Steyer, R., Mayer, A., Geiser, C., & Cole, D. (2015). A theory of states and traits—Revised. *Annual Review of Clinical Psychology*, *11*, 71–98.

Stieger, M., Flückiger, C., Rüegger, D., Kowatsch, T., Roberts, B., & Allemand, M. (2021). Changing personality traits with the help of a digital personality change intervention. *Proceedings of the National Academy of Sciences of the United States of America PNAS*, *118*(8), e2017548118.

Streeter, C., Whitfield, T., Owen, L., Rein, T., Karri, S., Yakhkind, A., . . . Jensen, J. (2010). Effects of yoga versus walking on mood, anxiety, and brain GABA levels: A randomized controlled MRS study. *Journal of Alternative and Complementary Medicine*, *16*(11), 1145–1115.

Strickland, L. H. (1997). Who? V. M. Bekhterev? A field theorist? *SAFT Newsletter*, *13*(1), 2–3.

Strickland, L. H. (2001). Introduction. In *L. Bekhterev's collective reflexology: The complete edition* (E. Lockwood & A. Lockwood, Trans.). (pp. 15–19). Transaction.

Stuart, A., Bandara, A. K., & Levine, M. (2019). The psychology of privacy in the digital age. *Social and Personality Psychology Compass*, *13*(1), 17519004–20191101.

Suh, E. M., Diener, E. D., & Updegraff, J. A. (2008). From culture to priming conditions: Self-construal influences on life satisfaction judgments. *Journal of Cross-Cultural Psychology*, *39*(1), 3–15.

Sullivan, H. (1953). *The interpersonal theory of psychiatry*. W. W. Norton.

Sulloway, F. (1996). *Born to rebel: Birth order, family dynamics, and creative lines*. Pantheon.

Summers, J. (2021). Alligator attack: Utah zoo worker saved by guests. *Latin Post*. https://www.latinpost.com/articles/151552/20210817/alligator-attack-utah-zoo-worker-saved-guests.htm

Sunesh-Kumar, P. N. S., Anish, P. K., & Biju, G. (2015). Risk factors for suicide in elderly in comparison to younger age groups. *Indian Journal of Psychiatry, 57*(3), 249–254.

Sutherland, S. (2014). How yoga changes body and mind. *Scientific American, 25*(2). http://www.scientificamerican.com/article/how-yoga-changes-the-brain/

Tabarrok, A. (2015, September 16). What was Gary Becker's biggest mistake? *Marginal Revolution.* http://marginalrevolution.com/marginalrevolution/2015/09/what-was-gary-beckers-biggest-mistake.html

Tafarodi, R., Lo, C., Yamaguchi, S., Lee, W., & Katsura, H. (2004). The inner self in three countries. *Journal of Cross-Cultural Psychology, 35*(1), 97–117.

Tafarodi, R., Shaughnessy, S. C., Yamaguchi, S., & Murakoshi, A. (2011). e reporting of self-esteem in Japan and Canada. *Journal of Cross-Cultural Psychology, 42*(1), 155–164.

Tafarodi, R., & Swann, W. (1996). Individualism-collectivism and global self-esteem: Evidence for a cultural trade-off. *Journal of Cross-Cultural Psychology, 27*, 651–672.

Talhelm, T., Zhang, X., Oishi, S., Shimin, C., Duan, D., Lan, X., & Kitayama, S. (2014). Large-scale psychological differences within China explained by rice versus wheat agriculture. *Science, 344*(6184), 603–608.

Tarde, G. (1903). *The laws of imitation.* Holt.

Taves, A. (1999). *Fits, trances, and visions: Experiencing religion and explaining experience from Wesley to James.* Princeton University Press.

Taylor, F. W. (1911). *The principles of scientific management.* Harper.

Taylor, S. E. (1983). Adjustment to threatening events: A theory of cognitive adaptation. *American Psychologist, 38*(11), 1161–1173.

Taylor, S. E. (1989). *Positive illusions: Creative self-deception and the healthy mind.* Basic Books.

Taylor, S. E. (2000). Psychological resources, positive illusions, and health. *American Psychologist, 55*(1), 99–109.

Taylor, S. E., Sherman, D., Kim, H. S., Jarcho, J., Takagi, K., & Dunagan, M. (2004). Culture and social support: Who seeks it and why? *Journal of Personality and Social Psychology, 87*(3), 354–362.

Thaler, R. H., & Sunstein, C. R. (2021). *Nudge.* Yale University Press.

Theoduloz, G. (2017). Relevance of rorschach test in assessment of psychopathological symptoms and executive functions. *Journal of Neuropsychology, 10*(2), 89–105.

Thorndike, E. L. (1911). *Animal intelligence: Experimental studies.* Macmillan.

Thorne, A., & Nam, V. (2009). The storied construction of personality. In P. Corr & G. Matthews (Eds.), *The Cambridge handbook of personality psychology* (pp. 491–505). Cambridge University Press.

Thornton, J. (2019). WHO report shows that women outlive men worldwide. *The BMJ.* https://www.bmj.com/content/365/bmj.l1631

Tindle, H., Chang, Y., Kuller, L., Manson, J., Robinson, J., Rosal, M., & Matthews, K. (2009). Optimism, cynical hostility, and incident coronary heart disease and mortality in the Women's Health Initiative. *Circulation, 120*(8), 656–662.

Tindle, R. (2021). Improving the global reach of psychological research. *Discover Psychology, 1*(5). https://doi.org/10.1007/s44202-021-00004-4

Tishler, C. L., Reiss, N., & Rhodes, A. (2007). Suicidal behavior in children younger than twelve: A diagnostic challenge for emergency department personnel. *Academic Emergency Medicine, 14*(9), 810–818.

Tolman, E. C. (1932). *Purposive behavior in animals and men.* Century.

Tolman, E. C. (1948). Cognitive maps in rats and men. *Psychological Review, 55*(4), 189–208.

Tori, C. D., & Bilmes, M. (2002). Multiculturalism and psychoanalytic psychology: The validation of a defense mechanisms measure in an Asian population. *Psychoanalytic Psychology, 19*, 701–721.

Tosi, J., & Warmke, B. (2016). Moral grandstanding. *Philosophy and Public Affairs, 44*(3), 197–217. https://philpapers.org/rec/JUSMG

Traeger, L. (2013). Distraction. In M. Gellman & J. R. Turner (Eds.), *Encyclopedia of behavioral medicine* (pp. 610–611). Springer.

Triandis, H. (1989). The self and social behavior in different social contexts. *Psychological Review, 96*, 506–520.

Triandis, H. (1994). *Culture and social behavior.* McGraw-Hill.

Triandis, H. C. (1996). The psychological measurement of cultural syndromes. *American Psychologist, 51*(4), 407–415.

Tromholt, M. (2016). The Facebook experiment: Quitting Facebook leads to high levels of well-being. *Cyberpsychology, Behavior, and Social Networking, 19*, 661–666.

Trull, T. J., & Sher, K. J. (1994). Relationship between the five-factor model of personality and axis I disorders in a nonclinical sample. *Journal of Abnormal Psychology, 103*(2), 350–360.

Tsytsarev, S. V., & Krichmar, L. (2000). Relationship of perceived culture shock, length of stay in the US, depression and self-esteem in elderly Russian-speaking immigrants. *Journal of Social Distress and the Homeless, 9*(1), 35–49.

Tucker, W. H. (2009). *The Cattell controversy: Race, science, and ideology.* University of Illinois Press.

Turing, A. (1950). Computing machinery and intelligence. *Mind, 50*, 433–460.

Turner, J. F. (1920). *The frontier in American history.* Henry Holt.

Tutty, L., Rothery, M., & Grinnell, R. (1996). *Qualitative research for social work.* Allyn & Bacon.

Tversky, A., & Kahneman, D. (1973). Availability: A heuristic for judging frequency and probability. *Cognitive psychology, 5*(2), 207–232.

Tversky, A., & Kahneman, D. (1974). Judgment under uncertainty: Heuristics and biases: Biases in judgments reveal some heuristics of thinking under uncertainty. *Science, 185*(4157), 1124–1131.

Tversky, A., & Kahneman, D. (1982). Judgments of and by representativeness. In D. Kahneman, P. Slovic, & A. Tversky (Eds.), *Judgment under uncertainty: Heuristics and biases* (pp. 153–160). Cambridge University Press.

Twenge, J. (2017). Have smartphones destroyed a generation? *The Atlantic.* https://www.theatlantic.com/magazine/archive/2017/09/has-the-smartphone-destroyed-a-generation/534198/

Twenge, J. M., Joiner, T. E., Rogers, M. L., & Martin, G. N. (2017). Increases in depressive symptoms, suicide-related outcomes, and suicide rates among U.S. adolescents after 2010 and Links to increased new media screen time. *Clinical Psychological Science, 6*(1), 3–17.

Tyrer, P., Coombs, N., Ibrahimi, F., Mathilakath, A., Bajaj, P., Ranger, M., . . . Din, R. (2007). Critical developments in the assessment of personality disorder. *British Journal of Psychiatry, 190*, 51–59.

Tyrer, P., & Johnson, T. (1996). Establishing the severity of personality disorder. *American Journal of Psychiatry, 153*(12), 1593–1597.

Umanah, U. (2020). Teachers college votes to remove eugenicist's name from building. *Ivyletter.* https://ivyletter.substack.com/p/breaking-teachers-college-votes-to

UN Free and Equal. (2022). Lesbian, gay, bi, trans, intersex and queer (lgbtiq+) women. https://www.unfe.org/wp-content/uploads/2022/03/UNFE-LGBTIQ-Women-Factsheet.pdf

United Nations for LGBT Equality. (2015). LGBT rights: Frequently asked questions. http://bit.ly/1RwMHAZ

United States Census Bureau. (2021). National single parent day: March 21, 2021. https://www.census.gov/newsroom/stories/single-parent-day.html

Vaihinger, H. (1952). *The philosophy of "as if."* Routledge. (Original work published 1924)

Valsiner, J., & Lawrence, J. (1997). Human development in culture across the life span. In J. W. Berry, P. R. Dasen, & T. S. Saraswathi (Eds.), *Handbook of cross-cultural psychology: Basic processes and human development* (Vol. 2, pp. 69–106). Allyn & Bacon.

Van de Vliert, E. (2006). Autocratic leadership around the globe: Do climate and wealth drive leadership culture? *Journal of Cross-Cultural Psychology, 37*, 42–59.

Van Gestel, L. C., Kroese, F. M., & De Ridder, D. T. D. (2018). Nudging at the checkout counter–A longitudinal study of the effect of a food repositioning nudge on healthy food choice. *Psychology & Health, 33*(6), 800–809.

Värnik, P. (2012). Suicide in the world. *International Journal of Environmental Research and Public Health, 9*(3), 760–771.

Vassilieva, J. (2016). *Narrative psychology: Identity, transformation, and ethics.* Springer.

Vassiliou, V., & Vassiliou, G. (1973). The implicative meaning of the Greek concept of philomoto. *Journal of Cross-Cultural Psychology*, *4*(3), 326–341.

Vealy, R., & Perritt, N. (2015). Hardiness and optimism as predictors of the frequency of flow in collegiate athletes. *Journal of Sport Behavior*, *38*(3), 321–388.

Veenhoven, R. (2008). Sociological theories of subjective well-being. In Eid & R. Larsen (Eds.), *The science of subjective well-being: A tribute to Ed Diener* (pp. 44–61). Guilford Press.

Ventegodt, S., Thegler, S., Andreasen, T., Struve, F., Bassaine, L. Enevoldsen, L. , & Merrick, J. (2006). Clinical holistic medicine: Psychodynamic short-time therapy complemented with bodywork. A clinical follow-up study of 109 patients. *The Scientific World Journal*, *6*, 2220–2238.

VerBruggen, R. (2019). The real housewives of America: Dad's income and mom's work. *Institute for Family Studies.* https://ifstudies.org/blog/the-real-housewives-of-america-dads-income-and-moms-work

Verhallen, A., Renken, R., Marsman, J., & Ter, H. G. (2019). Romantic relationships breakup: An experimental model to study effects of stress on depression (-like) symptoms. *PLoS ONE*, *14*(5). https://bit.ly/3UcQ1b7

Verhulst, B., Eaves, L., & Hatemi, P. (2012). Correlation not causation: The relationship between personality traits and political ideologies. *American Journal of Political Science*, *56*(1), 34–51.

Verhulst, B., Hatemi, P. K., & Martin, G. (2010). Personality and political attitudes. *Personality and Individual Differences*, *49*(4), 306–316.

Vernon, P. (1969). *Intelligence and cultural environment*. Methuen.

Vich, M. A. (1988). Some historical sources of the term "transpersonal." *Journal of Transpersonal Psychology*, *20*, 107–110.

Virkkunen, M. (1983). Insulin secretion during the glucose tolerance-test in anti-social personality. *British Journal of Psychiatry*, *142*, 598–604.

Volavka, J., Crowner, M., Brizer, D., Convit, A., Van Praag, H., & Suckow. (1990). Tryptophan treatment of aggressive psychiatric patients. *Biological Psychiatry*, *28*, 728–732.

von Mayrhauser, R. (2002). The mental testing community and validity: A prehistory. *American Psychologist*, *47*, 244–253.

Vygotsky, L. (1933, April 20). *Kriticheskie vozrasta* [Critical periods]. Leningrad Pedagogical Institute's Archive.

Vygotsky, L. (2005). Myshlenie i rech [Thought and language]. In *Psychology of the individual's development*. Smysl. (Original work published 1934)

Wade, N. (2015). *A troublesome inheritance: Genes, race, and human history*. Penguin Books.

Wairaven, G. (2013). *Health and poverty: Global health problems and solutions*. Routledge.

Wang, J., Korczykowski, M., Rao, H., Fan, Y., Pluta, J., Gur, R. C., . . . Detre, J. A. (2007). Gender difference in neural response to psychological stress. *Social Cognitive and Affective Neuroscience*, *2*(3), 227–239.

Wang, Y., Niya, M., Mark, G., Reich, S. M., & Warschauer, M. (2015). Coming of age (Digitally): Am ecological view of social media use among college students. In *proceedings of the 18th ACM conference on computer support and social computing* (pp. 571–582).

Warburton, N. (2012). *Philosophy: The Classics* (2nd ed.). Routledge.

Ward, L. (2021, April 7). Research suggests how robots could affect behavior. *The Wall Street Journal*, R5.

Watson, J. B. (1919). *Psychology from a standpoint of a behaviorist*. Lippincott.

Watson, J. B. (1927). Can psychology help in the selection of personnel? *J. Walter Thompson News Bulletin*, *129*, 113.

Watson, J. B. (1929). Should a child have more than one mother? *Liberty Magazine*, 31–35.

Watson, J. B., & Rayner, R. (1920). Conditioned emotional responses. *Journal of Experimental Psychology*, *3*, 1–14.

Watson, J. M. (2012). Educating the disagreeable extravert: Narcissism, the big five personality traits, and achievement goal orientation. *International Journal of Teaching and Learning in Higher Education*, *24*(1), 76–88.

Watson, P. J., Grisham, S. O., Trotter, M. V., & Biderman, M. D. (1984). Narcissism and empathy: Validity evidence for the narcissistic personality inventory. *Journal of Personality Assessment, 45*, 159–162.

Watts, T., Duncan, G., & Quan, H. (2018). Revisiting the marshmallow test: A conceptual replication investigating links between early delay of gratification and later outcomes. *Psychological Science, 29*(7), 1159–1177.

Weber, E. (1998). What folklore tells us about risk and risk taking: Cross-cultural comparisons of American, German, and Chinese proverbs. *Organizational Behavior and Human Decision Processes, 75*(2), 170–186.

Weiner, I. (2003). *Principles of Rorschach interpretation.* Lawrence Erlbaum.

Weinstein, L. B. (1989). Transcultural relocation: Adaptation of older Americans to Israel. *Activities, Adaptation & Aging, 13*, 33–42.

Weisberg, Y., DeYoung, C., & Hirsh, J. (2011). Gender differences in personality across the ten aspects of the big five. *Frontiers in Psychology.* Online Publication. http://www.ncbi.nlm.nih.gov/pmc/articles/PMC3149680/

Weissman, M. M., Markowitz, J. C., & Klerman, G. L. (2007). *Clinician's quick guide to interpersonal psychotherapy.* Oxford University Press.

Weiten, W., Dunn, D., & Hummer, E. (2011). *Psychology applied to modern life: Adjustment in the 21st Century.* Cengage.

Weizenbaum, J. (1976). *Computer power and human reason.* W. H. Freeman.

Wells, G., Howritz, J., & Seetharaman, D. (2021, September 15). Facebook knows Instagram is toxic for teen girls, company documents show. *The Wall Street Journal,* A1, A10–11.

Wertz, A., & Wynn, K. (2014). Selective social learning of plant edibility in 6- and 18-month-old infants. *Psychological Science, 25*(4), 874–882.

Wertz, J., Belsky, J., Moffitt, T. E., Belsky, D. W., Harrington, H., Avinun, R., Poulton, R., Ramrakha, S., & Caspi, A. (2019). Genetics of nurture: A test of the hypothesis that parents' genetics predict their observed caregiving. *Developmental Psychology, 55*(7), 1461–1472.

Whiting, B. B., & Whiting, J. W. M. (1975). *The children of six cultures: A psycho-cultural analysis.* Harvard University Press.

Wideman, T., & Sullivan, M. (2011). Reducing catastrophic thinking associated with pain. *Pain Management, 1*(3), 249–256.

Widiger, T. A., & Spitzer, R. L. (1991). Sex bias in the diagnosis of personality disorders: Conceptual and methodological issues. *Clinical Psychology Review, 11*, 1–22.

Widiger, T., & Oltmanns, J. (2017). Neuroticism is a fundamental domain of personality with enormous public health implications. *World Psychiatry, 16*(2), 144–145.

Willems, Y., Boesen, N., Li, J., Finkenauer, C., & Bartels,

M. (2019). The heritability of self-control: A meta-analysis. *Neuroscience and Biobehavioral Reviews, 100*, 324–334.

Williams, K. E., Ciarrochi, J., & Heaven, P. C. (2012). Inflexible parents, inflexible kids: A 6-year longitudinal study of parenting style and the development of psychological flexibility in adolescents. *Journal of Youth Adolescence, 41*(8), 1053–1066.

Wilson, D. (2017). Supervision of indigenous research students: Considerations for cross-cultural supervisors. *AlterNative: An International Journal of Indigenous Peoples, 13*(4), 256–265.

Wilson, G., & Rahman, Q. (2008). *Born gay: The psychobiology of sex orientation.* Peter Owen Publishers.

Wilson, K. (2014, August 6). Transgender at 10. *Willamette Week.* http://www.wweek.com/portland/article-22897-transgenderat10.html

Winter, J., & Teitelbaum, M. (2013). *The global spread of fertility decline: Population, fear, and uncertainty.* Yale University Press.

Wolfe, R. (1993). A common-sense approach to personality measurement. In K. Craik, R. Hogan, & R. Wolfe (Eds.), *Fifty years of personality psychology* (pp. 269–290). Plenum Press.

Wong, P. T. P. (2015). Meaning therapy: Assessments and interventions. *Existential Analysis, 26*(1), 154–167.

Wood, A. L., & Wahl, O. W. (2006). Evaluating the effectiveness of a consumer-provided mental health recovery education presentation. *Psychiatric Rehabilitation Journal, 30*, 46–52.

Wood, D., Harms, P., & Vazire, S. (2010). Perceiver effects as projective tests: What your perceptions of others say about you. *Journal of Personality and Social Psychology, 99*(1), 174–190.

World Health Organization. (2014). Mental health, poverty and development. http://bit.ly/1j7j4az

World Health Organization (WHO). (2022). *Suicide rates: Data by country.* WHO.

Wozniak, R. (1993). *The roots of behaviorism.* Routledge.

Wright, D. (2013, December 7). My unwelcome stranger [Web log post]. http://deniswright.blogspot.com.au/

Wrzus, C., & Mehl, M. (2015). Lab and/or field? Measuring personality processes and their social consequences. *European Journal of Personality, 29*(2), 250–271.

Wundt, W. (1916). *Elements of folk psychology: Outlines of a psychological history of the development of mankind* (E. L. Schaub, Trans.). Macmillan.

Xiubing, W. (2021). Some issues I have encountered on my path to becoming a psychoanalyst. *Psychoanalysis and Psychotherapy in China, 4*(2), 278–281.

Xu, J., & Harvey, N. (2014). Carry on winning: The gamblers' fallacy creates hot hand effects in online gambling. *Cognition, 131*(2), 173–180.

Yakunin, V. (2001). *Istoriya Psikhilogii* [A history of psychology]. St. Mikhailov.

Yang, M., Coid, J., & Tyrer, P. (2010). Personality pathology recorded by severity: National survey. *The British Journal of Psychiatry, 197*(3), 193–199. https://doi.org/10.1192/bjp.bp.110.078956 PMID: 20807963

Yeager, D. S., Henderson, M. D., Paunesku, D., Walton, G. M., D'Mello, , Spitzer, B. J, & Duckworth, A. L. (2014). Boring but important: A self-transcendent purpose for learning fosters academic self-regulation. *Journal of Personality and Social Psychology, 107*(4), 559–558.

Yip, P. S., Caine, E., Yousuf, S., Chang, S. S., Wu, K. C., & Chen, Y. Y. (2012). Means restriction for suicide prevention. *Lancet, 379*(9834), 2393–2399.

YouGov. (2022). Viewpoints on pronouns. *YouGov Poll: June 29 - July 4, 2022.* https://today.yougov.com/topics/society/articles-reports/2022/07/08/viewpoints-pronouns-yougov-poll-june-29-july-4-202

Young, J., Klosko, J., & Weishaar, E. (2006). *Schema therapy: A practitioner's guide.* Guilford Press.

Young, R. K. (1985). Ebbinghaus: Some consequences. *Journal of Experimental Psychology: Learning, Memory, and Cognition, 11*, 491–495.

Yuill, K. (2013). *Assisted suicide: The liberal, humanist case against legalization.* Palgrave.

Zanarini, M. (2009, October 6). Psychotherapy of borderline personality disorder. *Acta Psychiatrica Scandinavica, 120*, 373–377.

Zanarini, M. C., Frankenburg, F. R., Hennen, J., Reich, D. B., & Silk, K. R. (2005). The

McLean study of adult development (MSAD): Overview and implications of the first six years of prospective follow-up. *Journal of Personality Disorders, 19*(5), 505–523.

Zeidner, M., & Endler, N. (Eds.). (1995). *Handbook of coping: Theory, research, applications.* Wiley.

Zhou, J. N., Hofman, M. A., Gooren, L. J., & Swaab, D. F. (1995). A sex difference in the human brain and its relation to transsexuality. *Nature, 378,* 68–70.

Zimbardo, P. (2007). The lucifer effect: Understanding how good people turn evil. *The Journal of the American Medical Association, 298*(11), 1338–1340.

Žižek, S. (2015, January 10). Slavoj Žižek on the Charlie Hebdo massacre: Are the worst really full of passionate intensity? *New Statesman.* http://www.newstatesman.com/world-affairs/2015/01/slavoj-i-ek-charlie-hebdo-massacre-are-worst-really-full-passionate-intensity

Zmorzyński, S., Styk, W., Klinkosz, W., Iskra, J., & Filip, A. A. (2021). Personality traits and polymorphisms of genes coding neurotransmitter receptors or transporters: Review of single gene and genome-wide association studies. *Annals of General Psychiatry, 20*(1), 7. https://annals-general-psychiatry.biomedcentral.com/articles/10.1186/s12991-021-00328-4

Zuckerman, M. (1990, December). Some dubious premises in research and theory on racial differences in scientific, social, and ethical issues.

American Psychologist, 45(2), 1297–1303.

Zuckerman, M. (2007a). *Sensation seeking and risky behavior.* American Psychological Association.

Zwir, I., Arnedo, J., Del-Val, C., Pulkki-Råback, L., Konte, B., Yang, S., Romero-Zaliz, R ., Hintsanen, M., Cloninger, K., Garcia, D., Svrakic, D., Rozsa, S., Martinez, M., Lyytikäinen, L.P., Giegling, I., Kähönen, M.,

Hernandez-Cuervo, H., Seppälä, I., Raitoharju, E., & C. Cloninger, R. (2020). Uncovering the complex genetics of human temperament. *Molecular Psychiatry, 25*, 2275–2294.

INDEX